Information Systems and Qualitative Research

IFIP – The International Federation for Information Processing

IFIP was founded in 1960 under the auspices of UNESCO, following the First World Computer Congress held in Paris the previous year. An umbrella organization for societies working in information processing, IFIP's aim is two-fold: to support information processing within its member countries and to encourage technology transfer to developing nations. As its mission statement clearly states,

> IFIP's mission is to be the leading, truly international, apolitical organization which encourages and assists in the development, exploitation and application of information technology for the benefit of all people.

IFIP is a non-profitmaking organization, run almost solely by 2500 volunteers. It operates through a number of technical committees, which organize events and publications. IFIP's events range from an international congress to local seminars, but the most important are:

- the IFIP World Computer Congress, held every second year;
- open conferences;
- working conferences.

The flagship event is the IFIP World Computer Congress, at which both invited and contributed papers are presented. Contributed papers are rigorously refereed and the rejection rate is high.

As with the Congress, participation in the open conferences is open to all and papers may be invited or submitted. Again, submitted papers are stringently refereed.

The working conferences are structured differently. They are usually run by a working group and attendance is small and by invitation only. Their purpose is to create an atmosphere conducive to innovation and development. Refereeing is less rigorous and papers are subjected to extensive group discussion.

Publications arising from IFIP events vary. The papers presented at the IFIP World Computer Congress and at open conferences are published as conference proceedings, while the results of the working conferences are often published as collections of selected and edited papers.

Any national society whose primary activity is in information may apply to become a full member of IFIP, although full membership is restricted to one society per country. Full members are entitled to vote at the annual General Assembly, National societies preferring a less committed involvement may apply for associate or corresponding membership. Associate members enjoy the same benefits as full members, but without voting rights. Corresponding members are not represented in IFIP bodies. Affiliated membership is open to non-national societies, and individual and honorary membership schemes are also offered.

Information Systems and Qualitative Research

Proceedings of the IFIP TC8 WG 8.2 International Conference on Information Systems and Qualitative Research, 31st May–3rd June 1997, Philadelphia, Pennsylvania, USA

Edited by

Allen S. Lee,
McGill University
Montréal
Quebec
Canada

Jonathan Liebenau
London Schools of Economics
London
UK

and

Janice I. DeGross
University of Minnesota
Minneapolis
Minnesota
USA

SPRINGER-SCIENCE+BUSINESS MEDIA, B.V.

First edition 1997

Originally published by Chapman & Hall in 1997
MyCopy version of the original edition 1997

DOI 10.1007/978-0-387-35309-8

A catalogue record for this book is available from the British Library

Printed on permanent acid-free text paper, manufactured in accordance with ANSI/NISO Z39.48-1992 and ANSI/NISO Z39.48-1984 (Permanence of Paper).

www.springer.com/mycopy

Contents

PART THREE Illustrating, Experiencing, and Being Critical in Ethnography

PART FOUR Interviewing and the Interviewer

PART FIVE The Social and Political Context of IS

PART SIX Developments in Qualitative Methods

Program Committee

General Chairs:

Kenneth E. Kendall	Rutgers University, Camden, USA
Hans-Erik Nissen	Lund University, Sweden

Program Chairs:

Allen Lee	McGill University, Canada
Jonathan Liebenau	London School of Economics, United Kingdom

Organizing Chair:

Ken Peffers	Rutgers University, Camden, USA

Program Committee:

Soon Ang	Nanyang Technological University, Singapore
David Avison	University of Southampton, United Kingdom
Richard Baskerville	Binghamton University, USA
Richard Boland	Case Western Reserve University, USA
Claudio Ciborra	Institute Theseus, France
Sue Conger	Southern Methodist University, USA
Gordon Davis	University of Minnesota, USA
Amir Hartman	University of California, Berkeley, USA
Lynda Harvey	Curtin University of Technology, Australia
Juhani Iivari	University of Oulu, Finland
Lucas Introna	London School of Economics, United Kingdom
Marius Janson	University of Missouri, St. Louis, USA
Matthew Jones	University of Cambridge, United Kingdom
Julie Kendall	Rutgers University, Camden, USA
John King	University of California, Irvine, USA
Stephano Kluzer	ENEA, Italy
Kalle Lyytinen	University of Jyväskylä, Finland
M. Lynne Markus	Claremont Graduate School, USA
Michael Myers	University of Auckland, New Zealand
Ojelanki Ngwenyama	University of Michigan, USA
Hans Oppelland	Erasmus University, The Netherlands
Wanda Orlikowski	Massachusetts Institute of Technology, USA

Dan Robey	Georgia State University, USA
Ulrike Schultze	Case Western Reserve University, USA
Eileen Trauth	Northeastern University, USA
Duane Truex	Georgia State University, USA
Dick Welke	Georgia State University, USA
Susan Winter	University of Victoria, Canada
Chee-Sing Yap	National University of Singapore

1

Information Systems and Qualitative Research

A. S. Lee
McGill University
Montreal, Quebec, Canada H3A 1G5
Tel: (514) 398-4012
Fax: (514) 398-3876
E-mail: AllenLee@Management.McGill.ca

J. Liebenau
Department of Information Systems
London School of Economics
London WC2A 2AE England
Fax: 44 171 955 7385
E-mail: J.L.Liebenau@lse.ac.UK

Most mature social studies include both qualitative and quantitative methods in the normal course of research activities. Scholars may gain reputations based on one or the other, or in some cases on the combination of both. In fields such as sociology, psychology, history, political science, and even anthropology the balance has been struck; the rules are accepted. Business studies in general, and information systems in particular, have had a much harder time coming to terms with the balance. With so many colleagues using exclusively quantitative methods in business economics, in marketing, in accounting and even in organizational behavior, and other colleagues sticking strictly to formal methods in computer science and software engineering, we have had to fight an uphill battle at times. This volume is evidence of the maturing of information systems as a discipline which can recognize the place of qualitative along with quantitative research methods.

Qualitative research in information systems has been manifested in a wide variety of ways, as is exemplified in this volume. Since the 1970s, and arguably even before, systems researchers have looked to other disciplines to apply qualitative methods to problems such as decision making, users' responses to computing, and man-machine interfaces. Only recently, however, has it seemed necessary to try to define what qualitative research essentially is and even more urgently, to defend it against those who ignore or denigrate it. Qualitative research in information systems must in each instance reconcile two forces. The first is the technique and standard that is expected in the discipline from which the method is taken. The second is to ensure that the technique, or the associated theoretical baggage from that other discipline, does not diminish the information systems purpose and importance. This is not an easy task. Sometimes we feel that the issue at stake is so pertinent to information systems as a discipline that we can or should overlook or circumvent the standards that the contributing discipline applies. At other times we are so taken up by the techniques that have proven so effective in sociology, for example, that we lose sight of the information systems issues we started with. The papers in this volume, we believe, do not suffer from either of these shortcomings.

What links these papers is first and foremost a community of information systems researchers who have a set of shared interests. It is not so easy to characterize that common interest, especially since most authors personally know only a few of the other authors. One commonality is a commitment to information systems research of high quality. This distinguishes them from those who regard research to be an activity peripherial to teaching and consulting. Another feature is their willingness to attempt qualitative methods. Most of our authors have been engaged in other forms of research, and it would not be right to assume that all of them are devoted to qualitative methods alone. We see this as a strength, and further evidence of the new maturity which we are coming to accept.

The topic of information systems and qualitative research is problemmatic now in at least three ways: in the challenge which information systems poses to traditional research approaches; in the new diversity which is emerging; and in the way in which it calls into question the impact of previous qualitative work.

First, information systems [IS] phenomena have posed serious problems to traditional research approaches in the development of scholarly knowledge about IS. These phenomena have defied the power of traditional research approaches to explain how individuals, groups, organizations, nations and society as a whole can harness computer technology to serve humanity. In *Sciences of the Artificial*, Herbert Simon points out that once a bridge begins to strain under a load greater than it was designed to bear, observers can take advantage of the situation to learn about the materials with which the bridge was constructed and the manner in which it was built. A bridge functioning normally, however, would present no similar opportunity for observation and insight. In much the same way, IS phenomena have come to constitute a load greater than traditional research approaches, alone, were ever intended to bear. IS researchers employing these approaches have fallen short of being able to provide full and satisfactory accounts of the success, failure, effectiveness, efficiency, freedom, and subjugation that occur in instantiations of computer technology in everyday life. In this situation, it is not surprising that the focus of attention should shift, at least temporarily, from IS phenomena to the research approaches by which researchers come to try to understand these phenomena.

Two earlier meetings of Working Group 8.2 of the International Federation for Information Processing (in Manchester in 1984 and in Copenhagen in 1990) convincingly established that IS phenomena have stretched traditional research approaches to, and even beyond, their limits. These two meetings took advantage of the situation to throw open to question, and no longer assume or take for granted, what constituted the traditional research approaches. These approaches were typically those associated with the supposed natural science model of social science research and were labeled (often inaccurately) "positivist," "quantitative," "experimental," and "hypothetico-deductive." While there has been great success in applying natural science and engineering models to research into computer technology, they have been inadequate and inappropriate in explaining the human, group, organizational and societal matters which surround the use of information systems. These matters have come to constitute a load that natural scientists and engineers themselves never intended their research methods to bear.

The Manchester and Copenhagen meetings were milestones in the effort to inaugurate additional research approaches needed to explain and understand information systems. These meetings have lifted some of the burden for qualitative researchers to justify the need for or the legitimacy of their approaches. In the current volume, the authors proceed quickly, assertively and unapologetically to the next steps of applying and refining qualitative research approaches.

Second, as is reflected in these papers, there is an emerging acceptance of diversity in research approaches. Whereas the term "qualitative" once carried the connotation of "anti-positivist," there is qualitative research in this volume that draws confidently upon positivism or other forms of deductivist approaches. For some this is problemmatic, but for others it is expedient, or merely the approach which best seems to solve the problems of evidence gathering in their research domain. Paré and Elam conduct a case study which they say "adopts a positivist view of research in that it is based on predefined research questions, a consideration of *a priori* constructs, and . . . [develops] testable hypotheses." Process models and variance models, which are the subject of the paper by Shaw and Jarvenpaa, are used in a distinctly hypothetico-deductive manner. The supposed distinction between positivism and interpretivism is blurred by research such as that of Romm and Pliskin who demonstrate that the combination of data analysis techniques and situational interpretation are appropriate when trying to gain an understanding of "playing politics with e-mail." In personal correspondence with us concerning a reviewer's comment on her paper, Trauth responded, "I am more on the positivist side of the positivist-relativist continuum than Referee 10 . . . [and] for that I do not think I need to defend myself." In other words, qualitative IS researchers are proceeding with maturity and open minds, willing to adopt and adapt forms of positivism for qualitative research even though, at one time, self-styled positivist IS researchers had perjoratively and imperialistically dismissed all qualitative research as "unscientific." We read this acceptance of what was once seen as the archenemy of qualitative research as a sign that the domain of qualitative IS research has cast off its defensiveness, is secure in its development, and has already commenced a process of maturation. Similarly, the "hybrid models" of Shaw and Jarvenpaa, which constitute a refutation to and transgression of the previously rigid and non-overlapping categories of process and variance models, is a manifestation of an emerging acceptance of diversity. Gallivan explicates different approaches to triangulation using quantitative and qualitative methods that reveals diversity even within triangulation.

Third, there is the significance of the theme of evaluating qualitative research which underlies this volume. A distinguishing feature here is that we are deliberately reflecting on the accomplishments of qualitative IS research since the times of the Manchester and Copenhagen meetings. With this in mind, we invited M. Lynne Markus to give the keynote address at the Philadelphia meeting of IFIP 8.2, and we commissioned papers specifically to assess what various qualitative approaches have achieved since the mid-1980s. Markus's paper provides a grand tour of how well qualitative IS research has fared, and also how much more remains to be done.

The papers prepared for the Philadelphia meeting of IFIP 8.2 are both retrospective and contemporary.[1] The retrospective elements were to a large extent contrived. We indirectly commissioned four assessment pieces, one of which, the paper on ethnography by Prasad, appears here. This was arranged and edited by Wanda Orlikowski. Another commissioned work, arranged by Boon Siong Neo, is on case research and authored by John King and Lynda Applegate. As it is written in the form of hypertext, it does not appear in this volume, but is available on the world wide web via the home page of IFIP Working Group 8.2. The two remaining commissioned assessment papers on critical social theory and action research did not survive the rigors of the review process, but highlights of a special panel in the program on critical social theory will be made available on the world wide web. Fortunately, an excellent paper on action research came to our attention. Its author, Francis Lau, accepted our invitation to present it as one of the assessment papers at the Philadelphia meeting. In addition to the commissioned works, the paper by Shaw and Jarvenpaa includes a reflective assessment of twenty-eight IS studies that make use of process models, in addition to their own contribution to the process theory approach itself. Because of the quality and theme of that work, it too is being presented as one of the assessment papers.

A collection of papers of this sort could have been organized in a number of ways, and the current structure is by no means the only appropriate one. Two good alternatives to the one used in this book were suggested at a brainstorming session at the December, 1996, meeting of IFIP Working Group 8.2 just prior to the annual Interna-

---

[1]Sixty papers and panel proposals were submitted to this conference. Along with the program committee members and a few additional experts who served as the referees, we applied the same reviewing practices and standards as for journal submissions. Of the sixty submissions, we conditionally accepted twenty papers and one panel (by Kaplan, Lau, Aarts, and Forsythe). After revisions, we accepted them for publication in this volume.

tional Conference on Information Systems in Cleveland. For each of the three proposed ways of organizing the papers, the astute participants pointed out where the proposed categories were imperfect, suggested different categories under which certain papers could be classified, noted the overlap of some categories, and revealed where the given categories did not satisfactorily classify one or another paper. In one alternative, there were just three categories: methodological criticism, methods, and practice. Another organizing framework consisted of five categories, the first three corresponding to stages in the research process: theorizing, collecting, and analyzing. The other two stages would cut across these to gather papers which provide frames and those which express arenas. All such categorizations, including the one we are using, suffer from some unevenness and a lack of fit. Furthermore, scholars who submitted papers for publication in this volume did not have any of these categories in mind when they wrote their pieces.

The structure which you have before you does require some explanation. First, it is grounded on the presentational categories which the authors themselves imply through the content of their work. The result is a long list of headings, but it is comprehensibly ordered. The first, *Overviewing and Assessing Qualitative IS Research*, includes the specifically assessment papers, those by Prasad, by King and Applegate, by Shaw and Jarvenpaa, and by Lau, and also the grand-tour assessment paper by Markus. The next heading, *Interpretation and IS Requirements Definition* contains the papers by Davidson, by Urquhart, and by Westrup. *Illustrating, Experiencing, and Being Critical in Ethnography* gathers together papers by Harvey, by Myer, by Ruhleder, and by Trauth. *Interviewing and the Interviewer* brings the paper by Janson, Guimaraes, Brown and Taillieu next to the one by Mantelaers. Three papers addressing *The Social and Political Context of IS* are those by Sawyer, by Silva and Backhouse, and by Romm and Pliskin. *Developments in Qualitative Methods* is a grouping of specifically methodological papers by Ang and Endeshaw, by Garcia and Quek, by Introna and Whitley, by Vidgen and Braa, by Walsham, by Gallivan, and by Paré and Elam.

1 OVERVIEWING AND ASSESSING QUALITATIVE IS RESEARCH

In a sense, all Working Conferences of 8.2 are about qualitative research. The Philadelphia meeting is distinct, however, because of the purposely self-reflective and evaluative stance it takes on qualitative approaches and their history in the information systems field. Markus, in the text of her keynote address, celebrates the status of widespread acceptance of qualitative research in the world of information systems researchers and calls for qualitative researchers to accept diversity in research approaches amongst ourselves; however, unlike other calls to (or criticisms of) diversity in information systems research, Markus additionally identifies the need for a "convergence on content," where attention to technological details is needed not only to develop good understandings of information systems, but also to differentiate ourselves from other fields that are becoming increasingly interested in the study of information technology. King and Applegate, whose overview and assessment paper about case research is written in hypertext and is available through a pointer on a World Wide Web page at www.isr.uci.edu, also acknowledges the acceptance of qualitative approaches, but that "qualitative research is viewed as a privilege reserved for those with tenure"; presented in the form of a case itself, their paper allows the reader to examine not only the epistemological and methodological debates, but also the politics of research, with which an untenured Assistant Professor must struggle when pursuing qualitative research in information systems. Looking less at the political context of doing research and more at its content, Lau's paper provides a somewhat dazzling overview and assessment of action research in information systems studies reported in literature over the last 25 years; he concludes by proposing a contemporary information-systems action research framework as a conceptual foundation and practical guide for researchers and practitioners interested in action research for information-systems studies. Shaw and Jarvenpaa, in their overview and assessment of information systems studies, describe and categorize over a score of such studies; whereas the annotation of the studies is useful in itself as a guide to the literature, the paper by Shaw and Jarvenpaa is no less useful citing instances of studies that combine elements of both process-theory research and variance-theory research, where these instances refuting any claims that hybrid research (combining elements of both process and variance research) is undesirable or inferior. In the final paper in this section, Prasad provides an overview of ethnography as a methodology to study information technologies and contrasts ethnography with other commonly used qualitative field research methods; her paper delves into features of qualitative research that lead some to call it intensive: the concern for "thick description," the plausibility of accounts, and the cultural context and the immersion of the researcher.

2 INTERPRETATION AND IS REQUIREMENTS DEFINITION

The three strong papers on requirements definition provide an excellent model for how to apply qualitative methods to a mainstream systems development problem. Through longitudinal, in-depth, qualitative field studies of information systems delivery processes, Davidson shows not only how appropriate data are collected, she also explains how it can be analyzed, using techniques honed in the analysis of narrative. A different narrative approach is taken by Urquhart, who uses a form of grounded theory to structure the interpretation of a set of dialogues. These interactions between analyst and client are presented in the form of an unfolding plot where features of the encounter are redefined and presented to check with participants that their intent had been properly represented. Another view of users is presented by Westrup, whose concern is to develop the methods devised by Enid Mumford and those which have come to be known as the Scandinavian cooperative approach for capturing the underlying goals of participants in the process of systems development. Here the capturing process involves a reinterpretation of the expressions of differing participants in the systems development process.

3 ILLUSTRATING, EXPERIENCING, AND BEING CRITICAL IN ETHNOGRAPHY

Myers encourages us to see the advantages of ethnographic methods. They get behind the reasoning of the participants, they have the advantages of structuralist techniques, and they are nonjudgmental. Walsham, judging by his contribution to this volume, would claim that it is not quite so easy, but at least we can see from Myers how immersion techniques work from his brief description of one case. Harvey manages, without being unduely self referential, to reflect ethnographically upon ethnography and does so by the use of Orlikowski's early work in the field. Although there is a potential for loops within loops of self consideration, Harvey avoids this by linking her interpretation of the process of ethnography to both pedagogical and methodological reasoning. Again, it shows that there are no shortcuts to the process of "getting inside." Another approach to explaining the problem of getting inside is that of Trauth, who reflects upon her own heartfelt experiences and provides many useful methodological pointers to prospective newcomers to ethnography. Those pointers have to some extent been anticipated by Ruhleder and Jordan, who demonstrate excellent research methods in their application of video-based interaction analysis to ethnography.

4 INTERVIEWING AND THE INTERVIEWER

Good interviewing techniques have stood at the base of much successful qualitative research in many social studies disciplines. The papers by Mantelaers and by Janson, Guimaraes, Brown and Taillieu demonstrate how such best practices can be used within information systems research. Mantelaers takes us through the steps in part of the design of an interview-based system design procedure. Here the pitfalls of various approaches are described and the specific advantages of proper elicitation techniques are demonstrated. Good elicitation was necessary for the Colruyt case presented by Janson et al. By quoting at length from the interviews themselves, we can see clearly how far in-depth they were able to go. Readers of this volume will have the opportunity to assess the relationship between the explicitly ethnographical approaches covered in the preceding section with the technique based approach of these studies of interviewing.

5 THE SOCIAL AND POLITICAL CONTEXT OF IS

Silva and Backhouse believe that "qualitative research in information systems should be led by theories grounded in interpretive and phenomonelogical premises to make sense and to be consistent." Theirs is an application of actor-network theory which, with three appearances in this volume (see also the papers by Walsham and by Introna and Whitley), might be regarded as a trend, at least among qualitative researchers in Britain. Appropriately, longitudinal analyses have been adopted by Romm and Pliskin as well as Sawyer and Southwick as the means of charting changing political pressures in organizations.

6 DEVELOPMENTS IN QUALITATIVE METHODS

Actor-network theory reappears in Walsham's paper, which draws together its features to help us make sense of its increasingly awkward and inconclusive application to IS research. His proposals are explicit and would affect many procedural matters if they were to take hold, such as the encouragement of longer texts and more detailed case studies. He also stresses the real distinction between morally judgmental analyses and other forms of research. It is not all that easy to have it both ways. Vigden and Braa advocate a means of adapting action research so that it can become useful as a realistic research strategy through the "action case." This is an advantage to doctoral students and, through their clear guidelines, to those who would need well delineated research practices.

There are many surprising results scattered throughout the papers in this volume. However, perhaps the most surprising result can be seen in the aggregate of qualitative research in the 1990s. Here, finally, we see the end of meek and tentative forays into qualitative methods as applied to information systems. No longer do we have to look to a very small group of pioneers who import methods from elsewhere. Now we can claim that there is a healthy and highly productive element of the study of information systems which draws maturely upon the best of a wide range of social investigative techniques.

7 BIOGRAPHY

Allen S. Lee is the Paul Paré Professor of MIS at McGill University and a senior editor at *MIS Quarterly*. A theme throughout his research has been the advancement of qualitative, interpretive, and case approaches in information systems research and their constructive relationship to quantitative, positivist, and large-sample approaches. He has published in *MIS Quarterly*, *Organization Science*, *Human Relations*, *Information & Management*, and *The Computer Journal*. He earned his doctorate at the Massachusetts Institute of Technology, his master's degree at the University of California at Berkeley, and his bachelor's degree at Cornell University.

Jonathan Liebenau is a Senior Lecturer in Information Systems and Chairman of the Information Society Observatory at the London School of Economics and Political Science. He is editor of the *European Journal of Information Systems* and has written eight books, including *Understanding Information* (with James Backhouse, London: Macmillan, 1990) and *Information Technology Policies and Applications in Commonwealth Developing Countries* (with G. Harindranath, London: Commonwealth Secretariat, 1993). He concentrates on two areas, information technology and economic development, and theories of information.

Part One

Overviewing and Assessing Qualitative IS Research

2

The Qualitative Difference in Information Systems Research and Practice

M. L. Markus
The Claremont Graduate School
Claremont, California 91711-6190 USA
Tel: (909) 607-3151
FAX: (909) 621-8564
E-mail: markusm@cgs.edu

Abstract

Since the Manchester conference on research methods in Information Systems (IS) more than ten years ago, qualitative IS researchers have made great strides toward acceptance both within the IS field and in broader academic communities. This is a major collective achievement of which we all should be proud. Yet, we may well have reached the point of diminishing returns in this direction. While incremental improvement is possible and desirable, many of us are motivated by more ambitious goals. Therefore, I invite you to join me in undertaking three ambitious ventures: celebrating diversity in qualitative methods, converging on content in our field, and pursuing practicality in IS research. These complementary activities are worthy in their own right and promise important instrumental benefits to our community of research practice.

In discussing what he would like to see me do in this address, Allen Lee asked me to conduct a grand tour of how well qualitative IS research has progressed since the Manchester and Copenhagen meetings and, also, what remains to be done. To me, "grand tour" conveys two rather contradictory images: leisurely strolls among the ruins of former civilizations and blitzkreig bus trips of crowded tourist traps.

Neither of these images suits my current perspective on qualitative research in the IS field. Instead, I prefer the image of the newspaper sports page – online, if you prefer. I'm not a great sports fan, but the metaphor seems more apt than that of a grand tour. On the sports page, the past is largely forgotten except for epic victories and defeats, but yesterday's game and future contests are thoroughly critiqued.

1 THE SCORE

In this vein, I will spend little time paying homage to the past. I will single out few significant papers, methodological contributions, or heroic researchers. We have them, and I honor them. But what matters most to me now is how our record adds up and the contests we will enter in the future.

1.1 Past Wins

As I look back over the proceedings of the Manchester and Copenhagen meetings and the research published in IS over the same time frame, it is clear to me that qualitative research has won at least one major championship – academic acceptance, both within the IS field and within the larger domain of academic management studies. Today, most high-status members of the IS community acknowledge that qualitative research methods occupy an important niche along with formal modeling and quantitative empirical methods (survey and experiments). Qualitative studies and methodological essays dealing with qualitative methods increasingly appear in our conferences and journals. Some research articles employing qualitative methods figure among the seminal studies read by IS doctoral students. An increasing number of IS doctoral programs teach qualitative research methods and legitimize use of qualitative methods in dissertation research. Further, members of our field whose work is largely or exclusively qualitative in method have been granted promotion and tenure in their respective institutions, signifying that academics from other management disciplines also accept the legitimacy of qualitative IS research. Members of our field have been appointed to the editorial boards of journals in other fields. Other signs of acceptance can be noted.

As those of us who have been in the IS field for more than ten years know, achieving academic acceptance for qualitative research methods was no small feat. Winning this collective championship involved the deployment of at least three distinct talents. One was persuasion. Some of our heroes organized awareness building sessions at conferences and wrote book chapters and articles about qualitative methods. These activities exposed everyone in our field to qualitative research methods and made an increasingly persuasive case for the legitimacy of these methods in IS championship events, like promotion decisions and selection of papers for publication in "A" journals. A second contribution was demonstration. Others of our former and current stars showed through published accounts that qualitative empirical work produces valuable insights and explanations of IS phenomena and contributes to the development of theory. We each have our own favorite exemplars of qualitative IS research. A third contribution was elucidation. Champions in this last area studied the process of qualitative research and identified the elements that constitute or contribute to rigor. This type of contribution has enabled us to evaluate, improve, and teach qualitative research to others in various professional settings (e.g., research supervision and reviewing).

As in every recognized sport, qualitative IS research has its own Hall of Fame. At the same time, the role of the sport in the larger society –its functions of occupation, entertainment, and inspiration –is a collective achievement, not merely a function of its stars. Therefore, while I honor our heroes, I hope you will forgive me for not singling you out and dwelling on your triumphs. Instead, I would like us all to appreciate the magnitude of our collective achievement. And I would you to join me in planning our next championship events.

1.2 Future Contests

As I see it, we have gone just about as far as we can in the game we have been playing. We have achieved academic acceptance; what more can we expect to win in this arena? It seems unlikely to me that qualitative research will ever be accepted as inherently superior to formal and quantitative research methods, either in IS or in academic management research more broadly. Further, it does not even seem desirable to me that we should choose this ambition as our goal. After all, many well-regarded modern philosophers of science argue persuasively that there is no scientific basis for claiming the superiority of any scientific research method. While we should, I believe, continuously strive to improve our methods and thereby maintain our legitimacy, our future big victories must lie elsewhere.

I believe that we qualitative IS researchers have a unique opportunity to exhibit leadership in three important and related new contests. These new arenas are the celebration of diversity in qualitative research, convergence on content in our field, and the appreciation of practicality in IS research. For each, I will say what it is and why I think it is important.

2 THE CELEBRATION OF DIVERSITY IN QUALITATIVE RESEARCH

As you know, one of John van Manaan's books on methods is entitled *Varieties [plural] of Qualitative Research* (Van Manaan, Dabbs and Faulkner 1982). At the same time, I'm aware, as I'm sure you are, of several other books with very similar titles (Strauss and Corbin 1990; Miles and Huberman 1994) that nevertheless address only one of many possible varieties of qualitative research – different in each case.

This casual observation symbolizes for me a part of our game that needs radical improvement.

At one level, those of us who specialize in qualitative research know that there are qualitatively different types of qualitative research in terms of philosophy, technique, and output. Consider the fact that the organizers of this conference commissioned survey papers on four different methods:

- the case study strategy,
- ethnography,
- action research, and
- critical social theory.

To this list one could add grounded theory development, hermeneutic interpretation and phenomenological inquiry, among others. In addition, many researchers use qualitative data collection and analysis techniques in conjunction with other types of rigorous and legitimate academic inquiry (e.g., surveys, formal or qualitative theoretical essays).

At another level, it is my observation that the differences among these methods are neither widely understood by our non-qualitative research colleagues nor truly respected by us. I have experienced, and I know that others in this room have experienced, reviews from qualitative research colleagues with the criticism that the right qualitative research philosophy or method has not been used. For instance, in his introduction to the proceedings of this conference, Allen Lee reported the comment of one author who felt that she should not have to apologize for being a positivist.

This troubles me deeply. It is an indication to me that we do not practice what we preach. When we argue for the legitimacy of qualitative research relative to formal and quantitative empirical methods, we claim that no method is inherently superior to any other. But when we review the research of qualitative research colleagues, we "diss"[1] those who do not do qualitative research exactly as we do. To me, this is pure and simple prejudice and an indication that we have turned a scientific technique into a religion.

I think of research methods as analogous to languages, artistic media, and technologies. Yes, there are, alas, wars over language, as over religion, but does this make any one language right? With my culturally diverse doctoral students, it is easy to explain the value of learning different methods in terms of learning different languages: Some languages can express concepts that will not translate into others. Learning new languages gives us new windows on the world.

Art provides another useful analogy with research methods. Newer media, like acrylics, photography, and performance art, may take years to become accepted as "artistic" and may never achieve true parity in perceived "artistic merit" with established media like oils. Nevertheless, only a reverse snob would call the new media

---

[1]"Diss" is ebonic for "disrespect."

superior. They are simply different, offering unique and valuable ways of representing creative vision.

For this audience, the most compelling analogy should be between research methods and technology. From our own collective body of IS research, we know the dual enabling and constraining nature of technology. While technology helps us do some things better than we could do without it, it can also prevent us from doing other things. For those, we need different tools. Similarly, one research method can answer certain kinds of questions that others can't answer quite as well, but they also prevent us from asking questions that our methods can't answer. That is, in part, why I think we should all learn more than one method. And, if we who claim to understand qualitative research argue that there is only one right way to do it, we are deliberately blinding ourselves to many interesting and important research questions and phenomena.

I'm certainly not saying that "anything goes" in qualitative research, any more than I would say that anything goes in an experiment. When someone claims to have used the case study research strategy, I believe that we are all well within our rights (and obligations) as supervisors and reviewers to demand that the researcher apply the method rigorously as documented by the experts in that method. Significant deviations from the documented approach of a particular method require careful justification. On the other hand, we should never forget that new research problems may necessitate methodological innovations. (For scientific rigor, the features of innovative methods should be methodically justified in theoretical or empirical terms.)

The potential consequences of religious fervor (as opposed to scientific rigor) in the area of research methods are extremely negative. First, religious fervor stifles innovation. Second, it promotes unproductive conflicts and bad feelings within our relatively small community of researchers. Life is too short for this. Third, by failing to accept, or better yet, to celebrate the diversity among us, we unnecessarily risk our future evolutionary development. While life is short, extinction is eternal. Fourth, petty rivalries within our ranks distract us from fun and challenging opportunities to make positive contributions to the world at large.

3 CONVERGENCE ON CONTENT

Convergence on content is a second new contest which I propose that we as qualitative IS researchers should enter. By this I mean a concerted coming together of the disparate, even divisive, substantive factions in our field.

In the last few years I have heard many of our colleagues around the world express concerns about the signs of fragmentation in our field. One bit of evidence, frequently cited, is the emergence of small specialized conferences, such as WITS and

WISE[2], that entice some of us away from meetings intended to represent the larger community, such as ICIS or AIS[3]. WITS and WISE are scheduled to precede ICIS and so, in theory, do not directly compete with ICIS for attendance. However, I am told that some attendees in these specialized meetings do not attend ICIS, claiming that it has much less value for them. To my mind, this suggests that some of the institutions intended to represent our entire field have ironically become too specialized to do so. They have, in essence, evolved into internally homogeneous factions, not unlike the new groups that hoist their own flags.

Some of you will undoubtedly see these as natural events or even as positive developments. In most living systems, differentiation increases with size. In human systems, involvement and commitment tend to decrease with size. Therefore, the emergence of small, internally homogeneous subfields can be viewed both as an inevitable result of our success as a academic field and as an essential development for the well being of our members.

However, I am deeply concerned that our field may be, not merely differentiating, but splitting into disconnected parts. If so, the trend is neither inevitable nor desirable. In my view, the splintering of our field would be a tragic loss. If the schisms just involved methodological differences, they would be bad enough, for reasons I argued earlier. However, because methods limit what can be learned as well as enabling important other learning, the splitting also involves ideas and research content. Intellectual compartmentalization poses serious threats to any academic field, by reducing the stimulus for creative innovation and growth.

Right now, three broad subfields in IS are in danger of growing apart. One group consists of researchers who mainly employ economic methods to address macro-level issues in IT use, management, and impacts. A second group predominantly uses engineering approaches to IT design and development. A third group uses non-economic behavioral and social science methods (both quantitative and qualitative) to address mainly the micro-level problems associated with IS development and use. The diversity of content addressed within the IS field should be a great strength. But the splintering of our community could make diversity a great weakness, by cutting us off from each others' thinking and increasing the divisiveness among methods-based factions.

Let me discuss one area in particular where fragmentation in our field seems already to be having negative consequences. Many of the behavioral science IS articles I have read recently, regardless of whether they are quantitative or qualitative in method, have almost totally ignored technological details – the features, if you will

---

[2]WITS is the Workshop on Information Technology and Systems; WISE is the Workshop on Information Systems Economics.

[3]ICIS is the International Conference on Information Systems; AIS is the Association for Information Systems.

– of the information technology used in the studied settings. Why does this neglect of technology in behavioral IS research happen? Is it because technology is like the air we breathe, so pervasive that we hardly notice it? Is it because our focus on academic respectability and methodological excellence has distracted us from the substance of our field? Is it because we collectively reject materialism and embrace social construction, so that we "know" that technology itself does not matter?

Whatever the reason, the negative consequences are clear: Neither we nor others who read our work learn much about how variations in technology features shape human behavior. Further, we close ourselves off to opportunities to influence, and to learn from, other researchers and practitioners for whom technology details are the most interesting (if not the only important) aspect of IT. Finally, we unnecessarily expose ourselves to invidious comparisons with researchers in other fields (e.g., psychology and sociology) who are increasingly interested in IT. Put differently, I believe that we as members of the IS field have absolutely no comparative advantage in the study of behavioral issues related to IT unless we can draw handsomely upon a unique understanding of technological matters that elude most people in other fields.[4]

An example from the CSCW[5] field of the type of qualitative research I would like to read more frequently in IS involves a study of electronic calendaring systems. Grudin and a colleague studied user behavior around two different calendar programs and found that social practices varied with system defaults (Grudin and Palen 1995). I can think of only a few examples of behavioral IS research that exhibit a similar level of technological detail. Yet, a growing body of research (much of it done by people outside IS) suggests that technological details matter (Griffith and Northcraft 1994).

In my view, lack of technological detail in behavioral IS research is a sad reflection of harmful content divergence in our field. Yet, it's one thing for me to advocate our pulling together, and quite another when we starting talking about who should take the first step. I argue that the first step should be taken by those of us who study the social and behavioral issues in IS. I think that we have more to gain by joining our technologically (and economically) oriented colleagues than they have from joining us; conversely, we also have more to lose intellectually and politically from content divergence than they do. Further, I believe it is possible for us to move toward these colleagues without losing the perspectives, methods, and skills that make us special. As evidence, I cite the CSCW meetings, which exhibit high tolerance for both engineering and social scientific perspectives. At those conferences, the juxtaposition of different approaches has usually generated more innovation and excitement than it has

---

[4]Individually, of course, some of us may compete quite successfully with members of other fields.

[5]Computer-supported cooperative work.

conflict. In short, I am arguing that greater content convergence in our field (maintaining diversity of method) is a contest for us qualitative IS researchers to enter and play to win. The payoffs of even a modest success will include accumulation of knowledge, community strength, and greater practical contributions – the arena I'll discuss next.

4 THE APPRECIATION OF PRACTICALITY IN IS RESEARCH

A third new championship I think we should enter is the appreciation of practical knowledge. I am using the word appreciation in the dual sense of growth (as in real estate appreciation) and of admiration (as in art appreciation). By practical research, I mean academic research that seeks primarily to describe, qualify or measure, evaluate or interpret practice in publications for academics. I am deliberately contrasting practical research with theoretical research, which seeks primarily to build or test academic theory, and with practitioner research, which addresses practitioners' concerns and is written for practitioners. Therefore, by appreciation of practical research, I mean that we as an academic field should (collectively) consume, reward, and contribute more heavily to a literature about what is going on in practice than we do today.

Several objections are undoubtedly forming in your minds. I'd like to dispel some of them, so that we can focus on the ones that really count. I am certainly not saying that all of our collective research output should be practical in nature. I recognize that academic theoretical work is fun and interesting in its own right, and it is important for academic legitimacy, among other reasons. I am merely saying that we should think of our collective research output as a portfolio and that we should expand the portion of our portfolio allocated to practical research.

I am also not saying that none of our work should be devoted to writing directly for practitioners and researching issues that addresses their concerns. This, too, is important work, and we probably don't do enough of it now. However, I am suggesting that we as academics should value, as a legitimate academic contribution, rigorous research that describes and evaluates what is going on in practice, even if that work makes no immediate attempt to build or test academic theory. I believe we should do this because it supports our educational mission and because it is useful for both theoretical research and research for practitioners.

4.1 Educate Practitioners

Many of us are educators in professional schools as well as being researchers. We have a collective responsibility to help our students apply in practice the theories and skills we teach them in the classroom. But many of us face considerable challenges in discharging this responsibility. One is the high rate of change in technology and practice that quickly renders textbooks and teaching materials obsolete. Historically, such materials have been one of the most important sources – other than personal experience and the trade press – of shared academic knowledge about the state of practice. I am personally quite concerned about the consequences of this rate of change in our field.

Let me give you a personal example from own work. When I started in this field, it was widely considered "best practice" to build information systems to fit an organization's existing business practices. We knew that lack of fit between systems and business practices gave rise to inefficiencies and resistance. However, it was also known that automating existing business processes that were inefficient or ineffective was not a good idea, since this approach often failed to produce the desired business benefits. Eventually, this insight crystallized with some ideas about what makes business processes good or bad and came to be known as "business process reengineering." The new best practice was to streamline business processes before system development. Or, perhaps I should say, the new best practice was to build new systems after the business processes had been carefully reengineered.

In the meantime, however, a generational shift had occurred from mainframe and midrange architectures to client-server computing. Many companies discovered that this was a competence-destroying shift; a number of large client-server projects failed at great expense. Simultaneously, software development firms began marketing integrated enterprise software packages[6] in versions designed for the client-server architecture. The vendors claimed that these packages were very flexible – that is, capable of supporting a wide range of business processes – and that the packages incorporated the best practices in each functional area – that is, they were useful both after and before business process reeengineering. Many companies are now buying and installing these packages instead of developing their own client-server based administrative systems.

I recently studied three leading companies that had successfully installed such packages. As far as I can tell, their logic, which may well be today's best practice, can be summarized as follows:

> Don't always reengineer business processes first. Instead, purchase and install a leading enterprise software package with no modifications (if at all possible), even if this means changing business practices.[7] Chances are, you'll end up with a better business process than before because of built-in best practices, and you'll certainly have a more time and cost-

---

[6]Examples include SAP's R/3, Peoplesoft, and BAAN software.

[7]Installation of these packages involves filling in parameters in hundreds of tables but does not normally require writing or modifying software code. Modifying the code of an enterprise software package involves expense, delay, and risk; package vendors often refuse to provide ongoing support for packages that are modified by their purchasers.

effective installation than with either custom development or package modification. If the process still isn't as good as you'd like, reengineer and change the package set-up, again without modifying it, so that you can continue to rely on vendor maintenance and enhancement.

In short, if you are old-timer like me and if you accept this summary as a statement of today's best practice in IS, you will certainly agree that best practice in our field has changed considerably from what it was twenty, or even five, years ago.

So, what's the problem here? The problem is the lag between this view of current best practice and that which you'll find in many current textbooks and teaching cases. In many intro courses, we're still in a mentality of building custom software for unique organizational needs while the world around us is demanding that we find ways to satisfy unique needs with generic software and components. As one of my experienced students recently exclaimed, "I've been in this field 25 years, and I've just realized that everything we do is 'one off.' But the vendors are approaching things in an entirely different manner."

The mentalities we help to shape can last a very long time – the entire careers of some of our students. But the generations of technology are much shorter (on the order of ten years) and may be shrinking. If our academic appreciation of practice doesn't change as fast as practice, we may be preparing our students for certain and rapid career extinction, particularly at times of major technical discontinuities. Peter Keen and other respected industry observers have estimated that only about half of IS professionals imbued with the mainframe mentality can make the mental shift to client-server computing. Are we still teaching important aspects of the mainframe mentality – like one off development? If so, how long will it be before we can present an up-to-date perspective on practice? Five years, perhaps? If so, that is about the time, technology analysts tell us, we can expect to see full-blown emergence of the next computing architecture. We'll again be out of synch.

Please understand me, here. I know that most of your departments offer courses in the latest architectural concepts and technologies. My worry is that our collective understanding of practice is not state-of-the-art and that our students may be suffering as a result. Qualitative IS researchers can exhibit great influence in turning this situation around.

4.2 We Should Eat Our Own Dogfood

A second reason I believe we need to produce and consume academically legitimate practical research involves professional values. Knowledge about practice must go into the advice we give practitioners, and it is also an important ingredient in sound theoretical development and testing. If we believe our practical knowledge is good enough for practitioners and for theoretical researchers, we ought to be willing to prove this by consuming it, writing it for, and reading it, ourselves. In Microsoft

Corporation, this organizational value is known as "eating our own dogfood."[8] I'll add that if eating one's own dogfood is good enough for Microsoft, it should be good enough for us.

When I first began preparing this talk, I thought I would be speaking more about doing research for a practitioner audience. This is something that I care a good deal about, as a result of my own historical experience, my research for the Advanced Practices Council of SIM International, and more recently my research for the Financial Executives Research Foundation.[9] I have come to experience firsthand the great lack of credibility we academics have in the practitioner community. This credibility gap concerns me, because it affects our long-term economic well being and quality of work life as academics.

I asked myself how I would teach the skills of doing research for practitioners to doctoral students who lacked a strong background in practice or consulting. I reread two excellent books that I highly recommend, *Usable Knowledge*, by Lindblom and Cohen (1979), and *Methods for Policy Research*, by Ann Majchrak (1984). I realized what should have been obvious to me at the outset: to do good research that is intended to be useful to practitioners (as opposed to work that achieves the same result through serendipity), it is useful (if not essential) to think like a practitioner. For example, practitioners rarely get excited about theories that do not include variables that they can do something about. Ann Majchrzak calls these "malleable variables," and they are conspicuously absent from much academic IS research. Majchrzak explains that one of the first steps in good research for practice is learning how decisions related to the research topic get made, because this helps the researcher understand what kind of research results are likely to be used by practitioners.

So, my question then became "How would I teach IS doctoral students without significant practical or consulting experience to think like practitioners (as well as academics)?" This question produced the same sort of frustration I have felt when trying to teach IS or organizational behavior to students who entirely lack real-world business experience. I know that some of you excel at this, and I wish I knew how you do it.

It is clearly a challenge for us as academics to acquire and maintain both the academic and the practical mindsets, and it is even more challenging to teach them both effectively. I believe, however, that we need to try, and that developing the attitude of appreciation for practice would be a great start. In our culture, appreciation manifests itself in research activities, including writing, speaking, and reading

---

[8]In other words, Microsoft uses its own products whenever possible. Operating systems developers often work by "bootstrapping" – using the operating system under development as the development environment.

[9]The Advanced Practices Council is headed by Bob Zmud, who has written about the importance of research for practitioners in recent editorial statements in *MIS Quarterly*.

related works. I believe that we as IS academics need a literature about practice written by and for us. I call this literature practical research.[10]

4.3 What Is Good Practical Research?

If you agree that practical IS research fills important needs, you may still need to be convinced that it is something that we qualitative IS researchers should include in our portfolio of activities. I hardly need to convince you that this is something we can do: with some shift in mindset, perhaps, our methods are ideally suited to practical research. Instead, I'll try to show why we need to do it, because it requires skills we have and because it is something that no other group of professionals has the skills and incentives to do.

I will define practical IS research as the "scientific observation" of IS practice that is documented in the public domain, where "scientific observation" is defined as "deliberate search, carried out with care and forethought, as contrasted with the casual and largely passive perceptions of everyday life."[11] Kaplan goes on to note that "It is the deliberateness and control of observation that is distinctive of science, not merely the use of special instruments" such as telescopes or social science data-gathering devices. To these special instruments, I would add academic theory: the way in which we codify our understandings and communicate them to other scientists. Put differently, systematic observation of plants and animals is scientific, even in the absence of a theory to explain the observations. Similarly, research that systematically observes IS practice is a scientific contribution, even in the absence of explicit theory that predicts or explains the observations.

Contrasts with Other Contributions

Practical research is qualitatively different from other important contributions to knowledge made by academics and other professionals. However, it is superficially similar to some activities that we do not usually regard as academic or scientific. This similarity may cause some people to devalue practical research or fear that doing practical research would be disrespected. Fortunately, we qualitative IS researchers are trained to see through such distracting illusions. We of all people should see the uniqueness and importance of practical research.

Practical research differs from the development of teaching materials. Textbook and teaching case writers have different audiences and objectives than practical researchers. They write primarily for novices, rather than for people with substantial expertise; their goal is to convey basic concepts or to provide a shared context in

---

[10]Again, I contrast practical research with literature about practice for practitioners.

[11]Quote from Abraham Kaplan's "The Conduct of Inquiry," cited in Lindblom and Cohen 1979, p. 16.

which mutual discovery can occur. While researchers may obtain new insights from these words, their main research value accrues to their authors. By contrast, practical researchers write for other researchers. They generally omit details that novices need but experts know and include details that distract novices but interest experts.

Similarly, practical research differs from journalism. The genres of journalism can be loosely categorized as "news" – reportage of current events – and "features" – detailed exploration or analysis of events or news makers. In general, journalists write for the public-at-large or for the modal member of a specialist audience, rather than for experts. In many cases, journalists are not experts in the topics they report, although they are often much better informed than their average reader. By contrast, practical researchers are experts writing for other experts. They judge themselves by standards of argumentation and evidence that are qualitatively different than those journalists use. In addition, practical researchers subject their work to review by peers, who control access to publication venues.

Practical research also differs from consulting and contract research. Most consultation and contract research is proprietary, meaning that the funders can restrict the publication and dissemination of knowledge. Funders may, for example, have the legal authority to block publication, censor certain details, impose publication delays, select publication venues, impose heavy charges for research reports, etc. Further, they, rather than researchers, may dictate key terms of the investigation. By contrast, practical researchers are committed to publishing their findings in the public domain. While research subjects and collaborators may exert some influence over the terms of investigation, practical researchers usually retain control over major research design decisions.

Theoretical research also differs from pedagogy, journalism, consulting, and contract research. What, then, are the essential differences between theoretical and practical research? Theoretical research is committed to the development and testing of academic theory – a particular knowledge form in which academics codify their understandings, explanations, and predictions in abstract terms and concepts. By contrast, practical research emphasizes disciplined empirical observations and ordinary knowledge[12] about why things happen. Practical research honors concrete details, commonsense observations, and practitioners' rationales. It requires no immediate use of or contribution to abstract academic theory. On the other hand, practical research is not hostile or antithetical to theoretical research. Theoretical researchers will find practical research invaluable in theory development and in constructing sound tests of theory.

In other words, practical research is a qualitatively different type of academic contribution from theoretical research. Both are independently worthy of publication

---

[12]See Lindblom and Cohen (1979) for a good discussion of ordinary knowledge and its relationship to scientific knowledge.

and other forms of appreciation in our community. We should not expect that every academician will excel at both.

Examples of Practical Research Genres

To make the contrasts between practical research and other important contributions clearer, I'll give a few examples of practical research genres that are, I believe, sorely needed in the rapidly changing IS field.

Revelatory cases. When is a single descriptive case study or small sample survey an important scientific contribution? According to case study expert Robert Yin (1994), revelatory cases can be invaluable to the scientific community when they involve unique, highly inaccessible, or leading-edge situations. Examples in IS include first-in-the-world (or biggest or best) IT applications, unusual business processes, and previously unexamined user behaviors or strategies for managing information technology. My personal favorite example of work in this genre is Tom Malone's study (1983) of the files and piles in people's workplaces. The expert academic reader of that paper in that historical era could instantly grasp the significance of the contribution made by Malone's disciplined observations and could put his ideas to use without further empirical or theoretical work by Malone.

Dissertation committee chairs may always require their students to demonstrate competence in theoretical research. Nevertheless, it is hard to credit arguments that would exclude insightful, disciplined observations like Malone's as publishable scientific contributions. Peer reviewers of work in this genre should have no trouble generating evaluation criteria that match the methodological rigor they demand to the scope of the author's claims or to the importance of the topic.

Comparisons. A second genre of practical research consists of comparative studies that identify similarities and differences in application features, process flows, or management policies and practices against important theoretical or practical criteria. For instance, I have heard it said that certain enterprise software packages are better suited to certain types of organizations or business processes than others. This strikes me as an important empirical question within the intellectual domain of our field. I'd like to read in our literature about how different types of enterprise packages actually handle different types of business processes and the potential and actual implications for their adopting organizations.

My personal favorite study in this genre is a working paper by Chris Kemerer and a colleague on the mortgage loan application systems developed by different financial organizations. The authors subsequently published a theoretical paper using their case data (Hess and Kemerer 1994), but I've long believed that the original, more descriptive, paper was itself worthy of note (e.g., of publication). Again, I believe that it is possible for us to establish high enough standards for the peer review of such comparative studies that we can appropriately appreciate them as academic contributions.

I might add here that the disciplined comparison of IT products and services is perhaps the major arena in which practitioners would welcome input from academics.

Practitioners may well wonder whether the reports they read in trade publications have been influenced by advertising dollars. More important, they well may wonder how technical benchmarks interact or relate to important business criteria. It seems to me that IS academics, in general, and we qualitative IS researchers, in particular, are ideally positioned to make important contributions in this practical domain.

Evaluations. A third potentially important genre of practical research involves after-the-fact evaluations of various sorts: How usable was that software feature or package (and what can we learn from assessing it)? How effective was that application in various contexts? How effective were those implementation tactics or change processes? What impacts had that type of systems had?

We as qualitative IS researchers already know a great deal about usability, use, implementation, and impacts from a theoretical point of view. I'm not saying that we know all we need to know theoretically and that we shouldn't strive to know more. However, I'll wager that we collectively know more about these topics theoretically than we do empirically and practically. And I feel this hampers me personally in my teaching and research. I love to read disciplined observations of these phenomena, and I am personally impatient when theoretical material demanded by reviewers pushes out useful empirical detail from an academic article. Rather than increasing page lengths, I like us to have fora for both practical and theoretical work and to treat well executed practical research as a legitimate scientific contribution.

Conceptual essays. A fourth potentially important genre involves disciplined assessments of practice in light of existing theory or known best practice. Why, for example, do "Microsoft Secrets" (Cusumano and Selby 1995) represent a significant departure from the traditional IS system development life cycle, and what does this mean, if anything, for IS teaching and research? What is different, if anything, about the ways in which the CSCW and IS communities view the world, and why should we care? Interpretive analyses may apply academic theory, but they may equally represent disciplined factual or pre-theoretical arguments about the important practical issues in our field.

4.4 What Would it Take to Appreciate Practical Research

Appreciation is never having to say you're sorry for "exploratory research." All research is exploratory, even research that seeks to confirm or disconfirm theory. No one study is conclusive, no matter what its findings or who finds them. Confirmation and disconfirmation of theory are matters of consensus among scientists. In the absence of consensus, all research is exploratory. And in this context, practical research is every bit as much a contribution to the scientific enterprise as is theory development and testing. The real questions for all research should be "Is it important and interesting?" and "Is it well done?"

Practical research should by no means be everything we as IS academics do. Again, I see this as a portfolio allocation decision, and just to start discussion, I'll suggest that practical research – that is, research about practice by and for academics – should be roughly 30% of our collective portfolio, and research for practitioners should be maybe another 30%. Individuals will have portfolio allocation decisions, too, with some devoting 100% of their efforts to theoretical work, at least at certain stages of their careers. Others with different personal or institutional missions will allocate their efforts differently.

Clearly, my vision of appreciating practical research needs practical implementation steps. Most important in my view are publication outlets or tracks for practical research that we collectively value in assessing others' contributions. Appropriate criteria for peer evaluation of these works will emerge naturally once we have the joint commitment to them as important and interesting contributions to our science.

5 CONCLUSIONS

In this conceptual essay, I have argued that we played a great game yesterday. We won the major championship of academic acceptance. We should continue to play in this game and we should continue to play to win. However, because the big wins in academic acceptance are behind us, we have the opportunity now to find exciting new challenges and to develop new skills.

I have identified three important new arenas for us: celebration of our methodological diversity, convergence on our unique IS content, and appreciation for IS practice. Fundamentally, these three games all relate to one essential goal: respect for individual differences in talents and contributions. I hope that we qualitative IS researchers will enter all three games and play to win. The world needs us all and what we have to give.

6 REFERENCES

Cusumano, M. A., and Selby, R. A. (1995). "*Microsoft Secrets: How the World's Most Powerful Software Company Creates Technology, Shapes Markets, and Manages People*. New York: Free Press.

Griffith, T L., and Northcraft, G. (1994). "Distinguishing Between the Forest and the Trees: Media, Features, and Methodology in Electronic Communication Research." *Organization Science*, Volume 5, Number 2 (May), pp. 272-285.

Grudin, J., and Palen, L. (1995). "Why Groupware Succeeds: Discretion or Mandate?" *Proceedings of ECSCW '95*. Dordrecht, The Netherlands: Kluwer, pp. 263-278.

Hess, C. M., and Kemerer, C. F. (1994). "Computerized Loan Origination Systems: An Industry Case Study of the Electronic Markets." *MIS Quarterly*, Volume 18, Number 3 (September), pp. 251-275.

Lindblom, C. E., and Cohen, D. K. (1979). *Usable Knowledge: Social Science and Social Problem Solving*. New Haven, Connecticut: Yale University Press.

Majchrzak, A. (1984). *Methods for Policy Research*. Thousand Oaks, California: Sage Publications.

Malone, T. W. (1983). "How Do People Organize Their Desks? Implications for the Design of Office Information Systems." *ACM Transactions on Office Information Systems*, Volume 1, Number 1 (January), pp. 99-112.

Miles, M. B., and Huberman, A. M. (1944). *Qualitative Data Analysis: An Expanded Sourcebook*, Second Edition. Newbury Park, California: Sage Publications.

Strauss, A., and Corbin, J. (1990). *Basics of Qualitative Research: Grounded Theory Procedures and Techniques*. Newbury Park, California: Sage Publications.

Van Maanen, J.; Dabbs, Jr., J. M.; and Faulkner, R. R. (1982). *Varieties of Qualitative Research*. Newbury Park, California: Sage Publications.

Yin, R. K. (1994). *Case Study Research: Design and Methods*, Second Edition. Newbury Park, California: Sage Publications.

7 BIOGRAPHY

M. Lynne Markus is Professor of Information Science and Management at the Peter F. Drucker Graduate Management Center, The Claremont Graduate School. Her research focuses on the role of information technology in organizational design, performance, and change. In 1996, she visited ISEG at the Universidade Technica de Lisboa, Portugal, as Fulbright/FLAD Chair in Information Systems. Dr. Markus has also taught at the School of Accountancy and Business, Nanyang Technological University, Singapore, the John E. Anderson Graduate School of Management at UCLA, and the Alfred P. Sloan School of Management at MIT and has consulted with Arthur D. Little, Inc. She holds a B.S. in Industrial Engineering from the University of Pittsburgh and a Ph.D. in Organizational Behavior from Case Western Reserve University.

3

Crisis in the Case Study Crisis: Marginal Diminishing Returns to Scale in the Quantitative-Qualitative Research Debate

J. L. King
Center for Research on Information Technology
and Organizations (CRITO)
University of California
Irvine, California 92697 USA
Tel: (714) 824-5244
Fax: (714) 824-8091
E-mail: king@ics.uci.edu

L. M. Applegate
Harvard Business School
Baker West 182
Soldiers Field
Boston, Massachusetts 02163 USA
Tel: (617) 495-6362
Fax: (617) 496-2910
E-mail: lapplegate@hbs.edu

Abstract

The quest for legitimation of research approaches preoccupies many information systems researchers. Researchers who have adopted various forms of "qualitative" research seem particularly concerned about legitimating their work. This desire for legitimation is stimulated in part by ongoing debates about the nature of human understanding and the way we come to know about the world. In healthy circumstances this produces a useful, self-critical discussion that heads to improvements in the development and execution of research projects. Often, however, these debates are facades. They cover an underlying political struggle for position within the broad patronage structure of the academic world. Certain approaches are seen as "better" – more scientific, more rigorous, more formal, more pure – while others are marginalized as weak, journalistic, and even "atheoretical." These political dynamics are compounded by practical considerations (e.g., the length of time and cost required to conduct rigorous case research and the need for access to managers within companies) and the requirement for a researcher to have achieved a certain level of management and business sophistication to effectively collect and analyze qualitative data.

These realities serve as powerful barriers to case research for all academics. For doctoral students and nontenured faculty, these obstacles are often insurmountable. As a result, few doctoral programs teach students to conduct rigorous qualitative research and the body of knowledge on how to conduct and evaluate such research is not well developed. It is no surprise that qualitative research is viewed as a privilege reserved for those with tenure.

All of this comes at a time when the need for qualitative research is reaching crisis proportions. Faced with a fast-paced, rapidly-changing and complex environment, managers are placing increasing pressure on educational institutions to prepare students to deal with current business realities. Faculty are expected to be knowledgeable of the issues facing managers in the 1990s and to be able to offer solutions to these problems. They are expected to deal with these issues in a holistic manner, rather than segmenting knowledge along narrow functional and discipline-based lines. This type of knowledge is best developed through qualitative, field research that enables deep understanding of a complex phenomena. But, with the tenure clock ticking and a fundamental lack of the skills and understanding required to conduct this type of research, most untenured faculty are forced to fall back on traditional, quantitative research methods.

This paper presents the dilemma faced by an untenured faculty member who is deeply interested in a research problem that is best explored through case research. Through the struggles of the new Assistant Professor, the paper explores the epistemological, political and methodological debates that surround qualitative, case research. The paper is constructed for academic legitimacy in the information systems field. The paper is constructed as a hypertext document and is available in full on the World Wide Web. Access pointers can be obtained from the web site www.isr.uci.edu and can be searched for by the word "ducktest" in any of the commonly used search engines.

BIOGRAPHY

John L. King's current research focuses on the development of high-level requirements for information systems design and implementation. This research is informed by study of the ways in which organizational and institutional forces shape how information technology is developed (including what gets developed) and how the technologies that do get developed change the course of organizational and institutional behavior. The research draws on the fields of economics and other social sciences as well as the engineering sciences. The goal of the work is to improve the design of information technologies for both organizational and institutional usability, through better articulating the processes of requirements analysis, specification, and prototype creation. The work also informs policy and strategy development at the firm, sectoral, and institutional levels. Current projects include a study of institutional policies in shaping global and national information infrastructure in the U.S., Asia and Europe; a study of the evolution of systems requirements in intermodal transport and logistics; examination of California criminal courts as a venue of computer-supported cooperative work implementation; and study of the technical and institutional co-evolution of standards and technical infrastructure in global land-line and cellular telephony. Dr. King is Professor in both Information and Computer Science the Graduate School of Management at the University of California, Irvine, and is Editor-in-Chief of *Information Systems Research*, a leading academic journal published. He holds a Ph.D. in Administration from the University of California, Irvine.

Lynda M. Applegate is a Professor of Business Administration at Harvard Business School. The focus of her research and teaching is the impact of information technology on organizations, industries and markets. She has authored or coauthored two books, over 25 articles and over 140 business cases and related teaching materials (including videotapes and software) on this topic. Several of her papers have won awards as the best paper at leading information systems and management conferences and a number of her cases are HBS Publishing best sellers. Lynda is a senior editor for *MIS Quarterly*, an Associate Editor for *The Journal of Organizational Computing and Electronic Commerce*, and is on the editorial board of *Organization Science*. She is on the Board of Directors of MicroAge, Inc. and is on the Strategic Advisory Boards of Mainspring Communications (an Internet start-up) and the Alliance Analyst. Lynda was recently appointed to the Information Technology Council, an advisory board that assists the Congress in defining U.S. information policy.

4

A Review on the Use of Action Research in Information Systems Studies

F. Lau
Faculty of Business
University of Alberta
Edmonton, Alberta, Canada
Tel: (403) 492-5828
Fax: (403) 492-3325
E-mail: flau@gpu.srv.ualberta.ca

Abstract

This paper examines the use of action research in information systems (IS) studies reported in literature over the last twenty-five years. Thirty such field studies and discussion papers on information technology, system design/use or socio-technical systems were reviewed and compared with those from social science. Evolving patterns are noted among these IS studies in terms of their underlying assumptions, study designs and presentation styles. A contemporary IS action research framework is proposed as a conceptual foundation and practical guide for researchers and practitioners interested in action research for IS studies. Its implications in IS research and practice are discussed.

1 INTRODUCTION

Over the past twenty-five years, there has been a gradual shift from the predominately positivist view toward the use of alternative modes of inquiry in information systems (IS) studies. Among the pivotal milestones were the International Federation of Information Processing (IFIP) and Harvard Business School research colloquia held in 1984 at Manchester and Boston, respectively, where academics and practitioners discussed different approaches to understanding information systems and their implications in IS research and practice (Mumford et al. 1985; McFarlan 1985). These range from theorem-proving, laboratory experiments and survey research within the traditional positivistic realm, to case studies and field experiments that are more descriptive in nature, to such interpretive and emancipatory forms of inquiry as phenomenology and action research. From both colloquia there was a recognized need for alternative theory assumptions and methods to address the diversity of contexts and processes in IS research, and that prior beliefs of researchers and participants can influence what is observed and deemed significant.

Since that time, there has been a modest but growing number of IS publications on the use of alternative theories and methods to explore the organizational, behavioral and social consequences of information systems planning, development, adoption and use (Banville and Landry 1989; Checkland 1989; Lee 1989; Lacity and Janson 1994; Markus and Robey 1988; Orlikowski 1992; Walsham 1995). Perhaps the collective writings from the 1990 IFIP WG 8.2 Conference best epitomize the pleas for methodological pluralism in IS research through diverse approaches that range from grounded theory, action research, argumentative reviews, critical social theory, cooperative design, to hermeneutics (Nissen, Klein and Hirschheim 1991). Other examples of such IS studies include the use of grounded theory to examine the adoption and use of CASE tools (Orlikowski 1993), critical approach to changing accounting systems within organizational contexts (Laughlin 1987), multimethod investigation of managers' use of email through the information richness theory (Markus 1994), and ethnographic descriptions of the effects of new technology on management accounting practices (Jonsson and Gronlund 1988). While some IS researchers have suggested the use of these alternative approaches as complementary to those of positivism, others have advocated their adoption as the emerging interpretive paradigm to replace the so-called prevailing "positivism rhetoric" (Walsham 1995).

One such alternative mode of inquiry to be reviewed in this paper is action research, which has been used in the field of social science since the 1940s as a research strategy that integrates theory and practice through change and reflection (Argyris, Putnam and Smith 1985; Lewin 1947; Reason 1993a). With the emergence of multiple research paradigms and methodologies in IS, there is a need for researchers and practitioners to gain a better understanding of the various approaches in terms of their epistemological stance, how they are used in IS research, and their influence on IS practice. Such writings are found lacking for action research in IS. In this paper, we describe the evolving patterns of action research in IS and social science based on an exploratory review of related literature over the last twenty-five years. We then propose a contemporary IS action research framework according to the emerging varieties of action research observed. The intent of this framework is to provide a conceptual foundation and a practical guide for researchers and practitioners wishing to understand, review or conduct action research in IS studies. Implications of this framework on IS research and practice are also discussed.

2 THE LITERATURE REVIEW PROCESS

2.1 Literature Sources

A review of the literature on action research published over the last twenty-five years was conducted. The literature sources consisted of journals, conference proceedings, monographs and textbooks from the areas of business, health, education, and social science. The keywords used were action research, action inquiry, action science and cooperative inquiry – based on the terms used by Reason (1993a). These were then combined with the terms information systems, computer, technology and software to identify those publications where information technology was involved in the study. Over 600 action research related articles were found initially and categorized as one of action research field studies in IS, action research field studies in other areas, discussion papers on action research in IS, general discussion papers and books on action research, or discussion papers on IS research methodologies that included action research. For this study, we focused mainly on IS related action research field studies and discussion papers. Selected articles on the epistemology of action research, exemplary cases from a special issue of *Human Relations*, and subsequent critiques of these cases were also included for comparison. Based on these constraints, seventy articles were retrieved in time for the review. Of the articles obtained, twenty are action research fields studies related to information systems, information management, socio-technical systems, or software design/use; ten are discussion papers on action research in IS. The remaining are three articles on IS research methodologies that included action research, five exemplary action research cases from social sciences, eight critiques of these cases, and twenty-four discussion papers on action research in general. To observe the evolving patterns of action research over time, the thirty IS articles were organized into four periods for the review: 1971-80, 1981-85, 1986-90 and 1991-95.

2.2 Review Criteria

To provide a meaningful comparison of the different IS action research studies unveiled, a set of review criteria was established from writings on the pedagogy of qualitative research paradigms and the epistemology of action research. These are described below.

Pedagogy of Qualitative Research
A comprehensive pedagogy for qualitative research is provided by Denzin and Lincoln (1993) where they describe it as a process with five distinct phases: (a) the researcher's view and tradition; (b) the theoretical paradigms and perspectives; (c) the strategies of inquiry; (d) the methods of data collection and analysis; (e) the art of interpretation and presentation. In particular, Denzin and Lincoln contrast different

research paradigms according to their assumptions, criteria for evaluation, and type of narration used. For example, within the constructivist or interpretivist paradigm, the assumptions are based on substantive-formal theories, the evaluation criteria are typically those of credibility, transferability and confirmability, with case studies and ethnographic fiction as the most common types of reporting used. Within this pedagogy, action research is regarded as a research strategy or approach along with others such as ethnography, phenomenology and grounded theory. Different methods of data collection and analysis are available to the researcher ranging from the interview to direct observation, to the analysis of artifacts, documents and cultural records, to the use of visual materials or personal experience. As such, when addressing action research we should be aware of the five research phases and as a minimum consider the researcher's tradition, perspectives and theories as the underlying assumptions, his/her strategy for inquiry and data collection and analysis as the study methods, as well as the style of presentation used.

Epistemology of Action Research

The epistemological foundations of action research have been debated over the years by researchers in social science (Rapoport 1970; Hult and Lennung 1978; Susman and Evered 1978; Brown and Tandon 1983; Peters and Robinson 1984; Baburoglu and Ravn 1992; Robinson 1993; de Cock 1994). While the use of action research as a strategy of inquiry is undisputed, its epistemological basis as a research paradigm is open to question due to the different meanings that have been attributed to the concept over time. For instance, Peters and Robinson suggest a weak and a strong version of action research depending on whether it is used as a research strategy or a theory of social science. Both versions share the characteristics of being change-focused, collaborative and an iterative process. However, the strong version also requires a commitment to an underlying philosophy of social science that is consistent with the researcher's tradition and beliefs.

Various types of action research with different emphases and traditions have also been described in literature (Rapoport 1970; Hult and Lennung 1978; Reason 1993a). Lewin is widely recognized as the originator of action research based on his work on group dynamics and bridging of social theories and practice. Perhaps one of the most comprehensive definitions of action research was provided by Hult and Lennung:

> Action research simultaneously assists in practical problem-solving and expands scientific knowledge, as well as enhances the competencies of the respective actors, being performed collaboratively in an immediate situation using data feedback in a cyclical process aiming at an increased understanding of a given social situation, primarily applicable for the understanding of change processes in social systems and undertaken within a mutually acceptable ethical framework.

Participatory action research is a form of action research that involves practitioners as both subjects and coresearchers. It emerged from the work with oppressed peoples in the Third World during the 1940s where they learned to help themselves (Brown and Tandon 1983; Reason 1993a), but has since been applied in a variety of organizational settings across Europe, North America and Australia (French and Bell 1990; Whyte 1991; McTaggart 1991). In participatory action research, participants solve problems for themselves by setting their own research agenda, collecting and analyzing the data, and controlling over use of the results and the whole process. Action science is yet another form of action research pioneered by Argyris, Putname and Smith (1985) that places the emphasis on understanding participants' behaviors as theories-in-use versus their beliefs as espoused theories, and the use of single and double-loop learning for self improvement (Argyris and Schon 1989). Action learning stems largely from the work of Revans (1980; 1983a; 1983b; 1983c) that advocates group participation, programmed instructions, spontaneous questioning, real actions, and experiential learning within different social and organizational contexts.

According to this brief review on the epistemology of action research, it is necessary for the researcher to distinguish the type of action research used and its historical context from which the purpose, focus, theory and methods of the study are based. Within an IS context, Checkland (1991) also suggests the need for an intellectual framework to guide the research, and to clarify such methodological details as the role of the researcher, the process of problem diagnosis, the nature of the intervention, the extent of reflection and learning intended, and whether there is to be new knowledge to be gained.

2.3 Bases for Comparison

Based on the criteria presented above, we chose to review action research for IS in the following sequence. First, we examined the role of action research in IS over the past twenty-five years based on its extent of usage, the type of action research adopted and the IS area addressed. This was followed by a review on the explicitness of the research approach in terms of their underlying assumptions, study methods and presentation styles. Next, we analyzed the so-called diagnosis-action-reflection cycle that is the most unique aspect of action research by contrasting the respective components and how they are described in these articles. We then compared these IS articles with those selected from social science for similarities and differences. Finally, these findings were used as the basis to construct our contemporary IS action research framework and to discuss its implications on IS research and practice.

3 EVOLVING PATTERNS OF ACTION RESEARCH IN IS

3.1 Role of Action Research in IS

The role of action research in IS can be gauged from the number and patterns of such articles published, the types of action research adopted, the IS areas addressed, and the trends noted over the past twenty-five years from these three areas. Note that these parameters have been adapted from those used by Benbasat (1985) and Hamilton and Ives (1982) in their discussion of IS research methodologies.

IS Related Action Research Publications

The types of journals where the IS action research articles were published are listed in Table 1. Note that the journals in which these articles were published vary widely, with no apparent dominance from any single source. In fact, their subject areas span vastly different disciplines ranging from business, education, and health to social and public service. Of interest is that none of the articles appeared in such mainstream IS journals as the *MIS Quarterly*, *Information Systems Research*, *Communications of the ACM*, or *European Journal of IT*. Nor were there any articles in *Organization Science* and *Management Science*, often considered the alternate sources for many of the scholarly IS publications. Only one article was published in the *Journal of MIS* (Levine and Rossmoore 1993), with five others from the two IFIP Conference Proceedings in 1985 (Sandberg 1985; Wood-Harper 1985) and 1991 (Checkland 1991; Ngwenyama 1991; Jonsson 1991), respectively.

Types of Action Research in IS

Table 2 summarizes the types of action research adopted in the thirty articles. Less than half of these articles included a definition such as those provided in this review. Ten remaining articles cited action research in their paper but had minimal to no clarification on the approach used. For example, Jonsson and Solli (1993) described an action research project to investigate the effects of individually designed financial reports on managing costs in public organizations. While they reviewed the epistemological status of case studies, the use of action research as a strategy of inquiry was assumed understood by the reader and not explained. Of the two studies that cited action learning as the basis for their training (Blennerhassett 1988; Wood-Harper and Flynn 1983), neither offered a definition of what they meant by the term. Seven other articles defined action research in ways that seem to contradict our understanding of the types of action research presented. To illustrate, Gibson (1975) labeled his implementation project to deploy computer-based facility planning models into banks as action research but he equated it with participant observation, which is often associated with ethnographic studies.

Areas of IS Addressed

The IS areas addressed by the thirty articles can be grouped into four broad categories similar to those proposed by Galliers and Land (1987): IS theories and methods; systems development; use of information and/or systems; socio-technical systems. The category for IS theories and methods consists of two discussion papers on the epistemology of action research in IS (Checkland 1991; Ngwenyama 1991). The category for systems development includes eleven articles covering the areas of analy-

Table 1 Distribution of IS studies involving action research reported in the literature over the past twenty-five years and sorted by journal in alphabetical sequence.

Name of Journal	1971-80	1981-85	1986-90	1991-95	Total
Accounting, Organizations and Society	1	1			2
ASIS Annual Meeting		1			1
Computer Methods & Programs in Biomedicine				1	1
Education for Information				1	1
Engineering Management International			1		1
European Journal of Operational Research				1	1
Health Progress			1		1
Human Communication Technology Meeting			1		1
Human Relations			1		1
Human Systems Management				1	1
Implementing Operations Research and Management Science	1				1
Information and Management				1	1
Information Systems Research: IFIP 1991				3	3
International Journal of Operations and Production management				1	1
Journal of Accounting and Public Policy		1			1
Journal of Applied Behavioral Science	1		1	1	3
Journal of European Industrial Training			1		1
Journal of Management Information Systems				1	1
Journal of Occupational Psychology			1		1
Management Accounting Research				1	1
Organizational Change and Innovation				1	1
Research Methods in Information Systems		2			2
Technovation		1			1
The Computer Journal		1			1
Total	3	7	7	13	30

sis, design, development and implementation of information systems and decision support systems. Three of these studies (Earl 1978; Levine and Rossmoore 1993; Salmela and Ruohonen 1992) are based on action science with a focus on understanding conflicts among subjects brought on by the introduction of systems in organizations, while only one (Timpka, Sjoberg and Svensson 1995) explored collaboration between users and developers through participatory action research when designing complex systems. The remaining seven used action research mostly as a systems development methodology that provides reflection and learning with participants as users in place of conventional methods such as joint application design (Candlin and Wright 1992; Crowther 1985; Gibson 1975; Mirvis and Lawler 1983; Ngwenyama 1993; Wood-Harper 1985; Ziegenfuss 1987).

Table 2 Types of action research adopted.

Legends: "+" are articles where the meaning of action research is not defined or explaned; "*" are considered action science articles according to this review but were not declared as such by the authors; "?" are articles with questionable definitions for action research.

Type	1971-80	1981-85	1986-90	1991-95
Action Research	Gibson (1975)? Harris (1978)+	Mirvis and Lawler (1983)+ Crowther (1985) Rickards (1985)+ Sandberg (1985) Wood-Harper (1985)	Oakland (1986) Pava (1986)+ Cassell et al. (1988) Ziegenfuss (1987)? Liu (1990)+	Checkland (1991) Jonsson (1991)? Ngwenyama (1991) Nosek and Yaverbaum (1991)+ Candlin and Wright (1992) Cassell and Fitter (1992) Jonsson and Solli (1993)+ Badham, Couchman and Little (1995) Fox (1995)
Participatory Action Research				Timpka, Sjoberg and Svensson (1995)
Action Science	Earl (1978)*	Covaleski, Dirsmith and Jablonsky (1985)*	Calabrese and Acker (1987)*	Salmela and Ruohonen (1992)* Levine and Rossmoore (1993)
Action Learning		Wood-Harper and Flynn (1983)+	Blennerhassett (1988)+	Ngwenyama (1993)+

Trends for Action Research in IS

To observe the evolving patterns over the four time periods, the articles were sorted by the type of action research, type of study, appropriateness of the definition, and IS category. These are summarized in Tables 3a, 3b, 3c and 3d, respectively. One can see from Table 3a that the number of IS action research publications has increased steadily over the years, with the number of articles from 1991-95 almost double those of the previous five-year period. Similarly, Table 3b shows the number of IS action research field studies has increased dramatically during the last five years when com-

Table 3a The Number of articles published during the four periods by type. Note that four action science articles are suggested by this review only since they were not declared as such by the original authors.

Type	1971-80	1981-85	1986-90	1991-95	Total
Action Research	2	5	5	9	21
Action Science	1	1	1	2	5
Preparatory Action Research				1	1
Action Learning		1	1	1	3
Total	3	7	7	13	30

Table 3b The number of action articles published during the four periods by type of study.

Type of Study	1971-80	1981-85	1986-90	1991-95	Total
Field Study	3	3	4	10	20
Discussion Paper		4	3	3	10
Total	3	7	7	13	30

Table 3c The number of articles published during the four periods by definition.

Definition	1971-80	1981-85	1986-90	1991-95	Total
Minimal/No Definition	1	3	3	3	10
Conflicting Definition	2	1	2	2	7
Proper Definition		3	2	8	13
Total	3	7	7	13	30

Table 3d The number of articles published during the four periods by IS category.

IS Category	1971-80	1981-85	1986-90	1991-95	Total
IS Theories and Methods				2	2
Systems Development	2	3	1	5	11
Use of Information/Systems	1	2	2	4	9
Socio-technical Systems		2	4	2	8
Total	3	7	7	13	30

pared with the previous periods. From Table 3c, the proportion of articles that including included a proper definition for the type of action research used has also increased during the last five years. From Table 3d, the IS categories with the most notable increase in the number of publications over the last ten years are in systems development and use of information and/or systems. The patterns of publications suggest that, over the years, action research has not received much attention as an alternative strategy of inquiry in IS. Even with the increasing trends noted, thus far only twenty IS action research field studies have been reported during the past twenty-five years, and only two articles are on the epistemology of action research in IS. These patterns suggest a vastly under-exposed qualitative research methodology awaiting potential exploration by IS researchers and practitioners.

3.2 Explicitness of the Research Approach

The explicitness of the research approach used in the thirty articles can be described in terms of the differences in their underlying assumptions, the methods of study adopted and the variation in presentation styles, as summarized in Table 4. These parameters have been adapted from the five research phases (Denzin and Lincoln 1993) that are considered pertinent when describing qualitative research in IS.

Differences in Underlying Assumptions

According to Denzin and Lincoln, the researcher's assumptions are often shaped by his or her tradition and perspective. Hult and Lennung suggest there are three traditions of action research spanning different disciplines: a school tradition that focuses on teaching and learning mostly in the field of education; a community development tradition that helps advance the cause of under-privileged groups; an organization tradition intended mostly for effective design and development of organizations. As shown under "Assumptions" in Table 4, nine articles did declare their tradition: six are from organization design and three from community development. Of the six organization design articles, only Badham, Couchman and Little (1995) and Salmela and Ruohonen elaborated on how their action research was shaped by the tradition. Conversely, all three of the community development articles have made explicit their ideologies in advancing the cause of under-privileged groups in industrialized countries.

In terms of the researcher's perspective, seven of the thirty articles were declared by the authors as interpretive, three as critical. By being interpretive, the researcher is engaged in social construction of reality where he or she attempts to understand the social phenomena within a naturalistic setting (Jonsson 1991). For instance, Covaleski, Dirsmith and Jablonsky (1985) used action research to gather empirical evidence on the interpretations of and meanings attached to the actors' espoused theories on budgeting practices with a newly computerized budgeting system versus their actual

Table 4 Underlying assumptions, study methods and presentation styles used in the articles.

Legends: AL–action learning; AR–action research; AS–action science; PAR–participatory action research; CAL–collaborative action learning. "+" under Authors identifies the article as a field study; "?" under Methods indicates the suggested researcher role; "*" under Assumptions and Presentation indicates the label is suggested only.

Author	Assumptions	Methods	Presentation
Gibson (1975)+	Post-positivistic*	AR, participant observation grounded theory. Interviews, surveys, document review, statistics, two year study, single site, researcher as expert	Ethnographic exploratory case
Earl (1978)+	Not indicated	AR, AS. No information on methods	Essay with three illustrative cases
Harris (1978)+	Not indicated	AR. Questionnaire, site visit interviews, three month trial, multiple sites, researcher as expert?	Scientific report
Mirvis and Lawler (1983)+	Post-positivistic*	AR. Study/control groups, interviews, focus groups, surveys, correlational analysis, one year study, single site, researcher as expert?	Ethnographic, explanatory case*
Wood-Harper and Flynn (1983)+	Not indicated	AL. Feedback	Descriptive case*
Covaleski, Dirsmith and Jablonsky (1985)+	Interpretive	AR, AS. Interviews, observations, review of archival information, analysis of system, 3.5 year study, multiple sites, researcher as expert?	Ethnographic, explanatory case*
Crowther (1985)	Post-positivistic*	AR. Hypothesis testing, theory development, simulation	Essay
Rickards (1985)	Not indicated	Participative motivation as AR	Essay
Sandberg (1985)	Community development, critical	Socio-technical design, AR, praxis research. Continuing dialogue, scientific reflection proposed.	Essay

Table 4 (continued)

Author	Assumptions	Methods	Presentation
Wood-Harper (1985)	Interpretive, objective idealism	Multiview methodology, AR, hermeneutic analysis.	Essay
Oakland (1986)	Not indicated	AR. Observation.	Essay
Pava (1986)+	Organization design	AR, social technical system design. Survey, one year study, single site, researcher as collaborator?	Essay, illustrative, explanatory case
Calabrese and Acker (1987)+	Interpretive	AR, AS. Interviews, focus groups, > five year study, single site, researcher as expert?	Explanatory case*
Ziegenfuss (1987)	Not indicated	AR as data collection method.	Essay
Blennerhassett (1988)+	Not indicated	AR, AL. Interviews, participant observation, questionnaire, pre/post comparison over one year, single site, researcher as collaborator?	Descriptive case*
Cassell et al. (1988)+	Community development	AR. Discussion groups, interviews, surveys, site visits, content analysis, 18 month pilot, multiple sites, researcher as collaborator	Explanatory case
Liu et al. (1990)	Organzation design	AR; no other details.	Essay
Checkland (1991)	Interpretive	AR, soft system methodology.	Essay
Jonsson (1991)+	Interpretive	AR. Interviews, site visits, observations, four years for first case and one year in second case, single sites, researcher and collaborator.	Essay with two illustrative cases
Ngwenyama (1991)	Critical	AR, AL. Participant observation, audio/video taping, interviews, action experiments, participant written cases proposed. Theory-in-use models, ladders of inference and cognitive maps as data analysis tools.	Essay

Table 4 (continued)

Author	**Assumptions**	**Methods**	**Presentation**
Nosek and Yaverbaum (1991)+	Organization design	AR. Interviews, surveys, three year study, single site, researcher as expert?	Explanatory case
Candlin and Wright (1992)+	Not indicated	AR, joint system design. Structured interviews, feedback to clients and sponsors, < one year study, single site, researcher as expert.	Explanatory case*
Salmela and Ruohonen (1992)+	Organization design	AR, longitudinal study. Interviews, review of documents and feedback seminar, two year study, multiple sites, researcher as expert?	Ethnographic, explanatory case
Jonsson and Solli (1993)+	Interpretive.	AR, AS. Observations, interviews, review of reports, study over one year, multiple sites, researcher as expert?	Ethnographic, explanatory case
Levine and Rossmoore (1993)+	Post-positivistic,* interpretive	AS. Interviews, role-play, document analysis, observation, site visits, three month study, single site, researcher as expert.	Ethnographic, explanatory case
Ngwenyama (1993)+	Not indicated	AR, holographic organization theory, communicative action theory, AL, CAL. Diaries, audio records and notes of post-development discussions, six week study, single site, researcher as collaborator.	Essay, illustrative, exploratory case
Badham, Couchman and Little (1995)+	Organization design, critical	AR, organizational ethnography, longitudinal study, multiple sites, researcher as collaborator	Essay with two illustrative cases
Fox (1995)	Organization design	Socio-technical system design, AR	Essay
Timpka, Sjoberg and Svensson (1995)+	Not indicated	PAR, action design. Interviews, project diaries, field notes, participant observation, video recordings, five year study, single site, researcher as collaborator	Explanatory case

behaviors as theories-in-use routines. Of the three critical articles identified, two are essays on the role of action research in IS and its influence on automating the workforce, respectively (Ngwenyama 1991; Sandberg 1985). The third is a field study (Badham, Couchman and Little 1995) to introduce team-based manufacturing through radical action to help participants control their own situation.

In implementing a new strategic financial information system, Levine and Rossmoore claimed to be interpretive by emphasizing their insight on human behaviors and conflicts caused by automation. However, their approach follows more of a post-positivistic stance (Denzin and Lincoln 1993) with their desire to develop and test theories and to subject their findings to the criteria of falsifiability and generalization. In total, four articles are considered post-positivistic in this review with their focus on traditional theory development and testing, but were not declared as such by the authors.

Methods of Study Adopted

While most of the thirty articles cited action research as their strategy of inquiry, eleven also combined it with one or more alternative strategies that range from organizational ethnography, longitudinal study, soft systems methodology, socio-technical system design, to evaluation research. These are summarized under "Methods" in Table 4. Only a few of these articles elaborated on their combined research strategies. For example, in adopting a longitudinal action research design, Salmela and Ruohonen described their study process to include ongoing interviews and feedback seminars with participants to compare findings over a two-year period. Of the twenty IS field studies listed, sixteen included information on their research sites, subjects, background, and methods of data collection. Only seven involved multiple departments/units as their site; twelve others were conducted within a single organization, while one was unspecified. The length of these field studies ranged from three months (Harris 1978; Levine and Rossmoore 1993) to five years (e.g., Timka, Sjoberg and Svensson 1995) with one to two years as the most frequent duration cited (e.g., Blennerhassett 1988; Jonsson and Solli 1993). Different data collection methods were used with varying levels of details provided – interviews, participant observation, questionnaires, focus groups, site visits, field notes, document review and video-recording. Only three articles mentioned their analytical methods, being one of correlational analysis (Mirvis and Lawler 1983), content analysis (Cassell et al. 1988) or tabulation of quantitative results (Gibson 1975). Less than one half of the field studies explicitly mentioned the respective roles of the researcher and participants, which ranged from having the former as an expert resource (e.g., Candlin and Wright 1992) to the latter as collaborators and coresearchers (e.g., Badham, Couchman and Little 1995).

Variation in Presentation Styles

Considerable differences are also noted in the style of presentation among these thirty articles. As seen under "Presentation" in Table 4, the most common form of reporting is case study found in nineteen of the articles. This is followed by ten essays and one scientific report. Based on Yin's classification (1994), case studies may be exploratory, descriptive or explanatory depending on the research question, the extent of control over actual behavioral events, and the focus on contemporary versus historical phenomena. Of the nineteen case studies reported, twelve are considered explanatory where they explain the causal links in real-life interventions and effects. Two cases are descriptive in that they describe an intervention in detail and the real-life context in which it occurred. Two others are exploratory in nature where the intervention being investigated has no clear single set of outcomes. The remaining five are essays with brief cases included for illustrative purposes only. It should be noted that our categorization of the types of case studies reported is only suggested, as many authors did not make any distinction of the type used in their paper.

Six of the case studies are written as ethnographic fiction, where dialogues from participants are included as part of the interpretation. However, none of the authors acknowledged the use of ethnographic writing in their paper. Perhaps our best example is the study on social use of financial information by Jonsson and Solli, where extensive quotes from participants and events are included, some of which they referred to as organizational story-telling. The most unique form of reporting is that of a play put together by participants for stakeholders on the needs of unemployed people (Cassell and Fitter 1992).

Trends in the Research Approach

The patterns of assumptions, study methods and presentation styles for the thirty articles over the four time periods are summarized in Tables 5a, 5b, and 5c, respectively. In Table 5a, if one were to include the community development tradition as critical based on their similar ideological stance, to regard the organization design articles as interpretive in nature, and to distinguish those publications that are considered post-positivistic by this review, then the number of articles where the underlying assumptions were mentioned has increased steadily during the last five years. From Table 5b, one can see that the use of one or more departments and/or units within a single organization as the study site is more common than those spanning multiple organizations, although this gap appears to be narrowing within the last five years. On the other hand, the role of the researcher has shifted over the years from that of an expert resource to a collaborator, with the participants playing an increasing role in the research process. In terms of the length of the field studies reported, both short-term studies of less than one year and longitudinal studies of three years or more are noted within the last five years. As for the presentation style, one can see from Table 5c that the methods of reporting for action research in IS have remained largely the same over the years, with case study still being the preferred method of presentation. There is, however, an increase in the number of illustrative and ethnographic case studies reported in the last five years. As a whole, the action research approach adopted in IS has become more explicit and open over the years.

Table 5a The number of action research articles published during the four periods by underlying assumption. Note: "Critical" includes articles with community development tradition, while "Interpretive" includes the organization design tradition; articles listed as post-positivistic are suggested by this review only and not declared as such by the original authors.

Assumption	1971-80	1981-85	1986-90	1991-95	Total
Not Indicated	2	2	2	3	10
Post-positivistic	1	2		1	4
Interpretive		2	3	5	10
Critical		1	1	3	5
Total	3	7	7	13	30

Table 5b The number of action research articles published during the four periods by study design. Note that two thirds of the researcher roles cited are suggested only and not declared by the original authors. Legend: N/A–not applicable or unknown.

Design		1971-80	1981-85	1986-90	1991-95	Total
Study Site	Single	1	2	3	6	12
	Multiple	1	1	1	4	7
	N/A	1	4	3	3	11
Researcher Role	Expert	2	2	1	4	9
	Collaborator		1	3	6	10
	N/A	1	4	3	3	11
Length of Study	< 1 year	1			3	4
	1-2 years	1	2	3	2	8
	≥ 3 years		1	1	3	5
	N/A	1	4	3	5	13

Table 5c The number of action research articles published during the four periods by style of presentation. Note that the ethnographic style is only suggested by this review and not declared by the original authors.

Presentation Style	1971-80	1981-85	1986-90	1991-95	Total
Scientific Report	1				1
Essay		4	3	4	10
Case Study					
Illustrative	1		1	3	5
Exploratory				1	1
Descriptive		1	1		2
Explanatory			2	3	5
Ethnography*	1	2		3	6
Total	3	7	7	13	30

3.3 Diversity in the Research Process

According to Checkland (1991) and Ngwenyama (1991), the most unique aspect of action research as a strategy of inquiry is in its iterative process of problem diagnosis, action intervention, and reflective learning by the researcher and participants. These are summarized in Table 6 for the thirty articles and discussed in detail below.

Choice of Problems and Issues

Under "Problem" in Table 6, one can see that the scope of the problems addressed among these articles vary widely, ranging from the lack of welding expertise within an engineering firm (Candlin and Wright 1992) to the need for an action-oriented change strategy in high-technology and production management for an entire country (Oakland 1986). Despite such diversity, the nature of these problems can be categorized as one of improving the development of organizations and communities through collaborative actions and reflections, overcoming resistance to change by reconciling between espoused and in-use theories held by participants, or training users to enhance the level of their information and systems knowledge. While all ten discussion papers described particular concepts such as socio-technical system design as their proposed framework, only twelve of the twenty field studies included the use of theories, concepts or research themes to guide the problems being investigated. Six of these articles contain theories on human behaviors or organizational/community improvement when introducing new systems (Cassell et al. 1988; Jonsson and Solli 1993; Jonsson 1991; Mirvis and Lawler 1983; Pava 1986; Badham, Couchman and

Table 6 Problems, actions, and reflections described in the articles. "+" under Author indicates a field study; "*" under Problem identifies articles where theories or concepts are cited; "**" under Action identifies articles with specific interventions; "?" under Reflection identifies articles with general reflections cited.

Author	Problem	Action	Reflection
Gibson (1975)+	Improvement for election of branch bank sites	Develop and implement a computer-based planning model; monitor its usage by staff	Implementation affected by staff attitude. Actions interfered with observation; results difficult to replicate and generalize?
Earl (1978)+	Inability to accommodate organizational learning	Used prototyping to design systems	Double-learning can break down barriers.
Harris (1978)+	Staff improvement to enhance patient satisfaction	Staff designed and conducted questionnaire, reviewed feedback.	Staff improved service, evaluated outcomes and offered guidelines
Mirvis and Lawler (1983)+	Lack integrated system on staff feedback/performance; lack public reporting of work life*	Staff participated in development of system; managers encouraged to use data; firm published indicators	System use affected by managers; public reporting created problems; required commitment?
Wood-Harper and Flynn (1983)+	How analysis and design is viewed with objective realism	Tried methods on practical cases with experienced and novice analysts	IS evolution needs methodology, intentions, assumptions of analyst
Covaleski, Dirsmith and Jablonsky (1985)+	Need budgeting system for information reporting and use*	Implemented system after extensive consultation with users	Traditional and emergent theories of budgeting influenced users?
Crowther (1985)	Problems in systems analysis	Focus on change in people and value through experiment	Checklist of viewpoints on analysis for third world countries
Rickards (1985)	Different approaches to addressing innovation	Participative thinking proposed; use of process consultants/facilitators	Participative approach deals with ill-defined problems; learned knowledge through experience

Table 6 (continued)

Author	Problem	Action	Reflection
Sandberg (1985)	Limited union role in planning socio-technical systems	Independent union actions to build up competence, mobility, negotiation	Need for praxis and centralized research on technical choices
Wood-Harper (1985)	How analysis and design is viewed with objective idealism	Tried methods on practical cases with experienced and novice analysts	IS evolution needs methodology, intentions, assumptions of analyst
Oakland (1986)	Improve high technology production management and resource utilization	Joint collaboration, emphasis on practice, shared values, change agent	Need action research with measurements on a dynamic system that changes when studied
Pava (1986)+	Improve socio-technical system design, e.g., customer support*	Conducted business, technical, social analysis; provided recommendations	Customer support improved; update to socio-technical system design concept/method proposed?
Calabrese and Acker (1987)+	Access, socio-technical aspects of online catalog systems	Users participated in development of an electronic journal delivery system	New organizational relationship is part of innovation/reinvention?
Ziegenfuss (1987)	Research needed to deal with major issues in healthcare	Develop research information system to collect data on service, patient characteristics, cost outcome	A see and learn approach needed for learning in continuing organizational development
Blennerhassett (1988)+	Senior civil service managers had little experience with IT*	Interviews/workshops conduct to define learning contents; different learning methods used**	Evaluated effects with managers positive on learning, attitude, behavior, organizational effects
Cassell et al. (1988)+	Information poverty in unemployed community*	Group defined needs and evaluation framework; trained on computers; collaborated between three sites**	Increased self-confidence, effectiveness dependent on ability of sites to adapt needs
Liu et al. (1990)	Technology affected organization of work and character of social relations	Organize open process with explicit collective learning and qualitative objectives	New organizational programs for organization design and action research needed

Table 6 (continued)

Author	Problem	Action	Reflection
Checkland (1991)	Humans can act to change phenomena investigated	Declare an intellectual framework for action research	Alternative to positi-visitic research with explicit methodological framework
Jonsson (1991)+	Information overload, lack of control in social welfare units and automobile production*	Group solved problems within control; managers trained to design reports; interviewed on use of information	Managers/groups increased control through dialogue, action and problem solving?
Ngwenyama (1991)	Use of critical social theory in IS research and practice	Use action science with action experimentation, hypothesis testing	Dialectic needed between practice oriented research and critical theory
Nosek and Yaverbaum (1991)+	Managers to improve decision making on IS development	Six planning/implementation phases; strategy, prototyping, interviews, feedback, development, training	Product judged successful; advantages and obstacles identified?
Candlin and Wright (1992)+	Improve welding knowledge through an expert system	Client defined problem, initiated actions, researcher collected/ clarified information**	Need to formulate theory on system as testable proposition in prototyping
Cassel and Fitter (1992)+	Gap between waged/ unwaged in computer resource/skills	Provided IT resources for unwaged in their local community	Feedback at operational, strategic and policy levels
Salmela and Ruohonen (1992)+	Contradiction in managing units, inadequate expertise and change in work conditions*	Document review and interviews to find contradictions, new system proposed to management**	Changes identified/ proposed; follow-up?
Jonsson and Solli (1993)+	Financial management and professionalism incompatible*	Managers trained on accounting and cost report design; monthly talk with controllers on financial performance**	Meaning, explanation and trust needed to understand actions?
Levine and Rossmoore (1993)+	Obsolete systems prevented new market, products and services*	Management redefined mission, strategy to develop new system	Staff acted on theory-in-use; conflict on whether project was strategic or technical?

Table 6 (continued)

Author	Problem	Action	Reflection
Ngwenyama (1993)+	Lack inventory, customer order tracking information*	End-user teams developed systems, conducted discussions for learning	Needed policies on standards, roles, incentives, commitment?
Badham, Couchman, and Little (1995)+	Automation effects on unions; need for human-centered work organization*	Work groups formed to involve users; created flexible systems, network to transfer knowledge/experience	Defined problems/needs, provided recommendations
Fox (1995)	Need to consider technical and social systems of an organization for effective organization design	Conduct systems scan, technical analysis, social analysis, quality of working life and interpersonal/group deliberation considerations	Staff seek more meaningful empowerment, greater productivity and viability in organizations
Timpka, Sjoberg and Svensson (1995)+	Hypermedia systems complex requiring collaboration*	Participatory design/evaluation of system through action design method	Need for codevelopment, respectful attitude for hierarchy?

Little 1995), while three are on conflict resolution (Covaleski, Dirsmith and Jablonsky 1987; Levine and Rossmoore 1993; Salmela and Ruobonen 1992). Three others are on enhancing user knowledge based on communicative action theory (Ngwenyama 1993), a content-centred learner model (Blennerhassett 1988), and organizational learning (Timpka, Sjoberg and Svensson 1995), respectively. The remaining eight field studies are mostly based on some stated objectives to solve certain practical problems, such as the need for a new form of systems analysis in third-world countries proposed by Crowther (1985) taking into account the lack of scarce resources and access to technology.

General Versus Specific Interventions

As seen from "Action" in Table 6, the types of actions proposed or implemented in these articles also vary tremendously, ranging from a specific intervention (e.g., Jonsson and Solli 1993), to a series of related tasks (e.g., Badham, Couchman and Little 1995), to that of an action-oriented learning or systems methodology (e.g., Wood-Harper and Flynn 1983). In some instances, the actual interventions implemented are not explicitly defined since they are assumed understood through the problem diagnosis and proposed solutions described by the authors (e.g., Calabrese and Acker 1987; Mirvis and Lawler 1983). This is particularly true with the ten discussion papers, where the need for action interventions is expressed at the conceptual level only and not further elaborated. Only five studies provided sufficient details on the action interventions implemented. For instance, Jonsson and Solli described their main intervention as the monthly accounting talks with managers from six social agency units where the duration, intensity and scope of such talks increased over time as the managers became more confident in using the cost information within a social context. In studies where action research is used as a systems development methodology, the interventions generally consist of defining user requirements, conducting systems analysis, and designing the new system with the collaboration of participants as the intended users (e.g., Candlin and Wright 1992; Nosek and Yaverbaum 1991).

Extent and Level of Reflections

The most important aspect of action research is the reflection phase of the study process, seen under "Reflection" in Table 6, where the researcher and participants engage in collective interpretation of the findings and contemplate what can be learned from the experience. Such reflection may be iterative in nature depending on the problem and interventions involved, but should always be conducted in a way that Checkland (1991) refers to as "methodologically explicit" in order for the results to be coherent and potentially transferable. Of the twenty field studies, those that are full-length case studies (fifteen in total) included a fair amount of details on lessons learned. On the other hand, while the five essays with illustrative cases are descriptive in conveying their theories or general experiences, there were few reflections that were directly from the case cited.

Finally, as part of reflection and learning, there is also an expectation of new knowledge to be generated as a by-product of the research process. For some researchers, this form of new knowledge represents local or tacit experience of the participants that can improve the practice of the organizations involved (e.g., Badham, Couchman and Little 1995). With others such as Agyris, Putnam and Smith and Ngwenyama (1991), this process should result in the development of new theories and knowledge that can be generalized and validated. In-depth discussions of generalized knowledge are noted in twelve of the twenty field studies. One such example by Covaleski, Dirsmith and Jablonsky (1985) on the role of traditional and emergent budgeting theories in understanding budget-related behaviors from a computerized state geriatric accounting system. From the resulting behaviors as manifested through an interplay of the participants' espoused views and in-use routines, Covaleski, Dirsmith and Jablonsky generalized on the shortcomings of double-loop learning and advocated "a triple-loop level of accounting for how accounting is to be accounted." As for the remaining field studies, most have included discussions of their experiences based on local tacit knowledge gained through the problem-action-reflection cycles in their study. Admittedly, the differences between local, tacit experience and generalized new knowledge are sometimes difficult to discern from these articles.

Table 7 The number of action research articles published during the four periods by research strategy. Legend: N/A–not applicable or unknown.

Strategy	1971-80	1981-85	1986-90	1991-95	Total
Framework					
Theories/Concepts		2	3	7	12
Objectives	3	1	1	3	8
Discussion papers		4	3	3	10
Problem					
Improve Conditions		4	6	6	18
Overcome Conflicts	2	1		2	4
Enhance User Knowledge	1	2	1	4	7
N/A				1	1
Action					
Specific Interventions			2	3	5
Related Tasks/Methods	1	4	2	6	13
N/A	2	3	3	4	12
Reflection					
Local Knowledge	1		2	3	6
Generalization	1	4	1	6	12
N/A	1	3	4	4	12

Trends in the Research Process

Table 7 summarizes the action research strategy in terms of the type of framework, problem, action and reflection from the thirty articles over the four time periods. One can see from "Framework" of Table 7 that the proportion of articles with explicit theories, concepts or objectives has increased over the last five years. While the most common problems addressed are still to improve the condition of organizations and communities as seen from "Problem," there has been an increasing number of studies that deal with overcoming conflicts and enhancing user knowledge during the last five years. From "Action," one can see that, over the years, the majority of the articles either did not reveal their actions or have described them as a series of related tasks or a systems methodology. Only five articles within the last ten years have provided sufficient details on the specific interventions undertaken. As for "Reflection," there has been an increase in the number of articles during the last five years with some form of generalization that contributed to the creation of new knowledge in IS.

Overall, while the use of action research in IS has matured over the years, more theoretical and empirical studies on different IS problems with explicit methodological details are needed to enrich our understanding of the action research process.

3.4 Comparison of Action Research in Social Science

A special 1993 issue of *Human Relations* containing five exemplary action research cases and six critique articles of these cases in a subsequent issue were compared with the IS articles for similarities and differences in terms of their methodologies. By doing so, we hope to gauge the current status of action research in IS relative to that in social science.

Exemplary Action Research Cases and Critiques

To introduce these exemplary cases, Elden and Chisholm (1993) first reviewed the characteristics of classical action research as having purposes and value choice; a real-world contextual focus; change based data and sense making; participation in the research process; knowledge creation and diffusion. In contrast, the five exemplary cases represent divergent forms of action research that are different in the level of system engaged in the change process; the degree of formal organization of the research setting; the extent of openness in the research process; the goals and purpose of the research effort; the role of the researchers. Overall, these emergent varieties of action research are far more complex in terms of their multi-level focus that spans organizations, communities and regions, the use of a variety of self-design and participatory methods, as well as the duration of studies that are typically staged over a four to five year period. While the cases by Levin (1993), Ledford and Mohrman (1993b and Engelstad and Gustavsen (1993) have emphasized on the development of large regional and national networks as new forms of organization for economic and work reform, the work of Greenwood, Whyte and Harkavy (1993) and of Brown (1993) is more focused on the direct participation of those affected as coresearchers and their engagement in knowledge diffusion and organizational learning.

Six critiques with contrasting viewpoints on the exemplary cases were published in a subsequent issue of *Human Relations*. While Bartunek (1993) and Ledford and Mohrman (1993a) praise the conceptual contributions of these cases and the need for such exemplars, others are more critical on their lack of details, the extent of participant engagement, and the notable absence of any effort to validate the new knowledge generated (Mangham 1993; Reason 1993b; Heller 1993; Gustavsen 1993). However, these reviewers also acknowledged the difficulty of having to condense such complex longitudinal studies into a mere twenty pages of writing, and the need for publishing these cases.

Classical Versus Emergent IS Action Research

In comparison, the patterns of evolution as seen in the thirty IS action research articles are somewhat different. For example, many of these IS studies would fall under what Elden and Chisholm refer to as classical action research with their focus on a specific problem within an organization or community through the use of a single study site where the researcher played the role of an expert in the process. Instead of dealing with increasingly complex problems and issues spanning multiple levels of communities and regions as suggested in the emergent approach, many of the recent IS action research field studies have focused on systems development and use of information and/or systems in organizations and communities, where the appropriate and effective use of a specific system within a particular socio-technical context is investigated. This difference is probably due to the fact that many of the technological solutions reported are intended for specific problems within an organization or community. It is from within such specific settings that the social interpretation of the meanings and effects of the technologies are constructed and determined, respectively. Nevertheless, there has been a small but increasing number of IS studies over the last ten years that are of the emergent variety described through their use of multiple organizations, participants as collaborators, and longitudinal design of three or more years in duration. In particular, four of these IS articles have addressed socio-technical systems and technological innovations in ways that are close to the multi-level focus cited in the exemplary cases (Oakland 1986; Liu et al. 1990; Badham, Couchman and Little 1995; Fox 1995). Interestingly, even though there has been an increased recognition in the collaborative nature of the research process, only one of the thirty IS articles has formally adopted the term participatory action research. Conversely, the use of action science to resolve conflicts in organizations, while inferred in at least four of the IS articles, is not mentioned anywhere in the special issue of *Human Relations*. Such contradictions suggest a need to reconcile the different types of action research that exist to explore their potential integration as new forms of action research not previously attempted.

Differences in Methodological Details

The methods of study and reporting for the thirty IS articles and the five exemplary cases are also worthy of discussion. For instance, the basic concept of action research is assumed understood in all five cases and not explained. Their description of the research process and findings is mostly through detailed exposition on different phases of the studies over time, which consisted of a series of problem diagnoses, action interventions and reflective learning cycles. The writings are mostly in the form of condensed essays with no dialogue from the participants. Such patterns are notably different than the thirty IS articles. For example, many of the IS articles reported the use of multiple research strategies and data collection methods. Instead of the condensed style of writing as seen in the five cases, many of the IS articles have also adopted a case study approach where multiple dialogue passages are presented. Perhaps the most significant difference is the emphasis in IS to be explicit with the theoretical assumptions and research approach. This reflects the immature status of action research in IS relative to social science, where it is better understood and accepted. Perhaps such emphasis is pertinent for the emerging interpretivism rhetoric (Walsham 1995) in IS as there can be multiple research paradigms and methodologies requiring clarifications for the untrained. Where the two disciplines share a similar problem is in the length of their publications, which is typically restricted by the journals. This can present a conflict especially in extended IS studies where the tradition of action research writing is narrative in nature, requiring detailed descriptions of the events being reported.

4 A CONTEMPORARY IS ACTION RESEARCH FRAMEWORK

Based on the characteristics of action research in IS seen over the past twenty-five years and the emerging varieties of exemplary action research observed in social science, a contemporary IS action research framework that integrates the so-called classical and the emergent approach is proposed. The intent of this framework is to provide a conceptual foundation and a practical guide for researchers and practitioners interested in understanding, reviewing or conducting action research for different areas of IS. An argument is put forth in that neither the epistemological status of action research nor its methodological details are well-established in IS at present. There are also variations of the classical and emergent forms of action research in IS similar to those observed in social science as demonstrated from the thirty IS articles. To advance the use of action research in IS, an integration of the two forms is needed as the contemporary approach to address the increasingly complex role of information systems, technological innovations and socio-technical systems in groups, organizations and societies. Such integration can take on combinations of features from the narrowly focused classical action research and the more open emergent approach depending on the context of the study, its research focus, the involvement of the participants, and the expected outcome.

There are four distinct dimensions to this proposed framework: (a) the type of action research used and its focus; (b) one's tradition and beliefs as the underlying assumptions; (c) the process involved including its research theme, the level of organization involved, the extent of change intended and the researcher role; (d) the style of presentation adopted. For each of these dimensions, a range of options exists for the researcher or practitioner to adopt a unique strategy along a continuum that spans the classical action research at one end to the emergent approach at the other. Also included are reference sources from the thirty IS articles to be used as representative cases to illustrate the concepts involved. The components for this framework in terms of its four dimensions, the contrasting classical-emergent approaches, and their reference sources are shown in Table 8 and elaborated below along with its intended usage.

Table 8 A proposed contemporary IS action research framework.
Legend: C–classical, E–emergent.

Dimension		Classical	Emergent	Reference Source
Type and Focus	Action Research	Change information system related practice, create new information system related knowledge from experience	Change social practice with a socio-technical system or a technological innovation, create new general knowledge from experience	C–Mirvis and Lawler (1983) E–Badham, Couchman and Little (1995)
	Action Science	Resolve conflict in the use of a specific information system	Resolve conflict within a socio-technical system or technological innovation	C–Covaleski, Dirsmiith and Jablonsky (1985) E–Levine and Rossmoore (1993)
	Participatory Action Research	Participants as collaborators to change practice or resolve conflict related to a specific information system	Participants as collaborators to change social practice, resolve conflict in a socio-technical system or technological innovation	C–Pava (1986) E–Timpa, Sjoberg, and Svensson (1995)
	Action Learning	Provide experiential learning for users of a specific information system	Provide experiential learning for users of a socio-technical system or technological innovation	C–Wood-Harper and Flynn (1983) E–Blennerhassett (1988)
Assumptions	Interpretive	Social construction of reality for use of a specific information system	Social construction of reality in a socio-technical system or technological innovation	C–Covaleski, Dirsmith and Jablonsky (1985) E–Badham, Couch-man and Little (1995)
	Critical or Community Development	Improve human conditions through actions and a specific information system	Improve human conditions through actions and socio-technical systems or technological innovation	C–Cassell et al. (1988) E–Badham, Couch-man and Little (1995)
	School or Organization Design	Improve effectiveness with a specific information system	Improve effectiveness with a socio-technical system or technological innovation	C–Pava (1986) E–Fox (1995)

Table 8 (continued)

Dimension		Classical	Emergent	Reference Source
Process	Research Theme	Start with an IS theory, concept or objective as the intellectual framework, with research process largely predetermined	Start with a theory or objectives but open to change; process and theories evolve over time	C–Covaleski, Dirsmith and Jablonsky (1985) E–Badham, Couch-man and Little (1995)
	Level of Organization	Involve a single group or organization with well-defined purpose, structure, process and boundary	Involve multiple groups, organizations and communities with loosely defined purpose, structure, process and boundary	C–Jonsson and Solli (1993) E–Badham, Couch-man and Little (1995)
	Extent of Change	A specific IS problem from which a specific action, set of tasks or a methodology is implemented; change within existing context	A complex socio-technical problem from which a set of related actions or tasks is implemented; change includes underlying context	C–Jonsson and Solli (1993) E–Badham, Couch-man and Little (1995)
	Researcher Role	Researcher as expert, participants as subjects	Researcher as collaborator, participants as co-researchers	C–Mirvis and Lawler (1983) E–Timpka, Sjoberg and Svensson (1995)
Presentation	Case Study –Full Length	Study on development or use of a specific system; may be exploratory, descriptive or explanatory	Study on a socio-technical system or innovations; may be exploratory, descriptive or explanatory	C–Covaleski, Dirsmith and Jablonsky (1985) E–Cassell and Fitter (1992)
	Case Study –Illustrative	Discuss development or use of one or more specific information systems; include field studies for illustration	Discuss introduction of one or more socio-technical systems or innovations; include field studies for illustration	C–Jonsson and Solli (1991) E–Badham, Couch-man and Little (1995)
	Essay– Epistemology and/or Usage	Discuss action research as a mode of inquiry for information systems	Discuss action research as a mode of inquiry for socio-technical systems and innovations	C–Checkland (1991) E–Ngwenyama (1991)

4.1 Type and Focus Dimension

As seen from the "Type and Focus" dimension in Table 8, the type of action research adopted by the researcher/practitioner would influence the focus of the study as one of change in practice, conflict resolution, participant collaboration or experiential learning. Under the classical approach, the study would typically involve the development or use of a specific information system to solve a particular IS related problem. In the emergent approach, the study is more likely to introduce a complex socio-technical system or a technological innovation that includes different information systems and processes leading to fundamental changes in social practice and its underlying context. The development of a human resource information system by Mirvis and Lawler is an example of classical action research where the effects of a system on an organization and its staff are explored. In contrast, the instigation of a complex team-based manufacturing system by Badham, Couchman and Little in the manufacturing industry is an illustration of the emergent approach that changes the culture of an industry as a whole through the introduction of a technological innovation. For action science, participatory action research and action learning, their corresponding reference sources have also been identified in Table 8 for both the classical and emergent approaches.

4.2 Assumptions Dimension

From the "Assumptions" dimension, one may adopt an interpretive or critical perspective based on the beliefs of the researcher/practitioner, or choose from one of the community development, school/organization design traditions. Within our framework, the community development tradition and critical perspective are considered equivalent according to their ideological stance, whereas the school and organization design traditions have similar beliefs except for their intended settings. Under the classical approach, the focus is on the social meanings of a specific system and/or its use to improve human condition or organizational effectiveness within a firm. The respective reference sources are the interpretation of a budgeting system for a state geriatric department by Covaleski, Dirsmith and Jablonsky, the ideological stance by Cassell et al. to implement computers in a community center for self-improvement of the unemployed, and the introduction of a customer support system by Pava to improve the effectiveness of a computer firm. In the emergent approach, the interpretation of social change and desire for improvement are much more complex with the introduction of a socio-technical system or a technological innovation. Examples of this latter approach include the use of socio-technical analysis as a method to improve organization design by Fox, and the combined interpretive and critical perspectives in team-based manufacturing as technological innovations by Badham, Couchman and Little. In both studies, the nature of the problems, actions and reflections are more far-reaching than those described under the classical approach.

4.3 Process Dimension

In the "Process" dimension, the research theme refers to the inclusion of theories, concepts or objectives as the intellectual framework to guide the research process. Under the classical approach, such themes are usually predetermined and well-established by the researcher with only minor changes or refinement expected. An example is the budgeting behaviors of staff within an organization described by Covaleski, Dirsmith and Jablonsky, where the accounting and budgeting theories are well laid out at the beginning of the study. The emergent approach is much more open in that usually only a broad theme is stated, with the research agenda subjected to change as the research progresses. This is illustrated with the team-based manufacturing study by Badham, Couchman and Little, where the intended outcome of the project is stated only as broad objectives. In terms of the level of organization and the extent of change involved, the classical approach typically is concerned with a single group or organization such as the social service units of a government department (Jonsson and Solli 1993) where their financial management is improved through the introduction of an information reporting system with little change to the organization. In the emergent approach, the level of organization usually would involve multiple groups, organizations or communities. The extent of change would go beyond the current practice resulting in a fundamental shift within the underlying organizational context as in the creation of team-based manufacturing cells as new forms of organizations by Badham, Couchman and Little. The role of the researcher and participants in the study under the classical approach would have the researcher as the expert, as in the study by Mirvis and Lawler on the introduction of a human resource information system and its effects on staff. On the opposite end is the hypermedia development project by Timpka, Sjoberg and Svensson as the emergent approach whereby the researcher is a collaborator in the research process, with the participants taking control of the research agenda, process and outcomes as partners, collaborators and coresearchers.

4.4 Presentation Dimension

In the "Presentation" dimension, the researcher/practitioner may choose to write the action research report as a case study or essay regardless of the approach adopted. For case studies, they may be full-length or illustrative in style with or without direct quotes from the participants. Depending on the research objective, the study may be exploratory, descriptive or explanatory in nature. For essays, they may be on the epistemology of action research in IS and/or its usage within a given IS context. In classical action research, these cases or essays would refer to specific information systems, whereas, in the emergent approach, typically one or more complex socio-technical systems or technological innovations are involved. Examples of full-length and illustrative case studies in classical action research are the deployment of a budgeting system by Covaleski, Dirsmith and Jablonsky and the two short cases on social use of information by Jonsson and Solli, respectively. Those for the emergent approach include the full-length case on introducing computers to the unemployed by Cassell and Fitter and the illustrative case to automate the tax department by Badham, Couchman and Little. For essays on the epistemology of action research in IS, the article by Checkland (1991) is more classical with its focus on information systems research and practice, while the one by Ngwenyama (1991) is more of the emergent variety with an emphasis on value-laden change in social practice through the deployment of socio-technical systems.

4.5 Intended Use of the Framework

The contemporary IS action research framework presented above provides researchers and practitioners with a comprehensive scheme to consider when contemplating action research in IS. To illustrate, when planning an IS study, one may choose a particular type of action research such as action science with conflict resolution as the focus. Depending on the organization and participants involved, the research may take on a critical perspective aimed at empowering the employees at the workplace in a classical sense through the deployment of an integrated information system. However, an emergent process may be adopted where the research theme and extent of change are only loosely defined at the outset to evolve over time, with the participants playing an active role in the research and influencing its outcome. This is just one hypothetical example of how an IS study can take on features from both the classical and emergent approaches to become a hybrid, contemporary form of action research in IS.

Our proposed framework can also provide researchers/practitioners with the pertinent criteria to judge what may constitute good action research in IS. For novices or outsiders wishing to understand its use as a strategy of inquiry in IS, the framework allows one to systematically examine a given study along the four dimensions to review how action research is used. For those interested in conducting action research in IS, the framework provides an comprehensive template to guide the study design, the research process and its reporting. The framework outlines an initial pedagogy for a new, contemporary form of action research in IS that can be refined over time by experienced researchers and practitioners as the insiders.

5 IMPLICATIONS ON IS RESEARCH AND PRACTICE

The use of action research in IS can be a rewarding experience yet a challenging one at the same time. For those who aspire to make a difference in the field of IS, action research provides a unique opportunity to bridge theory with practice, allowing one to solve real-world problems while contributing to the generation of new knowledge. This overcomes much of the criticism by Keen (1991) that IS as a self-defined discipline has become overly preoccupied with theories, methods and publication to have any significant influence on the business community where major IS decisions are made. From this review, it is clear that action research can provide the type of pragmatism needed in IS research through its focus on change and improvement in practice. At the same time, action research can contribute to new knowledge on the consequences of IS through intellectual reflection and learning of the changes instigated. With the increasingly complex role of information technology as a key enabler of social change that can lead to new forms of organizations and communities, the use of such an action-oriented methodology should improve our understanding of real-world problems through "doing" and experiential learning through "afterthought." In particular, our proposed contemporary IS action research framework can serve as a practical guide for both insiders and outsiders to recognize and engage in good action research in IS.

For those interested in intensive IS research methodologies, action research presents an alternative mode of inquiry to the traditional positivistic approach in studying IS. With its emphasis on change that is process oriented by nature, action research can be a very effective way to collect a rich set of qualitative data from the field not available otherwise. Using this research approach, new ways of research design need to be derived taking into account such issues as the research context, its practical focus, the role of the participants, the intended outcome, and the need for theory contribution. If social change is context-bound, as suggested by Walsham (1993), then the creation of relevant knowledge should be "a direct result of local dialogue, where action research will become a central research strategy" (Sandberg 1985). As such, action research in IS should not be assessed according to existing evaluation criteria for IS research that is aimed more at positivistic approaches by statistical means using a restricted set of variables. With the emerging interpretivism rhetoric in IS research, such intensive methodologies as action research will undoubtedly assume a more important role in years to come. Hopefully, our proposed framework can provide an initial pedagogy for a new contemporary form of IS action research as part of the intensive IS research methodologies to be refined over time.

6 CONCLUSION

At the 1995 ICIS Conference in Amsterdam, Baskerville (Lee et al. 1995) outlined the criteria for acceptable IS action research to include: a real need for change; theory-based iterative problem-solving; genuine collaboration with participants; and honesty in theorizing research from reflection. The literature review and the contemporary IS action research framework presented in this paper provide a useful foundation and guide for researchers and practitioners in ways that are consistent with the aforementioned criteria. Specifically, the articles included in this review provide a rich historical account for those wishing to understand the use and evolution of action research in IS studies over the past twenty-five years. Also, the suggested framework provides a comprehensive template for use when reviewing or conducting IS studies based on such an approach. Looking ahead, the major challenges in IS action research will be the need for a better understanding of this strategy of inquiry within an IS context, increased use of this contemporary form of action research in the field, and the ability of researchers and practitioners to recognize and publish such exemplars in mainstream IS journals.

7 REFERENCES

Argyris, C.; Putnam, R.; and Smith, D. M. (1985). *Action Science: Concepts, Methods, and Skills for Research and Intervention.* San Francisco: Jossey-Bass Publishers.

Argyris, C., and Schon, D. A. (1989). "Participatory Action Research and Action Science Compared." *American Behavioral Scientist*, Volume 32, Number 5, pp. 612-623.

Baburoglu, O. N.; and Ravn, I. (1992). "Normative Action Research." *Organization Studies*, Volume 13, Number 1, pp. 19-34.

Badham, R.; Couchman, P.; and Little, S. (1995). "Getting Smart: Developing an Action Research Approach to the Integrated Management of Technical and Organizational Innovation." *Human Systems Management*, Volume 14, pp. 91-104.

Banville, C., and Landry, M. (1989). "Can the Field of MIS be Disciplined." *Communications of the ACM*, Volume 32, Number 1, pp. 48-60.

Bartunek, J. M. (1993). "Scholarly Dialogues and Participatory Action Research." *Human Relations*, Volume 46, Number 10, pp. 1221-1233.

Benbasat, I. (1985). "An Analysis of Research Methodologies." In W. MacFarlan (Editor), *The Information Systems Research Challenge.* Proceedings of Harvard Business School Colloquium. Boston: HBS Press, pp. 47-85.

Blennerhassett, E. (1988). "Research Report: Management Learning Groups: A Lesson in Action." *Journal of European Industrial Training*, Volume 12, Number 8, pp. 5-12.

Brown, L. D. (1993). "Social Change Through Collective Reflection with Asian Nongovernmental Development Organizations." *Human Relations*, Volume 46, Number 2, pp. 249-274.

Brown, L. D.; and Tandon, R. (1983). "Ideology and Political Economy in Inquiry: Action Research and Participatory Research." *Journal of Applied Behavioral Science*, Volume 19, Number 3, pp. 277-294.

Calabrese, A. M., and Acker, S. R. (1987). *Information System Design: A Case Study in the Generation of Innovations.* Meeting of the Human Communication Technology Interest Group, International Communication Association, Montreal, Canada.

Candlin, D. B., and Wright, S. (1992). "Managing the Introduction of Expert Systems." *International Journal of Operations and Production Management*, Volume 12, Number 1, 1992, pp. 46-59.
Cassell, C., and Fitter, M. (1992). "Responding to a Changing Environment." In D. M. Hosking and N. Anderson (Editors), *Organizational Change and Innovation: Psychological Perspectives and Practices in Europe*. London: Routledge, pp. 288-304.
Cassell, C.; Fitter, M.; Fryer, D.; and Smith, L. (1988). "The Development of Computer Applications by Non-employed People in Community Settings." *Journal of Occupational Psychology* , Volume 61, pp. 89-102.
Checkland, P. B. (1989). "Soft Systems Methodology." *Human Systems Management*, Volume 8, pp. 273-289.
Checkland, P. (1991). "From Framework through Experience to Learning: The Essential Nature of Action Research." In H-E. Nissen, H. K. Klein, and R. Hirschheim (Editors), *Information Systems Research: Contemporary Approaches and Emergent Traditions*. Amsterdam: North-Holland, pp. 397-403.
Chisholm, R. F., and Elden, M. (1993). "Features of Emerging Action Research." *Human Relations*, Volume 46, Number 2, 1993, pp. 275-298.
Covaleski, M. A.; Dirsmith, M. W.; and Jablonsky, S. F. (1985). "Traditional and Emergent Theories of Budgeting: An Empirical Analysis." *Journal of Accounting and Public Policy*, Volume 4, pp. 277-300.
Crowther, W. (1994). "Considering Complex Objectives and Scarce Resources in Information Systems Analysis." ASIS Annual Meeting, Las Vegas.
DeCock, C. (1994). "Action Research: In Search of a New Epistemology?" *International Journal of Management*, Volume 11, Number 3, pp. 791-797.
Denzin, N., and Lincoln, Y. S. (1993). "Entering the Field of Qualitative Research." In N. Denzin and Y. Lincoln (Editors), *Handbook of Qualitative Research*. London: Sage Publications, pp. 1-17.
Earl, M. J. (1978). "Prototype Systems for Accounting, Information and Control." *Accounting, Organizations and Society*, Volume 3, Number 2, pp. 161-170.
Elden, M., and Chisholm, R. F. (1993). "Emerging Varieties of Action Research: Introduction to the Special Issue." *Human Relations*, Volume 46, Number 2, pp. 121-142.
Engelstad, P. H., and Gustavsen, B. (1993). "Swedish Network Development for Implementing National Work Reform Strategy." *Human Relations*, Volume 46, Number 2, pp. 219-248.
Fox, W. M. (1995). "Sociotechnical System Principles and Guidelines: Past and Present." *Journal of Applied Behavioral Science*, Volume 31, Number 1, pp. 91-105.
French, W. L., and Bell Jr., C. H. (1990). *Organization Development: Behavioral Science Interventions for Organization Improvement*, Fourth Edition. Englewood Cliffs, New Jersey: Prentice Hall.

Galliers, R. D., and Land, F. F. (1987). "Choosing Appropriate Information Systems Research Methodologies." *Communications of the ACM*, Volume 30, Number 11, pp. 900-902.

Gibson, C. F. (1975). "A Methodology for Implementation Research." In R. L. Schultz and D. P. Slevin (Editors), *Implementing Operations Research/Management Science*. New York: American Elsevier Publishing Co., pp. 53-73.

Greenwood, D. J.; Whyte, W. F.; and Harkavy, I. (1993). "Participatory Action Research as a Process and as a Goal." *Human Relations*, Volume 46, Number 2, pp. 174-192.

Gustavsen, B. (1993). "Action Research and the Generation of Knowledge." *Human Relations*, Volume 46, Number 10, pp. 1361-1365.

Hamilton, S., and Ives, B. (1982). "MIS Research Strategies." *Information and Management*, Volume 5, pp. 339-347.

Harris, R. T. (1978). "Improving Patient Satisfaction Through Action Research." *Journal of Applied Behavioral Science*, Volume 14, Number 3, pp. 382-399.

Heller, F. (1993). "Another Look at Action Research." *Human Relations*, Volume 46, Number 10, 1993, pp. 1235-1242.

Hult, M. and Lennung, S. (1978). "Towards a Definition of Action Research: A Note and Bibliography." *Journal of Management Studies*, Volume 17, Number 2, pp. 241-250.

Jonsson, S. (1991). "Action Research." In H-E. Nissen, H. K. Klein, and R. Hirschheim (Editors), *Information Systems Research: Contemporary Approaches and Emergent Traditions*. Amsterdam: North-Holland, pp. 371-396.

Jonsson, S., and Gronlund, A. (1988). "Life with a Sub-contractor: New Technology and Management Accounting." *Accounting, Organizations and Society*, Volume 13, Number 5, pp. 512-532.

Jonsson, S., and Solli, R. (1993). "Accounting Talk in a Caring Setting." *Management Accounting Research*, Volume 4, pp. 301-320.

Keen, P. G. W. (1991). "Relevance and Rigor in Information Systems Research: Improving Quality, Confidence, Cohesion and Impact." In H-E. Nissen, H. K. Klein, and R. Hirschheim (Editors), *Information Systems Research: Contemporary Approaches and Emergent Traditions*. Amsterdam: North-Holland, pp. 27-49.

Lacity, M. C., and Janson, M. A. (1994). "Understanding Qualitative Data: A Framework of Text Analysis Methods." *Journal of Management Information Systems*, Volume 11, Number 2, pp. 137-155.

Laughlin, R. C. (1987). "Accounting Systems in Organizational Contexts: A Case for Critical Theory." *Accounting, Organizations and Society*, Volume 12, Number 5, pp. 479-502.

Ledford, G. E., and Mohrman S. A. (1993a). "Looking Backward and Forward at Action Research." *Human Relations*, Volume 46, Number 10, pp. 1349-1359.

Ledford, G. E., and Mohrman, S. A. (1993b). "Self-Design for High Involvement: A Large-Scale Organizational Change." *Human Relations*, Volume 46, Number 2, pp. 143-174.

Lee, A. S. (1989). "A Scientific Methodology for MIS Case Studies." *MIS Quarterly*, Volume 13, Number 1, pp. 33-50.

Lee, A.; Baskerville, R.; Liebenau, J.; and Myers, M. (1995). "Judging Qualitative Research in Information Systems: Criteria for Accepting and Rejecting Manuscripts." In J. I. DeGross, G. Ariav, C. Beath, R. Hoyer, and C. Kemerer (Editors), *Proceedings of the Sixteenth International Conference on Information Systems*. Amsterdam, pp. 367.

Levin, M. (1993). "Creating Networks for Rural Economic Development in Norway." *Human Relations*, Volume 46, Number 2, (46:2), 1993, pp. 193-218.

Levine, H. G., and Rossmoore, D. (1993). "Diagnosing the Human Threats to Information Technology Implementation: A Missing Factor in Systems Analysis Illustrated in a Case Study." *Journal of Management Information Systems*, Volume 10, Number 2, pp. 55-73.

Lewin, K. (1947). "Frontiers in Group Dynamics. I. Concepts, Method and Reality in Social Sciences: Social Equilibria and Social Change." *Human Relations*, Volume 1, pp. 5-41.

Liu, M.,;Denis, H.; Kolodny, H.; and Stymne, B. (1990). "Organization Design for Technological Change." *Human Relations*, Volume 43, Number 1, pp. 7-22.

Mangham, I, L. (1993). "Conspiracies of Silence? Some Critical Comments on the Action Research Special Issue, February 1993." *Human Relations*, Volume 46, Number 10, pp. 1243-1251.

Markus, M. L. (1994). "Electronic Mail as the Medium of Managerial Choice." *Organization Science*, Volume 5, Number 4, pp. 502-527.

Markus, M. L., and Robey, D. (1988). "Information Technology and Organizational Change: Causal Structure in Theory and Research." *Management Science*, Volume 34, Number 5, pp. 583-598.

McFarlan, F. W. (Editor) (1985). *The Information Systems Research Challenge*, Proceedings of Harvard Business School Colloquium. Boston: HBS Press.

McTaggart, R. (1991). "Principles for Participatory Action Research." *Adult Education Quarterly*, Volume 41, Number 3, pp. 168-187.

Mirvis, P. H., and Lawler, E. E. (1983). "Systems Are Not Solutions: Issues in Creating Information Systems That Account for the Human Organization." *Accounting, Organizations and Society*, Volume 8, Number 2/3, pp. 175-190.

Mumford, E.; Hirschheim, R.; Fitzgerald, G.; and Wood-Harper, T. (Editors) (1985). *Research Methods in Information Systems*. Amsterdam: North-Holland.

Nissen, H-E.; Klein, H. K.; and Hirschheim, R. (Editors) (1991). *Information Systems Research: Contemporary Approaches & Emergent Traditions*. Amsterdam: North-Holland.

Ngwenyama, O. K. (1991). "The Critical Social Theory Approach to Information Systems: Problems and Challenges." In H-E. Nissen, H. K. Klein, and R. Hirschheim (Editors), *Information Systems Research: Contemporary Approaches and Emergent Traditions*. Amsterdam: North-Holland, pp. 267-280.

Ngwenyama, O. K. (1993). "Developing End-users' Systems Development Competence: An Exploratory Study." *Information & Management*, Volume 25, pp. 291-302.

Nosek, J. T., and Yaverbaum, G. (1991). "Overcoming Obstacles to University and industry Synergy in Information System Education: Lessons from Action Research." *Education for Information*, Volume 9, 1991, pp. 3-19.

Oakland, J. S. (1986). "Production Management and High Technology in the United Kingdom." *Engineering Management International*, Volume 3, pp. 269-278.

Orlikowski, W. J. (1992). "The Duality of Technology: Rethinking the Concept of Technology in Organizations." *Organization Science*, Volume 3, Number 3, pp. 398-427.

Orlikowski, W. J. (1993). "CASE Tools as Organizational Change: Investigating Incremental and Radical Changes in Systems Development." *MIS Quarterly*, Volume 17, Number 3, pp. 309-340.

Pava, C. (1986). "Redesigning Sociotechnical Systems Design: Concepts and Methods for the 1990s." *Journal of Applied Behavioral Science*, Volume 22, Number 3, 1986, pp. 201-221.

Peters, M., and Robinson, V. (1984). "The Origins and Status of Action Research." *Journal of Applied Behavioral Science*, Volume 20, Number 2, pp. 113-124.

Rapoport, R. N. (1970). "Three Dilemmas in Action Research." *Human Relations*, Volume 23, Number 4, pp. 499-513.

Reason, P. (1993a). "Three Approaches to Participative Inquiry." In N. Denzin and Y. Lincoln (Editors), *Handbook of Qualitative Research*. London: Sage Publications, pp. 324-339.

Reason, P. (1993b). "Sitting Between Appreciation and Disappointment: A Critique of the Special Edition of Human Relations on Action Research." *Human Relations*, Volume 46, Number 10, pp. 1253-1270.

Revans, R.W. (1980). *Action Learning: New Techniques for Management*. London: Blond & Briggs.

Revans, R. W. (1983a). "Action Learning: Kindling the Touch Paper." *Management Decision*, Volume 21, pp. 3-10.

Revans, R. W. (1983b). "Action Learning: Its Terms and Character." *Management Decision*, Volume 21, pp. 39-50.

Revans, R. W. (1983c). "Action Learning: The Skills of Diagnosis." *Management Decision*, Volume 21, pp. 46-54.

Rickards, T. (1985). "Making New Things Happen: An Interpretation of Observed Innovation Strategies." *Technovation*, Volume 3, 1985, pp. 119-131.

Robinson, V. M. J. (1993). "Current Controversies in Action Research." *Public Administration Quarterly*, Fall, pp. 263-290.

Salmela, H., and Ruohonen, M. (1992). "Aligning DSS Development with Organization Development." *European Journal of Operational Research*, Volume 61, pp. 57-71.

Sandberg, A. (1985). "Socio-technical Design, Trade Union Strategies and Action Research." In E. Mumford, R. Hirschheim, G. Fitzgerald, and A. T. Wood-Harper (Editors), *Research Methods in Information Systems*. Amsterdam: North-Holland, pp. 79-92.

Susman, G. I., and Evered, R. D. (1978). "An Assessment of the Scientific Merits of Action Research." *Administrative Science Quarterly*, Volume 23, Number 4, pp. 582-603.

Timpka, T.; Sjoberg, C.; and Svensson, B. (1995). "The Pragmatics of Clinical Hypermedia: Experiences From Five Years of Participatory Design in the MEDEA Project." *Computer Methods and Programs in Biomedicine*, Volume 46, pp. 175-186.

Walsham G. (1993). *Interpreting Information Systems in Organizations*. Chichester, England: John Wiley & Sons.

Walsham G. (1995). "The Emergence of Interpretivism in IS Research." *Information Systems Research*, Volume 6, Number 4, pp. 376-394.

Whyte, W. F. (Editor) (1991). *Participatory Action Research*. Newbury Park, California: Sage Publications.

Wood-Harper, A. T. (1985). "Research Methods in Information Systems: Using Action Research." In E. Mumford, R. Hirschheim, G. Fitzgerald, and A. T. Wood-Harper (Editors), *Research Methods in Information Systems*. Amsterdam: North-Holland, pp. 169-191.

Wood-Harper, A. T., and Flynn, D. J. (1983). "Action Learning for Teaching Information Systems." *The Computer Journal*, Volume 26, Number 1, pp. 79-82.

Yin, R. K. (1994). *Case Study Research: Design and Methods*. Second Edition. London: Sage Publications.

Ziegenfuss Jr., J. (1987). "Research Information Systems are Paths to High-Quality Healthcare." *Health Progress*, October, pp. 50-53, 82.

8 BIOGRAPHY

Francis Lau is an assistant professor in the Faculty of Business at the University of Alberta where he teaches information technology to undergraduate and MBA students. His research interests include the planning, development, implementation and evaluation of information systems in healthcare. His background consists of a Ph.D. in medical informatics, an MBA, a M.Sc. in medical bacteriology, a B.Sc. in medical laboratory science, and over twelve years of systems consulting experience within the health industry.

5

Panel – The Impact of Action Research on Information Systems

R. Baskerville
Binghamton University, USA

M. Myers
University of Auckland, New Zealand

P. A. Nielsen
Aalborg University, Denmark

T. Wood-Harper
Salford University, UK

This panel will discuss the impact of action research methodology on the field of information systems (IS). Action research is often discussed as a paragon of qualitative methods, but how has this method made a significant difference in our understanding of the interaction between information systems and the organization?

The panel will take as a point of departure Francis Lau's paper, "A Review on the Use of Action Research in Information Systems Studies." This paper analyzes a broad spectrum of published IS action research. The panel will consider the impact of this body of research along three dimensions: the impact on IS development (ISD) methods, the impact of IS research methods, and the impact on the goals and objectives of information technology practice. Richard Baskerville will open the panel with a quick overview of the history of action research. This will be followed by three brief presentations. Trevor Wood-Harper will describe the impact of action research on ISD methods. Michael Myers will focus on the impact of action research on IS research methods. Peter Axel Nielsen will describe the effects of action research on IS practice, especially focusing on the changes in Scandinavia.

Following these presentations, the audience will participate in an open discussion of the paper and the impact of this research on the field of IS.

6

Process Models in Information Systems

T. Shaw
University of Texas at Austin
Austin, Texas, United States
Tel: (512) 502-9976
E-mail: shaw@mail.utexas.edu

S. Jarvenpaa
University of Texas at Austin
Austin, Texas, United States
Tel: (512) 471-1751
E-mail: sjarvenpaa@mail.utexas.edu

Abstract

The classic story of the blind men and the elephant teaches us that in order to fully understand something, we need to observe it from more than one perspective. In this paper, we extend the range of perspectives available for researchers by developing a typology of models. The typology is based on the process-variance dichotomy suggested by Mohr (1982). A selection of empirical IS research is classified with the typology, resulting in the identification of four distinct hybrid models. The research using these four forms is able to make valuable contributions to our knowledge of IS, refuting Mohr's claim that hybrid models are inferior to pure process and variance models. The analysis of the IS research using the typology is combined with a series of interviews with process researchers to yield a collection of implications for researchers interested in studying process or hybrid models.

The reason for our existence in the business school is to provide prescriptions to managers on how to improve things. Only the process approach can lead us to these prescriptions.
(statement by an IS researcher experienced in the study of process models)

1 INTRODUCTION

The classic story of the blind men and the elephant teaches us that to fully understand something we must observe it from more than one perspective. This lesson applies to examining researchers as well. To understand a construct, Campbell and Fiske (1959) suggest examining multiple traits using multiple methods. Likewise, Markus and Robey (1988) identified alternative perspectives for structuring research models in the field of information systems. They contrasted process and variance models, building on the earlier work of Mohr (1982).

Markus and Robey called for further study of process models. A process model attempts to explain the occurrence of an outcome by identifying the sequence of events preceding it. Despite the encouragement, process models are underrepresented in both IS and organizational journals (Markus and Robey 1988; Monge 1990; Orlikowski and Baroudi 1991). Rather, IS researchers tend to study variance models, which are models that explain the variability of a dependent variable based on its correlation with one or more independent variables.

Monge (1990, p. 407) offered an explanation for the imbalance between these two perspectives when he wrote that "the organizational and social sciences generally lack the conceptual tools with which to develop dynamic theories."[1] Our purpose in this paper is to develop such a conceptual tool: a typology of research models that includes not only process and variance forms, but also those that lie between these two extremes.

The process-variance typology is valuable for a number of reasons. First, it will help IS researchers understand the distinction between process and variance models by identifying the key dimensions along which they differ. Also, the categories in the typology will identify the range of options available to IS researchers when structuring models. These options, many of which are hybrids of process and variance models, were not addressed by Mohr or Markus and Robey. Rather, they defined process and variance models as the two extreme, or pure, forms of models. Mohr (p. 35) suggests these two pure forms are the ideals that researchers are (and should be) trying to achieve: "One does, however, detect in social research a striving, though implicit and imperfect, toward process theory and variance theory as distinct modes

[1]Monge used the terms *process* and *dynamic* interchangeably when discussing types of theories.

of explanation—a striving that deserves to be reinforced." While Mohr chose to focus his discussion on these two extremes, he recognized that the kinds of models researchers actually build and study usually lie somewhere in between. By developing a typology based on the pure process and variance models, we hope to better understand the hybrids that combine features of both.

The second objective of this paper stems from another comment from Monge (1990, p. 426): "[an] explication of how to develop process stage theories, hypotheses, and research would enrich the organizational literature." We contend that such an explication would also enrich the IS literature, and we will make a first step toward this by categorizing a selection of empirical IS research using the process-variance typology. One exemplar of the process form and each hybrid form will be examined in depth to uncover its unique ability to contribute to our understanding of IS issues. By analyzing the IS literature using the typology we will not only identify the types of models that have been studied by IS researchers, but also infer a series of practical implications, or lessons, for IS researchers interested in empirically studying processes. These lessons are further enriched by a series of interviews we conducted with the authors of the research categorized with the typology.

The remainder of this paper is organized into four sections. The second section develops the typology. The third section categorizes empirical IS research with the typology. The fourth interprets the categorization of research and presents a series of implications for IS researchers. The paper concludes with the discussion of process and hybrid models in IS research. This discussion highlights the role of process models in qualitative research.

2 DEVELOPMENT OF THE PROCESS-VARIANCE TYPOLOGY

The process-variance typology is consistent with a nominal theoretical typology (Rich 1992). It is nominal, rather than ordinal, because the categories simply name different types of models and the categories are not nested in a hierarchical pattern. The typology is theoretical in that the initial categories are defined prior to examining the data (i.e., the empirical IS literature), and this definition is based on existing theory.

The theoretical framework underpinning the typology is the discussion of process and variance models presented by Mohr and again by Markus and Robey. While there are other perspectives on studying processes, such as those from Abbott (1983, 1992) and Monge, both Mohr and Markus and Robey are more widely accepted among scholars, particularly in the IS community. The Social Science Citation Index lists 62 citations of Markus and Robey through April 1996. Many of these are from mainstream IS publications, such as *MIS Quarterly* and *Information Systems Research*. Mohr has been cited 97 times, in areas as diverse as communication, psychology, accounting, political science, and gerontology. Taken together, the three articles by Abbott (1983, 1992) and Monge have only been cited 49 times. Most of these citations are of Abbott's work, which are primarily from sociology journals. Given the greater number of citations of Mohr and Markus and Robey, the diversity of fields that have cited Mohr, and the number of IS journals citing Markus and Robey, we consider the dichotomy of process and variance models presented by these authors to be an appropriate and legitimate basis for the process-variance typology.

One of the first steps in the development of a typology or taxonomy is the selection of the "operational taxonomic unit, or the object of classification" (Rich 1992, p. 765). As argued earlier, the objects to be classified in this typology are research models. Lave and March (1975, p. 3) define a model as "a simplified picture of a part of the real world." The two essential characteristics of models—concepts and relationships—form the basis for identifying the dimensions that differentiate one category in the typology from the next. Three dimensions emerge from the following analysis of Mohr's process-variance dichotomy.[2] The three dimensions allow for eighteen distinct types of models, ranging from pure process to pure variance. These configurations are listed in Table 1.

2.1 Concepts

The first dimension, *concepts*, is based on the nature of the concepts forming the research model. The concepts in a variance model are variables that can take on multiple values (Mohr 1982), often labeled independent or dependent variables. In contrast, the concepts of a process model are events or possibly states. Often considered binary, their value is either on or off; they either occur or do not. Rather than labeling these independent and dependent variables, Mohr called the beginning and end of a process model the precursor and the outcome, respectively.

Examples of variables include the level of conflict experienced by a group prior to using GDSS technology (Sambamurthy and Poole 1992), the degree to which users perceive a new information system as a threat (Newman and Sabherwal 1989), the level of satisfaction users feel toward an IS (DeSanctis et al. 1991), and the degree to which IS personnel intend to leave the organization (Gupta and Gupta 1990). A precursor event might be the existence of top management sponsorship (Markus

---

[2]We have purposely omitted from the typology one of the factors Mohr discussed: the logical relationship between concepts. Each event in a process model is alleged to be *necessary* for the subsequent events to occur, while a change in the value of the independent variable is *necessary and sufficient* for the dependent variable to change. These ideas are based on assumptions of causality that are both abstract and philosophically debatable. It is not our intention to enter into this debate. Rather, we contend that the logical relationship between concepts as described by Mohr does not contribute significantly to our understanding of the different forms of models. Including this as a dimension of the typology adds complexity with little in return. Omitting it maintains the simplicity of the typology without sacrificing its ability to help us make sense of research models.

Table 1 Process-Variance Typology.

Sequential	Concepts	Predictable	Type of Model
Sequential	Events	No	PROCESS
		Yes	HYBRID
	Mixed	No	HYBRID
		Yes	HYBRID
	Variables	No	HYBRID
		Yes	HYBRID
Temporal	Events	No	HYBRID
		Yes	HYBRID
	Mixed	No	HYBRID
		Yes	HYBRID
	Variables	No	HYBRID
		Yes	HYBRID
Non-temporal	Events	No	HYBRID
		Yes	HYBRID
	Mixed	No	HYBRID
		Yes	HYBRID
	Variables	No	HYBRID
		Yes	VARIANCE

1994) or the implementation of a new information system (Markus 1983; Joshi 1991). One cannot have more or less of these factors; they either are or are not. An outcome might be the withdrawal of commitment to an IS project (Newman and Sabherwal 1996) or a change in the nature of an organization (Orlikowski 1993, 1996).

There are three distinct values that the *concepts* dimension of the typology can assume. First, all of the concepts can be defined as events, which would be consistent with a pure process model. Second, all can be defined as variables, as in a pure variance model. Finally, the concepts can be a mix of variables and events. Such a model would be classified as a hybrid.

2.2 Relationships of Concepts

The second dimension for distinguishing models is the temporal and sequential relationship of the concepts. Mohr implies that sequential and temporal are synonymous. In a process model the events are sequential; one occurs after another. Indeed, a sequential relationship is temporal because there is some time gap between the occurrence of events. However, a temporal relationship need not be sequential. If a research model is based on the measurement of the same concept at two points in time, it makes sense to call it temporal, but not sequential.

This conceptualization implies that a sequence can only occur between two *different* concepts. A temporal, non-sequential relationship exists between two instances of the same concept. A time-series model such as $X_t = f(X_{t-1})$ is an example of this hybrid form. The third value this dimension can assume is non-temporal, which is consistent with a pure variance model. In such a model the variables coexist simultaneously; there is no temporal and therefore no sequential relationship between independent and dependent variable.

Mackay and Elam's (1992) study of spreadsheet usage incorporates a sequential relationship among spreadsheet tasks. The sequence begins with the formulation of a plan in the mind of the spreadsheet user. The plan is manifested when the user invokes the desired spreadsheet commands, using either the keyboard or the mouse. Following invocation, the user can execute the command. These events must occur in this order; execution cannot occur without prior invocation, nor can invocation occur without prior formulation. Another event, abandonment, can occur at any point of this sequence.

This dimension of the typology is called *sequential*, and it can assume a value of "sequential," "temporal," or "non-temporal." We have chosen the label "sequential" because Mohr emphasized sequence over time in his discussion of process models.

2.3 Predictability of the Relationship

The last dimension of the typology is based on the predictability of the relationship between concepts. The path from one event to the next in a process model is probabilistic, or subject to random external forces that may cause the path to deviate. The path is inherently unpredictable. The relationship between variables in a variance model is not affected by such random forces, so it is consistent over time. The relationship is thus predictable. This *predictable* dimension of the typology can assume a value of "yes" or "no."

The spreadsheet example introduced above (Mackay and Elam 1992) includes unpredictable relationships from one event to the next. The progression through the sequence of spreadsheet tasks is influenced by the users' spreadsheet and domain experience, and there may be multiple sequences that can accomplish the same task, so two users may select different paths. Also, some users may prefer to invoke a series of commands before executing one, while others may execute the first command they invoke. These factors make it difficult, if not impossible, to accurately predict the sequence of events in the spreadsheet usage model. The process is inherently uncertain.

The relationships in Abdel-Hamid's (1989) model of IS project management is based on predictable, fixed relationships among variables. The simulation program used to study this system dynamics model can be run repeatedly based on the same initial starting conditions and result in consistent outcomes each time. Although this model includes predictable relationships among variables, the relationships are also sequential, making this a hybrid rather than a variance model.

3 CLASSIFICATION OF EMPIRICAL IS LITERATURE

The process-variance typology was used to categorize and analyze a selection of empirical IS research. The publications searched to compile this research database included *MIS Quarterly*, *Journal of Management Information Systems*, ICIS *Proceedings*, and *Information Systems Research* for the last six years (1989–1996). We selected those empirical articles whose title, abstract, or introduction suggested they were consistent with at least one of the three dimensions of process models in the typology. Other studies were identified through bibliographic databases, reference searches using keywords such as *process theory*, and personal correspondence. We limited the search to the period following Markus and Robey's 1988 *Management Science* article. Articles were removed from the database if, after closer inspection, they failed to satisfy at least one of the criteria of process models. The research database thus includes "pure" process models and those in the hybrid range between process and variance, but no "pure" variance models.

The appendix explains how each study was interpreted using the typology.[3] Because few of the authors explicitly described their work in terms of process or

---

[3]This lengthy appendix is included so readers of this paper can better understand how the various process-related studies were interpreted and categorized. The detailed abstracts are intended to allow even those who have not read these studies to determine if our interpretation is legitimate. Most importantly, this level of detail is intended to support the replicability of our categorization.

variance models, each model was essentially reconstructed within the parameters of the three dimensions. The resulting interpretations lead to the categorization listed in Table 2. This shows the majority of the models in the "pure" process category, that based on an unpredictable sequence of events.

3.1 Process Model

Orlikowski's (1996) study of emergent, situated change is an exemplar of process models. While some process models are stated in general terms, this model focuses on the particular events within a single organization. Orlikowski uses primary and secondary sources of qualitative data and a grounded theory analysis method to derive this ideographic model. The model describes five metamorphic phases in the evolution of work within the customer service department of a large organization. Each phase consists of deliberate and emergent changes in the work of managers and customer service specialists, as well as unintended outcomes. Since the overall model is so comprehensive, this review will only cover a portion of it: Metamorphosis III.

This phase begins with a deliberate change in specialists' practices. They enter, document, process, and transfer service calls electronically. Prior to this, some of these tasks were performed manually. This change initiated an emergent change in specialists' practices as they started to interact electronically within the department. This resulted in proactive collaboration, as well as the unintended consequence of decreased face-to-face interaction. The increased collaboration produced ambiguity about electronic "help giving" (unintended consequence), which in turn resulted in the development of help protocols (emergent change) and increased problem solving effectiveness (unintended consequence). The collaboration also initiated an emergent change among managers; they changed the evaluation criteria to recognize these new behaviors.

As the preceding paragraph implies, Orlikowski's (1996) process model tells a rich and detailed story about the changes taking place within a single organization. A variance model might be able to capture a piece of this story, such as the relationship between increased collaboration and help-giving ambiguity. However, this relationship would not have been evident if Orlikowski had not built the process model describing this organizational change. Describing the qualitative data as a series of sequentially interconnected events and interactions, which essentially tells the story of this organization, yields valuable insight that would be difficult if not impossible to capture in a variance model.

3.2 Hybrid Model I

Only four types of hybrid models were observed in the research database. The first of these hybrid forms violates Mohr's warning about mixing variables and events in the same model, but is otherwise consistent with a process model. The examples

Table 2 Categorization of Empirical IS Research.

Sequential	Concepts	Predictable	Empirical IS Research
Sequential	Events	No	Joshi 1991 Mackay and Elam 1992 Markus 1983, 1994 Newman and Noble 1990 Newman and Sabherwal 1996 Orlikowski 1993, 1996 Orlikowski, Yates, Okamura and Fujimoto 1995 Poole and Holmes 1995 Robey and Newman 1996 Sabherwal and Robey 1993, 1995 Sen, Vinze and Liou 1994 Tyre and Orlikowski 1994 Vicinanza, Mukhopadhyay and Prietula 1991
Sequential	Events	Yes	—
Sequential	Mixed	No	Newman and Robey 1992 Newman and Sabherwal 1989 Sambamurthy and Poole 1994
Sequential	Mixed	Yes	—
Sequential	Variables	No	Poole and DeSanctis 1992 DeSanctis, Poole, Lewis and Desharnais 1991
Sequential	Variables	Yes	Abdel-Hamid 1989 Abdel-Hamid and Madnick 1989 Gupta and Gupta 1990
Temporal	Events	No	—
Temporal	Events	Yes	—
Temporal	Mixed	No	—
Temporal	Mixed	Yes	—
Temporal	Variables	No	—
Temporal	Variables	Yes	Galegher and Kraut 1994 Orlikowski and Yates 1994 Soh, Ang and Neo 1994
Non-temporal	Events	No	—
Non-temporal	Events	Yes	—
Non-temporal	Mixed	No	—
Non-temporal	Mixed	Yes	—
Non-temporal	Variables	No	—
Non-temporal	Variables	Yes	—

within this hybrid form use variables to measure attributes of the process as it unfolds. Newman and Sabherwal's (1989) model of information systems development includes two contextual variables that affect and are affected by the relationship between users and IS developers. These contextual variables include the degree to which users perceive the new IS to be a threat, along with the balance of power between users and IS developers. The sequence of events comprising the ISD process structures the dynamic relationships that are studied. The events include a project proposal, MIS design and development, MIS implementation, and MIS evaluation. The model yields four potential scenarios for the information systems development process: cooperation, conflict, MIS-dominated, and user-dominated. In the conflict scenario, for example, the new system is perceived as a threat and power is equally distributed between the two groups. Users will try to resist the new system or negotiate with MIS for an acceptable outcome. MIS will try to increase their power so they can force the system on users, or they will try to negotiate. The outcome of these behaviors at each stage of the development process can change the nature of the contextual variables, so what started as a conflictual process can end as a cooperative one, for example.

The relationships among some of these concepts can be described using variance models. For example, the relationship between the contextual factors and the four scenarios can be tested with quantitative data and variance methods. However, such data and methods would not be able to recognize or explain how the process can change over the life of the project. For example, a variance model cannot explain how resistance from users changed a conflictual process to a user-dominated one, or how the resulting efforts to increase the power of the MIS department in turn led to a cooperative strategy. This is the kind of rich scenario that requires a process-oriented model. However, a pure process model also misses some of the richness of this story, as it fails to capture the contextual factors that influence and are influenced by the behaviors of users and developers. Newman and Sabherwal's (1989) story thus requires a model that includes a sequence of events situated within a context described by variables.

3.3 Hybrid Model II

Another hybrid form of model is based solely on variables while maintaining the sequential and unpredictable relationship among these variables. Poole and DeSanctis (1992) examine GDSS-supported group processes using such a model. The study looks at the relationship between GDSS restrictiveness and microlevel structuration processes, and the relationship between structuration processes and a group outcome, the change in consensus. The specific events comprising the group process (i.e., the behaviors of the group members) are not specified in the model, which distinguishes this form of model from the previous form. Data describing behavior is collected and analyzed, but instead of focusing on each behavioral instance as an event, the behaviors are categorized and counted to yield variables describing the group process. A sense of sequence is maintained because the three variables-context, process, and outcome-occur in order. The relationship among these concepts is implicitly unpredictable because the process involves complex interpersonal behaviors.

Poole and DeSanctis found that groups which faithfully appropriated the services of the GDSS had a larger change in consensus following the group process. Increased restrictiveness of the GDSS also affected the way groups appropriated the GDSS technology. Because of the focus on variables, this research model resembles a variance model more than the others discussed so far. However, the nature of the research questions demands a model that incorporates sequence. Each concept in the model occurs at a different point in time, so a pure variance model is inadequate for this purpose. A pure process model is also inadequate, as it is not able to accommodate the variable nature of each concept. Poole and DeSanctis thus demonstrate an effective appropriation of process and variance model attributes, blended into the kind of hybrid research model that best fits their study.

3.4 Hybrid Model III

The third hybrid form combines predictable relationships between variables into network configurations. These networks are comprised of multiple variables and are studied using the system dynamics methodology, a formal system for studying complex relationships among a series of sequentially and predictably related variables. Each pair of concepts in a system dynamics model resembles a variance model, except there exists an explicit time lag between the independent and dependent variables. Also, the complex network pattern suggests a variable that plays the role of independent variable in one pair can be the dependent variable in another pair.

Abdel-Hamid and Madnick (1989) develop such a systems dynamic model of the software development process. The model includes twenty-two variables collected into four categories: human resource management, software production, control, and planning. The recursive nature of the network is evident in the following selection from the software production process. The concepts in this selection are learning, actual productivity, and the software development rate. Learning is positively related to actual productivity, which is positively related to the software development rate, which in turn is positively related to learning. So the more one learns, the more one learns. However, these variables are involved in relationships with other variables, so this self-reinforcing loop may be dampened by other factors.

Abdel-Hamid and Madnick arrive at several interesting conclusions following a simulation analysis of the system dynamics model. One such conclusion is that too little or too much spending on quality assurance dramatically increases the cost of a software development project. The simulation model suggests a 10% to 20% spending level is optimal. This kind of result is not possible with a pure variance or process model. Neither form is well suited for the complex, recursive, self-reinforcing relationships among so many variables.

3.5 Hybrid Model IV

The final hybrid form can be described as a temporal pattern. It consists of a single variable measured at various points in time. The relationship between one observation and the next is not as important in this kind of model as the overall pattern formed by the observations. A temporal pattern is thus best suited to describe a particular phenomenon, rather than explain or predict it.

Soh, Ang, and Neo (1994) developed a temporal pattern model of application portfolio development. They counted the number of business areas being automated in each of 215 organizations over the span of twenty-one years. They examined the overall pattern for the entire sample, comparing patterns for high and low performing organizations. They found that most automation is completed early, within the first two years, and the pattern tapers off rapidly. There are periodic bursts of automation later, usually around year 5 or 6, but the activity does not approach the high levels of the initial automation period. While this model is purely descriptive, it does describe automation in a way that variance and process models would have missed. Because both pure forms emphasize the relationship between *different* variables or events, they are not well suited to describing the changing levels of a single variable.

In the introduction we noted Mohr's suggestion that researchers should strive to build "pure" models, consistent with either the process or variance forms. After classifying empirical IS research into the process-variance typology, we have observed four distinct deviations from these pure forms. Each hybrid form is able to answer a research question or arrive at a conclusion that would not be possible from a pure process or variance model. So rather than failing, as Mohr implied, these models succeed at furthering our knowledge of important IS issues, such as information systems development, technology-supported group processes, IS staffing, and technology adoption.

4 PRACTICAL IMPLICATIONS FOR IS PROCESS RESEARCHERS

The classification of research models into the typology required close scrutiny of the process literature, which resulted in insight on the practical issues facing process researchers. These implications are supplemented through a series of interviews with a convenience sample of the authors whose papers are included in the review. The interview protocol and respondents are listed in Figure 1. These interviews are intended to tap the stories behind the research, the reality of studying processes that may not be evident from simply reading the literature. The remainder of this section presents the lessons we learned from the review and classification process, as well as the results of the interviews. These lessons are organized around a generic model of the research process: research question, model building, validation of the model, and report writing.

Interview Protocol:

1. How did you get started using a process approach to research?
2. How would you recommend someone start with this approach?
3. Are there any readings you would recommend, any exemplary applications of the process approach?
4. What do you see as the challenges and limitations of the process approach?
5. When is it appropriate to use the process approach?
6. How can the process approach complement the variance approach?
7. Do you think the process approach is more or less risky than the variance approach and why?
8. Does the process approach yield research that has inherently more or less practical value and why?

Respondents:
Kailash Joshi, University of Missouri, St. Louis
Allen Lee, McGill University
Mike Newman, University of Manchester
Scott Poole, Texas A&M University
Daniel Robey, Georgia State University
Rajiv Sabherwal, Florida International University
V. Sambamurthy, Florida State University
Christina Soh, Nanyang Technological University, Singapore

Figure 1 Interview Protocol and Respondents.

4.1 Research Question

The review implies that a wide range of questions can be addressed through the study of process or hybrid models, and these questions can be focused at any level of analysis. At one extreme is Joshi's equity-implementation model, which describes a cognitive process taking place inside a user's head. Similarly, the system dynamics model developed by Gupta and Gupta includes cognitive processes that result in intentions to leave the organization. Other studies deal with interpersonal or group-level issues, such as GDSS usage (DeSanctis et al. 1991), communication patterns (Orlikowski and Yates 1994), systems development (Abdel-Hamid and Madnick 1989; Newman and Robey 1992; Newman and Sabherwal 1989, 1996; Robey and Newman 1996; Sabherwal and Robey 1993), and power (Markus 1983). Some studies looked at the relationship between individuals and technology (Tyre and Orlikowski 1994; Orlikowski et al. 1995; Markus 1994). Finally, at the other extreme, some process studies examined organization-level issues (Orlikowski 1993; Soh, Ang and Neo 1994).

The process researchers interviewed agree with the broad applicability of process models and their hybrid forms. One said,

> *I wouldn't rule out any area of research. The process approach has good scope. For example, it would work with something like outsourcing. Something that involves how decisions are made.*

Another researcher hinted at the blurred line between process and variance models, suggesting the two may be complementary,

> *You can attack a variance research question from a process perspective, provided you recast the question into process terms. The general question can be the same, though.*

Despite this flexibility, we were warned not to apply process models to all research questions,

> *I think we should use as simple a model as possible. Processes are inherently underlying everything that can be explained with a variance approach, but we don't have to include these processes into our theories. We can freeze the process into variables. We wouldn't want to include theories about electrons into the wiring diagrams of a house!*

4.2 Model Building

The review suggests both inductive and deductive methods are feasible when studying process or hybrid models. Orlikowski (1993) follows the inductive approach in her model of CASE tool adoption. Most process research, however, follows what Miles and Huberman (1984) call the conceptualist approach, in which the researcher develops a model deductively based on extant literature and then tries to confirm and refine the model based on data from the field. Similarly, Eisenhardt (1989) acknowledges the value of specifying constructs prior to collecting data in a case study research. The conceptualist approach strengthens the empirical grounding of the resulting theory and provides the researcher with some framework for collecting and interpreting data.

The value of the conceptualist approach is recognized by the experienced process researchers, one of whom said,

> *Process research requires lots of theory building at the outset. The hardest thing is to find a theory in process terms. Theories in the literature tend to be phrased in variance mode, so you'll need to recast them first into process terminology.*

Others emphasized the importance of understanding the real world process over the need for an *a priori* theory. For example, one said,

> *If you don't understand the real world process, you won't know what data to collect, and you won't know what to do with the data.*

Another implied that this understanding may be arrived at inductively, by conducting preliminary research:

> *If there's not much prior work to build on, then you'll need to muck around first, maybe by doing some factor research. That'll define what you need to explain.*

4.3 Model Validation

Both qualitative and quantitative data can be used in validating the model. Some of the exemplars of using qualitative data are Orlikowski's (1993) two case studies on CASE tool adoption and use, Markus' (1983) case on power and IS implementation, and Newman and Sabherwal's (1996) case on commitment to IS development. Other process studies use quantitative data. For example, DeSanctis et al., in addition to using data from meeting transcripts and computer log files, use quantitative data collected from groups using and observing the use of GDSS. Soh, Ang and Neo use retrospective, quantitative data collected in a large cross-sectional survey to build their temporal pattern of IT adoption. These examples suggest that process models can be built or tested with either qualitative or quantitative data.

The respondents to the interviews agree that qualitative and quantitative data are appropriate for the study of processes. One researcher said,

> *One myth my students seem to have is that you shouldn't measure anything if you're doing process research. Measurement is fine, and it might help you learn more about the process that's taking place. It definitely has a place, again depending on your research question.*

Another was more specific about the kind of data and methods that might apply to the study of processes,

> *Reconstructing quantitative, longitudinal data—called process mapping—can give you a better understanding of what's happening over time.*

Despite the variety of options available to process researchers, there is a significant disadvantage to collecting process data. One researcher noted,

> *The risks are mainly in the data collection. Access to longitudinal data is a big challenge. It takes a lot of work to hang in there and to get consistent data over time. And the time it takes to collect data increases as the level of analysis increases, say from groups to organizations. The processes take longer to unfold. This is a real disincentive for junior faculty.*

Because the data can take both qualitative and quantitative forms, it follows that the data analysis methods can also. Orlikowski's (1993) CASE tools study uses qualitative methods. On the other hand, Soh, Ang and Neo use statistical methods to develop and analyze a temporal pattern of IT adoption. Sabherwal and Robey (1993) use optimal matching techniques and cluster analysis, both quantitative methods, to create an empirical taxonomy of IS implementation processes.

One researcher we interviewed produced a broader list of potential analysis methods,

> *There's a wide range of methods that might be required: time series analysis, event series analysis, Markov analysis, other Stochastic methods, non-linear dynamic modeling, simple qualitative phase mapping, and case studies. Not all of these methods are equal, though. It depends on the research question.*
>
> *Given all the methods that process research can require, it takes a broad background, and the ability to select the right ones. Otherwise you'll be putting the wrong foot into the right shoe, or the right foot into the wrong shoe.*

Even if a process researcher is able to select the right method and apply it correctly, he or she has the further challenge of convincing reviewers that the methods are sound. One researcher offered this warning and recommendation,

> *Process research is risky for the same reason case studies are. The issue has more to do with data interpretation than with process. I think there's an inbred bias toward quantitative research, which means process studies take more effort. Because of this you especially need to keep good records of what you're doing. You need an audit trail, in case your findings are not surprising, or are too surprising. You've got to be able to explain your methods.*

Another researcher summarized the challenge succinctly,

> *One has to present the illusion of being as rigorous as in variance research.*

4.4 Report Preparation

The review of research models uncovers a diversity of research questions and model types. It is not surprising that the writing styles differed significantly as well. There does not appear to be any consensus on the format of a process research paper. This point is also noted by some of the interviewees, one of whom said,

> *Writing the paper is more difficult because there are no standard models to follow, and expectations are less clear. It's kind of like storytelling. To be good at variance research requires an engineering or science background. But to be good at process, you almost need to come from the arts, or English, or philosophy.*

Even if the paper is well-written, the response from reviewers may not be positive. Three of the process researchers suggested this may be the result of the knowledge gap, the absence of "conceptual tools," that this paper is intended to address:

> *Our education system is not geared toward process, but variance. For example, when people look at stage models they tend to focus on the stages. But the real key is the transition between stages, and the mechanism underlying this.*

When one of my earlier process papers was being reviewed, one of the referees said he didn't believe in this approach. Another interpreted it as a form of variance study. So I'd believe there's a lack of understanding. People just haven't been trained to look at processes, so your paper almost needs to educate the reviewers.

People generally have trouble understanding processes. They don't understand that it's not the same as giving out questionnaires. You know you have an inexperienced reviewer when he or she asks for operationalizations of your process variables. So it's important to boil terms down so people can understand them, into things like life cycles.

Several of the researchers felt this state of affairs is improving. One said,

The reception has been better recently, largely because I think more people are familiar with that Markus and Robey article. So while it's difficult to publish process research, the situation is improving.

The final implication for IS researchers, and perhaps the most encouraging, is raised by several of the experienced process researchers. In spite of the laborious publication process, the process researchers have received highly positive responses from practitioners. Three researchers posed different explanations for this reception:

I'm convinced that processes are more practical, because it's easier to visualize them than variance relationships. It's hard to change an independent variable, but activities and events... it's easier to make them happen.

Practitioners don't care much about quantitative results. That doesn't have much value for them. They want insights, not correlations. They want explanations that they can relate to... logical arguments they can use to convince themselves that some explanation makes sense.

Being able to explain how and why is important, it's what people want to know. So perhaps there's more prescriptive potential with the process approach.

However, not everyone is convinced that the impact of process research is a result of the contributions it can make. One researcher said,

I don't think process studies have any more practical value, at least not based on their contributions. They have the same advantages as case studies. There's a real feel that you get, and practitioners find that more interesting. So they'll tend to read it before they'll read a variance paper.

Finally, process studies seem to have a positive impact in the classroom, as one researcher commented:

Students find this more practical than R^2's of .40 or so. They're not interested in how things are associated, but in how to get from here to there.

5 DISCUSSION AND FUTURE IMPLICATIONS

This paper extends the process-variance dichotomy presented by Mohr and Markus and Robey. This extension identifies four alternative, or hybrid, forms of models and gives examples of each. This is particularly interesting since Mohr (p. 61) suggested these hybrid forms were undesirable:

> Theoretical propositions may sometimes not be recognizable as being in either of the two categories because they are actually somewhere in between. This tendency to blur the distinction...contributes to the frustration of theory. It becomes an obstacle, a distraction, a derailer of purpose.

The evidence from our review of process models refutes this claim. Not only did the pure process models make valuable contributions, but also the hybrid models. These hybrids successfully explained key IS issues relating to GDSS use, information systems development, technology adoption, and IS staffing. The hybrid models fit the research questions and allowed the researchers to arrive at conclusions that would have been difficult using any other form of model. The typology thus plays an important role in identifying the range of options available to researchers, all of which stem from the process-variance dichotomy.

Some issues were studied using both pure and hybrid models, and sometimes multiple forms of hybrid models. This suggests that researchers have a great deal of flexibility and discretion when forming their research models. When defining concepts, a researcher can focus on the occurrence of an event, such as the establishment of guidelines governing the relationship between users and information technology (Orlikowski et al. 1995). The nature of these guidelines can vary in terms of formalization and flexibility. The establishment of guidelines can thus be a variable by looking inside the event to see the different values it can assume. The appropriate level of abstraction, and the appropriate definition of such a construct, will depend on the nature of the research question and the intentions of the researcher. The specification of relationships among concepts is likewise in the control of the researcher.

This flexibility extends to a broader scale. Some of the researchers we interviewed suggested that the research question placed limits on the type of model and methods used. This may be so, but the review of process-oriented studies suggests that within a broad research issue a number of models and methods may be complementary. Sabherwal and Robey (1995) demonstrate this when they combine process and variance perspectives in a single study of information systems development. By using two different models to study the same issue, they are able to explain more of the IS development process than either perspective could alone.

The typology has the potential to help IS researchers in a number of ways. It is particularly important for qualitative IS researchers to understand the structure of process and hybrid models, as qualitative research is intimately concerned with process. Several qualitative research scholars explicitly address this relationship between qualitative methods and process. Both Dey (1993) and Merriam (1988) agree that describing processes is a key step in the analysis of qualitative data.

Merriam adds that qualitative researchers are more interested in processes than outcomes or products. Others are most specific, relating particular methods to the study of processes. For example, Creswell (1994, p. 71) suggested that the case study, a popular qualitative research methodology in the IS field (Orlikowski and Baroudi 1991), is appropriate when one wants to "explore a process." Strauss and Corbin (1990) established the relationship between process and the grounded theory method. They said linking sequences of action and interaction (i.e., describing a process) is an essential part of any grounded theory analysis.

These qualitative scholars agree that the study of processes is integral to qualitative research. The process-variance typology can support the description of processes by providing a consistent vocabulary for developing and writing about process-oriented models. Such a vocabulary will help qualitative researchers in IS to communicate more clearly using their models. Explicitly identifying the form or structure of one's research model in uniform terms can help others to make sense of the model. Improving communication between scholars in this way can in turn facilitate the accumulation of knowledge in the IS field.

The process-variance typology can also help IS researchers who are interested in studying processes to understand the forms that process models can take, and the areas in which it is reasonable to relax Mohr's strict guidelines. The eighteen categories in the theoretical typology map the full range of options available in building models. The five types of models observed in the IS literature map what has been done by IS researchers. One possibility for future research would be to stretch this set of empirical types and develop a new form of model that studies a process in a new way. For example, it would be interesting to identify the environmental conditions that make a process unpredictable, so that controlling for these conditions would lead to a predictable process model. Alternatively, one might try to develop a model comprised of events in a non-temporal, predictable relationship. Perhaps there exists a set of events that consistently occur simultaneously. In such a case, when one event occurred, we would know with confidence that the others did as well.

The motivation underlying the development and application of the typology is the advocacy of further process-oriented research in IS. Given the young age of the IS discipline, we believe it is an important time for exploration rather than convergence. As Cannella and Paetzold (1994, p. 332) argue, "the evolution of knowledge requires fuzzy boundaries and a tolerance for (if not acceptance of) a plurality of paradigms." Premature convergence on a single perspective, such as variance models, limits the progress of knowledge. One researcher shared with us compelling cases in support of process models in information systems:

> *Think about a football game. The score alone doesn't tell you much. Unless you look at the game itself, you won't understand why the outcome occurred. And with systems, the results are even less clear, making it that much more important to look at the process. Unless you look at the process, it's impossible to untangle the events or history that altered the trajectory, that led to the outcome you're studying.*

6 REFERENCES

Abbott, A. (1983). "Sequences of Social Events: Concepts and Methods for the Analysis of Order in Social Processes." *Historical Methods*, Volume 16, Number 4, pp. 129-147.

Abbott, A. (1992). "From Causes to Events: Notes on Narrative Positivism." *Sociological Methods & Research*, Volume 20, Number 4, pp. 428-455.

Abdel-Hamid, T. K. (1989). "A Study of Staff Turnover, Acquisition, and Assimilation and Their Impact on Software Development Cost and Schedule." *Journal of Management Information Systems*, Volume 6, Number 1, pp. 21-40.

Abdel-Hamid, T. K., and Madnick, S. E. (1989). "Lessons Learned from Modeling the Dynamics of Software Development." *Communications of the ACM*, Volume 32, Number 12, pp. 1426-1438.

Campbell, D. T., and Fiske, D. W. (1959). "Convergent and Discriminant Validation by the Multitrait-Multimethod Matrix." *Psychological Bulletin*, Volume 58, pp. 81-105.

Cannella, A. A., Jr., and Paetzold, R. L. (1994). "Pfeffer's Barriers to the Advance of Organizational Science: A Rejoinder." *Academy of Management Review*, Volume 19, Number 2, pp. 331-342.

Creswell, J. W. (1994). *Research Design: Qualitative and Quantitative Approaches.* Thousand Oaks, California: Sage.

DeSanctis, G.; Poole, M. S.; Lewis, H.; and Desharnais, G. (1991). "Using Computing in Quality Team Meetings: Initial Observations from the IRS-Minnesota Project." *Journal of Management Information Systems*, Volume 8, Number 3, pp. 7-26.

Dey, I. (1993). *Qualitative Data Analysis: A User-Friendly Guide for Social Scientists.* London: Routledge.

Eisenhardt, K. M. (1989). "Building Theories from Case Study Research." *Academy of Management Review*, Volume 14, Number 4, pp. 532-550.

Galegher, J., and Kraut, R. E. (1994). "Computer-Mediated Communication for Intellectual Teamwork: An Experiment in Group Writing." *Information Systems Research*, Volume 5, Number 2, pp. 110-138.

Gupta, Y. P., and Gupta, M. C. (1990). "A Process Model to Study the Impact of Role Variables on Turnover Intentions of Information Systems Personnel." *Computers in Industry*, Volume 15, pp. 211-238.

Joshi, K. (1991). "A Model of Users' Perspective on Change: The Case of Information Systems Implementation." *MIS Quarterly*, Volume 15, Number 2, pp. 229-242.

Lave, C. A., and March, J. G. (1975). *An Introduction to Models in the Social Sciences.* New York: Harper & Row.

Mackay, J. M., and Elam, J. J. (1992). "A Comparative Study of How Experts and Novices Use a Decision Aid to Solve Problems in Complex Knowledge Domains." *Information Systems Research*, Volume 3, Number 2, pp. 150-172.

Markus, M. L. (1994). "Electronic Mail as the Medium of Managerial Choice." *Organization Science,* Volume 5, Number 4, pp. 502-527.
Markus, M. L. (1983). "Power, Politics, and Mis Implementation." *Communications of the ACM,* Volume 26, Number 6, pp. 430-444.
Markus, M. L., and Robey, D. (1988). "Information Technology and Organizational Change: Causal Structure in Theory and Research." *Management Science,* Volume 34, Number 5, pp. 583-598.
Merriam, S. B. (1988). *Case Study Research in Education: A Qualitative Approach.* San Francisco: Jossey-Bass.
Miles, M. B., and Huberman, A. M. (1984). *Qualitative Data Analysis.* Newbury Park, California: Sage Publications.
Mohr, L. (1982). *Explaining Organizational Behavior.* San Francisco: Jossey-Bass.
Monge, P. R. (1990). "Theoretical and Analytical Issues in Studying Organizational Processes. " *Organization Science,* Volume 1, Number 4, pp. 406-430.
Newman, M., and Noble, F. (1990). "User Involvement as an Interaction Process: A Case Study." *Information Systems Research,* Volume 1, Number 1, pp. 89-113.
Newman, M., and Robey, D. (1992). "A Social-Process Model of User-Analyst Relationships." *MIS Quarterly,* Volume 16, Number 2, pp. 249-265.
Newman, M., and Sabherwal, R. (1996). "Determinants of Commitment to Information System Development: A Longitudinal Investigation." *MIS Quarterly,* Volume 20, Number 1, pp. 23-54.
Newman, M., and Sabherwal, R. (1989). "A Process Model for the Control of Information System Development Projects." In J. I. DeGross, J. C. Henderson, and B. R. Konsynski (Editors), *Proceedings of the Tenth International Conference on Information Systems,* Boston, pp. 185-197.
Orlikowski, W. J. (1993). "CASE Tools as Organizational Change: Investigating Incremental and Radical Changes in Systems Development." *MIS Quarterly,* Volume 17, Number 3, pp. 309-340.
Orlikowski, W. J. (1996). "Improvising Organizational Transformation over time: A Situated Change Perspective." *Information Systems Research,* Volume 7, Number 1, pp. 63-92.
Orlikowski, W. J., and Baroudi, J. J. (1991). "Studying Information Technology in Organizations: Research Approaches and Assumptions." *Information Systems Research,* Volume 2, Number 1, pp. -27.
Orlikowski, W. J., and Yates, J. (1994). "Genre Repertoire: Structuring of Communicative Practices in Organizations." *Administrative Science Quarterly,* Volume 39, Number 4, pp. 541-574.
Orlikowski, W. J.; Yates, J.; Okamura, K.; and Fujimoto, M. (1995). "Shaping Electronic Communication: The Metastructuring of Technology in the Context of Use." *Organization Science,* Volume 6, Number 4, pp. 423-444.

Poole, M. S., and DeSanctis, G. (1992). "Microlevel Structuration in Computer-Supported Group Decision Making." *Human Communication Research,* Volume 19, Number 1, pp. 4-49.

Poole, M. S., and Holmes, M. E. (1995). "Decision Development in Computer-Assisted Group Decision Making." *Human Communication Research,* Volume 22, Number 1, pp. 90-127.

Rich, P. (1992). "The Organizational Taxonomy: Definition and Design." *Academy of Management Review,* Volume 17, Number 4, pp. 758-781.

Robey, D., and Newman, M. (1996). "Sequential Patterns in Information Systems Development: An Application of a Social Process Model." *ACM Transactions on Information Systems,* Volume 14, Number 1, pp. 30-63.

Sabherwal, R., and Robey, D. (1993). "An Empirical Taxonomy of Implementation Process Based on Sequences of Events in Information System Development." *Organization Science,* Volume 4, Number 4, pp. 548-576.

Sabherwal, R., and Robey, D. (1995). "Reconciling Variance and Process Strategies for Studying Information Systems Development." *Information Systems Research,* Volume 6, Number 4, pp. 303-327.

Sambamurthy, V., and Poole, M. S. (1992). "The Effects of Variations in Capabilities of GDSS Designs on Management of Cognitive Conflict in Groups." *Information Systems Research,* Volume 3, Number 3, pp. 225-251.

Sen, A.; Vinze, A.; and Liou, S. F. T. (1994). "Role of Control in the Model Formulation Process." *Information Systems Research,* Volume 5, Number 3, pp. 219-248.

Soh, C.; Ang, S.; and Neo, B. S. (1994). "Building the Application Portfolio: A Process Analysis." In J. I. DeGross, S. L. Huff, and M. C. Munro (Editors), *Proceedings of the Fifteenth International Conference on Information Systems,* Vancouver, pp. 407-418.

Strauss, A., and Juliet, C. (1990). *Basics of Qualitative Research: Grounded Theory Procedures and Techniques.* Newbury Park, California: Sage.

Tyre, M. J., and Orlikowski, W. J. (1994). "Windows of Opportunity: Temporal Patterns of Technological Adaptation in Organizations." *Organization Science,* Volume 5, Number 1, pp. 98-118.

Vicinanza, S. S.; Mukhopadhyay, T.; and Prietula, M. J. (1991). "Software-Effort Estimation: An Exploratory Study of Expert Performance." *Information Systems Research,* Volume 2, Number 4, pp. 243-262.

7 BIOGRAPHY

Thomas Shaw is a Ph.D. student in Information Systems at the University of Texas at Austin. His research focuses on the use of process models to study IS issues and on how IS managers make decisions about the ethical issues they face. Mr. Shaw studied at the State University of New York at Binghamton and the State University of New York at Albany prior to attending UT. He has work experience in banking, journalism, and education.

Sirkka L. Jarvenpaa is professor of information systems at the University of Texas at Austin. Her current research projects focus on global information technology, electronic commerce, and the use of IT in radical organizational transformations. Dr. Jarvenpaa serves as the senior editor for *MIS Quarterly*. She is an associate editor for several other journals. Dr. Jarvenpaa received her Ph.D. from the University of Minnesota in 1986.

Appendix
Reconstructing the Process Literature Based on the Process-Variance Typology

Abdel-Hamid 1989
Abdel-Hamid and Madnick 1989
Abdel-Hamid (1989; Abdel-Hamid and Madnick 1989) developed a system dynamics model to explain how human resource, planning, and control issues are interrelated with the management of software development. Like all systems dynamics models, this one consists of variables linked via invariant, predictable relationships. When variable X changes, variable Y will subsequently change. Sequence is incorporated into the model in the form of time lags between variables. There are twenty-two concepts in this model, including learning, actual production rate, perceived project size, turnover rate, hiring rate, and forecasted completion date. The recursive network of relationships is too complex to reduce to a narrative sequence.

DeSanctis, Poole, Lewis, and Desharnais 1991
DeSanctis et al. studied the use of group decision support system (GDSS) technology. The input-processes-output form of the model is consistent with adaptive structuration theory. The relationship between input and output is unpredictable because the intervening processes are characterized by emergent social interaction, which is subject to random influence and fluctuations. All of the constructs in model are defined as variables, but their configuration in the input-output form makes them sequential. The concepts in the model include 1) extent of GDSS use, 2) types of GDSS features used, 3) initiation of use, 4) instrumental uses, 5) use sentiments, and 6) satisfaction of GDSS. Their sequence involves three steps: (1,2), (3,4,5), (6).

Galegher and Kraut 1994
Galegher and Kraut describe the level of activity during group writing projects. They divide activity into four tasks—planning, drafting, revising, and socializing. All four

of these tasks can be taking place simultaneously, or in any order, so in this sense the model is not sequential. However, the model traces the proportion of the group performing each task on each day of the two-week writing projects, so it can be considered a temporal pattern of variable levels. No random external forces are identified, and the authors observe a consistent pattern over time that implies a degree of predictability in the process. The concepts in the model include planning activities, drafting activities, revising activities, social activities, coordination difficulty, perceived fairness, satisfaction with workgroup, meeting quality, total communication, and perceived project quality. Since this model is temporal, the concepts are not related sequentially. The first four concepts are studied as temporal patterns, and the remaining variables describe outcomes of the process.

Gupta and Gupta 1990

Gupta and Gupta's system dynamics model explains how human resource policies affect role perceptions and employee turnover within an IS department. The analysis of Abdel-Hamid and Abdel-Hamid and Madnick applies to this study, as well. The model consists of variables related sequentially and predictably. The variables include outgoing rate of commitment, level of new policy effort allocation, pool of IS personnel, new policy decay, and more than a dozen others. As with Abdel-Hamid and Madnick (1989), the sequences are too complex to describe textually.

Joshi 1991

Joshi's Equity-Implementation model tells the story of why resistance to IT implementation occurs. It suggests that cognitive processes lead to perceptions of inequity which in turn trigger behavior to resolve these feelings. It considers the implementation of IT as the precursor event leading to resistance behavior. The intervening events include the reevaluation of one's equity position relative to self, organization, and peers; the perception of inequity; and finally action to resolve any perceived inequity. This sequence of events can lead to other outcomes, such as perceptions of equity, so the path is unpredictable. As the process is largely cognitive, the timeframe is much shorter than any other of the process studies reviewed in this paper. The concepts in order are: IT implementation, reevaluation of equity, perception of inequity, and actions to resolve inequity. This last step may involve resistance behavior.

Mackay and Elam 1992

Mackay and Elam study problem solving with decision aids. The decision makers can be either experts or novices in spreadsheet use, and experts or novices in the task domain. Mackay and Elam develop four models of problem solving, based on these four precursor conditions (for example, spreadsheet expert/task novice is considered a binary condition, consistent with an event). Solving the problem in the experiment is the event marking the outcome of the process. The intervening steps are associated with using the decision aid (Lotus 1-2-3). They include formulation, invocation, execution, and abandonment of spreadsheet command sequences. These steps are related sequentially and unpredictably because one event will not always follow the other. The concepts in this model in order include the initial spreadsheet/domain expert condition, the formulation, invocation, execution, and possible abandonment of spreadsheet commands, and the resolution of the spreadsheet task.

Markus 1983

Markus' analysis of resistance to IT focuses on political processes. The model begins with the distribution of power and information throughout the organization, which is a binary state (consistent with an event). The intervening events include IT implementation and a perceived redistribution of power and information. Depending on how these changes are perceived, resistance may subsequently occur. The outcome is based on perceptions and social processes, so it might not occur. The model is thus unpredictable. The sequence of events leading to resistance takes place over time, as illustrated in the case study used to examine this process model. The concepts in the model, in sequence, are the initial distribution of power and information, the implementation of IT, the perceived redistribution of power, and potential resistance behavior.

Markus 1994

Markus explained why managers adopted a lean communication medium (electronic mail) in a particular organization. The model is based on social definition theories, which assert that the concepts of top management sponsorship and socialization mechanisms are necessary to maintain a target behavior. Sponsorship and socialization precede the target behavior. All of these factors can be considered events, as they are either present or not. The relationship is unpredictable because we cannot determine in advance if the precursor conditions will lead to the outcome. While the path between precursor and outcome does not lead through any intermediate events, one does precede the other, so the model is sequential.

Newman and Noble 1990

Newman and Noble incorporated four process models—learning, conflict, political, and garbage can—into their study of information systems development. Each model begins with a state that involves some imbalance between users and analysts, either in knowledge, interests, or power. These states are followed by interactions between users and analysts, which might consist of educating, discovering and resolving conflict, using political tactics, or dumping problems and solutions into the process. These interactions are considered behaviors that either occur or do not, so they are events. The models conclude with outcomes such as user acceptance, an acceptable solution, a solution that satisfies the most powerful party, or some random outcome. The sequential path from one event to the next is uncertain, so it is unpredictable.

Newman and Robey 1992

Newman and Robey's process framework provides a structure for explaining the leadership of a systems development project. There are four types of leadership, one of which is present at the beginning of the project. The ISD process is punctuated by encounters between IS and users that result in acceptance, equivocation, or rejection of the initial leadership condition. The outcome in the framework is the leadership style under which the project is completed. The constructs are considered variables because they encompass a range of possible values. The framework is unpredictable because the path from start to finish can deviate at any point based on the social interactions between users and IS. The concepts in this model include leadership, episodes, and encounters. The sequence includes beginning leadership, encounter, episode, (repeat encounter-episode sequence), and finally the ending leadership pattern.

Newman and Sabherwal 1989

Newman and Sabherwal explained how the information systems development (ISD) process changes over the life of a project. The four stages in the model—proposal, design, implementation, and evaluation—occur in a fixed sequence. The relationship patterns between users and IS during each stage are based on two contextual variables—the system's perceived threat to users and the balance of power between users and IS. The model thus includes a mix of events and variables. The values of these contextual factors, and consequently the nature of each stage of the ISD process, are affected by unpredictable and inconsistent social processes. The concepts in this model include the four ISD stages and the two contextual factors.

Newman and Sabherwal 1996

The model of commitment developed by Newman and Sabherwal explains how and why commitment to an ISD project changes over time. There are really two models embedded within this, representing two kinds of changing commitment. One begins with a state of commitment and moves toward the withdrawal of commitment, while the other reverses the direction. The broader model encompassing these two is unpredictable because the nature of commitment throughout the life of the project cannot be determined in advance. Commitment is influenced by four sets of intervening factors (project, psychological, social, and structural), which must form a particular configuration or state in order for commitment to change. The sequence of events linking the two models includes making initial commitment, ensuing events, withdrawal of commitment, ensuing events, making commitment to a new approach. The ensuing events concepts involve a reconfiguration of the contextual factors. In the first, linking commitment and withdrawal, social and structural determinants are reduced. In the second, psychological and project determinants are increased.

Orlikowski 1993
Orlikowski's process model explains how and why the consequences of CASE usage emerge from CASE adoption. The precursor events include articulating the IS problems and formulating the expected benefits of CASE. The existence of these events does not ensure that the intermediate events will occur, so the model is unpredictable. The events associated with CASE adoption and use are followed by the final outcomes of the model, which include reactions from system developers, IS managers, and clients. The high-level concepts in this model include conditions for adopting and using CASE tools, adopting and using CASE tools, and consequences of adopting and using CASE tools. These three concepts influence and are influenced by three contextual factors relating to the environment, organization, and IS.

Orlikowski 1996
Organizational transformation can be an emergent, continuous process based on both intentional and unintentional changes in individual practices. The process model explaining how and why this occurred in one organization begins with the introduction of a new technology, which over the course of three years changed the organization's structures and practices. The intervening stages include deliberate and emergent changes in the practices of both managers and the specialists in the customer support department of this organization. Orlikowski grouped these changes into five phases to facilitate her explanation; she actually considers the three year change process to be continuous. Each step in the chain of events may have led to different outcomes, so the process was unpredictable. This model includes too many concepts to list here, but a short selection (presented in sequence) from Metamorphosis I includes entering calls electronically, documenting process electronically, searching electronically, re-using knowledge, and developing guidelines for knowledge evaluation.

Orlikowski and Yates 1994
Orlikowski and Yates explain how communication patterns and conventions (called genre repertoires) changed over the course of a project to define a technical standard. The initial pattern was adopted from pre-project norms, which changed to result in a different pattern at the completion of the project. Over time, specific events and emergent milestones in the project, such as distribution of various drafts of the technical manual, initiated shifts in the communication patterns. Since these events are the result of complex social processes they could not be determined in advance, so the model is unpredictable. The model consists of four temporal patterns, one for each genre (memo, dialogue, proposal, and ballot). These four genres are the concepts in the model.

Orlikowski, Yates, Okamura, and Fujimoto 1995
The technology-use mediation cycle explains how the relationship between users and technology is influenced by organizational actors. Following the establishment of this

relationship (i.e., technology and the guidelines for its use are introduced), a series of reinforcement and adjustment events take place. An example of a reinforcement event is training users in the features of the technology; an adjustment event can be a modification of the rules or guidelines to facilitate use of the technology. These events shape institutional properties, which in turn enable future events in a cycle consistent with structuration theory. The periods of reinforcement and adjustment are punctuated by episodic changes, such as the addition of new features to the technology. The specific events within the mediation cycle are the result of social and organizational processes, so it is not possible to predict their nature or timing. The concepts in this model include establishment, reinforcement, adjustment, and episodic change.

Poole and DeSanctis 1992

Poole and DeSanctis explain group processes using a model comprised of variables. The concepts (in sequence) include the restrictiveness of the GDSS or manual system used by the group, characteristics of the structuration processes followed by the group, and the change in consensus that resulted from the process. The variables describe the events in the sequence of GDSS use, so the model is sequential. This sequence is dictated by emergent social processes, which makes it unpredictable.

Poole and Holmes 1995

Poole and Holmes looked at group processes from a variety of perspectives, one of which involved building models of the decision development process. They used flexible phase mapping to form clusters of similar sequences, and from these clusters identified decision paths followed by the groups in their study. The stages in each path are binary events, consisting of activities such as problem definition, solution confirmation, and process reflection. The step from one stage to another is unpredictable, because the next step can be in one of a number of directions. The concepts in the model are phases in the decision-making process: problem analysis, problem critique, orientation, criteria development, solution development, solution approval, solution critique, and integration. These phases can occur in any sequence, and can be repeated during the decision making process, so there is no one path from start to finish.

Robey and Newman 1996

Robey and Newman developed a process model explaining an IS project in one particular firm. They used their ISD process framework (Newman and Robey, 1992). The model begins with an analyst-led ISD approach and ends with a joint-led approach. The intervening process is composed of social encounters which lead to acceptance, rejection, or equivocation episodes. Each encounter is an event that leads to its subsequent episode. For example, the evaluation of a new product (encounter 14) led to the rejection episode that followed. The path from one encounter to the next is unpredictable because of the social processes and organizational dynamics leading to each encounter. The concepts are too numerous to list, but some of the initial concepts in the sequence that occurred include: proposal to begin, acceptance, Jess appointed as project director, equivocation, organization of users, equivocation, sign-off on systems requirements, and then acceptance.

Sabherwal and Robey 1993

Sabherwal and Robey develop several models of the IS development (ISD) process using student case studies that have been coded and then quantitatively analyzed. The six models are each composed of a series of events. The path from start to finish can lead to other events at any point, so the sequences are unpredictable. The most prevalent of the six *ideal* models, called *In-house Trial and Error*, begins with the submission of a proposal and proceeds through approval or authorization, assignment of personnel to the project, project definition, assessment of performance, performance problems, physical system construction, training, resistance, and physical system construction, before concluding with performance problems.

Sabherwal and Robey 1995

Sabherwal and Robey build on their earlier empirical taxonomy (see Sabherwal and Robey 1993), so the characteristics of these models are identical to those described above. This study is an effort to blend variance and process approaches in one study. They calculate a variable measuring the participation of key actors in the IS implementation process and use this variable to define clusters of stage models. This variable does not change the nature of the stage models — they are still unpredictable sequences of events. Rather, the variable describes a characteristic of each stage model. See above for an example of one of the processes.

Sambamurthy and Poole 1994

Sambamurthy and Poole developed a model explaining how groups manage conflict. The process begins with some level of conflict and ends with some level of consensus, both of which are variables. The intervening steps have characteristics of both events and variables, but the variables seem to dominate. Conflict resolution occurs when two activities take place—differentiation and integration. These could be considered events, but Sambamurthy and Poole imply they are variables because each can occur to a greater or lesser degree. However, differentiation must precede integration, so the model is sequential. The degree to which differentiation and integration occur is bundled into a variable called confrontiveness, which has four levels. This variable is operationalized by examining the pattern of events that occur during the group's interaction. Since these events map to a larger construct that can take on different values, the intervening construct in this model is considered a variable. The intervening process is unpredictable because the events in the conflict management process can occur in a variety of patterns; the occurrence of one event does not determine the next. The concepts in this model include task and group characteristics, level of existing conflict, communication and consensus support, conflict management, and quality of group outcomes. Conflict management consists of the confrontiveness concept, which is further divided into differentiation and integration. The primary sequence of events includes level of existing group conflict, conflict management process, and quality of group outcomes.

Sen, Vinze and Liou 1994

The model developed by Sen, Vinze and Liou looks at model formulation—the process of "developing mathematical abstractions for a real world problem" (p. 220). There are nine different controls that experts use to regulate the reasoning process during model formulation. These controls are events that either happen or do not. One control will start the process, others will intervene, and finally one will conclude model formulation. The path through the model formulation process is unpredictable because it cannot be defined in advance; it is emergent. The events in the process are linked sequentially. The controls include formulation planning, formulation goal setting, formulation component postulating, evaluating the formulation, problem decomposition, problem boundary determination, problem replanning, reasoning direction, and formulation component focusing.

Soh, Ang and Neo 1994

Soh, Ang and Neo describe the average number of business areas that were computerized each year by a sample of 215 large organizations. This is a variable that is measured over time. There is a temporal relationship to this model, because each level of computerization is followed by a subsequent level in the next year. The model that results from this study suggests that the pattern of computerization can be predicted. The concepts in this model include the number of business applications automated in a given year and the performance of the organizations responding.

Tyre and Orlikowski 1994

Tyre and Orlikowski's process model of technological adaptation explains why the amount of adaptation activity drops so significantly from its high level immediately following implementation. Implementation is the precursor event that leads to the outcome, which is the temporal pattern of adaptation. The model explaining this pattern conforms to the requirements of a process model. The intermediate states and events that tend to extinguish adaptation include production pressure, routinization of behaviors, changing expectations to match experiences, and erosion in team membership. Other events, such as problems with the technology or new product requirements, can initiate temporary upward spikes in the level of adaptation. The timing of these events over the life of a certain technology cannot be determined in advance, so the model is unpredictable. This explanation of how and why adaptation diminishes so quickly implies that a short window of opportunity exists for adaptation soon after the implementation of a new technology. The process involves cycles of adaptation and routine use.

Vicinanza, Mukhopadhyay and Prietula 1991

Vicinanza, Mukhopadhyay and Prietula developed two process models of the strategies experts use to estimate the effort required to complete a software development project. They used a process tracing technique on verbal protocol data. They described the strategies on both abstract and detailed levels. On the abstract level, one involves the identification of the software team's productivity rate, followed by an estimation based on that rate. The other starts with the identification of a referent project (or analog), then the estimation based on that referent. The detailed models are in the form of flowcharts, consisting of events and decision points. The decision points suggest the process is unpredictable, as it can diverge at these points in the sequence.

7

Systems of Meaning: Ethnography as a Methodology for the Study of Information Technologies

P. Prasad
Faculty of Management
University of Calgary
Calgary, Alberta, Canada
Tel: (403) 220-8803
E-mail: prasad@acs.ucalgary.ca

Abstract

This paper explores the implications of using ethnography as a methodology to study information technologies. It outlines the principal distinguishing characteristics of ethnographies by contrasting this methodology with other commonly used qualitative field research. It traces the philosophic roots of ethnography in symbolic anthropology and stresses the methodology's concern for thick description, plausibility of accounts, the cultural context and the immersion of the researcher. The paper also illustrates how the methodology can contribute to our understanding of Information Systems by discussing a few studies in this genre. It concludes by highlighting some recent dilemmas facing researchers in the ethnographic tradition.

1 INTRODUCTION

The recent qualitative turn in social science research has left unquestionable imprints on the discipline of information systems. The work of Markus (1983), Lee (1994), Orlikowski (1991; 1993), Kling and Iacono (1984), Walsham (1993) and others in this tradition is too well known to require elaboration here. While many qualitative researchers in the IS field concentrate on the analysis of electronic text and systems design (Lee 1994), others have resorted to indepth field studies of the implementation and adoption of information systems, relying primarily on the use of participant observation as a method of data collection (Orlikowski 1993; Ruhleder, Jordan and Elmes 1996). In the IS field, as in most others, the term *ethnography* has become the label of choice to designate qualitative fieldwork involving a sizeable amount of on-site observation.

The central contention of this paper is that the term ethnography holds distinct connotations for communities of scholars, thereby triggering specific expectations about its conduct and presentation which may not apply equally to all forms of qualitative fieldwork. As reviewers of qualitative work become more sophisticated, distinctions between ethnographic studies and other forms of qualitative fieldwork become more apparent and therefore more institutionally relevant (Wolcott 1995). A well-done piece of qualitative work can sometimes be faulted because of certain unwarranted claims to be ethnographic. It is therefore becoming increasingly necessary to understand the distinctions between different traditions of qualitative research and to grasp the specific connotations held by the term ethnography itself. Simultaneously, the practice of ethnography is increasingly being subjected to much debate and redefinition in disciplines such as anthropology and communication. The nature of assumptions undergirding ethnographies, the methodological expectations, and ethical stances adopted by researchers are all areas of growing intellectual contestation. For those of us who are users of this methodology, a renewed understanding of recent debates is likely to be of great relevance.

In this paper, a personal interpretation of the methodology of ethnography, focusing in particular on how it is distinctive rather than similar to other forms of qualitative fieldwork, is presented. While some might dispute the specific stance taken here, sharpening rather than broadening the concept of ethnography will ultimately offer us a more relevant methodology for understanding information systems. In sum, this paper attempts to do the following:

(a) broadly distinguish between ethnography and other forms of qualitative fieldwork,
(b) understand the complex set of anthropological traditions within which ethnography is rooted,
(c) present key features of ethnography as a methodology,
(d) discuss ethnographic applications to the study of information systems, and
(e) discuss contemporary dilemmas and debates confronting ethnographers.

2 ETHNOGRAPHY AND QUALITATIVE FIELDWORK

In most peoples' minds, the term ethnography denotes some form of in-depth fieldwork invariably employing participant observation, often used in combination with interviews or document analyses. From this perspective, ethnography is understood predominantly as a mode of data collection involving the development of close connections with subjects and situations being studied. While ethnographies would certainly imply all of these things, they also stand for something more. In this regard, it may be more useful to conceptualize ethnography as a *methodology* rather than a method which is linked to specific world views and approaches to understanding reality. The term methodology is used to designate the intricate set of ontological and epistemological commitments that a researcher brings to his/her work. Method, on the other hand, refers to the actual set of techniques and procedures used to collect and analyze data. Needless to say, one's choice of methodology eventually drives one's use of method. In this paper, the meaning and implications of using ethnography as a methodology for the study of information systems will be outlined.

Following the initial enthusiasm for qualitative research, several attempts have been made to sort out both the subtle and more obvious differences within diverse qualitative traditions (Hamilton 1993; Morgan and Smircich 1980). While these authors have alerted us to many fine distinctions between qualitative genres such as symbolic interaction, hermeneutics and structuralism, it may be useful to spend some time understanding one central distinction between different forms of qualitative fieldwork. This is the distinction between *realist* qualitative fieldwork and *interpretive* qualitative fieldwork, with ethnography (as a methodology) being clearly connected to the latter.

Briefly, we can think of realist traditions as holding relatively uncomplicated views of the world. At heart, realists believe that prolonged detached observation yields an accurate picture of reality. The underlying assumption behind realist fieldwork is that extended periods of observation accompanied by careful note-taking will result in an authentic assessment of the social situation under study. In essence, this view *privileges* the perspective and position of the researcher over that of the subjects being studied because it holds that ultimately the researcher's objective assessment of any social situation (given the right deployment of method) is a superior one.

Interpretive fieldwork (to which the methodology of ethnography is historically linked) is more concerned with understanding social situations from the standpoints of participants present within them. While interpretive fieldwork shares with realist fieldwork a strong predilection for extended observation and rich detail, it is always concerned with the process of *cultural sense-making* within any social situation. It is therefore, a mistake (although one made all too frequently) to think of ethnography solely in terms of depth of involvement (Wolcott 1995). Most qualitative traditions automatically imply a concern for depth of involvement. The crux of ethnography however, rests on the nature of that involvement which would emphasize *a focus on local interpretations* (Geertz 1973) and grasping the native point of view (Agar 1992; Schwartzman 1993). Anthropologists employ a somewhat useful terminology to underscore this distinction: that of *etic* versus *emic* research (Headland, Pike and Harris 1990).

At its most extreme, etic research implies that the researcher adopts a more exogenic approach to the field, avoiding close involvement with participants and trying to stay clear of presenting all but objective assessments of the situation. A classic study of IS change in the etic tradition is the longitudinal field study of an organization's adoption of electronic data processing equipment by Mann and Williams (1960). The authors spent months observing a technological change process, but commented on the event from a distant and detached perspective. Methodologically, ethnography clearly does not belong to the etic tradition. Coming from an emic or more endogenic perspective, it stresses what are often referred to as "native-view paradigms" (Gregory 1983) or reality as understood by the participants within it. Barley's (1988) study of CT scanners, for instance, is an appropriate example of an emic (ethnographic) study of technological change which takes into account the cultural sense-making and practices of organizational inhabitants in understanding a process of technical innovation.

It needs to be emphasized that the etic/emic distinction in the ethnographic tradition is no where as cut and dry as the preceding discussion might suggest. For example, as Van Maanen (1987) has pointed out, a number of realist field studies in the etic tradition claim to use ethnographic methods. First of all, it makes more sense to think of etic and emic research as lying on a continuum rather than being diametrically opposed to each other. Second, another way to sort out some of these ambiguities is to resort again to the distinction between method and methodology. Thus, many field studies that are obviously located within the etic tradition often use ethnographic methods, such as lengthy participant observation, and pay considerable attention to minute details. However, methodologically, these studies would still adhere primarily to etic objectives, depicting a more observer-based view of the situation being studied. Further, while the etic/emic distinction provides some clues to grasping the nature of ethnographic work, there is still much more to ethnography than its endogenic inclinations. To fully understand its complex characteristics, an appreciation of the anthropological tradition in which it is rooted is probably quite useful.

3 THE ANTHROPOLOGICAL ROOTS OF ETHNOGRAPHY

As a technique, ethnography has been developed, polished and perfected within the discipline of anthropology, from which it has since been exported to many social scientific fields including information systems research. While the discipline of sociology often lays claim to it, historically, as Schwartzman (1993, p. 1) points out, ethnography is the "trademark of cultural anthropology." It therefore makes sense to understand some of its historical intellectual antecedents. First of all, ethnography belongs to the subfield of anthropology originally known as cultural anthropology, and more recently referred to as symbolic anthropology. Unlike other fields within anthropology, notably structural-functionalism and evolutionist anthropology, symbolic anthropology tries to understand human action within cultural systems of meaning. Tracing its roots back to the work of Margaret Mead and Ruth Benedict, researchers within this field have traditionally used ethnography as a way of understanding "others" on their own terms.

While symbolic anthropology's initial focus was on "primitive" cultures in distant lands, its approach has, in the latter half of the twentieth century, been extremely influential in shaping the study of a multitude of other issues of interest to contemporary social scientists including political processes (Bailey 1965), organizational interactions (Gregory 1983; Van Maanen and Kunda 1989) and patterns of modern consumption (Campbell 1987; Sherry 1990), to name only a few. In fact, it is possible to assert that hardly any aspect of contemporary life is now exempt from a cultural lens that relies on the methodology of ethnography.

This more recent absorption with cultural and symbolic approaches owes much to the work of Clifford Geertz, whose ideas will be briefly sketched out in the remainder of this section. Few scholars occupy as prominent a place in the field of symbolic anthropology as Geertz, whose main contribution lies in his attempt to theoretically mingle an understanding of human meaning and social action. To Geertz (1973), all human action is suspended in *webs of significance* which in turn are embedded in cultural codes and contexts. In other words, one can understand social situations only through appreciating the *meanings* they hold for people in a given culture. These meanings, in turn are always enacted through innumerable symbolic actions and artifacts such as ceremonies, rites, folklore, ritual, etc., which have an overall stable quality. Thus, for Geertz, one can only comprehend social processes through a cultural-symbolic lens that is engaged in searching for the local meanings or interpretations of relevant actors.

Geertz's evocative but somewhat over-used term for this kind of analysis is *thick description*, a phrase that has come to be employed almost synonymously with ethnography. While thick description is often used in more realist qualitative research to denote nothing more than rich detail, the term, in the Geertzian tradition, has far deeper connotations. In fact, Geertz's main concern was to alert ethnographers to the problems of analyzing social interactions without resorting to the local interpretations and cultural contexts of key participants. In his much celebrated essay on ethnography and thick description, Geertz (1973) highlights the difficulties confronting ethnographers who have to make sense of social events from the observation of simple actions. The illustration he uses is that of the wink. How, Geertz asks, can we discern from simple observation the difference between an eyelid twitch (involuntary physical movement) and a wink (voluntary conspiratorial act)? Further, the wink itself could have multiple connotative layers and could signify different things when engaged by different actors. After all, as Geertz pursues, an individual could be parodying a wink by an acquaintance, in which case his own wink becomes a burlesque rather than a conspiratorial act. Geertz's overall point is quite simple. Detailed observation of actions alone may not always provide a meaningful view of the situation. Rather, uncovering the multiple complex layers of local meanings or sorting out the structures of signification is what yields a comprehensive and insightful picture of any social circumstance being studied. Ethnography, therefore, in Geertz's (1973, p. 43) own words, is like "trying to read a manuscript – foreign, faded, full of ellipses, incoherencies, suspicious emendations and tendentious commentaries, but written not in conventionalized graphs of sound but in transient examples of shaped behavior."

Symbolic anthropology and the ethnographic method have had other recent influences as well, notably Mary Douglas, James Clifford and others. Since the scope of this paper does not permit a detailed discussion of their ideas, some of their contributions will be taken up when we discuss the more current dilemmas and debates confronting ethnographers in the social sciences.

4 CENTRAL CHARACTERISTICS OF ETHNOGRAPHY

Despite its dynamic and continuously changing nature, it is still possible to understand ethnography as constituting certain key elements. As Wolcott (1995), Frake (1983), and others assert, it is necessary to keep in mind that the methodology of ethnography refers simultaneously to a perspective, an approach, a set of procedures and a manner of presentation. More specifically, ethnographic research is not only about data collection and analysis, but also about writing and presenting one's findings. Some key (and mostly shared) elements that would characterize a study as being ethnographic are discussed below.

4.1 The Use of Thick Description

Ethnographers are firm believers in the use of thick description to uncover and analyze data. As discussed earlier, thick description (Geertz 1973) refers primarily to a researcher's development of understanding out of the sense-making and schemas of local participants. The key concept used in arriving at thick descriptions is that of meaning. When out in the field, ethnographers try to understand any situation based on the meanings that it holds for relevant social actors. These meanings may sometimes be shared; sometimes they may be contradictory and contested. It is the ethnographer's task to uncover and present these multiple meanings and their complex connections with each other in the course of analyzing any social event.

Too often, field workers are tempted to look only for shared meanings and agreements, or to present the views of more powerful and influential individuals and groups. Ethnography would insist on understanding multiple realities and uncovering the often complex sets of meanings associated with them. Thus, typically, in an ethnographic piece of writing, we can be faced with completely differing visions of reality based on different participants' interpretations of any situation. A good ethnographer will present these different interpretations and try to incorporate them into his/her analysis. It is in the skillful weaving of these contradictions and complexities that a thick description can be produced.

4.2 The Cultural Context

Ethnographers are strongly wedded to understanding events and social interactions within a specific cultural context, whether it is a Sumatran island, a shopping mall or a professional law firm. The key focus here is on how specific cultures and subcultures shape both the interpretations and interactions of subjects being studied. The significance of cultural understanding to ethnography cannot possibly be over-emphasized. Given its anthropological genesis, ethnography seeks to locate actions within cultural circumstances. What this implies is a focus by researchers on cultural practices such as rituals, myths, taboos, etc., that guide everyday action in any situation.

While it is easy to view "foreign" and distant cultures as having these obvious cultural trappings, ethnographers would insist on understanding our own everyday lives in the same terms. Berg's (1985) study of technological change in a Volvo plant and Barley's study of a new CT scanner are exemplars of ethnographic approaches that are concerned with cultural processes. Berg's research explains the rise of what he terms as a "techno-culture" in a Swedish plant out of the traditional culture of craftsmanship that still pervaded the company. He argues that the strength of this new techno-culture could be best understood only by paying attention to some of the corporate myths that were compatible with this new subculture. Barley's work examines how the implementation of a new CT scanner was accomplished through many ritualistic processes that even led to the emergence of technological superstitions around the new system. In both studies, the authors' analyses of the technologies are distinctly influenced by cultural concepts such as myths, ritual, heroes, etc.

4.3 Immersion and Connection

Ethnography is almost synonymous with getting close to one's field. The careful development of close connections with one's subjects is a hallmark of ethnographic research (Agar 1980). In the anthropological tradition of the early twentieth century, field workers would spend extended periods of time in distant lands, where they frequently learned the language of the people they were studying. In our contemporary settings, familiarity with language remains as important as before. Ethnography implies not only understanding the jargon and terminology of the people one is studying, but also using this language in the writing of one's research to convey a flavor of the situation to readers. Golden-Biddle and Locke (1993) point out that ethnographies are often evaluated favorably when they convey a sense of authenticity to their readers. Accomplished ethnographers will insert phrases and comments made by their subjects to illustrate key points in their analysis. Van Maanen's (1973) well-known study on the socialization of policemen is remarkable in part for the way in which the reader begins to appreciate the world of the rookie cop through the language used by many of the policemen.

Ethnography also implies a high level of familiarity with the field itself. Thus, the ethnographic tradition strongly favors the method of participant observation where researchers spend extended periods of time in the site, and sometimes even take on the roles of inhabitants within the site. Using an ethnographic approach calls for the cultivation of some degree of informal intimacy with the people being studied. Anthropologists often develop especially close relationships with one or two individuals, whom they refer to as informants, who clue the researcher into the more subtle and informal dynamics present in any social situation.

4.4 The Plausibility of Accounts

In describing the nature of ethnography, Golden-Biddle and Locke (1993), Rosen (1991), Wolcott (1995), Frake (1983), and others point out that producing an ethnography is as much about writing as it is about data collection and analysis. In other words, ethnographic research substantially involves a commitment to presenting one's findings in a way which is often described as providing a *plausible account*. Plausible accounts refer to ethnographic writings that are convincing not only because they pay attention to detail, but because the overall narrative incorporates the viewpoints of multiple actors and ties these together in a culturally coherent and articulate fashion. Thus, a great deal of effort necessarily goes into learning the form and style of ethnographic writing (Van Maanen 1987). Many features can contribute to the plausibility of the research narrative including the development of a strong story line, evidence of the researcher's own involvement in the field, a sense of historical context and a coherent weaving of disparate events within the field. Above all, an ethnography is ultimately judged also on its ability to offer convincing explanations of action in a particular culture or subculture, be it ancestral worship among the Yungur or obsessive relationships with computers among hackers at MIT. In doing this, ethnography is also primarily committed to *insight* over prediction. Ethnographers are more concerned with providing "authentic" explanations of human behavior and action than tightly forecasting specific events. While a powerful and plausible ethnographic account may well suggest that certain groups are likely to adopt certain patterns of action, that is not the main focus of ethnographic inquiry.

Creating a plausible account is also accomplished by inviting readers to see themselves in solidarity with the text's assertions (Golden-Biddle and Locke 1993). Skilled ethnographers make appeals to readers by connecting the topic or situation being researched to the everyday life worlds of readers themselves. In doing so, ethnographers establish insightful linkages between their own findings and parallel issues concerning readers.

4.5 Privileging Local Knowledge

The purpose of ethnography is not the generation of universalistic knowledge in the form of what social scientists often refer to as grand theory. Many variants of traditional management theory and some forms of Marxist analysis would fall within this category of grand theory. In essence, grand theorists seek to understand human action through a set of universally applicable lenses. Typically, therefore, their understanding of specific events are mediated by broad intellectual categories such as race, status, class, and human nature. Ethnographers are almost unanimously opposed to any form of grand theorizing. Their epistemological position is one that squarely privileges local knowledge, and therefore sees theory building as being engaged in the development of what Geertz (1973) refers to as "particular truths" regarding a situation or phenomenon. For an ethnographer, grand theories conceal far more than they reveal because, in their zest for developing generalizable knowledge, they miss the local interpretations and cultural context that ultimately constitute such knowledge. Further, it is only through our understanding of *microscopic* interactions that any attempt to comprehend macro-structures is at all possible.

5 ETHNOGRAPHY AND THE STUDY OF INFORMATION SYSTEMS

The foregoing discussion has probably made quite obvious the fact that an ethnographic approach to understanding information systems cannot merely be equated with a qualitative stance. First of all, an ethnographic approach would regard information technologies as *systems of meaning*, i.e., as cultural artifacts holding multiple meanings for different people, and simultaneously being located within a broader cultural system of meaning. With the assistance of fieldwork done in the ethnographic tradition, we can better understand how to study information systems from this methodological standpoint. This section takes a close look at how some researchers of information systems have employed an ethnographic perspective. The field examples selected here illustrate rather vividly the contributions of an ethnographic methodology. The choice of studies discussed here in no way implies that other ethnographic studies have little to offer. While many other competent examples of ethnographic research can be found, the scope of this paper does not permit a detailed discussion of all of them.

The anthropological tradition within which ethnography is situated treats any technology as a cultural artifact accomplishing specific functions in different cultural milieus, and often reflecting and structuring social practices. Typically, ethnographers would adopt a more problematic understanding of technology, seeing it as having both functional and symbolic properties. In fact, the discipline of anthropology is filled with studies that illustrate the complex role of technologies in different societies. Most of these studies clearly demonstrate that technologies often fulfill far more than instrumental roles. They are often ceremonial (Berns 1990), reflect the myths of the culture that designs them (Harrison 1982) and can be used as mechanisms of social control (Berns 1990; Joerges 1989). When computer technologies are studied in this more ethnographic fashion, we are confronted with a more complex set of insights than studies that treat them merely as functional instruments designed to accomplish certain specific purposes.

Turkle's (1984) extraordinary ethnographic study of the intricate connections between computers and the human spirit falls within this genre. Turkle spent extensive periods observing and interviewing different populations in contemporary society including children, working men and women, hackers, etc., with a view to understanding the multiple subjective connotations held by the computer in today's society. Her project, in her own words, was to arrive at a portrait of the computer as an "evocative object" rather than solely a technical one. Turkle's study is not only richly detailed, but offers us, through an understanding of what the computer means to society, a better appreciation of the culture in which it is located. In her remarkable study, we see how computers take on various personifications in the minds of small children and adult hackers, and how they come to stand for democratic hopes in a society constantly searching for new alternatives to governance. In her complex analysis, Turkle never ignores the cultural context within which computers are located. Her discussion of the identification of personal computers with the personal politics of the 1960s helps explain some of their popularity in the late 1970s and 1980s. As she notes, "Personal computers became symbols of hope for a new populism in which citizens would band together to run information resources and local government" (Turkle 1984, p. 172).

In this study, we see how an ethnographic consciousness alerts readers to appreciating information technologies as symbolic and cultural objects that are also defined in part by the historic moments in which they are situated. Her discussion of the MIT hacker culture with its obsessive and intimate relationships to information technology reveals a masterful appreciation of cultural currents shaping these human-computer relationships. Her work constitutes good ethnography because of its analytic depth, its relentless search for cultural explanations, and its appreciation of computers as a fundamentally symbolic object. Other ethnographies of information technology in this genre are Pfaffenberger's (1989) study of personal computers and Prasad's (1993; 1995) studies of the anthropomorphism of computers in a medical center. The latter study (Prasad 1995), in which approximately nineteen months were spent observing an organization's transition to computerization, documents the multiple ways in which the new technology was anthropomorphized by local organization members. In a careful recording of local terminology and language to demonstrate how the personification of computers was socially constructed, the researcher was trying to keep within the spirit of the ethnographic tradition, in part, because it pays so much attention to the computer system as a meaningful object. The study also tried to provide cultural explanations for this phenomenon and probed not only the local culture of the organization but also looked at comic books, TV shows, magazines and other vehicles of popular culture to enhance our understanding of how computers become personified in the workplace.

In these studies, the ethnographic approach results in an understanding of computer technology as cultural and symbolic object/artifact. This kind of analysis can easily be extended to different forms of information technologies such as groupware, expert systems, electronic communication and so on. The central focus of such inquiry would be on the multiple meanings evoked by these different systems and the implications such systems of meaning had for the use and misuse of these technologies.

In a slightly different oeuvre are the ethnographic studies of Barley (1988) and - Zuboff (1988), both of whom were explicitly concerned with processes of change triggered by the introduction of new information systems. Barley's study was an in-depth longitudinal ethnography of two organizations and their radiology departments in which a new CT scanner was introduced. Zuboff's study looked at the process and outcomes of computerization in eight different organizations including pulp mills, an insurance company, a telecommunications firm, a bank and a pharmaceutical company. Barley's work is a remarkable piece on alterations in the social organization of work following technological change. His work offers many insights, one noteworthy one being the ritualization whereby individuals in social situations become comfortable with new and often disquieting technologies. The ethnographic lens is used here not only to dictate methods of observation but also to root the analysis in cultural concepts such as ritual and magical thinking to understand technological processes.

Zuboff's work needs little introduction. Her extensive use of participant observation in eight different organizations, which she studied over a period of five years, stands out as an exemplar of ethnographic inquiry. Her insights regarding information technology's Janus-like capacity to both informate and automate work is consistently informed by the subjective experiences of different organizational participants as well as the historical-cultural context of white collar work and its symbolic status. Her work is ethnographic because she does not treat technological change as a one-dimensional phenomenon, but locates it within other *webs of significance* such as authority relationships, the symbolic value of work, and the texture of oral versus electronic communication. Zuboff's work again offers guidelines for ethnographers of information systems by suggesting different cultural backdrops (e.g., organizational hierarchies, oral culture) against which their studies can be conducted.

6 DILEMMAS/DEBATES FACING ETHNOGRAPHERS

Despite (or perhaps because of) its growing popularity, ethnography has more recently been wrestling with several dilemmas regarding the role and responsibilities of the researcher, the conduct of the study and the presentation of the findings. While the debates are, for the most part, far too complex to be discussed in detail here, three major issues confronting ethnographers will be presented. They are the degree of researcher covertness, dilemmas of deep immersion, and the representation of subjects in the final writings of the researcher.

6.2 The Overt/Covert Debate

Anyone embarking on an ethnographic study needs to be aware of the debate around the ethics of using covert forms of observation. While many early anthropologists were too conspicuous within the sites they were studying to attempt any form of clandestine research, once ethnography was transferred to studying one's immediate social situation, the option of using covert methods became quite popular. One can find innumerable studies in which researchers took on certain roles such as meat packers (Thompson 1983), Pentecostal church members (Homan 1980), and even mental patients (Caudill 1952) without disclosing their identities to the people being studied.

Needless to say, this mantle of secrecy in ethnography has been subjected to much criticism in recent years. The obvious objection to this kind of clandestine observation is that the researcher might violate certain privacy considerations and be privy to some types of information that would have been unavailable if the ethnographic intentions had been openly disclosed. While it is quite easy to make certain personal decisions based on ethical considerations regarding the adoption of covert versus overt participation methods, ethnographers often find that the lines between openness and secrecy can become very blurred in actual field settings.

In my own study of computerization in a health maintenance organization (HMO), I began with the explicit and fully disclosed intention of studying how the process of computerization transformed the nature of work in the organization. After spending a few months in the organization, I began to feel that the symbolism associated with the change process was a far more interesting and worthy research project. When I attempted to communicate this changed focus to the HMO manager, I was received with blank stares and a response that my earlier focus was much more relevant to the organization itself. I eventually decided to effect a compromise by studying both angles, although I kept my interest on technological symbolism more to myself.

Several months after successfully defending my dissertation, I was engaged in a discussion on workplace resistance with several colleagues. One of them asked me if I had in fact found any resistance to the computerization process that I had been studying. The discussion led me to return to my field notes and interview transcripts, which I examined quite closely for instances of workplace resistance. Not only did I find several instances and discussions of resistance, I began writing about this issue with a greater passion than ever before. My point here is quite simple. When I started my work, my research intentions were completely different than when I finished. People in the organization were well aware that I was looking at changes associated with computerization. However, when I completed the study, I became more interested in an area which I had not disclosed to them for the simple reason that I had no intention at that time of studying resistance. Yet, it is entirely possible that had I disclosed such intentions, I might have been excluded from the site and made employees so self-conscious that I might not have found out much about resistance at all. Was my ethnography then, in fact, a covert project?

The answers to this question are obviously not that simple. Many ethnographers will frequently find themselves in similar situations in which their ostensible and original research focus becomes diverted into something quite different which they may or may not be able to disclose. Second, ethnographers periodically stumble on confidential material which may pose potential damage to certain individuals and groups. Here again, several ethical decisions may have to be made regarding the researcher's own responsibility to breach certain confidences. One thing is for sure: in embarking on ethnographic research, simplistic moral platitudes condemning all forms of covert research are certainly rendered more problematic.

6.2 Dilemmas of Immersion

Ethnography automatically implies some level of deep immersion in the culture one is studying. More recently, ethnographers have been seriously wrestling with what exactly is meant by the notion of immersion, and with what obligations this may leave us. As many ethnographers point out, becoming a part of the culture one studies may not always be either possible or desirable (Geertz 1973; Wax 1983). As Geertz argues, only romantics and spies want to become completely identified with another culture. For most ethnographers, the goal is more often one of learning enough about a site and its inhabitants so that we can present an authentic interpretation of their own experiences of their life worlds. However, even this level of comfortable familiarity is never easy to obtain. "Going native," to use a somewhat obsolete anthropological term, requires a genuine commitment to learning about others, as well as, on some occasions, a deliberate attempt to "perform" the role of the native. As Wax (1983: 197) suggests,

> Perhaps good fieldwork is more like playacting than most of us are willing to admit. Respondents rarely resent a fieldworker's "acting like them" or "learning their ways" as long as a fieldworker makes it clear that he knows he is only playing a part and that his newly acquired skills do not entitle him to any privileges which they are not willing to offer him.

Yet, even developing this kind of understanding usually involves gaining the trust of one's subjects (Rosen 1991; Wax 1983). This ability to establish and maintain trust in a field setting while simultaneously being committed to authentically reporting on the same situation is always, at best, a precarious practice. Achieving some level of successful immersion means that people will confide in the researcher or reveal aspects of their personality and life which they would not share with most other people. Ethnographers who then write about these more intimate or confidential experiences in an indiscreet or instrumental fashion seriously rupture trusted relationships and leave very negative feelings in the communities that were being studied.

One way of managing this process more delicately is to share one's proposed findings with some of one's subjects. While they might not always agree with the researcher's interpretation, they are likely to feel less exploited and to voice their disagreements with the researcher's findings. In many cases, this can further refine a researcher's narrative and turn it into an even more plausible account. The central issue here is that people resent having their experiences and relationships objectified in research articles, especially when the researcher has been regarded as a trustworthy member of their community. One way in which ethnographers can minimize this problem is by writing about people in a way that is more empathetic and human, rather than in the clinical language of the social sciences. Here again, anthropological narrative is a useful way in which ethnographers can talk about people in less commodified ways.

6.3 Dilemmas of Representation

The preceding discussion leads neatly into a more recent controversy around the way in which ethnographers represent individuals, groups and cultures in their writings. In the last decade or so, ethnography (along with other forms of academic writing) has been severely critiqued for the many cultural biases which pervade it. As Van Maanen (1995) asserts, ethnography is now on trial for its unreflective adherence to scientific principle, its hidden prejudices, and its frequent incapacity to incorporate marginal voices into its narrative form. In other words, ethnographers in anthropology, sociology, communication and other disciplines are engaged in seriously reexamining the tenets that guide their writings and influence their storytelling methods.

No longer is it sufficient to merely tell a good story (Rosaldo 1989; Van Maanen 1995). Ethnographers are now grappling with the kind of values that implicitly shape their own storytelling and reevaluating the agendas that undergird their own research. In particular, anthropologists are exploring how ethnographies can speak more respectfully of less privileged groups (e.g., third world cultures) and bring in the voices of marginal groups (e.g., women, the poor). This debate is also forcing ethnographers to come to terms with their own privilege *vis a vis* some of their more powerless subjects and to recognize that the ethnographic project itself is embedded in a web of power relations (Behar 1993).

While these concerns might seem esoteric to researchers of information systems, a little reflection would suggest that is not really the case. In our own work, we are constantly representing both powerful groups (e.g., systems designers and senior management) and less powerful ones (e.g., clerical workers and data entry operators). How we represent these diverse groups, their concerns, and their arguments is what the issue of representation is all about. For instance, students of systems design are often unwittingly disrespectful of those who resist technological change. Many studies will either dismiss such resistance as an outcome of pathological or ignorant beliefs (Nord and Jermier 1994) or treat it solely as a problem to be overcome. Those who resist new information systems are often regarded as old fashioned, wary of progress, or ignorant and are implicitly represented as less knowledgeable and therefore to be taken less seriously. The current debates on representation alert ethnographers of technological change against taking such stances. At the very least, they also clue us into thinking about how we can meaningfully talk about people whose opinions are tacitly considered less knowledgeable.

Some questions they force upon us are

- How should we speak about resistance and resistors?
- Why are we so quick to treat resistance so pejoratively?
- How do we make space in our research for the voices of resistors to be heard?

While the answers to these questions are obviously not simple, they force us to wrestle with these and other problematic issues.

7 SOME CONCLUDING THOUGHTS

Today, few would oppose the use of qualitative methodologies for the study of information systems. In a post-positivist world, where multiple qualitative approaches such as ethnomethodology, ethnography, hermeneutics, and deconstruction are clamoring for our attention, we need to be increasingly clear about the implications of specific methodological choices. In this paper, an attempt was made to clarify some key implications in employing ethnography as a methodology for the study of information systems. In doing so, the intent was to dispel some of the confusion surrounding the term and to show how the methodology of ethnography was different rather than similar to many other popular genres of qualitative fieldwork. Such a stance is useful because researchers using the term become more cognizant of its implication and they will have a better sense of the ethnographic tradition, which primarily implies a constant engagement with the notion of culture. Too often, aspiring ethnographers, while paying attention to detail and immersion, ignore the cultural context which is at the heart of the ethnographic project. What this paper has tried to stress is that the lens of culture provides an analytic standpoint that is distinct from other qualitative traditions such as realist case methodology, semiotics, and phenomenology.

Further, it is probably evident by now that a major strength of ethngoraphy lies in its ability to lend itself easily to disciplinary hybridity, or what Geertz (1980) has termed the "blurring of the genres" whereby insights from literary theory, history and other disciplines can be woven into ethnographies of information systems. However, as the paper has also stressed, ethnography, while immensely attractive and insightful, is not an easy methodology to practice. While most people are familiar with the rigor it demands in terms of data collection, few pay sufficient attention to the theoretical orientation it demands or the complex issues it raises in the process of writing and researching. Yet, to anyone who has engaged in an ethnographic project, the insights it offers are often sufficient compensation for the emotional and intellectual demands it imposes. Certainly in a field such as MIS, still lacking a substantial ethnographic voice, its contribution would make its rigorous practice a worthwhile effort.

8 REFERENCES

Agar, M. H. (1980). *The Professional Stranger: An Informal Introduction to Ethnography*. New York: Academic Press.

Agar, M. H. (1992). *Speaking of Ethnography*. Newbury Park, California: Sage Publications.

Bailey, F. G. (1965). *Stratagems and Spoils: A Social Anthropology of Politics*. Oxford: Basil Blackwell.

Barley, S. R. (1988). "The Social Construction of a Machine: Ritual, Superstition, Magical Thinking and Other Pragmatic Responses to Running a CT Scanner." In M. Lock and D. Gordon (Editors), *Knowledge and Practice in Medicine: Social, Cultural and Historical Approaches*. Boston: Kluwer Academic Publishers, pp. 497-540.

Behar, R. (1993). *Translated Woman: Crossing the Border with Esperanza's Story*. Boston: Beacon Press.

Berg, P. O. (1985). "Techno-Culture: The Symbolic Framing of Technology in a Volvo Plant." *Scandanavian Journal of Management Studies*, Volume 4, pp. 237-256.

Berns, M. C. (1990). "Pots as People: Yungur Ancestral Portraits." *African Arts*, Volume 23, 23: 50-60.

Campbell, C. (1987). *The Romantic Ethic and the Spirit of Modern Consumerism*. London: Basil Blackwell.

Caudill, W. C. (1952). "Social Structure and Interaction Processes in a Psychiatric Ward." *American Journal of Orthopsychiatry*, Volume 22, pp. 314-334.

Clifford, J., and Marcus, G. E. (1986). *Writing Culture: The Poetics and Politics of Ethnography*. Berkeley: University of California Press.

Frake, C. O. (1983). "Ethnography." In R. M. Emerson (Editor), *Contemporary Field Research*. Boston: Little Brown, pp. 60-67.

Geertz, C. (1973). *The Interpretation of Cultures*. New York: Basic Books.

Geertz, C. (1980). "Blurred Genres: The Refiguration of Social Thought." *The American Scholar*, Volume 49, p. 165-179.

Golden-Biddle, K., and Locke, K. (1993). "Appealing Work: An Investigation of How Ethnographic Texts Convince." *Organization Science*, Volume 4, pp. 595-616.

Gregory, K. L. (1983). "'Native View' Paradigms: Multiple Cultures and Culture Conflicts in Organizations." *Administrative Science Quarterly*, Volume 28, pp. 359-376.

Hamilton, D. (1993). "Traditions, Preferences and Postures in Applied Qualitative Research." In N. Denzin and Y. Lincoln (Editors), *Handbook of Qualitative Research*. Thousand Oaks, California: Sage Publications, pp. 60-69.

Harrison, S. (1982). "Yams and the Symbolic Representation of Time in a Sepik River Village." *Oceania*, Volume 53, pp. 141-162.

Headland, T. N.; Pike, K. L.; and Harris, M. (1990). *Emics and Etics: The Insider/Outsider Debate*. Newbury Park, California: Sage Publications.

Homan, R. (1980). "The Ethics of Covert Methods." *British Journal of Sociology*, Volume 31, pp. 46-59.

Joerges, B. (1989). "Romancing the Machine: Reflections on the Social Scientific Construction of Computer Reality." *International Studies of Management and Organization*, Volume 19, pp. 24-50.

Kling, R., and Iacono, S. (1984). "Computing as an Occasion for Social Control." *Journal of Social Issues*, Volume 40, pp. 77-36.

Lee, A. S. (1994). "Electronic Mail as a Medium for Rich Communication: An Empirical Investigation Using Hermeneutic Interpretation." *MIS Quarterly*, Volume 18, pp. 143-157.

Mann, F. C., and Williams, L. K. (1960). "Observations on the Dynamic Nature of a Change to Electronic Data Processing Equipment." *Administrative Science Quarterly*, Volume 5, pp. 217-256.

Markus, M. L. (1983). "Power, Politics and MIS Implementation." *Communications of the ACM*, Volume 26, pp. 430-444.

Morgan, G., and Smircich, L. (1980). "The Case for Qualitative Research." *Academy of Management Review*, Volume 5, pp. 491-500.

Nord, W., and Jermier, J. (1994). "Overcoming Resistance to Resistance: Insights from a Study of Shadows." *Public Administration Quarterly*, Volume 17, pp. 396-409.

Orlikowski, W. (1991). "Integrated Information Environment or Matrix of Control? The Contradictory Implications of Information Technology." *Accounting, Management and Information Technologies*, Volume 1, pp. 9-42.

Orlikowski, W. (1993). "CASE Tools as Organizational Change: Investigating Incremental and Radical Changes in Systems Development." *MIS Quarterly*, Volume 17, pp. 309-339.

Pfaffenberger, B. (1989). "The Social Meaning of the Personal Computer or Why the Personal Computer Revolution Was no Revolution." *Anthropological Quarterly*, Volume 61, pp. 39-47.

Prasad, P. (1993). "Symbolic Processes in the Implementation of Technological Change: A Symbolic Interactionist Study of Work Computerization." *Academy of Management Journal*, Volume 36, pp. 1400-1429.

Prasad, P. (1995). "Working with the 'Smart' Machine: Computerization and the Discourse of Anthropomorphism in Organizations." *Studies in Cultures, Organizations and Societies*, Volume 1, pp. 253-265.

Rosaldo, R. (1989). *Culture and Truth*. Boston: Beacon Press.

Rosen, M. (1991). "Coming to Terms with the Field: Understanding and Doing Organizational Ethnography." *Journal of Management Studies*, Volume 28, pp. 1-24.

Ruhleder, K.; Jordan, B.; and Elmes, M. B. (1996). "Wiring the 'New Organization'." *Proceedings of the Annual Meetings of the Academy of Management*, Cincinnati, August.

Schwartzman, H. (1993). *Ethnography in Organizations*. Newbury Park, California: Sage Publications.

Sherry, J. F. (1990). "A Sociocultural Analysis of a Midwestern Flea Market." *Journal of Consumer Research*, Volume 17, pp. 13-30.

Thompson, W. E. (1983). "Hanging Tongues: A Sociological Encounter with the Assembly Line." *Qualitative Sociology*, Volume 6, pp. 215-237.

Turkle, S. (1984). *The Second Self: Computers and the Human Spirit*. New York: Simon and Schuster.

Van Maanen, J. (1973). "Observations on the Making of Policemen." *Human Organization*, Volume 32, pp. 407-418.

Van Maanen, J. (1987). *Tales of the Field: On Writing Ethnography*. Chicago: University of Chicago Press.

Van Maanen, J. (1995). "An End to Innocence: The Ethnography of Ethnography." In J. Van Maanen (Editor), *Representation in Ethnography*. Thousand Oaks, California: Sage Publications, pp. 1-35.

Van Maanen, J., and Kunda, G. (1989). "'Real Feelings': Emotional Expression and Organizational Culture." *Research in Organizational Behavior*, Volume 11, pp. 43-103.

Walsham, G. (1993). *Interpreting Information Systems in Organizations*. New York: Wiley.

Wax, R. H. (1983). "The Ambiguities of Fieldwork." In R. E. Emerson (Editor), *Contemporary Field Research*. Boston: Little Brown, pp. 191-202.

Wolcott, H. F. (1995). "Making a Study more Ethnographic." In J. Van Maanen (Editor), *Representation in Ethnography*. Thousand Oaks, California: Sage Publications, pp. 79-111.

Zuboff, S. (1988). *In the Age of the Smart Machine: The Future of Work and Power*. New York: Basic Books.

9 BIOGRAPHY

Pushkala Prasad is an associate professor at the University of Calgary where she teaches organization theory, qualitative methodology and management skills. Her research interests are in the areas of technological symbolism, resistance to computerization, workplace diversity and philosophies of research methods. Her work has been published in a number of journals including *Academy of Management Journal* and *Journal of Management Studies and Organization Science*. She has just coedited a book entitled *Managing the Organizational Melting Pot: Dilemmas of Workplace Diversity*. She recently was named an Ascendent Scholar by the Western Academy of Management. Professor Prasad has been a visiting professor at the Helsinki School of Economics and at Lund University in Sweden.

8

Panel – Assessing Critical Social Theory Research in Information Systems

O. Ngwenyama
University of Michigan, USA

G. Davis
University of Minnesota, USA

K. Lyytinen
University of Jyväskylä, Finland

D. Truex
Georgia State University, USA

P. Cule
Georgia State University, USA

The Critical Social Theory (CST) program of information systems research is now just over a decade old. Although the number of researchers associated with the CST program are few, they have had a disproportionately larger impact on the field than other research communities. The main reason for this disproportionate impact can be found in the intense and incisive radical critiques of the foundational assumptions of our field that CST researchers have conducted. These radical critiques have helped to open up the theoretical debate on IS research and point out new directions for future inquiry. But as we turn the century, new challenges are emerging. New information technologies (IT) are rapidly invading all social forms of life, impinging upon the daily experiences of individuals and radically changing the relationship between people and IT. Like no other research program, the CST approach is based on the ideals of emancipation from blind technological rationality and uses of IT that enhances freedom and justice. How then will the CST research program respond to developments in new information technologies which have the potential to be intensively oppressive?

This panel brings together leading CST-IS researchers and, in keeping with CST tradition, opposing voices to ensure critical self-reflection and debate. The debate and discussion will examine the emergence of new socially transformative information technologies and the role of CST research in helping to shape the future.

Ojelanki Ngwenyama will chair and moderate the panel. He will make introductory remarks that set the panel agenda and closing remarks that tie together the panelists' comments. Kalle Lyytinen will outline the basic tenets of critical social theory and its short history and impact on the theoretical foundations of IS research. Gordon Davis will provide a critique of the critical social theory approach and provide a more general perspective on how CST fits in the mosaic of IS research. Duane Truex will outline some of the important social issues that are emerging around new information technologies and suggest how some of these can be carefully examined and understood from a CST perspective. Finally, Paul Cule will open the debate on the future of CST research in the context of new emerging information technologies.

Part Two

Interpretation and IS Requirements Definition

9

Examining Project History Narratives: An Analytic Approach

E. J. Davidson
College of Business Administration
University of Hawaii, Manoa
Honolulu, Hawaii 96822, USA
Tel: (808) 956-6657
Fax: (808) 956-9889
E-mail: DAVIDSON@busadm.cba.hawaii.edu

Abstract

Scientific interest in human beings' ability and propensity to construe reality through narrative constructions has increased since the 1970s. Although narrative processes have been addressed in the organizational literature, little research attention has yet been given to the role and function of narratives in organizational efforts to develop, implement, and apply information technology. An analytic approach drawn from Mishler (1986b) for the analysis of project history narratives found in research interviews is described. Three project history narratives collected during a field study of systems development are analyzed using this approach. Differences in sensemaking and interpretation revealed in the analysis of each informant's story and comparison of the analysis of multiple stories are discussed. Insights that narrative analysis may provide into the social cognitive worlds of participants in IS development and its applications in IS research are then considered.

"I learned that it's unsafe to say anything much about narrative, because if a poststructuralist doesn't get you a deconstructionalist will."
"Some Thoughts on Narrative" by Ursula K. LeGuin, 1980

1 INTRODUCTION

In *Actual Minds, Possible Worlds*, Bruner (1986) contrasts "two modes of cognitive functioning, two modes of thought, each providing distinctive ways of ordering experience, of constructing reality" (p. 11). Paradigmatic thinking is characterized by the well-formed argument, principled hypothesis, generalized causes, and procedures to empirically test its "truthfulness." Narrative thought, on the other hand, "deals in human or human-like intention and action and the vicissitudes and consequences that mark their course" (p. 13). Its measure is "lifelikeness."

Narrativizing is the interpretive process though which human beings make sense of their experiences by accounting for human actions and intentions in the course of events that occur over time. Human experiences, and memories of them, are typically framed in a narrative form (Bruner 1990). In a narrative, events, actions and accounts of actions move through time and are organized in a way that demonstrates connectedness or coherence to a goal state or end point (Gergen and Gergen 1986). The organization of actions and events accounts for actors' reasons for their acts and implies causes for happenings (Sarbin 1986). Bruner (1990) contends that deviations from canonical cultural patterns are mitigated or made comprehensible in this way, making narratives "especially viable instruments for social negotiations" (p. 55). Narrativizing experience by telling stories is often a collaborative activity between the narrator and listeners, in which the interpretation embodied in a story is tested and adjusted (Boje 1991; Robinson and Hawpe 1986).

Research interest in human beings' ability and propensity to construe reality through narrative constructions has increased since the 1970s in disciplines such as anthropology, linguistics, philosophy, literary theory, and psychology (Howard 1991; Sarbin 1986). Bruner (1990) has characterized scientific interest in narrative as a "renewed cognitive revolution" concerned with interpretation and meaning-making, and Sarbin has proposed narrative as a root metaphor for psychology. Not surprisingly, research interest in narrative processes has extended to the domain of organizational studies. Much of this research has addressed stories as objects which symbolize aspects of organizational culture (Clark 1972; Martin et al. 1983; Martin and Meyerson 1988; Wilkins 1984), internal conflicts (Gabriel 1991; Hansen and Kahnweiler 1993; Mumby 1987), or change efforts (McConkie and Boss 1986). Other researchers have examined the role of storytelling in organizational sensemaking and problem-solving (Boje 1991; Brown and Duguid 1991; Mitroff and Kilmann 1975). More recently, Tenkasi and Boland (1993) have called for empirical research on the day-to-day organizational process of narrativizing experience as a way to examine meaning making and learning in organizations, and Boland and Tenkasi (1995) have posited that narrativizing experience is fundamental to organizational learning and innovation in knowledge-intensive firms.

Despite the growing interest in narrative processes in the organizational literature, little research attention has yet been given to the role and function of narratives in organizational efforts to develop, implement, and apply information technology.[1] Yet these complex social activities, eloquently described here by Bansler and Bødker (1993), require the kind of sensemaking and social negotiations which narrativizing experience enables:

> Problems are ill-defined more often than not. Objectives and goals are vague, changing, and often in conflict with one another. In most cases the design process is one of collective inquiry and search where several actors, in cooperation or conflict, define relevant problems and possible solutions – doing so more or less simultaneously. Problems and ends can not be taken as givens, they are negotiated and clarified during the design process. [p. 173]

A field study of information systems development examined how project participants communicated their knowledge, assumptions, and expectations to negotiate a shared understanding of information systems (IS) requirements (Davidson 1996). Creating and maintaining accounts of actions and events in the IS development projects were critical sensemaking processes that shaped participants' interpretation of IT requirements and influenced their decisions about the design and implementation of IT artifacts. This interpretive process of narrativizing experience was evident both in informants' retrospective accounts of project events during research interviews and in project members' interactions during day-to-day project activities as they reacted to and accounted for events that affected the development project.

These findings are described in detail elsewhere (Davidson 1996). The goal here is to describe an analytic approach for examining such narratives, to illustrate its application in the analysis of project history narratives collected during the field study, and to consider how narrative analysis may inform our understanding of the social cognitive worlds of participants in IS development activities. In this endeavor, we rely primarily on Mishler's (1986a, 1986b) work on narrative analysis of interview data, which is reviewed in the next section.

2 ANALYZING NARRATIVES IN INTERVIEW DATA: AN OVERVIEW

In *Research Interviewing: Context and Narrative*, Mishler (1986b) reviews and critiques various methodological approaches for analyzing narratives produced in the context of research interviews. He first considers methods that focus on the analysis of structural components of narratives. Citing the work of Labov and Waletzky (1967) and Labov (1972), Mishler notes that the focus of their analytical method is identification of narrative clauses or "complicating actions" within the text of a story. Narrative clauses are those clauses which depend on a strict sequential ordering for

[1]See Boland and Schultze (1995) for one example.

their meaning. For example, in the sequence of clauses "The dog bit Mary, and Mary cried," the meaning of the clause "Mary cried" is implied by its temporal ordering after the clause "The dog bit Mary." Nonnarrative clauses, which may also occur in a narrative account, include a narrator's abstract or summary of the story's point, orientation or contextual information, evaluative comments, the result or resolution of actions, and a coda or return to the conversation from the story. Mishler comments that this method of categorizing portions of a narrative text into structural categories is similar to content analysis methods used in qualitative data analysis and therefore should be accessible to researchers familiar with these methods.

In his critique of the Labov-Waletzky's model, Mishler notes that, although temporal ordering is given theoretical importance, the model focuses on further categorization and analysis of the evaluative components of a story. He reviews Labov's (1982) solution to this apparent paradox, in which a higher level of abstractions is achieved by characterizing the narrative clauses in terms of the social meanings of the events to which they relate. Using Goffman's concept of a Move, the skeletal outline of narrative clauses is transformed into a highly abstract sequence of Moves to reveal patterns of social positioning in interaction.

Drawing next on the work of Agar and Hobbs (1982), Mishler considers how the structure of content in a narrative may reveal implicit meaning. In this approach, the narrator's intentions and narrative strategies to produce a coherent account are examined in terms of coherence relations among utterances or narrative segments. In the Agar-Hobbs model, there are three general types of coherence which impart a form of unity to a narrative text: (a) global coherence, which relates to the speaker's overall plan or intent for the narrative; (b) local coherence, which refers to the function of an utterance within the immediate text segment; and (c) themal coherence, which suggests the narrator's assumptions, beliefs, and goals that reoccur throughout the narrative. Examining how coherence is manifest in a narrative reveals aspects of the structure and content of the narrator's cognitive world. Mishler concludes that the researcher cannot avoid applying his own cultural understanding in this interpretive process and, in this way, enlarging the text with his or her own knowledge, values, and beliefs. His conclusion is similar to the position taken by Polanyi (1989) in her analysis of cultural values and beliefs in conversational stories.

Mishler contends that the influence of the interaction context in a research interview on informants' production of narrative accounts has been largely ignored or has not been systematically addressed in these types of research approaches. Instead, the researcher is "written out" of the context with the assumption that he or she has had no significant influence on the production of the narrative. Drawing on the work of Paget (1982, 1983) and Bell (1983) on life history interviews, Mishler suggests that narratives are a joint production of interviewer and interviewee which reflects ongoing shifts in the reciprocal dual roles of interviewer/interviewee and listener/narrator. He concludes that systematic analysis of the interview context contributes to a more adequate interpretation of the narrative's meaning.

How a narrative is identified and how it is bounded in the text of an interview influences interpretation of the narrative. In the Labov-Waletzky model, narrative and nonnarrative portions of an interview are separated and attention is focused on the narrative statements. In the Agar-Hobbs model, all portions of the text potentially contribute to the coherence and the interview (or major portions of it) are treated as one narrative. In Bell's approach to life history narratives, stories are bounded within the interview and linkages between stories or episodes are examined.

Despite these methodological differences, Mishler (1986a, 1986b) suggests that a richer interpretation of a narrative is made possible by considering the insights available from all of the three approaches (structural, meaning, and interaction analysis). In the analysis of a text segment from a research interview, he first uses the Labov-Waletzky model to classify portions of the narrative as orientation, the narrator's abstract, complicating actions or narrative clauses, and resolution or outcome (Mishler 1986a). By making inferences informed by the model, he identifies the core narrative as the narrator's "point" in the story. He then applies Labov's method (1982) to summarize the narrative clauses into a highly abstract plot sequence of Moves (an offer-refusal-counteroffer sequence) through which threats to social status are reduced. Using the notions of global and themal coherence from the Agar-Hobbs model, Mishler then considers how various segments of the text relate to the narrative as a whole and, through this analysis, he interprets the narrative as the informant's attempt to present himself according to a cultural ideal (being a self-reliant and responsible person). Mishler notes that both the production of the narrative and his interpretation of it depended on the shared recognition of cultural values between interviewer and interviewee. Finally, Mishler assesses the interaction context of the research interview, which he characterizes as bordering on an adversarial struggle for control of the interview. The interviewee evaded direct answer to some questions, digressed with many stories and concealed relevant information that would be unflattering to him.

In his sequential application of the three analytic approaches, Mishler (1986a, 1986b) does not attempt to integrate the methods. Nor does he claim to have arrived at one, true interpretation of the narrative account. Instead, he demonstrates that narratives are multifaceted, and that using a variety of analytic lenses provides deeper insight into their multiple meanings as well as into the assumptions and values which inform meaning making through narrative construction. The narrative analytical approach used here to examine project history narratives is modeled on Mishler's three-steps of structural, meaning, and interaction analysis. The next section describes the current application of these methods in detail.

3 ANALYZING PROJECT HISTORY NARRATIVES: A METHODOLOGICAL APPROACH

The narratives examined in this paper are drawn from interview data collected as part of a year-long field study of requirements definition activities during information systems development (Davidson 1996). The research was conducted at Group Health, Inc. (GHI), a nonprofit health care insurance company in the eastern United States. For several years before the research project began and throughout the study period, GHI experienced major changes in its market. Executives at the company responded with new strategies, organizational restructuring, new product introductions, and IS development initiatives aimed at improving management information. A year before the study began, GHI executives outsourced the entire IS operations and development functions to an IT vendor, Information Systems, Inc. (ISI). Not surprisingly, this organizational context posed significant challenges to project teams that were developing and implementing large-scale information systems.

One of the projects examined at GHI was the INFOSYS project. The project involved building a relational database of historical data from transaction processing systems and implementing a purchased software package, the INFOSYS system, which contained analytical algorithms and had a client-server based, graphical user interface (GUI). During its three year history, the project had gone through a number of episodes in which project activities were halted or the project was redirected. Data on the INFOSYS project was collected over a four month period from project files and documents and through retrospective interviews with thirty informants at who had some involvement in the project, either as team members, sponsors, developers, or potential users. In interviews, a semi-structured interview protocol was used to ask informants to reflect on their understanding of the project and the IT application, their own and others' actions, and events in the organization that they believed had affected the project. Interviews were audio taped and transcribed.

In many instances, the informant's response to questions took the form of an extended narrative history of the project, in which they told stories about major events and episodes in the project, identified key actors, attributed goals and motives to these actors, and so on. Methodological decisions must be made about how to identify and bound such narratives (Mishler 1986b). No attempt to treat the entire interview as one narrative was made. Instead, the interview text was considered a series of narratives, some of them with multiple episodes, interspersed with nonnarrative interchanges and information. Interest then was in those sections of the interview in which the informant narrated portions of the INFOSYS project history, although both narrative and nonnarrative clauses within these sections were examined.

To illustrate this approach to narrative analysis, in this paper we examine the narrative accounts of the origins of the INFOSYS project from three key informants: the project manager, the project sponsor, and a GHI executive. In interviews, these informants were asked to describe, from their perspective, how and why the INFO-

SYS project got started. Each individual had a unique perspective on the project's origins which reflected not only their experiences with project activities but also their knowledge, assumptions, and expectations about the project's purpose and definition, technology development strategies, desirable features of the IT application, problems or opportunities at GHI to be addressed through the technology, and so on. The full text of the narrative accounts, extracted from the interview transcript, are documented in Appendices A, B, and C respectively.

Following Mishler's (1986a, 1986b) example of a three-phased examination of structure, meaning, and interaction context, the first step was the structural analysis of the project history narrative. To identify structural components, each informant's narrative account was divided into segments of partial sentences, complete sentences, or strings of sentences which contained distinctive information. To classify segments, the four structural components used by Mishler (1986a) – orientation, the narrator's abstract, complicating actions or narrative clauses, and resolution or outcome – were considered as well as the narrator's perspective, actors identified in the narrative, the problematic situation articulated by the narrator, and the goal/problem solution perceived by the narrator (see Table 1). These categories better fit the data in the problem-solving narratives analyzed. They also reflect Bruner's (1990) four "crucial grammatical constituents" of narrative cognitive processes: 1) goal-directed action by humans; 2) a sequential order to events and states moving through time; 3) a sense of the canonical and the exceptional or noncanonical; and 4) a narratorial voice or perspective.

The results of this first step of the structural analysis are summarized in Exhibits 1, 2, and 3. A next step was to develop an abstract of the actions and events which constituted the story line. Unlike Mishler (1986a), Goffman's Move concept was not used to create the plot abstract, because the concept of a Move, which relates to the structure of interpersonal interactions, was not the focus of this research. Instead, the narrative accounts examined were stories of the problem-solving activities of individuals and groups in an organizational setting. To develop the abstract of the underlying plot sequence, generic descriptions of the actions or events described were used. For example, action clauses such as "a few of us went around and looked at different alternative ways of doing this" or "we explored doing it on our own or going with and outside vendor" were characterized generically as "a search for alternative solutions."

In the next analytic step, the Agar-Hobbs model for coherence relations was used to examine how various narrative segments conveyed unity to the narrative account of the project's origins. In this step, segments which did not directly contribute to the plot sequence or were parenthetical in the movement of the plot, such as orientation and contextual information, were particularly revealing. Segments that had global and themal coherence provided insights into how the informants made sense of the events and actions depicted in their accounts, the meaning they attributed to them, and key assumptions and expectations they drew on to attribute meaning to actions and events. Comparisons among the three narrative accounts highlighted individuals' assumptions as well as shared assumptions.

Table 1 Classification Categories for Narrative Segments.

Category	**Description**
Narrator's abstract	Segments in which the narrator summarizes the events and outcome of the story. An abstract is not always present.
Narrator's perspective	Segments or use of language (e.g., "I" or "we" versus "they") in which the narrator reveals his or her perspective on events in the narrative.
Orientation/contextual descriptions	Segments in which the narrator provides contextual information which does not contribute to the movement of action through time. These are not always present.
Actors	Segments or use of language (e.g., "I" or "we" versus "they") which indicate who carried out actions or contributed to events depicted in the narrative.
Problematic situation	Segments in which the narrator describes his or her perceptions of the noncanonical or exceptional circumstances which motivates actions described in the narrative.
Goal/problem solution	Segments in which the narrator describes his or her perceptions of how the problematic situation could be or was resolved.
Actions and events	Narrative clause segments: • Actions are activities that occur during the time span of the narrative that have a strict temporal sequencing. • Past actions or flashbacks serve as orientation clauses. • Events are recognized changes in state, such as completion of an activity or arriving at a decision point.
Outcomes	Segments in which the narrator describes the perceived outcome of actions and events, such as resolution of the problematic situation by achieving the goal.

The last step in the narrative analysis was to assess how the interaction context may have affected the informant's production of the narrative account. The goal in each interview was to elicit open-ended responses to questions and the informant was generally encouraged to answer as he or she was inclined. However, by using a semi-structured interview protocol, the informant's narratives were guided to topics of interest in the study. Thus, the informant's narrative was a response to the questions asked and to how their response was guided. The relationship of the researcher with the informant at the time of the interview and how this may have influenced his or her decision about what information to relate was then considered.

In the next section, the application of the three step analytical approach to three narrative accounts of the origins of the INFOSYS project is illustrated. For brevity in presentation, the analysis of the project manager's account is discussed in detail and then the analysis of her account is compared and contrasted with the analyses of the project sponsor's and executive's accounts.

4 HOW DID THE INFOSYS PROJECT GET STARTED? THE PROJECT MANAGER'S NARRATIVE

In response to a request that she describe how the INFOSYS project got started, the project manager described her experiences with and perceptions of the events and activities that led to the formulation of the project (see Appendix A). Following the methodology described above, the structural components of the narrative were analyzed first. The results of this analysis are documented in Exhibit 1.

The structural analysis focused on the identification of the narrative clauses and creation of an abstract of the plot sequence through which the narrator organized her explanation for her own and others' actions. The sequence of events in the problem-solving plot abstract revealed through this analysis were i) identification of a problem or need, ii) evaluation of alternative solutions, and iii) selection of an alternative. In the first problem-solving sequence, *"there was a need identified to be able to provide accounts with some access to their own data"* (lines 45-6), alternative solutions were considered (lines 47-51, 55-6, 57), and the best solution (INFOSYS) was chosen (lines 58-60, 61-64). The problem-solving plot was complicated, however, by the unexplained failure of management "a couple levels up" to support the project in this first project episode (lines 65, 66-67), resulting in a temporary ending to the story (line 68). The story continued in the next episode with a second problem-solving sequence in which a major customer's request for the INFOSYS software created a new need (lines 75-79; 80-82; 84-86), alternative solutions were again evaluated (lines 91-92), and INFOSYS was finally selected as the best alternative (lines 93-100). The outcome of this episode was GHI's commitment of resources to acquire and implement the software (lines 101-106).

In the analysis of meaning, the local, global, and themal coherence of segments in the narrative were considered. Take, for example, the informant's entree into her story of the INFOSYS project's origins: *"Really, there have been several fits and starts"* (line 15). This utterance was locally coherent, functioning as a transition from the interviewer's question (lines 10-13) into the informant's story. It was globally coherent, serving as the abstract for the informant's story and setting the stage for the informant's lengthy account of project episodes that followed. Additionally, this ut-

Exhibit 1 Structural Analysis of Project Manager's Narrative.

Narrator's Abstract:	"Really, there have been several fits and starts..." (line 15)
Narrator's perspective	"I was in the account reporting department" (line 17) "There was a...systems team that I managed..." (lines 20-21) "So I didn't hear anything else about it for a while." (line 69) "...so I wasn't involved in the actual going around and interviewing vendors at this point..." (lines 88-89) "And I was a part of that uh...effort..." (line 107)
Orientation/ contextual descriptions:	In lines 21-27 the informant uses a scenario to describe the account reporting process. In lines 52-54 the informant mentions a related IS initiative. In lines 70-74 the informant describes the organizational change affecting her area. In line 83 the informant refers to the outsourcing of the IS department.
Actors:	"I" (project manager); "we" (unspecified group); "a few of us" (line 47); "a couple of levels [managers]" (line 65); RBC (lines 75, 80, 94, 98); marketing reps (line 80) "a team...at a higher level" (line 87); "Dave...people at his level" (line 90)
Problematic solution:	In lines 28-44, the informant uses a narrative scenario to describe the inefficiencies of the account reporting process. ("But the problem that we saw...")
Goal/problem solution:	"and we were looking at providing accounts with some access that they could have to their own data" (lines 18-19)
Actions and events	"So there was a need identified..." (lines 45-46) "...a few of us that went around and looked at...alternatives..." (lines 47-51) "So we had explored doing our own thing..." (lines 55-56) "We had interviewed several different companies" (line 57) "...we had gone over to their office and had seen the product..." (lines 58-60) "And it got to a certain point..." (lines 61-64) "I think it kind of bumped up a couple of levels..." (line 65) "then it came back down..." (lines 66-67) "And, at that point we heard from RBC..." (lines 75-79) "And the marketing reps...started contacting different people..." (lines 80-82; 84-86) "They went out and interviewed a few vendors..." (lines 91-92) "...so it kind of came down to well, INFOSYS is the best thing..." (lines 93-100)
Outcome:	"We kind of went 'bye.'" (In line 68, the informant describes an intermediate outcome.) "So at that point, a team was put together...to look at this and negotiate a contract..." (In lines 101-106, the informant describes the final outcome of these episodes.

terance had themal coherence with the informant's depiction of her own and other's long struggle to overcome problems and disruptions that delayed, halted, or altered the course of project activities. Thus, she implied that there was no simple answer to the question of how and why the INFOSYS project got started but that the answer lay in its *"fits and starts."*

In a similar manner, other segments of the narrative were analyzed. Some segments were only locally coherent. For example, the informant's statement in line 17 (*"I was in the account reporting department"*) served primarily to clarify the narrator's perspective in the actions described in lines 18-19 *("and we were looking at providing accounts with some access")*. Such segments were of less interest in the analysis of meaning than segments that were globally or themally coherent. Two merit special attention here.

In the narrative segment in lines 28-44, the project manager stated her perception of the problematic situation, clearly introduced with the verbal cue *"but the problem that we saw,"* and using the pronoun "we" to imply that her perception of the problem had been shared with others. The informant's dramatization of the problem through a narrative scenario of the inefficient and frustrating reporting process suggested that this segment was of particular importance to the narrator's purpose in the narrative. It had global coherence, because it provided the motivation the actions and events that led to acquisition of the INFOSYS system. It also had themal coherence, expressing themes that reoccurred throughout the project manager's narrative of the INFOSYS project about the desirability of having end-users access data directly and the advantages of freeing programmers from producing the reports. Her articulation of the reporting problem also related to her interpretation of the INFOSYS technology, with its GUI interface, as the technology which would allow GHI to *"provide accounts with some access to their own data"* (lines 45-46).

Related to her articulation of the problematic situation in this segment is the project manager's dismissal of one of alternative solutions in lines 52-54 (*"You know, we had been building our own repository. But didn't, you know, have the friendly front-end type thing"*). At first glance the informant appeared simply to provide contextual information that related to her preceding statement, that alternative solutions to the reporting problem were being explored including the *"build or buy option"* (lines 48-51), and the following statement, that the team had decided on *"going with an outside vendor"* (lines 55-56). However, consideration of the global and themal coherence of this segment with other parts of the narrative suggested other meanings implicit in this statement. The segment was globally coherent with the underlying plot sequence of problem identification, evaluation of alternatives, and selection of the best alternative, suggesting that this alternative (using the in-house developed system) had been given due consideration but dropped because it lacked *"the friendly front-end type of thing."* Themal coherence with the project manager's depiction of the INFOSYS software package as the only viable solution (lines 93-100) was also evident, particularly later in the interview when she emphasized the importance of the graphical user interface (GUI) feature of the INFOSYS software.

In the last analytic step, the influence of the interaction context on the project manager's production of the narrative account of the origins of the INFOSYS project was assessed. The context was a formal research interview conducted with the project manager. Formal aspects of the setting were evident in note taking and recording of the interview and in guiding of the discussion with questions. By telling her story, the project manager fulfilled her agreement to provide information about project events for the research project. Her narrative account reflected the request (lines 1-6) that she describe the project from her own perspective and relate project events to other happenings in the company. In doing so, she meticulously specified which events she had participated in and which she had only second hand knowledge of (see narrator's perspective in Exhibit 1). However, a degree of rapport with the project manager had been established earlier after several informal meetings with her to discuss including the INFOSYS project in the research project at GHI and in informal discussions about similarities in professional background and personal circumstances. As she told her story, she appeared to take advantage of the opportunity to relate her experiences with this frustrating project to an informed and sympathetic listener. After clarifying what information was being requesting (line 8), she largely ignored the suggestion that she skip the details to describe how and why the project got started (lines 10-13) and instead proceeded with a 1600 word, detailed narration of project events. By shifting from the role of interviewer to listener and not interrupting, the researcher cooperated with her assumption of the authority to tell the story of the project in her own way, that is, through the story of its *"fits and starts."*

Through these analytic steps, a fuller interpretation of the possible meanings of the informant's narrative of the origins of the INFOSYS project was achieved. Her problem solving plot implied the rational and objective nature of the actions which lead to purchase the INFOSYS package. Her story became not that of yet another over-budget, over-schedule IS development project but one of a lengthy and difficult struggle by herself and others to solve a long-standing problem at GHI and to satisfy important customers. The epic-like proportions of her story were even more strongly evident in her later accounts of incidents in which the villain-like outsource organization temporarily *"killed"* the project or attempted to *"sabotage"* it. Given these insights into her story, questions arise about the assumptions, values, or beliefs that informed the project manager's narrativizing of actions and events in the INFOSYS project. What do they tell us about her social cognitive world? To what extent was her interpretation shared by others? Comparing the results of the analysis of the project manager's narrative to the analyses of the project sponsor's and executive's accounts highlighted similarities and differences in the narrative structure, in the structure of content and the implications for meaning of the narratives, and the influence of the interaction context. In this way, individual assumptions, values, and beliefs which informed their meaning making became clearer, as did the extent to which these assumptions were shared with others at GHI.

5 HOW *DID* THE INFOSYS PROJECT GET STARTED? A COMPARISON OF ACCOUNTS

The summary of the structural analysis of the INFOSYS project sponsor's and the executive's narrative are provided in Exhibits 2 and 3, and the full text of the interview segments are contained in Appendices B and C respectively. Not surprisingly, there were differences evident in the three accounts. Each informant constructed an account of the origins of the INFOSYS project using his or her own experience with and knowledge of project events. The project manager's narrative reflected her involvement in the day-to-day operation of the project. The perspective of the project sponsor was consistent with his responsibility for a variety of MIS support activities in the accounting and actuarial departments. The executive's perspective was that of a senior manager concerned with the company's standing with competitors and customers.

Beyond these expected differences, comparison of the structural analysis of the three accounts indicated other interesting variations in the narratives. Interestingly, each of the three informants articulated the problematic situation which motivated the actions and events in their narrative differently. The project manager's narrative focused on the inefficient utilization reporting process as the problematic situation and its resolution by giving accounts direct access to data. In her story, INFOSYS emerged as the best choice among alternative solutions. The project sponsor's narrative suggested that the project grew out of a long-acknowledged desire at GHI to have a data warehouse or MIS system. Providing the INFOSYS software package in response to the RBC, Inc.'s request was then *"a fast way to jump start"* into having an MIS (lines 47-49 in Exhibit 2). In his narrative, the executive stressed recognition of an opportunity to gain competitive advantage by excelling in analytical utilization reporting for customers (lines 37-39, Exhibit 3), and he perceived the answer to be the technology provided by INFOSYS, Inc.

Although these diverse interpretations of the problematic situation intersected in the rationale for GHI's decision to acquire the INFOSYS package, each informant identified different actions and events that led to this decision. The plot sequence in the project manager's narrative was a problem identification/alternative evaluation/selection sequence of events. The project sponsor's narrative was generally consistent with the project manager's account, but it differed in the details of actions and events noted. He briefly mentioned the first episode in which GHI personnel evaluated the INFOSYS package (lines 13-15, Exhibit 2) and then, noting RBC's action (line 16), he dramatized RBC, Inc.'s request that GHI purchase INFOSYS with a paraphrase (lines 17-21) and gave his own explanation of the logic of RBC's request (lines 22-36) which provided the impetus for the project. In the plot sequence in this narrative, there was no evaluation of alternatives. Instead, a change trigger was acknowledged (lines 16), information was gathered (line 37), and an opportunity was recognized (lines 38-42) to satisfy a long-standing goal of having an MIS.

Exhibit 2 Structural Analysis of Project Sponsor's Narrative.

Narrator's Abstract:	"...so we saw it as, although an expensive way, a fast way to jump start us into a management information situation." (lines 47-49)
Narrator's perspective:	Narrator's participation in the events is implied through his first-person plural narration of events (lines 7, 10, 37, 38, 47).
Orientation/ contextual descriptions:	In lines 11-12, the informant describes the IS organization.
Actors:	"We" (unspecified) and "I" (lines 7, 10, 37, 47) RBC, Inc. (line 16) "I and the IS people I was working with" (line 38)
Problematic situation:	"We were, we had been talking for years about a data warehouse, an MIS system..." (lines 7-9)
Goal/problem solution:	In lines 37-42, the informant cites INFOSYS as the solution to the need for an MIS. In lines 22-36, he outlines the logic of GHI's decision to provide the system for its customer, RBC. In lines 39-42, he links this approach to the goal of having an MIS. In lines 43-47, he qualifies to what extent INFOSYS is a solution to the MIS issue.
Actions and events	"...we were talking about it (an MIS) about two and a half years ago" (line 10) "...and INFOSYS was one of the, was something that was looked at but not looked at seriously" (lines 13-15) "...and then RBC came along..." (line 16; lines 17-21 describe RBC's request) "So, we looked at INFOSYS..." (line 37) "...[we] saw it as a solution to...the RBC issues...and a quick way to jump us into having a management information system" (lines 38-42)
Outcome:	"...so we saw it as, although an expensive way, a fast way to jump start us into a management information situation" (lines 47-49)

Similarly, the executive's narrative was not inconsistent with the Project Manager's, but it provided details of actions and events that reflected his interpretation of the problematic situation as an opportunity to gain competitive advantage with customers. He began his narrative by setting the stage with a description of a marketing consultant's report on customer's interest in utilization reporting, an event not mentioned by either the project manager or project sponsor. His implication that in-house capabilities had been considered but dismissed (lines 49-52) was consistent with the project manager's account. However, the plot sequence evident in his narrative was one of environmental scanning (lines 8-9), organizational assessment (lines 44-48), reaction to environmental triggers (lines 77-81; 82-84; 92-93), information gathering (line 85, 91) and competitive action (line 99). In this narrative sequence, he inserted

Exhibit 3 Structural Analysis of Executive's Narrative.

Narrator's Abstract:	"Obviously, an opportunity for somebody to do it well" (lines 40-41)
Narrator's perspective:	"When I first came here back in '91" (lines 7-8) "So, I was part of a group of folks here" (lines 42-43) "XYZ expressed the interest before I got here" (lines 69-70)
Orientation/ contextual descriptions:	In lines 8-17, the informant describes a market survey of GHI's customers. In lines 66-68, the informant describes customer's interest in INFOSYS. In lines 69-76, the informant describes an earlier event in which customer XYZ acquired INFOSYS. In lines 86-90, the informant cites the CEO's support for INFOSYS.
Actors:	"I" and "we" (unspecified); "two or three of us" (line 43) RBC (lines 77-84)
Problematic situation:	"...nobody in the marketplace did it well. Nobody..." (In lines 18-29, the informant describes customers' interest in account reporting. In lines 30-35, he clarifies which accounts are affected, and in lines 37-39, he states that no providers are satisfying customers.)
Goal/problem solution:	"INFOSYS, on the other hand, has a tool..." (lines 53-65 describe why the software company has a solution to the perceived opportunity)
Actions and events:	"...we had just completed some work with the Dryer poll people" (lines 8-9) "We kind of did a quick look" (line 44; lines 45-48 clarify what was examined) "We didn't have anything" (line 49; lines 50-52 clarify what actually existed) "and RBC went out and looked at it" (lines 77-81) "and they asked us if we would be interested in acquiring it..." (lines 82-84) "So we took a look at it [INFOSYS]" (line 85) "We all looked at it [INFOSYS]" (line 91) "and they also had just announced the product for the desktop..." (lines 92-93, with clarification in lines 94-98) "and so we went out and acquired the license..." (line 99)
Outcome:	"and it turned out we were either the second or third largest company in the country...to pull the data down to the PCs for our accounts" (lines 100-104)

a rationale for using the INFOSYS package (lines 53-65 in Exhibit 32) and flashbacks to earlier actions by RBC, Inc. (lines 67-68) and another customer (lines 66, 69-76) which supplemented his interpretation of the competitive opportunity (lines 18-29).

Earlier, the local, global, and themal coherence of the project manager's narrative abstract to consider the meanings implicit in her narrative were examined. Differences in the narrative abstracts of the project sponsor and executive suggested that the three informants attributed different meanings to the events that led to the formulation of this project. The project sponsor's narrative abstract in lines 47-49 (*"So we saw it as...a fast way to jump start us into a management information situation"*) was locally coherent with his preceding remarks about the INFOSYS package (lines 38-46) and globally coherent with his intent to tell the story of the project's origins that contradicted the assumption that the request by RBC, Inc. was the impetus for the project. By subsuming the influence of RBC, Inc. in the decision to acquire INFOSYS to the long-standing goal of having an MIS system (lines 7-10), his narrative summary integrated his explanation of events. Themal coherence was evident throughout the interview in his assertions that there had been an understanding that INFOSYS would serve as the basis for an MIS system at GHI, Inc.

The executive's narrative abstract in lines 40-41 of Exhibit 3 (*"Obviously, an opportunity for somebody to do it well"*) suggested yet a third interpretation of the events that lead to the formulation of the project. This statement was locally coherent with the preceding opportunity description and globally coherent as a transition from the recounting of background events that set the stage for the problem definition to the description of activities that led to the selection of INFOSYS. The statement also had themal coherence with the executive's conclusion about the outcome of the story, that GHI became one of the first large companies to *"pull the data down to the PC's for our accounts"* (lines 100-104).

Although it is not possible to completely understand the dynamics at work in the context of a research interview, assessing the degree to which the interaction settings may have influenced production of the narrative accounts is useful when considering the import of these differences. Earlier the interaction context in the project manager interview was described. It is important to note that the project sponsor's narrative was a response to a more pointed question about whether the INFOSYS project had originated in RBC's request. His narrative can be seen as a refutation of this assumption. Because the rapport was not as strong as with the project manager and because the research project had been authorized by one of his opponents in the controversies surrounding the INFOSYS project, his construction of the narrative account may also have been motivated by his desire to depict the INFOSYS project as a broad-based IS solution. The interaction context in the interview with the executive was yet again different. Initially, the executive sponsored the research project at GHI, and the researcher had met with him on three other occasions and had conducted an earlier interview. As a senior executive at GHI, he apparently had nothing to lose or gain through his interview with me, and the tone of the interview was one of helpfulness and information sharing.

Having considered the possible influence of the interaction context on production of these informants' narrative accounts of the origins of the INFOSYS project, substantive differences revealed through the narrative analysis remain. The three informants did have different perspectives on the project, but they were working with roughly the same "facts." This was evident in similarities in their accounts, such as the first, informal evaluation of the INFOSYS package and the influence of RBC, Inc. However, each narrator constructed a different story to account for actions and events that lead to the formulation of the INFOSYS project. The three informants used different problem-solving plot sequences to organize the actions and events, which implied different causal relations among actions and events. They offered different explanations of the problematic situation that motivated the INFOSYS project and attributed different meaning to the events in the project. Differences in their ways of narrativizing an account of the project's origins may have reflected their ongoing need to make sense of and account for the issues each faced related to the project. After the long delayed pilot for RBC, Inc. was implemented, various user groups began placing demands for implementation of software features and data sources, and the project manager was still struggling to set and maintain a direction for implementation of the INFOSYS software and database. The project sponsor, on the other hand, had fought budget battles with the outsourcing company, ISI, Inc., to fund development beyond the RBC pilot installation and, at the time of the research interview, he was contesting the claim of a subsidiary's IS group to have a superior MIS/warehouse product. Although the executive depicted INFOSYS as a strategic technology and concluded his narrative with the assertion that GHI was one of the first large companies *"to pull data down to the PC's for our accounts,"* this aspect of the technology had never been implemented and, in fact, the INFOSYS system was not being used even by RBC, Inc. However, the executive had recently assumed responsibility for technology initiatives with customers and providers, and his story of this earlier incident, though inaccurate in fact, supported his call to extend use of the PC feature to a variety of customers.

Through the systematic narrative analysis of each informant's story and comparison of the analysis of multiple stories, such differences in sensemaking and interpretation become evident. In the next section, the insights that narrative analysis may provide into the social cognitive worlds of participants in IS development are considered more generally and we discuss how narrative analysis may inform IS research.

6 DISCUSSION

The structural analysis of informants' stories described in this paper provides a systematic way to summarize key aspects of lengthy narrative accounts that often occur in research interviews. By identifying and isolating narrative clauses, generic plot sequences that underlie the sequence of actions and events identified by the narrator and that guide his or her interpretation and presentation of events are revealed. Plot sequences used by multiple informants may then suggest prototypical rationales which IS participants apply when they account for and interpret the meaning of organizational activities through which information technologies are developed, implemented, and used. In the three narratives of the origins of the INFOSYS project considered here, narrators' variations on the problem-solving plot suggest several interesting questions. Why did the project manager's narrative include the evaluation of alternatives in the problem-solving plot, whereas the project sponsor's and executive's narratives did not? Does their selection of different plots indicate differences in perspective, in organizational role, in power and authority? Would they use different plot sequences to organize their recounting of events in different circumstances?

Consideration of the local, global, and themal coherence of segments of a narrative guide the analyst's assessment of the possible meanings of the narrative. Identification of statements with themal coherence may indicate aspects of the organizational context that influenced the narrator's interpretation. For example, interjections by both the project manager (*"there's no ISI at this point,"* line 83) and the project sponsor (*"MIS, before they were outsourced,"* line 12) in their recounting of events referred to the outsourcing of the IS organization at GHI. Their parenthetical interjection of this contextual information indicated not only the importance this organizational change had for their understanding of the INFOSYS project but also signaled its influence on IS participants' interpretation of systems development activities at GHI. Recognition of the coherence function of such statements within a narrative depend in part on their familiarity with the organizational context. In this case, knowledge of the controversies surrounding the IS outsourcing facilitated perception of the global and themal coherence of statements about outsourcing in INFOSYS project history narratives.

In some ways the narrative analysis approach presented here, particularly the classification of narrative segments as structural components, is similar to more familiar approaches for content analysis of qualitative data. Mishler (1986a) notes, however, that "the distinctive feature of narratives is that they refer to meaningful and coherent courses of action, with beginnings, middles, and ends" (p. 248), and this distinction is preserved when the narrative is analyzed *as a narrative*. In contrast to a content analysis in which sections of text are categorized and compared across informants to identify recurring themes, narrative analysis addresses substantial portions of a single text (or a whole text) as a unit. The sequential ordering of the data in the text is preserved in the structural analysis, and the relationships between segments of the narrative are explicitly addressed in the analysis of coherence that may be of interest to the researcher.

Because narrative constructions display the dynamic ordering of events, they are particularly significant in the construction of empirically grounded, dynamic theories of social processes (Mishler 1986a). There has been increasing research interest in developing such process models for IS development and implementation activities (Markus and Robey 1988; Newman and Noble 1990; Newman and Robey 1992; Sabherwal and Robey 1993). The narrative analysis approach presented here could inform the development and specification of social process models, particularly when data is collected primarily through retrospective interviews and the researcher must reconstruct events. A narrative analysis approach will not, of course, result in the one, "true" account of a project. Informants' narratives do not necessarily relate to real events and certainly relate them from the narrator's perspective (Mishler 1986b). Even when data from informants' narratives are triangulated with other data sources such as observational data or documentary evidence, differences in the interpretation of actions and events are possible. However, narrative analysis can provide detailed insights into individual informants' understanding of project events and highlight similarities and differences in interpretations among informants.

This approach was used here to examine social cognitive processes such as knowledge sharing and sensemaking in IS development. As noted in the methodology section, the interview data examined in this paper was drawn from a research project on social negotiations around IT requirements definition (Davidson 1996). One area of research results suggested that narrativizing their experiences with IS development projects was a critical sensemaking process for participants, that they developed their understanding of the project, their own and others' roles, and of requirements for the IT application being developed by constructing and maintaining a narrative account of the project's history. Individuals built and updated their narrative account by reflecting on events and actions and by discussing possible implications with other knowledgeable organization members. A shared narrative account evolved among individuals who had similar experiences with the project and who engaged in joint-sensemaking activities through discussion and analysis of events. Shared aspects of the narrative account were evident in common elements of individuals' project history stories and in the "official story"[2] conveyed to newcomers to the project or to outsiders. To extend this research, the narrative analysis approach described here is being applied to further analyze how project participants used narratives to communicate and share assumptions about requirements for the IS application, to make sense of changes at GHI, and to understand the implications of change for IS requirements. Structural analysis of the narratives obtained through retrospective interviews highlights actions and events of interest, for example, change triggers that influenced stakeholders' interpretation of requirements. Comparing the analysis of informants' stories indicates points at which key stakeholders reached agreement about IS requirements or recognized differences in assumptions.

The analysis of narratives, aside from its value in IS research, has applications for IS practice. Tracking narratives and examining changes that occur over time is a viable way to examine meaning making and organizational learning (Tenkasi and Boland 1993). Examining evolving project history narratives could highlight how events have been interpreted or misinterpreted (from a given perspective) and what has been learned, or should be "unlearned" (again, from a given perspective) about a project experience. Comparing and contrasting narratives, and perhaps positing new narratives, could surface tacit assumptions about what is canonical and what is noncanonical in the IS development context. In this way, as Boland and Tenkasi

[2]Schank (1990) uses the term "official story" to denote the sanitized account sanctioned by those in authority. The term is used more broadly here to denote commonly accepted and shared accounts of key project events. These accounts may or may not be sanctioned by those in authority.

suggest, narratives could serve as boundary objects among the diverse stakeholders who must collaborate to successfully develop or implement IS in organizations by promoting perspective taking and organizational learning.

7 CONCLUSIONS

Developing, implementing, and using information technology applications in organizations is a complex social activity. It is often characterized by ill-defined problems or vague goals, conflict and power struggles, and disruptions that result from pervasive organizational change. Narrativizing experience in such an organizational context is undoubtedly fundamental to sensemaking and social negotiations. Narrative analysis is an approach that can inform our understanding of these activities. However, applying narrative analytic approaches in IS research poses a number of challenges.

Narrative analysis is an interpretive endeavor in which the analyst draws on his or her familiarity with broad cultural knowledge and values in the analysis (Mishler 1986b; Polanyi 1989). Although interpretive research has been gaining legitimacy and acceptance in the world of IS research (Walsham 1995), researchers will be challenged with the question of how the validity of a narrative interpretation can be assessed. Mishler (1986b) suggests that the question of validity should become one of assessing the plausibility of the analyst's interpretations, compared to other possible interpretations. The researcher must carefully and explicitly detail the steps taken in data collection and analysis, paying particular attention to the researcher's influence on, and participation in, the creation of a narrative, to the selection (and exclusion) of materials for analysis, and to the researcher's theoretical orientation and assumptions which enter into the analysis.

Of course, these comments apply to any rigorous methodological approach to data analysis. However, narrative analysis poses particularly tough challenges. For example, the researcher must decide whether he or she assumes that "all telling" is narrative in form or that narratives are one of many forms for "telling" (Mishler 1986b). The answer to this question will guide decisions about how to identify and bound narratives within an interview text and will influence the interpretation that results. Rather than striving for the one correct interpretation, multiple interpretations are not only possible but desirable to enrich the understanding of possible meaning in the narrative. For critics and reviewers unfamiliar with narrative analysis, the explication of multiple interpretations may discredit all accounts. There are practical difficulties as well as theoretical and methodological issues. Data collected through research interviews is voluminous, and texts may contain many interwoven and partial stories. Analysis is a time-consuming process, and adequate presentation of results may require more space than in often allowed in publishing outlets such as conference proceedings and journals. Analyses which focus on small sample sizes to allow for these difficulties are likely to be criticized as being unrepresentative or idiosyncratic.

Despite these challenges, narrative analysis holds the promise of informing our understanding of information systems development and use in an organizational context in unique and interesting ways. The analytical approach discussed in this paper suggests some ways in which these issues may be addressed and illustrates the insights that may be gained as a result.

8 REFERENCES

Agar, M., and Hobbs, J. (1982). Interpreting Discourse: Coherence and the Analysis of Ethnographic Interviews." *Discourse Processes*, Volume 5, pp. 1-32.

Bansler, J., and Bødker, K. (1993). "A Reappraisal of Structured Analysis: Design in an Organizational Context." *ACM Transactions on Information Systems*, Volume 11, Number 2, pp. 165-193.

Bell, S. (1983). "Narratives of Health and Illness I: DES Daughters Tell Stories." Unpublished paper.

Boje, D. (1991). "The Storytelling Organization: A Study of Story Performance in an Office-Supply Firm." *Administrative Science Quarterly*, Volume 35, pp. 106-126.

Boland, Jr., R., and Schultz, U. (1995). "From Work to Activity: Technology and the Narrative of Process." In W. Orlikowski, G. Walsham, M. Jones, and J. I. DeGross (Editors), *Information Technology and Changes in Organizational Work*. London: Chapman and Hall, pp. 308-324.

Boland, Jr., R., and Tenkasi, R. (1995). "Perspective Making and Perspective Taking in Communities of Knowing." *Organization Science*, Volume 6, Number 4, pp. 350-372.

Brown, J., and Duguid, P. (1991). "Organizational Learning and Communities-of-Practice: Toward a Unified View of Working, Learning, and Innovation." *Organization Science*, Volume 2, Number 1, pp. 40-57.

Bruner, J. (1986). *Actual Minds, Possible Worlds*. Cambridge, Massachusetts: Harvard University Press.

Bruner, J. (1990). *Acts of Meaning*. Cambridge, Massachusetts: Harvard University Press.

Clark, B. (1972). "The Organizational Saga in Higher Education." *Administrative Science Quarterly*, Volume 17, pp. 178-184.

Davidson, E. (1996). *Framing Information Systems Requirements: An Investigation of Social Cognitive Processes in Information Systems Delivery*. Unpublished Ph.D. Dissertation, Massachusetts Institute of Technology.

Gabriel, Y. (1991). "Turning Facts into Stories and Stories into Facts: A Hermeneutic Exploration of Organizational Folklore." *Human Relations*. Volume 44, Number 8, pp. 857-875.

Gergen, K., and Gergen, M. (1986). "Narrative Form and the Construction of Psychological Science." In T. Sarbin (Editor), *Narrative Psychology: The Storied Nature of Human Conduct*. New York: Praeger Publishers, pp. 22-44.

Hansen, C., and Kahnweiler, W. (1993). "Storytelling: An Instrument for Understanding the Dynamics of Corporate Relationships" *Human Relations*, Volume 46, Number 12, pp. 1391-1409.

Howard, G. (1991). "Culture Tales: A Narrative Approach to Thinking, Cross-Cultural Psychology, and Psychotherapy." *American Psychologist*, Volume 46, Number 3, pp. 187-197.

Labov, W. (1972). *Language in the Inner City: Studies in the Black English Vernacular*. Philadelphia: University of Pennsylvania Press.

Labov, W. (1982). "Speech Actions and Reactions in Personal Narrative." In D. Tannen (Editor), *Analyzing Discourse: Text and Talk*. Washington: Georgetown University Press.

Labov, W., and Waletzky, J. (1967). "Narrative Analysis: Oral Versions of Personal Experience." In J. Helms (Editor), *Essays on the Verbal and Visual Arts*. Seattle: University of Washington Press.

LeGuin, U. (1989). "Some Thoughts on Narrative." *Dancing at the Edge of the World: Thoughts on Words, Women, Places*. New York: Grove Press, pp. 37-45.

Markus, M. L., and Robey, D. (1988). "Information Technology and Organizational Change: Causal Structure in Theory and Research." *Management Science*, Volume 34, Number 5, pp. 583-598.

Martin, J.; Feldman, M.; Hatch, M.; and Sitkin, S. (1983). "The Uniqueness Paradox in Organizational Stories." *Administrative Science Quarterly*, Volume 28, pp. 438-453.

Martin, J., and Meyerson, D. (1988). "Organizational Cultures and the Denial, Channeling, and Acknowledgment of Ambiguity." In L. Pondy, R. Boland Jr., and H. Thomas (Editors), *Managing Ambiguity and Change*. New York: Wiley, pp. 93-125.

McConkie, M., and Boss, W. (1986). "Organizational Stories: One Means of Moving the Informal Organization During Change Efforts." *Public Administration Quarterly*, Volume 10, Number 2, pp. 189-205.

Mishler, E. (1986a). "The Analysis of Interview-Narratives." In T. Sarbin (Editor), *Narrative Psychology: The Storied Nature of Human Conduct*. New York: Praeger Publishers, pp. 233-255.

Mishler, E. (1986b). *Research Interviewing: Context and Narrative*. Cambridge, Massachusetts: Harvard University Press.

Mitroff, I., and Kilmann, R. (1975). "Stories Managers Tell: A New Tool for Organizational Problem Solving." *Management Review*, Volume 64, Number 7, pp. 18-28.

Mumby, D. (1987). "The Political Function of Narrative in Organizations." *Communication Monographs*, Volume 54 (June), pp. 113-127.

Newman, M., and Nobel, F. (1990). "User Involvement as an Interaction Process: A Case Study." *Information Systems Research*, Volume 1, Number 1, pp. 89-113.

Newman, M., and Robey, D. (1992). "A Social Process Model of User-Analyst Relationships." *MIS Quarterly*, Volume 15, Number 2, pp. 249-266.

Paget, M. (1982). "Your Son is Cured Now; You May Take Him Home." *Culture, Medicine and Psychiatry*, Volume 6, pp. 237-259.

Paget, M. (1983). "Experience and Knowledge." *Human Studies*, Volume 6, Number 2, pp. 67-90.

Polanyi, L. (1989). *Telling the American Story*. Cambridge, Massachusetts: MIT Press.

Robinson, J., and Hawpe, L. (1986). "Narrative Thinking as a Heuristic Process." In T. Sarbin (Editor), *Narrative Psychology: The Storied Nature of Human Conduct*. New York: Praeger Publishers, pp. 111-125.

Sabherwal, R., and Robey, D. (1993). "An Empirical Taxonomy of Implementation Processes Based on Sequences of Events in Information System Development." *Organization Science*, Volume 4, Number 4, pp. 548-576.

Sarbin, T. (1986). "The Narrative as a Root Metaphor for Psychology." In T. Sarbin (Editor), *Narrative Psychology: The Storied Nature of Human Conduct*. New York: Praeger Publishers, pp. 3-21.

Schank, R. (1990). *Tell Me a Story: A New Look at Real and Artificial Memory*. New York: Schribner.

Tenkasi, R., and Boland, Jr., R. (1993). "Locating Meaning Making in Organizational Learning: The Narrative Basis of Cognition." *Research in Organizational Change and Development*, Volume 7, pp. 77-103.

Walsham, G. (1995). "The Emergence of Interpretivism in IS Research." *Information Systems Research*, Volume 6, Number 4, pp. 376-394.

Wilkins, A. (1984). "The Creation of Company Cultures: The Role of Stories and Human Resource Systems." *Human Resource Management*, Volume 23, Number 1, pp. 41-60.

9 BIOGRAPHY

Elizabeth J. Davidson is an Assistant Professor in the Department of Decision Sciences at the College of Business Administration of the University of Hawaii, Manoa. Her research has focused on investigations of social cognitive processes in the development and implementation of information technology applications in an organizational context. In recent work, she has examined the role of narratives and metaphors as sensemaking devices in requirements definition activities. Dr. Davidson received her Ph.D. in Information Technologies from the Sloan School of Business at MIT in 1996.

Appendix A
Text Segment from Interview with the INFOSYS Project Manager

1 Q: So I guess what I'd like to do is just have you
2 tell me again
3 from your perspective
4 how the project got started
5 and how it relates to other things that have
6 happened in the company.
7
8 A: OK [p] and going back to the very beginning?
9
10 Q: Yeah, and you don't necessarily have to go
11 through a lot of the details.
12 I think Tim went through kind of the timing but,
13 how it got started and why?
14
15 A: Rally, there have been several fits and tarts
16 and [p] most distant one in my mempry is um [p]
17 I was in the account reporting department
18 and we were looking at providing accounts with
19 some access that they could have to their own data.
20 Um [p] you know, at that point there was a...a
21 systems team that I managed
22 and there were analysts that actually took the data
23 that we produced and wrote the narrative that went
24 along with the report, and that type of thing. And
25 there were standard reports that went out to accounts.
26 And there are also special requests, ad-hoc kinds of
27 things that came in.
28 But the problem that we saw was that for some of
29 the major accounts, we had many people doing or
30 at least one dedicated person doing benefits design
31 type things. Um...that they would submit a
32 complicated request. It would go through the
33 marketing area, and the marketing area would come
34 to the analyst. The analyst would be interpreting
35 this request and then put in a data request to the
36 programmers. And the programmer would program
37 something, give it back to the analyst and the
38 analyst would write something up and then it
39 would go back to marketing and then finally back
40 to the account. What the account really requested
41 and what they received in the end, most of the time
42 either wasn't exactly the same or they realized that
43 yes, this is what they requested but it really wasn't
44 what they wanted underneath.
45 So there was a need identified to be able provide
46 accounts with some access to their own data.
47 And at that point um [p] there were few of us that
48 went around and looked at a different ... a couple of
49 different alternative ways of doing this.
50 And [p] in terms of, you know, the ... the build or
51 buy option, whatever.
52 You know, we had been building our own data
53 repository. But didn't, you know, have the friendly
54 front-end type thing.
55 So we had explored doing our own or um ... you
56 know, going with an outside vendor to do that.
57 We had interviewed several different companies.
58 One of the companies was INFOSYS.
59 And we had gone over to their office ...
60 and had seen the product, whatever.
61 Um [p] and it got to a certain point, and when it
62 started to get, you know, 'We did our analysis that
63 this is the company,' you know, 'We'd like to look
64 at this company more,' or whatever,
65 I think it kind of bumped up a couple of levels
66 and then came back down like, 'Well no, we really
67 don't want to do this at this point,'
68 and we kind of went 'bye.'
69 So I didn't here anything else about it for a while.
70 Um [p] a couple of years later um [p] well .. yeah,
71 after this time period, account reporting became
72 part of actuarial. Which was actuarial and
73 underwriting. And the analysts actually started to
74 report for the underwriters.
75 And, at that point we heard from RBC,
76 which is our major local account, that they were
77 interested in having this kind of capability in order
78 to look at their own data and do some analysis
79 themselves and that sort of thing.
80 And the marketing reps um .. who were RBC's,
81 started contacting different people in the actuarial
82 area and the IS area at that point;
83 there's no ISI at this point in time,
84 and saying 'Well gee, we should look at a few
85 vendors out there ... um...but they really seem to
86 like INFOSYS.'
87 So, a team that was at a higher level than myself
88 so I wasn't involved in the actual going around and
89 interviewing vendors at this point.
90 That was more Dave and um ... people at his level.
91 They went out and interviewed a few vendors and
92 figured out what was going on, whatever.
93 One of the major competitive vendors was a vendor
94 that RBC had already been doing business with and
95 wasn't too pleased with.
96 So it kind of came down to well, INFOSYS is the
97 best thing out there um .. at this point.
98 You know, maybe, they [RBC] really like it.
99 They've seen it and they really like it
100 and maybe we should look into INFOSYS.
101 So at that point, a team was put together
102 of people from actuarial, underwriting, account
103 reporting, um ... and IS
104 to sort of, you know, look at this and negotiate a
105 contract and, you know, build a system and um ...
106 an interface to INFOSYS and all that.
107 And I was a part of that uh ... effort ...

Appendix B
Text Segment from Interview with the INFOSYS Project Sponsor

1 [Q]: A number of people have kind of told me the
2 story about INFOSYS in that they said RBC was
3 looking at it. They contacted GHI. Is that how you
4 think the project got started?
5
6 [A]: Yeah.
7 We were, we had been talking for years about a data
8 warehouse, an MIS system for, probably going on
9 a decade pretty soon
10 and we were talking about it two and a half years ago
11 and some new people had been brought on and
12 MIS, before they were outsourced,
13 and INFOSYS was one of the, was something that
14 was looked at,
15 but not looked at seriously
16 and then RBC came along
17 and said, "We have looked at this. We want to
18 access our own data. We want you to give that to
19 us and oh, by the way, we looked at this product on
20 our own but it is too expensive for us to buy, but
21 we would like you to give it to us."
22 And there is, and we probably, we can give it to
23 them at a lesser cost than they could buy it
24 themselves, because buying it themselves was two
25 hundred thousand dollars a year, so it is very [p]
26 and I think that that is something that INFOSYS
27 recognizes and that's why they developed this an
28 insurance carrier system, knowing that it was
29 getting too expensive, for other than the biggest
30 accounts, to go out and provide this service to
31 individual accounts. If they sold it to carriers then
32 carriers could use it internally and also sub-license
33 it out to accounts. It would be another marketing
34 channel and if we do put it out on an account's
35 desktop, likely they will pay a sublicense fee to
36 INFOSYS so they still gain some income.
37 So, we looked at INFOSYS
38 and I and the IS people I was working with back at
39 the time saw it as a solution to the, a quicker
40 solution to the RBC issue and also a quick way to
41 jump us into having a management information
42 systems.
43 Although it wouldn't satisfy all of our needs, it
44 would satisfy the biggest area of demands, which
45 were claims, cost utilization reporting, enrollment
46 reporting,
47 so we saw it as, although an expensive way, a fast
48 way to jump start us into a management information
49 situation.

Appendix C
Text Segment from Interview with GHI Executive

1 **[Q]:** I talked to almost thirty people or so on
2 this project now and your name has started to
3 come up with, "Sam was involved with that."
4 Can you tell me just a little bit about what
5 your, and how you were involved in this?
6
7 **[A]:** Sure. When I first came here back in
8 '91, we had just completed some work with
9 the Dryer poll people.
10 They do a survey every year and they look at
11 the seventeen major factors that drive
12 corporation's decisions around who to
13 purchase health care from and one of the
14 issues in the way and there's tons of issues, a
15 lot of them around cost, as you know,
16 network, quality of care, and you know, all
17 that junk.
18 One of them was, especially for the self
19 insured customers, was account reporting,
20 access to the information so that they know,
21 on a fairly frequent basis, how well their
22 health care provider is performing on their
23 behalf, so that it is not a surprise once a year
24 at renewal but there's a fairly consistent and
25 current flow of information between health
26 care providers and the buyer,
27 and that came up as a very high need in
28 almost all large companies during the Dryer
29 survey
30 and there is a moderate need in the middle
31 size companies. It's kind of off the screen
32 for small companies. First of all, most of
33 them aren't self insured and second of all,
34 they have got fairly standard products and
35 they have fairly standard pricing.
36 So we said that,
37 oh, and the other data point was that there
38 was nobody in the marketplace that did it
39 well. Nobody.
40 Obviously, an opportunity for somebody to
41 do it well.
42 So, I was part of a group of folks here, a
43 group meaning, only two or three of us.
44 We kind of did a quick look.
45 What do we provide? A, what do we have
46 available for data that could drive a reporting
47 capability that would get us to work [?fast]
48 and quickly.
49 We didn't have anything.
50 We had some very old technology and large
51 data bases that had questionable integrity and
52 they were hard to get at.
53 INFOSYS, on the other hand, as a tool, has
54 been in the business for, I don't know,
55 fifteen years and their tool that does things
56 like account reporting which was the first
57 product we bought has the advantage of
58 having a lot of clinical knowledge and clinical
59 protocol built in, so there is a lot of stuff in
60 there that could, quote, interpret the data on
61 behalf of the viewer of the data. So, you are
62 not just getting raw data and you have to go
63 figure it out. They really give you a lot of
64 structured queries and reporting techniques
65 that allow you to analyze the data
66 and one of our biggest accounts, XYZ
67 and then RBC,
68 had expressed an interest in INFOSYS.
69 In fact, XYZ expressed the interest before I
70 got here.
71 They became so enamored with the tool that
72 they went out and bought it themselves, and
73 we were providing historical claim data for
74 XYZ so that they could do their own
75 reporting.
76 So we weren't even in the loop on that
77 and RBC went out and looked at it
78 and they wanted to acquire it but the
79 acquisition cost, they couldn't justify it. It
80 was something like three hundred thousand
81 for the license and they couldn't justify it
82 and they asked us if we would be interested
83 in acquiring it and letting them be the guinea
84 pig.
85 So, we took a look at it
86 and also Tom Smith [CEO] had had some
87 experience with it in [his previous position]
88 and he was very impressed with the product
89 so we kind of had an in house testimonial to
90 it.
91 We all looked at it
92 and they also had just announced the product
93 for the desktop of an account,
94 for an account to pull its own data right down
95 to its own PC and use PC based tools to do
96 its own reporting fairly quickly, easily and
97 much cheaper than doing it at the mainframe
98 level,
99 and so we went out and acquired the license
100 and it turned out we were either the second or
101 third largest company in the country to
102 acquire the license, to run the software
103 ourselves and to pull the data down to the
104 PCs for our accounts.

10

Exploring Analyst-Client Communication: Using Grounded Theory Techniques to Investigate Interaction in Informal Requirements Gathering

C. Urquhart
Department of Information Systems
University of Melbourne
Parkville, Victoria, Australia
Tel: +61 3 9344 9248
Fax: +61 3 9349 4596
E-mail: c.urquhart@dis.unimelb.edu.au

Abstract

This paper describes a case study in client-analyst interaction during the requirements gathering phase. The focus of this work is a discussion of interactional tactics used by analysts and clients to facilitate shared understanding and agreement and how this may impact on conceptualization of information systems. The paper also describes in detail methodological issues encountered when analysing conversational data and how these issues were resolved by application of grounded theory techniques allied with other qualitative techniques. Finally, the paper gives some suggestions as to how the findings could assist current practice in systems analysis, particularly with regard to how systems analysts might better structure their interactions.

1 INTRODUCTION

The requirements definition phase of an information systems project is of necessity a problematic process, founded as it is on a very unreliable technique: human communication. The oft heard cry of the practitioner – "users don't know what they want" – contains at least a grain of truth when analyst-client communication can properly be characterized as cross-cultural communication, where use of unfamiliar language that is domain specific on both the part of the analyst and the client can create a barrier to communication. Most cross-cultural studies take culture to be shared knowledge of how to behave and recipes for understanding experience in specific ways (Barnett and Kincaid 1983). Viewed from this perspective, it can be seen how users and analysts might be perceived to come from different cultures. It has also been stated that miscommunication events *between* cultures are essentially of the same type as *intra* cultural encounters, and that the problem is perhaps made salient by those differences (Banks, Ge and Baker 1991).

Previous research on analysts and clients has found many differences between the two groups in the areas of beliefs, attitudes, personalities and motivations (Pettigrew 1974; Gingras and McLean 1982; Green 1985; Kaiser and Bostrom 1982; Benbasat, Dexter and Manther 1980; Ferret and Short 1986).

The issue of communication between client and developer has been identified as a major factor impacting on systems development for two decades, since ineffective communication was found to be negatively correlated with project success (Edstrom 1977). In 1994, the Australian Computer Society devoted a whole issue of its practitioner magazine to the problem of communication with users (Kennedy 1994). In longitudinal studies over ten years of researching computing professional characteristics (Dengate, Cougar and Weber 1990), computing professionals have been characterized as having low social needs, resulting in a need for communication skills training. The authors of that study felt there had been no improvement in the area of communications skills during the lifetime of the study.

Those studies that have explored analyst-client communication by studying analyst-client pairs (Tan 1989; Guinan 1988) have variously identified rapport, client communication skills, analyst performance skills, communication competence and frame flexibility as factors in successful interactions. Tan found that communication satisfaction was determined by perception of rapport rather than goal achievement. Goal achievement was not found to be positively linked to communication satisfaction – for example, both parties may have found the communication successful even though it did not achieve their original goals.

Given that the starting point of all requirements gathering is a verbal interchange between analyst and client, then it is not unreasonable to assert that how communication skills are employed will have a significant bearing on perceptions between client and analyst. Systems requirements verbalized by the client will be encoded into a set of system requirements by the analyst. This in turn becomes the reality of the new system. If the initial precepts on which the system is based are false or inaccurate, then there is every possibility of system failure.

The case study described in this paper is an attempt to explore how that communication takes place, and how the analyst and client work toward a shared perception of requirements. Of necessity, the words they use, and how they use them, represent the starting point. Language forms have been described by Candlin (1985) as

> the surface realization of those communicative strategies involved in the interactive procedures working amongst those various social, contextual, and epistemological factors...identified as crucial to the process of communicative inference and coherence.

In an analyst-client interaction, a shared perception of requirements is essentially the crux of the matter and arguably the most important outcome. It is also most difficult to observe or measure, given Candlin's point that language is merely the surface realization of communication and that there are a number of "underground" processes to be considered when examining the communicative inference and overall coherence of an interaction. Coherence is said to be the extent to which a discourse "hangs together," in terms of how relevant successive utterances are to those that precede them and to the concerns of the discourse as a whole (McLaughlin 1984). Communicative inference is much more complex, concerned with how people assign meaning to what they hear and how they make sense of information they receive. There are many views of how this might occur: for instance, the field of symbolic interactionism contends that meaning is constantly negotiated between individuals in the form of symbols (Wood 1982). In cognitive theory, Dervin (1983) puts forward a sense-making approach which assumes information to exist to a significant degree internally and assumes users of information to be making sense of it literally on a moment by moment basis. Bateson (1972) evolved a theory of framing behaviors based on levels of abstraction. Watzlawick, Weakland and Fisch (1974) extended this concept through to the notion of a *reframe* – essentially the meaning attributed to a situation is altered while the concrete facts remain the same. Guinan, in her study of analyst-client interaction, defined the concept of "perceptual correspondence" – where interactants assume they are seeing things the same way – and posited that this occurred through problem framing and reframing.

The case study described in the following pages was designed to explore analyst-client interaction from a processual perspective. Previous studies (Guinan 1988; Tan 1989) attempted to measure certain analyst behaviors and link them to outcomes. Neither study considered contextual factors or the *process* by which an analyst and client might come to an agreement. Furthermore, as both studies were quantitative in nature, there was little opportunity to examine analyst-client dialogue at the micro level or to consider how perceptual correspondence might develop over the lifetime of the interaction.

The case study has as its general focus the question "*How* do analysts and clients reach a shared understanding of system requirements?" More specifically:

- what conversational tactics do analysts and clients use to build up a joint picture of the system under discussion? and
- what conceptual schemas do analysts and clients employ with regard to systems?

By looking at the participants' interpretations of the interaction and other data sources, it should also be possible to ascertain which of these tactics and schemas are helpful to analysts and their clients.

2 METHODOLOGY

This section of the paper describes how the case study was designed, the motivation for that design, how grounded theory techniques were chosen as the main qualitative tool of analysis, and how they were applied to this particular case study. When encountering qualitative analysis for the first time, one is struck by both the number of methods and the difficulty of analyzing and presenting large amounts of data. The objective of interpreting the data in such a way that it allows people who have not directly observed the phenomena to obtain a deeper understanding of it, without applying a pre-existing theory to the data (Feldman 1995) is a formidable one. This objective requires a thorough examination of the most appropriate research method and careful consideration of how best to present the findings.

2.1 Case Study Design

The case study described in the paper is one of a series of six case studies employing multiple data sources. These data sources include a videotaped interaction between the client and the analyst, a review of that interaction (also videotaped), and audio recordings of individual interviews with both the client and analyst (before and after the interaction). Two questionnaires were also used – one a rapport measure, the other attempting to measure conversational sensitivity of the individuals concerned. According to Yin (1984), case studies can involve single or multiple cases and numerous levels of analysis. The case study design incorporates triangulation and has as its main focus the interaction which takes place between analyst and client. The interaction in each case discusses a real life case of systems requirements, and takes place at either the analyst's workplace or the client's workplace. This paper focuses on the qualitative analysis of the videotaped interaction and its review.

The multiple data sources have been chosen to give as many insights into the interaction as is feasible and to assist in theory generation. The review of the videotaped interaction by the participants is an important element of the case study as it enables a multiple interpretation of the realities of the interaction; similarly, individual interviews enable both participants to articulate what realities they are bringing to the interaction. The post interaction interview also gives insights into outcomes as the participants perceive them. Videotaping enables consideration of nonverbal factors and paralinguistic features. The rapport measure is a standard instrument which enables yet another view of the interaction. The measure of conversational sensitivity (Daly, Vangelisti and Daughton 1987) gives an indication of whether the participants are predisposed to pick up on hidden meanings in conversation and was itself developed using grounded theory techniques.

2.2 Conducting the Case Study

All six case studies were carried out in the public sector in Tasmania. IS managers were approached and asked if systems analysts in their employ were carrying out development work and would be willing to participate in the research project. The criteria for inclusion in the project were that the development work had to be at an initial stage (generally the first or second meeting between analyst and client about the development work in question) and that the interaction to be videotaped should either be about the development of a new system or a substantial amendment of an existing system. Several potential cases were rejected on the grounds that all the initial requirements had already been gathered.

Participants were asked to furnish a one page description before the planned discussion. The purpose of this was to both ensure that the interaction fell within the definition of informal requirements gathering and to give insight into initial individual perceptions. The objectives of the study – to investigate how analysts and clients reach agreement – were clearly spelled out as were assurances of confidentiality. Videotaping of interactions seemed to present no difficulty from the participants point of view : in practice, those who were initially nervous soon forgot the camera's presence. Videotaping seems to have little impact on anxiety and responsiveness, as evidenced by nonverbal behaviors generally held to be beyond interactants' control (Weimann 1981).

Motivations for joining the study varied. Some analysts were encouraged to do so by their managers, and others felt they would benefit by examining their communication style. Clients were attracted by the opportunity to review the video tape and discuss the process from their perspective.

2.3 Deciding on a Method of Analysis

There are many ways of analyzing spoken texts and a number of approaches were considered before settling on the use of grounded theory technique. These approaches come from diverse fields and all offered the possibility of different insights on the data. These were evaluated from two perspectives: whether the approach drew on all features of the case study and whether the philosophy of the approach imposed pre-existing theories of interaction. There may be special features of analyst-client conversation, as a phenomena in a professional setting, that may not be served by adopting a purely social interactional approach. Requirements gathering represents a bounded situation which has some standard features and the overt objective is not to socially interact but to converse in order to solve a given problem.

Previous studies (Guinan 1988; Tan 1989) employed content analysis according to a strict predetermined coding scheme. Conversational analysis is a much used approach and focuses on discovering structures and orderliness in interaction (Psathas 1995). Goffman (1967, 1981) did much pioneering work in this area and introduced many new concepts for describing interaction. However, use of conversational analysis, while very informative about social structures and giving a processual perspective, was not appropriate for two reasons. First, its orientation toward social relations gives limited insight into how a client and analyst might reach agreement in a professional sphere. Second, the adjacency pair concept means that analysis is confined to pairs of sentences rather than examining a temporal whole.

Discourse analysis sets a broader agenda (Coulthard 1985) and incorporates diverse elements such as consideration of tonality and speech acts, but much of the analysis occurs at a micro level rather than considering how an interaction might evolve. In both discourse and conversational analysis, there are also elements of orderliness imposed on the data which can amount to the application of a preexisting theory. However, McLaughlin's work on topics and conversational coherence gives some guidance as to how people structure conversations and this may be important when considering how people might manage an interaction in requirements gathering.

Ethnomethodology, with its emphasis on social meaning and tacit knowledge, might be considered a suitable approach, but again its focus on social-cultural rules might not reveal all there is to know about the process by which analysts and their clients reach shared understanding.

The field of semiotics, which studies systems of signs and has been claimed to treat all cultural processes as processes of communication (Eco 1976), would be a way of exploring client-analyst communication by examining denotive and connative meanings of terms used in system requirements. Using a semiotic approach, however, would not give as many insights as to the processes which analyst and client might employ. Using a deconstructionist approach could also be an option, especially with its aim of seeing words in context and examination of changing contexts on meaning (Manning 1992). However, as in the case of using semiotics, using this approach might restrict consideration only to meaning rather than the process by which that meaning is reached.

As has been pointed out by Candlin when reviewing the field of discourse analysis, structural and processual approaches to analysing texts, while very different, cannot be easily abstracted from each other and this dilemma is not easily resolved.

2.4 Reasons for Using Grounded Theory Techniques

Grounded theory method (Glaser and Strauss 1967; Glaser 1978, 1992; Strauss 1987; Strauss and Corbin 1990) is a "qualititative research method that uses a systematic set of procedures to develop an inductively derived theory about a phenomenon" (Strauss and Corbin 1990, p. 24). Because it does offer well signposted procedures, it has some attraction for a researcher using qualitative techniques for the first time. More importantly, it is a general style of doing analysis that does not depend on particular disciplinary perspectives (Strauss 1987) and, therefore, would seem to lend itself to information systems research which can be described as a hybrid discipline. The goal of grounded theory in seeking a theory that is compatible with the evidence, that is both precise and rigorous, and capable of replication (Neuman 1994) is also an attractive one. It also has the benefit of producing theory intimately tied with the evidence, so that the resultant theory is likely to be consistent with empirical observations (Orlikowski 1993; Eisenhardt 1989).

Grounded theory method also requires that the researcher demonstrates theoretical sensitivity (Glaser and Strauss 1967; Glaser 1978) by being well grounded in technical literature as well as from personal and professional experience and in collection and analyses of the data (Strauss and Corbin 1990). At the same time, the inductive nature of grounded theory techniques encourages researchers to steer their thinking *out* of the confines of technical literature and avoid standard ways of thinking about the data (Strauss and Corbin 1990). The interplay between emergent theory and technical literature comes to the fore when extending generalisations from the study. This is achieved by either integrating supplementary or conflicting analyses into the theory by including them as categories or conditions, or criticising them in terms of what has emerged (Strauss 1987).

As use of grounded theory analysis is founded on the premise that the generation of that theory at various levels is indispensible for a deep understanding of social phenomena (Glaser and Strauss 1967; Glaser 1978), it seems particularly suitable for a case study aimed at exploring how systems analysts and their clients reach agreement. It is also useful for understanding contextual and processual elements (Orlokowski 1993) that constitute the main focus of this case study.

2.5 Applying Grounded Theory Techniques to the Case Study

First, the transcript of the interaction was subjected to *open coding*. This is essentially a line by line examination of the data to generate concepts or codes. The exercise is extremely time consuming but yields many rich concepts for the next phase. Open coding quickly forces the researcher to break apart and fracture the data analytically, leading to grounded conceptualization (Strauss 1987). *Axial coding*, examining codes in terms of the coding paradigm of *conditions, interaction among the actors, strategies and tactics,* and *consequences* (Strauss 1987), was then carried out. The use of this paradigm enables the researcher to link subcategories to a category in a set of relationships and also enables further dimensionalisation of categories (Strauss and Corbin 1990).

It should be noted at this point that Glaser (1992) has criticised the paradigm in particular and the publishing of strict procedures in general (Strauss 1987, Strauss and

Corbin 1990). Glaser regards the paradigm as "forced conceptualization" of data and says categories should be allowed to emerge naturally. (Further discussion of this area of important disagreement between the co-originators of grounded theory will be provided in later sections.) Strauss does point out that the procedures outlined should be thought of as rules of thumb, rather than hard or fixed rules, and advises researchers to study these rules of thumb, use them, and *modify* them in accordance with the requirements of the research.

2.6 Applying the Paradigm and the Adaptation of Grounded Theory techniques

During axial coding, the application of the paradigm to the open codes was used selectively. It was viewed not only as an aid to understanding the relationships between open codes and emergent categories, but also as a means of drawing some preliminary distinctions in the data. When examining the open codes generated from the transcript, using the paradigm of *conditions, interaction among the actors, strategies and tactics,* and *consequences,* it was found that the open codes tended to fall into one of two areas: those associated with *interaction* aspects (interaction among the actors, strategies and tactics) or those associated with the *conceptualization* of the information system (conditions and consequences). This drew a natural distinction in the data and also allowed the research questions to be addressed in a straightforward manner. *Interaction* and *conceptualization* can also be thought of as emergent core categories. Obviously there was an element of choice in applying the paradigm in this way. For instance, some conditions and consequences could be found among interactional aspects, but it was found that the vast majority of conditions and consequences did apply to the conceptualization of the information system (the topic under discussion), rather than how the discussion was managed vis-à-vis interaction. That the data naturally fitted the paradigm in this manner, rather than being forced, supports its selective application in this particular case.

The methodological question of whether to start with predetermined categories or to start with line by line coding is one that confronts all qualititative analysts. Dey (1993) recommends a middle order approach, where some broad distinctions are drawn initially, based on fairly common sense categories. Analysis can then proceed in either direction, toward subcategorization or linking and integrating the middle order categories. In this case study, rich concepts were yielded using line by line coding, and the subsequent application of the paradigm in a selective fashion enabled a focus on the research questions.

The application of the paradigm in this manner gave an additional benefit, as the distinctions made go some way to abstracting the processual/structural dichotomy evident in discourse analysis. Attention can be given to the social processes by which analyst and client reach agreement and structural analysis of the text can give insights as to how an analyst and client might jointly conceptualize an information system.

The relationship between the emergent core categories, and subcategories, can be regarded as the interplay between social processes and how the dialogue itself is structured as a consequence. Another way of viewing this distinction is to say that what is of interest in this study is how the participants manage the interaction, and how the management of that interaction impacts on the subsequent conceptualization of the information system.

Table 1 illustrates how the paradigm was selectively applied, with some sample codes that were generated during the open coding phase.

Table 1 Application of Paradigm to Open Codes.

Emergent Core Category	Paradigm Items	Samples of Initial Open Codes
Interaction	Interaction among the actors Strategies and tactics	acting out, imagining, vivid description, posited action, prop, reframe
Conceptualization	Conditions Consequences	information source, information type, document ref, computer system ref, clerical system ref, information link, process identification, condition, client action

While using the paradigm to consider relationships it became clear that an alternative way of examining relationships between sub categories had to be sought. As the paradigm had also been used to draw distinctions in the data, it became more complex to apply when considering relationships between codes. For instance, it is difficult to think of *conditions* as both pertaining to the information system under discussion and also pertaining to interactive social processes; yet clearly causal and other relationships exist between the two.

Spradley's (1979) domain analysis was used to assist formulation of relationships between codes and categories. Spradley defines a *domain* as an organizing idea or concept, akin to a category in grounded theory methodology. These domains can contain "folk" terms, used by the members of the social setting, analytic terms generated by the researcher and relevant theories, and mixed domains containing folk terms to which the researcher adds other terms. In grounded theory methodology, these translate into "in-vivo" codes used by the participants, the concepts generated by the researcher during open coding, and theoretical sensitivity demonstrated by using terms from the technical literature.

In addition, Spradley provides *semantic relationships* that can exist between domains. The benefit of using these semantic relationships was that they allowed a finer grained analysis of relationships between codes. They enabled an extension of causal conditions, intervening conditions and consequences given in the later version of the paradigm provided by Strauss and Corbin. These nine semantic relationships vary from strong causal relations to those that specify characteristics. The nine relationships are *a kind of, is a part of/a place in, is a way to, is used for, is a reason for, is a stage of, is a result/cause of, is a place for, is a characteristic of.* Other than the references to place which presumably are important for studying social settings, these relationships seem to offer enough variation to cover most kinds of connections between categories, but are comprehensive enough to offer ease of use.

An alternative route would have been to use one or two of the theoretical coding families advanced by Glaser (1978). There are eighteen families proposed in all, some of which would be applicable. Spradley's semantic relationships would seem to cover at least some of the informing ideas of these families. It is proposed to use some of these theoretical codes when extending the theory to other case studies, if further application of Spradley's relationships prove not to cover all possible eventualities.

Another view of the coding process is presented in Figure 1. Here the emergent core category of *conceptualization* contains three subcategories, actions, processes and information, found to be key to conceptualizing information systems in the case study. Two of these subcategories, actions and information, have subcodes represented in the boxes. Actions and information are seen as having a relationship with processes. No subcodes were generated for processes, as processes were seen as being at a higher level of abstraction than either actions or information. The emergent core category of *interaction* is here entitled interaction tactics and some subcodes for this category are provided. The relationships A, B, C, and D use Spradley's relationships and are seen as initial theories as to the nature of the relationships between the core categories and subcategories. Some of the subcodes represented in the boxes have relationships between themselves as well as with the subcategories. The advantage of using Spradley's domain analysis is clear: it prevents consideration of codes as purely hierarchical and so allows the consideration of all types of relationships and the generation of a rich theory. Instances of codes, categories and subcategories are illustrated by examples of dialogue found in the findings section of the paper.

2.7 Using Analytic Memos and Integrative Diagrams

During the axial coding phase, integrative diagrams and analytic memos were used to consider relationships between codes and to develop theory. The use of analytic memos and integrative diagrams are suggested by Glaser and Strauss, Glaser (1978), Strauss, and Strauss and Corbin and are viewed as critical for theory development. They should be utilized throughout the lifetime of the project and Strauss and Corbin go so far as to suggest that sparse use of these tools will result in a theory which lacks density. Use of analytic memos provide an opportunity for the qualitative researcher to think aloud, explore new categories, integrate borrowed concepts, and establish the grounding of concepts. Analytic memos are a generic tool in qualitative research (Neuman 1994), and are not confined to use in grounded theory method. In this case study, they were found to be most helpful when considering how codes might be

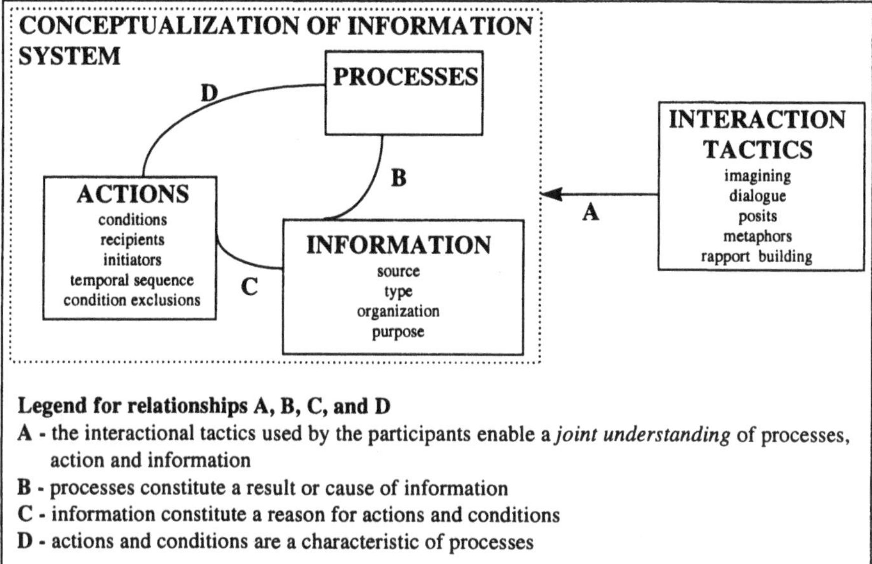

Figure 1 A View of Initial Core Categories and Subcategories Generated by Axial Coding.

grouped and what relationships existed between them. In addition, it was found useful to illustrate emergent concepts by relating back to instances in the data to ensure that the emerging theory was truly grounded. Appendix 1 gives an excerpt of an early analytic memo on the interaction of clerical and computer systems in the case study.

Integrative diagrams were used extensively during the axial coding process to assist understanding of relationships between codes and grouping of codes, and to bring together various analytic clusters (Strauss 1987). Spradley's relationships in domains were assigned between various clusters. An example of an integrative diagram pertaining to interactional aspects is reproduced in Appendix 2. Note that this diagram makes a distinction between those interactional tactics used when gathering information and those used to facilitate understanding. This distinction is described in a further analytic memo on tactics; briefly, participants have a battery of tactics that they use depending on the difficulty of the subject matter.

3 FINDINGS

Presentation of the findings in this case study presented some challenges as how best to give readers a feel for the case study data, given the limited space afforded by an academic paper. When presenting qualitatively analyzed data, there is the problem of whether to weave interpretation and description together or allow them to stand as separate entities (Wolcott 1990). Wolcott advises the presentation of a descriptive account without heavy handed or intrusive analysis. The nature of qualitative research lends itself to multiple interpretations of the data. There is also the objective of giving a feel for how the participants construct meanings and create interpretations (Neuman 1994) to take into account. Communications researchers in general seem to take a highly selective approach to the presentation of their data, and this has been criticised on the basis of providing an insufficient database on which to build rules (McLaughlin 1984) or theory. When presenting grounded theory studies, researchers are advised to opt for a narrative chronology where categories and subcategories are related to the story line (Strauss 1987).

The findings, therefore, have been presented as chronological episodes from the interaction, together with illustrations of analytic concepts generated by applying grounded theory techniques to the dialogue being described. These analytic concepts are represented in italics. It also attempts to incorporate idiographic or thick description (Wolcott 1990. Neuman 1994) by not only illustrating analytic concepts but also incorporating a narrative or story line.

Episodes in this context can be regarded as akin to subtopics in the transcript. In practice, it is relatively straightforward to identify topic shifts. Planap and Tracy (1980) demonstrated that this can be done with a high degree of reliability by most people. In their study, twenty subjects were asked to read transcripts and view videotapes, and twenty subjects to read transcripts. Reliabilities for topic shift were quite high: .926 in the first case, .919 for the second. The videotape did not assist much in identifying topic shift, verbal cues seemed sufficient.

The episodal approach used here also allows readers to develop an understanding for how the interaction moves through distinct phases in terms of building rapport and seeking solutions. It also allows the actors to speak in their own voices and allows for multiple interpretations (both important goals for interpretative research). The concepts that are italicised generally refer to open codes or subcategories rather than full categories. Where appropriate, commentary has been added as to how these relate to emergent core categories.

Another reason for opting for this mode of presentation is that contextual and processual factors are a focus of the case study. Episodal presentation urges the reader to consider the interaction in the context of its larger temporal whole.

3.1 Interactional Tactics and the Conceptualization of an Information System

Throughout the episodes presented below, two clear themes relating to the emergent core categories are evident.

First, the *interactional tactics* employed by the analyst and client to facilitate the discussion at hand are found throughout the interaction. Episodes 1 and 2 illustrate how the analyst and client agree on the objectives of the discussion and how to discuss those objectives. Episode 4 demonstrates how the analyst uses *posits* for *information gathering*, and Episode 5 illustrates a battery of tactics utilized to *facilitate understanding* of the problem. An integrative diagram giving the relationships between some of these categories is found in Appendix 2.

Second, how the *conceptualization of the information system* proceeds is also demonstrated by Episodes 1 through 6. In Episode 3, we see the identification of various *information types* by the analyst. In Episode 5, the consideration of *conditions*, and *actions* associated with various *processes* or *functions* is evident.

All open codes, subcodes and categories in the findings are represented in italics to assist the reader.

An additional advantage of presenting the case study in episodes is that it becomes clear that the *conceptualization* is intimately intertwined with *interactional tactics*. Without appropriate tactics, it is difficult to gain appropriate information for conceptualization. Without appropriate conceptual tools, it is difficult to make sense of the information gained.

Episode 1: "Basically we're looking at..."

The analyst commences his interview of the client by saying

> What I've done...I've drawn up, a little, sort of a couple, of points from when we talked last...when you gave me an overview of the system.

In addition to providing a starting point for the conversation, the analyst seems to be trying to gain trust by using the tactic of *deprecation* – what he has drawn up is only "a little," "sort of," "a couple" of points and therefore is not threatening. The use of personal references is also interesting – "we" spoke last and "you" gave the overview of the system, the inference being one of *joint ownership*.

The analyst then proceeds to outline what he perceives as the *function* and *purpose* of the system.

> Basically what I've sort of got down here is the database is about keeping statistics of approved and nonapproved students, for a Student Grants Scheme.

The client confirms this; so far she has said very little.

The analyst goes on to outline a possible objective for the conversation. It is interesting to note that, perhaps not unreasonably, his primary focus is on the computer database rather than the clerical scheme it supports, and his signalling of the intention that the "improving" be a *joint ownership* exercise by the use of "we."

> Basically we are looking at...how the database works and possibly some of the points we are thinking about improving...you know, recording of information.

At this point the client interjects

> You've got by school have you?

She seems to be checking that this issue is within the *scope* of objectives being outlined for the amendment. The analyst confirms this, and also mentions a number of other *functions* or *processes* and "general things we are thinking about as we are going along." It can be seen that this episode sets the template for what is to be discussed, but that the interactional tactics used to manage the discussion are still evolving.

Episode 2: "Maybe if you can give me a bit of a run down"

Here the analyst and the client come to an agreement as to how to discuss the problem, having agreed on what the general objective is. This episode represents an interesting negotiation, as it illustrates how two people resolve the issue of possibly conflicting ideas on how to conduct the process. The analyst starts by saying

> But to get to that sort of point what I've got to...we need to try and work out, or I need to work out what the actual database does and how it functions at the moment?

There is a pronoun shift from "we" to "I" as the analyst makes clear what his personal objective for the interaction is but also requests *joint ownership*. Again it is interesting to note in the light of later interaction that the stated area of analyst interest is the database. Most of the subsequent interaction, in fact, hinges on the relationship between the database and the clerical procedures it supports, as later episodes will show. But to return to the present episode, the client agrees to his statement and the analyst then goes on to make clear the intended outcome of his objective:

> So we'll be able to look at umm what changes we can make to improve things?

The concept of "improvement" has now been mentioned by the analyst twice in the space of a minute's conversation, and the frequent use of "we" indicates his intention that this be a *joint ownership* exercise. He then goes on to suggest a process by which things can get started:

> So maybe, maybe to start that out, start that off, maybe if you can give me a bit of a...rundown just to

The client's reaction is rather surprising, she interrupts with

> Mmm, I actually just printed a copy of the range for you...for you to have a look at.

The client may be simply *offering information*, or suggesting a different process. It may be the latter, given the remark immediately following:

> Umm would you like me to go through the procedures we have at the moment step by step or?

The analyst responds with

> Yeah that might be, well just as an overview, well just as I said before we've got it's for approved reports statistics for approved or nonapproved applicants.

There are several possible interpretations of this remark – the analyst seems to be *reparcelling* the clients suggestion to be more in line with his previous suggestion for conducting the discussion – "well just as an overview." The restatement of systems *functions* may be an indication of what he perceives the baseline of the conversation.

The client then responds by giving a *reason* for those system functions:

> Mmm. The reason we need that is because we pay the schools.

The analyst asks if the database helps with assessment of students; the client says it does not and states her desire for a *process* in this area.

> That would be good, if we could get a process...but it's quite involved.

It is not clear at this stage whether the client is *conceptualizing* the notion of a *process* as a *computerized* process or a *clerical* one. By looking at the overall context of the conversation, one can probably assume the former but at this stage it is not clear.

What is evident is that by the end of this episode, both analyst and client have put forward their objectives, and they have (almost) agreed on how to proceed.

Episode 3: "If you could just go through the information"

In this episode, the analyst and client start to discuss information utilized and generated by the computer system. The analyst makes a *request for information* by saying

> All right, if you could just go through the information you get from schools...and the sort of information you put into the database, so then you've got a list of files that you keep...umm paper records.

Later he adds

> I just need to get an idea of what's, what you get from schools and what you actually put into the database.

So here the analyst is delineating between the various *information types*, held in the database or on paper, and its various forms (files, records) and *source* (from schools).

The client imposes a temporal order on things by starting from the beginning - consistent with her offer to go through step by step. She says:

> Each applicant has an application form which is submitted directly to the school, they can't come directly through us because the schools have a recording mechanism too.

The analyst takes the opportunity to establish the *ownership* of the *function* or *process* of assessment by asking

> Is it the schools that basically do the assessment?

She replies and gives an insight to the *actions* that the school carries out.

> No. We do the assessment. They gather the information...and collect the application forms.

Episode 4: "You too"

This episode is notable as it is where *rapport building* is evident between analyst and client. They are after all only three and half minutes into the conversation. The client is explaining the *conditions* and *information types* associated with an *action*. She explains:

Umm because they (the parents) need both to apply, the application form and the verification of income...and that can be by umm a tax assessment notice.

She then drops into an aside, and says laughingly:

That's if they've done their tax return – not like me!

The analyst replies:

Right. I haven't done mine yet.

She says:

No, I haven't done mine yet,no. You too...

and then drops seamlessly back into the previous topic:

or by a statement of pension or benefit

After *rapport building*, the interaction seems to flow more easily, as evidenced by what follows immediately afterward. The analyst says:

Right. So what, what sort of information do they send back to you, so you guys in Student Assistance can assess them?

The language "you guys" denotes an informality that was not present before. The following exchange illustrates a speeding up of the transfer of information from client to analyst, as they repeatedly confirm or agree to what the other has said. It is also interesting to note that in the first statement the analyst makes, there is an effort made to express the function of the system in the client's language:

Analyst: Right, do the assessment, decide whether they are eligible for the scheme.

Client: That's right, so that when the school receives the applications summarize each applicant on a form we have devised...so that is their record of the number of applications they've received

Analyst: Right.

Client: ...and who the students are.

Analyst: So, so they then send that summary of information do they?

Client: Yes with the application forms.

The analyst starts using an *interactional tactic* at this point, which is readily identifiable all through the interaction – he makes *posits* or *suppositions* about the system based on the information.

Episode 5: "So what happens when?"

This episode occurs approximately twenty minutes later in the interaction. By this time, the client and analyst have established a rapport with each other and are working jointly to establish the current role of the database supporting the Student Assistance Scheme and associated *clerical processes.*

This episode gives a number of examples of the analyst determining which *actions* are associated with which *conditions* and *information* when discussing the database and associated procedures. This episode also demonstrates instances of *reframing*, where either the client or analyst reframe the existing facts as stated to draw new conclusions about what is being discussed, and in doing so progress the interaction

(Watzlawick, Weakland and Fisch 1974). This episode has been chosen to illustrate various *tactics*, such as *imagining* and *narrative*, that the analyst and client use to assist each other in understanding. It also amply illustrates the complexities of procedure that can exist when a computer system interfaces with a clerical system.

The analyst starts off by saying:

> So what happens when you actually receive back something, like a review, umm application or some more information?

The client replies:

> Its then reassessed. And then we have to...

The analyst interrupts with a *posited action*.

> So you have to go to the paper files?

The client confirms that this is the case, and goes on to explain the *actions* that are carried out and some associated *conditions*:

> We actually put all reviews in a separate file, but we still yeah have to go back to the paper files, and when its being reviewed...to change the detail. You know, that its now been approved.

The analyst pursues this last point and makes a *consequential query* about the actions:

> If they were approved...what would happen to them then?

The client replies:

> We'd have to notify them that it's been approved, and the school.

The analyst *reframes* the facts in the following manner:

> So, through a, through a reply. And if they are still not approved, I guess you'd still have to send them back a reply.

The *reframe* enables the analyst to put forward another *posited action*, which proves to be accurate. The analyst is also trying to pin down a *temporal sequence* for the action and isolate the *condition* for the reply. This piece of dialogue is also interesting as it is evident that the analyst is thinking aloud, and quickly enough to formulate a subsequent query on the basis of the reframe.

The analyst and client continue to follow through the chain of *actions* associated with a review:

> Analyst: So once you get a review back, you're going to have to send them a letter regardless of what the outcome of that review is.
> Client: Well we usually we notify the school.
> Analyst: Oh, right.
> Client: Because, its, its...apart from code ones, they're usually not approved, until we receive information, so we...the main thing is to notify the school, if its subsequently been approved.

Various *action outcomes, action justifications* and *action initiators/recipients* are identified, and generally the *action* is associated with a *condition* – in this example a review having taken place. A *condition exclusion* is identified "apart from code ones."

A few sentences later, something happens as the client continues to explain what occurs during the review process:

Analyst: Does the school go back and...
Client: Well, they would then say, yeah, they would then say, oh yes you've been approved, the department has...because they...as far as the client is concerned, they are not approved.

Apart from the way the client anticipates the analyst's query, her statement is interesting as it illustrates how she is literally *imagining* what takes place, to the extent of assigning *dialogue* to the school. She uses the same tactic a few sentences later:

> It's sort of back to square one, yeah, they, the client will quite often, say, come into the school and say, oh, I sent in more information to the Department can you tell me if I've been approved yet?

The analyst picks up on the same tactic, albeit in a more informal vein:

> I imagine the student coming in and giving the headmaster a big serve or something – why haven't I been approved!

As the analyst actually uses the word imagine, *imagining,* therefore, indicates an "in-vivo code" (Strauss 1987) where the term is taken from or derived directly from the language used by the actors themselves. In vivo codes have analytic usefulness as they are often used precisely by the participants, and they often have very vivid imagery.

Episode 6: "We need just to have a look"

This episode is the final episode of an interaction that has lasted for approximately thirty five minutes; the participants have been asked to wind up. The analyst says:

> Yeah, what we probably need to do now is really have a look at the database...so I can get a look at how its actually working, because it's a bit.... Now I've got a fairly good understanding of the processes you want to have...seeing the information that's on there in real life I guess.

These statements illustrate a number of interesting points: the analyst's use of "we" to indicate *joint ownership* of future action associated with improvement, an objective advanced early on in Episode 1. There is explicit acknowledgment of the clients requirement for computerisation of various processes. The references to "really," "actually," and "real life" seem to indicate a need to confirm what information has been gathered here, or maybe is an implicit reference to all the "imagining" that has taken place.

The analyst goes on to outline in concrete detail what should take place next time they meet:

> Maybe just having a look from the start, maybe just walk through what would happen if you got a bunch of applications and a batch summary sheet. What you'd put in, what would happen if someone is approved, obviously you would tick them on the sheet and their number...but what happens if someone is not approved? The letters you'd produce and that sort of thing.

The analyst is clearly still very engaged with what *actions*, *conditions* and *information* are associated with various *processes*.

The client responds with something of a *reframe* and is evidently trying to make sure that the analyst takes into account the need for solutions. She responds with

> Yes, that's what it needs...refining... so that if we do have a client ringing up and saying have I been approved, we can, you know, find it, or the number if a school rings up and says has this person been approved. We can look it up, some sort of reference to the name.

The analyst does not immediately appear to pick up this point, and instead mentions a technical dimension of the problem:

> [Because] you've got alot of, twenty seven thousand applicants, so it's alot of information going through there.

Another interpretation of this remark is that the analyst is indicating that he understands it to be a large problem for the client in terms of complexity of information processing.

Subsequent dialogue shows that the analyst both appreciates the problem and is prepared to proffer a solution:

> Analyst: And maybe for all the ones that aren't approved, we will have to look at the numbers, maybe looking at the current year's database.
> Client: Yeah.
> Analyst: I guess we can get it from the statistics, the codes two and four, umm aren't kept in there, I mean the nonapproved codes one.
> Client: Yes, and twos and fours, that's the problem area actually.
> Analyst: Which means, they, which makes it harder if someone phones up.
> Client: That's right.
> Analyst: And that's the reason you have to go to the paper file.
> Client: We've got to go to the file and say you weren't approved because of so and so.

After demonstrating that he understands the consequences of the problem to the client, he offers a way forward and a possible solution:

> Analyst: So probably have a look at the total numbers of those, and see if it is feasible, possibly, to keep some sort of indication, maybe just the reference number of the approval code?
> Client: Yeah.
> Analyst: ...or the status or something like that?
> Client: Sounds exactly what we need.

And so the interaction ends, with both parties in concordance as to the nature of the problem. Over the course of the interaction, they have clearly adopted a joint problem solving approach and have enjoyed working through the problem together. One only has to contrast Episode 1 with Episode 6 to appreciate both the depth of understanding of the problem that has developed between participants and also how informality has increased and assisted with the exchange of information and solutions.

3.2 Reviewing the Videotape

The analyst, client and researcher review the videotape of the interaction. The researcher stops the tape at approximately five minute intervals and asks each participant in turn to tell her what they think is happening in that particular frame. Most of their comments focussed on *interactional tactics* and how *conceptualization* proceeded as opposed to specific comments about individual statements they made. For example, the analyst comments about Episode 5:

> I think what would have been really useful, looking at that, was maybe if we had used the whiteboard or something...I think my notetaking was a bit suspect. It would have been a lot better if I'd have to really try and say what was happening on a piece of paper in nice clear symbols to tell what was going on. Umm I think my concentration was starting to wane a bit there and I was starting to lose the plot, trying to follow that.

The client added:

> Yeah we really needed a flow chart, you know, from this to this.

The analyst replied:

> That's something I really should have tried, to do something like that there.

Later he says:

> And it probably would have been worthwhile just to take a few minutes out and write what's been happening.

About Episode 6, the client makes an interesting comment about the difficulty of describing detailed procedures and her expectation of his understanding.

> I didn't explain alot of it very well...like the codes two to four are actually not approved until they...we get the forms back from the parents and I didn't even explain that. Assumed that they would, you notify the schools, they notify they are not approved at the...yeah. It's sort of an internal process you wouldn't be expected to understand.

The analyst comments on the difficulty of processing the information from his perspective:

> Just looking at my notes it isn't really clear the information we've actually come up with and we are into such a really, fairly complex area, and I'm trying to rely on the information I have already got and trying to remember what we've already, what I should already know, what we've already found out...and applying it to our situation.

These comments about the difficulty of the process notwithstanding, in subsequent individual interviews both participants rated the interaction as having gone "very well."

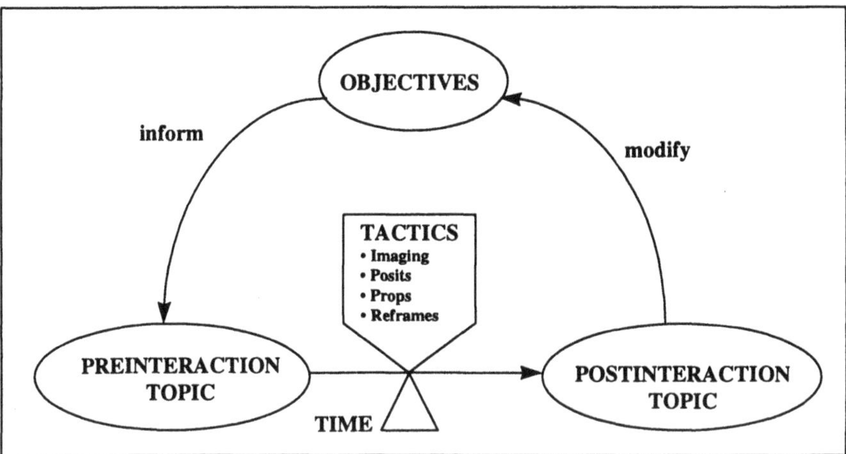

Figure 2 The Role of Tactics in the Interaction.

3.3 The Role of Tactics in Determining Objectives

Another way of perceiving how tactics might have operated within this interaction is shown in Figure 2.

Figure 2 demonstrates how the tactics employed by both participants influence the topic – in this case, possible modification to the Student Grants scheme – and how this subsequently modifies the objectives for the interaction put forward by the participants.

Tactics act as a "valve" (this notion is borrowed from general systems theory) to enable the topic to evolve over a period of time. This concept of topic – which in itself is a very abstract concept – is a local one, where a chain of topics evolve with each successive utterance (McLaughlin 1984). It was by using this principle that the transcript was divided into episodes.

How objectives change throughout can best be illustrated by the following excerpts from the interaction. Referring back to Episode 1 the analyst outlines a possible objective for the interaction:

> Basically we are looking at...how the database works and possibly some of the points we are thinking about improving...you know, recording of information.

At the end of the interaction, the objectives have been transformed into a possible solution:

Analyst: So probably have a look at the total numbers of those, and see if it is feasible, possibly, to keep some sort of indication, maybe just the reference number of the approval code?
Client: Yeah.
Analyst: Or the status or something like that?
Client: Sounds exactly what we need.

4 CONCLUSION

Presented in this paper is a detailed examination of the evolution of a research methodology used to investigate analyst-client interaction and a rich description of what took place between an analyst and client in the case study. In addition, some initial analytic concepts derived directly from the data are offered. As such, the contribution of the paper can be judged from a number of perspectives.

First, the methodology put forward demonstrates the need to tailor the research method to the object of investigation and how the data and analytic concepts interact in an iterative fashion. The process of coding, establishing relationships, and understanding a phenomena at the micro level warrants full explanation as it is integral to a full understanding of the data. In addition, Strauss and Corbin recommend that special procedures be explained in order to enable to help readers judge the overall adequacy of the research. Wolcott claims that qualitative researchers no longer have to justify their methods, but they can and should give insights into how the data gathering was conducted and ensure that generalisations made are made with care.

Second, the emergent core categories and subcategories put forward assist generation of a theory as to how analysts and their clients tackle requirements gathering. By generating a rich description of the findings, there is the benefit of close contact with the data and gaining an insight into how the participants come to agreement regarding system solutions, what interactional tactics they use, and how they conceptualize information system elements such as actions, conditions and processes.

Finally, the analytic concepts generated in this case study, *interactional tactics* and *conceptualization of information system*, together with their associated subcategories, enable a demonstration of how analyst and client reach agreement. The interactional tactics of *reframing*, *imagining*, *props*, and *rapport building*, are used in the case study interaction to aid conceptualization of an information system. Use of these tactics during episodes of interaction to conceptualize an information system demonstrate how the two core categories are interrelated. The concepts of *actions*, *processes* and *information* and associated subcategories in the case study offer an insight into the conceptual schemas used by analysts and their clients with regard to information systems.

The following two sections of the paper assess the use of grounded theory methodology in this case study and consider how the findings might assist current practice in systems analysis.

4.1 Evaluating the Use of Grounded Theory Methodology

When evaluating the use of grounded theory techniques in this case study, it could be asked whether this is truly a grounded theory study or a case study that borrows from these methods to structure qualitative analysis. To some extent, this evaluation depends on whether one regards slavish following of procedures as a hallmark of a grounded theory study, and indeed whether one regards these procedures as the only way to do a grounded theory study. In the light of serious disagreement (Glaser 1992) between the co-originators of grounded theory (Glaser and Strauss 1967) about published procedures (Strauss 1987; Strauss and Corbin 1990), conformity to these procedures should probably not be a paramount consideration for evaluating grounded theory studies. However, this is not to say that the procedures followed should not be open to evaluation.

Given Glaser's (1992) criticism of the publication of such procedures, and Strauss's injunction to modify procedures as appropriate, use of procedures is clearly a moot point. Glaser regards the use of the paradigm as "forcing" the data, rather than allowing core categories to emerge naturally. Certainly use of the paradigm in this case study was not forced; either the data fitted or it did not. Because of that lack of fit, other ways of considering relationships were sought, resulting in the use of Spradley's semantic relationships.

Another way of evaluating the use of grounded theory in the case study is to use Strauss and Corbin's seven criteria for judging a grounded theory study in *conjunction with* Glaser's (1992) response to those criteria.

The Canon of Reproducibility. Strauss and Corbin state that a researcher using the same methods ought to be able to come up with the same theoretical explanation. Glaser (1992) challenges this by saying that a substantive grounded theory continues generalising a process to continue its fit and work and relevance. While full conceptual description might require replication, it is difficult to reproduce grounded theory as it is fluid and changeable.

Clearly, in this case study, the theory is evolving, and replication at this time is difficult. In this researcher's opinion, this does not gainsay the use of technical literature to supplement or contradict analyses.

The Canon of Generalizability. Strauss and Corbin state that a grounded theory study is generalisable to specific situations only. Glaser (1992) points out that taking a process-based view rather than a unit based view should enable generalization from a substantive theory with limited scope to a process of larger scope based on its ability to fit, work and be relevant. Processes are not only durable and stable over time but can also account for change over time (Glaser 1978), and may have wider implications. One possibility for this study then is to see if the process of negotiation between analyst and client resembles the process of negotiation in other professional fields.

Criterion 1: Are concepts generated? This criterion assesses whether the concepts are grounded in the data, or at least if technical or common sense categories are applied to the data. Clearly the case study fits this criterion.

Criterion 2: Are the concepts systematically related? This criterion asks if conceptual linkages have been made and if they are grounded in the data. The case study gives many examples from the data of linkages between concepts and so fits this criterion.

Criterion 3: Are there many conceptual linkages and are the categories well developed? Do they have conceptual density? This criterion asks if the categories and subcategories are tightly linked and whether the categories are theoretically dense in terms of their properties. Although it has not been possible to completely demonstrate theoretical saturation (Strauss 1987) in this paper due to confines of space, the open coding process and axial coding resulted in categories of dense properties with many dimensions. It could be argued that the selective application of the paradigm meant there were less linkages, but applying Spradley's domain analysis ensured that the links made were exhaustive. Therefore, the study could be viewed as fitting with this criterion in spite of the unorthodox manner in which the paradigm was used.

Criterion 4: Is much variation built into the theory? This criterion states that a feature of grounded theory is that it specifies variations in the theory, and establishes more than a few conditions, actions and consequences related to the phenomena under study. While multiple interpretations of the data are given in the findings, these have yet to be fully explored. This case study is one of a series of six on the same phenomena. The categories and codes put forward in this case study are being applied to other case studies. Further instances of conditions, actions and consequences will be found, codes further dimensionalised, and more variations discovered. The emergent theory is constructed in such a way that these variations can be easily incorporated.

Criterion 5: Are the broader conditions that affect the study built into its explanation? This criterion specifies that the analysis should not be so "microscopic" as to disregard "macroscopic" sources such as economic conditions, social movements, trends, cultural values and so forth. Glaser (1992) regards this criterion as a good example of "forcing" the data rather than allowing concepts to emerge. Clearly, incorporation of macroscopic sources is problematic in a study that focuses on the analysis of interaction.

If language is indeed the surface realization of social and contextual processes (Candlin 1985), then some of the analytic concepts from the dialogue do implicitly include some of these broader conditions. For instance, the way the systems analyst conceptualizes various elements of the information system in the case study is founded in previous experience and training and this information is contained in one of the data sources. Similarly, the client's reference to the department in Episode 5 reveals something of the culture of the department. The focus of the case study on interaction tactics and conceptualization means that these are considered first and foremost. The use of broader conditions here can be seen as a means of providing alternative explanations for the phenomena observed. This is the purpose of having multiple data sources in the case study.

Criterion 6: Has process been taken into account? This criterion asks if identifying movement and change in the form of process is considered. Given that the case study has a processual focus and that the findings are presented in such a manner as to reflect the passage of time, it must be assumed that this criterion has been satisfied.

Criterion 7: Do the theoretical findings seem significant and to what extent? This criterion states that a grounded theory study can fail to produce findings of any significance if the grounded theory "canons" or procedures are applied without imagination or insight. This would seem to be a further caution against following the method without fully understanding the requirements of the research. Analytic ability, theoretical sensitivity, sensitivity to the subtleties of the interaction and sufficient writing ability to convey the findings are required from the researcher. In addition, the data has to be fully drawn upon and data collection has to be sufficient. The design of the case study, with its multiple sources, should ensure that the data is fully examined from differing perspectives. Theoretical sensitivity, analytical procedures, sensitivity to subtleties of interaction and writing to convey findings are all demonstrated in this paper. The findings at this time do seem to fit within some of Glaser's (1992) criteria in being parsimonious, relevant and having a satisfactory fit with the data.

Strauss and Corbin also point out that the above criteria should be regarded as guidelines rather than fixed, and that new areas of investigation require that procedures and evaluative guidelines be modified to fit the circumstances of the research. The work presented falls into this category as procedures have been modified in accordance with the focus of the research. Given that most discourse analysis either addresses structural *or* processual aspects due to the sheer difficulty of analysing large amounts of dialogue, it could be said that Criterion 5 in particular is not entirely appropriate for a study of this nature. For instance, broader conditions such as social movements can be regarded as only having a marginal impact on the detailed business of *how* analysts and clients reach agreement. This research not only examines social processes but also how a standard professional task – requirements gathering – interacts with it. How the system is conceptualized is at least as important as the social processes used.

The criticism of Criterion 5 notwithstanding, Strauss and Corbin do recommend that readers should be apprised of how exactly the study departs from the given criteria. This section performs that function, so that readers can evaluate the case study with reference to those criteria.

4.2 How the Findings Might Assist Current Practice

Some systems analysis texts (Kendall and Kendall 1995) provide excellent advice to a systems analyst engaged in requirements gathering with regard to setting up interviews, use of information sources, use of metaphors in interpreting organisational literature, and structuring interviews. However, detailed consideration of social processes is unfortunately given scant treatment in most traditional systems analysis textbooks. This is surprising, given the impact of social processes on project failure (Edstrom 1977; DeMarco and Lister 1987; Rothfeder 1988; Kennedy 1994). Perhaps this not too surprising when one considers that current teaching of systems analysis has but a short time within an undergraduate program to convey many technical concepts, which the systems analyst must possess in order to design an information system. In other words, attention is given to *conceptualization* of an information system rather than the *interactional tactics* required to elicit the information upon which the conceptualization is based. As this case study has demonstrated, these two issues are intimately intertwined. It is difficult for systems analysts to perform well if they are not competent at both. It is interesting to note that all the analysts involved in the six case studies felt communication with clients to be an important issue and one where they felt detailed examination would be helpful. This perhaps indicates that they felt more skilled at conceptualization than interactional tactics.

The findings from this case study could assist current practice in the following ways.

Use of reframes. Reframing is a powerful interactional tactic that influences conceptualization. If systems analysts were aware of reframing in general and the concepts of problem identification, forward reframes and reparcelling in particular, they would become sensitive to how the labeling of an object or an idea using certain words influences the joint perception of an information system. In a previous study, Guinan concentrated on framing rather than reframing and suggested outcome framing (suggesting goals), backtrack framing, pointers, an "a if" frame, and metaframing (looking at the issues as a whole). Some of these concepts have been coded differently in this study, and it was difficult to find instances of some of them. As this study looks at how shared meaning evolves between an analyst and a client, reframing is an important category as it represents a tactic by which meaning changes throughout the interaction.

Use of props. Systems analysts are not given much advice in systems analysis texts as to the use of props except with regard to prototyping input. Most systems analysts stumble on to the use of props such as finding whiteboarding a good way to work with a client. If the use of props was to be formally discussed, systems analysts would become aware of a range of possibilities to aid communication between themselves and the client. Consideration of props in a formal manner would also demonstrate the different ways people process information. Some clients who do not react well to data flow diagrams, for instance, might react better to other mechanisms.

Use of imagining and associated tactics. If systems analysts were to be formally trained in "stepping through" a process to the extent of using metaphors, acting out and vivid description, they would gain greater insights into the processes being discussed. Certainly this tactic worked well for the analyst and client in this case study. This was to some extent dependent on the analyst being able to enter into the client's mode of thinking. Perhaps systems analysts should also consider how best to do this. The notion of entering into another person's mode of thinking carries with it an implicit assumption that multiple views of a system are possible. The consideration of linguistic views in current data modelling research (Milton and Keen 1996) reflects the importance of multiple views as an issue in analyst-client communication.

Rapport building and joint ownership. The role of *rapport building* in eliciting information, and the importance of *joint ownership* of solutions, was clearly illustrated in this case study, yet systems analysis texts do not pay much regard to either issue. Previous studies (Guinan 1988; Tan 1989) regarded rapport as an important variable in analyst-client interaction. In other types of interviewing (Dwyer 1992), rapport is regarded as an important element. This case study demonstrated that information processing between analyst and client speeded up after the establishing of rapport. Similarly, the tactic of *joint ownership* ensures that solutions are jointly owned and this is important in ensuring the success of an implemented system. Systems analysts need to be aware of the role of such tactics in interaction in gaining information and cooperation.

Use of the concepts of actions, processes and information. By consciously labeling actions, processes, information and associated conditions, the conceptualization of an information system during an interaction could be greatly strengthened. A supporting document (or prop) requiring this identification could be used throughout the interaction. Such a document would have to be very carefully designed so as not to stifle interaction. One of the remaining case studies, not described in this paper, used a supporting form to structure the discussion, but it had a unexpected effect on the interaction as the client was not conversant with the concepts therein. An alternative way of using these concepts would be for the analyst to explain to the client how they can be used to build up a joint picture of the information system.

Summary. By looking at how these emergent concepts could be applied to current practice, it becomes clear that the contribution of this case study comes from its detailed examination of interaction. The value of these concepts would come from their *explicit* use and teaching to systems analysts. Most systems analysts are not aware of the tactics they employ or how they impact on the shared perception of an information system. Therefore, it can be seen that the emergent core categories of interaction tactics and conceptualization, together with their associated categories, provide valuable insights that can be incorporated into current practice.

4.3 Further Work

A problem when analysing discourse is the interrelated nature of the structure of the text and the social relationships it represents (Candlin 1985). Therefore, when attempting to discover how participants reach shared perceptions regarding a system, one is of necessity decoding the social process that allows this to take place. Nevertheless, it is hoped that further work on the relationships between core and subcategories will allow an examination of how shared meaning is built up between participants. This probably requires a more detailed examination of temporal factors, of which the narrative of the interaction in the six episodes presented constitutes a first step. At first glance, the structure of the interaction fits the sequence advanced in an earlier paper of task definition, problem framing, interpretation, agreed definition and possible solutions, and final agreement (Urquhart 1995).

This paper does not address the role of nonverbal signals and intonation to the development of shared understanding. Halliday (1979) points out that intonation acts as a means of saying different things and that if you change the intonation of a sentence you change the meaning. Nonverbal elements are said to comprise 75% of human communication (Dwyer 1992), yet a surprising amount of discourse analysis is done on written words as opposed to spoken words. When dealing with something as complex as human communication, it is difficult to address all elements: the size of the data analysis task probably contributes to this tendency to specialise in one direction or the other. One issue here is that nonverbal elements are said to contribute to conversation structure (McLaughlin 1984) and this may be of importance in professional interactions such as analyst-client conversations where the outcome is important and related to a specific task.

This research is no exception: the majority of the analysis has been done from transcripts of the videotaped interaction as a practical necessity. However, the researcher has periodically checked the videotape, where the meaning intended by the participant is unclear or where the code assigned seems problematic, in order to gain further information by examination of nonverbal indicators or tone of voice. In addition the review of the videotape, itself on videotape, has acted as a further cross check. This case study would benefit from a separate analysis of nonverbal signals and paralinguistic features.

To conclude, this case study provides some valuable insights into interactional tactics and how these interrelate with conceptualization of information systems. Examination of other data sources associated with the case study will further extend the emergent theory as presented here. Examination of the remaining case studies will provide alternative explanations, will confirm or challenge the theory, and will further saturate categories. The final aim is to provide a robust theory of how analysts and their clients reach shared understanding. Given the importance of requirements gathering to successful information systems, it is hoped that the emergent theory put forward here will contribute to current systems analysis practice.

5 ACKNOWLEDGMENTS

The author would like to thank the participants for giving their time so willingly and allowing data about their conversation to be shared in this paper. Thanks are also due to the Information Systems Group at the University of Tasmania and colleagues at the University of Melbourne for comments on earlier drafts. I am indebted to referees of IFIP 8.2 for their helpful and constructive feedback. Finally thanks are due to Chris Greaves and Frances Separovic for their numerous and helpful proof reading suggestions.

6 REFERENCES

Banks, S. P.; Ge, G.; and Baker J (1991). "Intercultural Encounters and Miscommunication." In N. Coupland, H. Giles, and M. J. Wiemann (Editors), *Miscommunication and Problematic Talk.* Newbury Park, California: Sage Publications.

Bateson, G. (1972). *Steps to an Ecology of Mind.* New York: Ballintine.

Barnett, G. A.,and Kincaid, D. L. (1983). "Cultural Convergence: A Mathematical Theory." In W. Gudykunst (Editor), *Intercultural Communication Theory: Current Perspectives* . Beverley Hills: Sage Publications.

Barrett, R. A., and Davis, B. C. (1986). "Successful Systems Analysts Hone Their Communication Skills." *Data Management*, Volume 24, Number 4, April, pp. pp 18-21.

Baronas, A. K., and Louis, M. R. (1988). "Restoring a Sense of Control During Implementation: How User Involvement Leads to System Acceptance." *MIS Quarterly*, Volume 12, Number 2, March, pp. 111-123.

Benbasat, I.; Dexter, A. S.; and Mantha, R. W. (1980). "Impact of Organizational Maturity on Information System Skill Needs." *MIS Quarterly*, Volume 4, Number 1, pp. 21-34.

Candlin C.N (1985). Preface, *An Introduction to Discourse Analysis* by Malcom Coulthard , Gen Series Editor C.N Candlin, 2nd Edition, London: Longman, p. ix.

Coulthard, M. (1985). *An Introduction to Discourse Analysis.* Second Edition. London: Longman.

Daly, J. A.; Vangelisti, A. L.; and Daughton, S. M. (1987). "The Nature and Correlates of Conversational Sensitivity." *Human Communication Research*, Volume 14, Number 2, Winter, pp. 167-202.

DeMarco, T., and Lister, T. (1987). *Peopleware: Productive Projects and Teams.* New York: Dorset House.

Dengate, G.; Cougar, J. D.; and Weber, R. (1990). "Motivational Characteristics of Australian Information Systems Personnel." *The Australian Computer Journal*, Volume 22, Number 3, August 1990.

Dervin, B. (1983). In S. Ward and L. Reed (Editors), *Knowledge Structure and Use: Implications for Synthesis and Interpretation.* Philadelphia: Temple University Press, Philadelphia, pp. 154-183.

Dey, I. (1993). *Qualitative Data Analysis: A User Friendly Guide for Social Scientists.* London: Routledge.

Dwyer, J. (1992). *The Business Communication Handbook.* Third Edition. Englewood Cliffs, New Jersey: Prentice Hall.

Eco, U. (1976). *A Theory of Semiotics.* Bloomington, Indiana: University of Indiana Press.

Edstrom, A. (1977). "User Influence and the Success of MIS Projects: A Contingency Approach." *Human Relations*, Volume 30, Number 7, pp. 580-607.

Eisenhardt, K. M. (1989). "Building Theories from Case Study Research." *Academy of Management Review*, Volume 14, Number 4, pp. 532-550.

Feldman, M. (1995). *Strategies for Interpreting Qualitative Data*. Newbury Park, California: Sage Publications.

Ferratt, T. W, and Short, L. E. (1986). "Are Information Systems People Different: An Investigation of Motivational Differences." *MIS Quarterly*, Volume 10, Number 4, pp. 377-387.

Gingras, L., and McLean E. R. (1982). "Designers and Users of Information Systems: A Study of Differing Profiles." In M. Ginzberg and C. A. Ross (Editors), Proceedings of the Third International Conference on Information Systems. Ann Arbor, Michigan, December.

Ginzberg, M. J. (1981). "Early Diagnosis of MIS Implementation Failure: Promising Results and Unanswered Questions." *Management Science*, Volume 27, Number 4, pp. 459-475.

Glaser, B. G. (1978). *Theoretical Sensitivity: Advances in the Methodology of Grounded Theory*. San Francisco: Sociology Press.

Glaser, B. G. (1992). *Basics of Grounded Theory Analysis: Emergence versus Forcing*. San Francisco: Sociology Press.

Glaser, B. G., and Strauss A. (1967). *The Discovery of Grounded Theory: Strategies for Qualitative Research*. Chicago: Aldine Publishing Co.

Goffman, E. (1967). *The Presentation of Self in Everyday Life*. New York: Doubleday Anchor Books.

Goffman, E. (1981). Forms of Talk,. Oxford: Basil Blackwell.

Guinan, P. J. (1988). *Patterns of Excellence for IS Professionals: An Analysis of Communication Behavior*. Washington: ICIT Press.

Green, G. I. (1985). "Perceived Importance of Systems Analysts Job Skills, Roles and Non-Salary Incentives." *MIS Quarterly*, Volume 13, Number 2.

Halliday, M. (1979). *Language as a Social Semiotic*. London: Arnold.

Kaiser, K. M., and Bostrom, R. P. (1982). "Personality Characteristics of MIS Project Teams: An Empirical Study and Action Research Design." *MIS Quarterly*, Volume 6 Number 4, December, pp. 43-60.

Kendall, K. E., and Kendall, J. E. (1995). *Systems Analysis and Design*. Third Edition. Englewood Cliffs, New Jersey: Prentice Hall.

Kennedy, S. (1994). "Why Users Hate Your Attitude." *Informatics*, February.

Manning, P. K. (1992). *Organizational Communication*. New York: Aldine de Greyter.

McLaughlin, M. L. (1984). *Conversation: How Talk is Organized*. Newbury Park, California: Sage Publications.

Milton, S., and Keen, C. (1996). "Linguistic Information Systems Modeling." *Proceedings of the Seventh Australasian Conference on Information Systems*, Volume 2, University of Tasmania, pp. 473-484.

Neuman, W. L. (1994). *Social Research Methods*, Second Edition. Old Tappan, New Jersey: Allyn and Bacon

Orlikowski, W. J. (1993). "CASE Tools as Organizational Change: Investigating Incremental and Radical Changes in Systems Development." *MIS Quarterly*, September, pp. 309-340.

Palmer, R. (1969). *Hermeneutics*. Evanston, Illinois: Northwestern University Press.

Pettigrew, A. M. (1974). "The Influence Process Between Specialists and Executives." *Personal Review*, Volume 3, Number 1, Winger, pp. 24-30.

Planap, S., and Tracy, K. (1980). "Not to Change the Topic but..: A Cognitive Approach to the Study of Conversation." In D. Nimmo (Editor), *Communication Yearbook 4*. New Brunswick, New Jersey: Transaction.

Psathas, G. (1995). *Conversion Analysis*. Newbury Park, California: Sage Publications.

Rothefeder, J. (1988). "It's Late, Costly and Incompetent – but try Firing a Computer System." *Business Week*, pp. 164-165

Spradley, J. (1979). The Ethnographic Interview. New York: Holt, Reinhart and Winston.

Strauss, A. (1987). *Qualitative Research for Social Scientists*. Cambridge, England: Cambridge University Press.

Strauss, A. and Corbin, J. (1990). *Basics of Qualitative Research*. Newbury Park, California: Sage Publications.

Tan, M. (1989). *An Investigation into the Communication Behaviours of Systems Analysts*. Unpublished Ph.D. Thesis, University of Queensland.

Urquhart, C. (1995). "Factors in Analyst-Client Communication in Requirements Definition." *Proceedings of Pan Pacific Conference on Information Systems*, National University of Singapore.

Watzlawick, P.; Weakland, J.; and Fisch, R. (1974). *Change Principles of Problem Formation and Problem Resolution*. New York: W.W. Norton.

Weimann, J. M. (1981). "Effects of Laboratory Videotaping Procedures on Selected Conversation Behaviors." *Human Communications Research*, Volume 7, pp. 302-311.

Wood, J. (1982). Human Communication: *A Symbolic Interactionist Perspective*. New York: CBS College Publishing.

Wolcott, H. (1990). *Writing Up Qualitative Research*. Newbury Park, California: Sage Publications.

Yin, R. (1984). *Case Study Research*. Newbury Park, California: Sage Publications.

7 BIOGRAPHY

Cathy Urquhart is a lecturer with the Department of Information Systems at the University of Melbourne. Prior to entering academe in 1990, she worked as a systems analyst in the public sector in the United Kingdom. She has taught at the University of Luton in the UK and at the University of Tasmania in Australia. She is currently completing her Ph.D. thesis in the area of analyst-client communication in requirements gathering. Her research and teaching interests encompass grounded theory, soft systems methodology, system development methodologies, management of information systems and project management.

Appendix 1
Excerpt from Early Analytic Memo

AM1 2/8/96

The interaction between Clerical and Computer Systems in Case 1

When trying to draw an integrative diagram covering system(s) and processes, I was struck by the fact that I had no relationship between the clerical and computer systems discussed, when in fact this issue is at the heart of the interaction in case 1, and probably many other interactions between systems analysts and their clients. The relationship I came up with was one of *scope* – how many processes does the computer system cover, and at what point does the clerical system pick up the job and pick up output from the computer system and process it clerically. All through the interaction, one can see the analyst trying to distinguish what is carried out by the database (computer system) and what is carried out by clerical processes and other generic computer systems such as word processing and spreadsheets.

The analyst asks early on in the interaction:

29 "does the database help you with the assessment of those?"
31 "It's just to record the statistics basically?"

And the client clearly by a "process" means a computerized process:

34 "that would be good, if we could get a process"

One quick way for the analyst to start to delineate is to look at where the storage of information is located – he asks

39 "and the sort of information you put into the database, so then you've got a list of files that you keep, umm paper records"

So I would deduce that one of the implicit objectives (I can't find anywhere where it is stated explicitly, the closest being line 7 about "improvement" and line 550 where a process of some sort is offered) is the extension of the scope of the current system. I suspect that quite often when an existing computer system is discussed, it is with this underlying agenda, as generally the client wishes to discuss some amendment that constitutes an extra process, and thereby an extension of functionality. Sometimes the amendment may be a streamlining of an existing process. So it is an interesting question as to whether all interactions about existing systems can be characterized in this way, or indeed do they only get to formal discussion if it's recognized that the client is asking for something outside the normal scope of the system (perhaps this is seen as a "big" amendment that needs a "big" discussion)

Appendix 2
Example of Integrative Diagram on Interaction Tactics 29/9/96

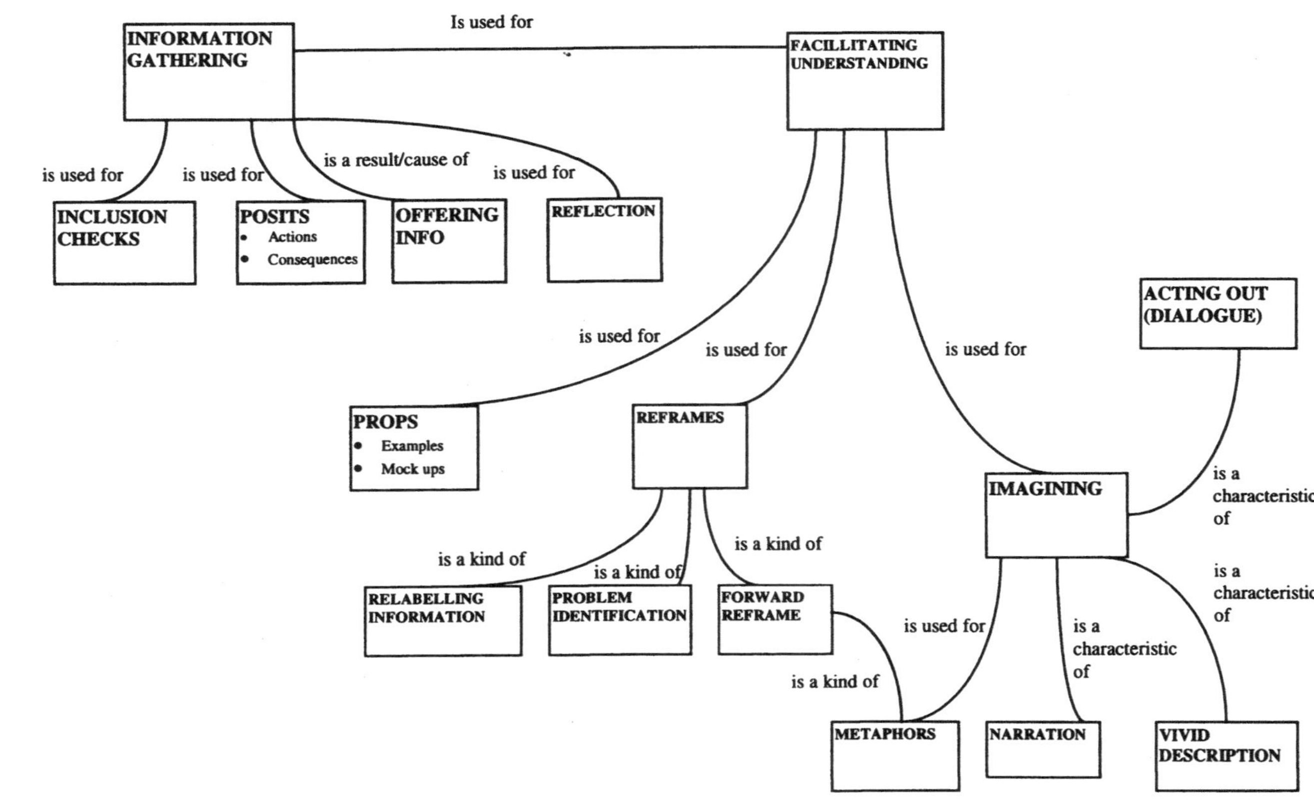

11

Constituting Users in Requirements Techniques

C. Westrup
Department of Accounting and Finance
University of Manchester
Manchester M13 9PL, England
Tel: +44 161 275 4007
Fax: +44 161 275 4023
E-mail: Chris.Westrup@man.ac.uk

Abstract

This paper explores the concepts of the "user" and "user participation" in the information systems (IS) literatures. It argues that categories such as future IS users are constituted by the processes of systems development such as requirements analysis techniques. The upshot of this argument is straightforward: qualitative research should not naively deploy categories such as users without acknowledging the considerable work that has gone into their constitution. This is not just an important academic nicety: constituting categories such as users and developers is shown to be a major concern of those engaged in systems development because it facilitates control of this process. The paper examines two well known approaches to systems development that involve users: ETHICS/QUICK-ethics and the Scandinavian cooperative approach, to show their constitutive effects. While agreeing that user participation is desirable, this paper makes four points that compromise many of the ambitions of user participation in systems development. First, that user participation is engaging in a political process in which issues of representation are central; second, that users (and systems developers) are categories constituted by these processes of systems development; third, that the users' ability to speak for the organization is usually limited; and finally, that users need to be wary of how information technology is represented to them by developers. Through these arguments, this paper seeks to contribute to the issue of researching IS by showing difficulties in the very *vocabularies* of systems development.

1 INTRODUCTION

Calls for the use of qualitative research in information systems research have appeal, not least in a common recognition of shortcomings in a simple reliance on quantitative techniques. But, as we witness in so many areas of life, agreement on the shortcomings of others often conceals differences among those who agree. This paper seeks constructively to critique some categories that are used to describe systems development from a qualitative perspective to show how techniques are implicated in constituting categories such as users. This argument has important consequences for how user participation may be achieved in systems development and two well known approaches to user involvement are examined: ETHICS/QUICKethics and the Scandinavian cooperative approach. The argument here is that these approaches are one formulation of attempts to negotiate what is attributed to the technical (computers, systems developers, computer science) and the social (organizations, users, and social theory). Although user participation is important, these approaches are important resources in configuring the entities they claim to represent, be they organizations, users, computers, or developers. This is an exploration of requirements in information systems theory but the findings of this paper have practical import for situations in which requirements are being established: requirements in practice. An outline of the theoretic approach will be given before discussion of the practical and theoretic issues raised in relation to requirements analysis. This discussion paves the way for a detailed examination of how, in theory, two approaches constitute categories such as users (and developers).

2 TECHNIQUES AND THE FORMULATION OF THE TECHNICAL AND THE SOCIAL

Our starting point is that neither technology nor social forces (technological or social determinism) can be invoked as causal agents in the development of information systems. In contrast we propose, drawing on Latour, that they are outcomes of relations of attribution that distribute the conception of the social and the technical (Latour 1987). This implies that neither the technical (as information technology) nor the social (as organizations) have essential qualities that remain unchanging; rather, what is seen as technical and as social changes over time and in different contexts. Requirements techniques have been developed to link organizations with information technology and *vice versa* and those involving users will be analyzed to see how they distribute the conceptions of the social (as users, organizations and the like) and the technical (as computers, developers). One formulation of the relationship between the social and the technical is to have users as the key exponents of what the organization wants and what the organization does (spokespersons for the social). Systems developers are taken as spokespersons for the technical, the information technology whose workings and deployment remain unseen (see Figure 1). To determine what the users' requirements might be, they must participate in the formulation of requirements and developers must cooperate and communicate with them to produce requirements.[1]

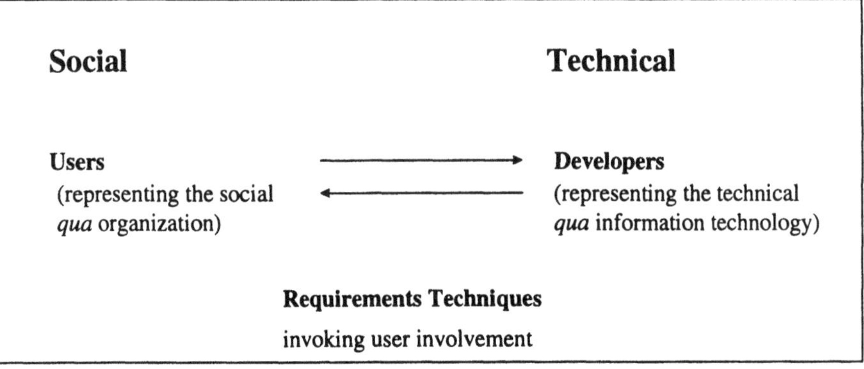

Figure 1 Users and Developers as Representatives of the Social and the Technical.

One of the features of a requirements technique is that it seeks to represent and inscribe the social (*qua* organizations) in such a way that it becomes capable of being circulated and recombined while maintaining its inscription. For example, data flow diagrams are inscriptions of processes recognized in the social. They represent the organization and may be taken elsewhere and recombined in different forms so that developers are able to create information systems which "fit" that representation of the organization. However, each inscription is a translation of what was recognized into a different formulation. The more successful the translation, the less it is seen as such and instead we consider that we are accurately/realistically depicting what was there. When inscriptions are created that can circulate, be combined, and remain intact, then it is possible for a network of relations to be produced which link people/actors in various sites (see Figure 2). Put simply, unless these inscriptions are produced, it is extremely difficult to develop requirements and "successful" information systems.

---

[1] This is but one formulation of these relations. Other approaches formulate the relationship as between organizations and technology; information required and requirements techniques; and social theory and computer science (see Westrup 1996).

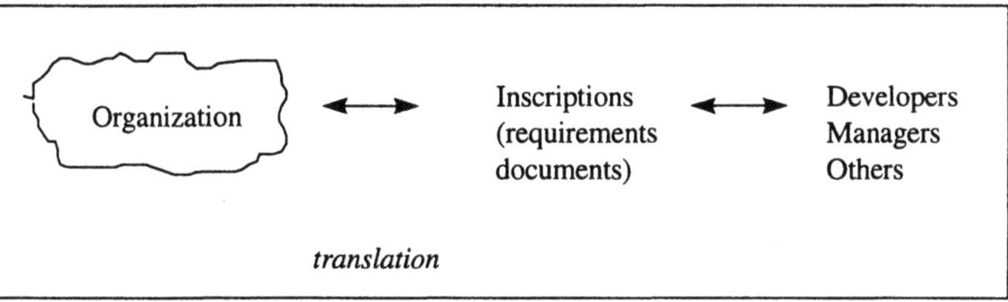

Figure 2 Requirements Specification: A Translation of an Unclear Organization into Inscriptions that may then Circulate Elsewhere.

3 WHO ARE USERS (AND DEVELOPERS)? A PRACTICAL PROBLEM AND THEORETIC ISSUE

Discussing requirements analysis in terms of social and the technical is rather abstract. In many situations of systems development, the categories of organization and information technology are treated as unproblematic and no requirements analysis techniques are used. However, we have a considerable literature on the failures of information technology and one outcome has been to emphasize the importance of the user and their participation in systems development. Various techniques have been created to produce conditions in which user participation is a key feature of requirements analysis. Before examining these techniques, it is important to explore the notions of user and designer and their interrelationship. When the question "what is a user" is asked, it is clear that, prior to the conception of an information system, no such category exists. In the literature on systems development, the word user is widely employed, but if an information system has not actually been implemented then the term user is, at the very least, an aspiration and does not refer to an actual state of affairs. What this demonstrates is that employing the term user is already creating a relationship between a posited information system and the social. The social is being taken as comprising of users, be they compliant, enthusiastic or recalcitrant, that are constituted by a relationship of using a potential computer system. In other words, an assumption is made manifest that the social may be described accurately in terms that relate it to a perception of the technical.

In the information systems literatures, the term user has not referred to a similar group of people. In the Garmisch conference on software engineering in 1968, users were considered to be those who used computer hardware; in other words, those who developed software for and ran computers in organizations – a category that would now be called developers (Naur and Randell 1969, pp. 40-41). In different countries it is recognized that users may refer to different groupings. The clearest distinction is the employment of user in the USA as opposed to Scandinavia (Carmel, Whitaker and George 1993). As Carmel , Whitaker and George put it:

> An unambiguous definition of "user" is impossible. The North American reader understands "user" to mean any non-IS/technical individual in an organization who is affected by the system – this includes managers. The Scandinavian reader understands "user" to mean any operational worker who is affected by the system - this does *not* include managers. [p. 40]

As we find that the term user is both referential, in terms of systems development, and mutable, in terms of time and space, it invites us to consider how the user is produced.

3.1 A Practical Problem

The question of who or what is the user is often a very practical problem for those developing computer systems. For what we term in-house development, the question is who can speak for those who will use the system; for those developing systems, either for other organizations or as products, the problem is more acute. Grundin (1991, p. 441) refers to obstacles to user participation drawn from the experiences of developers in producing computer systems for large numbers of organizations. The first obstacle is a "challenge in identifying appropriate users and groups." For example, developers produce a product for a market that will not have users until the information system is finished and marketed. A serious problem is found in "trying to identify specific or characteristic users" when choosing one user may "seem to eliminate other possibilities." A second difficulty is "obtaining access to users." Two issues arise here: the difficulty in contacting users and the problems that arise for developers when they do meet.

Grundin also identifies problems in motivating users to become involved, especially in large scale projects being developed over a number of years or where the outcome of the project is to threaten potential user's job security. Similarly, developers also have to be motivated to become involved with users due to a lack of empathy with nontechnical computer users or differences in values or work styles or because of the "slowness and imprecision that often accompanies user involvement."

Finally, Grundin poses another problem that of "trying to find the design team." He sets this problem in the context of interface design, but the problem can equally be applied to requirements in general:

> User involvement would be easier if one group had responsibility for all aspects of usability....But the "user interface," broadly defined, is not often the province of one recognizable team in a large product development company. The hardware is designed by one group, the software by another, the documentation by a third, and the training by a fourth. [p. 445]

The identification of problems such as these is not restricted to Grundin; in a widely cited study, Curtis, Krasner and Iscoe (1988) came to similar conclusions when they interviewed developers on large software development projects.

Although these studies show that user participation is a pressing problem for developers of computer systems, it raises issues of theoretic importance. Given the difficulty in identifying, isolating and communicating with users, how are users constituted as a group? Second, Grundin also shows that developers are not a homogeneous entity and that the mirror image of the question above is also pertinent: how are developers constituted as a group? The upshot of this is, and again a pressing issue illustrated by Grundin, how are the relations between developers and users to be controlled?

3.2 A Theoretic Issue

Woolgar (1991, 1994), as a consequence of spending a period as a project manager assistant in a microcomputer manufacturer, argued that the user is a social construction – the product of processes of delineation and definition. Woolgar proposes that preconceptions about users are more than just an interaction in a process of requirements definition; they are deeply held and "engrained in company culture" (Woolgar 1994, p. 213). As discussed above, it appears that this theoretic position accords with descriptions of what problems developers have faced in seeking user participation. However, Woolgar's report was restricted to the development of a piece of hardware for a potential market of users. In this instance it is plausible to argue that the user is configured through preconceptions of what users are and that users' actions will then be prescribed through having to follow instructions as to how to use the artefact so that the computer will work. This is obvious because, at the outset, for a new product no users exist as such. The question is whether we can extend this analogy of user as construct to other contexts of computer development. The answer is probably yes, although the means by which users are configured may be somewhat different.

One of the issues for those developing systems and seeking users is to find users who are representative of users in general. This is not only a problem for those developing generic software products, as shown by Grundin, but is shared by those developing systems for individual organizations or within organizations (contracted or in-house development). For the former the problem is, who represents the user? Is it definitely not the managers or information systems specialists but rather the computer users themselves, as Grundin supposes?

Even in projects developed within organizations, a similar issue arises: who will be users and how are they to be represented? The reasons why this is important are twofold. First, those developing systems seek a single source of requirements specification, as is suggested above, and second, those producing that requirements specification are expected to become more knowledgeable of designer concerns and develop requirements specifications accordingly. One of the ways to do this is to use techniques that involve users in development. Any involvement of users by definition makes visible parts of the social and brings them into a relationship with development. It is this participation of users that is constitutive of users. Users are not users until they are involved in development in some form. Requirements techniques organize so as to create users that will enable representation of the organization *qua* social.

How these techniques are designed and used are of importance to developers. If communication between users and developers is unregulated, then dangers are recognized of developers being side-tracked by unrepresentative user demands or users being put off by developers. The development of inscriptions to represent users' requirements is an important step in the process of control and one that is closely linked to the constitution of users. The capabilities of the inscriptions that are generated in terms of their mobility, immutability and combinability are important for developers because it is only when combinations of all three are present that they are capable of producing networks of stable relations among designers and also between designers and users. This brings us to the second point: developers are also constituted in this process. As Grundin has observed, who the designers are and how they are to be organized are important issues; ones that have been recognized since the late 1960s. Producing networks of relations that become teams of designers is due, in no small measure, to the circulation of inscriptions of requirements that have been made mobile, combinable and immutable. Put in this way, the importance of techniques and the inscriptions they generate in constituting users, developers and their interrelations, is hard to underestimate.

Finally, a consequence of focusing on users and designers is to present them as representative of the social and the technical respectively. What we find is the search for the end user as representative of the social and a focus on the developer, and in particular, the programmer as representative of the technical. Within this relationship, all others tend to be relegated to obstacles to communication between the two or to the clutter of nonuser components (Curtis, Krasner and Iscoe 1988; Grundin, 1991).

To assist in the analysis, two variations of relations between users as representing the social and developers as representing the technical are identified (see Figure 3). The first is termed user participation and the second dialogue with users. Both formulations share a presumption that users should/do speak for the organization *qua* social; however, a distinction may be may made as to how users and designers are seen as interacting. In the former, users are central and are actively engaged in processes/techniques that produce an inscription of the social. Developers are those who seek to align the information technology to that inscription, either by the provision of technical alternatives, as in the case of ETHICS (Mumford 1983), or in unproblematically incorporating the inscription into the technical as in Soft Systems Methodology (Checkland and Scholes 1990). In the category of dialogue with users, the expectation is that users and designers will work together in the production of requirements but that this process should entail techniques that produce inscriptions. This latter category is perhaps the most ambitious and comprises approaches such as the cooperative approach originating in Scandinavia and others proposing an emancipatory approach to systems development (Greenbaum and Kyng 1991; Hirschheim and Klein 1994; Murray and Willmott 1991).

Users speak for the social using requirements specifications	*Users speak for the social through dialogue and games*
Fitting the technical and the social together	*Aligning the technical to the social*
Requirements as a product of the requirements process	*Requirements as a process*
Techniques of user participation	**Techniques of dialogue with users**

Figure 3 Classifying Approaches to User Involvement in Requirements Analysis.

4 USER INVOLVEMENT: QUICKethics/ETHICS

Those approaches classified as user involvement approaches to the issue of requirements produce inscriptions for designers. Users are seen as important in speaking for the organization both in providing information about the organization and in participating in processes that may lead to a redefinition of the organization. The result of these processes is the production of an inscription (a requirements specification) that represents the organization and which may then be used by designers as representatives of the technical. The processes of user involvement are also processes engaged in the constitution of users so that they are seen as able to speak for the social. To do this, those in the organization have to be accepted as representatives of the social and seen as users. Second, users have to be organized so that they speak in terms that can be mobilized. In other words, they must be able to formulate their observations in a manner that is capable of translation into a representation which is immutable and mobile. Similarly, users must be organized so that they can read these inscriptions and comment on them. Finally, the outcome of these processes is an inscription that is, dependent on the context, immutable, mobile and combinable; it represents the organization and may then be used by developers who are seen both to represent information technology and to work in relation to the requirements produced by the processes of user involvement (see Figure 2). The requirements produced by these approaches are seen to be fixed for the medium term. In some approaches, such as ETHICS/QUICKethics, users speak for the organization, designers for information technology and the objective is to align them. In other approaches, such as soft systems methodology, the technical is to be aligned with the representation of the social produced by the methodology. The approach that will be examined in detail here is ETHICS/QUICKethics.

The ETHICS methodology was developed by Mumford in the late 1970s. It has become well known as a methodology of systems development that advocates user participation and, arguably, it is the best known methodology of user involvement in the information systems literature (Episkopou and Wood-Harper 1986; Ehn 1988; Flynn 1992; Hirschheim and Klein 1989, 1992, 1994; Jirotka and Groguen 1994; Mumford 1983, 1985, 1987, 1993, 1995; Mumford and Henshall 1983; Mumford and MacDonald 1990). It is because of the status of ETHICS as an exemplar of a methodology of user involvement that it is important to examine it in some detail.

Mumford's socio-technical approach has become influential but it is not without critics. The criticisms leveled at her approach can be split into two groups. First, it is argued that this approach neglects "asymmetrical relations of power" and assumes that the problem is one of communication between designers and users (Hirschheim and Klein 1992; Willmott et al. 1990). As Willmott et al. (p. 258) put it, this approach ignores "the understanding that meaningful dialogue and participation may be impeded or distorted by unfavorable material and ideological conditions." Others disagree with this appraisal: both Mumford herself (Mumford 1994) and Hirschheim and Klein (1994, p. 93), in a change of heart compared with their earlier analysis (Hirschheim and Klein 1992), propose that ETHICS "strives to realize the so-called 'ideal speech situation'." Second, ETHICS and, for that matter, soft systems methodology, have been criticized for placing "*a priori* classifications and categorizations of human behavior" on what is occurring in organizations and giving little guidance to analysts (Luff, Heath and Greatbatch 1994, p. 285).[2] Disagreeing with Luff, Heath and Greatbatch and contrary to their argument, the representation/classification capacities of ETHICS and also soft systems methodology are some of their greatest strengths for managing a process of requirements analysis through their capacity to provide agreed inscriptions of the organization, although it is likely that the representations furnished by ETHICS/QUICKethics will not accord with the analysis of video or ethnography.

Mumford (1985, p. 97) introduces the rationale for ETHICS as follows:

> It can be argued that the most important stage in systems design is the definition of systems requirements....It is essential for both the technical designers and the users of the new system to be absolutely clear on what they want the system to achieve. Only if systems requirements are clearly defined will the technical specialists have a set of required outputs against which they can match existing hardware and software. Similarly, only if systems requirements are clearly defined will users have a set of precise expectations of what they want the new system to help them achieve. These expectations should be specified as a set of objectives directed at improving personal and group efficiency, effectiveness, job satisfaction and the quality of working life. They will be attained through associating

[2] In other words, they ignore how activities are carried out in the workplace and rely instead on the accounts of those working there (see Jirotka and Groguen 1994, p. 6).

> new technology with new organizational structures and using both of these as a means of achieving these objectives.

This quotation shows some of the moves that are seen as important in ETHICS. First, the issue of requirements is positioned as between technical designers on the one hand and users on the other. The role of each is to produce clear definitions of what is required. Users speak for the social by furnishing designers with a set of "required outputs" while designers speak for the technical by assessing and matching the options of hardware and software. For the designers to speak effectively, they must have a defined set of requirements that represent the social. ETHICS provides mechanisms for users and, to a lesser extent, developers, to make visible what is social and what is technical. The social "should be specified" as objectives to be achieved in certain categories. ETHICS then provides instruments to measure (make visible) and evaluate (represent) the social in specific formulations. For example, job satisfaction is measured using a questionnaire. The supposition of ETHICS is that the technical and social constitute different domains, each of which needs to be associated, and that this may be accomplished through mechanisms employed by designers and users alike. As Mumford remarks,

> This design strategy can only be used if systems designers have a clear and comprehensive knowledge of the needs and behaviour of the user department. The involvement of users in the design process is seen by the author as the most effective way of achieving this knowledge. ETHICS facilitates such participation by providing a simple step-by-step method that can be used by non-technical staff to identify their efficiency, effectiveness and job satisfaction needs and problems. [Mumford 1985, p. 99]

This analysis of ETHICS/QUICKethics will focus on two issues: first, the means by which users are constituted and come to speak for the social; second, how designers are constituted and come to speak for the technical.

More recently, Mumford has produced a variant of ETHICS known as QUICKethics, which is described as "the front end of ETHICS" and is specifically designed for requirements analysis (Mumford 1995, p. 79). QUICKethics is portrayed as being able to assist in the following processes:

- Analyzing roles and responsibilities prior to considering information needs.
- Identifying and prioritizing information needs.
- Creating and applying a core information system as a preliminary to building or improving a larger one.

There is some confusion as to who should use QUICKethics; in some cases, Mumford (1995, p. 52) proposes that QUICKethics is used "to assist *managers* to define their information needs prior to the introduction of a management information system" (emphasis added), whereas, in other places, QUICKethics is seen as

> enabling the future users of a new system, or their representatives, if users form a large group, to work individually and as a group, thinking through

their roles and responsibilities and relating these to their information needs. [Mumford 1995, p. 95][3]

Almost in the next sentence, Mumford uses the term manager again. From this, it is clear that there is considerable ambiguity as to the relationship between managers and users and whether these two terms are interchangeable in QUICKethics. This issue goes to the heart of the criticisms raised above that Mumford fails to recognize power inequalities in the workplace. It is not that she does not recognize a concept of power but that she considers that the use of ETHICS is capable of ameliorating the situation (see Mumford 1995, pp. 55-62).[4] This is a rather Panglossian perspective. Although criticism is probably justified, it neglects the role of techniques in providing a representation of the social and it is this ability to organize an agreed representation of the social that is important for information systems development, be it from the perspective of a users or a managers.

The selection of users is not given much attention in QUICKethics; they are assumed unproblematically as either future users or representatives of future users.[5] Arguably, someone has to define who are future users and, in doing so, they exercise judgment as to what the bounds of the social are in a particular instance. This judgment is based on assumptions of how the social will be affected by the technical or, in other words, the constitution of the social is set by its expected relation with the technical. This judgement must be exercised regardless of whether managers or others or both are assumed as users. Although the social is taken as being comprised of users, it is the ability to describe the characteristics of users that is important in QUICKethics. Let us now look at ways in which QUICKethics defines users.

Mumford (1995, p. 94) argues that one of the problems of more traditional approaches to requirements analysis that use interviewing techniques is that "[it] has the major disadvantage of leaving the systems analyst with the task of integrating a number of different sets of needs."[6]

---

[3]As an example of QUICKethics, Mumford (1995) describes nurses creating the requirements for a new nursing information system.

[4]Mumford discusses approaches to participation and "work humanization" by Follett, Handy and the human relations school. She argues that ETHICS strives to reach a situation where "there is no place for regulation or coercion; everything should emerge from discussion and agreement' (p. 55), although she admits that it is only a "small step in the right direction" (p. 62).

[5]Elsewhere, in a discussion of participation, Mumford (1995, p. 20) suggests that "if consensus or representative design is used then, ideally, the design group should be democratically elected." This did not occur in the example of QUICKethics given in this text and this is considered to be a serious omission.

[6]Mumford ignores the claim of modeling techniques such as data flow diagrams, entity relationship diagrams or object oriented techniques in enabling different "sets of needs" to be compared and made coherent.

She considers that requirements analysis has to be a social process based on group discussion that "enables users to understand better the roles, responsibilities, problems and information needs of their colleagues" (p. 95). However, these roles, responsibilities, problems and information needs are not just elicited through discussion; QUICKethics provides activities to produce them. The primary means is a questionnaire that asks the manager/user to

> describe his or her work mission, key tasks, critical success factors and major problems. These are seen as *essential elements* of the managers' job. They are also almost certainly the most stable. They will only change if the manager experiences major changes of role and function.

QUICKethics then continues by an analysis of each key task based on the cybernetic model of a viable system developed by Beer (1981). This model represents the organization as comprising of five levels and it "assists the manager to examine systematically their roles and responsibilities" (p. 96). The questionnaire then

> asks each manager to use this job analysis to identify his or her information needs; to separate these into "quantitative" and "qualitative" needs, and to prioritize them into "essential," "highly desirable," and "useful." [Beer 1981, p. 96]

After completing the questionnaire, the managers/users meet for a two day session in which they discuss their mission, key tasks, critical success factors and principal problems and describe their essential information needs. Each manager/user's essential information needs are written up and "gradually, a picture of the group's essential needs is built up until agreement is reached that a viable core information structure has been achieved" (Beer 1981, p. 97).

Mumford argues that QUICKethics gives empowerment to users and allows both their knowledge to be used and their interests to be respected in the development of a new system. QUICKethics, Mumford suggests, enables organizations to learn how to learn by not only solving problems but through reducing or removing the factors that may have caused these problems in the first instance.

What QUICKethics provides are techniques which those who use QUICKethics, and thus potential users, engage in. Participants have to represent their work in relation to a work mission that comprises key tasks. Each key task has objectives, requires daily activities and needs information. In turn, a key task has critical success factors and problem areas, both of which require information. Finally, a key task has targets which also require information. QUICKethics is representing the work of users in a formulation that is seen as natural and systematic. It may appear that the QUICKethics questionnaire is no more than a systematic appraisal of people's work. However, it engages people to reformulate/translate their working experiences into answers that indicate the presence of these features. For example, the assumption is that everyone has a key mission and that, at worst, the problem is the articulation of an implicit key mission. It is assumed that such a mission must be comprised of identifiable tasks that in turn may be subdivided into daily activities. In other words, the questionnaire respondent, if the respondent is to engage in QUICKethics, is being configured into someone that is represented as working on a rational and systematic basis.

If engagement in completing the questionnaire in terms of these categories is a first translation, a second, and related, move is to cast each task, daily activity, problem, target, and critical success factor as being conditioned primarily on the presence or absence of requisite information. For example, a critical success factor may only be met if certain information is available. This configures the participant as engaged in systematic and rational work processes which necessitate the participant to be a user of information. Once this move has been made, then the role of participants is to create a list of essential information which is needed for their key tasks. As a consequence, the participant in QUICKethics becomes configured as a rational user of information to perform activities that are systematically related.

These users are taken as those who should speak for their activities on grounds of empowerment, participation and democracy. In other words, no one else has the ability to say what these users do but, on the other hand, the representations the social has been translated into enable a coherent picture of the organization to be created on the basis of information. In terms of inscriptions, the first move is to engage those in the workplace in the translation of their work into the vocabulary of cybernetics and a second is to represent these in terms of information needs. Once this has been done, an inscription can be produced which lists common information requirements. Such an inscription is, dependent on the context, a combinable immutable mobile and capable of both representing users and being used by developers. This process resolves the problem Mumford discusses of leaving the systems analyst with the task of integrating a number of different sets of needs. User participation has done this already. Users are configured in their engagement in QUICKethics and are seen as speaking for the social but the social as represented in the vocabulary of QUICKethics/cybernetics. However, once users have produced their information requirements, the users in turn may be represented by this inscription. At this point, the social is being related to the technical by the information it requires, a situation little different than orthodox requirements techniques, the differences being that the process by which that point has been reached and, secondly, the role assigned to developers.

This process, by which users come to be seen as representing the social, is dependent on the process of QUICKethics being seen as legitimate and useful. Hence the importance placed by Mumford in describing the utility of QUICKethics not only on democratic grounds but also on efficiency gains. If the utility of QUICKethics is questioned, then the status of the inscriptions that it produces may not be accepted as representative by others. For example, developers may wish to use analytic techniques such as data flow diagrams to represent the social mindful of Ackoff's warning against users defining their own information needs.

What of the designers and their place in QUICKethics? The process of QUICKethics and the inscriptions it produces are clearly designed in relation to a conception of the technical as capable of automating the social and thus being able to make the social more efficient. On the other hand, designers are not involved in the production of the representation of the social which is left as the domain of users.[7] The deployment of a computer system is seen as either being developed within the organization or though the purchase of a software package. In either case, the domain of the technical is seen as being represented by technical experts/developers who are able to talk about technology (Mumford 1995, p. 43). However, the role assigned to technology is twofold. First, it is seen as a factor as in the following quotation: "Technology is, of course, [a]... actor that can reduce or increase freedom" (Mumford 1995, p. 60). Second, technology is seen as supplementary to the social and it should be applied once the social has been reorganized: "Ideally, if work is to be fundamentally reorganized this should be done before the technical system is selected" (Mumford 1995, p. 43).[8] In short, QUICKethics does not dwell on the technical, leaving it as something that will be capable of delivering the information needs of users though the work of developers.

To conclude, the techniques and representational practices of QUICKethics in particular configure the user as representing the social in a vocabulary that enables immutable and mobile inscriptions to be produced. Of course, the characteristics of the inscriptions depend on the context in which they are deployed. Technology is left as a domain to be represented by developers and to be related to through the clear articulation of information requirements.

5 DIALOGUE WITH USERS: THE *COOPERATIVE APPROACH*

Approaches classified here as advocating dialogue with users share several characteristics. First, the presumption that the technical should be developed in relation to the social and not *vice versa*. Second, that those working within the social speak for the social. Third, that the process of requirements analysis is in itself misleading. Requirements are not seen as having a status that enables them to be captured and defined; rather it is more appropriate to consider requirements analysis as integral in a process of design of computing artefacts. Finally, it is taken as given that the way to create information systems is to have users as full partners in design (Greenbaum

---

[7]In ETHICS, the situation is more complex as designers and users may interact on a design team.

[8]This view of technology sits uneasily with Mumford's assertion that "everything that BPR (business process reengineering) offers is to be found in socio-technical design" (1995, p. 48). What ETHICS/QUICKethics does not acknowledge is a capacity for technology to transform organizations. The chameleon nature of ETHICS/QUICKethics is more apparent when elsewhere Mumford argues that this approach follows Habermas's dictums on the creation of communicative competence (Mumford 1994).

and Kyng 1991, p. ix). These assumptions differentiate them from the approaches termed here as user involvement in two respects. User involvement approaches, as their name suggests, involve users in the process of requirements production but they differ from dialogue with users' approaches in, first, assuming that a fixed set of requirements may be produced and, second, in presuming that the relationship between designers and users will be through the product of this process. In design by doing, there is an expectation that designers and users work together as equal partners in systems development and that requirements are integral to situated design and cannot simply be decontextualized into formal inscriptions.

The approaches classified here as dialogue with users are commonly known as either the cooperative design approach or as approaches to participative design (PD) (see ACM 1993; Greenbaum and Kyng 1991). Most of this work originated in Europe and has been associated with IFIP Working Group 9.1 on Computers and Work (see Clement and van den Besselaar 1993). More recently, there has been increasing interest in participative design in the United States (ACM 1993). Probably the best known influence on the development of these approaches has been work done in Scandinavia which has been reported in several books (Bjerknes, Kyng and Ehn 1987; Ehn 1988; Greenbaum and Kyng 1991). However, it has proved difficult to classify the Scandinavian approach within the information systems literature. On the one hand, Hirschheim and Klein (1992, pp. 325-326) describe them as complex and "not having transformed themselves into methodologies" and they propose that the approach itself has changed from a "radical structuralist" toward a more "neohumanist" paradigmatic affiliation while also changing name from the "collective resource" approach to one of "cooperative design." On the other hand, the very lack of cohesiveness of the cooperative design approach enables classifications to be developed that simply split it into a series of techniques that may be deployed as needed by systems developers (see Muller, Wildman and White 1993). Given this interpretative flexibility, the analysis is restricted to two well known sources: first, the book *Design at Work* that was produced, in part, to highlight key ideas in Scandinavian (and American) design (Greenbaum and Kyng 1991, p. ix) and, second, the experiences of the UTOPIA project[9] which is "probably the best known PD [participatory design] project" (Clement and van den Besselaar 1993, p. 30).

---

[9]The aim of the UTOPIA project was to build computer based tools and develop other skills for graphics workers in Nordic countries. It ran from 1981 to 1985 as a collaboration between graphic workers, computer and social researchers working with Scandinavian graphics work unions and funded by a variety of mainly government and academic sources (see Bødker et al. 1987; Ehn 1988, pp. 327-348). One objective was to produce a marketable technology for graphic design. This failed due to "a lack of technical competence within the company responsible for developing and marketing the software product" and "opposition from both management and the union of journalists" (Clement and van den Besselaar 1993, p. 34).

What interests us here are issues of the constitution of designers and users in the techniques of this approach. This is of special relevance given the importance attached to users as full partners in design.

Users, in this approach, are seen as

> not as one homogeneous group, but, rather, as diverse groups of people who have competence in work practices. Our perspective focuses explicitly on all the different groups of people using computers in their work, and not on the managers. [Greenbaum and Kyng 1991, p. 3]

This perspective on users is premised on the belief that work is fundamentally social and that work practice is comprised of situated actions. This means that workplace life is "not easily describable" (Greenbaum and Kyng 1991, p. 4) and that new techniques are needed to "capture this complexity, and to develop a more detailed understanding of its depth."

The way in which this complexity is to be understood is fourfold: mutual learning between users and designers about their respective fields, use of tools in design which are familiar to users, envisionment of future work situations so that users can experience emerging designs, and basing the design process in the practice of users. As Greenbaum and Kyng put it, cooperative design is

> an attempt to look at the development of computer systems as a process, where people as living acting beings, are put back into the center of the picture. A picture of the workplace, where the situations that people find themselves in, with all its conflict-laden social and political tensions, comes under close scrutiny.

The outcome of this is the observation that no method or universally applicable set of tools are available, rather that cooperative design depends on the situations in which it is applied.

What of designers? Greenbaum and Kyng (p. 20) propose to "refer to the technical people as designers in order to keep our eyes on the *process* of developing computer systems." Designers include the gamut of systems analysts, programmers, consultants, and systems engineers. In other words, their common characteristic is that they may speak for the technical. However, the cooperative approach views technology differently than other approaches. The assumption is that technology is a tool: "Computer systems are *tools*, and need to be designed to be under the control of the people using them."

Having introduced the conceptions of user, designer and technology in this approach, we proceed to describe some of the techniques used in design. Two of the more important in the UTOPIA project were the use of mock-up simulations of computer artefacts for users (design by doing) and, second, the use of an organizational design game to support discussions of existing and future work (design by playing) (Ehn and Kyng 1991; Ehn and Sjögren 1991).

Ehn and Kyng describe how they used cardboard models of printers and computers with drawings taking the place of the screen. They argue that users could not understand the descriptions given them using orthodox techniques. What they found is that if cardboard models of a possible system were produced, users could actively use them and the cardboard models were understandable, fun and cheap to produce. Ehn and Kyng argue that they were very successful in enabling users to envision what could be done; however, problems arose when users realized that a completed system would take some time to create. As Bødker et al. (1987, p. 257) remark, "the graphics workers who were used to rapid concrete results in their daily work, found that work progressed too slowly and was too abstract."

A second technique, called the Organizational Kit, was a game based on the traditional production flow in a newspaper and the artefacts and functions that were needed. Each item, artefact and function was represented by cards of different colours and shapes. The designers introduced the users to this game having first observed what the users did. The game was based around production at two newspapers, both computer based but with different work organizations. Ehn and Sjögren found that the game was a means to "create a common language, to discuss the existing reality, to investigate future visions, and to make requirements specifications on aspects of work organization, technology and education" (p. 252). They argue that social interaction came into focus using the game and that "existing hardware and software" were "more or less taken for granted" (p. 254). This, they suggest, shows that the basic problem is one of organizational change and not technology.

These brief descriptions of two techniques used in the UTOPIA project pose interesting issues in relation to conceptions of users, designers and the relationship between the technical and the social. First, techniques such as the Organizational Kit are produced by designers and played by designers and users. Both learn from this game but the rules of the game have been set up by the designers. So though users may speak for the social, they do so within the vocabulary constructed by developers. This game does not address the technical, which is taken as given, but it is probably open to designers to speak for the technical and open up possibilities for users if they so desire. Second, the choice of users is of importance. In part, this reiterates points made in relation to QUICKethics; the difference here is that the subsequent history of UTOPIA shows that both management and journalists refused to implement the proposed UTOPIA system. Managers had deliberately not been seen as users while journalists could be users but were not involved in the design. The upshot is that the users chosen to design the system were not contiguous with the users that were designed into the resulting system and, perhaps as a consequence, those not involved did not accept the new system. Put differently, UTOPIA techniques assisted in constructing a role of users not just through the creation of a UTOPIA artefact but also through techniques such as the Organizational Kit, which creates roles for those who act as player/designers, and subsequent design then produces a variety of other users who must interact with the new system if it is to work.

Third, some of the problems encountered above may be linked to the conception of technology as a tool. The tool metaphor emphases the relationship between tool and user in which the user is shaped by and may shape the tool as in the use of cardboard prototypes. However, this metaphor obscures characteristics that are often ascribed to the technical, such as the ability to make visible work processes and the capability to combine and mobilize that information. In other words, the designers' metaphor to enable the shaping of the technical through cardboard prototypes did not adequately represent characteristics of the technical.

So, we find a situation where, on the one hand, users were chosen and through techniques developed a vocabulary to describe the social but were unable to represent the social as subsequent problems with management and journalists imply. On the other hand, designers seek to represent the technical through techniques such as cardboard prototypes but are also unable to do so successfully. Their lack of success is shown by the inadequacy of the tool metaphor, by their inability to produce the actual technical artefact quickly and, finally, by the failure of the hardware/software manufacturer to produce a finished product.

It has been suggested here that designers were able to speak, if ultimately unsuccessfully, for the technical and that they are intimately involved in producing the vocabularies and techniques for describing the social. This ability leads to designers, as Ehn and Kyng (p. 194) put it, "as referees of the game: the gods that make the other players obey the given rules."

Not only are designers placed in this relation to those working in organizations and constituted as users but the characterization of designers is opaque. They are, it appears, a homogeneous group of people committed to doing the best for the users in the context of that project. Although this is laudable, it conceals any relationships between different designers; for example, who gets to speak to users and who codes the system? Perhaps this role taken on by developers is characteristic of the project based work where it derives, but its naiveté is striking and somewhat disquieting when we consider the concerns raised by Grundin and others discussed earlier on the heterogeneity of developers, the difficulties in managing the interaction between developers and users, and the demands on developers to be effective and efficient.

In summary, although it is difficult to characterize the cooperative approach which is avowedly nonmethodological, we may still draw some conclusions. First, although users speak for the social, we find that designers use techniques to develop vocabularies to describe the social for users. A problem arises in users being representative of the social because of what appears to be the conflictual and situated nature of the relations within it. Second, designers have created techniques that enable users to shape the technical as tool-like. Although designers speak for the technical, the composition of designers remains problematic as is their ability to speak for the production of technical artefacts. Finally, the characterization of the relations between the social and the technical as one as communication between users and designers is problematic. The source of difficulty does not appear to lie in what are unfavorable material and ideological conditions because it appears possible within the confines of these projects for resources to be available. Rather, it resides in the conflation of users as representing the social and designers as representing the technical. Each grouping may be able to interact successfully using a shared vocabulary, but it appears far more difficult for either grouping to continue to speak for either the social or the technical over longer periods of time as the experience of UTOPIA bears out.

6 DISCUSSION AND CONCLUSIONS

The argument presented here seeks to show how the categories of user and designer (let alone organization and information technology) are constituted by the techniques that seek to represent them. In other words, there are links between the organization of representation (requirements techniques) and the representation of the organization (requirements). This may appear to be an obvious comment, but drawing attention to it throws into stark relief some of the difficulties for those developing or using requirements techniques. As was found in science, representation is a form of intervention and what needs to be recognized is the extent of this intervention in any particular context. It is not that we can wish away the difficulty users may have in articulating their requirements but we need to recognize the extent to which the techniques that are used provide the vocabularies for them. This is a form of intervention that is subtle and far reaching and the translation that it entails may be extensive.

For those interested in research into systems development, the trajectory of developing yet better methodologies to resolve the problems of systems development has run its course. Ontological and epistemological analyses remain both difficult to apply in relation to methodologies and are, at base, philosophical. Indeed putting trust in methodology alone as a means of ensuring success in development is an act of faith that is unwarranted (cf. Hirschheim and Klein 1992). Not only are there a series of moves being made in the very constitution of these techniques – some of which this paper has attempted to illuminate – but we find that when it comes to requirements analysis in practice, methodologies are used as a resource and applied with considerable flexibility (see Westrup 1996).

Despite the arguments raised in this paper, user participation in systems development is both desirable and useful. Some of the difficulties that need to be addressed when user participation is invoked in systems development have been presented. Hopefully, the outcome will be that a more considered and indeed beneficial experience of user participation may be engendered. Four points arise from this analysis.

First, a recognition that user participation is engaging in a political process in which certain questions become central: who represents who; how are others to be convinced that this representation is legitimate; and how is that representation to be constituted? Using techniques of user involvement may help in addressing these issues but equally, and depressingly perhaps, more frequently the deployment of techniques displaces these questions and puts others in their place. For example, QUICKethics treats the issue of power relations in a naive (as empowerment) and often contradictory way (sometimes as emancipatory at other times like business process reengineering). This well known example of user participation does not do justice to the important issues of representation that its deployment raises.

Second, it is important to realize that users are constituted by the process of engagement in systems development. There is no pristine user awaiting the developer, and the particularity of any requirements analysis technique (as well as its deployment) will inevitably shape the types of user participation that occur. One of the prime difficulties is that once users are constituted as a group they are often unable to speak because they possess no legitimate vocabulary (in terms of systems development) that may be inscribed. Two moves have to be made: first, users have to acquire some representation of the technical and, second, they have to articulate their experience and understanding of the social in terms that may be inscribed. The latter is potentially extremely precarious as users frequently have to rely on others' (systems developers' or facilitators') vocabularies of the social in order that their experiences may be inscribed. For example, QUICKethics structures users' inscriptions of the social as a cybernetic system, while even in Scandinavian approaches to cooperative development we find that users have to gain insights into their work through the use of games created by developers.

Third, the limitations of users' ability to speak for the social *qua* organization needs to be recognized. It cannot be assumed, although it frequently is, that a homogeneous inscription of the social is going to be more than a construct of the development process. For instance, when detailed engagement with users has occurred in the cooperative approach we find that all aspects of the social just cannot be included. Those who are left out, be they managers, other elements of the workforce, or perhaps forces outside the organization, may act to compromise the users' claims to represent the social, especially as time elapses after the creation of the initial requirements. The experience of the UTOPIA project is a good example of this: the claims of the users to represent the social was shown to be deficient as both management and journalists failed to support the project. More wide-scale difficulties are often apparent when reviews of user participation projects are undertaken (see Clement and van den Besselaar 1993).

Fourth, users need to be wary of how the technical is represented to them and realize that any one metaphor or representation is at best limited and, at worst, misleading. Seeing a system being demonstrated should not lead to accepting its adequacy. As a representation of the technical, demonstrations are more akin to a theatrical performance whereas every eventual system in a working environment may perform in a very different way.

This paper has used a theoretic approach viewing the early stages of systems development as a process of representing organizations by having users speaking for them and technology by having developers as spokepersons. It attempted to show how these are practical difficulties in systems development not just theoretic issues and went on to show, in some detail, how requirements analysis techniques of user involvement attempt to resolve these problems. To aid the analysis, two types of user involvement were identified: user participation centered on the creation of requirements specifications (inscriptions) and dialogue with users which stresses far reaching communication between developers and users. In both categories, it was shown that the ambitions of user involvement are compromised by techniques which have to *constitute* users (and developers) while attempting to foster involvement.

What of the role of qualitative research? A consequence of this paper is that, in qualitative research, attention needs to paid to three issues. First, we must recognize that the vocabularies of research are problematic; terms such as users and developers have been constituted through a variety of processes of which requirements analysis techniques are one of the most important. Naive description of "what is there" is not an option in future qualitative research. Second, constructive critique of qualitative approaches is necessary and important. For example, although the active engagement of researchers in IS development is admirable, both theoretic difficulties and shortcomings in practice need to be identified and analyzed (see Westrup 1996). Finally, qualitative research needs to look carefully at the very concepts of technology and organization that are so frequently invoked. If, as has been argued, they are constituted and not unchanging, then many of the well known classifications in qualitative research into IS development will need fundamental rethinking (for example, Hirschheim, Klein and Lyytinen 1996).

7 ACKNOWLEDGMENTS

I would like to thank Brian Bloomfield, Geoff Walsham, and Hugh Wilmott for comments on a previous incarnation of this paper.

8 REFERENCES

ACM (1993). Special issue on "Participative Design." *Communications of the ACM*, Volume 36, Number 4.

Beer, S. (1981). *The Brain of the Firm*. Chichester, England: Wiley.

Bjerknes, G.; Kyng, M.; and Ehn, P. (1987). *Computers and Democracy*. Aldershot, England: Avebury.

Bødker, S.; Ehn, P.; Kyng, M.; Kammersgaard, J.; and Sundblad, Y. (1987). "A Utopian Experience: On Design of Powerful Computer-Based Tools for Skilled Graphic Workers." In G. Bjerknes, P. Ehn, and M. Kyng (Editors), *Computers and Democracy*. Aldershot, England: Avebury, pp. 251-278.

Carmel, E., Whitaker, R., George, J. (1993). "PD and Joint Application Design: A Transatlantic Comparison." *Communications of the ACM*, Volume 36, Number 4, pp. 40-48.

Checkland, P., and Scholes, J. (1990). *Soft Systems Methodology in Action*. Chichester, England: Wiley.

Clement, A., and van den Besselaar, P. (1993). "A Retrospective Look at PD Projects." *Communications of the ACM*, Volume 36, Number 4, pp. 29-37.

Curtis, B.; Krasner, H.; and Iscoe, N. (1988). "A Field Study of the Software Design Process for Large Systems." *Communications of the ACM*, Volume 31, Number 11, pp. 1268-1286.

Ehn, P. (1988). *Work-Oriented Design of Computer Artefacts*. Stockholm: Arbetslivscentrum.

Ehn, P., and Kyng, M. (1991). "Cardboard Computers: Mocking-It-Up of Hands-on-the-Future." In J. Greenbaum and M. Kyng (Editors), *Design at Work: Cooperative Design of Computer Systems*. London: Erlbaum, pp. 169-195.

Ehn, P., and Sjögren, D. (1991). "From System Descriptions to Scripts for Action." In J. Greenbaum and M. Kyng (Editors), *Design at Work: Cooperative Design of Computer Systems.* London: Erlbaum, pp. 241- 268.

Episkopou, D., and Wood-Harper, A. (1986). "Toward a Framework to Chose Appropriate IS Approaches." *The Computer Journal,* Volume 29, Number 3, pp. 222-228.

Flynn, D. (1992). *Information Systems Requirements: Determination and Analysis.* London: McGraw-Hill.

Greenbaum, J., and Kyng, M. (Editors) (1991). *Design at Work: Co-operative Design of Computer Systems.* London: Lawrence Erlbaum Associates.

Grundin, J. (1991). "Obstacles to User Involvement in Software Product Development, with Implications for CSCW." *International Journal of Man-Machine Studies,* Volume 34, pp. 435-452.

Hirschheim, R., and Klein, H. (1989). "Four Paradigms of Information Systems Development." *Communications of the ACM,* Volume 32, Number 10, pp. 1199-1216.

Hirschheim, R., and Klein, H. (1992). "Paradigmatic Influence on IS Development Methodology: Evolution and Conceptual Advances." In M. Yovits (Editor), *Advances in Computers,* Volume 34, pp. 294-392.

Hirschheim, R., and Klein, H. (1994). "Realizing Emancipatory Principles in Information Systems Development: The Case of ETHICS." *MIS Quarterly,* Volume 18, No., 1, pp. 83-109.

Hirschheim, R.; Klein, H.; and Lyytinen, K. (1996). "Exploring the Intellectual Structures of Information Systems Development: A Social Action Theoretic Analysis." *Accounting, Management and Information Technology,* Volume 6, Number 1/2, pp. 1-64.

Jirotka, M., and Groguen, J. (Editors) (1994). *Requirements Engineering: Social and Technical Issues.* London: Academic Press.

Latour, B. (1987). *Science in Action.* Milton Keynes, England: Open University Press.

Lei, Lei (1994). *User Participation and the Success of Information Systems Development: An Integrated Model of User-Specialist Relationships.* Ph.D. Dissertation, Tinbergen Institute Research Series, Number 73, Amsterdam: Thesis.

Luff, P.; Heath, C.; and Greatbatch, D. (1994). "Work, Interaction and Technology: The Naturalisitic Analysis of Human Conduct and Requirements Analysis." In M. Jirotka and J. Groguen (Editors), *Requirements Engineering: Social and Technical Issues.* London: Academic Press, pp. 259-288.

Muller, M.; Wildman, D.; and White, E. (1993). "Taxonomy of PD Practices: A Brief Practitioner's Guide." *Communications of the ACM,* Volume 36, Number 4, pp. 26-27.

Mumford, E. (1983). *Designing Human Systems for New Technology: The ETHICS Method.* Manchester, England: Manchester Business School.

Mumford, E. (1985). "Defining System Requirements to Meet Business Needs: A Case Study Example." *The Computer Journal,* Volume 28, Number 2, pp. 97-104.

Mumford, E. (1987). "Sociotechnical Systems Design: Evolving Theory and Practice." In G. Bjerknes, P. Ehn and M. Kyng (Editors), *Computers and Democracy* Aldershot, England: Avebury.
Mumford, E. (1993). "The ETHICS Approach." *Communications of the ACM*, Volume 36, Number 4, p. 82.
Mumford, E. (1994). "Technology, Communication and Freedom: Is There a Relationship?" In R. Baskerville, S. Smithson, O. Ngwenyama, and J. DeGross (Editors), *Transforming Organizations with Information Technology*. Amsterdam: North Holland, pp. 303-322.
Mumford, E. (1995). *Effective Systems Design and Requirements Analysis: The ETHICS Approach*. London: Macmillan.
Mumford, E., and Henshall, D. (1983). *Designing Participatively: A Participative Approach to Computer Systems Design.* Manchester, England: Manchester Business School.
Mumford, E., and MacDonald, B. (1990). *XSEL's Progress: The Continuing Journey of an Expert System*. Chichester, England: Wiley.
Murray, F., and Willmott, H. (1991). "The Communication Problem in Information Systems Development: Toward a Relational Approach." In J. I. DeGross, I. Benbasat, G. DeSanctis, and C. M. Beath (Editors), *Proceedings of the Twelfth International Conference on Information Systems*. New York, December, pp. 83-92.
Naur P., and Randell, B. (1969). *Software Engineering: Report on a Conference Sponsored by the NATO Science Committee, Garmisch, October, 1968*. Brussels: NATO.
Westrup, C. (1996). *Requirements Analysis: In Theory and Practice.* UNpublished Ph,D. Thesis, UMIST, England.
Willmott, H.; Mouritsen, J.; Flensburg, P.; and Elkjaer, B. (1990). "Systems Developers: Preoccupations, Knowledge and Power." In J. I. DeGross, M. Alavi, and H. Oppelland (Editors), *Proceedings of the Eleventh International Conference on Information Systems*. Copenhagen, December, pp. 257-264.
Woolgar, S. (1991). "Configuring the User: The Case of Usability Trials." In J. Law (Editor), *A Sociology of Monsters: Essays on Power, Technology and Domination*. London: Routledge.
Woolgar, S. (1994). "Rethinking Requirements Analysis: Some Implications Research into Producer-Consumer Relationships in IT Development." In M. Jirotk and J. Groguen (Editors), *Requirements Engineering: Social and Technical Issues.* London: Academic Press, pp. 201-217.

9 BIOGRAPHY

Christopher Westrup is a lecturer at the Manchester School of Accounting and Finance at the University of Manchester. His interests are in the interrelationship between advanced information systems and organizations both in their development and their use.

Part Three

Illustrating, Experiencing, and Being Critical in Ethnography

12

A Discourse on Ethnography

L. Harvey
School of Information Systems
Curtin Business School
Curtin University of Technology
Perth, Western Australia 6001, Australia
Tel: 09 351 7685
Fax: 09 351 7685
E-mail: harveyl@cbs.curtin.edu.au

Abstract

Ethnography is an approach to social inquiry developed by anthropologists and recently adopted by interpretive information systems researchers. In recent debates in anthropology, radical changes regarding appropriate approaches to ethnography have been presented. This paper looks at those changes and applies the debate to interpretive information systems research. The key assumption in this paper is that information systems is a discipline that is changing within a socio-historical context. Looking at interpretive information systems research as an emergent area in the discipline of information systems, an analysis is conducted of a product of the socio-historical context in order to illustrate the flux of changes which appear to be happening. These changes are related to the debates on ethnography in anthropology. The product of socio-historical disciplinary change which is analyzed is an unpublished Ph.D. thesis completed in the United States in 1988 (Orlikowski, 1988). The analysis is carried out through a textual re-reading of this thesis, concentrating on genres as indicators of flux in ideological changes regarding the move from an essentially realist genre to what may be described as a more evocative, or postmodern, genre. The importance of discourse and genre textuality is discussed. The aim in this paper is demonstrate how information systems researchers act within socio-historical contexts which reflect disciplinary changes. The argument is that information systems researchers can benefit from reflecting upon their work in context and that the reflection provides a critical approach which complements the evaluation of research quality from philosophical principles. The view that the information systems research discipline is a historically-dependent social construction with evolving methodological principles is supported.

1 INTRODUCTION

Interpretive information systems research is emerging as an acceptable body of inquiry within the information systems discipline (Walsham 1995). Walsham argues that there are a number of approaches to interpretive research emerging, including that of ethnography (Orlikowski 1991a; Davies and Nielsen 1992; Myers 1994). In the interpretive research area, the information systems discipline has adopted ethnography from anthropology, seemingly by adopting ethnographic approaches used in the study of organisations (Orlikowski 1991a). Ethnography has the potential for contributing to the exploration of information systems research issues (Zuboff 1988; Orlikowski 1991a, 1992a; Lee 1993; Harvey and Myers 1995; Avison and Myers 1995) and has been discussed at workshop presentations in regard to this potential (Orlikowski 1991b; Lee 1992; Davies 1993).

The growing interest in ethnography indicates that it is worthwhile to investigate the adaptation of ethnography into information systems research. This requires a recognition that ethnography is a changing methodology both within source disciplines and, through adaptation, within the discipline of information systems. In this paper, the changes are presented and discussed but not in order to investigate ethnography as a set of rational principles. Instead, the investigation takes a historical and contextual perspective, looking at ethnography's emergence at one point in history. The purpose of doing so is to demonstrate that the adaptation of ethnography shows ambiguity and inconsistency in its assumptions as seen in the montage of genres expressed in an ethnographic text. The argument is that the ambiguity and inconsistency are not a sign of a poor quality ethnographic text but, rather, that they are an indicator of the struggle of expression which comes from writing an ethnography during a time of adaptation and change. The indication is that all research writings, including ethnographic texts, are dependent upon the socio-historical contexts of information systems knowledge development. Arguably, it seems important to recognize this dependency both when writing an ethnography and when reviewing ethnographic texts.

The genre adopted in this paper is that of a critical commentator, deconstructing an information systems ethnographic text. It is recognized that any deconstruction is itself a rewriting of a text. In this manner, the author is declaring an invitation to the reader to take part in a textual discourse, seeking to involve the reader in the debate while considering both the text under deconstruction and, eventually, the text of this paper. This is an essentially textual perspective seeing the reader as text interpreter, the author(s) as text constructor(s), and the analytical investigator as text deconstructor (Derrida, translated by Spivak, 1976). However, this paper also looks to texts within contexts in order to explore the historical context of a text. The purpose is to perform an act of reflexivity (Lawson 1985) which seeks to critically explore assumptions regarding cohesion in knowledge domains. The criticality of reflexivity adopted in this paper stems from a postmodern view which seeks to explore the ambiguity, uncertainty, discontinuity and diversity often denied in rational analyses of history. In this paper the view taken of history in relation to the disciplinary body of knowledge called information systems is closer to a genealogical view (Foucault 1979; Preston 1991) than to a view of history as singular in rationality, linear in temporality and discoverable in a factual manner.

The primary purpose of this paper is to demonstrate the importance of historical contexts in the writing of an interpretive information systems ethnography. The broad historical context is that of the information systems discipline during the adaptation of an approach from another discipline. In adaptation, one discipline decontextualizes an approach from the debates of its source discipline and then recontextualizes it within its own ongoing disciplinary body of knowledge. A secondary purpose is to return to the debates in the source discipline's historical contexts in order to contribute to the debates on ethnography in the adapted context of information systems research.

After the initial introduction to the debates on ethnography in the source discipline of anthropology, an information systems ethnography is selected and reread in order to illustrate the issues arising from the source debates. The chosen text is taken as a representation of a novice text, being an unpublished Ph.D. thesis, and is chosen to provide initial illustrations of the struggles of using ethnography. It has been selected because:

- it illustrates the adoption of ethnography to information systems research at a particular point in the history of that research,
- it uses an already adapted approach to ethnography, organizational ethnography, which is then adapted again to the information systems area, recognizing that this may have provided a means for genre exploration not otherwise available,
- it was completed by an information systems researcher rather than by a researcher from a source discipline in ethnography, and
- although originally a novice text, it is now recognized as an important qualitative information systems research thesis as shown by subsequent writings which have originated from the thesis and have had important impact in the interpretive information systems research community (Orlikowski 1991a, 1992b; Walsham 1995).

This acceptance of a Ph.D. work as a central contribution to the field of information systems research indicates the relative lack of more advanced works from senior peers in the discipline prior to Orlikowski's ethnography. Although some anthropologists and historians had written ethnographic theses on information systems topics, there is a noticeable lack of Ph.D. theses from the information systems discipline at that time. The most commonly cited information systems ethnography is Zuboff (1988), which is a doctoral ethnographic work conducted as an organizational researcher rather than as an information systems researcher. The Ph.D. thesis by Orlikowski is seemingly the first notable doctoral ethnography produced in the United States by an information systems researcher. This indicates the potential historical significance of the chosen text.

The Orlikowski Ph.D. text is deconstructed through an analysis of genres which are argued to show shifts in the acceptability of schools of thought, most noticeably the shifts from a realist perspective to an impressionist one. The socio-historical contexts of the writing of the thesis are then introduced in order to interpret something of the shifts. The purpose of this is to show how genres vary in knowledge transition and is not to criticise the text for inconsistency. On the contrary, the text is shown to be a good example of a postmodern decalage of genres, indicating shifts which are likely to lead to further genre inconsistency as new debates arise during the process of knowledge change in the information systems research community. The genre inconsistency is a sign of non-determinism in a postmodern knowledge era. This is consistent with the values of postmodernism. The conclusion of the paper discusses the importance of reflecting upon socio-historical contexts when both writing and reading an ethnographic text as a contribution to information systems research.

2 A BRIEF SUMMARY OF ETHNOGRAPHIC DEBATES

Due to the obvious spatial limitations of this paper, the debates from the source discipline of anthropology have to be presented extremely briefly and are summarized due to the assumption that many of the readers will not have had first hand knowledge of them.

The main philosophical dimensions of ethnography have centered around the intention of the ethnographer to represent a culture. The assumptions often expressed are that cultures have hidden logics which can be uncovered by an intelligent observer who immerses herself/himself into the membership of that culture. The ethnographer seeks to decipher the code which makes up the logic of that culture, always standing by the assumption that there is a single, dominant logic to any culture. The codes to be deciphered are in the form of rituals, language, dress, community and family structures and political and economic practices. The ethnographer as informed observer then writes an ethnography which represents the culture as a logical system of rationalities, values, beliefs and actions. The purpose of conducting an ethnography is to uncover this logical system as the ethnographer attempts to minimize the intervention effects of searching for this system (Evans-Pritchard 1940; Geertz 1963; Sahlins 1972; Leach 1976; Cohen 1982).

Geertz (1973) challenges the assumptions of ethnography as a means of uncovering culture. He argues that the act of conducting an ethnography is essentially an interpretive act. This acceptance of interpretivism at the point of observation has challenged ethnographic practices which concentrate on gathering examples of cultural behavior while interposing a theoretical model of a system of logic, attributing this model to the situation and not to the theorist observing the situation (Atkinson 1992). Marcus and Fischer (1986) take the debate further, while still adopting a genre of scientific discourse, discussing the changing nature of anthropological research. Within sociology and philosophy, the rise of postmodernism has also challenged assumptions regarding the treatment of culture as a rational object (Lyotard 1984; Kroker and Cook 1988). Diversity of interpretation has emerged at this time as an alternative to representation (Clifford and Marcus 1986).

The representation school of thought views culture as something that can be captured, decoded and represented as a theoretical model, leading to the writing of ethnographic texts as if they represent a reality. This is described by Van Maanen (1988) as a realist tale. Although somewhat simplistic in its analysis and presentation, the Van Maanen text provides a useful initial introduction to ethnographic debates by categorizing ethnographies into three distinct types which he names as three tales. These are the realist tale, the confessional tale and the impressionist tale. From a broad interpretation, the realist tale describes ethnographies which seek to represent a culture. The realist ethnographic texts are non-reflexive and so lack a critical dimension in relation to the author's construction of the text. The confessional tale appears to be a transitional form of writing, away from realism and toward post-modernism, as expressed through the intensive acceptance of the need for authorial subjectivity. The impressionist tale seeks to evoke impressions of the events in the reader, to consider the creative act of developing a text as a discourse between reader and writer. Comparing the three categories, the primary differences between approaches to ethnography can be summarized as points along a continuum. At one end is ethnographer as scientist, seeking to uncover, decode and represent a culture. At the other is ethnographer as artist, seeking to explore the experiences of belonging to a culture and seeking to develop a text which invites the reader to relive those experiences through evoking images in the discourse between the writer and the reader. The writer expresses the experience to try to evoke that experience in the reader and this is how the ethnographer's experience of a culture is transferred into a text. Considering the ethnographer as scientist, the important discovery is the system of logic. In the case of the ethnographer as artist, the important act is the reflexive writing of a text. With one the challenge is to discover while with the other the challenge is to write evocatively. This distinction is further explored below.

2.1 The Ethnographer's Interests

Observation versus creation is central to the differences between the genres as is the authorizing of the text. Observation which does not declare the interests of the writer is authorizing a text to be a discourse of authority. Conversely, a text which declares the interest of the writer and brings that to the fore as critical to the attempt to evoke experiences is authorizing the text as an open debate, inviting the reader to contribute to the process of experience evocation. The ethnographic text differs dramatically depending upon which of the opposing ends of the spectrum is adopted. Most ethnographic texts are likely to fall between the two ends and many will be a mixture of genres along the continuum.

An ethnography is fundamentally a writing (graphy) of a culture (ethno). It is always a text that illustrates the researcher's interests and cannot simply be a recording of a stream of events in a situation. The ethnographer selects from the situation those aspects of interest to her/him. This selection process is important as it shapes how the ethnographer will interact with those in the field and then, subsequently, how the ethnographer will choose to write the ethnographic text. This simple point has been central in debates on ethnography. Early ethnographic texts give the reader the impression that the fieldworker simply observed what happened in cultures in a neutral manner and then recorded the observations in order to represent the culture in detailed models. The ethnographer's intent is placed in the background which gives the author an unchallenged authority when writing the ethnographic text and claiming that it is a representation of a culture (Clammer 1984; see also Van Maanen's discussion on realist tales [Van Maanen 1988, pp. 45-72] and Geertz's discussions of Malinowksi's posthumous confessions [Geertz 1983, pp. 55-59]). During the last two decades, there have been critical debates in anthropology which deny that authority and demand that ethnographers challenge their own assumptions regarding their intentions and write their ethnographic texts in a critical and reflexive voice (see the debates in Clifford and Marcus 1986). The writing of an ethnographic text is currently viewed in anthropology as an inescapably political act where the ethnographer is seen as purposefully selecting from the setting a story to be told. Texts are written with the voice of recognition that the telling of that story can also change either the situation or others' attitudes toward that situation.

2.2 Genres

In writing an ethnography, the author is no longer considered the authoritative controller of the interpretation of the text. The relationship between author, reader and text has been at the center of debates on ethnography. It is now recognized that there are many different genres in ethnographic writings (Marcus 1980; Clifford and Marcus 1986; Geertz 1988; Van Maanen 1988; Hammersley 1990; Atkinson 1992). These genres represent a continuing shift over the last two decades accentuated by the debates on what is acceptable as an ethnographic genre.

At the risk of further over-simplification, an illustration of extremes in the genre debate is now presented, moving from the seemingly acceptable genre found earlier in the debates into what is now arguably viewed as the desired genre. The contrast gives an impression of clarity in change. This is illusory as the change has not necessarily been smooth, nor has it been universal. The dangers of using a "categorize and contrast" approach to the presentation of history are obvious and the reader needs to remain aware of the simplification this creates. The reader also needs to recognize that, in constructing this text, the author has purposefully chosen this particular view of history.

Genre 1: Ethnographer as Scientist

An ethnographic text can simply be presented as a description. Its primary purpose may be to represent something to do with culture. A good descriptive writing would challenge the writer to represent as close to the actual event or situation as possible. This form of writing (representation) is evaluated on its depth and accuracy of representation. Theory is introduced by framing the representation as a system of logic and the disciplinary reasoning appears to be to find universals of logic systems from the analyses of comparative cultures. The reader's potential for interpretation is minimized as the writer seeks to control the ambiguity of the representative text.

To show the rigor in the representation, the writer is expected to confer with those involved in the event or with responsibility for the situation being represented. This form of ethnography assumes that authoritative knowledge lies with informants in situations and that the ethnographer's task is to represent the culture in which the informant exists.

The key issues for the ethnographer are in collecting adequate data from accurate sources and in using triangulation to develop a representation that truly represents what is being written about so that those who are not able to have access to that culture can understand it from the ethnographer's text.

In information systems research, this form of ethnography may represent events such as the implementation of a new system and the resultant change. There would be a key informant, probably in the form of a senior IT manager, and the ethnographer would have delivered an interpretation of the event back to a group of people in the situation in order to confirm that the representation is an accurate portrayal of events. The ethnographer is unlikely to challenge the authoritative capabilities of either those in the context or herself/himself as author.

This form of ethnography can be described under the realist tale as categorized by Van Maanen. The genre of a realist tale reads with the authority of a scientific script in that the author treats her/his textual representation as an objective account with the language being third party ("the analyst designed a system") rather than first party ("I saw the analyst's work and interpreted it as a design for a system"). Realist tales also adopt a documentary style as if the author is reporting on the micro-level aspects of an event in such a way as to discover something not obvious but hidden.

The author of a realist ethnography presents herself/himself as essentially outside the situation, observing, recording and analyzing rather than actively involved in the creation of the representation of that situation. In this way, the realist approach mimics the laboratory context of the scientist who observes and records in order to analyze and represent in the form of a model that can be generalized to other contexts.

The ethnographer mines the situation for minute details that wait for her/his intervention and do not change form when discovered. Meaning is merely hidden in symbols and the ethnographer seeks to discover it and decode the symbols.

The realist position is seemingly acceptable, and commonly found within information systems ethnographies. The problems of adopting a realist stance become more obvious when the debates from the source disciplines are addressed. Geertz (1988) presents a detailed argument against a realist stance, calling for a recognition of the ethnographer's active part in authorizing a text as opposed to viewing the ethnographer as the recorder of a culture. This argument is developed and supported by later ethnographers who adopt a critical or postmodern perspective (Clifford and Marcus 1986; Tyler 1986; Kroker and Cook 1988; Clough 1992; Myers 1994; Harvey and Myers 1995). By adopting a realist voice, information systems researchers will be obliged to actively deny the arguments made against this voice by the ethnographers cited above. As we are addressing the argument from a historical and contextual perspective, no claim can be made in an absolute manner against a realist stance. Instead, the claim is being made that information systems researchers who choose a realist position are choosing to reject the debates from the most recent historical ethnographers within the context of anthropological research. This acceptance indicates that information systems ethnographers choose to view their ethnographic contributions to the discipline as beyond the critiques of the anthropological ethnographers. If it is the case that the realist voice remains dominant within information systems research, then it follows that information systems ethnography is choosing to separate itself from anthropological ethnography at this point in history. The contexts become purposefully distinct and the adaptation becomes limited.

In order to show the distinctions more clearly, a polarized perspective to the realist tale is presented below.

Genre 2: Ethnographer at Play

At the other extreme to the realist perspective, an ethnography can be a means for evoking the imagination. The primary purpose here is not to represent but to involve the reader in an evocative experience which the writer puts forward. The writer then invites the reader to join with her/him in the experience of the interpretation.

With this approach, no two interpretations are ever expected to be the same as all readers are going to be different. Also, this approach fundamentally values history, the history of the context and the history of the writing/reading experience. Every new reading of the text is a new interpretation. The ethnographic text is never static and so does not seek to be an ultimate representation. Instead, the text is intended to be a tale that evokes ideas and images and which brings forward experiences. This is similar to what Van Maanen refers to as an impressionist tale.

Writers of this type of ethnography would see themselves as a critical part of the tale and would seek to write the text in that attitude. The language is likely to be subjective with first person referencing, talking of experiences and seeking to find imaginative ways of evoking the experiences in the mind of the reader. This may be by using analogies, allegories, poetry, or even music to seek to invoke an experience in the reader (Newman 1989). The writer is aiming to share the interpretive experience which is unfolding while critically challenging personal views on the situation.

The "text" can take many forms and is often intentionally obtuse (Baudrillard 1988). The aim is to leave purposeful space for ambiguity to develop so that readers can construct their own interpretations from the images put forward. This form of ethnography sees "art as experience" as being the guiding model for the writing of the ethnographic text. The text is more likely to read like a novel than like an objective report.

The purpose of this form of ethnography is to embellish the material so that experiences can emerge. Simply representing a culture is not treated as worthwhile in and of itself. The ethnographer has a responsibility to expand upon the text of the situation in order to invite the reader into a discourse with the text. When this experience is entered into, the reader can step out of the obvious, consider the absurd and then return to the obvious with fresh eyes. The process allows for novelty rather than just for representation.

This perspective is often referred to as postmodern ethnography. Tyler describes postmodern ethnography as "a fantasy reality of a reality fantasy whose aim is to evoke in reader and writer alike some intimation of a possible world already given to us in fantasy and commonsense" (Tyler 1986, p. 134).

The postmodern ethnography reads as a novel, is often disjointed, building upon many experiences which are juxtaposed. The concern of the author is more with aesthetics than with objective representation as she/he invites the reader-writer discourse in a historically-dependent contextual world. The evocation of the history and contexts through juxtaposition of experiences is the important criterion for judging the success of the ethnography. The success is not in representing a reality but in evoking a discursive experience. It is more concerned with creative play than with scientific discovery. It also accepts the essentially political nature of that play and does not neutralize the notion of knowledge by claiming that it can be apolitical. Hence, a postmodern ethnography is often concerned with the political nature of discourse both within situations and within texts which discuss situations, i.e., ethnographic writings. Lyotard (1984) provides a clear and thorough treatise on postmodernism. Lyotard's (1989) short summary of debates in postmodernism is also helpful in clarifying the problems with interpreting this genre.

In summary, the first extreme presented here seeks to represent in an objective format by *drilling down* into data. It appears to be highly analytical. The second extreme seeks to evoke an imaginative discourse by *moving out* from the text of the situation in order to explore alternatives before returning to the text, treating this as a discourse between text, writer and reader. The discourse is, at each reading, a further reconstruction of the text. It appears to be highly creative. The first extreme adopts a scientific reporting genre and the second extreme adopts an "artist at play" genre. The artist's genre tends to be heavily involved in debates concerned with the politicizing of texts, calling upon postmodernist social theory to enhance those debates (see the preface in Kroker and Cook 1988).

3 REVISITING AN INFORMATION SYSTEMS ETHNOGRAPHIC TEXT

In this section, Orlikowski's Ph.D. thesis is deconstructed (Orlikowski 1988). The thesis, being an unpublished text, demonstrates the struggles of writing a doctoral work thatis the source by which the author is examined as a competent new researcher. In retextualizing Orlikowski's text, the purpose is to discourse with the reader concerning Orlikowski's contribution within the information systems research context of 1988.

At the start of the thesis, the term genre is used to present the research area which is "the role of information technology in organizational processes" (p. 1). Taking that a genre is a style, often of literature, this simple introductory statement implies that the chosen research area adopts a textual form which is retextualized in the thesis. The use of the term genre indicates immediately that the thesis is presenting a different perspective than found at that time in information systems research.

The initial language of the thesis also breaks with tradition at that time in that the author uses first person when describing how the thesis will unfold. There is also discussion at many points throughout the thesis regarding what motivates the research, a highly subjective account when compared to the depersonalized accounts of information systems research in the journals at that time. Orlikowski uses the terms "we" and "ours" which invites the reader into a shared community, hence illustrating a postmodern voice and further denying the scientific genre of objectivity. Discussions are made of a "point of view" and a "standpoint" to show that the author is aware of the potential different readers of the thesis (p. 3).

After introducing the reader early in the thesis text to a subjective style, the latter part of this first chapter then reverts back to the more scientific reporting style. From section 1.3 to the end of the first chapter (page 6 through page 14), there is only one subjective reference to "I." More generally, the reference switches from the author as subject to the study as object using terms such as "this research," and "this research study." "The central concern of this research" is discussed instead of "I am concerned in carrying out this research with." Future research is discussed in relation to "findings established by this study" as if the study has a life independent of the author. Similarly, the description of the thesis is presented as chapters which conduct acts, e.g., "The chapter also presents a critique," thus depersonalizing the script and giving authority to the text rather than declaring that the author chooses to present a critique. Finally, this chapter discusses how "the research concludes" and the reader has lost the sense of direct interaction with the author.

A comparison between the objective reporting text and an alternative, subjective discourse, approach is shown below to illustrate the point.

Actual text (page 13): "This research study is premised on the notion that so little is known"

Alternative: "In carrying out this research, I was working on the notion that so little is known"

Actual text (page 13): "Future research will build on the framework and findings established in this study."

Alternative: "It may be that those who choose to enter this discourse in the future find some use for the interpretations and the frameworks which I have put forward in this ethnographic text."

Actual text (page 14): "The research then concludes with a discussion of the study's limitations"

Alternative: "As an arbitrary closure to our discourse, we can challenge the text to question the limitations of our interpretations"

The stylistic changes in this introductory chapter move from the subjective invitation from the author to the reader to take part in a discourse on the research puzzle, onto the objective presentation of the text as an authoritative and factual report on the knowledge argument. Even when the ethnographic fieldwork is discussed, this tension between two genres does not shift. The genre mix of adopting the stance of scientific reporting while using first person on occasion is retained throughout the thesis, at least until section 12.4 onward (final chapter, pages 439-446).

Up to the final sections, the text of the thesis reads as a realist tale, even though the first person is used on many occasions. This genre dominates despite the opening invitations and the use of first person. From page 439 onward, the genre moves away from a representative mode, through subjectivity and towards attempting to evoke impressions and experiences in the reader. The language changes occur when Orlikowski starts to reflect upon future research. The reader is given the impression that the author's controlled, objective reporting task is complete and so self-reflection and imagination can now be more freely expressed.

A small part of the final section of Orlikowski's ethnographic text is now deconstructed in order to show how a rereading of the text evokes an experience of the tensions between the various genres in her written text.

Orlikowski writes (all emphases are added by the author of this paper) "this study <u>represents</u> [*realist choice of word*] <u>but the first forays into a phenomenon</u> [*the romantic style of the artist*] that <u>I believe</u> [*subjective disclosure of the confessional*]." The thesis then continues with "<u>I intend</u> [*subjective disclosure of the confessional*] <u>pursuing</u> [*artist's genre: romantic metaphor of 'the chase'*] further indepth studies similar to this one to try and <u>obtain some verification</u> [*scientific reporting of the realist*] and <u>elaboration</u> [*the artist's genre of extension*] of <u>the findings</u> [*scientific genre – mining for the truth*] that <u>emerge</u> [*the artist's genre of interpretation*] from <u>this study</u> [*depersonalisation language of the scientific reporting of realism*] (page 439).

Orlikowski's thesis provides an evocative confusion for the interpretive reader. Despite the use of first person throughout the text, the thesis is presented as authoritative reporting. The thesis is a rational representation which then disturbs the reader by blending in the genre of subjectivity. The final section is the most evocative as the styles mingle and change. The reader is presented with a realist report of a situation which then switches and changes as the genre of artist emerges through an exploration of the implications of the text.

In order to situate the thesis as a text within a historical context, the deconstruction now extends beyond the text to seek to interpret how the contexts relevant to the writing of the thesis may have shaped and limited the genre switching.

3.1 History, Context and Text

Orlikowski's thesis was originally written in a particular time and shaped by related contexts. The contexts are discussed and then the deconstruction of the text is revisited to try and interpret why the thesis appears to work in different genres while being dominated by the realist's genre.

Context 1: Orlikowski's thesis is a Ph.D. thesis and, therefore, a traditional document in that it is written for an ancient purpose. That purpose has the full weight of many centuries of historical norms behind it, making it a highly authoritative norm. A Ph.D. is seen as a rite of passage where those who are nominated as gatekeepers for knowledge pass a judgment on the text (the thesis). That judgment will have wide-reaching repercussions on the future of the writer. The wider context of the writing of the thesis is the political context of academia.

Context 2: Orlikowski submitted the thesis as a candidate of the Leonard N. Stern School of Business, New York University. This prestigious business school is situated in a long established university with an international reputation for quality. The disciplinary implication is that a traditional university, and prestigious business school, would be likely to indicate to doctoral candidates a preference for traditional research during candidacy. Radical research would have to prove itself in a quality debate against traditional measures in order to ensure that high standards are maintained. Doctoral candidates, being disempowered novices, are least likely to be accepted for adopting radical research genres during a candidacy.

Context 3: The information systems research community in the United States did not appear to have a high acceptance of radical research methods in the late 1980s (Orlikowski and Baroudi 1991). Publications show that more radical approaches were accepted in European and Scandinavian writings rather than in American journals. A Ph.D. candidate is expected to publish from their research and so the choice to move outside of the traditional publication arena of the student's country would be a difficult one for a candidate to sustain. The publishing and career context in the United States is likely to caution the candidate against adoption of a radical voice.

Context 4: The chosen subject area of information systems and organizations does allow for a move into the area of organizational research. It is here that the study of organizational culture dominated in the late 1980s and that more radical critiques of the area were emerging (postmodernism was discussed in relation to gender and work, power relationships at work, etc.). Working in this context would allow the author of the thesis more freedom to explore the radical than in an information systems research context at that time.

The first three of these contexts are likely to have constrained Orlikowski's act of writing the Ph.D. text. This would be particularly true when any attempt is made to sustain a confessional or impressionist genre. The author was politically predisposed to occupy a realist stance while writing as a doctoral candidate in the historical context of the university, the country and the information systems research community. The fourth context allowed Orlikowski some room for exploration. It may even be that this context encouraged a more radical ethnographic voice in order to fit the thesis into the acceptable debate within anthropology and organizational research. The thesis represents a "radical" writing in a highly traditional knowledge domain and the montage of genres in the text evokes an image of the tension between the radical and the traditional.

4 CONCLUSION

The issue that arises for qualitative information systems research in using ethnography as an approach is whether the traditional is still dominating to an extreme. If it is, then the debates in anthropology in relation to ethnography which have occurred over the last two decades are unlikely to be allowed space in the discourse of information systems research. This means that any ethnographers who are also an information systems researchers are likely to live in a world of tensions when working on their texts. It also means that the ethnography-based information systems research produced is likely to be rejected by the source disciplines as naive, if not highly contentious.

Since 1988, there have been many instances of qualitative research which adopt ethnographic techniques being accepted into the information systems research domain. A highly selective few are referenced in this paper's introduction. The contexts in which Orlikowski's thesis was being developed are also likely to have experienced some form of historical shift. If these assumptions are reasonable, ethnography in information systems research will be open to the continuing adaptation of the debates from the source disciplines. If this is not the case, then information systems ethnographies are becoming disassociated from the source disciplines, indicating that information systems is a traditional discipline with a preference for a scientific genre as opposed to a postmodern genre. This would make the historical context difficult for those ethnographers within information systems research who would choose to adopt a postmodern stance, declaring the intention of the ethnographer in a more self-reflective and critical manner and attempting to deconstruct the political nature of ethnographic texts.

A critical or postmodernist stance challenges assumptions when looking at sense-making in organizations. Questions are asked such as

- What is the writer assuming an information system is seen to be in the context being visited?
- What are the selected assumptions regarding intervention in the issues in which the ethnographer may be involved?
- Does the ethnographer ignore the criticisms from individuals who tell them they are incorrect in their interpretations, instead choosing to argue for the discovery of a system of logic, claiming that this is essentially hidden from those within the situation?
- Are the representative ethnographers denying the images that they experience because they are in conflict with what is taken to be a logical system?
- Does the creative act of looking for alternative images seem too artistic, i.e., too far removed from scientific research?
- Does the ethnographer consider that a representation should be constructed rather than actively creating a discursive text as a discourse with those in the situation and future readers?

All these questions are challenges for information systems ethnographers who may find themselves in genre confusion. The extent of the persistence of that confusion is likely to depend upon the historical shifts of information systems research as a disciplinary domain of knowledge.

In this paper, a text has been deconstructed in order to show flux in historical genre changes. The main purpose has been to demonstrate the importance of history and context in the writing of an ethnographic text. Reading a text as a representation of knowledge, disembodied from history and context, is a highly restrictive form of inquiry. It limits the inquiry to a confined appreciation of the rationality of theoretical principles. These can only be fully appreciated when placed in historical contexts, that is, when appreciated as an essentially political act of writing. Critically reflecting on the historical contexts of a text allows for a fuller appreciation of both the concepts of that text and their wider relationship as expressed forms in an emerging and changing body of knowledge known as a discipline. Information systems ethnographies can be more fully appreciated for their contribution to the information systems discipline when interpreted both in history and in context. This includes a consideration of the histories and contexts of both writing an ethnography and of the subsequent readings of an ethnographic text.

It is hoped that we have succeeded in this paper in both our primary purpose of demonstrating the importance of historical contexts in ethnographic writing and in our secondary purpose of furthering the debates on ethnography in the adapted context of information systems research.

5 POSTSCRIPT

This postscript is written as a commentary on the historical and contextual shaping of this text to date. In writing this postscript, the intention is not to criticize the reviewers of the paper but to critically reflect on the discourse which has already occurred between the author, the reviewers as readers and the deconstructed/reconstructed text of this version of the paper.

The original draft of this paper was a mixture of the subjective and the objective voices. The reviews indicated a range of problems with the genre and voice of that script. It will be noticeable to the alert reader that the genre of this version of the paper is observational, seeking to avoid the obvious dominance of a postmodern voice, particularly as this is the preferred voice of the author. This has occurred through following all the indicated requirements of the reviewers. All references to authors' first names have been removed (as explicitly requested) as have all personalizations of the script. It is only in this postscript commentary that a critical self-reflection of this text as a discourse within a historical context has been attempted.

One review expressed strong value judgments against the critical postmodern genre discussed here. Value-laden statements were made which evoked a clear distaste for the postmodern stance, even though the reviewer is obviously well-versed in ethnography. The second review showed a concern with the difficulty of writing in a consistent genre while critically being reflective, recognizing how challenging self-reflective writing is and also providing useful and helpful comments. The third review was immediately accepting of the script while also fundamentally challenging assumptions in the text and providing helpful comments. Together, the three reviews demonstrated various degrees of unease in accepting a text which does not comply with an assumed tradition in interpretive information systems research. With respect to the reviewers, and in recognition of the socio-historical context in which I am currently writing, I have changed the obvious genre of the paper while retaining much of the challenge and debate. This indicates further concerns for ethnographers in information systems research who are keeping abreast with the debates in the source discipline while attempting to contribute to the information systems research discipline.

It is also recognized by myself, as author, that the original version of this paper was far less sophisticated than this version and that the change is due to the contributions from the reviewers. What has been removed, in all areas apart from this section, is the highly subjective and purposefully creative style of this author, an exploratory style which is preferred by the author as a postmodern writer and ethnographer.

A deconstruction of the original text, the reviews and the reconstructed text is likely to give a further indication of the 1996 historical context of interpretive information systems research in relation to debates on ethnography as is the placing of this text against other texts in the conference. This author suspects that a decalage of genres and tales will be present in the conference, indicating the fertile nature of the debates in this disciplinary area.

6 REFERENCES

Atkinson, P. (1992). *Understanding Ethnographic Texts.* Newbury Park, California: Sage Publications Qualitative Research Methods Series 25.

Avison, D. E., and Myers, M. D. (1995). "Information Systems and Anthropology: An Anthropological Perspective on IT and Organizational Culture." *Information Technology and People,* Volume 8, Number 3, pp. 43-56.

Baudrillard, J. (1988). *America.* London: Verso.

Clammer, J. (1984). "Approaches to Ethnographic Research." In R. F. Ellen (Editor), *Ethnographic Research: A Guide to General Conduct.* Londo: Academic Press, pp. 63-85.

Clifford, J., and Marcus, G. E. (Editors) (1986). *Writing Culture: The Poetics and Politics of Ethnography.* Berkeley: University of California Press.

Clough, P. T. (1992). *The Ends of Ethnography.* Newbury Park, California: Sage.

Cohen, A. P. (Editor) (1982). *Belonging: Identity and Social Organisation in British Rural Cultures.* Manchester, England: Manchester University Press.

Davies, L. (1993). "A Workshop on Two Techniques for Qualitative Analysis: Interviewing and Evaluation." In J. . DeGross, R. P. Bostrom, and D. Robey (Editors), *Proceedings of the Fourteenth International Conference on Information Systems,* December 5-8, Orlando, Florida, p. 399.

Davies, L. J., and Nielsen, S. (1992). "An Ethnographic Study of Configuration Management and Documentation Practices in an Information Technology Center." In K. E. Kendall, K. Lyytinen, and J. I. DeGross (Editors), *The Impact of Computer Supported Technology on Information Systems Development.* Amsterdam: North Holland Press, pp. 179-192.

Derrida, J. (1976). *Of Grammatology,* translated by G. Spivak. Baltimore: John Hopkins University Press.

Evans-Pritchard, E. (1940). *The Nuer: A Description of the Modes of Livelihood and Political Institutions of a Nilotic People.*

Foucault, M. (1979). *The History of Sexuality, Volume One: An Introduction.* Middlesex, England: Penguin.

Geertz, C. (1963). *Peddlers and Princes.* Chicago: University of Chicago Press.

Geertz, C. (1973). *The Interpretation of Cultures.* New York: Basic Books.

Geertz, C. (1983). *Local Knowledge: Further Essays in Interpretive Anthropology.* New York: Basic Books.

Geertz, C. (1988). *Works and Lives: The Anthropologist as Author.* Cambridge, England: Polity Press.

Hammersley, M. (1990). *Reading Ethnographic Research: A Critical Guide.* London: Longman.

Harvey, L. J., and Myers, M. D. (1995). "Scholarship and Practice: The Contribution of Ethnographic Research Methods to Bridging the Gap." *Information Technology and People,* Volume 8, Number 3, pp. 13-27.

Kroker, A., and Cook, D. (1988). *The Postmodern Scene: Excremental Culture and Hyper-Aesthetics*. Basingstoke, England: Macmillan Education.

Lawson, H. (1985). *Reflexivity: The Post-Modern Predicament*. London: Hutchinson.

Leach, E. (1976). *Culture and Communication*. Cambridge, England: Cambridge University Press.

Lee, A. (1992). "A Workshop on Two Techniques for Qualitative Data Analysis: Action Research and Ethnography." In J. I. DeGross, J. D. Becker, and J. J. Elam (Editors), *Proceedings of the Thirteenth International Conference on Information Systems,* December 13-16, 1992, Dallas, Texas, pp. 305-306.

Lee, A. (1993). "Electronic Mail as a Medium for Rich Communication: An Empirical Investigation Using Hermeneutic Interpretation." In J. I .DeGross, R. P. Bostrom, and D. Robey (Editors), *Proceedings of the Fourteenth International Conference on Information Systems*, December 5-8, 1993, Orlando, Florida, pp. 13-22.

Lyotard, J.-F. (1984). *The Postmodern Condition: A Report on Knowledge*. Manchester, England: Manchester University Press.

Lyotard, J.-F. (1989). "Defining the Postmodern." In L. Appignanesi (Editor), *Postmodernism: ICA Documents*. London: Free Association Books.

Marcus, G. (1980). "Rhetoric and the Ethnographic Genre in Anthropological Research." *Current Antrhopology*, Volume 21, pp. 507-510.

Marcus, G. E., and Fischer, M. J. (1986). *Anthropology as Cultural Critique: An Experimental Moment in the Human Sciences*. Chicago: The University of Chicago Press.

Myers, M. (1994). "A Disaster for Everyone to See: an Interpretive Analysis of a Failed IS Project." *Accounting, Management and Information Technology*, Volume 4, pp. 185-201.

Newman, M. (1989). "Revising Modernism, Representing Postmodernism." In L. Appignanesi (Editor), *Postmodernism: ICA Documents*. London: Free Association Books.

Orlikowski, W. J. (1988). "Information Technology in Post-Industrial Organizations: An Exploration of the Computer-Mediation of Production Work." Unpublished Ph.D. thesis, Leonard N. Stern School of Business, New York University, New York.

Orlikowski, W. J. (1991a). "Integrated Information Environment or Matrix of Control? The Contradictory Implications of Information Technology." *Accounting, Management and Information Technologies*, Volume 1, Number 1, pp. 9-42.

Orlikowski, W. J. (1991b). "A Workshop on Two Techniques for Qualitative Data Analysis: Analytic Induction and Hermeneutics." In J. I. DeGross, I. Benbasat, G. DeSanctis, and C. M. Beath (Editors), *Proceedings of the Twelfth International Conference on Information Systems*, December 16-18, 1991, New York.

Orlikowski, W. J. (1992a). "Learning from Notes: Organizational Issues in Groupware Implementation." *Proceedings of the Conference on Computer-Supported Cooperative Work (CSCW'92).* New York: ACM Press.
Orlikowski, W. J. (1992b). "The Duality of Technology: Rethinking the Concept of Technology in Organizations." *Organization Science*, Volume 3, Number 3, pp. 398-427.
Orlikowski, W. J., and Baroudi, J. J. (1991). "Studying Information Technology in Organizations: Research Approaches and Assumptions." *Information Systems Research*, Volume 2, Number 1, pp. 1-28.
Preston, A. M. (1991). "The 'Problem' in and of Management Information Systems." *Accounting, Management & Information Technologies*, Volume 1, Number 1, pp. 43-70.
Sahlins, M. (1972). *Stone Age Economics.* London: Tavistock.
Tyler, S. A. (1986). "Post-Modern Ethnography: From Document of the Occult to Occult Document." In J. Clifford and G. E. Marcus (Editors), *Writing Culture: The Poetics and Politics of Ethnography.* Berkeley: University of California Press.
Van Maanen, J. (1988). *Tales of the Field: On Writing Ethnography.* Chicago: The University of Chicago Press.
Walsham, G. (1995). "The Emergence of Interpretivism in IS Research." *Information Systems Research*, Volume 6, Number 4, pp. 376- 394.
Zuboff, S. (1988). *In the Age of the Smart Machine.* New York: Basic Books.

7 BIOGRAPHY

Lynda Harvey is professor of Information Systems and Head of the School of Information Systems at Curtin University of Technology in Perth, Australia. She specializes in the application of ethnographic research methods to the investigation of information systems in organizations. She has worked as a management consultant advising on change management issues as well as having been in academia in England and Australia for over twelve years. Lynda is associate editor of *Information Technology and People.* She has coauthored a book and numerous research papers on information systems management in organizations. She has been an active member of IFIP 8.2 for ten years.

13

Achieving the Research Goal with Qualitative Methods: Lessons Learned along the Way

E. M. Trauth
College of Business Administration
Northeastern University
Boston, Massachusetts 02115 USA
Tel: (617) 373-2759
E-mail: trauth@neu.edu

Abstract

The limitations of exclusive use of quantitative methods for social science research in the information systems field have led to increasing interest in qualitative alternatives. However, qualitative methods present their own challenges. The challenge addressed in this paper is that of keeping the methodology focused on the research goal rather than existing as an end in itself. Three different research projects employing qualitative methodologies carried out in three different countries – the United States, Ireland and The Netherlands – are used to explore some of the issues and lessons learned about the use of qualitative methods in pursuit of the research goal.

1 INTRODUCTION

As the limitations of quantitative methods for social science research in the information systems field have come to be recognized, increasing attention is being paid to the richness and variety available from the alternative approaches offered by qualitative methods. While qualitative methods address some of these limitations, they are not without their own issues which can impede the research effort. In the interests of contributing to our understanding of the benefits and challenges of qualitative research, in this paper I address some of the issues which I have faced in employing qualitative methods and in attempting to keep the methodology focused on the research goal. In doing so I draw upon three research projects from which I have extracted the challenges and lessons that are presented here. Because of the belief that the researcher cannot be removed from that which is being studied, I have written this paper in the first person.

2 THE USES OF QUALITATIVE METHODS

The issues and lessons that I present in this paper are those I have learned over the course of conducting several field studies that have employed qualitative methods wholly or in part. Before discussing these issues and lessons, I will briefly describe the three research projects and how qualitative methods were employed.

2.1 The Education of IS Professionals

In this study, our research team employed qualitative methods in conjunction with quantitative methods to explore recent changes in the IT industry and the ensuing fit between the skills and knowledge needed by industry and the academic preparation of IS professionals.[1] The role of qualitative methods was to complement quantitative methods. While we used qualitative methods throughout the project, we used them exclusively at the initial and concluding stages of this project. The methods included both face-to-face and telephone interviews, open forums and a series of focus groups. Additionally, the research team was constructed in such a way as to represent a variety of viewpoints on the IS field – professors, IS managers and consultants – so that we could also employ participant observation.

Following the dissemination and analysis of a mailed survey we engaged in member checking with representatives of the group from whom we were collecting data – chief information officers – by presenting our initial findings at forums in which we could collect feedback. Member checking, as explained by Ely et al. (1991) and Lincoln and Guba (1985) is a method of establishing credibility whereby the researchers check interpretations with the people who are being studied. We found member checking to be beneficial in helping us interpret our data. For example, there were times when the quantitative data yielded what appeared to be conflicting results. Through the devices of participant observation and member checking, we received help in deriving possible explanations for these contradictions. One obvious shortcoming of member checking arises when the respondents' and the researchers' interpretations are in conflict. This was not the case in this project, however. Rather, member checking helped to enhance interpretation of the results.

---

[1]A complete description of this study can be found in Trauth, Farwell and Lee 1993.

2.2 Societal Influences and Impacts of an Emerging Information Economy

In this second study, which is still in process, I am using qualitative methods exclusively and I am the sole investigator. I am examining Ireland's industrial policy of economic development through inward investment by information technology (IT) multinational firms as well as through the development of an indigenous IT sector. My interest is in examining the *influence* of societal factors on the shape of the IT sector in Ireland as well as the *impact* of this sector on Irish society.[2] Because of the scale and duration of this study, most of the examples I use in this paper are from this project.

I am studying the information workplace by means of participant observation of and interviews with IT workers and managers. In conducting this study, I am engaging in participant observation at both the micro and the macro levels (see Jorgensen 1989; Becker and Geer 1969). During the period in which I conducted the interviews with IT workers, I spent considerable time in fourteen IT firms in Ireland. Half of these are multinational (American) firms and half are Irish firms. On these site visits, I was able to observe the work environment, atmosphere and management style, all of which I was also discussing with the respondents during our interviews. This was the micro level of participant observation.

In order to place the information obtained from these interviews in a larger context, I also collected information about Irish culture, society, economy and public policy. I did so by means of participant observation,[3] interviews, and documentary analysis. At this macro level of participant observation, living and working in Ireland and communicating with Irish people enabled me to observe and directly experience Irish culture and to compare this information with what I was hearing in my interviews. Through subsequent time spent in Ireland, I have continued to observe Irish culture and society.[4] Additional relevant information about Ireland has been obtained from interviews with those outside the IT sector, public policy documents and social commentary found in Irish newspapers, magazines and books about Irish society,

---

[2]This study in its early stages was the subject matter of a paper presented at the 1990 IFIP Working Group 8.2 Conference on Research Methods (Trauth and O'Connor 1991). Descriptions of specific aspects of this study can be found in three additional papers by Trauth (1993, 1995, 1996b).

[3]During the first year of this research project in which the interviews with IT workers were conducted, I lived and taught in Ireland.

[4]As will be explained in more detail later, data collection is still going on through my return visits to Ireland and ongoing communication with selected informants. Thus participant observation is still occurring.

history and culture. This information has been used in determining which societal factors to explore in my interviews, to refine the coding categories and subcategories and to put into a broader perspective what I learned from my interviews.[5]

2.3 Influence of Societal Factors on the Diffusion of Information Technology

The third application of qualitative methodology was an exploration of the influencing role of societal factors in the diffusion of a new technology. The setting for this study was The Netherlands and the particular information technology was electronic data interchange (EDI) (Trauth, Derksen and Mevissen 1993). The purpose was to learn about the roles that public policy, national economy, culture and societal infrastructure can play in enhancing or inhibiting the organizational adoption of this particular information technology.

Our research team[6] used the qualitative methods of open-ended interview, participant observation and documentary analysis. The respondents in our study included technology vendors, corporate users, policy makers, and researchers and consultants who have worked on EDI implementations. I participated in each of the semi-structured interviews accompanied by one of my two coinvestigators.

3 METHODOLOGICAL CHALLENGES AND LESSONS LEARNED

In this section, I draw upon these three research projects to share some of the lessons learned during the actual application of qualitative methodologies. These lessons derive from the methodological challenges I encountered over the course of the projects. It is these challenges which I would like to address in this section. Content analysis of research journals which I maintained during the projects[7] revealed the presence of several methodological themes which emerged from my own research. The issues embedded in these themes arose throughout all phases of the research projects from model creation to data collection to data analysis to presentation of

---

[5]For example, in analyzing my data on women in the IT sector, I used documentary analysis to compare my findings with those of Irish researchers working in the area of IT and gender. I found that my conclusions concurred with those of one of the researchers and diverged from those of the other (see Harris 1989; Jackson and Barry 1989).

[6]The other two members of the team are Dutch.

[7]I did not maintain a research journal while conducting the study of the education of IS professionals. However, I did compile extensive notes on each phase of the data collection, both qualitative and quantitative, and noted issues that I encountered along the way.

results. To the extent that they are generalizable to other contexts, they can provide useful guidelines for those conducting similar research. The challenges can be conceptually organized around three themes: objectivity, flexibility and linearity. Within each are the lessons I have learned along the way.

3.1 Objectivity

This theme is about how my own training in positivist thinking and quantitative methodologies has served as an obstacle to my work. My own education taught me that objectivity is the hallmark of good science, that standing apart and conducting consistent measurements is the proper way to ensure validity. A dilemma I faced in these research projects was how to cope with the subjectivity that is an inherent part of qualitative methods. Part of this challenge was learning to be comfortable in my dual role. On the one hand, I needed to fully participate in my context in order to collect and interpret information. Yet I also felt the need to remain apart from this context in order to be able to note and process what I was experiencing and learning. I felt the need to maintain some psychic space around myself for reflection and analysis. It has been referred to in the literature of ethnography as *staying strange* (Hammersley and Atkinson 1983).[8]

Lesson 1: Becoming "Self Conscious" and Questioning Assumptions

In the case of the Irish study,I was an outsider to the culture who was collecting data for a limited period of time. Therefore, I was not able to identify or fully understand all the cultural nuances I was experiencing. Consequently, I have had to develop mechanisms for compensating in some way. To do this, I have sought alternative viewpoints on both the factors under study and on my interpretations. In this way I am seeking to evaluate both the data collected and the resulting interpretations and conclusions.

Additionally, remembering that the presence of the researcher influences the data collection, I sometimes wondered about the extent to which the respondents were simply telling me during interviews what they thought I wanted to hear. I wondered about the extent to which they were "packaging" their responses to me. I wondered how much I could believe what they were telling me. My response to this reliability issue has been to rely upon the consistency of responses across respondents and triangulation in order to ensure multiple perspectives on each topic (Jick 1979).

One source of alternative viewpoints on the phenomenon came through my social network. I found myself turning to various Irish and American friends and colleagues as a sounding board for the cultural factors I was identifying and exploring. Even though – or perhaps especially because – these individuals tended not to work in the IT sector, they were able to provide different perspectives than those offered by

---

[8]I will return to the controversy about this notion in the Epilogue.

respondents or from those I was developing. When it came time to interpret and present the results of my analysis, once again I have relied upon a form of member checking. I have had informal conversations and have sought feedback on paper drafts from colleagues in Ireland and in the Irish studies community in the US.

A related issue is the need to constantly question myself as a source of data, to question my own assumptions. This heightened sensitivity to context helped me to develop of posture of being "self conscious," to use the words of a British respondent who was working at an American firm in the west of Ireland. He said that he is self conscious in the sense that he reflects on his reactions. Since he had only recently come to the Republic from Northern Ireland he was very attuned to the cultural experiences I was having. Indeed, several times throughout my visit at his firm he would stop by my interview room to share his thoughts with me.

Halfway through my research year in Ireland, I was asked to give a research seminar at the university where I taught. I reluctantly agreed. My hesitation was that I had just begun to conduct my interviews and felt that I had little by way of valuable conclusions or insights to offer. The experience impressed upon me the importance of questioning my own assumptions. The first assumption to be questioned was that giving a seminar would be a one-way communication event. Instead, the experience became an opportunity for me to articulate some of my assumptions and initial perceptions and to receive feedback on them. While the audience of Irish faculty and students was not hostile, neither was it overly supportive of what I was doing.[9] It was not until they learned more about the thrust of my research, that they began to set aside their own assumption that the purpose of my research was to glamorize the presence of American multinational firms in Ireland. Their challenging questions influenced me to question what I was thinking and assuming and perceiving as much as I may have influenced them.

In the case of my research in The Netherlands, I did not have the same issues to overcome. My task was easier in some respects and more challenging in others. For several reasons I remained more in the outsider role. Since I do not speak Dutch and because I lived in The Netherlands for a shorter period of time than I did in Ireland, I was not as acclimated into the Dutch culture as I was in Ireland. In addition, because I was working with two individuals from that culture I could rely more on their perceptions to help me interpret data. On the other hand, I had to be alert to the biases and assumptions they brought to bear on their interpretations. In the IS education project, there were three different cultures represented in the project: the academic, the consulting and the practitioner. Throughout the phases of our research project, we used our different positions in the IS field to challenge each others' assumptions, interpretations and conclusions.

---

[9]At the time, there was an antimultinational sentiment in some quarters of Irish society and this viewpoint was represented in the audience in attendance at my seminar.

Lesson 2: Getting Close to People

Early on in my year in Ireland, I noted in my journal concern that I was perhaps enjoying myself too much and wondered whether I was staying distant (aloof was how I termed it) enough during the interview process. As the year wore on, I became more comfortable with the idea of enjoying myself during my research and even becoming friendly with some of the respondents in my study. However, as I became more comfortable with the people and the country, I continued to be aware of the issue of just how familiar I should become.

One respondent – an American woman – observed that the sense of familiarity can be deceptive. She pointed to the absence of markers of cultural difference (such as race or language) that signal foreignness. Hence, while I may have become more comfortable with Ireland and Irish people, they may not have felt the same toward me. One Irish respondent with whom I spoke toward the end of my year told me that there probably was a period of assessment during which colleagues and acquaintances were checking my values to see if they fit with theirs, observing how I reacted in certain situations, and identifying my personality traits to see if they were acceptable.

During the last month of my stay in Ireland, I had two occasions on which I wondered if I had crossed the line and become too familiar in my surroundings. In both instances, I had engaged in a lively discussion in which I exchanged views about such charged topics as gender, contraception, abortion and religion with individuals with whom I had spent a fair amount of time over the course of the year. In noting their reactions to my views when we differed, I was brought back once again to the issue of balancing distance and familiarity. I concluded that achieving the proper balance has both ethical and methodological dimensions.

When I reflected upon my experience of interacting with people whose views were different from mine, I noted that when these others controlled the flow of information, when I was primarily a passive listener, our interactions were fine. As I became more comfortable with these people and began to open up and share more of my own personality with them, I felt a tension develop. As I was becoming closer to these people as friends, I wanted to reveal more of myself to them. In reflecting on these two situations, I wondered (methodologically) whether I had been too much my own person and not enough the researcher, and as a result, was running the risk of alienating these informants. But I also wondered (ethically) whether it was proper to be so much the researcher in my interactions that these aspects of my persona had not emerged sooner.

3.2 Flexibility

Two months into my year in Ireland, I noted in my research journal that I felt I was moving about aimlessly and had yet to establish a coherent research design. I expressed discomfort about my research process that seemed to be out of control. I recorded similar sentiments at the early stages of my Dutch research. The important lesson I learned is that, when using qualitative methods, the more alien the context, the more important flexibility becomes. I learned that the researcher has to be prepared to embrace the data when it is presented regardless of the location, intention or source.

Lesson 3: Giving Up Control

In the Irish project, one example of not controlling the time or location of research occurred through my encounters with a couple of Irish families who befriended me. I was frequently invited to their houses for a Sunday afternoon. When I would arrive, I never quite knew what new things about Ireland I would learn or how I would be learning them. I just began to expect the unexpected. I had similar experiences in The Netherlands. Since my study of the diffusion of EDI involved examining aspects of Dutch society, relevant data was obtained during a weekend outing or during a conversation in the cafe after work or in the middle of work on another project.

Another time that I had to cope with not being in control was during my on-site interviews in Ireland. My initial reaction when I found that there were questions I did not get to ask was to wonder if I should perhaps establish a priority among my list of items and adhere rigidly to it. Alternatively, I thought perhaps I should just be more flexible and allow the flow of the discussion to guide me. I gradually developed a comfort level with doing the latter. Entries in my Irish research journal throughout the interview process registered concern about wanting to control the interview process, to make certain I was covering all the topics during each interview. I was feeling obsessed about the methodology. What I was struggling with was the acknowledgment that – contrary to what I may have been taught or how research projects are written up for publication – the qualitative data collection process was not something over which I had complete control. I would need to go back and reassess the data over and over again. If I tried to control the responses too much, I would perhaps get *data I sought* but I would not have the *information I needed.* I would be missing the opportunity to gain unplanned insights. Indeed, several cultural factors that became part of my study were initially introduced by the respondents themselves.[10]

Allowing the respondent rather than the interview protocol to drive the discussion was very useful particularly before I had a complete list of the societal factors I wanted to study. I had to remind myself that the number of respondents – eighty-five – ensured that in totality all of the topics would be covered, that consistency would assert itself in the end. However, at times I had to resist the urge to have breadth of treatment at the expense of depth. I sometimes had to fight against the urge to cover all the topics superficially rather than fewer topics in greater depth.

---

[10]Examples are "This is Ireland," social class, island mentality, British management style, attitude toward time, the family.

Since I was able to apply to my research in The Netherlands the methodological lessons I was learning in Ireland,[11] I had less anxiety about consistency across each respondent. In fact, covering all the items in the interview protocol during the Dutch interviews was more the exception than the norm!

Lesson 4: Always Working

By giving up control over the circumstances of data collection, I soon recognized that I was always working. In one entry in my Irish research journal, I noted that during a dinner party I had obtained valuable background information about a particular firm I wanted to include in my study. In wishing that I had brought along my tape recorder, I was recognizing that my research goes on continuously. I noted that I had to become more prepared to take advantage of all opportunities to learn more about what I was studying.

For example, during one of my early on-site interviews, the Irish human resources manager at one of the American firms was stiff and formal during our conversation in his office. I had difficulty during the interview getting him to open up about his cultural impressions. He seemed to want to stick with official law and policy. At the end of the conversation, over coffee in the canteen, he loosened up considerably. (I was also not taking notes.) After being very careful about his cultural commentary in his office, in the canteen he proceeded to share a variety of impressions about Irish culture and even went so far as to provide cultural commentary about people in other European countries! This particular experience sent a strong message to me that I did not control where or when the "research" would occur and that I needed to be ready to seize the opportunity when it arose.

The reality of always working means that a conversation in a restaurant or a pub, cafe or dinner party is quite often a source of research data. One day, an Irish faculty colleague invited me to join her and a guest speaker in her class at the local pub. Her guest speaker is an Irish film maker and I was invited not because of my research project but simply because I was friendly with this colleague. As it turned out, this man was able to offer me considerable cultural insights that were quite valuable to my research.

In The Netherlands, I had the experience of finding useful information for my EDI study while I was engaged in other work. One time I was invited to give a presentation at another Dutch university on some research I had done on a totally different topic. During conversation with the faculty members afterward, I learned that one of their colleagues could provide very valuable information regarding our research project. Eventually, this person was added to our set of respondents.

An extension of always working is taking advantage of social networks both to find contacts for interviews and for purposes of cultural observations. In Ireland, one rich

---

[11]I began the research in Ireland in 1989 and undertook the research in The Netherlands in 1992.

source of research contacts happened quite unexpectedly through my participation in the American Women's Club. This organization is comprised of two types of women. One type is the wife of a multinational executive. These women tend to be in Ireland three to five years while their husbands are setting up the subsidiary of an American IT firm in Ireland. The other type of woman is married to an Irish man and lives permanently in Ireland. The initial contact at several of the firms at which I conducted interviews occurred at social functions of this organization. The Irish people I met through dinner parties and other social functions were a rich source of cultural commentary and counterpoint to my developing impressions. In The Netherlands, my position on the faculty of a university helped me to identify respondents. Several recommendations about respondents came from faculty colleagues or others at the university where I taught.

Lesson 5: Collecting both Data and Metadata

Early into my round of interviews at the IT firms in Ireland, I had an experience which pointed out the importance of having sensitivity to contextual metadata. In reflecting on an interview with an Irish worker at an American plant, I noted that I had to be vigilant in order to be able to respond to the exigencies of the particular context I was in at any given moment. In this particular situation, the respondent was – at age forty-eight – the oldest worker at the plant. He was nervous upon first meeting me. As the human resource manager introduced me and briefly explained my research project, the man stood there shifting his weight from one leg to the other, pulling out of the back pocket of his jeans and fumbling with a rolled up copy of the three page summary of my research project which I had sent to the managing director. As I watched this man, I tried to put myself in his place. He had been made redundant three times already and had only been at this particular firm a matter of months. Now here he is, being asked by senior (American) management to talk with this American woman! A quick assessment of the situation led me to decide not to even *ask* if I could use a tape recorder, something I normally did at the beginning of each interview.

A similar situation which called for heightened sensitivity to context occurred at another American firm. This firm was experiencing financial difficulties and redundancies were a distinct possibility. In both my collection and interpretation of data from this firm, it was important for me to recognize that this atmosphere of diminished resources and layoffs was generating considerable insecurity which could, in turn, influence respondents' perceptions and be reflected in answers given during the interviews.

Perhaps the most poignant experience that I had with data and metadata was the interaction that I had with several female respondents. The type of interaction I had with several of the women whom I interviewed was both a surprise and a puzzlement. As a rule, I found the interviews with female respondents more difficult than those with males. Some women were merely abrupt and not inclined to be introspective about cultural factors. A few bordered on resistant. One woman bristled in the course of my collecting background demographic data when I asked what part of Ireland she was from: "I thought this wasn't going to be anything personal!" she replied. I was aware of working extremely hard to get her to open up to me. I believed myself to be successful when she began to smile part way through the interview. By the end, she said maybe she would be in Boston some day and I could sign a copy of the book I was going to write. Another woman kept me waiting quite a while beyond the agreed upon interview time of five o'clock. When I was finally escorted into her office, she looked at her watch and informed me that she could only spare thirty minutes (after both she and her boss agreed beforehand that we could talk for ninety). Through all of these interactions, I came to recognize that observing the respondent and the context during the interview process provided a rich source of metadata to accompany the data I was collecting.

3.3 Linearity

This last theme encompasses issues that speak to the way in which the methods are applied. The challenges associated with linearity are about letting the research flow naturally, as it needs to in pursuit of the research goal. They are about letting the research goal determine the way in which the research is conducted. While this may seem like a fairly obvious point, I encountered several temptations and pressures grounded in "conventional" scholarship to do otherwise. This theme contains lessons for definition of scope, sources of data and identification of respondents, data collection and analysis procedures, and coding schemes.

Lesson 6: Fitting the Method to the Model
The research project I conducted in Ireland was one that I had waited several years to undertake. From the beginning, I was very clear about the research goal – to depict and analyze the emerging information economy in Ireland – even if I wasn't completely sure how I would go about reaching it. As I was working to develop my research model to fit that goal, I encountered well-meaning suggestions to do something different. This advice seemed to be driven more by methodological convenience than by a desire to help me further the research objective I had in mind.

According to Yin (1989), a case study is an empirical inquiry that investigates a contemporary phenomenon within its real-life context, when the boundaries between phenomenon and context are not clearly evident and when multiple sources of evidence are used. My project fit this definition in that I intended to use on-site interview and observational data as well as internal and published documents. Unlike typical business case studies, however, in which a *single company* is the object of study, the scope of my case study was to be much larger in that it would be an *industry-level* case. In addition, I would be employing ethnographic techniques. However, since conventional IS case research is conducted with the unit of analysis being a company, conventional wisdom (and scholarship) was directing me toward that end. This occurred in the form of well-meaning advice given to me as I was trying to develop my research model. Rather than try to help me develop the methodology that would enable me to achieve the research goal that was of interest to me, I was advised to pursue other research goals in the interest of methodological ease. In one instance, I was asked to change the title of a paper I had written because a reviewer claimed my scope was too large to be considered a case study.

I do not believe I would have been able to obtain the rich viewpoints that I have received had I used the smaller scope of a single firm case study. When I explained to colleagues that my interest was the IT sector as a whole, not a single company within it, I was advised to send a mailed questionnaire to a large number of firms. Although this option is one way of addressing the scope aspect of my research, it would not have furthered my research goal since the set of factors that I wanted to examine needed to be developed in grounded fashion (Strauss 1987). At this point – having identified and documented the societal factors of interest – I could perhaps engage in an in-depth case study of workers at a single IT company and examine those factors in action. If I were interested in a different outcome, I could have conducted a mailed survey of a large number of firms. The picture I wanted to paint, however, required a qualitative approach and a canvas as large as the entire country. In my view, this lesson is especially important because it has implications not only for the conduct of our own research but also how we educate and advise future scholars. The message is to make sure not to get the (methodological) cart before the horse (research goal).

Lesson 7: Beginning at the Beginning

Early in my career, I had a conversation with a more senior colleague about a research project I had in mind that had to do with studying the relationship between information policy at the national level and corporate policy. He began to quiz me about how I would measure the "relevant variables." When I told him that I didn't think I knew how to think about his project in terms of measurable variables, he replied, "Well, then you're not yet ready to begin the research."

I had obviously internalized this admonition to some degree because about a third of the way through the year I lived in Ireland I was feeling frustrated with myself that so much time had gone by and I was just then starting my "research." I was thinking that the research would begin when the on-site interviews commenced. I held this view because I defined research as the conduct of the formal interviews. What I came to recognize is that research began the moment I first started to explore my themes. Gradually I became comfortable acknowledging that generating the questions in grounded fashion through participating in and observing the culture was also part of the research.

Some time after returning from my year in Ireland, as I was working on a paper about the IS education project, I received external validation of the lesson I had learned in Ireland. In reviewing our paper, the journal referees suggested that in writing up the results of our survey, we should reorient the paper to include more of the initial, qualitative results. Up until this point, we had viewed that work as preliminary or background research only.

Half of the lesson, here, is recognizing that while different phases may require different methods, research begins at the beginning. The other half of the lesson is that the research does not end with the analysis of data. The final piece is returning to the field for contextual validity. The reason for this final stage is that processed data can result in different interpretations. As a researcher, my assumptions, biases and motivations all influence the way in which I make meaning from that processed data. Going back to the context to receive feedback on my interpretations serves to enhance validity. In the case of the IS education project, we conducted structured feedback sessions in order to present our results, give our interpretation of the data, collect feedback on those interpretations and solicit alternative interpretations. In the case of the Irish project, I am employing two mechanisms for collecting this contextual feedback. One has been to present my findings to Irish studies scholars for critical review. The other is circulating drafts of my written work to selected respondents and other individuals for commentary.

Lesson 8: Staying True to the Research Goal

In the case of all three of these research projects, the identification and selection of respondents for the studies was something I expected to be rather straightforward; it was not. Because of the unexpected nature of the data collection in the Irish study, I not only changed my definition of when research begins or occurs but also who comprised the set of respondents. In the study, some after-the-fact inclusion of respondents occurred when I recognized that while a given exchange may not have been planned, it nevertheless provided insights comparable to those that were. For example, during one of my days spent interviewing at an American firm, a worker who I was not scheduled to interview had been designated by management as my luncheon companion. As we ate, I told her about my project and she, in turn, told me about her background, her work history, and gradually began to offer unsolicited comments on the items I was investigating in my interviews! Similar experiences happened in the Dutch study when casual conversations about electronic commerce or technology diffusion in The Netherlands turned into insightful comments directly relevant to my research project.

Once the on-site corporate interviews in Ireland were completed and I returned to the US for the data analysis phase, I encountered still other challenges to remaining true to my research goal. This new challenge had to do with how I would carry out the content analysis of the data. In considering my options for data analysis, one was to employ software that would search for certain keywords taken from the interview protocol and then retrieve surrounding text. To go that route would have considerably shortened the lengthy process of the alternative – and chosen – method of dividing transcripts into meaningful units or content chunks, creating coding schemes, coding each of these content chunks, and then loading them into a database for retrieval. There are two problems with using the first approach, however. The first is that the keyword is not as inclusive as the concept underlying it. For example, one of the themes about which I spoke with respondents is social class. This is an important factor in that social class governs in large part who goes to college to get the credentials to work in the information sector. The problem, however, was that people rarely used the words "social class" when speaking about it. Instead, they would comment indirectly by such means as mentioning a certain part of town as an indicator of social class. In some cases, as in this instance, I was soon able to discern during the interview that they were using code for social class. In other cases I was not. At the beginning of each interview, I collected data about the respondent's background including education. For quite a while I was puzzled by respondents' repeated reference to the particular religious order of nuns or priests who taught them until I learned that a Jesuit school, for example, had higher social standing than one run by the Christian Brothers! Thus, a significant amount of valuable data richness would have been sacrificed had I chosen the keyword route.

Once I had determined to code each content chunk for relevant categories, the next decision was which categories to use. My choice was either to use categories present in the interview protocol or to let the categories evolve from the data. I chose the latter. My rationale was that to do otherwise would be to overlook some of the unintended voices and messages present in my interviews. Maintaining consistency across transcripts when using evolving categories for data analysis, however, became a new challenge throughout the coding process. In the end I was satisfied with the meaning conveyed in the categories and the keywords.

4 CONCLUSION

After systematic reflection on my use of qualitative methods in these studies, I cannot say I have derived definitive answers about the rules of proper behavior in every situation. However, I have come to some conclusions which have influenced subsequent research. One is that as a researcher I cannot be removed from the context, nor should I want to be. I cannot be totally outside the setting and yet be successful in my research. In the case of the Irish study, several of the respondents have become close acquaintances; a few have become friends. To generalize from my own experience, I believe the answer is not for the researcher to remain apart from the context but rather to embrace it. At the same time, however, the researcher should constantly be conducting self examination with respect to assumptions, biases and motivations being used to interpret data; should make use of multiple perspectives and sources of data – and be open as to their source; and should obtain feedback while in the process of both collecting the data and interpreting it. Collecting and analyzing the data in this way speaks to the need for an iterative rather than a linear approach to the conduct of the research. This suggests that the neat outline be replaced with an evolving mosaic which is intended to serve the research model, not a predetermined methodology. I have learned that these approaches have been necessary if I am to achieve the goal for which the research was undertaken.

The challenge and the reward for letting the research goal drive the methodology is, for me, embodied in the interview experience I had with a young Irish woman who works for an Irish software firm. I first met her at the company site to introduce myself and schedule an interview. First, she wanted to think about my interview questions in advance of meeting with me, so I gave her a copy of the interview form. Then she suggested we meet outside work. I agreed and asked where she would like to meet and when, thinking she would suggest some coffee shop. Instead, she suggested a Dublin pub at six o'clock the following week. She then mentioned the names of three professors at the university where I taught and said they were all left of center in their political views.

As I prepared for my interview with her, I tried to sort through all the metadata contained in that initial conversation. One interpretation was that I was being tested. Perhaps her comments about the left-leaning tendencies of the professors was a test of my willingness and ability to set aside my American-business-professor persona and accommodate to a different setting. Alternatively, the interview-in-a-pub could have been an *acknowledgment* of my acceptance, given the focal point of pubs in Irish culture. Not knowing for sure, I substituted my normal interview attire for blue jeans, entered the pub and waited with a glass of Guinness in hand for my respondent. She brought along her sister and two young men who had been classmates in university. Then, for the next five and a half hours, I listened while the four of them talked quite frankly about Ireland, the culture, the IT sector and themselves. I ran the tape recorder until the tape ran out. In the semi-light with my Guinness glass constantly being refilled by my respondents, I took notes furiously until my notepaper ran out and I had to resort to writing on the back of my interview form! As I left that pub, I was certain that I had not worked as hard in any other interview, yet it was also one of the most rewarding experiences and clearly one of the richest interviews of the entire research project.

What I expected to learn as a result of my use of qualitative methods in these various research projects was about the subject matter at hand. What I did not expect was the additional learning about methodology and myself. The employment of these methods has been an opportunity for personal growth in helping me to question my assumptions and challenge my approaches. It has made me much more aware of the organic nature of change in general and learning in particular. Above all, I have been reminded that, as a researcher, not only do I not have all the answers, I don't know all the questions either.

5 EPILOGUE

As I have pointed out in this paper, one technique I have employed is member checking. With this technique, during the final stages of a research project the researcher shares preliminary insights and conclusions with either the participants in the study or those in a position to provide informed comments. Insofar as this paper represents a "research project" about methodology, it seems appropriate to obtain and respond to feedback about it. I would, therefore, like to respond to some of the questions about my methods and how I apply them that have not been completely addressed in the body of this paper. Some of these questions were raised in reviews of this paper; others have come from questions and comments during previous conference presentations. I have organized my responses to these questions around two themes: strangeness and reliability. In many respects, they derive from the same point: the unstable ground of subjectivity.

5.1 Strangeness

This theme is about conducting research as a stranger to the culture. It is a highly charged topic that evokes images of colonialism in which the stranger comes from the outside to "do" a foreign culture. I have addressed some of this in Lesson 2. But I would like to respond more fully to the notion of an outsider to the culture under study. To begin, I would like to quote from a paper which I delivered to a community of Irish scholars in 1996.

> In looking for some reference in my bookshelves recently, I happened upon a particular copy of a professional journal in my field of business information systems that caught my attention. The article was about the potential for gender-based discriminatory practices in information systems management and was written by two men. As a woman, my first reaction was, "Right! What can these two male authors tell me about gender discrimination in my field? As men, how would they be able to understand and represent the female experience?" Those silent words no sooner left my unmoving lips than I recalled the paper I was planning to write for this Irish studies conference on the topic of crossing cultures. In quick succession, my thoughts turned to an experience I recalled having just a couple of weeks after I had embarked upon a major research project in Ireland.
>
> Full of enthusiasm for my research project, I paid a courtesy call on a professor who was known to one of my Irish studies colleagues in the States whom I was told might be able to help me identify contacts for my research. After I gave a brief overview of my research project, he sat back in his chair, looked at me and said politely yet bluntly, "I don't know what you intend to do that's new. Everything you want to do has been done before." As a teacher I am used to thinking on my feet so I managed to recover from this pinprick to my research bubble. But during the ensuing months as I refined my research thesis and methodology, I was haunted by his remarks. By the time I embarked upon the on-site data collection, I had taken on those words as a personal challenge: to prove that although I was an outsider to the culture, nevertheless, I had something to contribute to the developing story of Ireland's information economy. [Trauth 1996a]

It seems to me that there are two aspects to the notion of strangeness that must be addressed. One is the justification for one who is not of the culture conducting a study of it. The best justification that I can give is that, in being alien to the culture, I am able to see assumptions and behaviors that might be more difficult for those in the culture to see. If one rejects the viewpoint that those outside the culture or group have no right to study it, then the challenge becomes one of capitalizing upon the strengths of being an outsider while being ever sensitive to the pitfalls of conducting contextual research as a stranger to it. So, having embarked upon a study of another culture, the next issue is whether and how much distance to maintain between myself and what I am studying.

As I have demonstrated throughout this paper, I have made a conscious effort to embrace the contexts in which I was conducting my qualitative research. Yet it is also true that I would never understand that context in the way that an insider would. My response has been to acknowledge this "otherness" and to take advantage of its benefit in helping me to maintain the analytical distance I needed. Hammersley and Atkins have talked about this "strangeness" as the hallmark of good ethnography.

> The comfortable sense of being "at home" is a danger signal. . . . There must always remain some part held back, some social and intellectual "distance." For it is in the "space" created by this distance that the analytic work of the ethnographer gets done. Without that distance, without such analytic space, the ethnography can be little more than the autobiographical account of a personal conversation. [Hammersley and Atkins 1983, p. 102]

In a later work, Hammersley (1992) acknowledges that, with the movement of ethnography toward relativism in recent years, this requirement for maintaining distance has diminished.

For my own part, I have come to see maintaining some distance as a necessary part of being self aware. This is not to say I did not participate fully in the context I was studying. Rather, to me it means attempting to bring into consciousness the emotional and intellectual reactions to experiences and observations. I interpret – and believe the value of – "strangeness" to be maintaining a psychic space in which I can make myself consciously aware of things that others might take for granted. In rereading methods books about this topic, I saw analogies with therapy, poetry and photography. In all these instances, one is totally "in the moment" yet also retains a space from which to frame the setting and reflect on it consciously in order to understand psychological forces, create a poem or take a photograph. My objective in maintaining strangeness is to engage in introspection while still engaging in routine activities.

5.2 Reliability

A second major theme, and one with which anyone doing qualitative research may be confronted, is establishing reliability. To those schooled in positivistic methods, the highest ideal of research is achieved through objective, value-free data collection and analysis which subsequent researchers can repeat with consistent results. The subjective nature of qualitative methods, in general, and ethnographic ones, in particular, therefore, calls for a totally different perspective on reliability. First, what does reliability mean in an ethnographic study? To me it means producing results that can be trusted and establishing findings that are meaningful and of interest to the reader. One measure is whether those familiar with the context can recognize in the results their own world of experience, whether the story being told "rings true" to them.

One hurdle I had to overcome in developing a comfort level with qualitative methods was fully accepting the fact that, as an observer, I can never be totally objective and judgment free. What I *can* do, however, is attempt to make observations without reading in my own biases and answers. Additionally, I can record my own introspection along with my interview and observational data. In my qualitative studies I accomplish this through journal writing. In my Irish study, I maintained two journals: a research journal and a personal journal. In the research journal, I recorded thoughts, feelings, experiences and anxieties more or less related to the research experience. Maintaining a personal journal is an ongoing activity in my life but one about which I am more diligent during foreign travel. When I embarked upon the research project, I had not expected my personal journal to be relevant to the research effort. But, then, I also didn't expect to be engaged in my "research" day and night either! Because of what I learned in my Irish experience, I maintained only one journal when I was conducting my research in The Netherlands.

In addition to developing self awareness about my biases, three other methods I have employed to establish reliability are consistency, triangulation and member checking. Consistency across respondents occurs when all or some group of respondents express similar views. On only a few occasions has there been complete consistency across respondents. What is more important to me is that groups of individuals represent consistent responses. When this occurs, I have greater confidence in my interpretations. Triangulation is employed to build confidence in my interpretation as well as to help me understand anomalies. One such anomaly occurred with respect to the Irish attitude toward education. I was having some difficulty in understanding the nature of responses to this question until I was able to place them in a larger context that included emigration patterns. When I did this, I could begin to see consistent responses emerging. A part of triangulation is also my participant observation. When my observations differ from what I am told in interviews, it gives me pause to consider the reason. In some cases I have been able to understand the anomaly; other times I cannot and must simply acknowledge the contradictions.

A final method for establishing reliability is member checking. Strictly speaking, this means going back to check interpretations with those who are being studied. I have employed it in a looser sense. As I discussed in the section on strangeness, since I am not of the Irish culture I am very sensitive about my perceptions of it. My interest in member checking is not so much to have the respondents agree with my perceptions as it is to have those of Ireland or more knowledgeable than me about the country evaluate my interpretations. Those from whom I have sought feedback include Irish studies scholars, individuals in Ireland who are not in the IT sector, and a few respondents with whom I have developed a personal relationship. My interest is in their reactions to the way I have interpreted cultural influences and impacts. In general, this has been a very affirming experience. I have had one experience, however, which raises an issue about this technique: what to do when the "members" disagree with your interpretation. This occurred with respect to a paper I wrote about women in the Irish IT sector. When I delivered the paper at an Irish studies conference, one Irish woman in the audience had a strong and negative reaction to my interpretations. Her response caused me to rethink what I had written. I went back to my transcripts and observational data and I thought again about how I reached the interpretations presented in my paper. In the end, I remained with my original interpretations. However, in the process I also discussed this experience with some of those who had witnessed it (there was a large group in attendance). In these discussions, I received help in understanding why this audience member might have reacted as she did. I also make a point of talking with this individual later in the conference. While I did not change my interpretations, the insights I gained did influence me to rephrase some aspects of them in later writings. In the Irish studies community, I have an ongoing support group that reads my work and offers critical commentary. I have found their comments to be invaluable in my efforts to establish reliability and personal confidence in my interpretations.

6 REFERENCES

Becker, H.,and Geer, B. (1969). "Participant Observation: A Comparison." In G. J. McCall and J. L. Simmons (Editors), *Issues in Participant Observation*. New York: Random House.

Ely, M.; Anzul, M.; Friedman, T.; Garner, D.; and Steinmetz, A. M. (1991). *Doing Qualitative Research: Circles within Circles*. New York: The Farmer Press.

Hammersley, M. (1992). *What's Wrong with Ethnography? Methodological Explorations*. New York: Routledge.

Hammersly, M., and Atkinson, B. (1983). *Ethnography Principles in Practice*. London: Tavistock Publishers, Ltd.

Harris, L. (1989). "Women's Response to Multinationals in County Mayo." In D. Elson and R. Pearson (Editors), *Women's Employment in Multinationals in Europe*. London: Macmillan Press, Ltd., pp. 144-164.

Jackson, P., and Barry, U. (1989). "Women's Employment in the Republic of Ireland: The Creation of a New Female Labour Force." In D. Elson and R. Pearson (Editors), *Women's Employment in Multinationals in Europe*. London: Macmillan Press, Ltd., pp. 38-59.

Jick, T. (1979). "Mixing Qualitative and Quantitative Methods: Triangulation in Action." *Administrative Science Quarterly*, Volume 24, Number 4, pp. 602-611.

Jorgensen, D. L. (1989). *Participant Observation: A Methodology for Human Studies*. Newbury Park, California: Sage Publications.
Lincoln, Y., and Guba, E. (1985). *Naturalistic Inquiry*. Beverly Hills, California: Sage Publications.
Strauss, A. L. (1987). *Qualitative Analysis for Social Scientists*. New York: Cambridge University Press.
Trauth, E. M. (1993). "Educating Information Technology Professionals for Work in Ireland: An Emerging Post-industrial Country." In M. Khosrowpour and K. Loch (Editors), *Global Information Technology Education: Issues and Trends*. Harrisburg, Pennsylvania: Idea Publishing Co., pp. 205-233.
Trauth, E. M. (1995). "Women in Ireland's Information Industry: Voices from Inside." *Eire-Ireland*, Volume 30, Number 3 (Fall), pp. 133-150.
Trauth, E. M. (1996a). "Issues with Ethnographic Research across Cultures: The Dilemma of Staying 'Strange' during Participant Observation." Annual Meeting of the American Conference on Irish Studies, Carbondale, Illinois. April.
Trauth, E. M. (1996b). "Societal Impact of an Imported IT Sector on Newly Industrializing Countries: Lessons from Ireland." In E. M. Roche and M. J. Blaine (Editors), *Information Technology Development and Policy: Theoretical Perspectives and Practical Challenges*. Aldershot, United Kingdom: Ashgate Publishing Ltd., pp. 245-261.
Trauth, E. M.; Derksen, F. E.; and Mevissen, H. M. (1993). "The Influence of Societal Factors on the Diffusion of Electronic Data Interchange in the Netherlands." In D. Avison, J. Kendall and J. I. DeGross (Editors), *Information Systems Development: Human, Social and Organizational Aspects*. Amsterdam: North-Holland.
Trauth, E. M.; Farwell, D.; and Lee, D. M. S. (1993). "The IS Expectation Gap: Industry Expectations versus Academic Preparation." *MIS Quarterly*, Volume 17, Number 3 (September), pp. 293-307.
Trauth, E. M., and O'Connor, B. (1991). "A Study of the Interaction between Information Technology and Society: An Illustration of Combined Qualitative Research Methods." In H-E. Nissen, H. K. Klein, and R. Hirschheim (Editors), *Information Systems Research: Contemporary Approaches and Emergent Traditions*. Amsterdam: North-Holland, pp. 131-144.
Yin, R. K. (1989). *Case Study Research: Design and Methods*. Newbury Park, California: Sage Publications.

7 BIOGRAPHY

Eileen M. Trauth is an Associate Professor of Information Systems in the Management Science Group of the College of Business Administration at Northeastern University. Her teaching and research interests include the societal, organizational and educational impacts of information technology, information management, national information policy issues, and global informatics. Her articles have appeared in numerous journals as well as several proceedings for the International Federation for Information Processing. She has published a textbook entitled *Information Literacy: An Introduction to Information Processing* and is completing work on a book about an ethnographic study of an emerging information economy. She has been a visiting professor in several countries, including Ireland where she was a Fulbright Scholar. Professor Trauth is a member of the Society for Information Management, the International Federation for Information Processing, and the Information Resources Management Association. Professor Trauth received her Ph.D. in Information Science from the University of Pittsburgh.

14

Capturing Complex, Distributed Activities: Video-Based Interaction Analysis as a Component of Workplace Ethnography

K. Ruhleder
Library and Information Science
University of Illinois
Champaign, Illinois USA
E-mail: ruhleder@alexia.lis.uiuc.edu

B. Jordan
Institute for Research on Learning
Xerox Palo Alto Research Center
Palo Alto, California USA
E-mail: jordan@parc.xerox.com

Abstract

Organizations increasingly carry out their work by relying on complex, distributed activities supported by a wide range of technologies for synchronous and asynchronous communication and collaboration. How do we capture complex, distributed activities? What tools do we use in settings where even a team of trained ethnographers could not comprehend, much less record, all the interplays between team members, the subtleties of a look or tone, the shifts in orientation to people or objects in the workspace? In this paper, we explore the use of video-based Interaction Analysis to extend the ability of traditional ethnographic methods for data collection and analysis. We draw on a study of a distributed organization's use of remote meeting technologies to illustrate how this approach contributes to the depth of insights to be garnered from workplace ethnography.

1 INTRODUCTION

Organizations increasingly find it necessary to engage in complex, distributed activities supported by a wide range of technologies for synchronous and asynchronous collaboration between geographically separated teams. These technologies include groupware, remote meeting technologies, and shared media spaces (c.f., Gaver 1992; Grudin 1994; Heath and Luff 1993). Developers and potential users of these technologies anticipate that they will profoundly alter the ways in which geographically distributed team members can work together. As a consequence, organizations are beginning to embrace them as a means for both fostering communication and managing the complexities inherent in distributed organizational forms (Hiltz and Turoff 1993, Sproull and Kiesler 1991, Ehrlich and Cash 1994).

Yet participation in electronic communities and work groups requires significant amounts of time and energy spent on learning the technology and integrating it into current organizational work practices (Bikson and Eveland 1990; Ruhleder, Jordan and Elmes 1996). The successful emergence and continued vitality of these virtual groups will depend on designers' abilities to understand complex work settings and to develop effective ways of supporting distributed work. The successful integration of these new technologies will also depend on the ability of organizational members to develop shared understandings of their applicability to local problems and new practices that incorporate these technologies (Eveland et al. 1994; Korpela 1994; Orlikowski and Gash 1994; Orlikowski 1993).

As researchers, what tools can we bring to bear on understanding the complex interactions between collaborative technologies and environments that span multiple physical locations and multiple organizational cultures? How do we analyze situations characterized by layers of activity, where multiple meanings are deeply embedded in each action and reaction? If we are to effectively contribute not only to the development and deployment of a new set of technologies, but to the establishment of a new paradigm of organization, we must continue to develop research methods and approaches that will allow us to gain a deep understanding of local work practices and the broader organization of work within a given enterprise.

We confronted these questions as we carried out a study of the headquarters of a distributed organization, The Holding Company (THC), which uses a variety of communication and information technologies to support work distributed across THC headquarters and ten business units. THC associates conduct the business of the organization through phone calls and face-to-face meetings, via electronic mail and shared databases, and with the support of remote meeting technologies including shared workspaces and video- and audio-conferencing. The members of THC headquarters and business units are constantly challenged with integrating these technologies in ways that effectively support the needs of their distributed teams.

In the sections that follow, we briefly discuss the role of workplace ethnography in organizational analysis and technology development. We then outline the contribution that one specific technique, Video-Based Interaction Analysis,[1] can make as a component of a broader ethnographic inquiry both as a technique for data collection and as the basis for in-depth multidisciplinary analysis. We describe how this technique contributes to conventional ethnographic analysis, and what new challenges and problems its use raises. In the final section, we draw on our field study to illustrate how this approach contributes to the depth of insights to be garnered from workplace ethnography (Ruhleder, Jordan and Elmes 1996).

2 WORKPLACE ETHNOGRAPHY

2.1 Workplace Ethnography

Ethnographic methods, originally developed by anthropologists as a means of studying exotic tribes (Malinowski 1922, 1979; Mead 1973, 1930), extend the methodological lenses typically used in IT research (Yates and Van Maanen 1996).[2] These methods provide us with a means of studying our own subcultures, including communities, professions, experiences, and organizations (c.f. Becker et al. 1977; Gladwell 1996; Gregory 1983; Ruhleder 1994, 1995; Star 1995; Suchman 1987; Wolcott 1973), Workplace ethnography approaches organizational communities from a holistic perspective, focusing on both formal and informal systems; and on myth, narrative and identity as well as product and process. The insights gained from ethnographic work can often shed light on organizational problems. For instance, when time is characterized as a social construction (Dubinskas 1988), the temporal structures experienced by different occupational groups within a single organization can be identified as a source of conflict (Barley 1988), and a source of tension between managers and designers becomes clarified by juxtaposing managerial perspectives of product design as a clear-cut trajectory with the designers' more fluid, iterative

[1]We use the term "Interaction Analysis" (capitalized) to refer to the particular method of analysis we have been using, while "interaction analysis" (lower case) or "analysis of interaction" refers to the domain of interest. This domain, of course, is one that concerns a great many theoretical and practical persuasions, e.g., symbolic interactionism, phenomenology, social psychology, and a variety of schools of therapy.

[2]See Van Mannen (1988), Chapter 2, for a brief history of ethnography and different approaches to fieldwork. The book also includes examples from his own work on the police force.

processes of shifting issues and representations (Bucciarelli 1994). Close study of work practices has uncovered the underlying mechanisms of local interpretation, integration, and adaptation of systems and artifacts (Gasser 1986; Markus 1994; Orlikowski and Gash 1994), and the resulting complexities of infrastructure (Star and Ruhleder 1996). Other ethnographic work has uncovered the social role representations and artifacts play, serving as boundary objects linking together multiple communities within and across organizations (Gerson and Star 1986).

With their central focus on the native/user, ethnographic workplace studies are increasingly becoming a source of insights not only for researchers but for organizational and technology designers as well (Beyer and Holtzblatt 1993; Blomberg et al. 1993; Ehn 1988; Jordan 1996b). Underlying much of this work is the view that learning and work take place within *communities of practice* (Lave and Wenger 1991), naturally occurring groups that arise more or less spontaneously around a particular task, technology or enterprise (Jordan 1996a). Within this perspective, the complexities of practice can best be understood by the thick description generated by a combination of observational and participatory methods (Darrah 1992; Brown and Duguid 1991; Holzblatt and Beyer 1995; Jordan 1996a; Orr 1986). In particular, these and other ethnographic techniques, including video analysis, can be used to understand and illustrate the complex ways in which collaborative activities are constructed and maintained, and the ways in which particular artifacts can support collaborative work (Dourish and Bellotti 1992; Heath and Luff 1991; Nardi et al. 1995; Suchman and Trigg 1991; c.f. also Button 1993; Greenbaum and Kyng 1991; Engestrŝm and Middleton 1993). Within CSCW, for instance, projects are often driven by extensive fieldwork that includes participant observation before the design phase and user participation during the design phase (Bentley, et al 1992; Hughes, Randall and Shapiro 1993; Shapiro, Tauber and Traunmüller 1996).

Ethnographic field work within organizational settings immerses the participant observer (the researcher) in the work practices and processes of the organization. Participant observers may sit in on meetings, talk formally or informally with various organizational members, obtain copies of documents, gather stories, watch events unfold, overhear comments (Lofland 1995). Questions arise *in situ,* just as the analytic framework arises out of the data itself, and field data may include interview transcriptions, field notes, meeting memoranda, sketches, even cartoons collected from cubicle walls. In some settings, the participant observer may be able to become a part of the organization by taking on some of the work, or by playing a legitimate role within the work setting. Including ethnographic techniques in the methodological repertoire when studying the workplace helps the researcher avoid, or at least guard against, several major pitfalls:

- they counteract the threat of irrelevance by focusing the study on naturally occurring work activities in real world settings;
- they guard against a "top-down bias," that is, a bias that privileges the views of managers and supervisors, by involving researchers in the daily life of workplace communities of practice;

- they enable researchers to capture both what people say and what they in fact do, something not easily accomplished with interview studies.

All of these factors are crucial if we are to develop a robust understanding of work practices and contribute to effective and beneficial technical development and workplace redesign.

Recently, additional challenges have emerged in workplace research. Increasingly it has to be carried out in distributed settings where distributed actors carry out coordinated work activities through synchronous or often asynchronous interaction via various communication media, including email and groupware. In addition to requiring tools and methods for representing these work environments, their transformation must be mapped over time to track the changes that occur as new technologies become integrated into local work practices. We believe that ethnographic methodologies can help address these kinds of issues.

In our own ethnographic work, we draw on the tradition of anthropological fieldwork (Garfinkel 1984; Naroll and Cohen 1973) and the techniques of grounded theory to guide our data collection and analysis (Glaser and Strauss 1967; Strauss 1986). Interaction analysis, the specific technique we address in this paper, has been shaped primarily by conversation analysis and ethnomethodology, but is also rooted in ethnography, sociolinguistics, kinesics, proxemics, and ethology. In the next section, we discuss how video-based interaction analysis fits into ethnographic work. Video-based data are subject to a variety of limitations: the camera operator's notions of what is significant and what is not invariably influence the kind of record produced and video equipment is inherently more restricted in its information processing capacities than a human observer's sensory apparatus. However, we feel that video-based data and video-based analysis can complement and extend conventional methods of data gathering and that the use of video-based Interaction Analysis can form an integral part of ethnographic work.

3 VIDEO-BASED INTERACTION ANALYSIS[3]

3.1 Doing Interaction Analysis

Video-based Interaction Analysis (IA), as outlined by Jordan and Henderson (1995), consists of the in-depth microanalysis of how people interact with one another, their physical environment, and the documents, artifacts, and technologies in that environment. Like ethnography in general, IA looks for orderliness and patterns in people's routine interactions, but operates at a finer level of detail than conventional ethnographic observation. As stated earlier, the roots of this technique lie in ethnography, sociolinguistics, kinesics, proxemics, and ethology, but it has been shaped most

[3] In the sections that follow, we draw heavily on Jordan and Henderson (1995).

consequentially by conversation analysis and ethnomethodology. The technique itself has emerged over the past twenty years as a distinct form of analysis.[4] It is well-suited to a wide variety of organizational settings in which people interact with a broad range of individuals and technologies. For instance, Jordan (1992) has used video data to explicate how authoritative knowledge is distributed in two highly technologized settings: an airline operations room, where knowledge is continually jointly produced, and a hospital setting, where it is vested in the technology and the physician.

Interaction Analysis involves several different types of activities on the part of the ethnographer or ethnographic team:

- *Ethnographic context.* Video taping is most productively done in conjunction with extensive ethnographic fieldwork. In the course of the fieldwork, specific interactions are identified for video taping. Participant observation, interviews, and the analysis of documents provide the contextual framework for selecting relevant interactions for video taping and furnish the background against which video analysis is carried out. In turn, the video data are analyzed as a component of the larger analytical effort. In studying THC, for instance, we learned about the importance of meetings between distributed teams. These collaborations are supported by remote meeting technologies, such as desktop conferencing, two-way video, and shared drawing spaces. The use of these technologies made it difficult for a single researcher to gather the salient data. As a consequence, we decided to videotape these kinds of interactions from both sides of the link.
- *Entry: permission and set-up.* Prior to the taping, the ethnographer must establish guidelines for confidentiality and obtain permission for video taping from the participants. The logistics of videotaping involve scoping out the setting, determining things like the optimal camera angles (see Figure 1) and how to change the tape unobtrusively, and making sure that the video equipment won't interfere with any other equipment used in the room during the course of the event or activity being taped.
- *Content logging and transcripts.* The next step is to create a content log of each tape containing summary listings of events. These logs provide an overview of the data corpus, and can be used for locating sequences for further analysis. Later on, they also serve as the basis for making transcripts of particularly interesting segments. Depending on the researchers' interests, transcripts may include both verbal and non-verbal interactions from the tape. Table 1 offers a sample of a content log, Table 2 offers a sample transcript of a meeting

[4]Jordan and Henderson describe the work of researchers in two of the laboratories associated with the development of Interaction Analysis, one at Michigan State University, which operated between 1975 and 1988, and one currently functioning as a joint venture between Xerox PARC and the Institute for Research on Learning (IRL).

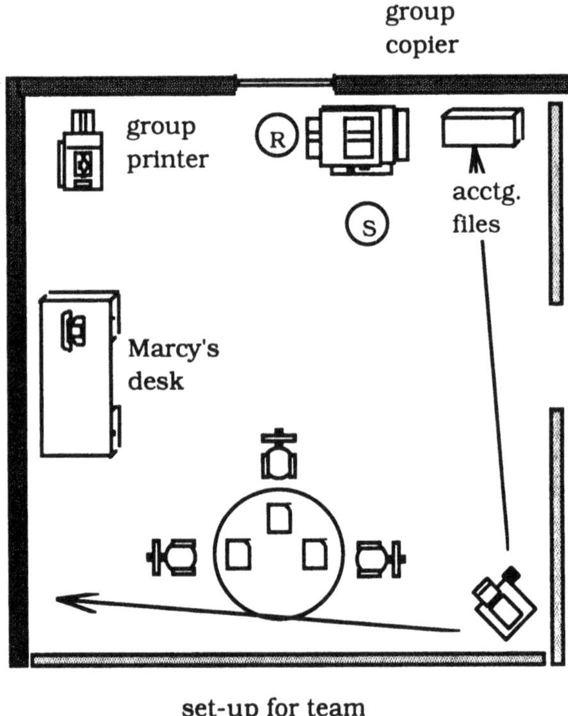

Figure 1 Sample Sketch with Camera Angle.

across two remote sites. An additional column can be inserted for notes, observations, links to other data, etc.[5]

- *Collaborative tape analysis.* A distinguishing feature of video-based IA is its reliance on multidisciplinary collaborative teamwork. Typically, a group of researchers convenes on a weekly basis for several hours of tape analysis where interesting sections of the tape are analyzed. Instead of using a preconceived coding scheme, analysts allow the categories to emerge out of a deepening understanding of the taped participants' interactions. In the course of multiple replayings, emerging patterns of interaction are checked against other sequences of tape and against other forms of ethnographic observations including field notes, interview transcripts, documentary materials, etc. Collaborative viewing

[5]Different researchers use different conventions for transcribing, usually determined by what depth of description is required for the type of analysis they are attempting to carry out.

Table 1 Sample Content Log.

The following is an excerpt from a content log. It lists a counter, the participants, and the activity in which they are engaged. This is a very broad-grained look at the activities on the tape, and is used to flag sequences of potential interest. For instance, we can identify sequences of technical set-up and accidental breakdown.

Counter	Participants	Activity	Notes
1:23:02		tape begins	
	D1	sets up computers for DTC; speakerphone on	
1:24:40	A4	announces that everyone is in	establish presence
1:24:53	D1	accidentally hangs up phone	tech breakdown
		calls THC	
1:25:30		speakerphone back on	
1:25:55	D1	leaves to find D3	
more set-up; waiting omitted			
1:27:22	D1, D3	enter room together	
	D1	introduces everyone a and begins meeting, explains agenda	beginning of formal meeting
1:28:00	D1	manipulates mouse and asks if screen is coming through (as is)	
	D1	gives introduction to presentation, what screens will be shown during DTC	
1:29:06	D1	explains that D2 will be taking over	
	D1, D2	switch chairs	change in primary speaker

helps neutralize the biases of the individual analyst while generating increasingly robust sets of analytic categories. Out of this collaborative analysis, the researchers construct an inventory of issues and hypotheses for further exploration.

Participants from the organization being studied are included in this collaborative viewing whenever possible so that they may contribute their insights.

Table 2 Sample Transcript.

The following is an excerpt from a transcript. It outlines the verbal and non-verbal activities on one side of a meeting in which some participants are listening to the action via speakerphone (hence the glances at the speakerphone). The transcript is an emerging object, and may be further expanded if, for instance, certain non-verbals take on greater importance over time.

Counter	Verbal	Nonverbal
1:28:13	D1: I just want to do an introduction quickly, OK, and then D2 will take it from this point	D1 looks at hisn otes D1 looks at D2 D1 looks at the screen D1 looks back at his notes
1:28:19	D1: Basically what we talked about was, was, the purpose of the system is to request and get access to data from the Walker system and	D1 looks at his notes D2 looks at D1
	D1: we've talked about data and how we're going to label it and those things and	D1 looks at his notes D1 makes a listing or outlining gesture with his hand on the table.
	D1: basically what this system, this is the mechanism to request the information	D1 reaches over to the mouse on "basically" D2 watches the screen
1:28:42	D1: We have something, a box up here called "project" and it's really no more than a way of tagging the requests, or grouping the requests a certain way. And what we're going to walk through is an example	D1 gestures briefly at the screen (to the box called "project") D1 looks at the speakerphone
	D1: of use, um, the quarterly balance sheet process as an example of walking through these screens.	D1 looks around D1 makes "presentation" gestures with his hands (as in, here is something for you) D1 looks back at the screen
	D1: So, I think I'll just let D2 take it, show you how it works, and get your feedback on this.	D1 and D2 trade places as he talks D2 moves to the computer and puts his hand on the mouse D1 picks up a folder from a table against the wall
1:29:11		D2 sits down D1 picks up his folder from a side table
1:29:13		D1 sits down
1:29:15	D2: OK, right off the bat as D1 mentioned we wanted to try to put together an application here that would hit on intuitiveness, I guess, to try to make it as easy as possible to get at the requests to the information that's on the [mainframe] system	D2 looks at screen D1 looks at screen D2 glances at notes D2 looks down at hands D1 looks down at hands D2 glances back and forth between screen, notes, and "nowhere"

Their contributions to the analysis help further elicit their view of the work world, forming an important counterpoint to the view of the ethnographic team and other researchers. Ideally, this joint analysis also provides a mechanism for feedback into the organization studied and might also lead to the construction of a "jointly told tale" (Van Maanen 1988:136ff) bringing together the voice of the ethnographer and the informant.

These activities are iterative and frequently overlap. Content logs generate potential tape sequences for analysis; tape analysis suggests further content logging and transcribing with emergent categories in mind. This, in turn, identifies new sequences for analysis, or suggests new venues for video taping.

3.2 Advantages of Video-Based Interaction Analysis

Under appropriate circumstances, video-based IA can form a powerful component of ethnographic workplace analysis for a variety of reasons:

- *IA creates a permanent data corpus.* Video data provides a rich[6] and relatively permanent primary record available for an unlimited number of viewings and listenings. Individuals and groups of researchers can return to the video record over time as questions change and hypotheses develop.
- *IA provides access to behavior invisible without replay technology.* Many of the phenomena of interest to us in workplace analysis emerge only on repeated viewing. In addition, a videotape can be played in slow or accelerated motion, thereby exposing otherwise invisible patterns in the movements of persons or artifacts. In a distributed setting, simultaneous video taping of events at multiple sites makes possible coordinating remote events for purposes of analysis. It allows us to understand what happens at site B contemporaneous with or following events at site A.
- *IA captures complex data.* Even for a trained observer, it is simply impossible to keep track of the overlapping activities of several persons with any accuracy or any hope of catching adequate detail. In multioperator workplaces, ethnographers are forever frustrated by the necessity to decide on whom to focus. Video is particularly useful in settings characterized by dense, concurrent

[6]We draw on Daft and Lengel (1986, p. 560) for our definition of *media* richness, believing that video-based data provides "multiple cues via body language and tone of voice, and message content...expressed in natural language." This contrasts with Lee's (1994) definition of the richness as "an emergent property on the *interaction* between the communication medium and its organizational context." From this perspective, the video tape itself can be rich or lean, depending on who works with it and how. For this reason, we strive for the richness of multiperson, multidisciplinary analysis.

dialogues and behaviors. It provides a level of detail that is unattainable for methods that rely on note taking or on-the-spot observational coding, allowing the analyst to later "pick apart" the complex interactions taking place.

- *IA counteracts certain forms of recorder bias.* Observers and interviewers invariably highlight important aspects and pass over what they consider to be at the time unimportant aspects of the activities they observe. The camera, on the other hand, records events as they happen, with consistent and known bias stemming from equipment characteristics such as available camera angle, audio recording levels, and the like.
- *IA counteracts bias of the individual analyst.* Multidisciplinary group analysis is particularly powerful for neutralizing preconceived notions on the part of individual researchers. It provides a critical corrective to the tendency to see in the interaction what one is conditioned to see or even wants to see. This is especially apparent when members of the organization being studied are included in these sessions.
- *IA avoids the say/do problem.* What people say they do and what they do in fact are not necessarily the same, which is why anthropological ethnography involves both asking questions and observing interactions. Field notes and other data can identify some discrepancies. Video recordings *approximate* the characteristics of direct observation of an event, thus providing optimal data on what really happened rather than particular accounts of what happened, such as people's recollections and opinions.
- *IA provides access to members' categories and world view.* Given that analysts have strong preconceived notions of what the world is like, it is often difficult to see when they differ from those of workplace participants. For example, we identified several sequences in which the accountants' questions weren't being fully answered by the developers, which we hypothesized might be explained by the imbalance in IS-user power relationships (c.f. Markus and Bjørn-Andersen 1987). In viewing these sequences, an alternate explanation emerged that suggested, instead, that the problem stemmed from different understandings of the role the application would play, rooted in different practices.
- *IA exposes mechanisms and antecedents.* Video provides process data rather than snapshot data. Since video records the phenomenon of interest in context, it is possible to ask about antecedents, varieties of solutions produced on different occasions, and questions of what led up to any particular state. While problems or breakdowns are often fairly obvious in workplace analysis, their antecedents may not be easily apparent. Video can help researchers and (where this is an option) participants look at and evaluate antecedents, potentially figuring out how to mitigate against particular chains of events.

3.3 Problems in Capturing and Analyzing Video-Based Data

Video-based Interaction Analysis, however, is not without its own problems and costs. A variety of issues have arisen for us and other analysts in the course of this kind of work:

- *Individuals are concerned about confidentiality.* In most settings, the people being videotaped are concerned about confidentiality: who will see the tapes, and will my performance be judged by my supervisor? Clarifying who will have access and the right of individuals to review and potentially erase any tape sequence forms an important part of the "up front" work the ethnographer must do. Our policy is that supervisors are not allowed to see video tapes of their subordinates unless explicit permission is granted and that anyone may request that any segment in which they appear be erased.
- *Companies are concerned about confidentiality.* In working in corporate environments, senior management may be concerned about the extent of researchers' access to sensitive information, and may not permit audio and video recordings in particular settings. Access needs to be clarified up-front and may be renegotiated over time. This may require going up the formal chain of command for authorization (Nardi et al. 1995).
- *Video-based Interaction Analysis is time consuming and expensive.* This point cannot be overstated. Beyond the cost of the equipment, this form of data collection and analysis requires substantial investment in trained personnel. The work of taping necessitates that someone intelligently set up and monitor the camera, as well as record supplementary field notes and collect relevant documentary materials. Similarly, the analysis ideally involves the on-going participation of a multidisciplinary team of analysts. The cost of all this can quickly become prohibitive.
- *Video-based data is difficult to work with.* A variety of annotation and analysis programs have been developed, including MacSHAPA® (Sanderson et al. 1994) and VideoNoter® (Roschelle and Goldman 1991), but no standards have emerged thus far and each has its limitations. Even with these tools, video records are clumsy to access, annotate, and integrate with other materials such as observer notes, key stroke data, or physiological or state measurements. However, emerging annotation and synchronization technologies promise to make this type of analysis easier in the future.
- *Incorporating screen-capture ups the ante on time, expertise and complexity.* Synchronous screen capture in settings where computing technologies or video monitors form a component of the interaction at hand suffer from all of the problems discussed above in terms of cost and necessary expertise. In addition, the elaborate technologies required for screen capture further complicate the problems of working with multiple streams of data.
- *Camera effects may arise.* The degree to which people are influenced by the presence of a camera is an empirical question that cannot be decided in principle

but must be investigated on each occasion of camera work. Evidence that the camera mattered to participants can sometimes be found on the tape itself in the form of visible monitoring of, or remarks about, the camera, particularly when there is some kind of breakdown or deviation from routine. Our experience shows, however, that people quickly habituate to the camera as they become engaged in their own work tasks, especially if there is no operator behind the camera.[7]

We may never be able to fully overcome some of these difficulties, and others will have to be addressed anew in each setting. Many of them, for example, confidentiality issues, arise in some form or other in all ethnographic work, whether or not videotapes form a part of the data corpus. Despite these difficulties, however, we believe that including the capture and analysis of video-based data as a component of ethnographic work is worth the effort for all of the reasons outlined in previous sections. It has helped us to understand the complex work environment at THC and, in particular, the ways its members rely on remote collaborative technologies to conduct their work over multiple distributed sites. In the following section, we provide examples of the analytic contributions of this technique.

4 APPLYING IA TO REMOTE MEETINGS

4.1 Studying a Geographically Distributed Organization

As mentioned above, we carried out an ethnographic study of The Holding Company (THC), which is using groupware and communication technologies to support a distributed work environment. THC headquarters manages ten business units distributed across the United States. LotusNotes® and remote meeting technologies such as LiveBoard® and PictureTel® are widely disseminated in order to facilitate interactions between headquarters and these geographically distributed holdings. THC associates freely combine groupware and nongroupware technologies to create different possibilities for remote group work, depending on the circumstances, the local availability of specific technologies, and the preferences of group members.

We carried out fieldwork over a period of four months, during which we collected data through unstructured interviews, participant observation at THC headquarters and several business units, and review of on-line and paper materials. All thirty-two headquarters associates, most of the seven temporary staff, and some members of the business units were interviewed at least once over the course of the four months. The

---

[7]This may not be surprising in corporate settings, where participants are familiar with computers, video cameras, and tape recorders, but was also found to be the case in settings such as the huts of Mexican village women, where Jordan videotaped births conducted with the assistance of a midwife and family members (Jordan 1993).

resulting dataset includes field notes, interview write-ups and partial transcripts, photographs, paper and electronic documents, and a set of video tapes capturing both sides of various small- and large-group remote interactions. Over the course of our field work, we were able to videotape four remote meetings, documented in a series of nineteen video tapes. We continue to develop and expand content logs, transcripts, and other documents relative to our analysis.

Our central concern in studying this organization has been the relationship between technology and everyday work practices, and the learning that has to take place in order to integrate technology and practices effectively and synergistically. Multiple factors, including local norms, physical infrastructures, and status differences influence who uses the remote meeting technologies, and to what purpose. Successful meetings require a great deal of preparatory work, including setting up, testing connections, and checking file formats when shared files are used. Teaching newcomers the mechanics of establishing a connection between two sites involves talking technically nonliterate individuals through an often ill-documented set of steps plagued by cryptic error messages. In addition to solving technical problems, remote meeting participants must figure out new ways of working together in settings with reduced context cues. We are interested in understanding how these issues interact with other aspects of organizational culture.

In our work, video-based IA has been extremely useful for pursuing hypotheses derived from other field data and for exploring a broad range of issues. These include issues of deep learning around technology, the interaction between competing paradigms in problem solving, and the distribution of authoritative knowledge across distributed workgroups. They also include the negotiation of local and global talk during the course of remote meetings, the ways in which particular technical arrangements shape participation frameworks, the role of infrastructure and local support staff in remote meeting facilitation and, finally, the ways in which distributed workgroups organize their interactions to exploit the positive affordances of remote meeting technologies and compensate for the negative ones.

Below, we draw on one particular example, the development of a relational database application to support the work of accountants at THC's headquarters, to illustrate some of the ways in which insights were generated by video analysis that most likely we would not have arrived at without this particular method.

4.2 Designing an Application for Accountants

One set of events we observed at THC was the interaction over time between two geographically distributed teams. A group of developers on the East Coast was designing a relational database application for accountants on the West Coast that would facilitate their access to information on a cumbersome legacy system. During ethnographic work, we observed two meetings between the teams, one face-to-face and one via PictureTel and LiveBoard, and recognized this as an opportunity for videotaping. We videotaped the following two meetings, one using PictureTel and

West Coast – Accountants: A1 is the most senior, A2 next, and A3 the most junior of the three. A1 initiated the process. A4 is a member of the IS staff. She set up the computer and the camera, then left as the formal meeting began.

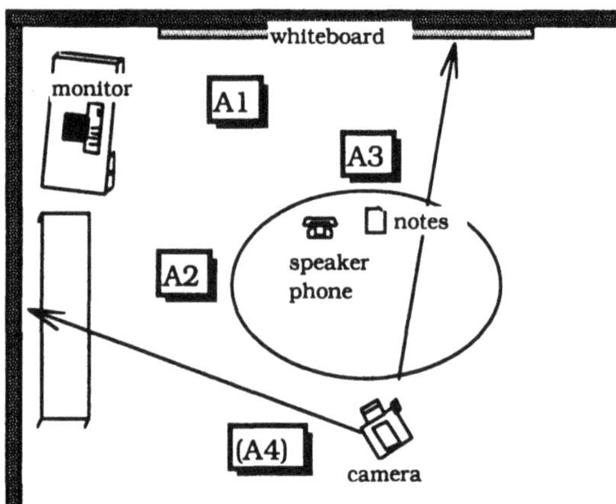

East Coast – Developers: D1 is the liaison with the accountants, D2 the project leader, and D3 a programmer. D4 is the ethnographer. She set up the room and the camera, and remained throughout the meeting.

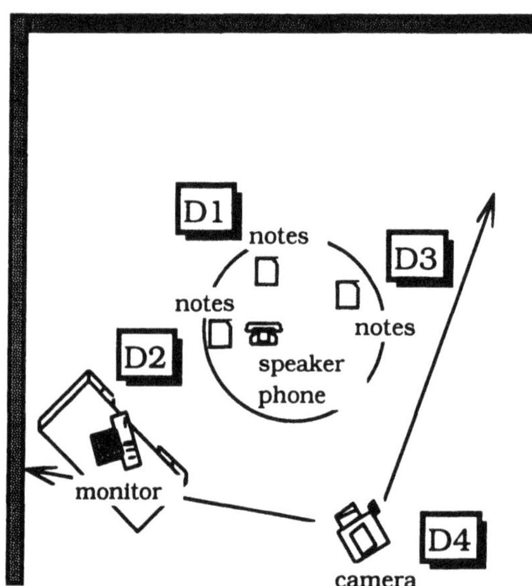

Figure 2 Sketches of the Two Meeting Sites.

one using a DeskTop Conferencing (DTC) application allowing the two groups to view and manipulate the same application prototype on their respective monitors.

We use the process of the development of this application and the dialogue around the prototype demonstration activities to illustrate some of the ways in which video analysis can lead to crucial insights not available through other methods. In particular, we draw on the fourth meeting in the series, during which DTC and a speakerphone provided an audio link and shared screen. Analysis of the video data helped us more fully understand how the distributed set-up disturbed premeeting alignment activities, how the activities of other group members influenced asking and answering questions across the link, and how groups moved from and integrated local work and global work. Figure 2 presents sketches of the two sites.

4.3 Disturbance in Premeeting Alignment Activities

Premeeting activities are so much a part of an on-going practice that participants hardly ever think about what they consist. These activities include both lighthearted banter and serious asides, catching up on prior history, readying papers and props, and choosing places to sit. It is only in distributed meetings that taken-for-granted activities become apparent in their absence and unaccustomed activities are added. For instance, participants have to pay attention to setting up and maintaining the link even as they try to carry on both serious and lighthearted premeeting exchanges. Furthermore, where visual and to some extent auditory context clues are lacking, premeeting exchanges can become strained and burdensome. For example, a joke in face-to-face interaction unifies people in a joint activity (laughter) and focuses attention, thereby allowing a meeting to start with eyes and ears on the chairperson. This breaks down if the other side doesn't hear the joke, either due to limitations of the technology, or because the remote technologies precluded the teller from judging the appropriate point at which to insert the joke into the other side's on-going activities. Consider the following excerpt from a transcript of pre-meeting activities at THC (underlining indicates what the other side heard):

	West Coast		**East Coast**	
ctr.	**accountants nonverbal**	**accountants verbal**	**developers verbal**	**developers nonverbal**
1:02:08	all turn to look at A4, A3 goes toward camera to where A4 is standing	A4: Hey, you guys, can I show A3 here, just at the end...		
			D1: OK, is D3 here, or	D1 turns away from table toward D2
			D2: He's not here yet	D2 walks toward the table

1:02:15			D1: Let me just check on D3, if he's not there, we'll start the meeting, we'll just get moving.	D1 gestures first toward the speakerphone, then to D2 D1 leaves D2 looks at the screen, fiddles with his watch
1:02:22	A2 starts looking for his water bottle, takes his notepad off the table A1 watches A4 and A3	A4: Just take the one that's on and move it to off. I'll check when I get back.		D2 wanders out the door, then back in again
1:02:25	A3 sits back down	A3: I think I can handle that		D2 wanders out the door, then back
1:02:28	A2 tosses an empty cassette tape onto the table	A4: That's what I said yesterday		
1:02:33	A1 looks at phone A3 pulls phone closer to group	A1: OK? A3: We still connected?		
			D4: Can I hand you this chair?	D2 moves a chair
1:02:36	A3 looks at A4 A1 looks at the phone	A4: I think he was going to get D4, D1 was going to get D4.		
1:02:39		A4: D1?		
1:02:40	A3 leans toward the phone, everyone looks at the phone	A3: Who's there? Anyone there?		
(D4 clarifies who is on the East Coast. West Coast participants start to kid around, joking about whether or not someone bought a fancy car.)				
1:03:45		A3: Well, we're having a little disagreement between me and A1.		D1 walks in with D3 All look very serious
1:03:47	A2 grins at A4	A2: There's a wager.		
		A1: Don't tell everyone.		
		A2: Well, not really a wager.		

1:03:50	A1 glances over briefly, turns back to looking at the screen A2 and A3 are grinning	A1: Don't talk about it.		D1 sets down his folder D2 closes the door D3 prepares to sit down
1:03:54	A2 and A3 looking at screen A2 turns toward speakerphone		D1: All right, we're all set here, we got D3, D2 and myself.	D1 starts to sit down D2 sits down

On the accountants' side, A4 is busy showing A3 something (1:02:08)while A2 looks for a water bottle and A1 watches A4 and A3 (1:02:22). After they are done with that aspect of the set-up, A1 checks in with the other side with an "OK?" When there is no response, A3 asks if they are still connected or if the link has been broken (they haven't heard anything from the developers for a little over fifteen seconds). A4 then answers, "I think he [D1] was going to get D4" (1:02:36), making a wrong inference about the currently available participants. D4 and D2, meanwhile, are busy with their own concerns of rearranging the physical space for the meeting. They miss A1's "OK?" as well as A4's inaccurate inference about getting D4 and A4's query, "D1?" (1:02:39). It isn't until A3 makes a special effort to attract their attention and clarify availability ("Who's there? Anyone there?" 1:02:40) that the designers finally respond, after which premeeting activities can continue on both sides.

In the end, the formal part of the meeting begins abruptly. When D1 walks in with D3 (1:03:45), the designers are ready for the transition to the formal meeting while the accountants are still in the informal phase. D1 walks to the table, sits down, and begins at 1:03:54: "All right, we're all set here, we got D3, D2 and myself." What D1 cannot see is that the accountants are still in a relaxed mood as late as 1:03:50, joking about a bet on whether or not someone has just bought a fancy car, with A1 admonishing them not to talk about the wager and A2 and A3 grinning at him. And, conversely, they cannot see D1 return with D2 and D3 in tow. In a face-to-face setting, D1 might have used the joke as a transition point and a means of integrating the two sets of people, or the accountants might have abandoned the joke as he and the other developers entered. With neither side having access to information about the other side's readiness, however, the formal phase of the meeting begins abruptly. This exchange shows how setting up the technology, combined with the lack of visual and auditory cues, generates lumps and bumps in the alignment process that would not occur in face-to-face meetings.

While premeeting activities in face-to-face settings are generally a time of convergence, in this distributed setting the activities of the two sites remain disjointed. Traditional forms of note taking or audiotaping could have captured these actions independently, but it would have been difficult to "sync up" field notes across the two settings.[8] For researchers, the confirmation of the tapes allows them to make statements about the activities, interactions, and *reactions* (or, often even more significant, lack thereof) on both sides of a link. With the tapes, we know with a high degree of certainty what each side heard across the link and how they incorporated that into their own local activities.

4.4 Local Team Support for Discourse Across the Link

Group cohesion and mutual support for team members are important parts of effective teamwork, particularly when subgroups come together for joint meetings. Without it, a spokesperson or decision maker for a subgroup cannot effectively represent them, especially in real-time problem solving situations. In face-to-face meetings, participants show support (or lack of support) for one another's positions through gesture, gaze, and body orientation. In the following excerpt, we see a marked difference in the nonverbal support subgroup members show each other. In the segment that follows, members of the accountants' team propose positions to which other members do not fully subscribe, while the designers, on their side, appear to be engaged in the co-construction of a response that involves all members (underlining indicates what the other side heard).

	West Coast		**East Coast**	
ctr.	**accountants nonverbal**	**accountants verbal**	**developers verbal**	**developers nonverbal**
1:07:25	A3 glances down briefly A2 continues to look at screen	A2: <u>Yeah, is there a way to prioritize</u>		D2 grimaces D2 cocks his head, looks off into space and presses his lips together D1 leans his head back
1:07:29	A2 turns toward the speakerphone A1 continues to look at screen A3 continues to look at screen	A2: <u>when its queued, similar to the way [the main-frame application] works so that if you had something that you had to get through that was,</u>		D1 shakes his head D2 turns halfway between the phone and D1

[8]One would also need more sophisticated audiotaping equipment than the usual tape recorder, however, because it is almost impossible to clearly pick up what comes across a speakerphone. It is also easier to distinguish between multiple speakers and speakers with similar voices when audio is coupled with the visual cues of a videotape.

1:07:35	A2 turns back to the screen	A2: you know, a higher priority than, say, five or eight other jobs over there, or since it runs overnight.		D1 makes "hold off" gesture – holds up flat palm toward D2 – and shakes his head
1:07:39	A2 turns back to the speakerphone	A2: is that even an issue?		
1:07:40	A3 nods slightly A2 nods slightly and turns back to the screen A1 coughs	A2: Yeah	D2: Not an issue because it does one a night and pretty much everything that's in there will get executed.	D2 turns back toward the screen, then looks somewhere between the screen and the phone D1nods D1 looks at hands
1:07:46	A2 nods, looks at water bottle	A2: OK		D2 looks at phone D1 looks at phone
1:07:49			D2: Does that answer your question?	D2 looks at phone
1:07:50	A2 turns to speakerphone, then back to screen	A2: Yes, thank you.		
1:07:51	A2 drinks from water bottle		D2: OK, good. Moving along, as D1 introduced, the way we wanted to set up some wrappers around the actual requests themselves.	D1 looks up, turns toward screen D1 nods, grabs ankle again D2 reaches for mouse D2 looks back and forth
1:07:51			D2: we have immediately coming up in the view here in the projects box and in this example.	D2 moves mouse D1 plays with his hands D2 makes "offering" gesture with hands on "in this example," keeping hands close to his lap
1:07:51	A3 flexes his neck, glances briefly at his notes		D2: this is not a working program yet, so there's really no data behind it, this is just some hardcoded items here, just for example, for display purposes.	D2 makes brief "no, no" gesture with his hands still close to his lap on "this is not"

A2 begins to ask a question about how the application will relate to one aspect of their need for quick, ad hoc reports in response to questions from members of the executive team, "if you had something that you had to get through" (1:07:29). He ends his question, however, by admitting that it may be ill-founded ("is that even an issue?" 1:07:39). D2 answers, "Not an issue because it does one [run] a night." This is technically correct, but does not address the underlying problem: as currently set up, the application will not do the kind of on-demand reporting the accountants want. Why doesn't A2 then pursue his question? It is, after all, a legitimate issue, since it constitutes one of the key reasons for developing the application in the first place.

What is striking about this interaction when viewing the video tape is the difference in behavior on each side. When people speak in a group, they look to each other for support and encouragement. Neither the accountant who spoke, however, nor his two colleagues, look at each other during any part of this brief exchange. A1 and A3, in particular, continue to fixedly look at the screen during the entire interaction, with the exception of A3's brief downward glance at 1:07:25, leaving A2 without feedback from his team members. The developer's side, on the other hand, is far more active, with D2 grimacing at 1:07:25 as A2 starts to ask his question, an expression that is peripherally available to his boss, D1. He then looks at D1 (1:07:29) who shakes his head and appears to silently coach him on the answer (making a "hold off" gesture and shaking his head at 1:07:35). After obtaining verbal agreement from A2 that the issue has been addressed ("Does that answer your question?" 1:07:49 – "Yes, thank you," 1:07:50), D2 moves into the next section with D1 nodding his acknowledgment.

In this tape sequence, the video data alerted us to the fact that the lack of success of A2's question is foreshadowed in the failure of his team members to legitimize his question by a supportive focus of attention. Access to the videotapes enabled us to analyze how local group activity during cross-link question-answer sequences may display and legitimize differential authority and power. We might hypothesize from this sequence, for instance, that power is granted or withheld in real-time by the nonverbal actions of co-located team members, and that they signal support for further probing through body orientation, gesture and gaze. We might also hypothesize that these non-verbals help co-located group members maintain a sense of internal cohesion. For instance, later on in the videotape, D2 rolls his eyes at one of the accountants' suggestions and grins broadly at D1 and D3.

4.5 Local Work and Global Work

Gesture, gaze and body alignment, not available to the remote party, also accomplish silent "local work" in audio-only settings. We observed multiple instances in which people on one side of the link would signal to each other in various ways, showing each other notes, or even sketching out ideas and recommendations. This kind of local work allows each group to work through a problem and possible solutions. At the same time, it may prevent "global work" that is serious joint discussion around the potential solution space. Consider the following excerpt in which the accountants sketch out a private solution to a problem on their side of the link while the developers sketch out their own (underlining indicates what the other side heard; parentheses indicates something that seems to be an aside to the local group):

	West Coast		East Coast	
ctr.	**accountants nonverbal**	**accountants verbal**	**developers verbal**	**developers nonverbal**
2:02:36	A3 walks to screen, starts pointing to things on the screen A3 lowers voice	(A3: See, maybe what we'd rather have is this never changes, that never changes, then you want to pull those to the end, have these so when you come down you go straight down, and you, you're able to input that and hit		D1 nods slightly, looks at D3, who looks back at D1
2:02:48	A3 makes tabbing motions as he talks about hitting the tab key	(A3: tab to go to the next one, tab to go to the next one and the ones we don't use, record type and these two, put at the end so, because you rarely change those.)		D2 looks at D1, makes a back and forth gesture with the pen in his hand
2:03:01	A2 points to screen	(A2: ...they rarely change...they should go in after...)		D2 mouths something to D1
2:03:03		(A1: yeah, gotcha)		
[some discussion omitted]				
2:04:27	A3 goes to whiteboard	A2: Those should be the first items on there		
2:04:47	A3 starts listing items on whiteboard	(A3: CU, major, detail)		D2 cocks his head forward, "listening pose"?
2:04:53		(A1: and then the other items)	(D1: can you just have it tab to corporate unit)	D1 turns to D3, draws something in the air that looks like a screen layout
2:04:54	A2 glances at the screen, then back at A3	(A3: Wouldn't you want controlling entity next?)		D1 makes downward gesture

2:04:58		(A1: It doesn't...)		
2:04:59		(A2: Yes)	(D1: we can always go back, wherever the defaults go)	D1 makes a "flipping" gesture
2:05:00	A1 points to things on the screen A2 nods A3 turns away from the whiteboard	(A1: Only for your first piece of data, fill in all this stuff, the only thing you'll be changing is these three.)		
2:05:06	A2 circles things on the screen A3 watches A2	(A2: You'll be changing more frequently than you'll be changing these things.)		
2:05:10	A3 erases board A1 turns to speakerphone		D2: Hey, guys, we do have another idea here that we can set it up	D1 gestures to D2 to jump in
2:05:15	A1 turns back to screen A2 turns back to screen		D2: where the tab key will specifically go to only those items in a particular order that you want without even moving anything, we can do it that way also.	
2:05:24	A3 returns to stand near his chair		D1: And then you can use the mouse to position yourself on something else if you wanted to	D1 looks at D3
(D1 continues to outline a solution, which is eventually accepted by the accountants and does not involve moving items on the screen around.)				

The developers have just demonstrated how accountants will select items for a report, but the accountants are not happy with the way in which the selections are laid out on the screen. At 2:02:36, A3 lowers his voice and begins a private discussion with the other accountants, with the developers able to overhear parts of the accountants' emerging design solution (the text with dotted underlining) even though they cannot see what A3 is pointing to on the screen at 2:02:36. The accountants continue laying out their own solution, with A3 suggesting, "the ones we don't use, record type and these two, put at the end so, because you rarely change those" (2:02:48); A2 echoing the solution, "they rarely change ... they should go in after" (2:03:01); and A1 agreeing, "yeah, gotcha" (2:03:03).

After recognizing the problem (D1 nodding at 2:02:36), the developers begin to quietly sketch out their own solution, with D1 making eye contact with D3, then D2 starting to gesture with his pen (2:02:48) and mouthing something (2:03:01). This back-and-forth pattern continues without the accountants being aware of it. It may well be that they imagine the developers paying rapt attention to *their* emerging solution since they are producing their own talk in overhearable fashion. Instead, the developers are feeding off of this overhearable discussion to construct their own solution. At 2:04:47, the developers listen to the specific elements A3 lists ("CU, major, detail") that the accountants want as their first items on the screen layout. As the accountants continue overhearably, D1 quietly proposes an alternative to D3, "can you just have it tab to corporate unit?" (2:04:53), amplifying this and a further suggestion with gestures (2:04:53–2:04:52). Throughout this tape sequence, the developers speak softly enough that the accountants can't hear what they are saying. Their ability to overhear the accountants, however, allows them to jump in at a break in the action and propose the solution they have constructed ("Hey, guys, we do have another idea here" at 2:05:10). Their interruption closes off the accountants' construction of a solution and the accountants abandon the process. A3 erases the whiteboard he has been using (2:05:10) and returns to his chair (2:05:24), while A1 and A2 have already turned their attention to the screen (2:05:15).

This particular segment offers one example of how people move between local work and global work, and the role that overhearing can play. This kind of behavior can be recorded through conventional note taking, but not necessarily with sufficient detail about action, reaction, and timing on both sides to make comments about the role of local work, or form hypotheses about how such local work feeds into the global work of the group. The videotape helps us trace out the ways in which people move between the two types of work, and develop an understanding of the role which overhearing and the manipulation of voice can play in these settings.

The above examples illustrate some of the ways in which videotapes can supplement interviews and observations, becoming part of a larger data corpus from which insights can be drawn and through which hypotheses can be tested. They allow us access to certain kinds of information about an interaction, including the role of gesture, gaze, and body alignment, which are difficult to obtain by standard ethnographic methods. This is of particular benefit when dealing with interactions between remote sites where questions of alignment, of synching up, of shared understandings of openings and closings, topic changes, sequencing, and the like become paramount. Thus, video data help us ascertain how people move between informal and formal meeting segments in remote meetings, and how they move in and out of local work and global work when connected via an audio or audio-plus-video link. Other sequences we have analyzed helped us identify particular instances in which competing paradigms clashed, in which different understandings of the technologies led to an impasse, and in which the negative affordances of the technology led to breakdown.

5 ETHNOGRAPHY IN DISTRIBUTED WORK SETTINGS

While there is widespread, popular belief that the new communication technologies will magically link people across distributed sites, the nature of the linkage is not well understood. We believe that many of the issues confronting designers and high-level decision makers regarding their development and use cannot be illuminated without the detailed, rigorous kind of analysis that video-based Interaction Analysis can provide. What is clear is that the positive and negative affordances of the new communication technologies are going to affect established work practices and work processes and eventually organizational structures. Laboratory studies are valuable for studying well defined variables in these domains, but the opportunities and barriers these technologies generate in the work place need to be explored by looking in a systematic manner at the ways in which real users doing real work in real work sites employ them. One promising way to capture and analyze these activities is through video-based Interaction Analysis.

6 ACKNOWLEDGMENTS

This research at THC was sponsored by Xerox Palo Alto Research Center, the Institute for Research on Learning, and THC. We wish to thank the members of the IA labs for their ideas, suggestions and commentaries. We also appreciate the comments of several anonymous reviewers, and the suggestions of Allen Lee, in shaping this article.

7 REFERENCES

Barley, S. R. (1988). "On Technology, Time, and Social Order: Technically Induced Change in the Temporal Organization of Radiological Work." In A. Dubinskas (Editor), *Making Time: Ethnographies of High-Technology Organizations*. Philadelphia: Temple University Press, pp. 123-137.

Becker, H. S.; Geer, B.; Hughes, E.; and Strauss, A. (1977). *Boys in White: Student Culture in Medical School.* New Brunswick, New Jersey: Transaction Books.

Bentley, R.; Hughes, J.; Randall, D. Rodden, T.; Sawyer, P.; Shapiro, D.; and Sommerville, I. (1992). "Ethnographically-Informed System Design for Air-Traffic Control." *Proceedings of the Conference on Computer-Supported Cooperative Work.* New York: ACM Press, pp. 123-129.

Beyer, H. R., and Holtzblatt, K. (1995). "Apprenticing with the Customer." *Communications of the ACM*, Volume 38, Number 5, pp. 45-52.

Bikson, T. K.; and Eveland, J. D. (1990). "The Interplay of Work Group Structures and Computer Support." In. J. Galegher, R. E. Kraut, and C. Egido (Editors),

Intellectual Teamwork: Social and Technological Foundations of Cooperative Work. Hillsdale, New Jersey: Lawrence Erlbaum Associates, pp. 245-290.

Blomberg, J.; Giacomi, J.; Mosher, A.; and Swenton-Wall, P. (1993). "Ethnographic Field Methods and Their Relation to Design." In D. Schuler and A. Namoika (Editors), *Participatory Design: Perspectives on System Design.* Hillsdale, New Jersey: Lawrence Erlbaum Associates, pp. 123-154.

Brown, J. S., and Duguid, P. (1991). "Organizational Learning and Communities-of-Practice: Toward a Unified View of Working, Learning, and Innovation." *Organizational Science,* Volume 2, Number 1, pp. 40-57.

Bucciarelli, L. L. (1994). *Designing Engineers.* Cambridge, Massachusetts: MIT Press.

Button, G. (Editor) (1993). *Technology in Working Order: Studies of Work, Interaction and Technology.* London: Routledge.

Daft, R. L., and Lengel, R. H. (1986). "Organizational Information Requirements, Media Richness and Structural Design." *Management Science,* Volume 32, Number 5, pp. 554-571.

Darrah, C. (1992). "Workplace Skills in Context." *Human Organization,* Volume 51, Number 3, pp. 264-273.

Dourish, P., and Bellotti, V. (1992). "Awareness and Coordination in Shared Workspaces." New York: ACM Press.

Dubinskas, F. A. (Editor), (1988). *Making Time: Ethnographies of High-Technology Organizations.* Philadelphia: Temple University Press.

Ehn, P. (1988). *Work-Oriented Design of Computer Artifacts.* Hillside, New Jersey: Lawrence Erlbaum.

Ehrlich, K., and Cash, D. (1994). "Turning Information into Knowledge: Information Finding as a Collaborative Activity." *Proceedings Digital Libraries '94.* College Station, Texas. pp. 119-125.

Engeström, Y., and Middleton, D. (Editors) (1993). *Communication and Cognition at Work.* New York: Cambridge University Press.

Eveland, J. D.; Blanchard, A.; Brown, W.; and Mattocks, J. (1994). "The Role of 'Help Networks' in Facilitating Use of CSCW Technologies." In *Proceedings of the 1994 Conference on Computer Supported Cooperative Work.* Chapel Hill, North Carolina.

Garfinkel, H. (1984, c.1967). *Studies in Ethnomethodology.* Cambridge, England: Polity.

Gasser, L. (1986). "The Integration of Computing and Routine Work." *ACM Transactions on Office Information Systems,* Volume 4, Number 3, pp. 205-225.

Gaver, W. W. (1992). *The Affordances of Media Spaces for Collaboration.* New York: ACM Press.

Gerson, E., and Star, S. L. (1986). "Analyzing Due Process in the Workplace." *ACM Transactions on Office Information Systems,* Volume 4, Number 3, pp. 257-270.

Gladwell, M. (1996). "The Science of Shopping." *The New Yorker,* November 4, pp. 66-75.

Glaser, B., and Strauss, A. (1967). *The Discovery of Grounded Theory: Strategies for Qualitative Research.* Hawthorne, New York: Aldine de Gruyter.

Greenbaum, J., and Kyng, M. (Editors) (1991). *Design at Work: Cooperative Design of Computer Systems.* Hillsdale, New Jersey: Lawrence Erlbaum Associates.

Gregory, K. L. (1983). "Native-View Paradigms: Multiple Cultures and Culture Conflicts in Organizations." *Administrative Sciences Quarterly,* Volume 28, pp. 359-376.

Grudin, J. (1994). "Groupware and Social Dynamics: Eight Challenges for Developers." *Communications of the ACM,* Volume 37, Number 1, pp. 92-105.

Heath, C., and Luff, P. (Editors) (1991). "Collaborative Activity and Technological Design: Task Coordination in London Underground Control Rooms." *Proceedings of the Second European Conference on Computer-Supported Cooperative Work.* Amsterdam, The Netherlands.

Heath, C., and Luff, P. (1993). "Disembodied Conduct: Interactional Asymmetries in Video-Mediated Communication." *Technology in Working Order: Studies of Work, Interaction, and Technology.* London: Routledge, pp. 35-54.

Hiltz, S. R., and Turoff, M. (1993). *The Network Nation: Human Communication via Computer,* Revised Edition. Cambridge, Massachusetts: MIT Press.

Holtzblatt, K., and Beyer, H. (1993). "Making Customer-Centered Design Work for Teams." *Communications of the ACM,* Volume 36, Number 10, pp. 93-103.

Hughes, J.; Randall, D.; and Shapiro, D. (1993). "From Ethnographic Record to System Design." *Journal of Computer Supported Cooperative Work,* Volume 1, Number 3, pp. 123-141.

Jordan, B. (1992). *Technology and Social Interaction: Notes on the Achievement of Authoritative Knowledge in Complex Settings.* Palo Alto, California: Institute for Research on Learning.

Jordan, B. (1993, c. 1983). *Birth in Four Cultures: A Crosscultural Investigation of Childbirth in Yucatan, Holland, Sweden, and the United States,* Fourth Exanded Edition, revised by R. Davis-Floyd. Prospect Heights, Illinois: Waveland Press, Inc.

Jordan, B. (1996a). "Ethnographic Workplace Studies and CSCW." In D. Shapiro, M. Tauber and R. Traunmüller (Editors), *The Design of Computer Supported Cooperative Work and Groupware Systems.* Amsterdam: North Holland, pp. 17-42.

Jordan, B. (1996b). "Transforming Ethnography – Reinventing Research." In J. Schiestl and H. Schelle (Editors), *Groupware – Software für die Teamarbeit der Zukunft: Grundlegende Konzepte und Fallstudien.* Marburg, Germany: Tectum Verlag, pp. 200-212.

Jordan, B., and Henderson, A. (1995). "Interaction Analysis: Foundations and Practice." *The Journal of the Learning Sciences,* Volume 4, Number 1, pp. 39-103.

Korpela, E. (1994). "Path to Notes: A Networked Company Choosing its Information Systems Solution." In R. Baskerville, S. Smithson, O. Ngwenyama, and J. I.

DeGross, *Transforming Organizations with Information Technology*. Amsterdam: North-Holland.

Lave, J., and Wenger, E. (1991). *Situated Learning: Legitimate Peripheral Participation.* Cambridge, England: Cambridge University Press.

Lee, A. S. (1994). "Electronic Mail as a Medium for Rich Communication: An Empirical Investigation Using Hermeneutic Interpretation." *MIS Quarterly,* Volume 18, Number 2, pp. 143-157.

Lofland, J. (1995). *Analyzing Social Settings: A Guide to Qualitative Observation and Analysis,* Third Edition. Belmont, California: Wadsworth.

Malinowski, B. (1922). *Argonauts of the Western Pacific.* New York: E. P. Dutton, Inc.

Malinowski, B. (1979, c. 1927). *Sex and Repression in Savage Society.* London: Routledge and Kegan Paul.

Markus, M. L. (1994). "Finding a Happy Medium: Explaining the Negative Effects of Electronic Communication on Social Life at Work." *ACM Transactions on Information Systems,* Volume 12, Number 2, pp. 119-149.

Markus, M. L., and Bjørn-Andersen, N. (1987). "Power Over Users: Its Exercise by System Professionals." *Communications of the ACM,* Volume 30, Number 6.

Mead, M. (1930). *Growing up in New Guinea.* New York: Mentor Book.

Mead, M. (1973, c. 1928). *Coming of Age in Samoa.* New York: American Museum of Natural History.

Nardi, B. A.; Kuchinsky, A.; Whittaker, S.; Leichner, R.; and Schwarz, H. (1995). "Video-as-Data: Technical and Social Aspects of a Collaborative Multimedia Application." *International Journal of Computer Supported Cooperative Work,* Volume 4, Number 1, pp. 73-100.

Naroll, R., and Cohen, R. (1973). *A Handbook of Method in Cultural Anthropology.* New York: Columbia University Press.

Orlikowski, W. J. (1993). "Learning from NOTES: Organizational Issues in Groupware Implementation." *The Information Society,* Volume 9, pp. 237-250.

Orlikowski, W. J., and Gash, D. C. (1994). "Technological Frames: Making Sense of Information Technology in Organizations." *ACM Transactions on Information Systems,* Volume 12, Number 2, pp. 174-207.

Orr, J. (1996). *Talking About Machines: An Ethnography of the Modern Job.* Ithaca, New York: ILR Press.

Roschelle, J., and Goldman, S. (1991). "VideoNoter: A Productivity Tool for Video Data Analysis." *Behavior Research Methods, Instruments, and Computers,* Volume 23, Number 2, p. 219.

Ruhleder, K. (1994). "Rich and Lean Representations of Information for Knowledge Work: The Role of Computing Packages in the Work of Classical Scholars." *Transactions on Office Information Systems,* Volume 12, Number 2, pp. 208-230.

Ruhleder, K. (1995). "Reconstructing Artifacts, Reconstructing Work: From Textual Edition to On-Line Databank." *Science, Technology and Human Values,* Volume 29, Number 1, pp. 39-64.

Ruhleder, K.; Jordan, B.; and Elmes, M. (1996). "Wiring the 'New Organization': Integrating Collaborative Technologies and Team-Based Work." 1996 Academy of Management, OCIS Division. [URL: http://alexia.lis.uiuc.edu/~ruhleder/publications/96.academy.html]

Sanderson, P.; Scott, J.; Johnston, T.; and Mainzer, J. (1994). MacSHAPA and the Enterprise of Exploratory Sequential Data Analysis (ESDA). *International Journal of Human-Computer Studies,* Volume 41, Number 5, p. 633.

Shapiro, D.; Tauber, M.; and Traunmüller, R. (Editors) (1996). *The Design of Computer-Supported Cooperative Work and Groupware Systems.* Amsterdam: North Holland.

Sproull, L., and Kiesler, S. (1991). *Connections: New Ways of Working in the Networked Organization.* Cambridge, Massachusetts: MIT Press.

Star, S. L. (Editor) (1995). *The Cultures of Computing.* Cambridge, Massachusetts: Blackwell Publishers.

Star, S. L., and Ruhleder, K. (1996). "Steps Towards and Ecology of Infrastructure: Design and Access for Large Information Spaces." *Information Systems Research,* Volume 7, Number 1, pp. 111-134.

Strauss, A. (1986). *Qualitative Methods for Social Scientists.* Cambridge, England: Cambridge University Press.

Suchman, L. (1987). *Plans and Situated Actions: The Problem of Human-Machine Communication.* Cambridge, England: Cambridge University Press.

Suchman, L., and Trigg, R. (1991). "Understanding Practice: Video as Medium for Reflection and Design." In J. Greenbaum and M. Kyng (Editors), *Design at Work: Approaches to Collaborative Design.* Hillsdale, New Jersey: Lawrence Erlbaum Associates.

Van Maanen, J. (1988). *Tales of the Field.* Chicago: University of Chicago Press.

Wolcott, H. F. (1973). *The Man in the Principal's Office: An Ethnography.* New York: Holt, Rinehart and Winston.

Yates, J., and Van Maanen, J. (1996). "Editorial Notes for the Special Issue." *Information Systems Research,* Volume 7, Number 1, pp. 1-4.

9 BIOGRAPHY

Karen Ruhleder works in the interdisciplinary area of social informatics. Her research and teaching crosses the areas of information technology, the ethnography of information systems, and organizational theory. Her past work has included evaluations of the integration of scholarly workstations into humanistic and scientific disciplines. Current research projects focus on the impact of information and communication technologies on work practices and organizational design, especially the emergence of socio-technical infrastructures to support geographically-distributed collaborative work. She is particularly interested in the integration of information and communication technologies into distributed workgroups, and the emergence of virtual learning communities. The venues for her work have included both academic and corporate settings.

Brigitte Jordan is an anthropologist with interests in the participatory design of productive and supportive work settings. She has done research in industrial and pre-industrial communities in the US, Europe, and several developing countries, tracing the influence of social and technological innovations on work practice, quality of life, and organizational change. Her long-range research interests revolve around the changing nature of work and leisure under the impact of the new communication and information technologies and the consequent transformation of ways of life, societal institutions, and global economies. Current projects focus on understanding and improving complex work settings in the production and service sectors, the support of organizational learning, and tool building to support knowledge management and work redesign.

15

Critical Ethnography in Information Systems

M. D. Myers
Department of Management Science and Information Systems
University of Auckland
Auckland, New Zealand
Fax: 649 3737 430
E-mail: m.myers@auckland.ac.nz

Abstract
In recent years, there has been growing interest in qualitative research methods and their application to information systems. This paper discusses the nature and applicability of one qualitative approach to information systems research, called critical ethnography. Critical ethnography, informed by critical hermeneutics, is one of many possible approaches to ethnographic research. A critical ethnographic study of the development of an information system in mental health is reviewed.

1 INTRODUCTION

There has been growing interest in qualitative research methods and their application to information systems in recent years. The interest shown is a direct result of the emergence of a certain dissatisfaction with the state of information systems research in the late 1980s and early 1990s. At that time, the most common research methods used in information systems were surveys, laboratory experiments, and descriptive case studies (Alavi and Carlson 1992), which led some researchers to charge that IS research suffered from a lack of diversity (Galliers and Land 1987; Orlikowski and Baroudi 1991). Other researchers claimed that IS research was often superficial and somewhat faddish (Banville and Landry 1989), which is disturbing given the importance and impact of information technology in contemporary society.

Out of this situation came a call for methodological pluralism in information systems (Avison and Myers 1995; Banville and Landry 1989; Galliers 1991; Hirschheim and Klein 1989; Landry and Banville 1992). Landry and Banville suggested that no single method could ever capture all the richness and complexity of organizational reality, and that a diversity of methods, theories, and philosophies was required (p. 78). Orlikowski and Baroudi, likewise, argued that there was much that could be gained if a plurality of research perspectives was effectively employed to investigate information systems phenomena. They argued that any one perspective is always only a partial view, and unnecessarily restrictive. In line with these calls for methodological pluralism, qualitative (and also interpretive) research methods have gained prominence and been increasingly accepted by the IS research community in the last few years (Benbasat, Goldstein and Mead 1987; Walsham 1993, 1995b; Yin 1989).

The nature and applicability of one qualitative approach to information systems research, called critical ethnography, are discussed in this paper. Critical ethnography, which is one of many possible approaches to ethnographic research, has critical hermeneutics as its philosophical base (Power 1991). Critical ethnography is distinctive in its focus on the relationships among knowledge, culture, society and action (Thomas 1993). The usefulness of the critical ethnographic research method for IS researchers will be illustrated by looking at a critical ethnographic study of the development of an information system in mental health.

The paper is organized as follows. The nature of ethnographic research in general is briefly reviewed in the following section. This is followed by a discussion of critical ethnography in section 3. Section 4 looks at one critical ethnographic study in some depth, the development of an information system in mental health. Section 5 discusses the findings in the light of the research method used. The final section presents the conclusions.

2 THE NATURE OF ETHNOGRAPHIC RESEARCH

An important focus of much recent IS research has been on the social and organizational contexts of information systems design, development and application (e.g., Hirschheim and Newman 1991; Newman and Robey 1992; Walsham 1993). This work has led to the realization that information systems have a highly complex, and constantly changing, social context. It is in the exploration of that social context where ethnographic research comes into its own. The goal of ethnographic research is to improve our understanding of human thought and action through interpretation of human actions in context. For an ethnographer, the preferred way of contributing to an understanding of information systems in organizations is to investigate how they affect social interaction and the creation of shared meanings.

In more traditional positivist techniques, context is treated as either a set of interfering variables that need controlling, known as noise in the data, or other controlled variables, which are experimentally set up in order to seek cause and effect relationships (Harvey and Myers 1995). The context of a situation is seen as something that can be factored out of the analysis or operationalized as a variable. In ethnographic approaches, however, context is treated as the socially constructed reality of a named group, or groups, of social agents and the key task of observation and analysis is to unpack the webs of meaning transformed in the social process whereby social reality is constructed. For an ethnographer, the context is what defines the situation and makes it what it is. In positivist techniques, cause and effect are the main objects being sought, while in interpretive techniques, meaning in context is the most important framework being sought (Harvey and Myers 1995).

Because context is crucial to qualitative observations and analyses, techniques that explore contextual webs of meaning are important. The two most common qualitative field research methods for doing this are interpretive in-depth case studies (Walsham 1993) and ethnographies (Hutchins 1995; Star 1995; Suchman 1987; Wynn 1979, 1991; Zuboff 1988). Although there is no hard and fast distinction, the principle difference between the two depends upon the length of time that the investigator is required to spend in the field and the extent to which the researcher immerses himself or herself in the life of the social group under study. In a case study, the primary source of data is interviews, supplemented by documentary evidence such as annual reports, minutes of meetings and so forth. In an ethnography, these data sources are supplemented by data collected during participant observation on the part of the researcher over an extended period of time. The ethnographer "immerses himself in the life of people he studies" (Lewis 1985, p. 380) and seeks to place the phenomena studied in its social and cultural context. As Yin explains,

> Ethnographies usually require long periods of time in the "field" and emphasize detailed, observational evidence... In contrast, case studies are a form of enquiry that does not depend solely on ethnographic or participant observation data. One could even do a valid and high-quality case study without leaving the library and the telephone. [Yin 1989, p. 21-22]

The difference between an in-depth case study and an ethnography can be illustrated from the IS research literature. The ethnographic research method was used by Orlikowski (1991), who studied a large, multinational software consulting firm over eight months. Data was collected via participant observation, interviews, documents, and informal social contact with the participants. The in-depth case study method was used by Walsham and Waema (1994), who studied a building society for a period of two years. The principal method of data collection was in-depth interviews with a range of organizational participants. The researchers did not use participant observation.

In recent years, a small but growing number of information systems researchers have recognized the value of the ethnographic method for information systems research (Harvey and Myers 1995; Lee 1991; Lee, Baskerville and Davies 1992; Pettigrew 1985; Wynn 1991). Some of the early ground-breaking work was done by Wynn (1979) in her study of office conversations, Suchman (1987) in her study of the problem of human-machine communications, and Zuboff (1988) in her study of the automating and "informating" potential of information technology.

Since then, ethnography has become more widely used in the study of information systems in organizations, from the study of the development of information systems (Hughes, Randall and Shapiro 1992; Orlikowski 1991; Preston 1991; Suchman 1995) to the study of aspects of information technology management (Davies 1991; Davies and Nielsen 1992). Ethnography has also been discussed as a method whereby multiple perspectives can be incorporated in systems design (Holzblatt and Beyer 1993). For example, Bentley et al. (1992) conclude that ethnographic studies "are helpful in informing the systems design process and may produce insights which contradict conventional thinking in systems design" (p. 123).

In the area of the design and evaluation of information systems, some very interesting work has been taking place in a collaborative fashion between ethnographers, on the one hand, and designers, IS professionals, computer scientists and engineers on the other. This collaborative work is especially strong in the UK and Europe and is growing in the US (Star 1995). For example, one of the main projects of the group at Lancaster University (Hughes, Shapiro and Rodden) has been to use the ethnographic method to gain an understanding of human cooperation in air traffic control (Bentley et al. 1992; Hughes Randall and Shapiro 1992).

Having briefly reviewed the nature of ethnographic research in general and its use in the IS field, attention will now be given to the distinctive features of critical ethnography.

3 CRITICAL ETHNOGRAPHY

Although all ethnographic research is similar in the sense that the ethnographer is required to spend a significant amount of time in the field, there are many different schools or views within anthropology about ethnographic interpretation and there is critical debate within anthropology concerning the ethnographic research method (Van Maanen 1988). These different views about ethnographic research are relevant to the ethnographic study of information systems as they show the variety of approaches which have been adopted within the source discipline. Although unable to discuss this critical debate within anthropology in depth here, one of the landmark publications in this debate is the work of Clifford and Marcus (1986; see also Clifford 1988; Marcus 1992).

Sanday (1979) divides ethnography into the holistic, semiotic, and behavioristic schools of thought, and she further divides the semiotic school into thick description and ethnoscience. Each school of thought has a different approach to doing an ethnography. For example, most ethnographers of the holistic school say that empathy and identification with the social grouping being observed are needed; they insist that an anthropologist should "go native" and live just like the local people (e.g., Evans-Pritchard 1950; Cohen 1985). The assumption is that the anthropologist has to become like a blank slate in order fully understand local social and cultural practices. The anthropologist acts like a sponge, soaking up the language and culture of the people under study.

On the other hand, Geertz, the foremost exponent of the "thick description" (semiotic) school, says that anthropologists do not need to have empathy with their subjects (Geertz 1973, 1983, 1988). Rather, the ethnographer has to search out and analyze symbolic forms – words, images, institutions, behaviors – with respect to one another and to the whole that they comprise. Geertz argues that it is possible for an anthropologist to describe and analyze another culture without having to empathize with the people. He says that anthropologists need to understand the "webs of significance" which people weave within the cultural context, and these webs of significance can only be communicated to others by thickly describing the situation and its context.

An alternative to the above is the adoption of a critical perspective on ethnographic research, called critical ethnography. Critical ethnography has emerged as one important approach to ethnographic research (Marcus and Fischer 1986; Thomas 1983, 1993; Power 1991). For example, Forester (1992) used critical ethnography to examine the facetious figures of speech used by city planing staff to negotiate the problem of data acquisition. Myers (1987) used critical ethnography in his study of the independence movement in the Melanesian nation of Vanuatu.

The critical ethnographic approach to interpretive field research is discussed below. Since critical ethnography has critical hermeneutics as its underlying philosophical base, critical hermeneutics will be reviewed first.

3.1 Critical Hermeneutic

Critical hermeneutics is an integrative philosophical approach, combining interpretive and critical elements (Thompson 1981; Myers 1994, 1995). Critical (or dialectical) hermeneutics is an attempt to dissolve the boundaries between the interpretivist and critical research traditions, which have usually been seen as quite distinct (Orlikowski and Baroudi 1991). The philosophical basis for integration is provided by Bernstein (1983), who argues that there is common ground between the critical theory of Jurgen Habermas and the hermeneutics of Hans-Georg Gadamer. Hoy (1988), likewise, argues that it is possible to integrate the interpretive and critical approaches. Hoy finds that the writings of Paul Ricoeur provide such an integrative perspective.

What follows, then, is a description of critical hermeneutics as an integrative philosophical perspective. In this discussion, critical hermeneutics will be distinguished from "pure hermeneutics" as it has been traditionally represented.

Hermeneutics is the science of interpretation, concerned with analysis of the *meaning* of a text or text-analogue. The basic question in hermeneutics is "What is the meaning of a text?" (Radnitzky 1970, p. 20). Taylor says that

> Interpretation, in the sense relevant to hermeneutics, is an attempt to make clear, to make sense of an object of study. This object must, therefore, be

> a text, or a text-analogue, which in some way is confused, incomplete, cloudy, seemingly contradictory – in one way or another, unclear. The interpretation aims to bring to light an underlying coherence or sense. [Taylor 1976, p. 153]

The idea of a hermeneutic circle refers to the dialectic between the understanding of the text as a whole and the interpretation of its parts, in which descriptions are guided by anticipated explanations (Gadamern 1976, p. 117). As Gadamer explains, "It is a circular relationship....The anticipation of meaning in which the whole is envisaged becomes explicit understanding in that the parts, that are determined by the whole, themselves also determine this whole."

The idea of the hermeneutic circle can be applied to the way in which we understand an organization as a text-analogue. In interpretive research, the movement of understanding "is constantly from the whole to the part and back to the whole"; in other words, the more interviews we conduct and the more information we gather, the more we understand the organization as a whole and its constituent parts. This hermeneutic process continues until the apparent absurdities, contradictions and oppositions in the organization no longer appear strange, but make sense.

It follows from this idea of the hermeneutic circle that we have an expectation of meaning from the context of what has gone before. The movement of understanding "is constantly from the whole to the part and back to the whole" (Gadamer 1976b, p. 117). Ricoeur points out that "Interpretation... is the work of thought which consists in deciphering the hidden meaning in the apparent meaning, in unfolding the levels of meaning implied in the literal meaning" (Ricoeur 1974, p. xiv).

In the last ten years, hermeneutics has been taken up by researchers in the information systems area (e.g., Winograd and Flores 1987; Lee 1991, 1994; Boland 1985, 1987, 1991; Boland and Day 1989; Myers 1994, 1995). The principles of hermeneutics have been applied to analyses of the metaphorical nature of theories of information (Boland 1987) and to systems development (Hirschheim and Newman 1991). Hermeneutics is a recognized framework for the analysis of organizations (Bryman 1989), in particular when looking at organizational culture (Frost et al. 1985), and has been applied to the analysis of socio-technical interactions (Barley 1986).

There are different forms of hermeneutics, all concerned with the textual treatment of social settings, but not all concern themselves with reflective critique of the meaning of interpretations derived from textual analyses. The early hermeneuts such as Dilthey advocated a "pure hermeneutics" which stressed empathic understanding and the understanding of human action from the "inside." As Radnitzky (1970, p. 20ff) points out, however, pure hermeneutics is uncritical in that it takes statements or ideologies at face value." He cites Gadamer as saying that "we don't have to imagine oneself in the place of some other person; rather, we have to understand *what* these thoughts or the sentences expressing them are *about*."

More recently, critical hermeneutics has emerged following the debates between Habermas and Gadamer (Gadamer 1976a; Ricoeur 1974; Thompson 1981; Myers 1995). There is a potential tendency to view interpretation as a closed and exact form, but critical hermeneutics recognizes that the interpretive act is one which can never be closed as there is always a possible alternative interpretation (Taylor 1976). In critical hermeneutics, the interpreter constructs the context as another form of text, which can then, of itself, be critically analyzed so that the meaning construction can be understood as an interpretive act. In this way, the hermeneutic interpreter is simply creating another text upon a text, and this recursive creation is potentially infinite. Every meaning is constructed, even through the very constructive act of seeking to deconstruct, and the process whereby that textual interpretation occurs must be self-critically reflected upon (Ricoeur 1974). The close relationship between critical hermeneutics and critical ethnography serves to "emphasize the sense in which all social inquiry is exploratory and open" (Power 1991, p. 338).

Critical hermeneutics also recognises that prejudice, prejudgement or prior knowledge plays an important part in our understanding. In positivist social science, prejudice or prejudgement is seen as a source of bias and therefore a hindrance to true knowledge; objectivity, according to positivism, is best attained if a social scientist adopts a value-free position and does not let biases interfere with his or her analysis. By contrast, hermeneutics recognizes that prejudice is the necessary starting point of our understanding. The critical task of hermeneutics then becomes one of distinguishing between"true prejudices, by which we understand, from the false ones by which we misunderstand" (Gadamer 1976b, p. 124). Of course, the suspension of our prejudices is necessary if we are to begin to understand a text or text-analogue. But as Gadamer points out, this does not mean that we simply set aside our prejudices. Rather, it means that we, as researchers, must become aware of our own historicality (p. 125). This awareness of the dialogue between the text and the interpreter is peculiar to contemporary hermeneutics. The earlier hermeneutic philosophers such as Dilthey ignored this dialogical relationship between the text and the interpreter and attempted to understand the objective meaning of a text in its own right.

3.2 Toward a Critical Ethnography

Adoption of critical hermeneutics as one's underlying philosophical position in ethnographic research leads to criticism of nondialectical views of ethnographic work. One such nondialectical position is that of the holistic school in ethnography. Ethnographers of the holistic school, in their attempt to "go native" and understand other cultures "in their own terms," in effect deny the glossing of those views by the interpretive act of the analyst. The end result is tantamount to a recourse to objectivity due to a taking for granted of the need for the critical analysis of the dialectics of the interpretive process. The role of the observer is treated as context-free, ignoring the fact that every interpretive exploration leads to a new understanding, thus rendering history as the most vital attribute of ethnographic analysis, the history of the material and the history of the interpretation. For example, in Zuboff's study of computer-mediated work, the historical nature of the ethnographic work was regarded as fundamental to the ethnographic work being carried out. She argued that "history would offer only a brief window of time during which such data could be gathered" (Zuboff 1988, p. xiv).

The critical hermeneutic perspective thus openly recognises that understanding of an institutional context is not gained by the researcher suspending her or his prejudices. Rather, the ethnographer is encouraged to become critically aware of them, making them explicit in the process of learning about the organization.

The critical hermeneutic perspective leads to the recognition that any interpretive field research is a form of historiography. The researcher is essentially situated in history, the history of the situation and of the interpretation, and is also part of a wider set of social, economic and political relationships. One of the key tasks of a researcher is to be aware of the historical context in which research takes place and to critically reflect this onto the research process itself. In arguing for a reflexive anthropology, Kahn (1989) points out that the interpretation of culture(s) "is in fact part of a process of construction" and says that anthropologists themselves "are similarly part of a broader socio-historical process" (p. 22; see also Scholte 1972).

> To put the argument in another way, when I, or any other anthropologist, produces in text an account of another culture, what I am in fact doing is engaging in a process with a history. That history is the cultural product of a longstanding relation between "us" and "them" within which I and my "informants" are embedded. At the same time, the knowledge which I/we produce out of that relation – in my case for example the knowledge I might choose to term "Minangkabau culture," or "the meaning of mosque symbolism in a West Sumatran village," or whatever – is new knowledge in the sense that it does not pre-exist in West Sumatra, hard-wired as it were in the brains of the Minangkabau from time immemorial. It exists, and can only exist, in the relationship between Minangkabau and the West. [Kahn 1989, p. 16]

This awareness of the importance of history leads to criticism of the "ethnographic present," a standard device used by many anthropologists to describe social and cultural practices. The ethnographic present gives the (false) impression that the activities being described have always existed from time immemorial. The use of such phrases as "the development process starts out each September" or "all the members of the development team do not participate" gives the distinct impression that such activities have taken place since the world was created. The ethnographic present is thus ahistorical, and neglects to mention when these activities were instituted. The ethnographic present ignores how human actions are always situated in history.

Although critical ethnography is distinctive, it does not stand in opposition to other forms of ethnographic research. Rather, it is a type of reflection about the relationships among knowledge, culture, society and action (Thomas 1993). "Critical ethnographers describe, analyze, and open to scrutiny otherwise hidden agendas, power centers, and assumptions that inhibit, repress, and constrain. Critical scholarship requires that commonsense assumptions be questioned" (Thomas 1993, pp. 2-3). In a critical ethnography, the critical analysis moves beyond the immediate narrative of the subjects to the broader processes within which the narratives are embedded. Further guidelines for doing critical ethnography can be found in Thomas (1993).

4 A CRITICAL ETHNOGRAPHIC STUDY OF THE DEVELOPMENT OF AN INFORMATION SYSTEM IN MENTAL HEALTH

A critical ethnographic study of the development of an information system in mental health will now be reviewed. This ethnographic study, conducted by Young (1995) under the supervision of Michael D. Myers at the University of Auckland, was concerned with the development of an information system in mental health. This information system, developed during 1994 and the first part of 1995, was developed for Mental Health in one of the Crown Health Enterprises in New Zealand. The ethnographic research took place over a period of ten months, from April 1994 to January 1995. The ethnographic material was collected via participant observation, structured and unstructured interviews, unpublished documents (such as minutes of meetings), and newspaper and magazine reports (Young 1995). Some information about the health sector in New Zealand and the organization will be summarized first, with the objective of setting the specific IS project within its broader social and historical context. This will be followed by a discussion of one of the key issues which emerged during development.

4.1 The Health Sector in New Zealand

The New Zealand health care system is made up of public, private and voluntary sectors that interact in financing and providing medical care. Total expenditure on health care in New Zealand of NZ $4,873 million in 1989/90 was funded in the proportions of $4,150 million by the government, and $723 million by the private sector (Danzon and Begg 1991). Funding was provided by the Department of Health, Accident Compensation Corporation (ACC), budget allocations and levies, individuals, private insurance premiums, insurance managed by employers and other organisations (such as unions), as well as out-of-pocket payments by patients.

New Zealand's public hospitals, which number around 175, are mostly administered by Crown Health Enterprises (CHEs). These public hospitals provide around 23,000 beds or about 80% of the total hospital beds in New Zealand. Services are provided to inpatients at zero monetary cost although costs are incurred in terms of waiting for an appointment for treatment, as well as waiting times once appointments have been made, and limitations in the quality of service provided to patients (Danzon and Begg 1991). There is a NZ $31 charge per visit for outpatients.

The public sector, through the Ministry of Health, provides free treatment for all New Zealand citizens at public hospitals, long term care and public health services. Private hospitals have evolved to provide services not adequately provided by the public sector, notably elective surgery and geriatric care. The voluntary sector includes such organizations as the Intellectually Handicapped Society, Plunket Society, Family Planning Association, Salvation Army and the Crippled Children Society. Some of these receive government assistance (Danzon and Begg 1991).

The health sector in New Zealand has, over the years, undergone many changes in administration and information technology. The changes have been somewhat more radical in recent years with major changes to the social and political structure of the New Zealand Healthcare system. In 1991, the New Zealand Government signaled a major reform to the health system, the key to which was the so-called "purchaser-provider split." Under this arrangement, the existing Area Health Boards were dismantled and replaced by a combination of Regional Health Authorities (RHAs) and Crown Health Enterprises (CHEs). The RHAs became responsible for the purchase of health care from institutions and practitioners within its region (Clausen, Domney and Pederson 1992). Crown Health Enterprises (CHEs) and community trusts became responsible for the provision of health services to the community (Upton 1991).

The main objective of the government's reform was to introduce competition into the health sector in the hope that this would reduce costs and improve the productivity of the health industry. In essence, the government created a competitive market whereby the RHAs purchase health care services from providers who compete with each other. However, the introduction of market principles into the health arena was strongly opposed by most other political parties and many doctors and nurses. Doctors and nurses often vented their anger and frustration at the reforms in the mass media, arguing, for example, that patients should not be viewed as customers. For them, the word customer was suggestive of a more impersonal kind of relationship based on the payment of a fee, as contrasted with the word patient, which for them implied a more personal kind of relationship based on concern for a person's well-being.

Nevertheless, with the emergence of a competitive market being a foregone conclusion, senior management in the CHEs saw the need to develop new information systems to help them compete for contracts. Senior managers realised that accurate cost and output information as well as information relating to service quality measures were needed if their organization was to be successful in the competitive bidding process (Myers and Young 1995). These newly developed information systems thus became one of the key instruments by which senior management could achieve the purported benefits of the government's reforms.

4.2 The Organization

Sky City Health (a pseudonym) is a Crown Health Enterprise in a New Zealand city, providing health services to the public. Sky City Health's vision statement reads as follows:

> Through innovation and dedication to the service of our patients, we will provide health care solutions that are measured as successful by the patient, the health care team and the organisation.
>
> To provide successful health care solutions we need to provide the right care, in the right amount, at the right time and in the right setting.

The organization has introduced the concept of shared values. The shared values include patient and user focus, professionalism, integrity, taking personal responsibility, service orientation, teamwork, innovation, communication, confidentiality and cultural sensitivity.

Sky City Health used to have a very hierarchical organizational structure, but in recent years this has become somewhat flatter. The chief executive officer is responsible to a board of directors. Five general managers report to the CEO, one of whom is the group manager for mental health services. Information services has no group manager; instead it comes under the responsibility of the general manager for finance and commercial (Myers and Young 1995).

4.3 Information Services

Information services is a separate unit in Sky City Health responsible for overseeing all information systems projects. he IS unit has identified three key critical success factors in relation to the successful implementation of information technology:

- Alignment of IT strategy with the organization's business plan.
- To put in place an architecture providing flexibility in case of future business change.
- Not to continue with current business practices that are inconsistent with new technology and/or new systems.

Other issues that have been identified as important are using information technology to add value to the organization, treating information technology as an asset, automating critical and commonly used parts of the existing medical record, and recognising quality service.

At the time of the research, information services used a project plan document to ensure a consistent methodology for the implementation of all projects undertaken by Sky City Health. These projects mainly arise through their information systems strategic planning exercise, but may include any other information systems projects that arise from time to time.

The key areas of the project methodology are

- definition of responsibilities for implementation

- confirmation of the deliverables
- development of the project plan(s)
- meeting schedules
- change control
- purchase of the componentry
- monitoring of implementation
- acceptance
- project closure
- post project review

Generally, project teams are comprised of a project director, a project sponsor, a project leader and one or more project champions, business analysts and technical resource personnel (if appropriate). Other parties likely to be involved in the project include vendors.

As part of the project team framework, an information systems steering group has been set up to provide a forum for directing, monitoring and reviewing information systems projects. The meetings are held once a month. The members are drawn from senior management, clinical services disciplines, operations and management support, and information services (Myers and Young 1995).

4.4 The Mental Health IS Project

Mental health services in Sky City are split into two categories of health care users: inpatients and outpatients. Inpatients are health care users who are admitted to a facility and stay for more than four hours, whereas outpatients are referred from other services or general practitioners to a particular service and leave the service on the same day. Two hospitals provide inpatient services for adults, whereas outpatient services are provided in three areas of the community.

In 1993, a functional specification for a management information system for mental health was compiled, and a request for information (RFI) for a mental health information system was sent out to vendors in 1994. Some of the requirements were

- to improve the quality of care given
- to improve management reporting
- to improve communications
- to improve personal care
- to improve efficiency

A number of clinical issues were required to be addressed by the information system:

- There is a need to record information at a level determined by the health care providers (HCP).
- There is a need to record clinical information on an event-by-event basis where it is regarded as important by the recording HCP.

Following the receipt of responses to the RFI, vendors were put on a short list. Only vendors that could potentially deliver a complete solution (including administrative and clinical functions) were considered. However, after some evaluation it was concluded that there did not seem to be any vendor that could technically and functionally deliver a complete system. Of the vendors looked at, none of them could provide for Sky City Mental Health's specific requirements, nor did they comply with New Zealand regulations. In view of the fact that nothing suitable was found, it was decided by information services that it would be far cheaper and faster to develop an interim system inhouse.

After an information strategic steering group meeting and subsequently a board meeting, it was decided that the overall strategic IS direction would be to split the proposed solution into three parts: core/administration, clinical and casemix. A request for proposal would be issued to vendors for clinical solutions, while the core/administration functions for mental health would be developed inhouse by information services at Sky City Health. Casemix would be tendered for separately. Figure 1 depicts the structure of the proposed information systems architecture and shows how it would be split.

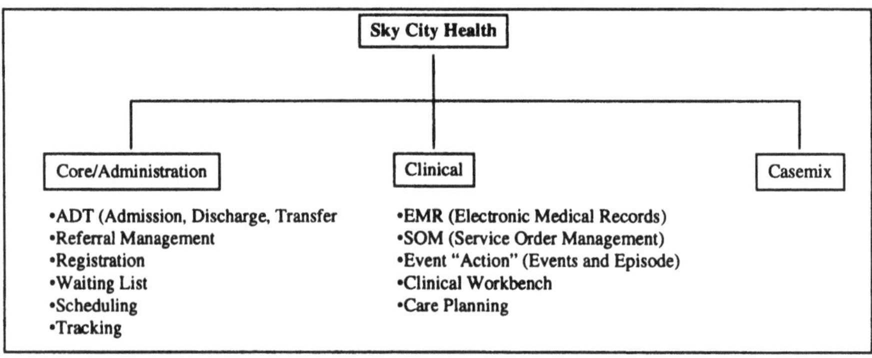

Figure 1 Sky City Health's IS Architecture (Adapted from Young 1995).

The core/administration functions to be covered by the inhouse IS project were the registration, referral, initial assessment, medical administration, tracking and exit modules. Added to that was a financial module dealing with the trust facilities currently provided by one of the hospitals for its health care users.

Consistent with the IS project methodology a project team for the mental health project was formed. The members of the project team represented all of the major stakeholder groups within Sky City Health's Mental Health services. The team consisted of the following: two project sponsors (group manager of mental health, and the clinical director); project leader – information services; project developer – information services; operations coordinator – group manager's office; medical records officer; psychiatrist district nurse – crisis unit; one clerical staff person; one psychiatrist; one charge nurse – acute service; one clinical psychologist. The project team had regular meetings once a week, after which the project leader reported to the project coordinator, who then reported to the IS manager, also on a weekly basis.

Throughout the course of the mental health project, the project team experienced a number of changes in membership. The project leader changed once and the project coordinator changed three times. Toward the end of the project, one of the user group members left the organisation and was replaced by two other users (the user group is discussed below). During the year the project developer from information services left and was replaced by a project developer from system support group to complete the project.

A user group composed of six members was formed in May 1994 to represent clerical staff and clinicians. The user group's role was to make sure that user requirements were considered throughout the project and to review the prototypes.

4.5 An Analysis of One Key Issue: Time-Based Costing

Space does not permit a full discussion of many of the issues which emerged during the project, therefore just one key issue will be discussed here: time-based costing.

It was suggested earlier that new information systems were proposed by senior management in many Crown Health Enterprises so that accurate cost and output information as well as information relating to service quality measures could be obtained. In Sky City Health, these information systems (of which the mental health system was but one) were seen as essential if the organisation were to be successful in the newly instituted competitive bidding process. The mental health IS project was thus intimately tied up with the government's reforms. The IS project was the means by which mental health in Sky City could be transformed into an effective and efficient business enterprise. In effect, the proposed mental health information system, to use the language of Broadbent, Laughlin and Read (1991), was a "steering mechanism" to steer the social system of mental health in a direction aligned to the goals of the New Zealand government. The new IS represented the introduction of market principles to the mental health arena.

However, significant numbers of clinical staff opposed the government's reforms in the health sector, and by implication the information systems that were to be developed to put these reforms into practice. Information services, charged by senior management with developing the new mental health IS, faced the problem of recruiting and retaining doctors and nurses to serve on the project team and on the user group. It was essential for doctors and nurses to participate in the development of the project if information services were to be consistent in their use of the IS development methodology. Participation was also seen to be essential if the new system were to be accepted by clinical staff.

In the mental health IS project, one important module was called "time-based costing." There was much discussion and major disagreements which centered around the development of the "time-based costing" module. Briefly, time base costing is the recording of hours utilized by clinicians, involving a costing report which can be used to estimate how much funding is required from the government. Senior management regarded time-based costing as an essential part of the new system, while many doctors and nurses saw this as a threat to their professional status and conditions of employment. Clinicians tended to see time-based costing as an attempt by management to treat them like factory workers.

In a user group meeting near the end of the project, the champion (a senior manager) explained time based costing to the clinical users as follows:

> There has been acknowledgment for some time that there hasn't been any measures of what we actually do. And this information is used by the financial department, which contract our services....[The lack of data] is more of a worry because, when one does hone in, you can't compare one home visit to another home visit – the number of variables could be huge. In mental health services in particular, our technology is our staff, not like radiology where you can talk about scans, you can attribute the amount of endorsers to the running of one X-ray, or one ultrasound or something like that. Our staff and staff time, that is the main cost driver for mental health ...I know there has been a history in the past to try and collect time based units, and that has certainly happened in other areas....So A and I sat down and tried to look at a way we could collect information based on time, that wasn't going to be unwieldy, not going to be difficult for staff and create major barriers....We are not talking about this as hidden information. What we see is a report coming up monthly – not that we are going to an individual level at this stage, it might be by professional group, or by location.

From the above statement, we can gather that this senior manager tried to minimize the importance of time-based costing to the clinical users (e.g., "we are not talking about this as hidden information"; "not that we are going to an individual level at this stage") while saying that it was very important for financial reasons. Senior management tended to regard the implementation of time-based costing as a certainty.

Interestingly, however, time-based costing was never included in the original user requirements document written in May 1994. Neither was it mentioned in the functional overview dated June 1994 or the updated user requirements of January 1995 (although it was mentioned verbally at a user group meeting). From the point of the view of information services, the project leader expressed the view that the issue was a business issue and not an IS issue. The onus would be on the user group to sort it out with management at a later date. The project leader stated that she preferred to have the time-costing module included later once the full system was in place. Clearly, both senior management and information services intended that the time-based costing module would be an integral part of the new mental health information system, but for political reasons the importance of this particular module was minimized and omitted from the initial user requirements documents.

The following is a transcript of a user group meeting when the time-based costing module was mentioned by the project leader from information services for the first time. The project leader had just informed the usergroup members that time-based costing should now be included in the official user requirements document.

User 1: So has that project been slipped into our brief as well?

IS: Yes, that will be included, and after tracking is the patient exit . . .

User 1: I am not happy actually with the time base costing going in . . .

IS: That is a very small module..

User 1: Well, we might think it is small, maybe it is small in terms of the thing we are bringing in. But when we take this product out to the users, that time base costing is going to seem this big, and the rest is going to seem this big, and they are going to be saying "Oh, so that's why they are setting up this thing!"

IS: No it is very small, it's just a print-out that's all.

User 1: I know, but . . .

User 2: You're worried about resistance.

User 1: I am worried about perceptions of what this whole project has been about, they are going to say this has been a big brother project. It's been a way to keep a track on us, so if I'm not performing they can sack me.

IS: No! What I get from time based [costing], the impression I got, costing is a report so we can get extra funding from the government.

User 1: I know what you are telling me P. What I am saying is, I brought this up the first time you mentioned it, that I thought it would not be a good idea, to be in this project, because people are going to see this whole project as being based around that particular item.

User 3: What we want is it to be taken on, and feel good about it, without feeling paranoid about it..

User 1: That's right.

User 3: Because they are already paranoid about it. . .

User 1: They are going to sabotage it.

U3: Yes, sabotage it or something.

(Transcript of user group meeting).

In the transcript from this meeting, we can see that the IS project leader tried to play down the significance of the time-based costing module (e.g., "it is very small, it's just a print-out that's all"), while at the same time acknowledging the business imperative for its use (e.g., "the impression I got, costing is a report so we can get extra funding from the Government"). The project leader also made it sound as if the introduction of the time-based costing module was inevitable ("Yes, that will be included"). The members of the user group, on the other hand, were surprised and annoyed that they had not been consulted earlier. As clinicians, they had ostensibly participated in the development of the system as user representatives, and until now the time-based costing module had not been mentioned. They were concerned that their fellow clinicians might perceive their participation in development as complicity in the introduction of time-based costing. Consequently, it was agreed at this same user group meeting (a little later on) that time-based costing should be kept as a separate module or introduced later when users had become accustomed to the system. The clinicians argued that the success of the mental health project could be jeopardized if time-based costing were introduced too early and users were not clearly aware of its purpose.

In a subsequent interview one user group member discussed the time-based costing module as follows:

> If time-based costing is put in, then it's going to be a problem with [the marketing of this system], because people are going to have a perception of what this computer system is all about....The perception has been, as an auditing service, as an accounting service, as a way of tracking people – I mean, that is the general sort of feeling about computers in organisations. In this system it [was not intended to be] that at all, but it could easily be perceived as such...I don't think it will be a problem, it will be brought up in the next meeting - we'll get it sidelined!

This clinician expresses the view that if the time-based costing module is included in the project, it will lead to significant problems in users' acceptance of it. The "general sort of feeling" among the clinical staff would be that computers are being used yet again to further control professional people. However, this clinician expressed confidence in his ability (and that of the other clinicians) to get the time-based costing module sidelined at the next meeting. This tactic was successful to a certain extent: the time-based costing module was still to be included, but at least it was agreed not to include it during the initial roll-out of the mental health information system.

Although a significant number of clinical staff opposed the government's reforms in the health sector, and by implication the information systems that were to be developed to put these reforms into practice, this was not true of everyone. Almost all the doctors and nurses chosen to be on the user group and project team were generally enthusiastic about the potential for information systems to improve clinical practice. These clinicians also tended to be sympathetic to the goals of both information services and mental health management. Also, while the project team members were drawn from various stakeholder groups (managers, IS, clinical and clerical users, etc.), the team members developed more of a loyalty to each other and to the project as time went on. The same process occurred within the user group. Despite the fact that the user group was theoretically supposed to represent users, the user group members started to identify more with each other and with the system as the project progressed. In other words, as members of the project team and user group continued to invest their time and effort in the development of the system, they developed more of a vested interest in it.

Seen in this light, the clinicians involved with the project were not opposed to the introduction of new information systems or time-based costing per se; rather, they were more concerned about how the project (and their involvement with it) would be perceived by their clinical colleagues. By being involved with the project as user representatives, they had given a certain amount of legitimacy to the development of the mental health information system. If time-based costing were to be included in the current project, not only would their peers question the legitimacy of the project, they would question their own credibility as well.

That there were developing coalitions of stakeholders (top management, information services, clinical and clerical users) as the system progressed throws into question one of the traditional assumptions of most critical management theorists: that organizational participants can be categorized into distinct groups and that these groups are opposed (often necessarily so) because of the underlying economic and power relations (e.g., Alvesson and Willmott 1992). An example of the latter is the (otherwise excellent) analysis by Broadbent, Laughlin and Read of the financial and administrative changes in the National Health Service in the United Kingdom. The authors assume that "performance-pay related managers" have interests which are distinct and opposed to those of doctors. They suggest that, whereas the former are interested in controlling expenditure and ultimately doctors' clinical practice, the latter are most of all concerned with clinical freedom.

As we have seen, the critical ethnographic research conducted by Young showed that not all doctors were opposed to the goals of management or to the mental health information system. The mental health information system was successfully implemented with the input and support of doctors and nurses on the project team and user group. This is not to say that all doctors and nurses supported the new information system, but the development of the system was legitimized by the support and participation of those who did. Even though those clinicians who participated in the project were unhappy with the attempt by management and IS to have the time-based costing module included in the initial roll-out of the mental health information system, they were not opposed to the system per se.

The previous discussion draws attention to the inherently political nature of information systems development and how terms such as user involvement and participation can mask the deeper political and cultural processes within which IS development is embedded. After the user group had succeeded in sidelining the time-based costing module to a later implementation date, the champion (a senior manager) commented:

> The usergroup felt that it was too much to ask the staff to get used to both the implementation of the information system and recording of their statistics in a new way.

Political opposition to time-based costing was thus reinterpreted by management as staff difficulty in adjusting to new information systems. The key problem was thus cleverly shifted from being one of system goals to the more politically neutral one of user acceptance.

5 DISCUSSION

In commenting on the critical ethnographic study reviewed above, a number of important points can be made.

First, the ethnographer was expressly situated in history. The system studied was intimately tied up with a wider set of social, economic and political relationships involving the New Zealand government's reforms of the health sector. The use of the ethnographic present to describe what the ethnographer saw and heard would have been nonsensical, given that the object of study was a moving target (an IS project). The ethnography was therefore written in the past tense (e.g., as soon as a meeting had finished, it was already history).

Second, the ethnography was critical in a number of ways. The ethnographer exposed the hidden agenda of senior management to introduce time-based costing despite not including this module in the initial user requirements document. Some commonsense assumptions about information systems development were also questioned, e.g., user involvement in this organization was as much about legitimizing the system as it was about obtaining user input. Further, the idea common in critical management studies that organizational stakeholder groups (such as management and doctors) are often necessarily opposed because of the underlying economic and power relations was shown to be somewhat simplistic. While this is true to a certain extent, it does not explain the support of those clinicians on the project team and usergroup for the mental health information system as a whole.

6 CONCLUSION

This paper has discussed the nature and applicability of a relatively new qualitative approach to information systems research called critical ethnography. Ethnographic research is a useful method for analyzing the institutional contexts of information systems practices, with the notion of context being the social construction of meaningful frameworks. When the form of ethnographic research known as critical ethnography is used (although this is not the only one), the findings can be scrutinized for otherwise hidden agendas, power centers and other taken for granted aspects of social reality.

This paper looked at one critical ethnographic study of the development of an information system in mental health. The new system was shown to contain within itself the hidden agendas of management, and more broadly of the New Zealand government. This study raises broader questions about the social and political nature of information systems development, such as the extent to which hidden agendas, power centers and managerial assumptions inhibit, repress and constrain user involvement and user participation. In the example of the specific IS discussed in this paper, the system penetrated most deeply into the social processes of cultural control (cf. Thomas 1993, p. 60; Orlikowski 1991).

7 REFERENCES

Alavi, M., and Carlson, P. (1992), "A Review of MIS Research and Disciplinary Development." *Journal of Management Information Systems*, Volume 8, Number 4, pp. 45-62.

Alvesson, M., and Willmott, H. (Editors) (1992). *Critical Management Studies*. London: Sage Publications.

Avison, D. E., and Myers, M. D. (1995). "Information Systems and Anthropology: An Anthropological Perspective on IT and Organizational Culture." *Information Technology and People*, Volume 8, Number 3, pp. 43-56.

Banville, C., and Landry, M. (1989). "Can the Field of MIS be Disciplined?" *Communications of the ACM*, Volume 32, Number 1, pp. 48-60.

Barley, S. R. (1986). "Technology as an Occasion for Structuring: Evidence from Observations of CT Scanners and the Social Order of Radiology Departments." *Administrative Science Quarterly*, Volume 31, Number 1, pp. 78-108.

Benbasat, I.; Goldstein, D. K.; and Mead, M. (1987). "The Case Research Strategy in Studies of Information Systems." *MIS Quarterly*, Volume 11, Number 3, pp. 369-386.

Bentley, R.; Rodden, T.; Sawyer, P.; Sommerville, I.; Hughes, J.; Randall, R.; and Shapiro, D. (1992). "Ethnographically-Informed Systems Design for Air Traffic Control." In *CSCW '92. ACM 1992 Conference on Computer-Supported Cooperative Work: Sharing Perspectives*. New York: ACM Press, 123-129.

Bernstein, R. J. (1983). *Beyond Objectivism and Relativism*. Philadelphia: University of Pennsylvania Press.

Boland, R. (1985). "Phenomenology: A Preferred Approach to Research in Information Systems." In E. Mumford, R. A. Hirschheim, G. Fitzgerald, and T. Wood-Harper (Editors), *Research Methods in Information Systems*. Amsterdam: North-Holland.

Boland, R. (1987). "The In-formation of Information Systems." In R. J. Boland and R. A. Hirschheim (Editors), *Critical Issues in Information Systems Research*. New York: John Wiley and Sons.

Boland, R. (1991). "Information System Use as a Hermeneutic Process." In H-E. Nissen, H. K. Klein, and R. A. Hirschheim (Editors), *Information Systems Research: Contemporary Approaches and Emergent Traditions*. Amsterdam: North-Holland.

Boland, R. J., and Day, W. F. (1989). "The Experience of System Design: A Hermeneutic of Organizational Action." *Scandinavian Journal of Management*, Volume 5, Number 2, pp. 87-104.

Broadbent, J.; Laughlin, R.; and Read, S. (1991). "Recent Financial and Administrative Changes in the NHS: A Critical Theory Analysis." *Critical Perspectives on Accounting*, Volume 2, pp. 1-29.

Bryman, A. (1989). *Research Methods and Organization Studies*. London: Unwin Hyman

Clifford, J. (1988). *The Predicament of Culture: Twentieth-Century Ethnography, Literature and Art*. Cambridge, Massachusetts: Harvard University Press.

Clifford, J. and Marcus, G. E. (1986). *Writing Culture: The Poetics and Politics of Ethnography*. Berkeley: University of California Press.

Clausen, J.; Domney, M.; and Pederson, M. (1992). "Auckland Area Health Board: The Enterprise Network." Unpublished MBA Working Paper, University of Auckland.

Cohen, A. P. (1985). *The Symbolic Construction of Community*. London: Ellis Horwood.

Danzon, P., and Begg, S. (1991). "Options for Health Care in New Zealand." Report for the Business Roundtable, Wellington, April.

Davies, L. J. (1991). "Researching the Organizational Culture Contexts of Information Systems Strategy." In H-E. Nissen, H. K. Klein, and R. A. Hirschheim (Editors), *Information Systems Research: Contemporary Approaches and Emergent Traditions*. Amsterdam: North-Holland.

Davies, L. J., and Nielsen, S. (1992). "An Ethnographic Study of Configuration Management and Documentation Practices in an Information Technology Center." In K. E. Kendall, K. Lyytinen, and J. I. DeGross (Editors), *The Impact of Computer Supported Technology on Information Systems Development*. Amsterdam: North-Holland.

Evans-Pritchard, E. E. (1950). *Witchcraft, Oracles and Magic among the Azande*. Oxford: The Clarendon Press.

Forester, J. (1992). "Critical Ethnography: On Field Work in an Habermasian Way." In M. Alvesson and H. Willmott (Editors), *Critical Management Studies*. London: Sage Publications.

Frost, P. J.; Moore, L. F.; Louis, M. R.; Lundberg, C. C.; and Martin, J. (Editors) (1985). *Organizational Culture*. Beverly Hills: Sage Publications.

Gadamer, H-G. (1976a). *Philosophical Hermeneutics*. Berkeley: University of California Press.

Gadamer, H-G. (1976b). "The Historicity of Understanding." In P. Connerton (Editor), *Critical Sociology: Selected Readings*. Harmondsworth, England: Penguin Books Ltd.

Galliers, R. D. (1991). "Choosing Appropriate Information Systems Research Methods." In H-E. Nissen, H. K. Klein, and R. A. Hirschheim (Editors), *Information Systems Research: Contemporary Approaches and Emergent Traditions*. Amsterdam: North-Holland.

Galliers, R. D., and Land, F. F. (1987). "Choosing Appropriate Information Systems Research Methodologies." *Communications of the ACM*, Volume 30, Number 11, pp. 900-902.

Geertz, C. (1973). *The Interpretation of Cultures*. New York: Basic Books.

Geertz, C. (1983). *Local Knowledge: Further Essays in Interpretive Anthropology*. New York: Basic Books.

Geertz, C. (1988). *Works and Lives: The Anthropologist as Author*. Cambridge, England: Polity Press.

Harvey, L., and Myers, M. D. (1995). "Scholarship and Practice: The Contribution of Ethnographic Research Methods to Bridging the Gap." *Information Technology and People*, Volume 8, Number 3, pp. 13-27.

Hirschheim, R., and Klein, H. K. (1989). "Four Paradigms of Information Systems Development." *Communications of the ACM*, Volume 32, Number 10, pp. 1199-1216.

Hirschheim, R., and Newman, M. (1991). "Symbolism and Information Systems Development: Myth, Metaphor and Magic." *Information Systems Research*, Volume 2, Number 1, pp. 29-62.

Holzblatt, K., and Beyer, H. (1993). "Making Customer-Centered Design Work for Teams." *Communications of the ACM*, Volume 36, Number 10, pp. 93-103.

Hoy, T. (1988). *Praxis, Truth, and Liberation*. Lanham: University Press of America.

Hughes, J. A.; Randall, D.; and Shapiro, D. (1992). "Faltering from Ethnography to Design." *CSCW'92 ACM : 1992 Conference on Computer-Supported Cooperative Work: Sharing Perspectives*. New York: ACM Press, pp. 115-123.

Hutchins, E. (1995). Cognition in the Wild. Cambridge, Massachusetts: MIT Press.

Kahn, J. S. (1989). "Culture: Demise or Resurrection?" *Critique of Anthropology*, Volume 9, Number 2, pp. 5-25.

Landry, M., and Banville, C. (1992). "A Disciplined Methodological Pluralism for MIS Research." *Accounting, Management and Information Technologies*, Volume 2, Number 2, pp. 77-97.

Lee, A. S. (1991). "Integrating Positivist and Interpretive Approaches to Organizational Research." *Organization Science*, Volume 2, pp. 342-365.

Lee, A. S. (1994). "Electronic Mail as a Medium for Rich Communication: An Empirical Investigation Using Hermeneutic Interpretation." *MIS Quarterly*, Volume 18, Number 2, pp. 143-157.

Lee, A. S.; Baskerville, R. L.; and Davies, L. (1992). "A Workshop on Two Techniques for Qualitative Data Analysis: Action Research and Ethnography." In J. I. DeGross, J. D. Becker, and J. J. Elam (Editors), *Proceedings of the Thirteenth International Conference on Information Systems*, December 13-16, Dallas, Texas, pp. 305-306.

Lewis, I. M. (1985). *Social Anthropology in Perspective*. Cambridge, England: Cambridge University Press.

Marcus, G. E. (1992). *Rereading Cultural Anthropology*. Durham, North Carolina: Duke University Press.

Marcus, G. E., and Fischer, M. M. (1986). *Anthropology as Cultural Critique*. Chicago: Chicago University Press.

Myers, M. D. (1987,). *Independens Long Vanuatu: The Churches and Politics in a Melanesian Nation*. Unpublished Ph.D. Thesis, University of Auckland.

Myers, M. D. (1994). "A Disaster for Everyone to See: An Interpretive Analysis of a Failed IS Project." *Accounting, Management and Information Technologies*, Volume 4, Number 4, pp. 185-201.

Myers, M. D. (1995). "Dialectical Hermeneutics: A Theoretical Framework for the Implementation of Information Systems." *Information Systems Journal*, Volume 5, Number 1, pp. 51-70.

Myers, M. D., and Young, L. W. (1995). "The Implementation of an Information System in Mental Health: An Ethnographic Study." *Proceedings of the Australasian Conference on Information Systems*, September 27-29, Perth, pp. 779-792.

Newman, M., and Robey, D. (1992). "A Social Process Model of User-Analyst Relationships." *MIS Quarterly*, Volume 16, pp. 249-266.

Orlikowski, W. J. (1991). "Integrated Information Environment or Matrix of Control? The Contradictory Implications of Information Technology." *Accounting, Management and Information Technologies*, Volume 1, Number 1, pp. 9-42.

Orlikowski, W. J., and Baroudi, J. (1991). "Studying Information Technology in Organizations: Research Approaches and Assumptions." *Information Systems Research*, Volume 2, Number 1, pp. 1-28.

Pettigrew, A. M. (1985). "Contextualist Research and the Study of Organizational Change Processes." In E. Mumford, R. Hirschheim, G. Fitzgerald, and A. T. Wood-Harper (Editors), *Research Methods in Information Systems*. Amsterdam: North-Holland.

Power, M. K. (1991). "Educating Accountants: Towards a Critical Ethnography." *Accounting, Organizations and Society,* Volume 16, Number 4, pp. 333-353.
Preston, A.M. (1991). "The 'Problem' in and of Management Information Systems." *Accounting, Management and Information Technologies*, Volume 1, Number 1, pp. 43-69.
Radnitzky, G. (1970). *Contemporary Schools of Metascience.* Goteborg: Scandinavian University Books.
Ricoeur, P. (1974). *The Conflict of Interpretations: Essays in Hermeneutics.* Evanston, Illinois: Northwestern University Press.
Sanday, P. R. (1979). "The Ethnographic Paradigm(s)." *Administrative Science Quarterly,* Volume 24, Number 4, pp. 527-538.
Scholte, B. (1972). "Toward a Reflexive and Critical Anthropology." In D. Hymes (Editor), *Reinventing Anthropology.* New York: Random House Inc.
Star, S. L. (1995). *Cultures of Computing.* Oxford: Blackwell.
Suchman, L. (1987). *Plans and Situated Actions: The Problem of Human-Machine Communication.* Cambridge, England: Cambridge University Press.
Suchman, L. (1995). "Making Work Visible." *Communications of the ACM,* Volume 38, Number 9, pp. 56-64.
Taylor, C. (1976). "Hermeneutics and Politics." In P. Connerton (Editor), *Critical Sociology: Selected Readings.* Harmondsworth, England: Penguin Books Ltd.
Thomas, J. (1983). "Toward a Critical Ethnography." *Urban Life,* Volume 11, Number 4, pp. 477-490.
Thomas, J. (1993). *Doing Critical Ethnography.* Newbury Park, California: Sage Publications.
Thompson, J. B. (1981). *Critical Hermeneutics: A Study in the Thought of Paul Ricoeur and Jurgen Habermas.* Cambridge, England: Cambridge University Press.
Van Maanen, J. (1988). *Tales of the Field: On Writing Ethnography.* Chicago: University of Chicago Press.
Upton, S. (1991). *Your Health and the Public Health: A Statement of Government Health Policy.* Wellington, New Zealand: Minister of Health.
Walsham, G. (1993). *Interpreting Information Systems in Organizations.* Chichester, England: Wiley.
Walsham, G. (1995a). "Interpretive Case Studies in IS Research: Nature and Method." *European Journal of Information Systems,* Volume 4, pp. 74-81.
Walsham, G. (1995b). "The Emergence of Interpretivism in IS Research." *Information Systems Research,* Volume 6, Number 4, pp. 376-394.
Walsham, G., and Waema, T. (1994). "Information Systems Strategy and Implementation: A Case Study of a Building Society." *ACM Transactions on Information Systems,* Volume 12, Number 2, pp. 150-173.
Winograd, T., and Flores, F. (1987). *Understanding Computers and Cognition: A New Foundation for Design.* Reading, Massachusetts: Addison-Wesley Publishing Co. Inc.

Wynn, E. (1979). *Office Conversation as an Information Medium.* Unpublished Ph.D. Dissertation, University of California, Berkeley.
Wynn, E. (1991). "Taking Practice Seriously." In J. Greenbaum and M. Kyng (Editors), *Design at Work.* Hillsdale, New Jersey: Lawrence Erlbaum.
Yin, R. K. (1989). *Case Study Research: Design and Methods.* Newbury Park, California: Sage Publications.
Young, L. W. (1995). *The Implementation of an Information System in Mental Health: A Critical Hermeneutic Interpretation.* Unpublished Masters Thesis, University of Auckland, Auckland.
Zuboff, S. (1988). *In the Age of the Smart Machine.* New York: Basic Books.

8 BIOGRAPHY

Michael D. Myers is senior lecturer in the Department of Management Science and Information Systems at the University of Auckland. He has an M.A. and Ph.D. in Social Anthropology from the University of Auckland. Before joining the university in 1989, he worked for IBM New Zealand Ltd. Dr. Myers is editor of the ISWorld Section on Qualitative Research.

Part Four

Interviewing and the Interviewer

16

Exploring a Chairman of the Board's Construction of Organizational Reality: The Colruyt Case

M. Janson
School of Business Administration
University of Missouri, St. Louis
St. Louis, Missouri 63121, USA
Tel: (314) 516-5846
E-mail: mjanson@umslvma.umsl.edu

T. Guimaraes
Tennessee Technological University
Cookville, Tennessee 38505, USA
Tel: (615) 372-3385
E-mail: TG5596@TNTECH.EDU

A. Brown
City University Business School
Frobisher Crescent, Barbican Center
London EC2Y 8HB, England
Tel: 44 017 477 8624
E-mail: A.P.Brown@CITY.AC.UK

T. Taillieu
Katholieke Universiteit Leuven
B3000 Leuven, Belgium
Tel: 32 16 32 6059
E-mail: Tharsi.Taillieu@psy.kuleuven.ac.be

Abstract

A qualitative exploration of Colruyt, a Belgian company that evolved from a one-store enterprise into Belgium's third largest food retail chain comprising some 120 stores, is presented. The company is unique on several dimensions: its managerial structures and business processes, its use of information technology, and its views of company rights, duties, and obligations concerning customers, employees, creditors, and government. During this interview, Mr. Colruyt,[1] Chairman of Colruyt's Supervisory Board, returns time and again to a single dominant idea: the use of information technology based communication to create new possibilities, organizational structures, and relationships among the firm and its employees, worker unions, customers, and suppliers. The qualitative exploration clarifies how societal, religious, historical, and linguistic beliefs unite to form a unique corporate environment. Because the contact time with the Chair of the Supervisory Board was limited to three hours, a qualitative approach was key to the success of an in-depth exploration of the company. Our analysis should be of interest to managers and academics who practice or study global business and business process reengineering.

1 INTRODUCTION

1.1 Qualitative Research Approach

This article presents the results of an interview-based study of Colruyt, a Belgian discount food chain, because it is an insightful example of qualitative research. According to Stake (1995), the essential difference between quantitative and qualitative research is that the former focuses on explanation and control whereas the latter centers on understanding complex interrelationships. Qualitative research has a longstanding tradition in diverse disciplines such as sociology, anthropology, public policy and education studies (Adler, Adler and Fontana 1987; Drummond 1994; Throngmorton 1993). However, the qualitative paradigm is not limited to the areas of study just listed. It is also the method of choice by many scholars for studying management and information systems phenomena (Aggarwal 1995; Thomas 1995). One of the most compelling qualitative studies we came across is Argyris' (1992) description of organizational learning.

The reason for selecting a qualitative approach was the limited time we had access to the company's chief executive officer. This left us no other tool than the semi-structured interview. A close reading of many of the executive's position papers

[1]Mr. Colruyt was the recipient of the 1993 Belgian Business Man of the Year Award.

dealing with social, political, and economic issues provided a solid basis for composing a set of well crafted interview questions. Furthermore, it was quite apparent from the aforementioned position papers that the executive very much thought in terms of broad philosophic, religious, economic, social, and political concepts. Our research put into perspective the company's chief executive's opinions by contrasting these with descriptive materials such as newspaper articles and company documents.

In the remainder of this the company's entry into the Belgian retail food industry in the 1960s is summarized and its adoption of informatization for corporate survival and success, its adaptation to a bilingual client base, programs for organizational and individual learning, use of a computer-based network for interpersonal communication, and its difficulties with several unions are described. In section 2, we discuss our qualitative research method. In section 3, we present with a minimum of commentary our interview with Mr. Jo Colruyt. The interview is organized into four themes and is, for the most part, presented in chronological order. In section 4, we discuss and analyze several of the issues raised during the interview. Finally, in section 5, we present the implications of the interview for scholars and practitioners interested in global business.

Those seeking to improve their chances of success in today's global market would do well to consider the experiences, thoughts, and opinions of someone who has survived under turbulent economic, social, and cultural conditions. In fact, the company has thrived under conditions that are unmistakably postmodern, characterized as they are by ambiguity, paradox, discontinuity, fragmentation, and contradiction.

1.2 Corporate Background

Mr. Jo Colruyt presided over the evolution of his original one-store enterprise into a highly profitable retail food chain currently comprising some 120 stores located throughout Belgium. The company's success is particularly noteworthy considering local business conditions: stringent and wide-ranging governmental regulations, domination of the retail industry by well-established large food retailers, paper-thin profit margins, strict hierarchical managerial structures, and worker representation by unions of diverging ideologies with extensive influence over local and national government.

Several issues stand out with respect to the company's evolution into what is now the third largest Belgian retail food chain. First, Mr. Colruyt's philosophical views were essential to the company's thirty year long business success. His views, which were rooted in a natural bent toward matters of the spirit, were shaped by his pre-World War II formal training in the Belgian Catholic school system and by his post-World II informal training in Marxism in Paris, France. As a result, before considering any action or strategy in his business, Colruyt focuses first on the cultural, behavioral, and communicative aspects.

A second emerging issue was Colruyt's realization of the need for worker participation, decision making, and empowerment. To effect these objectives, he needed to initiate cultural change on two fronts: a culture of blindly following directives had to be transformed into a culture of personal initiative, risk taking, and decision making; and relations with the union had to be managed by discourse attuned to the union's ideological persuasion.

A further example of his need to consider culture before embarking on organizational change is the fact that Colruyt stores are located in the Flemish-speaking and French-speaking parts of Belgium. According to Mr. Colruyt, language is a determining factor in an individual's cultural, educational, and political experiences. Thus, even though language is needed to establish understanding and consensus between individuals, it also places limits on what can be expressed and communicated. To help bridge the gap between Flemish-speaking and French-speaking individuals, professionally trained translators ensure that company documents are available to employees in both languages.

Another example of Colruyt's attention to culture was the shift toward full worker participation. It was greatly helped when employees realized that their livelihood and the firm's success were inextricably linked. As the firm expanded, great care was taken to ensure that new hires would fit in. Once hired, a person would enroll in any of the company's extensive range of training programs that, among other things, introduced employees to the corporate culture, built interpersonal communication and decision making skills, and offered personal development opportunities.

A third issue of importance is the use of IT throughout the company to support individuals in their day-to-day activities. One of the most intriguing examples of the supportive role of IT is a company-wide computer-based system for the dissemination of information. First, the system captures and permanently stores on optical disk all information flows among employees and among employees and individuals outside the company. Second, the system functions as an organizational memory which enables information retrieval in ways that are exceedingly helpful to employees' task performance. About 85% of the information stored by the system is available to any company employee, including union stewards, which is indicative of the openness under which the company operates.

The firm's innovative business practices, including job rotation, job enlargement and enrichment, and the extensive informatization of all essential business activities were never approved by the unions. During the early 1980s, individuals connected with the unions published a research monograph accusing the company of "Taylorism." The authors of this monograph sought to show that informatization of all essential company activities led to a work atmosphere fundamentally at odds with individual freedom and dignity (Adele et al. 1984).

Many employees at all levels within Colruyt reacted angrily to the unions' allegations. Although a minority of employees agreed with the unions' allegations, a vast majority disagreed with the unions' charges. Employees' reactions, whether critical or supportive of the company, were published in book form and made available to the public. The incident taught the company a valuable lesson: no longer a minor player, the company could not continue to focus solely on its internal operations but also had to give considerable attention to its public relations.

2 RESEARCH METHOD

Our project is a qualitative interview-based attempt at uncovering and making explicit the conditions and individual actions surrounding the creation and development of entrepreneurial initiatives concerning Colruyt. Hartwick and Barki (1994) elaborated the different objectives of confirmatory and exploratory research approaches. Confirmatory research seeks support for hypotheses which have been formulated using an a priori theory. These hypotheses are subsequently tested using data from carefully controlled experimental studies.

Exploratory research proceeds differently than confirmatory studies. Rather than relying on large randomly selected samples, exploratory analysis employs small convenience samples. Instead of using test statistics based on assumed probability distributions, exploratory analysis for the most part uses tabular and graphical data displays and other techniques for probing the data flexibly (McNeil 1977).

Exploratory analysis represents a first contact with the data and aims to isolate data patterns and features, and to uncover, clarify, and simplify a data structure (Velleman and Hoaglin 1981). The data acquire meaning within the analyst's frame of reference because he or she searches for a satisfactory structure by confronting the data with a variety of alternative models (which is to say: the model follows the data). In this spirit, exploratory data analysis is defined by Benzecri (1980) as a "method that extracts structure from data."

Before scheduling the semi-structured interview with Mr. Colruyt, we first fixed our project's goals. The semi-structured interview sought information on 1) the age of the business and changing business conditions, 2) the company's managerial structure, 3) the number of employees and their contribution to achieving company objectives, 4) the nature of the business and competition and current and future markets, 5) Colruyt's business clients and the services delivered, 6) the company's operating philosophy, 7) the balance between providing clients a quality service and offering workers meaningful work while realizing adequate returns on investment and staying ahead of the competition, 8) the company's use and acquisition of standard and special software and hardware (e.g., word processing, spreadsheet, and data base), and 9) the company's use of information technology to serve clients and manage and maintain the company's information systems.

The three hour interview took place at the company's headquarters in the City of Halle, Belgium. The interview was conducted by two of the co-authors and audio taped in Flemish. The two co-authors are equally proficient in Flemish and English. After its transcription to written text, the interview was then translated into English by one of the bilingual authors and carefully checked for accuracy against the original

Flemish version by the second bilingual author. Even though this article discusses the results of the interview with Mr. Colruyt, we did compare them with interviews conducted with other company personnel.

Sections of the interview's transcript are presented in chronological order. Only where absolutely necessary for clarity did we add explanations or rearrange words and sentences slightly. The interview is presented in six subsections including such topics as philosophy-driven management, instrumental rationality versus value rationality, worker empowerment and decision making, and information-driven strategy.

3 THE INTERVIEW

The opinions expressed during this interview cover a wide range of topics : the firm's relations with its customers, employees, unions, and governmental agencies. However, the *leitmotif* of the interview is how to fashion corporate strategies and modes of operating that are appropriate in light of contextual and cultural factors.

3.1 Philosophy-Driven Management

Mr. Colruyt is equally acquainted with the philosophical underpinnings of Christianity and Marxism. He attended Catholic schools until his eighteenth year. After leaving school, he lived in Paris, France from 1946 until 1947, where he joined a Communist cell organized by French university students. Concerning this important period in his life, Mr. Colruyt stated:

> While adjusting to Parisian life I also confronted Marxist philosophy. I immersed myself in the movement and worked diligently to understand its philosophy. In essence, I learned a completely new language [with which to interpret my life world]. The experience changed my entire way of thinking.

The revelation of Stalin's excesses and the Communist takeover of Czechoslovakia in 1948 motivated Mr. Colruyt to reject Communism. During discussion with his Communist counterparts, Mr. Colruyt was impressed by the intense rationality of the debates. He was equally impressed by the deep-felt need on the part of his Communist counterparts for human contact.

Mr. Colruyt further remarked that the Communist debating style took on additional importance when later in his career he was forced to confront members of the Communist union. He stated:

> During a fifteen-year period I had employees who were Marxist union members. I was able to keep the discussion with these employees going because I placed it in the context of Marxist ideology.

Later during the interview, Mr. Colruyt returned to the important task for both the company and the union to communicate with employees. In response to the question concerning communication with employees, Mr. Colruyt said:

> The company should keep the communication channels to the employees firmly in hand. Of course the unions should do likewise. But the unions should never get the exclusive right to communicating with the employees. As a company, you're lost if that were to occur! That is exactly what happened in the [Belgian] steel industry. Upper management started to feel superior vis-à-vis the working masses. The result: working people were informed solely by the unions. It was the deathblow for the steel industry, a real catastrophe!

Summarizing, we note that Mr. Colruyt's emphasis on communication, his interest in the workers' life world, and his penchant for rationality arose from his in-depth exposure to Roman Catholic and Marxist philosophical thought. Mr. Colruyt's remarks concerning the need for human contact expressed by his Communist counterparts foreshadow his later advice to temper rationality with a healthy dose of human emotion. Later during this interview, Mr. Colruyt returned to this topic.

3.2 Instrumental Rationality Versus Value Rationality

At different times during the interview, Mr. Colruyt often returned to the need for balancing rationality with emotionality. It clearly is an issue which holds his attention. Therefore, we followed up with the following questions:

M.J.: "You mentioned the rational aspect of Marxism. Would you say some more about rationality?"

J.C.: "I believe in launching and testing hypotheses and I view these as the only way to gain understanding. Hypotheses used to be formed by single individuals. Today, we need collective hypotheses which are created by groups consisting of twenty, fifty, or a hundred individuals. However, there are dangers associated with group hypotheses. Initial business success based on a collective hypothesis can turn into failure when the underlying assumptions no longer hold. Consider the unions: they have operated with the same hypothesis for fifty years. In today's world, that old hypothesis has lost much of its validity."

T.T.: "How do you debunk outworn collective hypotheses in the Colruyt organization?"

J.C.: "[You do that] in an atmosphere of open and frank discussion where there always exists the possibility that someone remarks, 'We have always analyzed this problem one way, how about looking at it differently?' The group builds a new Gestalt and suddenly one has two, three new hypotheses with which to interpret a situation. I feel most comfortable with three hypotheses; [because] that creates freedom, and freedom creates choice."

T.T.: "Marius Janson and I had a discussion yesterday on why you speak in terms of Marxist and other philosophies. Is it because you need a framework for making matters clear to others?"

J.C.: "Humans make sense of their world through abstract models; without these, reality is too complicated. [Similarly], to understand society one needs multiple models – economic theory, social theory, capitalism, Marxism, Maoism, and so on. I think these [philosophical systems] embody a collective intelligence which is activated by open and frank communication. Communication among individuals occurs at meetings, on the telephone, and by using Colruyt's computer-supported system for information dissemination (ISID). They are all keys to company success.

"Many individuals also learn to appreciate that multiple models imply freedom of choice. I'll demonstrate this point with a practical example – I attend steering committee meetings where teams present [their] modeling results. These presentations are first class, naturally. [But] to make decisions I need to shake up the assumptions that underlie the model. In fact I regard coming up with alternative assumptions is one of the very few talents that I have. The team may respond with 'Yes but these new assumptions invalidate our modeling results.' I ask the team to rework the problem using these new modeling assumptions. Then, after comparing the results of both models, I often suggest a third model. Well, you understand the team's reaction. . . what misfortune befell us with a boss like that! Changing assumptions does create ambiguity which makes some individuals very anxious. I try to reassure that anxious person by telling him that he has done a fine and marvelous piece of work. However, and this time just for the fun of it, let's reevaluate the problem using a different hypothesis. Frequently, the idea of being playful is sufficient to bring someone around and convince him that his professional prestige is not questioned. Well, at times even [the playful aspect] does not work."

In summary, Mr. Colruyt maintains that rational decision making is essential to the success of the business. However, rationality in isolation is insufficient; decision makers have to also consider human emotion and intuition. More importantly, Mr. Colruyt suggested a way to balance rationality with emotionality by making available to employees a wide range of company-sponsored seminars which focus on group dynamics, social and communication skills, assertiveness training, and so on.

Attending company-offered seminars raises the important issue of personal freedom because, even though the company does not force anyone to sign up for seminars against his will, every-day interaction with his colleagues who do attend seminars does place the non-attendee at a distinct disadvantage. In other words, it is debatable whether one can deal with emotionality in a seminar without also infringing on an employee's basic right to privacy.

The objective of these seminars is to enhance the individual's capacity for creating satisfactory interpersonal relations and achieving higher degrees of self-actualization.

The seminars focus on personal issues such as: Who am I? How do I interact with myself and others? In the words of Mr. Colruyt the seminars are not "American style," which is to say that their objective is not to create "winners."

The above paragraphs reveal that the Colruyt company seriously attempts to avoid invading the employees privacy but reaches this goal only partially. In fact, Mr. Colruyt concluded that inasmuch as employees change as a result of attending the seminars, the organization has to change as well:

> [A] person has to participate in a very real way, or else the individual is placed on the sidelines; or even worse – he is singled out or rejected! A nonparticipative individual gets run underfoot by a competitive environment. I would say that it is difficult for me to be definitive on this score. It strikes me that survey-based studies are needed to get a clearer insight into this issue.

As mentioned earlier, both rationality and emotionality are needed for decision making. Mr. Colruyt maintains that to do so calls for a feeling for humor to place situations in perspective. If someone during a decision-making meeting gets stressed out, much can be done with humor. This is exactly why sensitivity, assertiveness, and gestalt training are important. On the other hand, there are situations where all the sensitivity in the world just is inadequate; situations exist where it is necessary to pull out one's knife and ask "Well, what about it?"

3.3 Worker Empowerment and Decision Making

Earlier in the interview, Mr. Colruyt stressed balancing rationality and emotionality during decision making. During the ensuing questioning it became clear that the company has experimented without much success with several alternatives, such as the conflict and consensus approaches to decision making. Eventually the company settled on the following decision making rules:

1) Decisions are always made by a single individual.
2) The chair schedules the meeting. Meetings start and adjourn on time.
3) Decisions are never made during a meeting.

It should be stressed that decisions are always made by a single individual. The company has no faith in decision making by group consensus because these are always compromises and, according to Mr. Colruyt, have all the makings of a catastrophe! Throughout a meeting, the chair stays focused on "Is it necessary to make a decision? If so who will make that decision?" This could be the chair; however, it is also possible that someone else volunteers to take on the decision making responsibility. Decisions are never made during a meeting, because that would preclude careful contemplation.

Furthermore, all the affected individuals are informed of a decision before it is implemented. In other words, there is a grace period which enables feedback. Decisions that meet with adverse reactions are reconsidered and, where necessary, revised. When we discussed decision making, Mr. Colruyt returned to the topic of multiple models to represent reality. In this context, he commented on the company's decision making policy:

> Multiple models – yes I think that is the reality! Experience taught us that these [aforementioned] procedures are in tune with the mentality of the Flemish here in Brabant. You should take these regional differences into account. The procedures may not be in tune with the mentality of people in other regions of Belgium. In one region, decision making takes the form of a parliamentary debate. Individuals first stake out their positions during lengthy discussions which focus on individual principles. Stating one's principles, it is important! Only after that do we get around to considering the decision needed. It goes without saying that all this lengthens the decision making period.

This quote introduces an additional difficulty: decision making in a bilingual and multi-cultural environment. The two languages do cause problems because, according to Mr. Colruyt, language and words function as models. A concept represented in Flemish can be replaced by its French counterpart; yet that is not sufficient. It is of foremost importance to consider the nuances and shades of meaning which reflect upbringing, education, culture, and politics – and this is a job for language experts.

During meetings, each employee has the right to speak his native tongue and professional translators are present in cases where meeting attendees are not bilingual. Moreover, each memo written in Flemish is translated into French and vice versa. As a minimum requirement, members of upper management have to understand, but need not speak, Flemish and French.

Finally, we summarized the interview with this question:

M.J: "Mr. Colruyt, throughout the interview we returned time-and-again to: 1) open communication in all directions and accessible to all employees, 2) decisions are made by a single individual, and 3) any form of communication is stored in the company's information system for information dissemination. As a result, it seems to me, little room exists for defensive or offensive maneuvering such as posturing, deception, or any other form of molding reality. Yet in day-to-day situations such strategies seem necessary or, at any rate, are used by many. How does one motivate individuals not to use these ingrained ways of dealing with the day-to-day activities of getting along with life?"

While answering this question Mr. Colruyt retorted:

> Not to use these strategies? They might still be used! I have discussed matters from my point of view. Is what I told you the "reality"? It is no more than my model of the Colruyt organization. I stand behind my views, but I have no idea how other Colruyt members model their reality. Do you grasp the point – you must not assume that I know the organization!

3.4 Information-Driven Strategy

What sets the Colruyt Company apart from its competitors is a focus on informatization. Mr. Colruyt stated:

> We started with one discount store in 1965 with the deliberate adoption of information technology. Our thinking: the eventual arrival of large computers is a certainty and we therefore should organize the entire sales function around the computer. Using information technology in all business aspects required corporate structures that were based on a totally new business rationale and this made us different from our competitors who inserted information technology into already existing organizational structures where it then met with serious resistance if not outright hostility. Information technology in 1965 meant an IBM 360-20 in our headquarters and a tabulating machine in the store. Yet, even this primitive technology had important business consequences for employee selection, customer service, and product assortment. First, the employee we needed did not fit the mold of the traditional lady at the store's checkout because that person would be unable to work with the computer. Second, the tabulating machine at the checkout station made it possible to provide the customer a unique service: a detailed description of his or her purchases. Third, relying on information technology excluded certain products from our assortment – even today we do not sell items to which we cannot affix a bar code. Well, again, we were and still are different from our competition because we organized our business around information technology right from the start.

While continuing on this topic, Mr. Colruyt mentioned further that the company has an information technology supported contract with the customer: to be less expensive than its competition, under all circumstances and on every sales item. To this end, the company maintains a centrally located database on the pricing policies and promotional campaigns of every competitor located within a twenty mile radius of each of the 120 Colruyt stores.

What makes all this a reality is the large computer software application that Colruyt's MIS department has developed and implemented. It is maintained by twenty employees who track pricing policies and special sales promotion of the competition. The contract with the customer has important business consequences: our prices are not cost driven, they reflect the pricing policies of the competition. If the company can no longer beat the competition on price while making a profit, it drops the item from its assortment. Before taking this step, though, the suppliers are presented with an option: lower the price or lose Colruyt as a customer.

To keep software development costs down, the company starts most informatization projects at the request of the user – a checkout clerk, a district manager, or a store manager. The user describes how the information system will improve his job performance, calculates the system's contribution to the company's bottom line, estimates its development and annual system maintenance expenses, and specifies the financial resources he or she is willing to contribute toward the system's development. This request is then submitted to a steering committee comprising high level managers, end users, and information specialists.

For example, a marketing manager's request for an information system to help mount a publicity campaign is submitted together with a clear and straightforward cost-benefit analysis. The steering committee would find it difficult to reject a request for an information system that shows a positive cost-benefit analysis. The only concern left here is the believability of the cost-benefit figures. Ultimately, this issue is resolved by judging the reliability of the person behind the estimates. One can always determine a person's reliability by checking estimates for previous software projects.

The important implication of this method is the shift from centralized to decentralized decision making concerning informatization projects while retaining some measure of upper management control. However, Mr. Colruyt further stated that upper management can and, indeed, should delegate decision making to the lowest possible level. But upper management cannot and should not delegate accountability for the company's resource expenditures.

4 DISCUSSION

4.1 Social Theology

While Belgium has been at the center of social, economic, intellectual, and religious developments in Western Europe, it also has often been invaded by foreign armies and ruled by foreign governments. These experiences combined with certain ideas promulgated by the Catholic Church have profoundly affected the way Belgians view the issues discussed in this interview. Toward the end of the nineteenth century, Pope Leo XIII issued his *Rerum Novarum* encyclical letter (Newman 1979). In this pastoral letter, which was a direct response to issues raised by socialism, the Pope threw his support behind the emergent Catholic social movement.

The encyclical dealt with five topics: the right to private property, the role of the Church in social affairs, social action by the Church, responsibilities of the state, and the right of workers to form voluntary associations such as unions (Newman 1979). First, the encyclical supported the right to private property. Second, the Church concluded that without its active involvement no solution to the social questions posed by socialism would be possible. Third, the Church resolved that its care for man would include his earthly condition as well as his fate in the hereafter. Fourth, the Church rejected *laissez faire* economics and held the state responsible for protecting private property, regulating working conditions, and guaranteeing workers a fair and living wage. Finally, the Church accorded workers the right to voluntary association such as unions and Church societies became preoccupied with social action (Harte 1979).

The encyclical stressed rights as well as obligations; the Church admonished the employer to pay a living wage, respect the worker's human dignity, and to promote the worker's physical and moral welfare. Furthermore, the Church suggested that the employer temper rationality with charity by ensuring job security in the face of short periods of seasonally caused unemployment (Lowrey 1979). The encyclical counseled the worker to fulfill his obligations agreed to in the work contract. The worker is to refrain from idling on the job, coming late, leaving early, and committing similar unlawful acts. The Pope's (Giordani 1979) interest in labor relations emanates from the sanctified character of work: "Since work is the God-ordained means of man's subsistence, man has both the duty and the right to work."

The encyclical *Rerum Novarum* would have little effect on day-to-day work life were it not for the great influence that the Catholic Church has over large segments of Belgium's social life. In 1963, more than 80% of Belgian youths who had joined organizations were members of Catholic ones and 25% of Flemish business leaders belonged to the Catholic Association of Business Owners (Dierickx 1979). In 1963, the Christian Unions had over 800,000 members, whereas in the case of the Socialist Union the count was 700,000. Moreover, a 1984 survey by Harding and Phillips found that 72% of the Belgian population are Roman Catholic. These numbers show that, even today, Catholic ideas are at the center of cultural life in Belgium.

We think that several company policies at Colruyt are linked to the ideas presented above. For instance, the company's promise to best any competitor on price is taken very seriously and the company goes to extremes to ensure that this commitment is met. The Catholic norm being invoked here is that a promise should be kept. Another example is that it is standard practice for employees to do more than one job. For example, checkout clerks also restock shelves and upper level managers work their way up from the shop floor. Extensive job rotation and multiple work assignments indicate that any type of work has intrinsic value and fosters mutual respect among the employees.

4.2 Social Thought

If it can be assumed that both Colruyt and traditional food retailers are under the sway of identical religious, social democratic, and Marxist influences, then any differences between Colruyt and traditional food retailers arise as a result of the dissimilar interactions between the respective retail organizations and the sociocultural environment.

Tables 1, 2, and 3 present the most noteworthy differences between the two major food retail chain types for three categories: service, labor, and ideology. First, extensive informatization of all aspects of the company's activities enables Colruyt to offer customers products in prepackaged, easy to use quantities at significantly lower costs than any competing store thanks to a vast up-to-date and store-by-store computerized database (Table 1). Furthermore, the high degree of informatization of all sales activities enables daily reshelving of all Colruyt stores and leads to further reductions in inventory, spoilage, and transportation expenses.

Table 1 Customer Service.

Traditional Supermarket	Colruyt Discount Supermarket
• Wide product assortment offered in standard package sizes. • Inventory is replenished periodically. • Inventory is supply driven. • Stockouts are frequent.	• Extremely wide product assortment offered at low cost and in many different package sizes. • Inventory is replenished daily. • Inventory is demand driven using historical customer purchasing figures. • Stockouts are rare.
• Esthetically pleasing store interior. • The intended message – a pleasing store interior corresponds to quality products.	• Sober store interior lacking any but the most basic architectural features. • The intended message – a sober store interior enables low prices.
• Customer assistance is limited to friendly service at the checkout. • Average to long customer waiting times are the rule.	• Clients receive assistance throughout the store. • Clients are assumed capable of making rational purchasing decisions when provided the correct and right amount of information – product contents, product unit cost, and product preparation guidelines. • Short customer waiting times - during slack times some checkout clerks restock shelves and during busy times clerks assume checkout duties.
• Cost reductions are achieved by paying low wages, few benefits, and by using many part-time employees.	• Cost reductions are achieved by employing few but mainly full-time employees, by improving employee and organizational efficiency and effectiveness, and by bargaining for large-volume-based product cost reductions.

Similarly, in Table 2 it is shown that, in contrast to its competition, Colruyt new-hires are better educated, receive extensive on-the-job training, are empowered, handle significant levels of responsibilities, and perform multiple tasks. Full-time employee turnover and the number of part-time employees are extremely low. Low employee turnover in turn safeguards the investments in employee training and ensures a flexible work force with high levels of job familiarity and task preparedness.

Table 2 Labor Structure.

Traditional Supermarket	Colruyt Discount Supermarket
• Employees focus on a single task with a high degree of task demarcation.	• Employees focus on multiple tasks with a low degree of task demarcation.
• Employees have little formal education.	• Employees have much formal education – store clerks have high school diplomas, and managers poses university degrees.
• Little on-the-job training. • Little job rotation.	• Much on-the-job training. • An extensive company educational program – course offerings focus on organizational and inter-personal communication competencies. • An extensive job rotation policy.
• Limited worker job responsibility. • Limited worker empowerment. • A hierarchical management structure with decision making located at the top of the organization.	• Extensive worker responsibility – clerks perform multiple assignments ranging from checkout duty to reshelving and cleaning the store's interior. • Extensive worker empowerment – clerks decide when and how to perform their multiple job responsibilities. • A flat management structure with decision making throughout the organization.
• Limited job security for full-time employees. • No job security for part-time employees. • High employee turnover. • Homogeneous labor markets.	• Much job security for full-time employees. • Little employee turnover. • Heterogeneous labor markets.

Perhaps the most interesting items in the ideological category of Table 3 are postmodernism and deconstruction. Postmodern life is a fractured experience and consists of a series of indeterminates. Furthermore, as Abrams (1988), Holman and Harmon (1992), Lyotard (1992), and Sarup (1989) point out, language itself is problematic and subversive.

During the interview, Mr. Colruyt turned to postmodern ideas and conceptualized language as a "model" and contemplated assigning various meanings to words. Mr. Colruyt, in effect, stated that translating a French word into a Flemish word is not just a matter of consulting a dictionary. He remarked that one's language is the result, among other things, of one's upbringing, education, culture, and political experiences (Cottom 1989). Furthermore, while discussing his attending steering committee meetings, Mr. Colruyt mentioned making problematic the analyses presented by working groups. He did so by experimenting with the hypotheses underlying the analyses. Reality is fundamentally altered by assuming different vantage points. By their reactions, the working group members reveal their extreme discomfort with this fundamental change in reality.

Table 3 Company Ideology.

Traditional Supermarket	Colruyt Discount Supermarket
• Modernism informs the company's ideology – modernism is based on the concepts of instrumental rationality and value rationality. • Socialization of the individual into larger group entities.	• Postmodenism informs the company's ideology – postmodernism is based on the questioning of the grand narratives. • Attention is on the individual.
• Fordism – mass production and mass marketing of homogeneous products. • The aim is mass consumption of a limited assortment of products.	• Postfordism – small batch production of many heterogeneous products and niche marketing. • The aim is individualized production and selective consumption from among a very large assortment of products.
• Rigid organizational structures coupled with top-down command structures and bottom-up communicative structures. • The organizational structures are based on bureaucratic concepts. • Employees mistrust management.	• Flexible organizational structures couple with networked command and networked communicative structures. • The organizational structures are based on democratic concepts. • Employees trust management.
• Planning – short term. • Spatial centralization – product pricing on system-wide basis.	• Planning – long term. • Spatial decentralization – product pricing is determined on a store-by-store basis.
• Managerial decision making – consensus seeking. • Managerial decision making – rationalism.	• Managerial decision making – consent seeking. • Managerial decision making – deconstructionalism.

Note also Mr. Colruyt's closing statement: "I stand behind my views, but I have no idea how other Colruyt members model their reality. Do you grasp the point – you must not assume that I know the organization!" The sentence invites others to structure reality totally differently. Yet, his comment "I stand behind my views" implies that these multiple fractured experiences are all legitimate.

Deconstruction is a philosophical development that rejects the notion of objective truth or structure (Culler 1983; Derrida 1976, 1978; Holman and Harmon 1992). Deconstruction, which was first applied in linguistics, is the basis of several recent developments in textual criticism, political science, management theory, and information systems (Beath and Orlilowsky 1994; Leitch 1983; Taylor 1986). A critical notion of deconstruction is that any system of thought can be made to dissolve by the application of the very assumptions that underlie it.

On the topic of company relations with the unions, Mr. Colruyt remarked that his intimate knowledge of Marxist thought enabled him to establish and maintain a meaningful discussion. Mr. Colruyt uses Marxist rationality to make problematic the position of union leaders. Furthermore, the Colruyt company uses its computer-based communication system to make its negotiations, discussions, and correspondence with the unions available to the rank and file. In effect, the company subverts the possibility of any union posturing by its direct, frank, and "in your face" communication practices.

4.3 Informatization and Work Life

The effect of informatization on work life is controversial, with some being overly positive and others overly pessimistic (Dunlop and Kling 1990). Rule and Attewell (1990) claim the desire to make human and organizational behavior more rational and predictable is a frequent motivation for informatization. However, as pointed out by Dunlop and Kling, increased levels of efficiency and rationality usually benefit the owners and the stakeholders in the organization. That is to say, the interests of the workers and other members of the organization are, at best, overlooked. It would be easy to view the informatization efforts at N.V. Colruyt in negative terms (Adele et al. 1984). Thus, for example, the checkout information system automatically records customer service-times. At the end of a clerk's shift, the information system ranks these data on customer service-time. The clerk is then informed of the three highest ranked service-times. It is easy to see that this practice could lead to grave abuse (Attewell 1990).

Early on in the interview, Mr. Colruyt remarked that he accepted the positive and the negative implications of information technology. He argues time and again for the worker's right to privacy. To avoid privacy abuses, these service-time figures are not available to the clerk's direct supervisor (i.e., the store manager). Data access is restricted to the district manager and then only averaged on a store-by-store basis.

In paradoxical fashion, the company's openness once gave rise to privacy abuses. In a company directive, Mr. Colruyt discussed the balance between openness and potential abuse. In response to unauthorized information leaking to the press, some board members argued for restricting access to the company's computer-based information system for information dissemination. Mr. Colruyt disagrees with restricting information access. Instead, he proposes training employees in responsible use of information. In fact, he suggests that the drawbacks of restricting information access outweigh the risk of unauthorized information use (Colruyt 1985).

Colruyt practices informatization in a very participatory manner. Requests for information systems most frequently originate and are funded at the user level. In fact, system requests are initiated at the lowest managerial levels of the company and then developed with user oversight. It would be no overstatement to claim that system development is based on emancipatory principles.

We think that emancipatory principles are indeed an important weapon in the hands of workers who stand up for their rights and exert a meaningful influence over their work life. Over a two year period, we spent some twenty hours observing Colruyt stores and were impressed by the open, candid, and assertive manner of personnel behavior and comportment. Not everyone appreciates the assertive corporate culture. According to one employee, assertiveness at times crosses the border into aggressiveness, arrogance, and guilt by public opinion. However, most employees consider assertiveness a favorable trait and several clerks disclosed that it is acquired and encouraged in company-sponsored seminars and in day-to-day experience. One clerk expressed it succinctly in untranslatable Flemish but which approximates the English equivalent of "You have to stick up for yourself."

5 CONCLUSION

Despite his claims to the contrary, our qualitative research illustrates that Mr. Colruyt's ideas gave rise to an organization that is totally different from its competitors on several dimensions. As illustrated in Tables 1, 2, and 3, these differences greatly impact customer service, the company's labor structure, and its ideology. We show how a nation's cultural and religious values, and its historical experience, impact a company's operating philosophy, organizational structure, decision making, informatization, and value adding activities.

Our project demonstrates how qualitative research is a valuable instrument for uncovering contextual factors that may help or hinder organizational success. Hence, our interview-based study should be of interest to managers who face the demanding task of guiding their firm toward success in the turbulent global market.

6 ACKNOWLEDGMENT

This research project was supported in part by the Center for International Studies and the Office of Research at the University of Missouri-St. Louis, St. Louis, Missoui, USA, and by the Work and Organization Research Center at the University of Tilburg, Tilburg, The Netherlands.

7 REFERENCES

Abrams, M. H. (1988). *A Glossary of Literary Terms.* New York: Holt, Rinehart, and Winston.

Adele, B.; Martens, A.; Tordeur, G.; van der Smissen, E.; and van Muelenaer, G. (1984). *Dossier Colruyt.* Antwerp, Belgium: EPO.

Adler, P. A.; Adler, P.; and Fontana, A. (1987). "Everyday Life Sociology." In K. Plummer (Editor), *Symbolic Interactionism: Foundations and History.* Brookfield, Vermont: Edward Elgar, pp. 436-454.

Aggarwal, S. (1995). "Emerging Hard and Soft Technologies: Current Status, Issues and Implementation Problems." *Omega, International Journal of Management Science*, Volume 23, Number 1, pp. 323-339.

Argyris, C. (1992). *On Organizational Learning.* Cambridge, Massachusetts: Blackwell.

Attewell, P. (1990). "Big Brother and the Sweatshop: Computer Surveyance in the Automated Office." In C. Dunlop and R. Kling (Editors), *Computerization and Controversy: Value Conflicts and Social Choices.* Boston: Academic Press, pp. 236-256.

Beath, C., and Orlikowsky, J. (1994). "The Contradictory Structure of Systems Development Methodologies: Deconstructing the IS-User Relationship in Information Engineering." *Information Systems Research*, Volume 5, Number 4, pp. 350-399.

Benzecri, F. (1980). *Data Analysis.* Paris: Dunod.

Colruyt, J. (1985). "Information System for Information Dissemination and Confidentiality." In T. Penneman (Editor), *There are no Gentlemen Here, Sir.* Halle, Belgium: Druco, p. 238.

Cottom, D. (1989). *Text and Culture.* Minneapolis: University of Minnesota Press.

Culler, J. (1983). *On Deconstruction: Theory and Criticism after Structuralism.* Ithaca, New York: Cornell University Press.

Derrida, J. (1976). *Of Grammatology.* Baltimore: Johns Hopkins University Press.

Derrida, J. (1978). *Writing and Difference.* Chicago: Chicago University Press.

Dierickx, M. (1979). "Belgium." In P. A. Resch (Editor), *New Catholic Encyclopaedia.* New YorkL McGraw Hill, Volume II, pp. 245-249.

Drummond, H. (1994). "Too Little Too Late: A Case Study of Escalation in Decision Making." *Organization Studies*, Volume 15, Number 4, pp. 591-607.

Dunlop, C., and Kling, R. (1990). "The Dreams of Technological Utopianism." In C. Dunlop and R. Kling (Editors), *Computerization and Controversy: Value Conflicts and Social Choices.* Boston: Academic Press, pp. 14-30.

Giordiani, I. (1979). "In the Bible." In P. A. Resch (Editor), *New Catholic Encyclopaedia.* New York: McGraw Hill, Volume XIII, pp. 343-346.

Harding, S.; Phillips, D.; and Fogarty, M. (1984). *Contrasting Values in Western Europe.* New York: MacMillan.

Harte, T. (1979). "Papal Social Thought." In P. A. Resch (Editor), *New Catholic Encyclopaedia*. New York: McGraw Hill, Volume XIII, pp. 352-354.

Hartwick, J., and Barki, H. (1994). "Hypothesis Testing and Hypothesis Generating Research: An Example from the User Participation Literature." *Information Systems Research*, Volume 5, Number 4 (December), pp. 446-449.

Hofstede, G. (1980). "Motivation, Leadership, and Organization: Do American Theories Apply Abroad?" *Organizational Dynamics*, Volume 9, pp. 42-63.

Hofstede, G. (1991). *Cultures and Organizations: Software of the Mind*. New York: McGraw Hill.

Hofstede, G. (1993). "Cultural Constraints in Management Theories." *Academy of Management Executive*, Volume 7, pp. 81-94.

Holman, C. H., and Harmon, W. (1992). *A Handbook to Literature*. New York: MacMillan.

Leitch, V. B. (1983). *Deconstructive Criticism*. New York: Columbia University Press.

Lowrey, D. (1979). "Moral Obligations of Employers." In P. A. Resch (Editor), *New Catholic Encyclopaedia*. New York: McGraw Hill, Volume V, p. 328.

Lyotard, J. F. (1992). *The Post-Modern Explained*. Minneapolis: University of Minnesota Press.

McNeil, D. R. (1977). *Interactive Data Analysis: A Practical Primer*. New York: Wiley.

Newman, J. (1979). "Rerum Novarum." In P. A. Resch (Editor), *New Catholic Encyclopaedia*. New York: McGraw Hill, Volume XII, p. 387.

Poole, M. (1986). *Industrial Relations: Origins and Patterns of National Diversity*. Boston: Rouledge & Kegan Paul.

Rule, J., and Attewell, P. (1990). "What Do Computers Do?" In C. Dunlop and R. Kling (Editors), *Computerization and Controversy: Value Conflicts and Social Choices*. Boston: Academic Press, pp. 131-149.

Sarup, M. (1989). *An Introductory Guide To Post-Structuralism and Post-Modernism*. Athens, Georgia: University of Georgia Press.

Stake R. (1995). *The Art of Case Study Research*. Thousand Oaks, California: Sage Publishing.

Taylor, M. C. (1986). *Deconstruction in Context: Literature and Philosophy*. Chicago: University of Chicago Press.

Thomas, P. (1995). *The Social and Interactional Dimensions of Human-Computer Interfaces*. New York: University of Cambridge Press.

Throngmorton, J. A. (1993). "Survey Research as Rhetorical Trope: Electric Power Planning in Chicago." In F. Fischer and J. Forrester (Editors), *The Argumentative Turn in Policy Analysis and Planning*. Durham, North Carolina: Duke University Press, pp. 118-144.

Velleman, P., and Hoaglin, D. C. (1981). *Applications, Basics, and Computing of Exploratory Data Analysis*. Boston: Duxbury Press.

8 BIOGRAPHY

Marius Janson is Associate Professor of Management Sciences and Information Systems and Fellow in the Center for International Studies at the University of Missouri, St. Louis. He received his Ph.D. from the University of Minnesota. His current research interests center on social and international issues of information systems use. His articles have appeared in *Decision Sciences*, *Information and Management*, *Journal of Behaviour and Information Technology*, *Journal of Management Information Systems*, and *MIS Quarterly*.

Tor Guimaraes is the director of the Institute for Technology Management and holder of the Jesse E. Owen Chair of Excellence at Tennessee Technological University. Tor has a Ph.D. from the University of Minnesota and an M.B.A. from California State University, Los Angeles. In descending chronological order, he was Professor and Department Chairman at St. Cloud State University, and Assistant Professor and Director of the MIS Certificate Program at Case Western Reserve University. He has been the keynote speaker at national and international meetings sponsored by organizations such as the Information Processing Society of Japan, Institute of Industrial Engineers, American Society for Quality Control, IEEE, ASM, and Sales and Marketing Executives. He has consulted with many leading organizations including TRW, American Greetings, AT&T, IBM and the Department of Defense. With his partners throughout the world he has published over one hundred articles on technology management in leading journals.

Ann Brown is a graduate of the London School of Economics. She worked in the Central Operational Research Group of the British Steel Company before joining the City University Business School. She applied her early work on planning methods and investment appraisal to information systems before going on to develop a program of research on the subject of the management of IS/IT within organizations. She helped form the new group of practitioners and academics working in the subject of IS evaluation, being Chair for the first three European Conferences on the evaluation of IT, and Conference Chair for the Fourth European Conference of the evaluation of IT in 1997. Publications include journal papers, book and conference proceedings editorships, and short articles. Her current research is concerned with the impact of IS on organizational structure and work roles, and IS as a strategic resource.

Tharsi Taillieu is Professor of Organizational Psychology at the Catholic University of Leuven. He also teaches at the Tilburg Institute for Academic Studies, School of Management and Organization and School of Marketing, of Tilburg University where he worked for several years. He studied Industrial Psychology at the Catholic University of Leuven and received his Ph.D. from the Graduate School of Industrial Administration, Carnegie Mellon University. His current research concerns the nature of activities and work role of managers in settings where multiple parties collaborate in alliances and networks.

17

Acquiring Expert Knowledge on IS Function Design

P. Mantelaers
Faculty of Technical Mathematics and Informatics
Delft University of Technology
2600 AJ Delft, The Netherlands
Tel: +31 15 278 4427
Fax: +31 15 278 6632
E-mail: P.A.H.M.Mantelaers@is.twi.tudelft.nl

Abstract
Reorganizing the IS function can contribute to its efficiency and effectiveness. Management can choose from a large number of organizational options. This leads to uncertainty and a need for decision support. The knowledge of experts in this domain was elicited using think aloud protocols. Next the protocols were analyzed to derive guidelines that can be applied in practice. During the analysis, several techniques were tried. This knowledge acquisition process turned out to be very complex and labor intensive but it also was a rich source of information.

1 INTRODUCTION

Every organization in the private and in the public sector ought to (re)consider the organization of its IS function (ISF). From reports in professional periodicals it is shown that, in practice, many organizations reorganize their ISF. Applied research (e.g., Butler Cox 1991) shows that many organizations expect to adapt their ISF in the near future and have (repeatedly) done so. A more fundamental interest in this subject is apparent from articles in scientific journals (e.g., Swanson and Beath 1989) and from conference reports.

There are several reasons to change the organization's ISF: problems with efficiency or effectiveness, dissatisfaction with the ISF of users/customers within the organization, the desire to follow trendy developments, and reorganization to bring about other changes. A more fundamental development is the fact that an increasing number of organizations are becoming aware of the strategic value of information. A conclusion to be drawn from this is that an organization's ISF deserves more attention. Conversely, thinking about the organization's ISF may increase the insight into the strategic value of information.

With the extension of the number of possible solutions (through the loss of oppressive boundary conditions from the available technology and the informaticians available on the labor market), the organization's ISF problem has not become simpler or less important. Just as in designing information systems, in designing an organization's ISF it is always a matter of more than one solution. In principle, it is possible for various IS tasks to come to independent choices from all possible combinations of (de)centralization and (de)concentration. The answer to the question what would be the best alternative for a certain organization, will depend on specific circumstances.

This paper deals with the research approach I have chosen (Mantelaers 1995) to provide a scientifically justified contribution to answer the following practical question: "How can we design the most appropriate organization of the IS function for an organization in a certain situation?"

The ISF was the subject of the research. Its organization was considered within a certain organization to be defined beforehand. The external interorganizational organization problem was left out of consideration. *A priori* it was supposed to be known whether activities were executed inside or outside the organization. Another restriction was that only the design of the organization of ISF was taken into consideration and not the transition processes resulting from this. The organization, on behalf of which ISF had to be organized, is supposed to be known and fixed.

Three approaches were used to try to gain insight into an organization's ISF methodologies. First, directives for the organization of ISF were gathered from literature. In doing so, attention has been paid to general organization design theories (e.g., Douma and Schreuder 1992), to (methodologies for) information strategy planning (e.g., Turner et al. 1988), and to research in the organization's ITF field carried out by others (e.g., Bacon 1990). An analysis also has been carried out of the reorganization of ISF as it has, in the past, actually taken place within two organizations. The third and most important approach will be dealt with in this paper: the execution of a knowledge acquisition process.

This is an empirical paper that takes a qualitative approach in studying the design of the ISF. In section 2, the rough idea underlying the research approach will be explained. Section 3 focuses on the knowledge elicitation (selecting a method from the available knowledge elicitation methods), choice of experts and organizations and the setting of the experiments. The knowledge analysis (selection of and experiments with several analysis techniques) is covered in section 4. The results of the acquisition are summarized in section 5. Conclusions are drawn in section 6.

2 THE RESEARCH APPROACH

As indicated in Figure 1, there is, on the one hand, the problem of the design of the ISF. In this research, the design process is performed by experts. They collect information on the ISF and on its environment and use their expertise to come up with ideas to change the ISF in such a way that it reaches its goals better than before. On the other hand, there is the research problem: based on information about the ISF design processes by experts and on information from other sources, the researcher wants to draw conclusions (design a methodology) as to the improvement of future design processes.

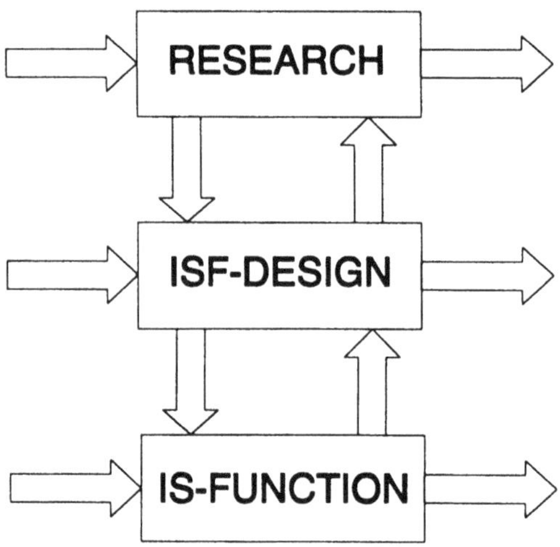

Figure 1 Two Control Problems: ISF Design and Research on ISF Design.

The essence of the research approach concerns the organization of the knowledge acquisition process (sections 3 and 4 deal with details regarding the elicitation and the analysis). The idea behind it is to invite three ISF experts to give their opinion on the way in which they would set up the ISF for three organizations (Rabobank Nederland, Fokker Aircraft and the Ministry of VROM). Each of these nine experiments (cells of the matrix in Figure 2) is first analyzed individually. The results have been compared together. In doing so, mainly similarities per organization (between experts) and per expert (between organizations) have been sought. Activities, concepts, and ways of thinking that are found in every experiment have are considered to be elements of a general approach. It is also possible that the analysis leads to general approaches for a certain (type of) organization or for a certain expert. The final result this research aims at is not a normative model that automatically leads to the best ISF, but a set of acceptable statements.

3 KNOWLEDGE ELICITATION

During the elicitation step knowledge is extracted from the expert and documented. During the analysis step this verbal data is analyzed, interpreted and modeled. This paragraph describes the knowledge elicitation. Several available methods are described (section 3.1) and from these, one is selected (section 3.2) and applied. The preparation of the experiments is covered in section 3.3 and their execution in section 3.4.

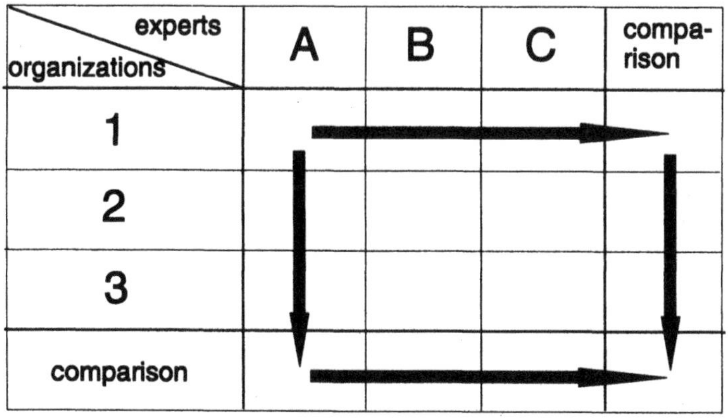

experts / organizations	A	B	C	compa-rison
1				
2				
3				
comparison				

Figure 2 Nine Experiments: Three Experts and Three Companies.

3.1 Available Elicitation Methods

Most expert knowledge cannot be observed directly but must be elicited from experts. The following list of most popular methods used in eliciting this knowledge is derived from Wijers (1991).

Interviewing. Interviewing is the most familiar method. It is widely used because it is relaxed and acceptable. Interviews are recorded question-answer sessions. There are two types of interview: unstructured and structured. Unstructured interviews closely resemble normal conversation. The method provides rough insight into domains. Structured interviews can be compared with interrogations. Knowledge engineers attempt to elicit knowledge about concepts or models by continuously soliciting clarifications, explanations, consequences and justifications. Interviews are effective in rapidly eliciting basic domain structures and when much of the knowledge explicit to experts can be elicited easily. Interviewing is unsuitable for eliciting detailed or poorly accessible domain knowledge and it relies heavily on uncued recall. Interviews especially encourage experts to speculate on and theorize about their cognitive processes.

Think aloud protocols. In these protocols, experts are asked to think aloud (or talk) about every thought and action while working on problems in their field of expertise. This verbalization is recorded and then typed out. The problems may be real or imaginary ones. It is argued that think aloud protocols do not change task performances, although they are slowed down. However, asking experts to explain why they are doing what they do requires them to attempt to access additional knowledge, which disturbs task performance.

Think aloud protocols are particularly suited to eliciting information about the whens and hows of the use of specific knowledge and to abstract the reasoning strategies and task decompositions that follow. Protocol analyses have the disadvantages of being time consuming and that, similar to interviews, knowledge engineers can only capture a series of verbal statements which must be converted to knowledge modules by an interpretative process of sifting, selection and re-representation. Furthermore, in think aloud protocols, knowledge engineers should be aware of the experts' inexperience in self-reporting and of the inaccessibility of proceduralized knowledge.

Think aloud protocols as defined above are known as concurrent protocols. Other forms of think aloud protocols are selective protocols, simulation by teletype and retrospective protocols (i.e., observation and review). Only part of the task is performed in a think aloud way in selective protocols. Simulation by teletype has been used in dialogues where experts could not be provided with completely specified problem statements in advance. The dialogues are held by teletype and both parties are asked to think aloud.

In retrospective protocols, task performances are recorded on audio or video. Reviewing the tape after having solved the problem, the experts are invited to comment on their thoughts and actions. However, retrospective protocols are not so reliable as concurrent verbalizations, because they depend too much on human memory and biases.

Introspection protocols. Introspection involves thinking aloud while solving artificial problems and is, therefore, unlike thinking aloud in problem solving because the process is not based on actual problems. Experts are encouraged to suggest feasible solutions, possibly relying on previous experience. Introspection protocols are shorter than think aloud protocols and contain many meta-descriptions and process comments. Introspection is effective in getting experts to sketch their views on the strategies they apply in problem solving, including their justifications.

Observational studies. Observations are similar to think aloud protocols but experts are not expected to think aloud while working. They can be recorded on video and could include telephone conversations. Observations are particularly useful in determining the experts' roles and activities in processes, but poor in establishing the applied reasoning strategies.

3.2 Method Selection

The initial idea was to use concurrent think aloud protocols using simulation by teletype as it was applied by Wijers. However, this was unanimously and independently rejected by the experts. They refused to work under such circumstances. The setting (see Figure 3) was considered to be too unrealistic to solve the defined problem. Given the type of problem, eye contact with the interviewees was considered to be indispensable. This puts constraints on the selection of the elicitation method.

From the available methods for knowledge elicitation, a combination of observation and think aloud protocols was chosen. Concurrent protocols and, additionally, retrospective protocols were used, however, in both cases selectively: during the task implementation, not every thought was expressed by the experts and afterwards not everything was explained. This method was completed by unstructured interviews.

In section 3.4, attention will be paid to the setting in which the experiments took place.

3.3 Preparing the Experiments

Selection of experts. To be qualified for participation in the research, the experts had to have had many years of experience in the field of the organization of the ISF, to be acknowledged as experts by professionals in the field of study, and to be prepared to reserve at least three times a period of two days for the research without being paid. The experts were told explicitly that this research did not aim at evaluating their individual advice. The advice and the processes preceding it would only be used as a means to come to conclusions about knowledge at a higher level. The top three of the list of acceptable expert-candidates agreed to take part in the experiments.

Selection of companies. With regard to the organizations, a certain spread was desired: both the private and the public sector had to be represented and, within the private sector, both physical and information-related transformation processes had to be involved. This spread was chosen because of the assumption that these distinctions in particular would influence the design of the ISF. Cooperating organizations would get three free-of-charge consultancy reports regarding their ISF by independent experts. However, employees, especially at higher levels in the organizations, had to

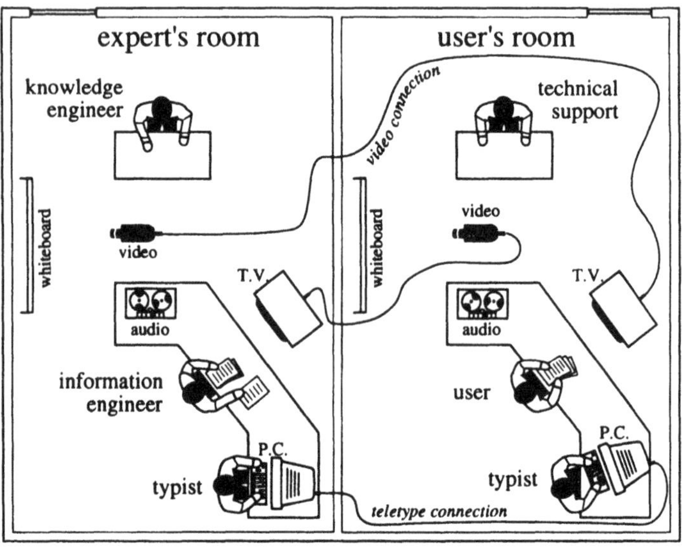

Figure 3 The Initial Idea (Wijers 1991).

be prepared to spend enough time on the project. They also ran the risk that employees not involved would get suspicious. We looked for organizations that recently reorganized their ISF. The experiments could, then, function more or less as an *ex post* evaluation of their transition.

Task to be fulfilled. Each experiment consisted of carrying out a consulting assignment in the field of ISF by an expert and was allowed to take two days at the maximum, inclusive of the formulation of the advice. In these two days, the expert could, in the presence of the researcher, have a number of interviews with functionaries of the organization in question. The whole experiment was registered on videotapes and audiotapes.

Selection of interviewees. The experts knew what they were expected to do but they did not know the names of the three organizations where they had to fulfill their mission. Informing them about their task was, of course, necessary to get their cooperation and also to offer them the opportunity to determine what functionaries they wanted to interview when performing their consultancy. The description of interviewees could only be done in general terms, due to the fact that the experts did not know the names of the companies. Two days were available for interviews. Taking into account that advice had to be formulated as well, about six interviews could take place in two days. This number was not considered to be a limitation by the experts. In close cooperation between the researcher and representative of each company and taking into account the requirements formulated by the experts, it was decided which persons were going to be invited to take part in the interviews. They all received a letter to explain the background of the experiment.

3.4 Execution of the Experiments

Information provided. From the research point of view, it was preferred to give the experts as little information as possible. This would prevent them from preparing their work without the researcher being present to record as much of the thinking process as possible. However, the experts had to be told what they were expected to do, otherwise they would not have cooperated and would not be able to determine who they wanted to interview.

The names of the companies were kept secret as long as possible. At the first company the experts only knew its name one hour in advance. At that point, they were given a document with general information about the organization (structure, information systems, number of employees, etc.) written by the researcher. They also received the interview schedule for the two days, including some background information about the interviewees. Due to time constraints, in the later experiments this information had to be provided to them the day before the experiment.

The interviews. This paragraph does not deal with the contents of the interviews but with the setting in which they took place. Not being able to have eye contact with the interviewees was unacceptable for the experts. Nonverbal communication was considered to be so essential in getting used to each other, in making interviewees feel comfortable, in influencing them or in the interpretation of their replies that the setting needed modification. The solution was to use an online video and audio connection between the two rooms. The setting of the experiment that was used for the first three experiments (with a large bank) is represented in Figure 4. A disadvantage was that it was impossible to think aloud during the communication with the interviewee. To compensate for this drawback, a time-out was introduced every twenty minutes by disconnecting the audio and video connection. During the time-out, the expert had the opportunity to think aloud about what happened until then and about the continuation of the interview. Some complementary questions were asked by the researcher. In the interviewee room, a research assistant was present to hear the opinion of the interviewee about the interview and the expert so far. He also asked the interviewee's opinion on differences between this expert and the other experts. These time-out conversations were only recorded on audio. Before starting an interview, the expert and his interviewee had a short opportunity to shake hands.

After the completion of the first three experiments, the setup was evaluated. According to all people involved, the whole process developed rather smoothly. The experts stated that the selected method of communication hardly hindered the communication. In spite of that, it was decided to put the expert and the interviewee in the same room. During time-outs, the expert and the researcher would go to an adjoining room. This new setting, which was applied from then on, is illustrated in Figure 5.

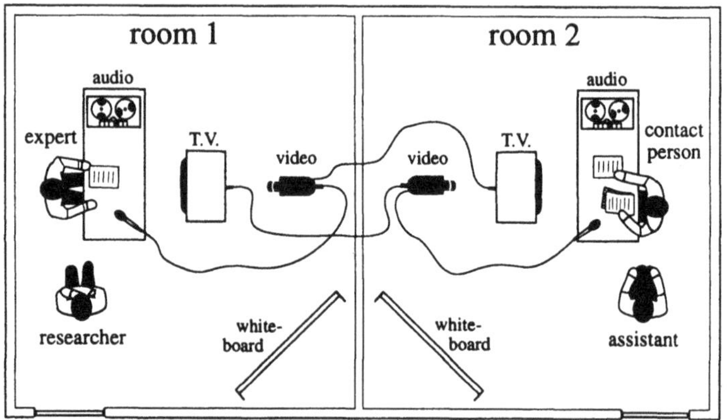

Figure 4 First Interview Setting.

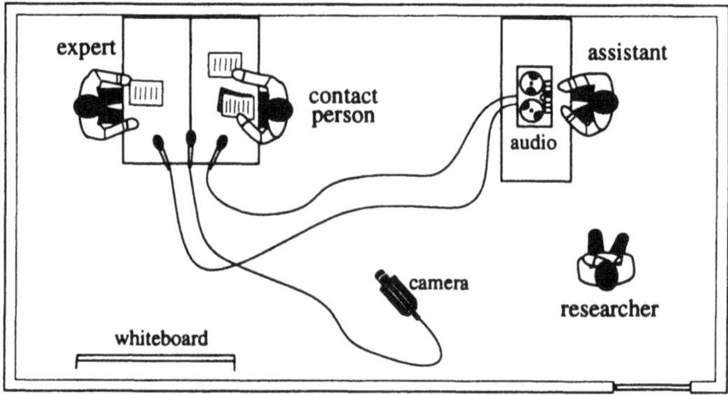

Figure 5 Second Setting.

The most important reason to change the setting was the idea that the clear presence of the video equipment might keep certain interviewees from providing certain information. In the new setting, video recordings were made as well, but the TV screens were no longer necessary and the location of the camera was less emphatic. The interviewee was placed with his back toward the camera. After being explained to the interviewees, the fact that the time-outs took place in another room was accepted by them as unavoidable from the perspective of the research objective.

The advice. Immediately after each experiment the expert was asked to formulate advice as to the IS function of the company involved. The experts used the notes they took during the interviews and their memory to recapitulate the most salient details of each interview. This formed another opportunity to register their ideas about important concepts, tasks and information while working on the design of the ISF. It also offered the researcher the opportunity to pose questions about the process. On the basis of the recordings of these conversations, the researcher formulated the advice and asked the expert to correct and complete it if necessary. The advice of the three experts was then presented to each company. They were presented as "a number of ideas" and it was emphasized that these ideas were just a by-product and not the main product of the process.

The transcripts. All conversations were recorded on audio and video tapes; time-out conversations were recorded on audio only. To make this material ready for analysis, all conversations had to be transcribed. This was not an easy task and was very labor intensive. The protocols were checked and corrected by the researcher. Having done this, 3,000 pages with conversations were ready to be analyzed.

4 KNOWLEDGE ANALYSIS

4.1 Introduction

The protocol transcriptions (on the basis of conversations recorded on audio and video tapes and transcribed literally) formed the starting point for the knowledge analysis. The aim was to isolate all knowledge that might be needed in solving the organization's ISF problem. In analyzing the protocol transcriptions and the representation of the knowledge to be drawn from it, it had to be taken into consideration that each experiment had to be described in such a way that mutual comparison of the results of the nine experiments was feasible. Next to that, the description ought to make it possible for the results to be used in practice by those who were considered to take decisions or make proposals about the organization of ISF (external advisors or someone from within the organization).

Within the knowledge analysis, Wijers distinguishes two tasks: interpretation (leading to a text model) and conceptualization (leading to a conceptual meta model). The text model is an intermediate step between the verbal data and the final conceptual meta model (see Figure 6). In the next section, it will be shown that this distinction is not applied very strictly.

4.2 Applied Methods

An important step is the choice of a method of analysis. Due to a lack of experience in this area, it was decided to experiment with different methods by trying them out rather extensively. In this section, these methods and the experiences with each method will be summarized. Not every method was carried out for a whole experiment. Sometimes the disadvantages of certain methods became clear very soon. This

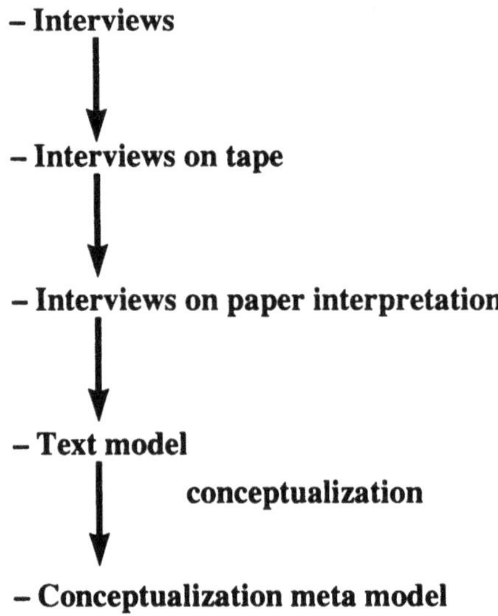

Figure 6 Knowledge Acquisition Tasks.

led to its immediate interruption. The original method was one that had been used before, within the Department of Information Systems at Delft University of Technology, to analyze expert knowledge in the area of information modeling (Wijers 1991; Verhoef 1993).

The use of the computerized tool Fragment. Fragment made it possible to perform both a task-oriented and a concept-oriented text analysis. The concept-oriented analysis meant that each text fragment had to be given a label, indicating of which concept this fragment was an instance and how it was related to other concepts. Concepts had to be chosen by the analyst. Fragment (a product of the Software Engineering Research Centre in the Netherlands) made it possible to generate reports with quantitative information on the protocols. This is a linear bottom-up approach that turned out to be rather labor intensive and it generated more pages of information than the 3,000 that formed the starting point for the analysis. The advantage of the approach was that it would afterwards be very simple to show that certain knowledge was indeed derived from the transcripts. Fragment does not support the creative step of determining what should be considered as a concept. Documenting instances of concepts took much more time than determining the concepts themselves. With a few thousand pages to go, very soon doubts came up as to the value added of the approach.

Direct representation in diagrams. Just like the previously described method, this method aimed at representing the information from the transcriptions in diagrams. The construction of a text-based model as an intermediate step in the process of producing a formal representation using diagrams was skipped. It was decided to make three rounds through the transcript of each interview to come to a task structure, a concept structure, and an overview of the directives used in each interview. As a next step, these products had to be consolidated for the experiment as a whole. This approach has been applied for one experiment. During the analysis, task structures and concept structures were made by paper and pencil. After that, computerized tools were used to make diagrams out of them. The disadvantage of this approach for the construction of concept structures was the fact that the contents of a certain concept structure were influenced by the sequence in which the concepts were discovered. For each interview, this approach sometimes led to more than three handwritten pages with concepts and relations between them. A diagram was "finished" when, due to space limits, it turned out to be impossible to add an extra concept. This linear modeling approach prevented an optimal clustering of concepts. For the task structure, this problem turned out to be less serious.

Categorize and summarize first. A number of categories (i.e., ISF, information processing, internal environment of the ISF, external environment) were delineated that made it possible to classify each part of the text. Next to the classification, each logical unit of text was summarized. All information in one category was used as a basis for the concept structure of that category. Through combination and consolidation these separate structures led to one structure for the interview as a whole. Although it was now possible to construct consistent diagrams more readily, this method also ended up with very large and complex representations with lots of interrelations. Constructing them in an objective way and within a reasonable amount of time remained a problem. Influenced by the fact that quite a lot of energy already had been spent without satisfactory results, doubts began to increase as to the usefulness of the produced diagrams. Their usability in practice would be limited because of their complexity. Was it possible to attain the goal of the knowledge acquisition process without these complex diagrammatic representations of knowledge in task and concept structures? It was not very realistic to expect that it would be possible to end up with an algorithm that would automatically lead to the best solution for the ISF. The domain being dealt with concerned strategic decisions with a wide scope. An overly structured and formalized way of representation to support this type of decisions would not be possible. The methods tested so far might be useful as a basis for computerized knowledge based systems but were not a feasible solution in the area of organization of the ISF.

Textual representation of types of knowledge. From the conviction that the diagrammatic way of representation demanded much energy that was not compensated by profit in terms of insight, the choice was made to make a textual representation per knowledge category instead. The following eight knowledge categories were distinguished.

- way of modeling: what does the expert want to know about an organization and its environment in order to get to know and to assess the organization, and in which terms does he express his view on the future organization of the ISF?
- way of diagnosis and design: how does the expert come to conclusions as to the present situation and how does he come to proposals for improvement?
- way of working: what activities does he perform in what sequence to come to a proposal for the design of the ISF?
- way of thinking: from which point of view does the expert act, what assumptions does he make?
- way of controlling: how does the expert manage the design process?
- way of supporting: what supporting tools does he use during the task execution?
- way of preparation: what does an expert know about the organization before he starts with the consultancy and what other knowledge turns out to be relevant during task execution?
- way of behavior: what else is important when working on the design of the ISF?

For the way of modeling, use was made of a categorization even more detailed than the one described in the previous approach. A linear approach was chosen to extract the information from the protocols. For each separate interview, the above knowledge categories were filled in. An incremental approach would have meant that from a certain interview only that information would be taken that was not covered by previously analyzed interviews. The advantage of the linear approach (which is more time consuming than an incremental approach) is that it would be possible in a later stage to make a comparison between different experts for each interview. The results of the analysis per interview for each expert were consolidated and restructured per knowledge category. This approach reduced the number of pages from more than 3,000 to about 450.

Aggregation of the way of modeling in core topics. Because of the interdependence between certain knowledge categories, is was not easy to make a bottom-up analysis of an experiment. When describing the way of diagnoses and design, for instance, it was clear that use had to be made of the information stored under way of modeling, which consisted of a rather long list of nouns. It was decided to stop producing this list. From then on, certain core themes were distinguished and the description of each theme would cover both the information on the way of modeling and on the way of diagnosis and design; guidelines that directly referred to the design and analysis of the ISF were kept separate. This new approach automatically led to analysis reports that would be more readable for outsiders. To perform this last change, the results per interview of the previous method were used as a starting point.

4.3 Comparing the Results

The individual reports (a total of 165 pages) of the nine experiments formed the basis of a mutual comparison, aiming at the discovery of correspondences between results of the nine analyzed experiments. Attention was also paid on gaining insight into the influence of the difference in type of organization upon the method followed by an expert and into the difference in methods applied by experts in one organization.

To allow for a better comparison of the way of design and analysis – guidelines directly regarding the ISF – they were categorized according to the contingency factors, design and goal parameters involved.

5 SUMMARY OF THE RESULTS

Although this paper focuses on the research approach, it is necessary for the assessment of this approach to summarize the research findings. The result (so far) of the research is phrased in terms of directives to be applied in practice for the design of the organization of ISF. As explained in section 2, the emphasis was on the acquisition of knowledge that the experts had in common. The summary of the results, in terms of guidelines, that is given in this section focus on that correspondence. It is not the goal of this paper, and it is impossible due to space limitations, to go into details of the results. The most important general conclusions will be given for each of the knowledge categories that are described in section 4.

For the subjects being most specific for the domain of the organization of the ISF (the way of thinking and the way of diagnosing and designing, as well as the way of modeling), this led to the following five main directives:

1. The design of the organization of the ISF has to take place from a dynamic and open system vision.
2. When organizing the vision, it has to be assumed that:
   - responsibilities ought to be integral;
   - changing the organization means changing information processing;
   - organizing is a continuous, reactive and pro-active activity;
   - the functioning of the organization depends more on people than on structure.
3. The vision of coordination ought to be that it is necessary in order to outweigh the disadvantages of self government.
4. Organizing ISF requires denoting goal variables, contingency factors and design variables. The most important contingency factors are the structure of the organization and the information related coherence between organization parts; the most important design variables are responsibilities, organizational place of the execution of activities and the procedure structure.

5. The directives for the organization of the ISF can be summarized as follows: make line management responsible for the internal working and the external tuning, and integrate the task execution in the primary process.

The five directives (for demands to be made upon ISF designers) in the sphere of the way of preparation, way of supporting, way of thinking, way of working, and way of controlling are more general in character:

- Applying practical experience in the right way is essential; (fore)knowledge is a useful addition here.
- A framework (based on experience) for the problem field is the best way of supporting; a good memory is an important aid.
- Flexibility as to the way of acting is essential for the acceptance of the designer by the organization, and so for his effectiveness.
- The main line in the way of working is to be characterized as a top-down search for signals being connected with the organization of the ISF, where getting acquainted, analyzing and designing strongly overlap.
- Using appropriate techniques influences the productive use of the time available for intelligence.

6 CONCLUSIONS

The think aloud protocol method was used to elicit the expert knowledge. During the subsequent analysis, a considerable amount of time and effort was invested in experimenting with several techniques (first a technique known from literature was used but after that several changes were introduced before arriving at the final approach) for analyzing the protocols. On the one hand, there is the conviction that a detailed analysis is unavoidable when one tries to disclose all the information that is hidden in the protocols. However, when you go through the protocols several times, the awareness increases that someone else (another researcher or the same researcher at another point in time) would have missed certain information drawn from the protocols or would have discovered additional information; next to that, one is less objective when one goes through a protocol for the second time. On the other hand, the time that can be spent on the analysis is limited and the marginal benefits of another round through the protocols are uncertain and will certainly decrease. This makes this trade-off rather difficult. A group of masters' degree students were asked to analyze parts of the protocols. Based on these experiences, it can be concluded that it might have helped (in more than one way) to do the analysis in parallel with another researcher.

Because of the detailed analysis, a considerable amount of time was spent on rather general knowledge (i.e., how does the expert treat the interviewee). Nothing of the findings in this area have been published elsewhere. However, this perspective ought not to be excluded in a research project aimed at practical problem solving. The factors mentioned influence the acceptance of both the designer and his conclusions by the interviewees.

The use of diagrams to map the applied concepts and the performed tasks was very labor intensive because an attempt was made – like my colleagues who applied the same method – to end up with perfect diagrams. This diverted attention, for a period, from the actual use of the diagrams. In fact, they turned out to be too complex for practical usage. The exactness they suggested was another disadvantage. The opinion obtained here is that the required way to document the intermediate and final results is plain text. Text wise intermediate results can be used – certainly by someone who wrote them and who took part in the experiments – to compare the results of the nine experiments and to formulate final conclusions.

The comparison of the results of the individual experiments turned out to be a rather complex process. It required the active availability of a large amount of information. Another problem was that the bottom-up approach, which was characteristic for the way of analysis of the individual transcripts, was not the required approach for the cross protocol analysis. A noticeable fact is that in this research information which at first sight was incoherent and different working methods of experts could be organized in a relatively small number of coherent directives. On the basis of this result, further research can be directed toward the development of a methodology for the organization of the information (systems) function.

In this research project, a qualitative approach was used. No attention was paid to the number of times certain things occurred during the experiments. Even *ex post* this is not considered to be a disadvantage. The aim was not to determine in a statistically justified way how often certain ideas occur with certain experts. The aim was to try to document everything worthwhile for answering the research question even if it occurred only once in one of the nine experiments.

The importance of the guidelines is that they result from the comparison of the individual results of nine experiments: they are common knowledge. It was out of the scope of this research to verify the results of the knowledge acquisition process in practice. For the same reason, the cooperating companies were not asked to give their opinion about the research findings. Next to that, the only conclusion that could eventually have been drawn from such an experiment is that a company partly or fully agrees or disagrees with three experts.

The rather general nature of the research results might lead to the question whether knowledge engineering in the domain of the ISF yields anything specific and useful to practitioners. Based on the evaluation of a series of lectures presented on ISF design to IT professionals from Dutch organizations, the answer tends to be positive.

Working in close cooperation with three experts in three organizations was very interesting and offered the opportunity to learn more about the design of the IS function than it is possible to transfer to others. Next to that, especially the struggle through the knowledge analysis process, contributed a lot to self knowledge.

7 REFERENCES

Butler Cox (1991). *Managing the Devolution of Systems Responsibilities*. Research Report 81, Butler Cox Foundation.

Bacon, C. J. (1990). "Organizational Principles of Systems Decentralization." *Journal of Information Technology*, Number 5, pp. 84-93.

Douma, S., and Schreuder, H. (1992). *Economic Approaches to Organizations*. Englewood Cliffs, New Jersey: Prentice Hall.

Mantelaers, P. A. H. M. (1995). *Information Capacity Engineering*. Doctoral Thesis (in Dutch), Delft University of Technology, Delft.

Swanson, E. B., and Beath, C. M. (1989). "Reconstructing the Systems Development Organization." *MIS Quarterly*, September, pp. 293-305.

Turner, W. S.; Langerhorst, R. P.; Hice, G. F.; Eilers, H. B.; and Uijttenbroek, A. A. (1988). *System Development Methodology*. Rijswijk, The Netherlands: Pandata B.V.

Verhoef, T. F. (1993). *Effective Information Modeling Support*. The Netherlands: Pijnacker.

Waterman, R.H., Jr.; Peters, T. J.; and Phillips, J. R. (1992). "The 7-S Framework." In H. Mintzberg and J. B. Quinn (Editors), *The Strategy Process*. Englewood Cliffs, New Jersey: Prentice-Hall.

Wijers, G. M. (1991). *Modeling Support in Information Systems Development*. Amsterdam: Thesis Publishers.

8 BIOGRAPHY

Paul Mantelaers is associate professor of information systems at Delft University of Technology, Department of Information Systems. After his graduation in 1974 from Tilburg University, he worked at the Dutch Central Bureau of Statistics, first as a national accounts statistician, later in the area of information systems design. In 1984, he joined Delft University of Technology and received his Ph.D. in 1995. He teaches information management and development of information systems. His principal research focus is on the design of the IS function and on the development and management of transnational information systems.

Part Five

The Social and Political Context of IS

18

Transitioning to Client/Server: Using a Temporal Framework to Study Organizational Change

S. Sawyer
School of Information Studies
Syracuse University
Syracuse, New York 13244-4100 USA
Tel: (315) 443-4473
Fax: (315) 443-5806
E-mail: ssawyer@cat.syr.edu

R. Southwick
School of Information Studies
Syracuse University
Syracuse, New York 13244-4100 USA
Tel: (315) 443-4473
Fax: (315) 443-5806
E-mail: rmsouthw@mailbox.syr.edu

Abstract

Research on the management of information systems has rarely conducted in-depth investigations on the problematic role of time in the development and implementation of these systems. When the research has done this, it has interpreted time in an objective, linear sense. This paper calls attention to the existence of not only the objective nature, but also the subjective nature of time in the organizational change surrounding the implementation of new information systems. This paper draws its empirical material from an on-going study of the implementation and use of distributed computing-based systems at a mid-sized university (MSU).

Implementing client/server networks illuminates three themes that contribute to the dual objective/subjective nature of time at MSU: (1) client/server computing is a complex web of technologies and involves people who are struggling to reach a stable, productive state; (2) the development of a client/server project is a discontinuous process; and (3) because of the number of stakeholders involved in the implementation of client/server systems, there are "temporal asymmetries" – that is, differences in how these people themselves perceive and experience time. For managers, to understand the subjective, perceptual nature of time can provide a managerial lever. For researchers, these temporal asymmetries make a difference to how data are collected and interpreted.

Research on the management of information systems has rarely conducted in-depth investigations on the problematic role of time in the development and implementation of these systems. Where the research has done this, it has interpreted that time is interpreted in an objective, linear sense (e.g., Robey and Newman 1996). The purpose of this paper is to illuminate the existence of not only the objective nature but also the subjective nature of time in the organizational change surrounding the implementation of new information systems. We draw our empirical material from an ongoing, multi-year study of the implementation and use of distributed computing-based systems at a mid-sized university (MSU). MSU is in the process of a campus-wide transition from a mainframe-computing architecture to a client/server architecture.

This paper's perspective of time as having a subjective, and not just objective, nature refers to how everyday people in their everyday lives actually experience time (Macey 1989; Friedman 1990). In most of the management and organizational literature, time is measured in divisible units that mark the passing of events – a Newtonian conceptualization. However, recent literature has acknowledged that time is also subjectively perceived (e.g., Vinton 1992). In this non-Newtonian conceptualization, everyday people in everyday life perceive time as shaped by what they are doing, whom they are with, and the numerous other factors that shape the everyday contexts in which they live. Consistent with this additional, perceptual nature of time is also the notion that time can move at different speeds, depending on the social context of the human actors. The issue of variable celerity has implications for both practitioners and researchers. For practitioners, the variations in subjective interpretations of time can be a source of managerial leverage as well as organizational dilemmas. For researchers, the variations affect how they would proceed in collecting and interpreting data.

1 THE DUAL NATURE OF TIME IN THE IMPLEMENTATION OF CLIENT/SERVER COMPUTING

The implementation of client/server computing, at least at our field site, illuminates three themes that contribute to the dual nature of time:

(1) Client/server computing is a complex web of technologies and involves people who are struggling to reach a stable, productive state. This complex web ties together multiple stakeholders, involving high levels of interdependence. These stakeholders are both within, and without, the organization that is implementing the distributed system.
(2) The development of a client/server project is a discontinuous process. The dependencies among stakeholders make possible many starts, stops, and redirections in the implementation effort.
(3) Because of the number of stakeholders involved in the implementation of client/server systems, there are "temporal asymmetries" – that is, differences in how these people themselves perceive and experience time. These differing perceptions and experiences can, in turn, create the potential for conflict between different groups of stakeholders.

To flesh out the three themes, this paper continues in five sections. The second section defines client/server computing and describes the research site. The third section part builds the case for the dual nature of time by drawing on the research literature relevant to our field work at MSU. The fourth section outlines our research approach. The fifth section presents our field observations, which we use in our attempt to provide rich, empirical illustrations of the three themes. Pulling back from the specifics of our case, the final section provides a general discussion on how to account for the dual perspectives on time.

2 TRANSITIONING TO CLIENT/SERVER COMPUTING AT MID-SIZED UNIVERSITY

Underlying the present research is our belief that distributed computing, embodied in technology such as client/server networks, represents a distinct and dramatic change in computing infrastructure. A computing infrastructure encompasses hardware systems, software systems, workers who serve these systems, and norms of use pertaining to these systems. In this way, computing infrastructures act as a web, tying an organization together (Kling and Scacchi 1982; Kling 1995).

2.1 Client/Server Computing

Client/server computing is currently the dominant model for new forms of distributed computing infrastructures. The technical architecture of client/server computing is substantially different from that of mainframe computing (Hall 1994). A fundamental premise of client-server computing is that the total capacity of the distributed servers and workstations exceeds that of the mainframes they replace. This is made possible by the ability of the technology to allow two or more computers to share the accessing, processing, and storing of data through cooperative and interactive use of software applications. Data-sharing imposes a heavy requirement on the technical capabilities of the network. This includes high-speed, broad-band data communication to connect clients with servers so the latter can run applications cooperatively. This new architecture moves software applications, and the associated processing of data, closer to the user (via the client software) and provides opportunities for computer processing that can be faster, more efficient, and more effective, hence improving the quality of service.

This broadening of computer processing – from centralized mainframes to an interconnected network of distributed computers – necessitates, in turn, significant organizational change. Physically distributing an organization's information processing capability has the consequence of also distributing the organization's information resources. From the organization's perspective, this means that the distribution of information, via technical innovation, will alter social and administrative practices (Zuboff 1988; Orlikowski 1991). In other words, changes in technology mean changes in the social definitions of what that technology is and what it does (Kling and Scacchi 1982).

2.2 Mid-Sized University

MSU is a private, research-oriented school. It enjoys high name recognition, nationally and internationally. MSU's administrative and organizational structures can be considered typical for American universities of nearly 18,000 students and nearly 3,700 employees. By 1993, three environmental factors had created a situation demanding MSU's attention. Those who administered MSU's computing infrastructure faced (1) an increasing workload required of MSU's mainframe systems, (2) a restrictive reliance on MSU's outdated legacy systems, and (3) a nearly unmanageable tangle of administrative and academic networks, characterized by overlapping links and disparate technologies.

These issues regarding computing are typical of most academic computing systems (Alpert 1985; El-Khawis 1995; McClure and Lopata 1996). Facing this scenario, MSU's CIO made the decision to revamp the computing infrastructure so as to take advantage of new client/server technology. The CIO reflected that this was "as much a decision on saving money as it was freeing ourselves from commitments we no longer wanted."

For two reasons, we viewed the situation at MSU to be especially favorable for studying organizational change in the context of a client/server implementation. The first is that, at the time of our decision to establish the research stream of which this study is a part, MSU was still in the relatively early stages of its multi-year implementation. Thus, we were presented with the opportunity to follow the project from the planning/design phase of implementation (pre-installation) through the eventual, actual use of the technology (post-installation). The second reason is that the technology implementation at MSU is organization-wide (campus-wide) in scope. The project called for a complete transition from the existing mainframe-dominated architecture to a client/server architecture, where the transition was targeted to span several years. In order to reach this objective, the project plan established many smaller department-specific projects (e.g., admissions, financial aid, etc.). The multi-project structure allowed us opportunities for research involving multiple levels of analysis within the organization and with vendors.

3 TIME

Given the turbulent and discontinuous environment for developing and deploying client/server computing in general, we believe that *time* can provide a common thread with which to organize observations and interpretations of client-server implementation. In this section of the paper, we examine how temporal elements help form the basis for our observations and interpretations.

Perhaps the most obvious influence of time in the transition to client/server computing at MSU derives from the fact that MSU's client/server initiative involves a perpetual process of product development. Participating in this development process are departmental system users, technologists within MSU, and external vendors (especially of client/server software). Time forms one structure in which the interaction among these groups unfolds.

Associated with the organizational process of deploying client/server computing, and the systems relying upon it, are artifacts that the organizational actors themselves use to impose administrative order. These are the tools of project management. The most obvious example is milestone charts, which are instruments for measuring time. Milestone charts also reflect a longstanding tradition in organizational studies, where time is understood to be a commodity that is objective, linear, homogenous, and divisible (partitionable by rational human mental process) and that has value commensurate with its divisible parts (Hassard 1996).

3.1 The Dual Nature of Time

With respect to our research, we recognize a problem in such conceptions of time. In the first place, the client/server project at MSU appears to be neither linear nor homogenous. As we will describe, project development at MSU has reflected discontinuity and turbulence. Individual client/server projects have often exhibited abrupt changes in direction (nonlinearity) and have not generally maintained a consistent pace (nonhomogeneity). This presents a problem for management instruments in which development (measured in objective time) is assumed to be incremental.

Gersick (1988 1989) has attempted to account for the nonhomogenous nature of time as it affects decision-making and problem-solving. Applying theory developed in natural science (Eldrege and Gould 1972), Gersick advances a model of "punctuated equilibrium" for group-level theory to explain the discontinuous, and apparently spontaneous, patterns and pace of activity exhibited in the course of group development projects. The punctuated equilibrium model differs from linear models of group activity in which processes are assumed to be linear and incrementally additive (Gersick 1989).

Gersick's model straddles the dual conceptions of time: objective time and subjective (socially constructed) time. This is also the case for Friedman and for Macey, who make distinctions between time as objectively measured and time as subjectively experienced. Bucciarelli (1988) posits two worlds in the temporal process of engineering design: an "object-world" defined by topicality and a "process-world" defined by social narrative. We may easily extend his analysis to the software development process. The object-world refers to the physical elements of computer technology, such as hardware and software. The process-world refers to the "world of dialogue and negotiation, of social exchange, laughter, gossip, banter – all that which is ever-present in design, but whose significance is generally discounted" (pp. 96-97).

Although research on the management of information systems has rarely conducted in-depth investigations on the problematic role of time in the development and implementation of these systems, the need to account for the socially defined aspect of time in order to bring about a successful systems implementation has been recognized for some time. In reflections on his experiences with software development projects, Brooks (1972) illustrates how traditional conceptions of time (i.e., as linear and additive) may lead to inaccurate hypotheses within the complexity of a social context. As reflected in the title of his book, *The Mythical Man-Month*, he relates how assuming that one might hasten the completion of a project by assigning more people to it was not only wrong, but also likely to produce the opposite effect. The lesson from Brooks is that, in software development projects, where social complexity interacts with the demands of system development tasks, success also depends on a recognition of social factors – among them, the way time is seen and structured by the participants themselves.

In addition to recognizing time as instrumental to the software development process, we also see it as an element in a conceptual framework for examining the power struggle among users, technologists, and vendors. Here, we refer to Barley's (1988) perspective on time which builds on the work of Zerubavel (1979, 1981). He examines the interaction of technology and organizational structure. His longitudinal study of radiology departments involved in new technology implementation serves to highlight that temporal order can structure the conflict between the technicians (as users) and the radiologists (as users). He posits a recurring dynamic between external, objective aspects of temporal order (structural) and its social constructedness (interpretive). Barley also makes a case for technology-based temporal order affecting the way individuals and groups interpret their work. He posits that temporal asymmetry may be a source of conflict between organizational groups.

Our perspective in the present research posits that management seeks stability and order in the deployment of information technology, or IT, resources. For this reason we prefer the term *synchronous* rather than *symmetrous*. In the implementation of client/server systems, we point to three sets of relations in which temporal perceptions may be asynchronous. The first exists between the vendors (the developers of software) and the technologists (members of the organization's information systems, or IS, group). The second exists between the vendors and the users. The third exists between the technologists and the users.

The first set of relations is new to the technologists at MSU. One of the directives regarding the client/server implementation was to buy software, not build it. The result has been that vendors are far more integral than previously to MSU's computing infrastructure. The technologists have become responsible for overseeing what they used to do for a living and their role turned into one of change agentry. With regard to the second set of relations, the asynchronous user/developer temporal relationship has always existed. However, because the developers (who are now vendors) are not co-located at MSU, it is now a relationship at a distance. The final set of relations, between the users and the technologists, has changed in that these two groups now share many of the same concerns. However, the long history between the two seems to mask some of the similarities they now share. In other words, the historical perception by users – that IS is not very responsive or accessible – is not changed by the fact that IS now includes them in every decision about the vendor packages. Users have trouble believing that IS has "the same vision."

These three sets of relations suggest a dual nature to time. As Jones (1988, p. 21) says, "All human events occur in time. But the character of those events and the time in which they occur vary widely from person to person, from culture to culture." Each set of the three sets of relations acknowledges the objective, measured chronology of time, but each also highlights the subjective and omni-present nature of time. Our observations confirm the presence of this subjective component. Further, we note the potential for temporal asymmetry to persist between developers and users of the client/server technology. This may have the effect of leading to inaccurate decisions in the users' evaluation of systems since perceptions of development time are structured according to traditional development cycles, rather than the rapid pace of client/server development. For instance, one vendor was selected over another because of a strong perception that this vendor was further along in the development cycle than the other vendors. One of the other vendors argued that "it is the nature of client/server in its present state that learning takes place through implementation."

We further extend this argument to suggest that the temporal asymmetries between developers and users creates a degree of control by developers over users (e.g., Markus 1983; Markus and Bjørn-Anderson 1987; Kling and Iacono 1984). Related to this point is that the user may maintain the perception that the length of time they are involved with a vendor is indicative of the degree of development of a product. In other words, they perceive a process which is linear and cumulative when it is, in fact, discontinuous and constantly reinitiated.

Because of the volatility of innovation in client/server technology, many applications persist in beta form. Weick (1990) has previously suggested that new technologies follow a pattern of development different from that of older technologies. The high level of mental interpretation and subsequent uncertainty in knowledge of the process serve to result in a situation in which "implementation often is the means by which the technology itself is designed" (p. 8). We see this as standard for client/server development. Beta versions of software are often the norm with upgrades occurring in beta-stage applications. As we will discuss, one of the vendors providing software for MSU releases a new version each month! This sets the stage for temporal discontinuities to persist. This means that the objective nature of time provides for measurement, even as the subjective nature of time sets the stage for conflict. This dual nature of time serves as a lens for interpreting our observations at MSU.

4 OUR RESEARCH APPROACH

In this part of the paper, we describe our research approach. Our motivations are concerned with documenting sequences of events and a process of change over time, rather than with attempting to capture organizational events as set of factors which relate to one another through causal interaction (Mohr 1982). We made the following four assumptions in conducting our research.

(1) Our perspective on change is social. While change may manifest itself in some physical form or artifact, we believe that, in order to develop useful knowledge of the phenomenon, it is necessary to elicit the socially constructed interpretations of the organizational actors which they develop through their social interactions (Markus 1983).

(2) An actor's interpretations are part of a larger, dynamic social context and, therefore, must be interpreted as situationally dependent. This perspective incorporates the social and physical aspects of computing into the concept of an infrastructure: the web of computing (Kling and Scacchi 1982; Kling 1995).

(3) The situationally dependent, socially interpreted foundation for social (organizational) action makes prediction based on a single event or a single actor's actions impossible. In other words, we take an emergent perspective on the relationship between information technology and the organization (Markus and Robey 1988).

(4) In taking an interpretive perspective, we believe that we, as researchers, cannot be detached from the social context. Therefore, our observations are necessarily subjective, and this has implications for the conduct of the research (Barley 1990).

Following the objectives and assumptions outlined above, we have employed a longitudinal, field-based methodology for studying organizational change at MSU. Zuboff (1988, p. 423) began her own discussion of her methodology by saying "Behind every method is a belief." Our belief is that longitudinal, *in situ* field work is an appropriate approach, well-suited for research that seeks to understand the evolving process of implementing new technologies. There has been an increased interest in longitudinal, field-based, and observer-centered research for the study of information technology in organizations (Kling 1980; Markus and Robey 1988; Pettigrew 1990; Lee and Markus 1995). There are many reasons for this emerging interest. Two of the most salient are (1) the limitations on what we know about technology's effects in organizations and (2) the speed at which technology changes (Van Maanen 1995).

4.1 Data Collection

In collecting data, we spanned individual and organizational levels of analysis. At the individual level, we looked at how client/server systems are being interpreted. At the organizational level, our interest was to see how these client/server systems affect the web of computing already in place at MSU. In doing this, we sought to emphasize the potentially differing perspectives that users, technologists, and vendors have. We began our fieldwork with a ten month period of gaining access to, and the confidence of, the site's employees. This early phase provided the context for the data collection and analysis in the current study.

We employed two primary methods for collecting data: interviews and observation. Interviews vary by level of structure, with most being semi-structured and open-ended. Typically these are taped and transcribed. All interviewees are asked if they mind being taped; if they are reluctant, we do not tape the interview. Our field notes record data collected from unobtrusive observations, from participation in committees and meetings, and from informal social interactions. There are two types of field notes for each observation: the first is a chronology of events and actions; the second is a more free-flowing account of perceptions, stories, and anecdotes. The chronology serves as a record of observations. The account serves as a record of the observer's perceptions. We also had access to formal documents and the archives of the client/server change. This includes e-mail, work records, and archival memos and reports. We used these materials to help establish our understanding of the context and organizational milieu.

4.2 Present Status

MSU initiated its mainframe-to-client/server transition project in February 1993. We commenced our research effort in February 1995. To date, our activities have centered on participation with, and observations of, committees formed to work on specific aspects of the client/server initiative; ongoing interviews with managers and workers (both IS and line); and document/records collection. This includes more than sixty hours of meetings and over fifty interviews (averaging about 65 minutes each). We also have more than 600 documents (e-mail, memos, handouts, and reports). Five people have participated in data collection, while two have been part of the project from its inception.

In the process of coordinating and tracking the data collection effort, we have made use of vignettes and stories to help develop an understanding of what we are observing. Through this informal effort, shared themes have been emerging. These take the shape of narratives and anecdotes, woven together from our data. Thus, these findings reflect an interim understanding, a valuable step in doing qualitative analysis (Miles 1979, 1990).

5 OBSERVATIONS FROM THE CLIENT/SERVER IMPLEMENTATION AT MSU

We began this paper by positing three related themes in the implementation of client/server computing that highlight the dual nature of time: (1) client/server computing is a complex web of technologies and involves people who are struggling to reach a stable, productive state; (2) the development of a client/server project is a discontinuous process; and (3) because of the number of stakeholders involved in the implementation of client/server systems, there are "temporal asymmetries" – that is, differences in how these people themselves perceive and experience time. These differing perceptions and experiences can, in turn, create the potential for conflict between different groups of stakeholders.

1. *Client/server computing is a complex web of technologies and involves people who are struggling to reach a stable, productive state.*

An underlying idea of client/server computing is that individual nodes on the network are able to exchange data, or facilitate the cooperative processing of data, in a direct, peer-to-peer relationship (Hall 1994). This stands in contrast to the idea of mainframe computing, in which computing activity is typically directed through, and controlled by, a centralized "master" processor. The individual nodes of the client/server network are typically computers which may run applications, provide access to databases, control printer activity, etc. In order for there to be direct, peer-to-peer connectivity there must be interoperability between the various hardware and software components (i.e., the architectures and platforms). This requirement poses a significant technical challenge.

In large part due to this need for interoperability, there is a fast-paced, continuous process of software development and redesign to fulfill the promise of client/server. New products necessitate modifications of old products, making this a seemingly self-perpetuating process. The breadth of innovation is accentuated by the fact that the concept of a computing network, especially in a technical sense, now commonly transcends organizational boundaries. The interest in Internet technology and the national information infrastructure (NII) has widened the scope of interoperability. This, in turn, has also contributed to accelerating the pace of product innovation.

In light of the frenzied pace of innovation in distributed computing, it becomes an even more daunting challenge for any organization to stay abreast of such technical change, and, consequently, to maintain technical integrity (interoperability) between the various segments of the broader organizational infrastructure. This accelerating pace sets the stage for temporal asymmetries to exist between vendors, users, and technologists. Technological developments have forced MSU's IS staff to shift its focus from mainframe systems to client/server systems, and the technological staff struggles to comprehend this new arena. The vendors, who have embraced the client/server architecture, are positioned to respond to these technological developments more easily than the IS staff at MSU. The users are the least able to keep pace, and this creates the potential for time-based conflicts.

Our observations to date suggest that, at this stage in the technological evolution of client/server computing, the transition from mainframe computing to client/server computing will continue to be challenging for all groups and individuals involved with the implementation project at MSU. This has been especially evident in the meetings of oversight committees where progress on individual subprojects appears to be continually undermined by the necessity to devote time to solve technical problems. For example, the director of the client/server implementation says of the weekly IT directors' meeting "I'm not comfortable, yet, with the directors. People talk about the technology, they talk about the budgets, they talk about the dynamics of [our] group. We never talk about the transition [the set of projects that are implementing the client/server systems]." The information center manager says "We don't plan, we don't pay much attention to anything but the new technology. [We] never talk about how to use it."

While this situation may not be unique or surprising, given the nascent state of client/sever technology, we believe that there are unique characteristics of this form of computing which compound the problem. In particular, the distributed nature of client/server applies to the social structure of the organization, not just to the spatial configuration of the physical technology. In other words, client/server computing enables a greater degree of freedom for technical independence within organizational subunits. Individual departments within MSU are adopting different strategies for computing, e.g., using WindowsNT instead of Novell as the network operating system. This makes it more difficult for the technologists, who are attempting to coordinate the computing infrastructure, to maintain a sense of control over it. As the director of the physical network states, "In some sense, [this is] the most strategic decision we made [i.e., allowing a department to break from the standard network configuration]."

2. The development of the client/server project is a discontinuous process.

Despite the techniques and instruments used by the IS department in its attempt to invoke or impose a temporally defined order for internal development efforts (such as PERT and Gantt charts), the actual client/server project at MSU is far from controllable. There are two reasons for this. The first is that development schedules now are controlled by the vendors, albeit with input from the technologists and users at MSU. The second reason is that applications often are not available on the market when MSU needs them.

Here, temporal asymmetries are created by expectations. MSU's users and technologists understand that the client/server market is evolving rapidly. However, the products that they need are not available. This creates a paradox in time: the quick pace of change is not providing what they need. For the vendors, the ability to respond to changing technology is moderated by their ability to produce products. This may be less about the technology than their own management skills, but the effect is that the users and technologists at MSU cannot keep up technologically. And the vendors cannot deliver products that are based on the technology they seem to know so well.

For example, MSU predicated its original project plan on having key student processing functions available in an integrated client/server system by Fall 1996. However, there were no viable products when they looked at the market in 1994. Since then, the two dominant players have moved at different speeds. The group MSU had chosen fell behind schedule and has recently bought out its contract. The other is about to bring a product to market, which MSU has decided to adopt. A second example is the continued need of a reasonably-priced security package that will provide single entry passwords to multiple applications. In the absence of this product, several other projects have been delayed.

These two examples also illustrate how the development and deployment of client/server infrastructure can proceed in fits and starts, with numerous changes in direction, rather than following a linear path of gradual and steady progress. MSU's project plans, and most deadlines, are flexible (and often not met). They are steadily revised to account for which products are ready and what sequence of dependencies between projects can be met. While this makes sense at a strategic level, for the users this translates into a steady discounting of any plans produced by the technologists (whether external vendors or internal IS). For internal IS, this puts them in a unique place: they know how hard it is to plan development yet they must act as overseers to vendors and as advocates for users. At the same time, they often serve as apologists for the vendors. The CIO, after visiting the senior management of one (severely delayed) vendor implementation said, "I'm sick of being their whipping boy."

As suggested above, many factors – internal and external to the organization – may contribute either to stimulate, retard, or even derail the development of client/server products. For example, software upgrades in this environment are frequent. One project has a new update to its software about every three weeks. From the vendor's perspective, they are developing software at breakneck speed and being responsive. The users interpret this as sloppy development. Furthermore, client/server systems often exhibit less stability than their mainframe ancestors. For the user, this creates a churning feeling. The lead implementor for a system with changes every three weeks calls it "computing on roller skates."

3. *Because of the number of stakeholders involved in the implementation of client/server systems, there are "temporal asymmetries" – that is, differences in how these people themselves perceive and experience time.*

One way to view these differing perceptions of time is to focus on the differences between groups. A temporal structure provides order to the daily conduct of work. Temporal structures show up in the rituals of coffee breaks, in how long meetings last, and in what it means to be early or late. These temporal structures are often implicit and so are not explicitly discussed when meeting with members of other groups (Barley 1988). For example, in speaking with various managers and administrators within MSU, we hear repeated reference to Fall 1997 as the target date for a complete transition from the mainframe system to a client/server computing system. This is the date originally set by the CIO to coincide with the termination of agreements with mainframe contractors. The temporal asymmetry that we perceive here exists between those who are most actively involved in the transition and those who are not. The former see this as a "drop-dead" date. The latter see this date as unreachable and, thus, flexible. Since this is never explicitly discussed, conflicts over the importance of different projects arise.

We have examined three groups' perspectives on development. The first two groups, vendors and MSU's IS staff, represent two subsets of the technologist's perspective. The vendors are building the client/server applications to be used at MSU, while the MSU IS staff are the computer and the network administration personnel (and their managers) who facilitate the integration of client/server applications into the existing computing infrastructure. The third group consists of the users who work with MSU's IS staff and MSU's vendors, so as to enable the integration of the client/server applications into the existing work life of the organizational units that will be using the systems.

Much of our data collection to date has focused on the technologists in the IS department, who have been attempting to form a bridge between the technology (personified through vendors) and their clients in the organization. These technologists are having to learn the client/server technologies even as the technologies are changing. The IS director of the implementation effort has said "we are one person deep at most skills. Sometimes we don't even have that." This means that very little is stable for the technologists. The greatest urgency is felt among the IS managers, the people ultimately responsible for a successful implementation. In their effort to implement successfully a large, complex, and often turbulent project, they struggle to convey this sense of urgency to others within and outside the organization. Vendors are also concerned with delivery of their product. But this delivery is set in the context of the vendor's overall needs, not MSU's. The users and their managers are interested in improvements that they have been led to expect. However, they have no interest in increased work or in "working hard so we can wait to change" says one senior administrator.

Users, who had grown accustomed to the stable, if limited, services in the mainframe environment, also do not know what to expect. Said one administrator, while learning about the data warehouse, "I'm not sure what this [system] can do. Nor am I sure what it can't. I just don't know." The support that technologists provided to users is not as certain in the new environment. And users do not know what to expect. This increased uncertainty for users as well as technologists is a new factor in their relationship at MSU.

6 IMPLICATIONS FOR RESEARCH: ACCOUNTING FOR TIME

Perhaps the most significant of temporal asymmetries is that the pace of time changes for each of these groups based on the issues confronting them. Vendors are rushing products, users are chafing at delays, and technologists are trying to mediate. And all three groups have differing temporal structures that define what rushing, chafing, and trying mean. Because perceptions of time are built from the social worlds in which these people live, these perceptions are implicit. Given the power of objective time measures, these subjective perceptions stay hidden. Still, objective time is a complication to the variations in subjective time. It is subjective time's temporal asymmetries that give rise to contentions among the three stakeholder groups. For managers, understanding the subjective, perceptual, nature of time can provide a lever. For researchers, these temporal asymmetries affect how data is collected and interpreted. These points are discussed in the following sections.

6.1 Time as a Lever for Managers

The temporal asymmetries which exist among vendors, users, and technologists can serve as a lever for managers in two ways. One point of leverage is to use the differing perceptions of time as a mechanism to instill urgency in the different groups by highlighting differences. These "artificial" crises are one form of short-term motivation. A second point of leverage is to use these temporal asymmetries as insulation. For example, vendors move slower than the technologists would like, regarding changes that the vendors make in the software. This is so the vendor can maintain control over its code. MSU technologists do the same with the users, explaining to these users how the extra time spent will result in better solutions.

6.2 Time and Data Collection

These observations on time's dual nature have implications for research in two ways. First, these findings suggest that the rapidly changing nature of client/server development deserves more attention. Second, these findings suggest that researchers must explicitly account for both objective and subjective time in data collection. These are discussed below.

The rapidly changing nature of client/server development deserves more attention. All implementations are unique, and the increased interdependence and number of stakeholders that client/server systems demands heighten this uniqueness. This means that the implications of the dual nature of time can be best understood in the field and not in an environment controlled by the researcher (McGrath 1988). This encourages observations and interviews across objective time as the basis of research on information systems implementation. However, while the employment of longitudinal research methods may be assumed to provide such an accounting, it may do so only in a limited way unless it is theoretically specified by the researchers prior to data collection (Monge 1990). Longitudinal methods may follow dynamic processes across time, rather than take snapshots, but do not necessarily incorporate a theoretic basis for time. Moreover, most social scientists see time in the Newtonian sense: metaphorically represented as an "arrow," imposing a linear order or sequence on events.

> Many social scientists have rather uncritically incorporated this orderly time of Newton into their own models, treating time as a background or hidden dimension. It becomes an attribute of the natural universe that is simply there (or "ticking away") as a parameter, marker, or line against which events and activities unfold in an orderly fashion and are then measured by the analyst. [Dubinskas 1988, p. 7]

Such an interpretation fails to account for time as a socially constructed phenomenon. In other words, time in this objective sense does not recognize that different individuals or groups may interpret the temporal structure of a given situation differently. Or, from our perspective, organizational members' reports concerning time may vary according to situational factors. It becomes important to understand the subjective nuance of this time in context.

Explicitly accounting for subjective and objective time in data collection. We had set out to capture a chronology of events: an objective accounting for time. What we have learned is that the interpretive nature of time provides another perspective on the way in which events transpire. This is what Bucciarelli calls the process world. We believe that a primary power of longitudinal research is the opportunity to focus on the subjective aspects of time. These nuances on time's subjective nature arise from reflecting on the data, from understanding the broader context, and from comparing narratives and observations across perspectives and levels of analysis. This can be better enabled by modifying data collection efforts in two ways. The first way is to more explicitly account for the time lines of the various constituents. The second way is to record perceptions of temporal asymmetries as part of the field notes following each observation.

More explicitly accounting for the time lines of the various constituents. To do this, we believe that a time line should be developed for each group. Doing this can highlight key assumptions and make explicit the way the different groups experience time. This provides a mechanism to compare the various perspectives both as they change as time passes and as they coexist with other constituencies' perspectives.

Recording perceptions of temporal asymmetries as part of the field notes following each observation. Our present method of completing field notes is to produce two sets. The first is a chronology (as we see it) of how the observation or interview proceeded. The second is a summary of our perceptions pertaining to that observation and our current thinking. In this second, more expository, set, we can more carefully record the ways in which time is presented or discussed in these observations/interviews. The goal is to describe better the temporal context; this effort should assist us in interpreting the process-world of time. In this state, the focus of the research needs to remain interpretive. Thus, while we continue to draw on existing work, this rapidity of change provides a chance to elaborate and extend our understanding of how change occurs in organizations (Vaughn 1992).

6.3 Client/Server: Technology or Metaphor?

Our position at the beginning of this study was that it is necessary to incorporate the rules, norms, values, and even the subjective perceptions of the people involved, not just the physical attributes of the system, in order to reach an understanding of the information technology. We made the distinction between technology, which has more to do with the hardware and software, and computing infrastructure, which we understand to include the social or cultural aspects as well. Our study to date has reaffirmed this definition of IT, extending the concept of infrastructure to embody time as one manifestation of socio-cultural life.

The new distributed computing technologies, represented by client/server in our work, present significant obstacles to understanding the effects of computing infrastructures on organizations. This is true for the designers and users of these systems and for organizational researchers. One recurrent question is "How will we know whether the impacts on the organization are caused by the client/server aspect of the technology?" The present findings suggest the irrelevance of such questions which imply a causal relationship between technology and organizational change (i.e., the technological imperative). The world of client/server is a world of metaphor (e.g., data warehouses and icons). Client/server is not a uniquely distinguishable technology; witness the difficulty one encounters in trying to obtain a consensus regarding its definition. For instance, when asked, one manager responded that client/server is "just one more icon on my screen."

In establishing how client/server computing is involved in organizational change, we began a chronology, tying events to a calendar to help organize and interpret them. This has helped us to understand how time is both a social construction and an objective measure (Berger and Luckmann 1967; Macey 1989). That is, time is both objectively measured – by the clock and calendar – and subjectively experienced – by both participants and researchers. For us, the differences in how people see time have arisen from attempts to see the world through their eyes, and this is the essence of interpretive work.

7 REFERENCES

Alpert, D. (1985). "Performance and Paralysis: The Organizational Context of the American Research University." *Journal of Higher Education*, Volume 56, Number 3, pp. 242-281.

Barley, S. R. (1988). "On Technology, Time and Social Order: Technically Induced Change in the Temporal Organization of Radiological Work." In Frank A. Dubinskas (Editor), *Making Time: Ethnographies of High-Technology Organizations*. Philadelphia: Temple University Press, pp. 123-169.

Barley, S. R. (1990). "Images of Imaging: Notes on Doing Longitudinal Fieldwork." *Organization Science*, Volume 1, Number 3, pp. 220-249.

Berger, P. L., and Luckmann, T. (1967). *The Social Construction of Reality: A Treatise in the Sociology of Knowledge.* Garden City, New York: Doubleday.

Brooks, F. (1972). *The Mythical Man-Month: Essays on Software Engineering*. Reading, Massachusetts: Addison-Wesley.

Bucciarelli, L. L. (1988). "Engineering Design Process." In Frank A. Dubinskas (Editor), *Making Time: Ethnographies of High-Technology Organizations*. Philadelphia: Temple University Press, pp. 92-122.

Dubinskas, F. A. (1988). "Cultural Constructions: The Many Faces of Time." In Frank A. Dubinskas (Editor), *Making Time: Ethnographies of High-Technology Organizations*. Philadelphia: Temple University Press, pp. 3-38.

El-Khawis, E. (1995). *Campus Trends: 1995*. Higher Education Panel Report, Number 85. Washington DC: American Council on Education.

Eldrege, N., and Gould, S. J. (1972). "Punctuated Equilibria: An Alternative to Phyletic Gradualism." In T. J. Schopf (Editor), *Models in Paleobiology*. San Francisco: Freeman, Cooper and Co., pp. 82-115.

Friedman, M. (1990). *About Time*. Cambridge, Massachusetts: MIT Press.

Gersick, C. J. G. (1988). "Time and Transition in Work Teams: Toward a New Model of Group Development." *Academy of Management Journal*, Volume 31, pp. 9-41.

Gersick, C. J. G. (1989). "Marking Time: Predictable Transitions in Task Groups." *Academy of Management Journal*, Volume 32, Number 2, pp. 274-309.

Hall, C. L. (1994). *Technical Foundations of Client/Server Systems*. New York: John Wiley and Sons.

Hassard, J. (1996). "Images of Time in Work and Organization." In S. R. Clegg, C. Hardy and W. R. Nord (Editors), *Handbook of Organization Studies*. London: Sage Publications, pp. 581-598.

Jones, J. (1988). "Cultural Differences in Temporal Perspectives: Instrumental and Expressive Behaviors in Time." In. J. McGrath (Editor), *The Social Psychology of Time: New Perspectives*. Newbury Park, California: Sage, pp. 21-38.

Kling, R. (1980). "Social Analyses of Computing: Theoretical Perspectives in Recent Empirical Research." *Computing Surveys*, Volume 12, pp. 61-110.

Kling, R. (1995). "Behind the Terminal: The Critical Role of Computing Infrastructure in Effective Information Systems' Development and Use." In W. Cotterman and J. Senn (Editors), *Challenges and Strategies for Research in Systems Development*. London: John Wiley and Sons.

Kling, R., and. Iacono, S. (1984). "Computing as an Occasion for Social Control." *Journal of Social Issues*, Volume 40, Number 3, pp. 77-96.

Kling, R., and Scacchi, W. (1982). "The Web of Computing: Computing Technology as Social Organization." *Advances in Computers*, Volume 21.

Lee, A., and, Markus, M. L. (1995). "Call for Papers: Intensive Research and Information Systems: Using Qualitative, Interpretive, and Case Methods to Study the Role of Information Technology in the Management and Use of Knowledge." *MIS Quarterly*, Volume 19, Number 1, pp. 125-126.

Macey, S. (1989). *The Dynamics of Progress: Time, Method, and Measure*. Athens, Georgia: The University of Georgia Press.

Markus, M. L. (1983). "Power, Politics, and MIS Implementation." *Communications of the ACM*, Volume 26, Number 5, pp. 430-444.

Markus, M. L., and Bjørn-Anderson, N. (1987). "Power Over Users: Its Exercise by System Professionals." *Communications of the ACM*, Volume 30, Number 6, pp. 498-504.

Markus, M. L., and Robey, D. (1988). "Information Technology and Organizational Change: Causal Structure in Theory and Research." *Management Science*, Volume 34, Number 5, pp.

McGrath, J. (1988). "The Place of Time in Social Psychology." In. J. McGrath (Editor), *The Social Psychology of Time: New Perspectives*. Newbury Park, California: Sage, pp. 21-38.

McClure, C., and Lopata, C. (1996). *Assessing the Academic Networked Environment: Strategies and Options*. Washington, DC: Association of Research Libraries.

Miles, M. (1979). "Qualitative Data as an Attractive Nuisance: The Problem of Analysis." *Administrative Science Quarterly*, Volume 24, pp. 590-610.

Miles, M. (1990). "New Methods for Qualitative Data Collection and Analysis: Vignettes and Pre-structured Cases." *Qualitative Studies in Education*, Volume 3, Number 1, pp. 37-51.

Mohr, L. B. (1982). *Explaining Organizational Behavior*. San Francisco: Jossey-Bass.

Monge, P. R. (1990). "Theoretical and Analytical Issues in Studying Organizational Processes." *Organization Science*, Volume 1, Number 4, pp. 406-430.

Orlikowski, W. J. (1991). "Integrated Information Environment or Matrix of Control? The Contradictory Implications of Information Technology." *Accounting Management and Information Technology*, Volume 1, Number 1, pp. 9-42.
Pettigrew, A. (1990). "Longitudinal Field Research on Change." *Organization Science*, Volume 1, Number 3, pp. 267-292.
Robey, D., and Newman, R. (1996). "Sequential Patterns in Information Systems Development: An Application of a Social Process Model." *ACM Transactions on Information Systems*, Volume 14, Number 1, pp.
Van Manaan, J. (1995). "Style as Theory." *Organization Science*, Volume 6, pp. 132-143.
Vaughan, D. (1992). "Theory Elaboration: The Heuristics of Case Analysis." In C. C. Ragin and H. S. Becker (Editors), *What is a Case: Exploring the Foundations of Social Inquiry*. Cambridge, England: Cambridge University Press.
Vinton, D. (1992). "A New Look at Time, Speed, and the Manager." *Academy of Management Executive*, Volume 6, Number 4, pp. 7-16.
Weick, K. E. (1990). "Technology as Equivoque: Sensemaking and New Technologies." In P. S. Goodman, L. S. Sproull and Associates (Editors), *Technology and Organizations*. San Fransisco: Jossey-Bass, pp. 1-44.
Zerubavel, E. (1979). *Patterns of Time in Hospital Life*. Chicago: University of Chicago Press.
Zerubavel, E. (1981). *Hidden Rhythms: Schedules and Calendars in Social Life*. Chicago: University of Chicago Press.
Zuboff, S. (1988). *In the Age of the Smart Machine: The Future of Work And Power*. New York: Basic Books.

8 BIOGRAPHY

Steve Sawyer is an Assistant Professor at Syracuse University's School of Information Studies. His research focuses on how people work together and how they use information technology. Present research includes investigating how software development can be improved through attending to the social aspects of working together and studying how people adapt to working with distributed computing applications (e.g., work-life in the era of client/server computing). Dr. Sawyer is a member of the INFORMS, IEEE, ACM, and USRowing.

Richard Southwick is a Ph.D. student at the Syracuse University School of Information Studies. Current research focuses on IT-based organizational change using longitudinal methods of inquiry. His dissertation research is in progress involving a study of academic libraries transitioning from mainframe to client/server technology. He is also interested in the information-seeking behaviors of users of information retrieval systems.

19

Playing Politics with E-Mail: A Longitudinal Conflict-Based Analysis

C. T. Romm
University of Wollongong
NSW 2522 Australia
Tel: 61 42+ 21 3707
Fax: 61 42+ 21 4289
E-mail: c.romm@uow.edu.au

N. Pliskin
Ben-Gurion University of the Negev
Beer-Sheva 84105, Israel
Tel: 972-7-6472203
E-mail: pliskinn@bgumail.bgu.ac.il

Abstract

Few studies have attempted to link e-mail use to power and politics. The purpose of this paper is to integrate issues of power and conflict into the research on e-mail. To frame the discussion, the paper starts from a review of the relevant writings on power and e-mail. The literature review is concluded with the assertion that contextual, temporal, and conflict management aspects should be incorporated into research on power in organizations. Following this assertion, one of the leading models on conflict management is introduced and used to analyze a case study. The case is presented as a play in three "acts." Each of the acts outlines a different set of conflict management strategies that were utilized by management and employees. The discussion synthesizes the analysis by demonstrating that a combined power and conflict management perspective can explain the playing of politics with e-mail.

1 INTRODUCTION

The last decade has seen an exponential growth in research on e-mail. At first, e-mail research focused primarily on the actual diffusion process (Pliskin 1989; Pliskin, Ball and Curley 1989; Pliskin and Romm 1990). More recently, aspects that relate to the effect of e-mail on organizations have been receiving considerable attention (Rice 1987, 1992, 1993; Rice and Aydin 1991; Markus 1994a, 1994b; Kling 1995). In recent attempts to explain e-mail diffusion and use, some researchers have recommended that concepts of power and control should be incorporated into e-mail research (Markus 1994b).

The purpose of this paper is, indeed, to integrate issues of power and conflict into the research on e-mail. More specifically, the research question that this paper addresses is how e-mail can support different organizational conflict strategies over time. To frame the discussion, the paper starts (in section 1) with a review of the relevant writings on power and e-mail. The literature review is concluded with the assertion that contextual, temporal, and conflict management aspects should be incorporated into research on power in organizations. Following this assertion, one of the leading models on conflict management is introduced. In section 2, the model is used to analyze a case study. The case is presented as a play in three "acts." Each of the acts outlines a different set of conflict management strategies that were utilized by management and employees. The discussion (in section 3) synthesizes the analysis by demonstrating that a combined power and conflict management perspective can explain the use of e-mail in organizational politicking.

2 THEORETICAL BACKGROUND

Some of the leading writers on power (Giddens 1985; Clegg 1995) indicate that one way to approach the literature in this area is to view it at as reflecting a conflict between two "voices": the Marxist, or critical voice, and the functionalist, or managerialist voice. While the Marxist, or critical voice, tends to side with employees, considering the struggle against management as legitimate and even desirable (Mezaros 1970; Gramsci 1971; Gamble and Walton 1972; Geyer and Schweiter 1981; Mann 1986), the functionalist, or managerialist voice, tends to side with management, viewing employees' use of power as illegitimate, disruptive, and potentially destructive to organizations (Bennis et al. 1958; Mechanic 1962; Hickson et al. 1971; Mayes and Allen 1977; Gandz and Murray 1980; Mintzberg 1984).

Much of the literature on organizational politics tends to take the perspective of the functionalist, or managerialist, voice. In fact, one of the most common definitions of politics in the management literature is *the unsanctioned or illegitimate use of power to achieve unsanctioned or illegitimate ends* (Mayes and Allen 1977; Gandz and

Murray 1980; Mintzberg 1984). This definition implies that politics is dysfunctional and aimed at thwarting initiatives that are intended to benefit the organization.

It should be noted that, taken together, the critical and the managerialist approaches have one thing in common: *they take sides*. Both have an implicit morality that sees *one group*, employees, in the case of the critical theorists, and management, in the case of the managerialist theorists, as right. As indicated by Clegg, this state of affairs calls for a new, integrative approach that could combine the two sides into one conceptual framework. The theoretical basis for such an approach can be found in Foucault's (1977, 1980) work, which suggests that truth (or knowledge) is relative and is a *product* of the power struggles that shape and define it.

The pioneering work on power and politics in information systems (IS) was undertaken more than a decade ago. Kling (1980) provided a starting point to this research by identifying six theoretical approaches that could explain resistance to the diffusion of information technologies: rational, structural, human relations, interactionist, *organizational politics*, and *class politics*. Building on Kling's work, Markus (1983) defined three major categories which can accommodate theories of resistance to diffusion: people-determined, system-determined, and interactionist. The main focus of her paper, however, was on one of the variants of the interactionist theory, i.e., the *political*. According to this variant, resistance is explained as a product of the "interaction of system design features with the intraorganizational distribution of power, defined either objectively, in terms of horizontal or vertical power dimensions, or subjectively, in terms of symbolism" (Markus 1983, p. 432). In other words, this theory predicts that information systems will be resisted by potential users if they cause a redistribution of power that either conflicts with the organizational structure (objective definition) or with the interests of individuals who are likely to lose power as a result of the implementation (subjective definition).

It is only in recent years that researchers have started to consider the social and political implications of e-mail. A review of the literature in this area reveals that much of it tends to focus on e-mail as a technology that *enhances work-related cooperation*. Thus, Finholt and Sproull (1990) investigated how e-mail can facilitate group decision making and bring about group unity and cohesion. Rice's series of studies (Rice 1987, 1992, 1993; Rice and Aydin 1991) were important in demonstrating the effect of networks on group behavior, with particular emphasis on how membership in networks affected members' attitudes to the new technology and promoted group innovation.

Another theme in the recent research on e-mail is the study of its role in supporting *social processes*. A major contribution in this area is Sproull and Kiesler's (1991) research. These authors were among the first to argue that e-mail has a democratizing effect on organizations. Other authors reported a series of dysfunctional attributes of e-mail, including flaming effects (Siegel et al. 1986; McGuire, Kiesler, and Siegel

1987), dis-inhibition, and de-individuation effects (Hiltz and Johnson 1989; Matheson and Zanna 1989). Markus (1994a), in a recent study on the negative effects of e-mail on social life at work, added to the list of the negative social effects of e-mail strategies such as "manipulative forwarding," "compulsive documentation," and "aggressive accountability games."

An emerging sub-theme within the research on the social uses of e-mail is the recent body of research on the role of e-mail as a *mobilizer of groups in conflict*. To date, much of the work in this area focused on public access systems (Lie 1990; Rogers, Collins-Jarvis, and Schmitz 1994; Van Tassel 1994). There is, however, some research on the social and political aspects of intraorganizational networks that has uncovered several uses and abuses of e-mail, including its potential use for managerial control (Winner 1992; Mantovani 1994), coalition building (Zuboff 1988, pp. 382-383), industrial relations (Pliskin and Romm 1996), and gender relations (Romm and Pliskin 1996a). The study that is presented here fits within this small but growing body of research.

As mentioned before, one of the major conclusions to be drawn from a review of the literature on power is that much of it *takes sides*. Summarizing the research on power, Clegg asserts that, to study this field in a meaningful way, one needs to (1) contextualize it in time and place, (2) adopt a systemic perception that examines more than one side, and (3) accept as a given that all sides in a power struggle are mutually dependent and equally capable of influence and manipulation. These three assumptions are the conceptual starting point for the analysis in this paper. Our analysis, which is based on an extensive case study, is highly contextualized. Also, by using a conflict management model as a basis for our analysis, we examine more than one side and avoid the danger of "taking sides." Thus, we contribute toward an integrative approach to the study of organizational power.

The model that is the basis for our analysis here was first proposed by Thomas (1976). It is considered the leading model in the literature on organizational conflict management, with most of the empirical research in this area based or related to it (Ruble and Thomas 1976; Filley 1975, 1978; Robbins 1974; Thomas 1993). The model uses two dimensions: cooperativeness (the degree to which one party attempts to satisfy the other party's concerns), and assertiveness (the degree to which one party attempts to satisfy his or her own concerns). Based on these dimensions, five conflict management strategies are identified: competition (assertive and uncooperative), collaboration (assertive and cooperative); avoidance (unassertive and uncooperative); accommodation (unassertive and cooperative); and compromise (mid-range on both assertiveness and cooperativeness). Figure 1 presents a pictorial description of the Thomas model.

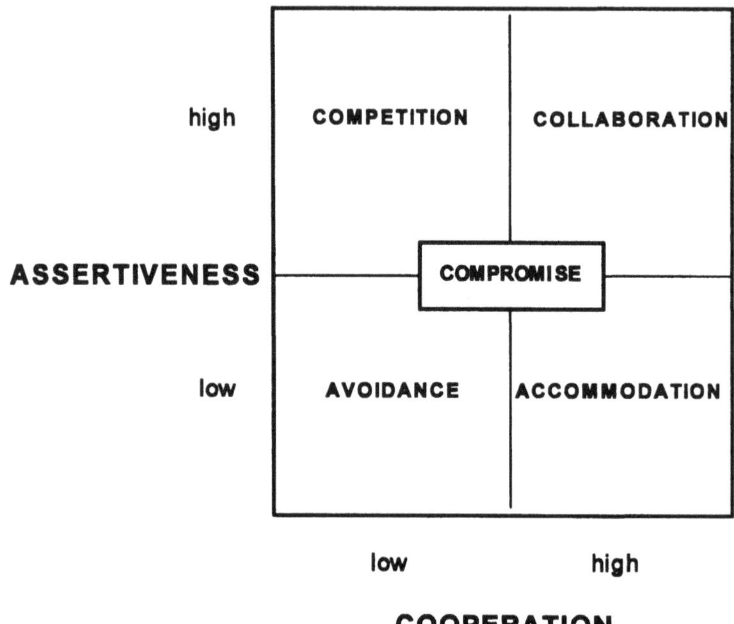

Figure 1 Conflict Management Model (based on Thomas 1993).

2 CASE STUDY

2.1 Methodology

The methodology of this study is based on the "integrative framework" developed by Lee in a series of papers on the use of qualitative research in management of information systems (Lee 1989a, 1989b, 1991, 1994). Lee's integrative framework is formally presented in his 1994 paper (pp. 146-147). It combines three types of "understandings": the subjective, the interpretive and the positivist. According to Lee, the three understandings are "far from being mutually exclusive and irreconcilable," in fact, "they may be utilized as mutually supportive and reinforcing steps in organizational research" (1991, pp. 355-363).

True to the spirit of Lee's model, the three types of understandings have been combined in our study in that (1) a case study that presents the points of view of a diversity of characters is the focal point of the paper (subjective understanding), (2) at the end of each "act," the case events are discussed and analyzed in a way that reflects the authors' interpretation of their meaning (interpretive understanding), and (3) the

Thomas conflict management model is used to explain the behavior of the characters and the major dynamics of the case events (positivist understanding). Another important source of insight for this study is the work by Lyytinen and Hirschheim (1988) and Hirschheim and Klein's (1989) on the application of critical theory to information systems development. In these papers, the authors introduced Habermas' (1974, 1984) notions of power and conflict into the analysis of information systems development via the conventions of stories, very much as we do in this paper.

Data for this study were collected by the authors at a university referred to here as UOR (the name of the university as well as the names of all characters in the case have been withheld to protect their anonymity; the names that are used are pseudonyms). Data was collected over three years (1993-1995), which overlapped with about half of the seven-year period during which the case events, including an e-mail implementation project, occurred (1988-1995). It should be noted that the authors, who reside in different continents and time zones, relied heavily on e-mail during the design of the study and the data analysis.

Textual analysis, questionnaires, and interviews were employed in the study. These were comprehensive and mutually supportive. For example, the interviews enabled cross checking of historical details extracted from the textual analysis of e-mail messages. To maximize reliability, both authors were involved in all data analysis activities. During data analysis, data from all sources pertinent to a particular event were analyzed and the interpretations of all interviewees for that event compared. Decisions regarding the events that were to be included in the case history were reached on the basis of a careful analysis of the data from the various sources and identification of major themes that were reflected in them. Only when an event was supported by data from all sources and when the two researchers were able to reach consensus on its validity was it included in the case history.

An important final stage of the analysis was the identification of the three major phases in the evolution of the conflict (presented here as "acts") and the main conflict management strategies utilized in each phase. The major criterion (Giddens 1985) used to decide when an "act" started was whether one or more of the two major groups of actors (management versus the rebels) *switched from one conflict management strategy to another.* The major means for validating decisions regarding the duration of the "acts" as well as the specific conflict management strategies used in the acts was a consultation process with a group of "judges." The judges (ten students taking a graduate research methods course in one of the two authors' universities) were provided with the case study as it is presented in this paper and were asked to assess it in terms of the conflict management model. The categorization of the various conflict management strategies, as well as the decision as to where the three acts started and ended are based on their consensus opinion.

Textual analysis: A variety of documents were collected at various stages of the e-mail implementation project. These included e-mail promotional materials, training transparencies, and minutes of relevant meetings. Textual analysis also included in-depth study of the organizational chart, hard and soft copy correspondence, newspaper clippings, and progress reports. A major source of data for the textual analysis was e-mail messages. Over 150 e-mail messages were made available to the authors by the key players in the case. The e-mail messages were analyzed using a specially constructed content analysis scheme. The scheme had both quantitative and qualitative aspects. The quantitative aspect included a recording of the number of e-mail messages broadcast by members of the two major groups (management and the rebels) as the case progressed. The qualitative aspect involved a thematic categorization of the issues discussed on e-mail by members of the two groups, with special emphasis on issues relating to the conflict.

Questionnaires: During the e-mail implementation, a survey assessing employee satisfaction was conducted by the "rebels" (see following sections for more details). The results from the survey were made available to the authors by the interviewees. These results provided valuable information that complemented and helped in cross-validating the qualitative data derived from the interviews.

Interviews: In-depth interviews with forty members of UOR were the most important source of data for this study.

During data collection, a semi-structured interview schedule, consisting of a series of open ended topics, was utilized. The questions gauged interviewees' memory of the case events, as well as their interpretation of the meaning of the events. Even though the interview schedule was semi-structured, an attempt was made to cover the same topics in all interviews. Issues on which interviewees disagreed received special attention. When such issues were identified, they were included in subsequent interviews, with a special attempt made to reach consensus among the interviewees in the two major groups (management versus the rebels) over these issues. In addition to gathering personal details (such as background information, career data, and future plans), interviewees were asked to describe the quality of their work life while the case events took place, relationships with other members of the organization, and areas of responsibility. The interviews, which lasted on average about ninety minutes, were all taped and transcribed for later analysis by the authors.

A similar data analysis scheme to the one used for the e-mail data was also used for the interview data. The scheme included a categorization of major themes in the interviews, with particular emphasis on issues relating to the conflict between management and the rebels.

Interviews were conducted over a period of three years (1993 to 1995). On average, two interviews were held with each interviewee over the three-year duration of the data collection process, bringing the number of interviews to over eighty. Members of three major groups were interviewed:

Main Parties to the Conflict

Top Management — Out of the eighteen interviewees that were members of the administrative staff, two were with the Provost and the Personal Assistant to the President can be seen as reflecting the views of top management.

The Rebels — Out of the twenty-two interviewees that were members of the academic staff, five were individuals who were closely associated with the "rebel" group (see following sections for description of these individuals). All five members of this group were Associate Professors. The "rebels" came from four different Faculties within the university.

Interested Observers

Mid-Management — Out of the eighteen interviewees that were members of the administrative staff, two can be categorized as representing mid-management. These interviewees included the Head of the Information Technology Unit (ITU) and the Head of User Services.

Non-Activist Academics — Out of the twenty-two interviewees that were members of the academic staff, fifteen were academics who were not directly involved in the conflict but who still had a strong interest in it. These individuals included two Associate Professors, ten Full Professors (including three Department Chairs and one Dean) and three Assistant Professors. This sample was derived from six different departments from all major divisions at UOR.

Indifferent Bystanders

Low Level Administrative Staff — Of the eighteen interviewees that were members of the administrative staff, who can be categorized as low level, seven were secretaries and seven were members of the Information Technology Unit (ITU). Each of the secretaries was from a different department, representing all major divisions at UOR. The seven ITU interviewees included the past and present coordinators of the e-mail project and five additional employees of the Unit.

Students — Out of the twenty-two interviewees that were members of the academic staff, two were Ph.D. students employed as research assistants.

As can be gathered from this presentation, data was collected from a variety of groups, representing six different perspectives. It should be noted, however, that even though data from all these groups was collected and analyzed, in this paper only the perspectives of top management and the rebels are highlighted. The other perspectives, which were useful for getting a complete picture for this study, offer material that can be further developed for future research and additional papers.

Case Events — Act 1

The E-mail Rebellion. UOR is a medium-sized university, with about 600 faculty members and about 8,000 students. It is centrally located within a densely populated, metropolitan area. Professor Stark, its president for more than a decade, had developed a reputation for being one of the most innovative academic leaders in the country, using the university as a laboratory for experimental new projects.

To support his innovative projects, Professor Stark introduced major changes in UOR's staffing. Within the first five years of his reign, he recruited a large number of new staff. Since the majority of the new recruits were highly qualified in their respective fields, they were often recruited at levels higher than Assistant Professor. This resulted in a large increase in the number of Associate Professors at UOR. To maintain a strong grip on the university, the President had insisted right from the start on full control over promotion and tenure procedures. As a rule, he or his right-hand man, the Provost Professor Selvi, chaired the promotion committees of all Associate Professors in the university. The President also maintained tight control over the promotion to Full Professor, making sure that the number of Full Professors within each department did not go beyond two Full Professors.

Toward the middle of 1988, it became apparent that the tight quota on the number of Full Professors was becoming a problem. Many of the "new" Associate Professors realized by then that their expectations of promotion to Full Professor within the foreseeable future were not going to be met. The position of Full Professor was filled in many departments by men and women who had no intention or retiring or moving to another university. Many of the "older" Professors had formal qualifications that were much below those of the "new" Associate Professors. Yet due to the President's quota system, it was clear that, until they retired, promotion of the "new" Associate Professors was impossible.

In this climate of innovation, on one hand, and growing resentment of the consequences of these innovations on the other, an e-mail implementation project was initiated late in 1988. The e-mail software was first piloted in the ITU for a few months. In the following year (1989), 100 administrators joined the e-mail experiment. Soon thereafter, a communication networking project was initiated to physically link all offices and other facilities in existing buildings to the central computer communication network. To facilitate the universal diffusion, a project manager was hired to head the e-mail implementation. She gradually approached individual departments, conducting training workshops for them. By the end of 1992, the project was declared a success, with all 1,200 potential users in UOR joining the network.

In early 1991, shortly after a critical mass of 800 users was achieved, a series of political events began to unfold. The trigger was an announcement by the Provost, on a routine departmental visit, that UOR's long-term objective was to "gradually abolish internal research grants." John Smith, an Associate Professor in the Faculty of Engineering, reacted by e-mailing, to all active network users on UOR, a memorandum that was critical of the financial conduct of the university. In response, the President electronically distributed a letter announcing a plan to create a forum of academics that would participate in strategic planning. Shortly thereafter, department chairs were notified (on internal university mail) of the date for the first meeting of the forum and the proposed agenda for the meeting.

Another Associate Professor of the Engineering Faculty, Sam Dover, accidentally came across the planning documents for the first forum. Following this, he e-mailed a series of provocative questions to the President, with copies to the campus-wide electronic distribution list. Dick Stone, an Associate Professor at the Faculty of Humanities and Social Sciences, responded to the messages of Professors Smith and Dover via e-mail, again with copies to the university-wide mailing list. He agreed that university resources were not allocated rationally.

During the weekend that followed, a letter written by a top official at UOR appeared in the local daily press. The letter accused Professors Smith, Dover, and Stone (hereinafter, the rebel group) with disloyalty to UOR. Professor Stone wrote a protesting response to the newspaper, sending e-mail copies to the university community. In his message, Professor Stone insisted that he had the right to express his opinion on a matter that was of utmost importance to the university community.

Early in 1992, the President fulfilled his promise to convene the planning forum. Since there was a rumor that one the rebels was going to use this forum to request the resignation of the President, the meeting was attended by most of UOR community, as well as by representatives of the local and national press. However, despite the expectations of an outburst of accusations, the agenda was followed to the letter, the debates were civilized, and the meeting dispersed without a vote of no-confidence against the President.

In the following months, even though there was no mention of the rebellion on e-mail, much was happening behind the scenes. The rebels had established an informal e-mail list that linked them with a group of Associate and Full Professors around the university. Two silent supporters of the rebels were the chairpersons of their departments. Although the rebels' supporters were not ready to express their views on e-mail, the growing network of supporters was significant enough to convince the rebels that the time had come to launch the second stage of their campaign. Believing that there was wide-spread discontent with the President's policies, they decided to conduct a survey that would document faculty dissatisfaction.

Toward the end of 1992, the survey was distributed on e-mail to all UOR faculty, with the request that responses be made by e-mail. The questionnaire covered a wide range of issues, including administrative procedures, promotion, and incentives. Once the results were analyzed, it became apparent that dissatisfaction among respondents was overwhelming. The results were distributed to all members of the community via e-mail. Attached to the results were comments by the rebels which made it clear that they saw the results as supporting their claims.

Almost immediately after the survey results were distributed, the President announced that a comprehensive review process encompassing all departments on campus was to commence immediately. The first targets of the review were the departments of the three rebels. The review process was swift. within weeks it became known that the report of the review committee was very critical of teaching, research, and administrative practices in the two departments. Following the publication of the report, the chairpersons of both departments announced their resignation. While one of the chairpersons was later reinstated, the other left the university, accepting a position in another part of the country.

Going back to the conflict management model that was presented in the previous sections, what conflict strategies can we identify in the first act? From the case data, it appears that the two sides, the rebels and management, were using two different strategies.

The Rebels — The rebels were clearly the initiators of the conflict in this act, applying what the model refers to as a "competitive" strategy, i.e., one that is low on cooperativeness and high on assertiveness. In a review of the literature on conflict management, Robbins et al. (1995) refer to this strategy as a win-lose approach. It is the most risky strategy in the conflict management repertoire because of its potential damage to long-term relationships between the parties to the conflict. It is, therefore, worth employing only when the stakes are high, the actor believes in his or her ability to Will, and the long-term effect on relationships is not considered important. In the first act of the case study these considerations may have been the underlying cause for the rebels' behavior. The rebels saw their situation as hopeless. At the same time, they believed that e-mail might be able to change the balance of power to their advantage. They saw the rebellion as a calculated risk that, with the help of e-mail, they just might win.

Management — Management was in a defensive position in the first act, applying what the model refers to as an "avoidance" strategy, i.e., one that is low on cooperativeness and low on assertiveness. In a review of the literature on conflict management, Robbins et al. determine this strategy to be preferable in cases where the actor feels helpless to assert himself or herself, or when the issue is not important enough to take a stand on. In the long run, this strategy causes considerable frustration because issues do not get resolved. Studying management behavior in the first act from this perspective, it appears that management chose not to openly counter-attack because it believed that the rebels enjoyed wide-spread community support. Given this is perception, an open conflict with the rebels was seen to be too risky. During the first act, management had not yet learned to use e-mail for its own political purposes, while the rebels found it useful for their political campaign.

Figure 2 presents a pictorial depiction of the conflict in Act 1. The figure not only indicates which conflict strategies were employed by the two sides, but also that a gap (represented by the arrow) existed between them. This gap relates to the disequilibrium of the system by the end of the first act, which led to further escalation of the conflict in the next acts.

Case Events — Act 2

Management Retaliates. Following the resignation of the two department chairpersons, the rebels became silent. Realizing that their supporters were not going to openly side with them against the President, they chose to refrain from using e-mail for any further expressions of dissent. However, even though the rebel group was no longer active, on-campus political activities on e-mail continued. Many members of the UOR community, including students, approached the campus e-mail list to exchange views and air concerns about controversial issues, including gender relations, racism, and student rights.

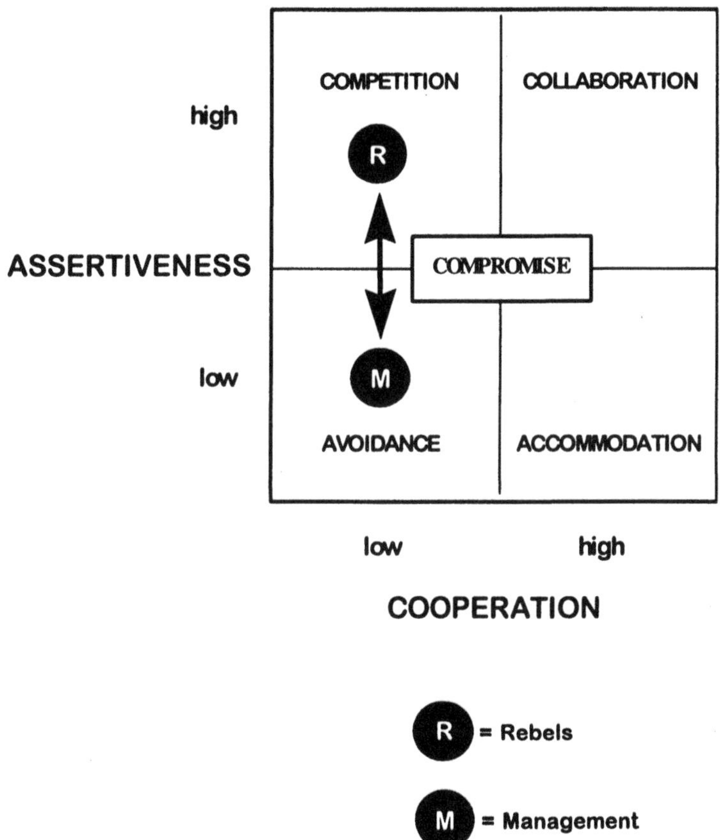

Figure 2 Act 1.

One particular message, distributed in late 1993, led top administration to change e-mail policies in a significant way. The message, which concerned the imminent introduction of a sexual harassment policy at the university, was highly sexist. It was sent anonymously from one of the Science Faculty labs by what appeared to be a student. Even though the letter was an isolated case, the university authorities used it as an excuse to introduce a new e-mail policy, which drastically curtailed student access to e-mail. It mandated that only students serving as research or teaching assistants for individual faculty members could be granted e-mail accounts and that those accounts would be valid for one semester only. Another change to e-mail policy involved restrictions on employees' use of the campus-wide distribution list. To restrict the use of the list, employees were informed on e-mail that the campus-wide list was intended only for dissemination of technical information such as dates of seminars and special events. Any controversial issues were to be sent to the university's newly created "Discussion List."

By the end of 1993, an e-mail code of practice was introduced. The code was compiled with the help of legal consultants. It stipulated a series of penalties for "misuse" of e-mail, ranging from fines to disconnection from the system. In extreme cases of misuse for "vilification of individuals, groups, or the university as a whole," the code stipulated legal action against the culprits. Failure to send an item to the "right" distribution list was also defined as a breach of the code that could result in the individual being disconnected from e-mail. A draft of the proposed code was distributed to all members of the university and, despite opposition to some of its sections by the rebel group and others, it became part of the university's body of rules and regulations.

Shortly after the introduction of the e-mail code of practice, the President decided to convene a meeting of all Associate Professors at UOR. The meeting, which was held in February 1994, was intended to address the Associate Professors' concerns and alleviate their fears that they had no future at UOR. At the meeting, three of the most vocal Associate Professors in the room were the rebels, Professor Smith, Professor Dover, and Professor Stone. Following the meeting the three rebels, who felt it had accomplished nothing, decided to renew their political activities.

On March 1994, the President sent an e-mail message to all members of UOR, announcing his resignation. The Provost, Professor Selvi, became Acting President. He remained in this capacity for the next few weeks, until the selection committee, which had been appointed by the university Board of Governors, had completed its deliberations, electing him as the new President.

In March 1994, the President sent an e-mail message to all members of UOR announcing his resignation. The Provost, Professor Selvi, became Acting President. He remained in this capacity for the next few weeks until the selection committee, which had been appointed by the university Board of Governors, had completed its deliberations, electing him as the new President.

Even though Professor Selvi was well-known around UOR, having served under Professor Stark for over five years, his leadership was not as widely accepted as his predecessor's. Within a short time after his appointment became known, several groups on campus tried to challenge his leadership. The most notable attempt was by UOR's academic union, who for years had been trying unsuccessfully to obtain concessions for their members from Professor Stark. Considering that the appointment of the new President was an opportunity to establish a "new order," the union declared that they wished to start negotiations on a new contract.

The negotiations on the new contract had reached a deadlock by the end of May 1994. The union responded to this by declaring, again on university-wide e-mail, that unless a breakthrough was achieved within the next few weeks, all academics at UOR would begin a general strike on the first day of the next school year, namely, in September 1994.

At the beginning of August 1994, Professor Smith sent an e-mail message to all members of the UOR community. The message was entitled "Promotion of the Unpromotables." It contained a plea to the university authorities, in particular, the newly appointed President, to address the problem of Associate Professors at UOR. In his message, Professor Smith claimed that the group of Associate Professors, who by now numbered eighty professors, included some of the most highly qualified individuals in the university and yet, because of the previous President's quota system, many of them had no career prospects. He demanded that the quota of two Full Professors per department be lifted to allow the promotion of more Associate Professors to Full Professor.

The only response to Professor Smith's e-mail message came from Mr. James Grace, the head of ITU. In an e-mail message, which was sent to Professor Smith two days after his "Promoting the Unpromotables" message, Mr. Grace reminded Professor Smith of the university e-mail code of practice. According to the code, messages that were intended to start a public debate were to be sent to the "Discussion List" and not to the campus-wide list. Mr. Grace concluded his message by maintaining that sending the message to the university-wide list was a breach of the code, punishable by disconnection from e-mail.

Even though Mr. Grace's message was not intended for wide distribution, Professor Smith decided to send it immediately to the campus-wide distribution list. Within minutes, the entire campus community was aware that one of its Associate Professors was under threat of having his e-mail disconnected. Professor Smith attached to Mr. Grace's original message a long message of his own in which he reiterated his previous points. He concluded his message by indicating that the university's threat to disconnect him from e-mail should be responded to by all members of the community, since it represented a most serious attack on academic freedom.

Within hours after Professor Smith's message appeared on e-mail, there was a response from Mr. Grace. This time, Mr. Grace sent his e-mail message to the campus-wide list. In his message, he expressed indignation at the fact that his "private" message to Professor Smith was forwarded to all UOR members. He insisting that the university was serious in its intention to impose the newly introduced e-mail code of practice and that no one, including Professor Smith, could get away with deliberately breaching the code. To make sure that all users were aware of the content of the e-mail code, a copy of the code was attached to Mr. Grace's message.

Shortly after Mr. Grace's message appeared on e-mail, there was a response from Professor Smith. Despite Mr. Grace's second warning, the message was again sent to the campus-wide list. In his response, Professor Smith reiterated the points that he had made in the first message. He concluded his message by stating that Mr. Grace's use of the e-mail code as a means for silencing him was not going to work and called upon all members of the UOR community to challenge the code by supporting the rebels' demands.

The next morning, when UOR academics turned on their e-mail expecting to get another message from Professor Smith, there was none. Instead, there was a message from Professor Dover, who informed the UOR community that, during the previous night, the university authorities had carried out their threat and disconnected Professor Smith from e-mail. Professor Dover concluded his message by urging members of the community who wanted to support the struggle of the Associate Professors to express their views on the university e-mailing list.

This, however, did not happen. In the next few days the only messages that appeared on e-mail were from university officials, particularly members of the university's Information Technology Unit. The messages supported Mr. Grace by maintaining that it was his duty to implement the e-mail code of practice, even if it meant disconnecting an academic from the system. All other members of UOR, despite their strong reactions to Professor Smith's disconnection, were reluctant to take a stand on the matter on e-mail.

Going back to the conflict management model that was presented in the previous sections, what conflict strategies can we identify in the second act? From the case data it appears that the two sides, rebels and management, were again using two different strategies.

Management — Management was clearly in an attacking position, applying what the model refers to as a "competitive" strategy. By the beginning of Act 2, management realized that the three rebels did not enjoy the wide community support that management had at first assumed they had. Management also realized that e-mail could be used not only for coalition building, as was demonstrated by the rebels in the first act, but also for top-down managerial control. The introduction and eventual enforcement of the e-mail code of practice was used to directly attack and punish the rebels, a strategy that management was not willing to risk in the first act. During the second act, this strategy was no longer seen as risky. In fact, it was probably perceived as advantageous, since it not only had the potential to punish the rebels, but also to deter others from following in their footsteps. Note that according to this deconstructive analysis (Boje and Dennehy 1994), management is assumed to have been willing to bear the long-term consequences of using a "competitive" strategy because, by the end of the second act, it was under the impression that the rebellion was totally suppressed.

The Rebels — The rebels seemed to have been in a defensive position in the second act, applying what the model refers to as an "accommodating" strategy, i.e., one that is high on cooperativeness and low on assertiveness. In a review of the literature on conflict management, Robbins et al. describe this strategy as one that is used when one party seeks to appease another. The motivation for such a strategy is often fear of retaliation by the other side. This has long-term negative consequences, since it may lead to bitterness and hostility on the part of the "self-sacrificing" party. The accommodation strategy of the rebels was reflected in the second act by their passive acceptance of the e-mail code of practice. Even though they were aware of its potential implications for their struggle and expressed strong views about the code on e-mail, they eventually chose not to oppose it in any significant way. From our interviews with the rebels, it appeared that the resignation of their department chairs was a major factor in their decision to accept the code. These resignations were an indirect signal that, if they persisted with their campaign, their positions could be threatened as well.

Figure 3 presents a pictorial depiction of the conflict in Act 2. The figure not only indicates which conflict strategies were employed by the two sides, but also that a gap (represented by the arrow) existed between them. This gap relates to the disequilibrium of the system by the end of the second act, which led to further escalation of the conflict in the third act.

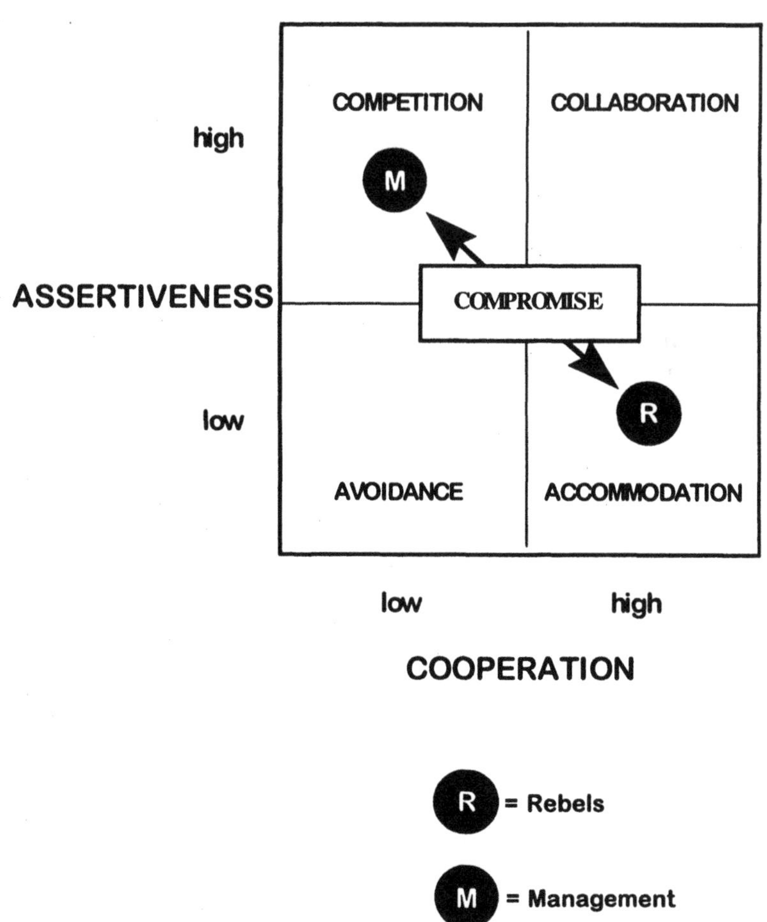

Figure 3 Act 2.

Case Events — Act 3

Finding a Common Ground. Within a week after its disconnection, Professor Smith's e-mail was reconnected. An announcement to this effect was sent by Mr. Grace on e-mail to all members of the UOR community. The message indicated that "the disconnection was temporary and intended as a warning to all members of the community who are intent on breaching the e-mail code of practice."

For the next few months, there were no further messages on e-mail from Professor Smith or the other two rebels. However, the three were very active behind the scenes. During September 1994, the rebels renewed their links with other Associate Professors who were involved in the activities of the first act. These included Professor Julia Robbins from the Faculty of Humanities and Social Sciences and Professor John Moor from the Faculty of Law.

During September 1994, the members of the group communicated extensively on e-mail, slowly consolidating their positions and formulating their ideas on future strategy. One of the first decisions the group made was not to let the promotion of Associate Professors be forgotten. Following this principle, Professor Robbins sent a supporting message to the University Discussion List. In her message, she listed the demands of Professors Smith and Dover and insisted that they should be seen as legitimate. A week later, a similar message from Professor Stone was sent to the University Discussion List. For the next few weeks, the group continued the practice of sending one e-mail message per week to the University Discussion List. Each message started by listing the names of all previous contributors, reminding the university community that the rebel group was slowly expanding. Each message was concluded with a call to the university authorities to take action on the Associate Professors' plight.

Another initiative that was much debated and then implemented by the group was to take their concerns directly to the President. Professor Smith was elected to represent the group. He met with Professor Selvi, but found that the President was reluctant to reconsider the policies of his predecessor. The meeting ended with Professor Selvi telling Professor Smith that if he felt frustrated at UOR, he should look for employment elsewhere.

Professor Smith informed his fellow activists of the meeting with the President, indicating that in view of the events that had transpired at the meeting, he felt that he should not lead the group. After some debate it was resolved that Professor Stone would be the formal spokesperson for the group.

As the new formal leader of the group, Professor Stone approached Mr. Grace with a request to help him establish an Associate Professors e-mail list. Mr. Grace was happy to oblige. Within a week, the first message appeared on the newly established Associate Professors list. It was sent by Professor Stone to all Associate Professors at UOR, calling on them to express their views on the proposed changes to the Full Professors quota. Contrary to the rebels' expectations, not much came out of this initiative. Very few of the eighty Associate Professors responded to the call. However, even though the majority of the Associate Professors were reluctant to be openly identified with the list, there were quite a few who expressed support by sending e-mail messages directly to the rebels.

One of the more prominent silent supporters of the group was Professor Graham Chandler, the Dean of the Faculty of the Humanities and Social Sciences. As a seasoned politician, he advised the group that the best way to proceed was to get the support of their faculties. Following Dean Chandler's advice, the rebel group decided to take their demands to the faculties. By the end of September 1994, Professor Smith was successful in passing a motion at a meeting of the Faculty of Engineering that supported the Associate Professors' demands. Two weeks later, Professor Robbins was successful in getting the Faculty of Humanities and Social Sciences to vote favorably on a similar motion. Both faculty resolutions called upon the university to lift its quota on promotions to Full Professor.

During September 1994, another set of events was taking place at UOR. As promised, on the first day of school, the union announced on the university-wide e-mail list that, in view of management's unwillingness to accept any of the union's demands, the union felt compelled to carry out its threat of a general academic strike. A one-day strike was called for the following Monday. Academics were urged not to attend lectures or carry on any other teaching-related activities during the one-day strike.

Contrary to the union's expectations, the strike was not a success. Many Professors actually crossed the picket lines on their way to lectures, insisting that the second week of the semester was too important to miss. Following the strike, the President announced on the university wide e-mail that in view of the union's unjustified strike, he was discontinuing negotiations with them. He called upon the university community to put pressure on the union to tone down their demands so that the negotiation process could be renewed and brought to a successful conclusion. Within a week, the university community was informed by the union, on university wide e-mail, that negotiations with management had been resumed.

While the dispute between the union and the President was going on, the group of rebels established its own contacts with the union. The head of the union suggested to the rebels that their demands could be added to the list of proposals that he and the other union representatives were negotiating with the President.

In early November 1994, Professor Chandler was successful in passing a resolution in Senate which supported the demands of the rebels. However, in view of the fact that several Full Professors strongly opposed the resolution, the President decided to appoint a special Quota Committee to study its actual implementation. The members of the Quota Committee were promptly elected, with six of the eight members on the committee being Full Professors. The Senate Committee was expected to complete its work in two weeks and to present its report to Senate on its last meeting before the Christmas break. By mid-December 1994, the Senate Committee had completed its work. In its report the committee recommended that the quota on the number of Full Professors be maintained, but extended to three Full Professors per department.

During 1995, all five members of the rebel group applied for promotion to Full Professor. While the applications of Professors Smith and Stone were denied, Professors Dover, Robbins, and Moor were promoted to Full Professor.

Going back to the conflict management model that was presented in the previous sections, what conflict strategies can we identify in the third act? From the case data it appears that, as the events of the third act unfolded, both sides moved toward one strategy collaboration.

The Rebels — In this act, the rebels were, again, the initiators of the conflict, but this time they applied, almost from the start, what the model refers to as a "collaboration" strategy, i.e., one that is high on both cooperativeness and assertiveness. In a review of the literature on conflict management, Robbins et al. refer to this strategy as a win-win approach. They see this strategy as almost as risky as competition, because it requires both sides to open up, disclose their true preferences, and admit their "bottom line." It is, however, potentially the most rewarding strategy because it can lead to solutions that are advantageous to both sides. It also promotes a long-term relationship between the two parties. Realizing that simply attacking management on e-mail (as they did in the first and second acts) was not going to work, in this act the rebels tried to mobilize support for their claims in other ways, namely, through joining forces with the union and by taking their campaign to the Faculties and the Senate. Most importantly, in contrast to presenting management with an ultimatum, this time they tried to identify a solution that would be acceptable to management: changing the Full Professors quota rather than getting rid of it.

Management — Management started this act with a competitive strategy, which was reflected in the President's refusal to negotiate with the rebels, and yet, toward the end of the act, management reverted to a collaboration strategy. This was reflected in the President's willingness to appoint a Senate committee that would draft the proposal for changing the quota of Full Professors and eventually in his willingness to implement the new policy. Note that, like the rebels, management also became aware, by the end of the third act, that e-mail was limited as a means of managerial top-down control. Faced with wide-spread disapproval of Professor Smith's disconnection from e-mail, management was compelled to reconnect him to the system. From this point on, management realized that using the e-mail code to suppress free expression was not going to succeed. A different approach, which involved listening to the rebels' demands and responding to them with an appropriate policy, was necessary.

Figure 4 presents a pictorial depiction of the conflict in Act 3. The figure indicates that, in this act, for the first time, the two sides were using the **same** strategy, thus closing the gap that existed between them in the previous two acts. The closing of the gap represented a change from the state of disequilibrium, which existed in the first two acts, to a state of equilibrium.

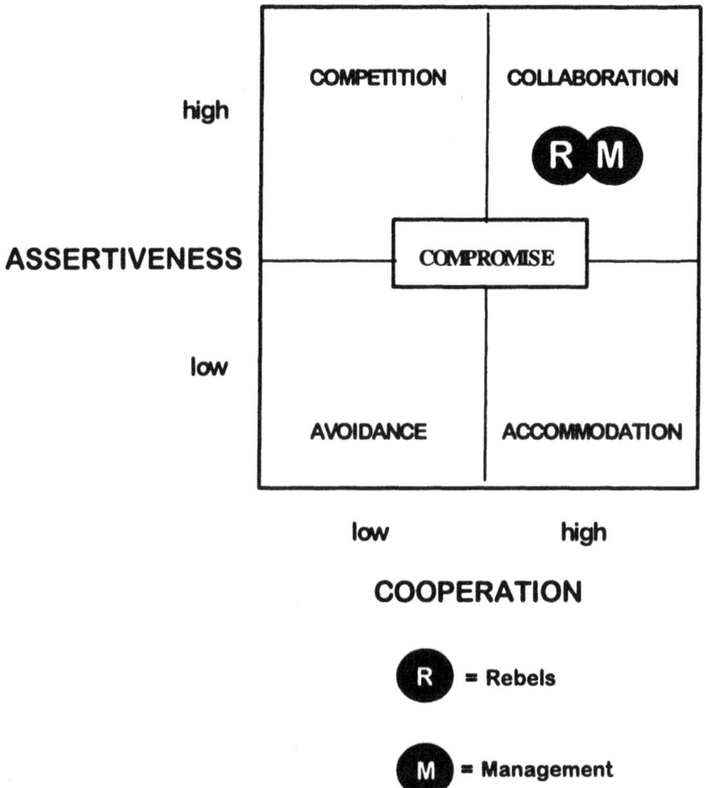

Figure 4 Act 3.

3 DISCUSSION AND CONCLUSIONS

The starting point for this paper was the literature on power and its implications for e-mail research. One of the major objectives of this study was to examine the use of e-mail for power and politics, with an emphasis on contextual, temporal and conflict aspects. As the previous sections have demonstrated, a contextualized, conflict-based, temporal approach is necessary if we are to understand the complexity of e-mail use in organizations. How can we synthesize the data in the three acts of the case study? Taken together, the acts seem to lead to several conclusions.

The first conclusion is that the evidence from the case demonstrates that e-mail can be considered a technology with strong political potential. As indicated by Romm and Pliskin (1996b), the usefulness of e-mail for political activity derives from its accessibility, speed, multiple addressability, recordabilty, processability, and routing. By virtue of its amenability to political use, e-mail can increase tensions between conflicting factions in an organization. Conflicts that may have existed before e-mail was introduced can be extenuated, polarized, and brought to a point of no return. In extreme cases, the coalition-building potential of e-mail can lead to fragmentation of an organization into several continually fighting coalitions. On the other hand, the potential of e-mail to be used for top-down control can lead to extreme suppression of employees and abuse of managerial power.

It should be noted that the data that has been presented here cannot conclusively *prove* that e-mail caused the events in the case. E-mail supported the conflict management strategies that were employed by management and employees, but did not cause the conflict itself. In fact, it can be argued that many of the events occurring in the case could easily have happened before e-mail was introduced and abused. What the evidence in this case suggests is that the introduction of e-mail may have been a moderating variable that made the events more likely to occur.

The fact that the effect of e-mail cannot be "proven" as the one factor explaining the events in the case is supported by recent theoretical assertions by Soh and Markus (1995) and by Robey (1995). As indicated by Soh and Markus, it is often impossible to demonstrate cause and effect relationships in IS research. Theories of process which focus on necessary conditions that bring about a given result are therefore preferable to theories of variance which focus on sufficient conditions that may or may not bring about a given result. A similar point is raised by Robey (1995, p. 61), who indicates that "Efforts to encompass contradiction in theory reveal the difficulty and futility of making simple predictions about the organizational consequences of information technology." Following this assertion, Robey advocates the adoption of less simplistic theories that put less emphasis on significant empirical associations between variables and more emphasis on plausible explanations of observed phenomena.

A second conclusion to be drawn from the case relates to the limits of the use of e-mail. As indicated in the case, the regulation of e-mail can expose the vulnerability to social scrutiny not only of employees, but also of management. By introducing the e-mail code of practice, management opened itself to further criticism by employees. The e-mail code of practice proved to be difficult, if not impossible, to enforce. In the long run, its introduction did **not** stop the social and political unrest at UOR, nor did it help the President gain popularity; rather it increased opposition. While the e-mail code of practice may have been useful in discouraging the rebels and their supporters from expressing their views on e-mail, it did not stop them from using other avenues for venting their frustrations in the long term.

The third conclusion to be drawn from our case is that e-mail can be put to different political uses. As we have pointed out in the analysis of the three acts, the use of e-mail by the two sides involved in the conflict was different in each of the three acts. In the first act, the rebels used "competition" while management was using "avoidance." In the second act, management used "competition" while the rebels were using "accommodation." It was only in the third act that both sides applied "collaboration" as their conflict management strategy.

How can the changes in the use of e-mail for conflict management be explained? As we have indicated in the analysis of the three acts, we believe that the changes in the use of e-mail for conflict management may reflect a learning process on the part of both the rebels and management. At the beginning of the case, the rebels were the first to learn that e-mail was an effective tool for coalition building. They chose to use the new technology because it had technical features that they saw as highly amenable to a large-scale campaign against the President. At this stage, management was not yet aware that e-mail could also be used to advance its own political objectives. In the second act, management learned that the new technology could be exploited for its own political purposes, i.e., for top-down control. Throughout the second act, it used the e-mail code of practice to regulate, curtail, and, eventually, deny the rebels access to e-mail. It was only in the third act that both sides had learned that using e-mail to intimidate, coerce, or overpower the other side was bound to fail. It was at this stage, therefore, that they considered using it to support a collaborative conflict management strategy.

Thus, the most important lesson to be learned from this case study is that, in the long-term, the different conflict management strategies to which e-mail lends itself may crystallize into a collaborative strategy. Even though this is only one case and cannot be extrapolated to all other possible e-mail supported scenarios, we believe that the explanation for the evolution of the conflict outlined may have general implications that go beyond this case. As we have indicated in the analysis of the three acts, when one side uses a competitive strategy, particularly when a new technology is used to support this strategy, the other side is likely to respond with a strategy that is low on assertiveness, namely, either "avoidance" (used in Act 1 by management) or "accommodation" (used in Act 2 by the rebels). Assuming that the two sides take turns in playing assertive and non-assertive roles in a conflict situation (as was the case here), both opponents will finally recognize that when one party is nonassertive, a disequilibrium is established which can only lead to another conflict. This realization is bound to result in a search for a strategy of conflict management that will allow both sides to be cooperative and assertive, namely, "collaboration." Once collaboration is established as the conflict management strategy, a state of relatively stable equilibrium is created, reducing the likelihood for further conflict.

This last point could have direct implications on the role of information systems practitioners in moderating the political use of e-mail in organizations. When e-mail is exploited politically in organizations, information systems professionals may be called upon to support one group of organization members against another. For example, a group of employees might ask for assistance in establishing an e-mail list with the intention of using the list to stage a political campaign against another group. In extreme cases, information systems professionals may be asked to disconnect from e-mail individuals or groups who are perceived by management to be politically disruptive. What position should information practitioners take in such events? Should they side with management? Should they side with employees? It remains for the information systems profession and society as a whole to debate, and perhaps legislate, the use and abuse of e-mail for political and conflict management purposes.

4 REFERENCES

Bennis, W. G.; Berkowitz, N.; Affinito, M.; and Malone, M. (1958). "Authority, Power, and the Ability to Influence," *Human Relations*, Volume 11, Number 2, pp. 143-156.

Boje, D. M., and Dennehy, R. F. (1994). *Managing in the Postmodern World: America's Revolution Against Exploitation*, Second Edition. Dubuque, Iowa: Kendall/Hunt Publishing Company.

Clegg, S. (1995). "Some Dare Call It Power." Paper presented at the APROS Regional Meeting on Power and Politics, University of Western Sydney, MacArthur, Sydney.

Filley, A. C. (1975). *Interpersonal Conflict Resolution*. Glenview, Illinois: Scott, Foresman and Company.

Filley, A. C. (1978). "Some Normative Issues in Conflict Management." *California Management Review*, Volume 71, pp. 61-66.

Finholt, T., and Sproull, S. (1990). "Electronic Groups at Work." *Organization Science*, Volume 1, Number 1, pp. 41-64.

Foucault, M. (1977). *Discipline and Punish: The Birth of Prison*. Harmondsworth, England: Penguin Press.

Foucault, M. (1980). *Power/Knowledge*. New York: Pantheon Books.

Gamble, A., and Walton, P. (1972). *From Alienation to Surplus Value*. London: Croom Helm.

Gandz, J., and Murray, V. V. (1980). "The Experience of Workplace Politics." *Academy of Management Journal*, Volume 23, Number 2, pp. 237-251.

Geyer, R. F., and Schweiter, D. (1981). *Alienation: Problems of Meaning, Theory and Method*. London: Routledge and Kegan Paul.

Giddens, A. (1985). *The Nation State and Violence*. Berkeley: University of California Press.

Gramsci, A. (1971). *Selections From the Prison Notebooks*. London: Lawrence and Wishart.

Habermas, J. (1974). *Theory and Practice*. London: Heinemann.

Habermas, J. (1984). *The Theory of Communicative Action: Volume One – Reason and the Rationalization of Society*. Boston: Beacon Press.

Hickson, D. J.; Hinnings, C. A.; Lee, C. A.; Schneck, R. E.; and Pennings, J. M. (1971). "A Strategic Contingencies Theory of Intraorganizational Power." *Administrative Science Quarterly*, Volume 16, Number 2, pp. 216-229.

Hiltz, S. R., and Johnson, K. (1989). "Experiments in Group Decision Making: Disinhibition, Deinidividuation, and Group Process in Pen Name and Real Name Computer Conferences." *Decision Support Systems*, Volume 5, pp. 217-32.
Hirschheim, R., and Klein, H. K. (1989). "Four Paradigms of Information Systems Development." *Communications of the ACM*, Volume 32, Number 10, pp. 1199-1214.
Kling, R. (1980). "Social Analysis of Computing: Theoretical Perspectives in Recent Empirical Research." *Computing Surveys*, Volume 12, Number 1, pp. 61-110.
Kling, R. (1995). "Social Relationships in Electronic Forums: Hangouts, Salons, Workplaces and Communities." In R. Kling (Editor), *Computerization and Controversy: Value Conflicts and Social Choices*. San Diego: Academic Press.
Lee, A. S. (1989a) "Case Studies as Natural Experiments." *Human Relations*, Volume 42, Number 2, pp. 117-137.
Lee, A. S. (1989b). "A Scientific Methodology for MIS Case Studies." *MIS Quarterly*, March, pp. 33-50.
Lee, A. S. (1991). "Integrating Positivist and Interpretive Approaches to Organizational Research." *Organization Science*, Volume 2, Number 4, November, pp. 342-364.
Lee, A. S. (1994). "Electronic Mail as a Medium for Reach Communication: An Empirical Investigation Using Hermeneutic Interpretation." *MIS Quarterly*, June, pp. 143-157.
Li, T. (1990). "Computer Mediated Communications and the Chinese Students in the US." *The Information Society*, Volume 7, Number 2, pp. 125-137.
Lyytinen, K., and Hirschheim, R. (1988). "Information Systems as Rational Discourse: An Application of Habermas' Theory of Communicative Rationality." *Scandinavian Journal of Management Studies*, Volume 4, Number 1/2, pp. 19-30.
Mann, M. (1986). *The Sources of Social Power, Volume 1: A History of Power from the Beginning to A.D. 1760*. Cambridge, England: Cambridge University Press.
Mantovani, G. (1994). "Is Computer Mediated Communication Intrinsically Apt to Enhance Democracy in Organizations?" *Human Relations*, Volume 47, Number 1, pp. 45-62.
Markus, M. L. (1983). "Power, Politics, and MIS Implementation." *Communications of the ACM*, Volume 26, Number 6, pp. 430-444.
Markus, M. L. (1994a). "Electronic Mail as a Medium of Managerial Choice." *Organization Science*, Volume 5, Number 4, pp. 502-527.
Markus, M. L. (1994b). "Finding and Happy Medium: Explaining the Negative Effects of Electronic Communication on Social Life at Work." *ACM Transactions on Information Systems*, Volume 12, Number 2, April, pp. 119-149.
Matheson, K., and Zanna, M. (1989). "Impact of Computer Mediated Communication on Self Awareness." *Computers in Human Behavior*, Volume 4, pp. 221-233.
Mayes, B. T., and Allen, R. W. (1977). "Toward a Definition of Organizational Politics." *Academy of Management Review*, Volume 2, pp. 674-678.

McGuire, T. W.; Kiesler, S.; and Siegel, J. (1987). "Group and Computer Mediated Discussion Effects in Risk Decision Making." *Journal of Personality and Social Psychology*, Volume 52, Numer 5, pp. 917-930.

Mechanic, D. (1962). "Sources of Power of Lower Participants in Complex Organizations." *Administrative Science Quarterly*, Volume 7, Number 3, pp. 349-364.

Mezaros, I. (1970). *Marx's Theory of Alienation*. London: Merlin.

Mintzberg, H. (1984). *Power In and Around Organizations*. Englewood Cliffs, New Jersey: Prentice Hall.

Pliskin, N. (1989). "Interacting with Electronic Mail can be a Dream or a Nightmare: A User's Point of View." *Interacting with Computers*, Volume 1, Number 3, pp. 259-272.

Pliskin, N.; Ball, L. D.; and Curley, K. F. (1989). "Impediments to Proliferation of Electronic Mail: A Study from the Users' Perspective." *Human Systems Management*, Volume 8, Number 3, pp. 233-241.

Pliskin, N., and Romm, C. T. (1990). "Design of Charging Mechanisms According to the Interaction between Information Technology Type and Diffusion Life Cycle Phase." *DataBase*, Volume 21, Number 3, pp. 34-40.

Pliskin, N., and Romm, C. T. (1996). "The Role of E-mail in an Industrial Dispute." *The Australian Journal of Information Systems*, Volume 3, Number 2, May, pp. 47-56.

Rice, R. E. (1987). "Communication Technologies, Human Communication Networks and Social Structure in the Information Society." In J. Schement and L. Livrou (Editors), *Competing Visions and Complex Realities: Social Aspects of the Information Society*. Norwood, New Jersey: Ablex, pp. 107-120.

Rice, R. E. (1992). "Contexts of Research on Organizational Computer-Mediated Communication." In M. Lea (Editor), *Contexts of Computer Mediated Communication*. Wheatsheaf, England: Harvester, pp. 113-144.

Rice, R. E. (1993). "Using Network Concepts to Clarify Sources and Mechanisms of Social Influence." In W. Richards, Jr., and G Barnett (Editors), *Progress in Communication Sciences*, Volume 12. Norwood, New Jersey: Ablex, pp. 43-62.

Rice, R. E., and Aydin, C. (1991). "Attitudes toward New Organizational Technology: Network Proximity as a Mechanism for Social Information Processing." *Administrative Science Quarterly*, Volume 36, June, pp. 219-244.

Robbins, S. P. (1978). "Conflict Management and Conflict Resolution Are Not Synonymous Term." *California Management Review*, Volume 21, pp. 67-75.

Robbins, S. P. (1974). *Managing Organizational Conflict: A Non-traditional Approach*. Englewood Cliffs, New Jersey: Prentice Hall.

Robbins, S. P.; Waters-Marsh, T.; Cacioppe, R.; and Millett, B. (1995). *Organizational Behavior Australia and New Zealand*. Sydney: Prentice Hall.

Robey, D. (1995). "Theories that Explain Contradiction: Accounting for the Contradictory Organizational Consequences of Information Technology." In J. I. DeGross, G. Ariav, C. Beath, R. Høyer, and C. Kemerer (Editors), *Proceedings of the Sixteenth International Conference on Information Systems*. Amsterdam.

Rogers, E.; Collins-Jarvis, L.; and Schmitz, J. (1994). "The PEN Project in Santa Monica: Interactive Communication, Equality and Political Action." *Journal of the American Society for Information Science*, Volume 45, Number 6, pp. 401-410.

Romm, C. T., and Pliskin, N. (1996a). "Battle of the Sexes on E-mail – Or is It?" *The Information Society Journal*, Forthcoming.

Romm, C. T., and Pliskin, N. (1996b). "Virtual Politicking: Toward a Theory of E-mail Use for Political Purposes within and between Organizations." In James L. Garnett and Alexander Kouzmin (Editors), *The Handbook of Administrative Communication*. New York: Marcel Dekker, Forthcoming.

Ruble, T., and Thomas, K. (1976). "Support for a Two Dimensional Model of Conflict Behavior." *Organizational Behavior and Human Performance*, Volume 16, pp. 145-155.

Siegel, J.; Dubrovksy, V.; Kiesler, S.; and McGuire, T. W. (1986). "Group Processes in Computer Mediated Communication." *Organizational Behavior and Human Decision Processes*, Volume 37, Number 2, pp. 57-187.

Soh, C., and Markus, M. L. (1995). "How IT Creates Business Value." In J. I. DeGross, G. Ariav, C. Beath, R. Høyer, and C. Kemerer (Editors), *Proceedings of the Sixteenth International Conference on Information Systems*. Amsterdam.

Sproull, R., and Kiesler, S., Editors (1991). Connections: New Ways of Working in the Network. Cambridge, Massachusetts: MIT Press.

Thomas, K. (1976). "Conflict and Conflict Management." In M. D. Dunnette (Editor), *Handbook of Industrial and Organizational Psychology*. London: Routledge and Kegan Paul.

Thomas, K. (1993). "Conflict and Negotiation Processes in Organizations." In M. D. Dunnette and L. M. Hough (Editors), *Handbook of Industrial and Organizational Psychology*, Second Edition, Volume 3. Palo Alto, California: Consulting Psychologists Press.

Van Tassel, J. (1994). "Accept-Yak, Do Talk Back: PEN, the Nation's First Publicly Funded Electronic Network, Makes a Difference in Santa Monica." *Wired*, Volume 2, Number 1, pp. 78-80.

Winner, L. (1992). "Silicon Valley Mystery House." In Michael Sorkin (Editor), *Variations on a Theme Park: The New American City and the End of Public Space*. New York: Noonday Press.

Zuboff, S. (1988). "The Panopticon and the Social Text." *The Age of the Smart Machine*. New York: Basic Books.

5 BIOGRAPHY

Celia T. Romm is an Associate Professor at the Department of Business Systems, University of Wollongong, Australia. She received her Ph.D. from the University of Toronto, Canada (1979). Her research interests lie in the areas of the impact of communication technologies on organizations, with particular emphasis on research on virtual communities, and on electronic commerce. Dr. Romm is currently completing a book titled *Virtual Politicking* (to be published through Hampton Press USA). She has published over sixty papers in refereed journals and chapters in collective volumes.

Nava Pliskin, from Ben-Gurion University in Israel, is a Thomas Henry Carroll Ford Foundation Visiting Associate Professor at the Harvard Business School. She holds Ph.D. and S.M. degrees from Harvard University. Her research, focused on longitudinal analysis of Information Technology impacts at the global, national, organizational, and individual levels, has been published in numerous journals.

20

Becoming Part of the Furniture: The Institutionalization of Information Systems

L. Silva
Department of Information Systems
London School of Economics and Political Science
London WC2A 2AE, England
Tel: 171 955 7641
Fax: 171 955 7385
E-mail: L.Silva@lse.ac.uk

J. Backhouse
Department of Information Systems
London School of Economics and Political Science
London WC2A 2AE, England
Tel: 171 955 7641
Fax: 171 955 7385
E-mail: J.P.Backhouse@lse.ac.uk

Abstract

The institutionalization of information systems allows managers in organizations to concentrate on and devote creative energy to their prime tasks. This paper argues that the process of deciding whether an information system is institutionalized or not can be understood better by examining its political dimension. We focus on the failure to institutionalize the London Ambulance Service information system. Our analysis unravels the political factors that influenced the system breakdown and its abandonment. In doing so, we propose a framework grounded on the interpretive tradition of research into information systems. The framework we are introducing will contribute to the understanding of power and institutionalization, in research into organizational information systems.

1 INTRODUCTION

In *The Prince*, Machiavelli asserts that fortune controls half of our actions, but that we can control the other half. We steer the ship of our lives in the sea of fortune. In steering our lives, we face the problem of distinguishing where the ship finishes and where the sea starts. In other words, how can we know which part of our lives we control and which we do not? There is no point in wasting effort trying to change factors that do not depend on us. It is better to identify them and then to prepare so their effects can be minimized. However, there is a point in putting effort into changing or influencing those factors that do depend on us. Organizations face similar problems when they try to introduce information systems: they want to know what they can do to stabilize an information system. Likewise, organizations would like to anticipate and be ready for those factors that can influence information systems but which organizations do not control.

The stabilization of an information system is its institutionalization. We can say that information systems become institutionalized when they are no longer considered as innovations but as unnoticed and unremarkable tools that people take for granted in doing their work. Institutionalized information systems are noticed only when they break down. An interesting question is, therefore, what makes an information system institutionalized? The institutionalization of information systems can be studied as the outcome of power relations, which may favor or hinder institutionalization. The purpose of this paper is to discuss how power relations hindered the institutionalization of a particular information system.

We propose a theoretical framework that presents the institutionalization of an information system as the outcome of power relations. The framework itself differentiates those relations that can be influenced by agents from those that can not. We illustrate the application of the framework by discussing the case of the collapse of the London Ambulance Service (LAS). In the discussion of this case, we highlight the power aspects that influenced the disaster of the LAS information system, such as the dominant strategies, the differences between managers and trade unions, and the inadequacies of the interpretation of the tasks performed by some of the LAS workers. The LAS case study, as the empirical data for this paper, illustrates the benefits of examining secondary sources as research material.

The study of the process of institutionalization of information systems is relevant for managers and practitioners. The benefits for managers of organizations are evident. If an information system becomes institutionalized, less effort is needed to manage it. Knowledge about the power base of the organization will also ease the management of change. Information systems analysts will also find it useful to know the power relations prevailing in the organization, because in this way they can design information systems not only according to users' requirements but also to users' interests. The framework we introduce might also be useful for researchers interested in the processes of institutionalization itself and the political aspects of information systems. It is widely accepted that information systems are social systems, and there is no doubt that studying how they become institutionalized, and also how they do not, should lead us to focus on those aspects that transform information systems from being innovations to being taken for granted as tools of work, which is what organizations and managers want them to be. The framework we propose could provide a starting point for those interested in researching organizational aspects of information systems such as legitimation, control, and politics. Moreover, we believe that qualitative research in information systems should be led by theories grounded in interpretive and phenomenological premises to make sense and to be consistent. The theoretical framework we are proposing in this paper has its roots in phenomenology. Because of that, we believe it will be consistent with qualitative and interpretive research in information systems.

The first section introduces the background of our proposal. Mainly, we discuss the relevant literature of power and information systems and introduce our conceptions on institutionalization. The second section explains our concept of power and introduces the framework, while in the third section we present the analysis of the LAS case. Finally the fourth section presents our conclusions. We hope that our focus on how information systems become institutionalized can help us in understanding what elements are susceptible to alteration, and therefore what we can change or manage, and what elements are independent.

2 BACKGROUND

The purpose of this paper is to propose a theoretical framework to explain the institutionalization of information systems. Our proposal considers that by focusing on the power phenomena linked to information systems we can understand the process of their institutionalization. In this section, we will introduce our stance regarding institutionalization in the context of organizations. We then discuss some ideas on power stemming from the social sciences that have influenced research on the political dimension of information systems.

2.1 Organizational Institutionalization

Institutionalization is the reciprocal typification of habitualized actions. Institutionalization is constituted by habits. Habits narrow the scope of choices; this constitutes a psychological gain. Institutionalized habits provide a stable background in which actions are often performed with a minimum of effort in decision making. Institutionalization frees energy that can be channeled to other areas. Institutionalization of information systems will open for managers of information systems opportunities for innovations in other areas (Berger and Luckman 1967). However desirable the state of institutionalization it cannot be created overnight. Institutions have a history, and it is the role of a researcher of information systems to understand and explain the process of institutionalization. We argue that institutionalization of information systems can be understood from a power perspective because institutions control and facilitate actions. In organizations, the institutionalization of an innovation, and in this case of an information system, will require effort and deployment of resources.

The process of institutionalization has been central for some researchers of organizational studies. According to Clegg (1990), there are two streams in the institutional school of organization studies, one from the east coast of the US, and the other from the west coast. Meyer and Rowan (1991), who are from the west, concentrate on the processes that lead to the institutionalization of rules, how they are brought into being, and particularly how they become legitimate. They follow the phenomenological approach to institutions of Berger and Luckman. DiMaggio and Powell (1983, 1991) in the east concentrate on how organizations structure themselves by taking elements from the environment; that is, how organizations adopt innovations and how to explain similarities among organizations. Although studying how organizations adopt information systems is an interesting topic, in this paper we will follow the west coast stream mainly for two reasons. First, because having phenomenology as its ontological stance, it makes it more suitable for interpretive and qualitative research; and second, because the focus of our research is on how information systems become legitimate and institutionalized within organizations.

2.2 Power and Information Systems

The study of power has been central in social and political sciences. Thus, almost every sociologist, anthropologist, or political scientist has her or his own view of power. However, we will discuss the dominant debate between voluntaristic and deterministic conceptions of power and the proposals to resolve this debate. We will briefly discuss the work of Lukes, Foucault, Giddens, Habermas, Latour, Callon and Law because they have influenced research on power and information systems. An exhaustive discussion of this debate is beyond the scope of this paper (for a more detailed discussion, see Clegg [1989] and Law [1991a]).

The voluntaristic approach to power in social sciences is exemplified by Lukes (1974). He focuses on the exercise of power and the interest of the individual. Thus, A is exercising power over B when A is affecting B against B's interests. This approach, although insightful, leads to the epistemological problem of how to determine interests without encroaching moral relativism. It is important to notice that voluntaristic approaches explain power adopting mechanical metaphors, such as one individual or group affecting directly other individuals or groups (see Clegg 1989). This conception of power is visible in some research in information systems, particularly the research focused on the politics of implementation such as Keen (1981) and Markus (1983). Markus and Bjørn-Andersen (1987) have based their work on Lukes in proposing a framework for the analysis of power exercised by information systems professionals over users.

In addition to the voluntaristic approach that focuses on agency for the exercise of power, other researchers have focused on how social structures exercise power. Perhaps one of the most influential social scientists moving from the agency and sovereign view of power is Foucault, who has abandoned mechanistic models of power. He has developed two concepts regarding power. First, Foucault (1972, 1980), in considering the relationship between power and knowledge, studied how knowledge is constructed, how it enacts domination and particularly how subjects take it as truth. Second, Foucualt (1977) developed the concept of disciplinary power, power depending upon surveillance. Administrative authorities carry out surveillance activities by collecting and holding information about society, its members and their actions. In organizational life, disciplinary power becomes associated with attempts to regularize activities in time and space. The latter concept has guided research on power and information systems, particularly that of Zuboff (1988) and Sewell and Wilkinson (1992), who have focused on how information systems can become instruments for exercising disciplinary power. he concept of power knowledge, on the other hand, is examined by Bloomfield and Coombs (1992) in mentioning how computer sciences have affected the way managers estimate the capabilities of information systems. The concepts of power and knowledge in Foucault's work and our view of institutionalization are not far from each other. This is because we aim at explaining the process of how an information system becomes objectivized and taken-for-granted knowledge.

Another significant set of ideas on power is in critical theory, which seeks emancipation from ideology. Habermas (1970, 1972, 1979), one of the critical theoreticians, argues that power distorts communication and therefore it hinders emancipation. Critical theory's focus on communication and power has made it an attractive theoretical ground for research in information systems. Habermas's influence is manifest in the works of Scandinavian researchers who have focused on how information systems can be instruments of emancipation (Bjerknes, Ehn and Kyng 1987; Bodker et al. 1987; Ehn and Kyng 1987; Friedman and and Cornford 1987). Hirschheim and Klein (1994) have modified an information systems methodology to achieve emancipation in the organization. Empowerment, as the result of implementing information systems, is the concern of Bloomfield and McLean (1995). However, their focus is still in the realm of information systems design and not on how they become institutionalized. We are not implying that research on the political features of implementation and design of information systems is irrelevant. On the contrary, we believe that our research is complementary to these efforts, because it is difficult to institutionalize a poorly designed information system or one whose implementation has been badly managed.

Giddens (1979, 1984) has offered a theory to solve the debate between structure and agency in proposing the concept of the duality of structure, which is a dialectical relation between agency and structure. The duality of structure explains how agents when acting draw on structures that can be of domination, interpretation or legitimation. Giddens' insights have been applied to the field of information systems by Walsham (1993) and Orlikowski and Robey (1991). Walsham argues for looking at how context and social process influence each other in analyzing the organizational impact of information systems. One of Walsham's contributions is to propose a framework based on structuration theory that explains the dialectical relation between information systems and organizations. Orlikowski and Robey introduced a concept of the duality of technology that recognizes the facilitative and constraining characteristics of information technology. They discuss the institutionalization of a productive tool for developing software but do not discuss fully the political factors that influence that institutionalization. The contributions of Walsham and of Orlikowski and Robey go beyond the relationship between analysts and users and the implementation of information systems. They offer a richer picture of the organizational impact of information systems by taking into account the dialectical relation between actions and structures.

Monteiro and Hanseth (1995) recognized the contributions of Orlikowski and Robey and of Walsham but at the same time point out the limitations of their scope. Structuration theory and the duality of technology do not account for the influence of social aspects on the design of technology. Monteiro and Hanseth maintain that neither Orlikowski and Robey nor Walsham describe the influence of social factors in the information systems they studied. For example, these applications of structuration theory do not lead to identifying how interests are inscribed in information systems and how technology makes social relations stable. To do so, Monteiro and Hanseth drew on actor network theory to explain the development of information infrastructures and the diffusion of standards. Their work comes close to explaining the institutionalization of information systems, although they do not focus on the political elements.

Actor network theory focuses on the relationships among science, society and technology (Law 1986, 1991b: Latour 1991; Callon 1991; Akrich 1992; Akrich and Latour 1992). One of the main premises of actor network theory is considering the social and the technical world at the same level. According to Callon (1986, p. 224),

> Translation is the mechanism by which the social and natural worlds progressively take form. The result is a situation when certain entities control others. Understanding what sociologists generally call power relationships means describing the way in which actors are defined, associated and simultaneously obliged to remain faithful to their alliances.

Actor network theoreticians subscribe to three epistemological axioms. First, the agnosticism of the observer that means that the observer avoids censoring and making ethical or moral judgements regarding the protagonists of their object of study. The second principle is the one of symmetry. This consists of describing scientific and technological issues in the same terms. The third principle is about free association. This implies abandoning all *a priori* differences between social and technological events. Actor network theory constitutes an alternative to dual conceptions of technology and society. As well as Monteiro and Hanseth, Vidgen and McMaster (1995) have applied the concepts of actor network theory, particularly from Latour (1987). These authors drew on Latour's ideas to check the limitations of other frameworks, such as the dualism of technology and society, to understand how information systems become black boxes in an organization. We associate the concept of information systems becoming black boxes with their institutionalizations. Bloomfield and Danieli (1995) have used concepts of actor network theory to analyze the exercise of power of information technology consultants over their customers. Sociology of translation is applied by Bloomfield and Best (1992) for analyzing power exercises during the development and implementation of information systems. This work is enlightening in the sense that one sees the political processes and political resources deployed by information systems consultants to exercise power over their customers. Power is a concept with many approaches and theories in social sciences, and it is our belief that some of these theories are not mutually exclusive but complementary. The circuits of power framework that we propose in this paper are an attempt to integrate the contributions that many social scientists have made in the study of power.

3 THE CIRCUITS OF POWER FRAMEWORK

In his book *Frameworks of Power*, Clegg (1989) carefully analyzes how social science has considered the concept of power. He discusses different frameworks and concepts to introduce his framework of circuits of power, which he claims includes most of the insights proposed by previous social scientists. Clegg argues that power is a relational concept. Hence, power is something that cannot be owned, and its exercise will depend on relations. Clegg uses the circuits metaphor to emphasize the relational nature of power. For him, social relations sustain, maintain, or transform power. The starting point for Clegg in analyzing power relations is the organization. The application of the circuit framework should lead us then to understand the relationship between the authority and politics of organizations. The circuits framework considers power as circulating in three different circuits: the episodic circuit, the social integration circuit, and the system integration circuit. The three circuits are linked by obligatory passage points (OPPs).

The three circuits of power represent three types of power. Clegg formulates these to move away from Lukes' three dimensional notion of power. The episodic circuit represents causal power which is the most apparent and most evident of the types of power (see Figure 1). Clegg derives his notion of episodic power from Dahl (1957). Dahl considers that A is exercising power over B when A gets B to do something B would not otherwise do.[1] However, Clegg maintains that A would not be able to exercise power over B if the standing conditions, which are constituted by resources, were not favorable to A (see Figure 1). The standing conditions are determined by the extant rules of meaning and membership that constitute the identity and position of the agencies in the organization. These rules of meaning and membership constitute the circuit of social integration and, without it, the understanding of episodic power would be incomplete. The third circuit, the circuit of system integration, carries facilitative power. This notion suggests that when A gets B to do something B would not otherwise do, A's power is facilitative because A is able to set and achieve collective goals. The focus of this circuit is domination because it concerns how agents comply with their duties in order to achieve collective goals. Clegg suggests that compliance is achieved by techniques of discipline and production. If successful, these techniques in the long term will become stable institutional fields or, as Clegg himself calls them, actor-networks. In this section we discuss each of the elements of the circuits framework.

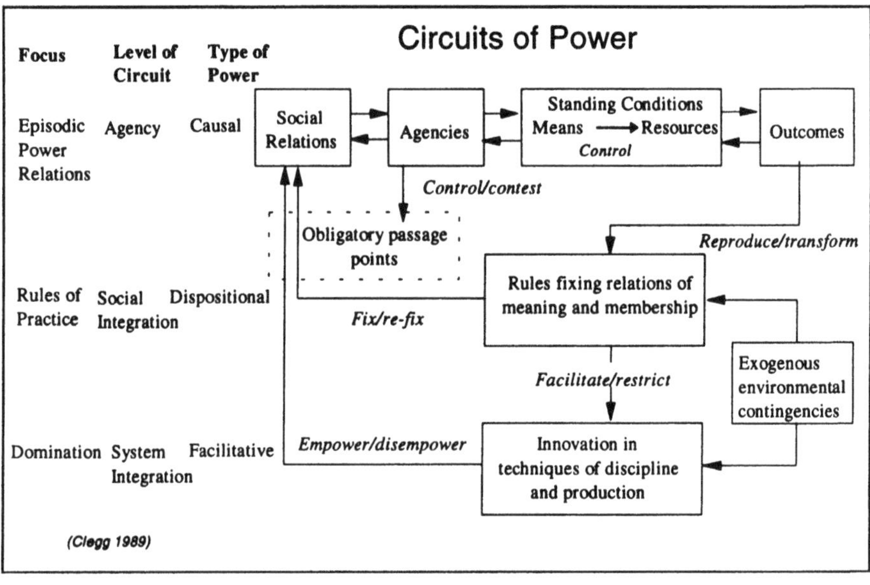

Figure 1 The Circuits of Power.

---

[1]This type of power is also known as "power over" (Law 1991) because A is exercising power over B.

3.1 Outcomes of the Circuits

Organizational information systems are constituted by different and heterogeneous elements. These elements could be tangibles like computers, telephones and printers. They can also be people, either managers or users, as well as procedures and knowledge associated with the tasks performed by the information system. An institutionalized information system will become a black box, in the sense that all its members and stakeholders may not notice how it operates. Most actions regarding an institutionalized information system will become predictable. Users will operate the system by applying knowledge that they take for granted, in the same way people use telephones and radios in the office. An institutionalized information system will be noticed only when it breaks down. To be institutionalized, all procedures and activities related to the information system should become a habit. Actions will be typified; this means that those performing the actions will play a role defined by the nature of the activities.

What is important is that most of the skills and the knowledge required to operate the information system will be made objective and external so they can be transferred to those who will eventually play the roles. Clearly institutionalized procedures and tasks in organizations are performed by roles and not by individuals, in the sense that whenever an individual leaves, the role can be filled smoothly. In our case study, the way the information system affected the performance of tasks in the organization will be analyzed when considering the circuit of social integration. Furthermore, any information system to become institutionalized will have to be legitimate. If the new practices or technology associated with the information system become illegitimate, then institutionalization will not occur. The legitimation of the information system will depend on the social integration circuit. The episodic circuit of power indicates that only those agents controlling resources will be able to achieve their desired objectives. However, the circuits of power diagram demonstrates that, in order to achieve their goals, those agents need to have fixed the relationship between the circuits of social and system integration. The fixing of these circuits will become an actor network, or an obligatory passage point. Obligatory passage points are constituted by cohesively connected roles with technical and social agents. The important implication here is that only those information systems resulting from the fixed circuits will become institutionalized. This is because the outcome of the circuits – the information system – will have an impact in the whole organizations. If an information system is not fixed as an obligatory passage point, its institutionalization will not be achieved, as it is illustrated in the LAS case study.

3.2 The Episodic Circuit of Power

This is the most evident of the circuits of power because it leads directly to tangible outcomes. Power is manifested here by agents[2] being capable of controlling resources and establishing alliances to produce their intended outcomes. Agencies and resources are its main elements. It is in this circuit where agents struggle to control resources. The arrows pointing to the right stand for agents acting to achieve their desired outcomes, while arrows in the opposite direction denote resistance. Those agents who successfully control resources will be those with a stronger power base: this is what the standing conditions represent in the figure. The power base of agents is given by the circuits of social and system integration that will be the focus of the following sections.

We have learned from Foucault that the outcome of any exercise of power will be actions. Developers and designers should, as the first step toward understanding power, identify and describe the intended outcomes of the information system in terms of actions. It is important to identify those actors who would execute the outcome, as well as those who would benefit. Finally, the analysis of the circuit will be complete when the resources required to carry out the outcomes are identified.

Organizations that succeed in implementing information systems are those able to arrange their circuits of power in such a way that agents will be capable of achieving their projected outcomes. We believe that looking exclusively at the circuit of episodic power is not enough to understand how organizations achieve this desirable state. Information systems will affect organizations in two ways. Information systems will affect the way jobs are performed, and they are going to change organizational norms, meanings, and membership of groups. The former concerns the circuit of system integration and the latter the circuit of social integration. Furthermore, change in either of the circuits of social or system integration should be fixed in obligatory passage points, which will be discussed in a later section.

3.3 The Circuit of Social Integration

Clegg (1989) defines social integration in terms of the relation between rules of meaning and membership. The analysis of this circuit will identify the legitimate (formal rules) and illegitimate (informal rules) dimensions of power within the organization. The recognition of the illegitimate dimension of power, or its dark side (Hirschheim and Klein 1994), is fundamental in performing a complete political appraisal of the organization.[3]

---

[2]Agency here does not only refer to human beings. Agents can be groups, organizations, animals, or machines (Clegg 1989).

[3]Mintzberg (1983) gives a negative connotation to the informal dimension of power. He refers to it as politics or illegitimate power. This moral position might hinder the objectivity of researchers or system analysts.

One of the reasons why information systems do not achieve their goals is the lack of fit between the new meanings arising from the new information system and the prevailing organizational rules and norms. In any organization, tension will arise as a consequence of the "lack of fit" between the institutional order and its material condition. The material condition is constituted by technology, techniques, and methods of production, whereas the core institutional order will be integrated by the values, beliefs, and norms already institutionalized in the organization. The lack of fit will be characterized by a type of strain stemming from the incompatibility between the institutional order and the material base (Lockwood 1964). In the case of this lack of fit, the material conditions, according to Lockwood, will engender social relationships and practices that can threaten the organization. The consolidation of these social relationships and practices will depend on the success with which managers are able to cope with the disintegrating tendencies within the organization. The circuit of social integration comprises the norms, rules, and meanings that give identity to particular groups and allow their integration. In other words, this circuit comprises what Lockwood called the core institutional order. The realization of this circuit will allow analysts and developers to incorporate in the system those characteristics required to make it fit in the organization.

3.3 The Circuit of System Integration

In the organizational context, system integration is the technological means of control over the material and social setting and the skills associated with these means (Lockwood 1964). Besides the material means of production, Lockwood includes in system integration the material means of surveillance. In short, we might say that system integration is constituted by techniques of production and discipline. System integration deals with facilitative power because the material conditions of production might empower or disempower agencies in their productive activities. The circuit of system integration is the major source of change in the circuits of power framework, particularly when the material conditions of production are altered; hence its relevance to our study. Changes in the circuit of system integration will entail new agencies, techniques and practices that the circuit of social integration might find difficult to resolve. That is why the introduction of computer-based information systems, insofar as they transform the circuit of system integration, will always be contentious. Success in implementation will depend greatly on the managerial ability to translate the new rules and norms implied by the system into pieces of discourse that other members of the organization can understand and accept. This could explain why participative methods for developing information systems might overcome implementation resistance more easily than other methods. User participation can be understood as a process through which the translation of the new rules and meanings is accomplished during the design and development stages of the system and not at the moment of implementation. In this way, participative methodologies integrate user interests and meanings to the system during its design and development.

The circuit of system integration is fundamental for understanding power relationships in information systems, not only because it provides an analytical tool for the way technology affects power relations, but also because it helps us to understand the way information systems can be shaped by power. To identify this circuit, analysts should focus on how information systems will be used as means of production, control, and discipline.

3.5 Obligatory Passage Points (OPPs)

Although this term might sound strange, this is the crux of the circuits of power. Whenever an innovation is introduced in organizations, it creates new meanings, and therefore disturbs the circuit of social integration. The new meanings are fixed in OPPs. An obligatory passage point is an actor network linked by discourses presenting the solution of a problem in terms of resources owned by the agent that proposes the OPP. Obligatory passage points will allow the formation of alliances and the control over resources that agents need to achieve their outcomes.

The concept of obligatory passage points was developed within the "sociology of translation" and actor network theory and developed by the French sociologists Callon and Latour (Callon 1986; Callon, Law and Rip 1986; Latour 1987). These theories attempt to provide a whole picture of power relationships. There are four "moments of translation": problematization, interessment, enrolment and mobilization.

Callon (1986) explains them in detail. The first step is problematization or how to become indispensable. Problematization is when, given a problem, one actor, through rhetorical means, presents the solution of that problem in terms of his or her resources. In this way, one group of actors defines an OPP. Following a successful problematization, the group of actors that experience the problem must be convinced that the only way to resolve their problem is by traversing the OPP. The second translation step is called interessment. After the identities of the actors and OPPs have been defined, the group of actors experiencing the problem must be isolated. This isolation consists of impeding other possible alliances or interference that might challenge the legitimacy of the OPP. If the interessment is successful, it will confirm the validity of the problematization and the alliances. The third translation step is enrolment. During this step, the alliances are consolidated through bargaining and making concessions. The fourth and final step is the mobilization of the allies. This mobilization implies that actors will become spokespersons of the groups they claim to represent. This step consists in determining the legitimacy of the spokesperson. The movement between each step is called displacement, which involves discursive practices. When displacement occurs, power is exercised. Information systems can be viewed as OPPs. For example, some commercial airlines practically force travel agents to use their reservation systems. Those airlines have converted their information systems in successful OPPs that travel agents must traverse if they want to sell airplane tickets.

Actor network theory and obligatory passage points have been the centre of criticism by sociologists of knowledge (see Collins and Yearley 1992a, 1992b; Callon and Latour 1992). One of the fundamental elements in the Collins and Yearley criticism of actor network theory focuses on the symmetry principle. The principle of symmetry, as discussed above, consists on describing human and non-human actors with the same vocabulary. While Callon and Latour claim that the symmetry principle avoids the ontological trap of reducing nonhuman actors to either natural objects or social constructions, Collins and Yearley suggest that, in actor network descriptions, only language changes but the story remains the same. Moreover, Collins and Yearley maintain that actor network descriptions are conservative and prosaic: conservative because they are limited to descriptions and narratives; prosaic because they lack commonsensical surprises.[4]

Despite their sharp critique, Collins and Yearly (1992a, p. 314) recognize that actor network theory could give an interesting account of the relationship between technology and society. Furthermore, they acknowledge that once actor network theory offers an explanation for non-human actors' behaviour it can contribute "to the detailed analysis of the relations of power between actors and networks (Collins and Yearley 1992b, p. 375). It is precisely because of these two virtues of actor network theory that Clegg introduced it in his circuits framework (see Clegg 1989, pp. 202-207). We believe that Collins and Yearley have a point when they ask actor network theoreticians to give explanations rather than descriptions, especially regarding nonhuman actors. In our case study, particularly when we deal with the failure of the information system, we will bear in mind their request to avoid prosaic descriptions by offering an explanation of the failure.

4 THE LONDON AMBULANCE SERVICE COMPUTERIZED INFORMATION SYSTEM

The London Ambulance Service (LAS) was selected as the case study to illustrate the circuits of power framework for various reasons. First, there is consensus about the failure of this information system. This eases our task because we do not need to argue that this was a failure as an information system. Second, the report of the independent inquiry (Page, Williams and Boyd 1993) is a public domain information and there are many reports and analyses about it. However, because our sources were secondary, we should be aware that we are dealing with interpretations of interpreta-

---

[4]Regarding Callon's (1986) paper on the scallops of St. Brieuc Bay, Collins and Yearly ask Callon to explain why the scallops rejected anchoring. Collins and Yearly argue that Callon's description of the scallops' refusal to anchor is not enough to understand why the scallops did not transit the obligatory passage point. It is in this sense that Collins and Yearly claim that anchor network descriptions are conservative and prosaic.

tions. We have been careful in selecting diverse sources to establish some degree of triangulation. In fact, secondary sources for the LAS case allowed us "to pan for gold," as Jarvenpaa (1991) calls it, with very good results.

The analysis of the case study is presented in the form of a narrative. We consider the elements of each circuit. Bearing those in mind, we then discuss what happened to the LAS information system. The idea is to identify all possible elements or factors that could have hindered the institutionalization of the information system. Our aim is not to arrive at a conclusion isolating a unique factor for the noninstitutionalization of the information system but to articulate an explanation covering all the possible political factors. The framework is a set concepts that will help researchers to collect, analyse, and interpret data and practitioners to identify elements and processes that hinder or favour institutionalization.

4.1 Analysis and Reinterpretation of the Case Study

During October and November 1992, LAS launched a computer-aided dispatch (CAD) information system. On October 29, news broke that the CAD system had collapsed. As a consequence, twenty people allegedly died (Beynon-Davies 1993). The system was reinstalled, but a week later the system crashed again. Immediately, the system was abandoned totally and manual procedures were again put in place. The chief executive officer of LAS announced his resignation. The British government reacted by ordering an independent inquiry. LAS managers had introduced the CAD system to change the organizational culture and to improve the overall performance of the service (Robinson 1994). This is why the history of the CAD system is relevant to our argument.

The CAD system was introduced in a context of financial and performance problems and poor industrial relations. By the time the CAD system was conceived, in the early 1990s, the British government wanted to transform the National Health Service (NHS) into an internal market. If this transformation were to be successful, the NHS would be characterised by more efficient and competitive services and operations. New management was appointed to LAS in 1990 and was put under pressure to improve performance and reduce costs (Hougham 1995). Information technology and computerized information systems were considered by the new LAS management to be techniques and strategies to solve their problems, and the decision to develop the CAD system was made. Of the bids submitted, the one selected was by System Options.[5] This company won the £1.1M contract for the system in June 1991. The offer was substantially below the one presented by IAL, a BT subsidiary, of £7.5M (Beynon-Davies 1993). Going for the cheapest offer was criticised by the report

[5]This was a small company without previous experience in developing systems of this magnitude. Hougham argues that the lack of experience in project management of this company was one of the main reasons for the collapse of the system.

inquiry (Page, Williams and Boyd 1993). Nevertheless, if the system had not failed, LAS managers might have been praised for saving public money. In this sense, by selecting the least expensive of the bids, they were doing their job of reducing costs and improving efficiency. Our theory of circuits of power suggests that the adoption of innovations in organizations responds greatly to environmental uncertainties rather than to a rationally based on calculations. Table 1 illustrates the influences of exogenous environmental contingencies on the circuits of social and system integration.

Table 1 Exogenous Contingencies Affecting Social and System Integration.

Exogenous Contingencies	System Integration	Social Integration
LAS crisis	Adoption of techniques towards cost-effectiveness	Redundancies and poor industrial relations
Managerial Discourses Available (strategies supported by IT)	Redesign of jobs Managers having more control over operations; Employees lose discretion	Uncertainty because of the new rules Changing traditional authority structures

The episodic circuit of power. This circuit focuses on the relationship between resources and outcomes. The new system was expected to improve the performance of the service, to reduce operational costs, and to change the culture of the organization. There were concerns about the quality of the service before the development of the system. A survey conducted by NUPE in 1992 revealed that only 13% of their members thought that they were providing a good service. The period of time, according to British standards, from the moment an ambulance is requested to the moment it arrives should be approximately fourteen minutes. LAS was far from matching this standard. It was thought by LAS managers that the introduction of a CAD system might produce a more efficient dispatching system that would result eventually in matching the standard. Table 2 presents the main elements in our analysis of the episodic circuit of power. We have highlighted the social relations that give identity to the agencies involved in the circuit of episodic power as well as their standing conditions. The power struggle dynamic between LAS management and staff is depicted in Figure 2. It can be appreciated that, despite having different goals, both agencies had one in common: the improvement of services.

In the context of the CAD system, looking exclusively at the episodic circuit of power gives us a picture where the strong position held by management, based on numerous resources and decision making, should have been enough to produce a successful information system. This assumption is supported by two theories of power in organizations: contingency (Hickson et al. 1971); and resource dependency (Pfeffer 1981). Contingency theory considers that power concentrates in centrality, i.e., the capacity of decision making whereas resource dependency theory relates power to control over resources. If managers had financial resources and were in the highest position of decision making, why did they not succeed in implementing the system? What type of power did they lack? It can be argued, using our framework terminology, that the circuits of system and social integration were not fixed in a successful obligatory passage point. These elements are not considered by contingency and resource dependency theories, and they are the main contribution of the circuits of power framework.

Table 2 The Episodic Circuit of Power.

Social Relations	Agencies	Standing Conditions	
		Means and Resources	**Targeted Agencies**
LAS CEO, Senior managers	LAS management	Authority, discretion on policies and plans, financial resources and control over financial and human resources	LAS staff and system developers
Dispatching personnel and ambulance crews	LAS staff	Execution of operations, discretion on operations, membership to trade union	LAS management especially on matters regarding their jobs
System Options	System Developers	Discretion on analysis, design, development and technical matters of the information system	LAS staff in making them use the system according to their specifications and control over the technological agents

The circuit of social integration. This circuit deals with rules of meaning and membership. The CAD system influenced the way employees interpreted management style. The emphasis on spending on technology and the overall LAS autocratic style of management were opposed by LAS unions, who wanted, instead, more training and new vehicles as well as more participation in the process of decision making (ALA 1991). The response managers gave to this position was to push ahead with the CAD system without union participation. Tension rose because the workforce interpreted these moves as a way of undermining the trade unions and concentrating decision making on top management.

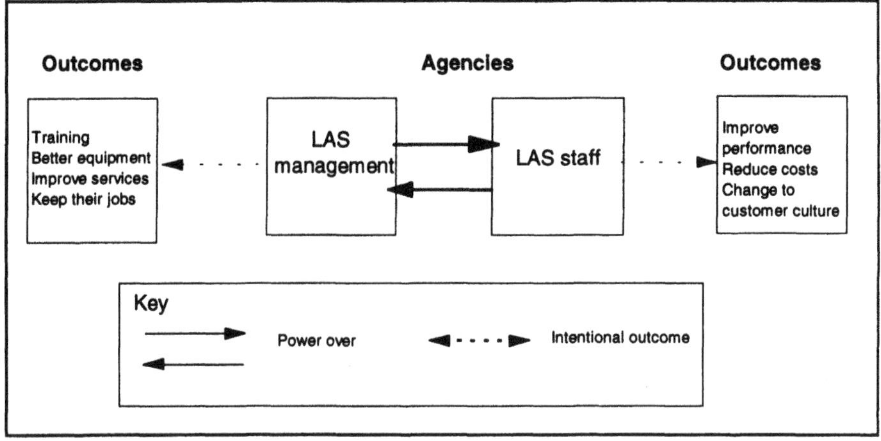

Figure 2 Power Struggle in LAS.

Table 3 The Circuit of Social Integration.

Discourse Affecting Rules of Meaning and Membership	Interpretation	
	LAS Management	**LAS Staff**
"LAS do not comply with national standards"	We need a new information system and new organiza-tional culture.	More training and better equipment. Better work conditions would im-prove performance.
"Introducing a new information systems"	The system will im-prove services and increase control over operations. Part of strategy to change culture.	Resources should be oriented to training and better equipment. Con-centrate control of op-erations on senior man-agement. Weaken trade unions
"Despite opposition and criti-cism management decides to move forward with the new sys-tem"	Trade unions do not co-operate. Intro-ducing the new sys-tem is crucial to achieve managerial objectives.	Maverick style of man-agement.

If workers interpreted the system as a threat to their identity and the existence of workers' organizations, managers interpreted workers' attitudes, actions and statements as a lack of collaboration and resistance. This added more pressure to managers, who instead of stopping and reflecting, surrendered to time pressure and decided to go ahead with the project. Resistance was outflanked by managers deploying their resources: money and authority for decision making. The new system reinforced the worsening industrial relations. Workers' attitudes might have only confirmed the belief of managers that the staff was the problem in LAS. Table 3 illustrates the contradictory interpretations of the discourses associated with the introduction of the new CAD information system. These contradictory interpretations hindered social integration, making it difficult for the LAS management to adjust their dispositional power to achieve the institutionalization of the system.

The new information system did not buttress social integration in LAS. The new rules stemming from the new tasks were not translated successfully into the system. Perhaps more importantly, the introduction of the system emphasized the gap and exacerbated relations between management and workers. It is unlikely in an organization, where social integration is low or characterized by conflict, that an information system – particularly if is interpreted as being a weapon of one group against another – can be consolidated and stabilized. In the case of LAS, the system required the total collaboration of the workforce to be successful. Developing and designing information systems needs not only technical but political skills.

The Circuit of System Integration. This circuit concentrates on techniques of control, discipline, and production. The major effect on control and discipline was found in the fact that discretion over deployment of ambulances was taken from the controllers and programmed into the new information system. Ambulances no longer responded to the judgement of controllers but to the calculations and orders produced by an information system. There were changes in the way tasks were classified and distributed. Before the introduction of the system, there were three divisions for dispatching ambulances: north-east, north-west, and south. Each of these divisions was managed by controllers who had a good knowledge of their section, in the sense that they knew those areas of London very well. This personal knowledge allowed them to identify, for example, when an accident was being reported twice. Thus, controllers would not send more than one ambulance to the same place. The inability of the CAD system to identify duplicate reports and the practice of sending more than one ambulance to the same incident was one of the reasons for the collapse in 1992. The design of the CAD system joined the three divisions and included rules for dispatching ambulances, so that the job of the controller, once the system was in place, was made redundant. The information system introduced new tasks and therefore new rules. These rules should have been translated effectively into the IS. The procedures and rules of calculation were introduced by information systems developers who apparently failed to capture the judgments and skills of the controllers. This inability of the system developers was one of the causes for the failure of the system. Table 4 shows the disruption caused to system integration by the new

CAD system. The organizational measures that accompanied the system, such as the elimination of the three geographical divisions and the substitution of the dispatchers, triggered those disruptions. In this table, we have highlighted the empowerment and disempowerment of agencies. It is not surprising that LAS staff perceived the CAD system as disempowering because it undermined their control over operations.

Table 4 The Circuit of System Integration.

Innovations in Techniques of Control and Production	Agencies	
	Empowered	Disempowered
New information systems	LAS management increased control of operations. System options won the contract.	LAS staff lost control over operations
Replacement of ambulance dispatchers	LAS management have more money for other plans. Weaken trade unions.	LAS dispatchers were made redundant. LAS staff morale went down.
Elimination of geographic divisions	[This did not empower anybody]	New system operators did not have control over dispatches.

The system replaced paper records and was installed without magnetic or paper backups (Robinson 1994). It was perhaps the time pressure and the lack of adequate supervision that made managers and system analysts overlook this elementary necessity. There is also evidence that training was not conducted properly. This was critical because the changes introduced were radical, especially in the way ambulances were dispatched and because staff of the central ambulances control were not well trained. For example, assistants and operators of the system were not taught how to cope with more than expected exception calls, a serious error in any system, unforgivable in a system on which people's life may depend.

Obligatory Passage Point. Obligatory passage points are actor networks linked by pieces of discourse whereby organizations translate the circuits of social and system integration in order to achieve outcomes. In the present case, the most evident and important obligatory passage point was the CAD information system. The CAD was an obligatory passage point linking and translating different actors such as management, market ideas, efficiency expectations, staff expertise, users, systems analysts and patients. If all these actors are translated successfully and their associations remain stable, then the obligatory passage point might be considered successful.

If all actors had remained faithful to their identities, alliances, and translations, then management would have achieved their objectives. The political atmosphere prevailing in the British government, pushing the NHS to an internal market, was represented in a system that was developed aiming at efficiency. The internal market ideology was translated into techniques and strategies enacted, in this case, by the managers of LAS. Staff expertise was inscribed in the system in the form of rules for allocation and dispatch of ambulances. Users of the system were also translated into the CAD. These translations were represented in the way system developers expected users to operate the system. For example, Mike Smith, Systems Director of LAS, said that the failure of the system was due to users not following the computer system instructions (*Daily Telegraph* 1992). Decisions made by systems analysts were inscribed into the system in other ways. Managers of LAS considered information technology to be fundamental in achieving the efficiency goals set when they were appointed. This consideration implies the belief that technology is a black box that can be safely left to expert technicians. System analysts were supposed to translate technology into the system in such a way that technology would do what it was told to do. In this sense, systems analysts were allegedly the representatives of information technology. The failure of November 4, 1992, was the result of a mistake: a programmer forgot to activate a routine that would maintain the memory of the system. Thus, designers and developers, the very representatives of technology, were "betrayed" by the technology itself. Poor translation also involved ambulance callers. One of the reasons given for the failure of the system was the excessive amount of exception phone calls. Ambulance requests did not traverse the OPP in expected ways. During that infamous night in October, 1992, LAS headquarters were flooded with 600 unexpected phone calls.

We might conclude that the translation of the actors in the obligatory passage point, the CAD system, failed. This might explain why, despite the fact that management had the power in terms of money and decision making, they failed to achieve their desired outcomes. If we recall Foucault's claimed characteristic of power, which is that power can be recognized in actions, we could say that successful outcomes through the use of technology can only be achieved by successful processes of translations. Successful translation will depend, then, on how faithful actors are toward their definition and their alliances.

5 CONCLUSIONS

In this case, successful translations would have been the result of managers reformulating strategies to create a common acceptable meaning for the new system. Furthermore, the project coordinator and LAS management should have identified exactly how the new system was to affect the way job processes and the tasks had been performed before the introduction of the system.

LAS management considered prematurely the information system as a black box with clearly defined inputs and outputs before it was institutionalized. The inputs were technology and financial and human resources, while the outputs were cultural change and improved performance. There is no doubt about the abject failure of this information system to alter the power structures of the LAS. We have applied the circuits of power framework and demonstrated that the system was a result of strategies and techniques prevailing in the government and within the organization. This analysis illustrates how the framework can shed light on the links between power and information systems. Perhaps more importantly it shows how risky it is to prematurely consider information systems as black boxes producing outputs, such as change in culture and power structures, without considering the social and system integration.[6]

The institutionalization of information systems, although desirable, requires great efforts from organizations, and it depends on many factors. The circuits of power framework is an attempt to encompass those factors in a theoretical model. The framework we have suggested could be useful for researchers interested in the political dimensions of information systems or in the processes of institutionalization in identifying those variables where collecting data is required. Furthermore, it can help researchers in analyzing and interpreting the data. Practitioners of information systems, either analysts or managers, can benefit from the framework and the example presented here when understanding their own systems in their own circumstances. The validity of an interpretive theory is difficult to establish. As Walsham (1993, p. 6) declares, "in the interpretive tradition, there are no correct and incorrect theories but there are interesting and less interesting ways to view the world." We hope the theoretical framework proposed here and the way we have applied it will be of interest to our readers and that the insights presented can serve the intersubjective process of theory building.

6 REFERENCES

Akrich, M. (1992). "The De-scription of Technical Objects." In W. E. Bijker and J. Law (Editors), *Shaping Technology/Building Society*. Cambridge, Massachusetts: MIT Press, pp. 205-224.

---

[6]We would like to pick up the point we made above about Collins and Yearly's critique of actor network theory. They also criticize actor network theory in the sense that tacit human knowledge cannot be translated onto nonhuman actors, i.e., actants. We believe that the disaster of the LAS information system shows the failure of information systems analysts and programmers in their attempts to inscribe on the system the tacit knowledge of the ambulance dispatchers.

Akrich, M., and Latour, B. (1992). "A Summary of a Convenient Vocabulary for the Semiotics of Human and Nonhuman Assemblies." In W. E. Bijker and J. Law (Editors), *Shaping Technology/Building Society*. Cambridge, Massachusetts: MIT Press, pp. 259-264.

ALA (1991). *London Ambulances: A Service in Crisis*. Pamphlet No. ALA, Association of London Authorities.

Berger, P., and Luckman, T. (1967). *The Social Construction of Reality: A Treatise in the Sociology of Knowledge*. London: Penguin Books.

Beynon-Davies, P. (1993). *The London Ambulance Service's Computerised Dispatch System: A Case Study in Information Systems Failure*. University of Glamorgan Pontyprid.

Bjerknes, G.; Ehn, P.. and Kyng, M. (Editors) (1987). *Computers and Democracy: A Scandinavian Challenge*. Aldershot, England: Avebury.

Bloomfield, B. P. (1990).

Bloomfield, B. P., and Best, A. (1992). "Management Consultants: Systems Development, Power and the Translation of Problems." *The Sociological Review*, Volume 40, Number 3, pp. 533-560.

Bloomfield, B. P., and Coombs, R. (1992). "Information Technology, Control and Power: The Centralization and Decentralization Debate Revisited." *Journal of Management Studies*, Volume 29, Number 4, pp. 459-484.

Bloomfield, B. P., and Danieli, A. (1995). "The Role of Management Consultants in The Development of Information Technology: The Indissoluble Nature of Socio-Political and Technical Skills. *Journal of Management Studies*, Volume 32, Number 1, pp. 23-46.

Bloomfield, B. P., and McLean, C. (1995). "Madness and Organization: Informed Management and Empowerment." In W. J. Orlikowski, G. Walsham, M. R. Jones, and J. I. DeGross (Editors), *Information Technology and Changes in Organizational Work*. London: Chapman and Hall, pp. 371-392.

Bodker, S.; Ehn, P.; Kyng, M.; Kammersgaard, J.; and Sundblad, Y. (1987). "A Utopian Experience: On Design of Powerful Computer-Based Tools for Skilled Graphic Workers." In G. Bjerknes, P. Ehn, and M. Kyng (Editors), *Computer and Democracy: A Scandinavian Challenge*. Aldershot, England: Avebury, pp. 251-278.

Callon, M. (1986). "Some Elements of a Sociology of Translation: Domestication of the Scallops and the Fishermen of St. Brieuc Bay." In J. Law (Editor), *Power, Action and Belief*. London: Routledge and Kegan Paul, pp. 196-233.

Callon, M. (1991). "Techno-Economic Networks and Irreversibility." In J. Law (Editor), *A Sociology of Monsters: Essays on Power, Technology and Domination*. London: Routledge, pp. 132-161.

Callon, M., and Latour, B. (1992). "Don't Throw the Baby Out with the Bath School! A Reply to Collins and Yearley." In A. Pickering (Editor), *Science as Practice and Culture*. Chicago: The University of Chicago Press, pp. 343-368.

Callon, M.; Law, J.; and Rip, A. (Editors) (1986). *Mapping the Dynamics of Science and Technology: Sociology of Science in the Real World.* London: The Macmillan Press Ltd.

Clegg, S. R. (1989). *Frameworks of Power.* London: Sage Publications.

Clegg, S. R. (1990). *Modern Organizations: Organization Studies in the Postmodern World.* London: Sage Publications.

Collins, H. M., and Yearley, S. (1992a). "Epistemological Chicken." In A. Pickering (Editor), *Science as Practice and Culture.* Chicago: The University of Chicago Press, pp. 301-326.

Collins, H. M., and Yearley, S. (1992b). "Journey Into Space." In A. Pickering (Editor), *Science as Practice and Culture.* Chicago: The University of Chicago Press, pp. 369-389.

Dahl, R. (1957). "The Concept of Power." *Behavioral Science,* Volume 2, pp. 201-105.

Daily Telegraph, 29 October 1992.

Dimaggio, P., and Powell, W. (1983). "Institutional Isomorphism and Collective Rationality in Organization Fields." *American Sociological Review,* Volume 48, Number 2, pp. 147-160.

DiMaggio, P. J., and Powell, W. W. (1991a). "The Iron Cage Revisited: Institutional Isomorphism and Collective Rationality in Organizational Fields." In W. W. Powell and P. J. DiMaggio (Editors), *The New Institutionalism in Organizational Analysis.* Chicago: The University of Chicago Press, pp. 63-82.

Ehn, P., and Kyng, M. (1987). "The Collective Resource Approach to Systems Design." In P. Ehn and M. Kyng (Editors), *Computers and Democracy.* Aldershot, England: Avebury, pp. 17-57.

Foucault, M. (1972). *The Archaeology of Knowledge.* London: Tavistock.

Foucault, M. (1977). *Discipline and Punish.* New York: Vintage Books.

Foucault, M. (1980). *Power/Knowledge: Selected Interviews and Other Writings 1972-77.* Brighton: Harvester Press.

Friedman, A., and Cornford, D. (1987). "Strategies for Meeting User Demands: An International Perspective." In G. Bjerknes, P. Ehn, and M. Kyng (Editors), *Computers and Democracy: A Scandinavian Challenge.* Aldershot, England: Avebury, pp. 137-162.

Giddens, A. (1979). *Central Problems in Social Theory.* London: Macmillan.

Giddens, A. (1984). *The Constitution of Society.* Cambridge, England: Polity Press.

Habermas, J. (1970). "Towards a Theory of Communicative Competence." *Inquiry,* Volume 13, pp. 360-375.

Habermas, J. (1972). *Knowledge and Human Interests* (J. Shapiro, Translator). Boston: Beacon Press.

Habermas, J. (1979). *Communication and the Evolution of Society* (T. McCarthy, Translator). Boston: Beacon Press.

Hickson, D. J.; Higgins, C. R.; Less, C. A.; Schneck, R. E.; and Pennings, J. M. A. (1971). "A Strategic Contingencies Theory of Intraorganizational Power." *Administrative Science Quarterly*, Volume 16, Number 2, pp. 216-229.

Hirschheim, R., and Klein, H. K. (1994). "Realizing Emancipatory Principles in Information Systems Development: The Case for ETHICS." *MIS Quarterly*, March, pp. 83-109.

Hougham, M. G. (1995). *London Ambulance Service* (Project Management Case Study No. PM696). Henley Management College.

Jarvenpaa, S. L. (1991). "Panning for Gold in Information Systems Research: 'Second-Hand' Data." In H.-E. Nissen, H. K. Klein, and R. Hirschheim (Editors), *Information Systems Research: Contemporary Approaches and Emergent Traditions*. Amsterdam: North Holland, pp. 63-80.

Keen, P. G. W. (1981). "Information Systems and Organizational Change." *Communications of the ACM*, Volume 24, Number 1, pp. 24-33.

Latour, B. (1987). *Science in Action*. Cambridge, Massachusetts: Harvard University Press.

Latour, B. (1991). "Technology is Society Made Durable." In J. Law (Editor), *A Sociology of Monsters: Essays on Power, Technology and Domination*. London: Routledge, pp. 103-131.

Law, J. (Editor) (1986). *Power, Action and Belief: A New Sociology of Knowledge?* London: Routledge and Kegan Paul.

Law, J. (1991a). "Power, Discretion and Strategy." In J. Law (Editor), *A Sociology of Monsters: Essays on Power, Technology and Domination*. London: Routledge, pp. 165-191.

Law, J. (Editor) (1991b). *A Sociology of Monsters: Essays on Power, Technology and Domination*. London: Routledge.

Lockwood, D. (1964). "Social Integration and System Integration." In G. K. Zollschan and W. Hirsch (Editors), *Explorations in Social Change*. London: Routledge and Kegan Paul, pp. 244-257.

Lukes, S. (1974). *Power: A Radical View*. London: The Macmillan Press Ltd.

Markus, M. L. (1983). "Power, Politics, and MIS Implementation." *Communications of the ACM*, Volume 26, Number 6, pp. 430-444.

Markus, M. L., and Bjørn-Andersen, N. (1987). "Power Over Users: Its Exercise by System Professionals." *Communications of the ACM*, Volume 30, Number 6, pp. 498-504.

Meyer, J., and Rowan, B. (1991). "Institutionalized Organizations: Formal Structure as Myth and Ceremony." In W. W. Powell and P. J. DiMaggio (Editors), *The New Institutionalism in Organizational Analysis*. Chicago: The University Press of Chicago, pp. 41-62.

Mintzberg, H. (1983). *Power In and Around Organizations*. Englewood Cliffs, New Jersey: Prentice Hall.

Monteiro, E., and Hanseth, O. (1995). "Social Shaping of Information Infrastructure: On Being Specific About the Technology." In W. J. Orlikowski, G. Walsham, M.

R. Jones, and J. I. DeGross (Editors), *Information Technology and Changes in Organizational Work.* London: Chapman and Hall, pp. 325-243.
NUPE (1992). *Ambulance Alert – A NUPE Report.*
Orlikowski, W., and Robey, D. (1991). "Information Technology and the Structuring of Organizations." *Information Systems Research,* Volume 2, Number 2, pp. 143-169.
Page, D.; Williams, P.; and Boyd, D. (1993). *Report of the Public Inquiry into the London Ambulance Service.* HMSO.
Pfeffer, J. (1981). *Power in Organizations.* Marshfield, Massachusetts: Pitman.
Robinson, B. (1994). *'And Treat Those Two Imposters Just The Same': Analysing Systems Failure as a Social Process.* Information Technology Institute, University of Salford.
Sewell, G., and Wilkinson, B. (1992). "'Someone to Watch Over Me': Surveillance, Discipline and the Just-In-Time Labor Process." *Sociology,* Volume 2, Number 6, 271-289.
Vidgen, R., and McMaster, T. (1995). "Black Boxes, Non-Human Stakeholders and the Translation of IT Trough Mediation." In W. J. Orlikowski, G. Walsham, M. R. Jones, and J. I. DeGross (Editors), *Information Technology and Changes in Organizational Work.* London: Chapman and Hall, pp. 250-271.
Walsham, G. (1993). *Interpreting Information Systems in Organizations.* Chichester, England: John Wiley.
Zuboff, S. (1988). *In the Age of the Smart Machine.* New York: Basic Books.

7 BIOGRAPHY

Leister Silva is a Ph.D. student in the Department of Information Systems at the London School of Economics and Political Science. He has coordinated several software and information systems projects for a research center of the Pan-American Health Organization. He has also worked for the same organization as an Information Systems consultant for the American region. His current research at the LSE is focused on the relationship between power and information systems in organizations. One of the objectives of this research is to develop a theoretical framework that would help to identify the relevant elements of the power phenomenon regarding information systems.

James Backhouse teaches in the Information Systems Department of the London School of Economics and Political Science (LSE). He writes widely for academic and commercial publications, advises international clients, and is consulting editor for a number of journals, including *Journal of Financial Crime.* A particular theme in his work has been the emphasis on understanding the role of semantics in communications and information, and his thesis refined an analytical tool, semantic analysis, which supports management and systems development activities. Since 1992, his research interests have extended to the field of information security, and he is now the Director of the LSE Computer Security Research Centre. The Centre focuses on the study of organizational and management aspects of the security and privacy of information systems.

Part Six

Developments in Qualitative Methods

21

Value in Triangulation: A Comparison of Two Approaches for Combining Qualitative and Quantitative Methods

M. J. Gallivan
Stern School of Business
New York University
44 W. 4th Street, MEC 9-77
New York, New York 10012 USA
Tel: (212) 998-0824
Fax: (212) 995-4228
E-mail: MGalliva@stern.nyu.edu

Abstract

This paper raises and pursues the question of why research utilizing mixed, quantitative and qualitative methods has been so strongly advocated, yet so little achieved. Following an overview of a range of solutions to the call for "ethodological pluralism," a conceptual framework for understanding the process and outcomes of mixed method research is advanced, and several research studies are used to illustrate the framework. The conceptual framework is based on two dimensions suggested by prior research. Specifically, the framework analyzes various outcomes that emerge from the research – such as different types of contradictions (Robey 1995) and also whether the two methods were employed *sequentially* or *independently*. The paper analyzes the relationship between these two dimensions of the framework, offering some possible reasons why mixed-methods studies in which the two methods are employed independently appear to lead to different outcomes.

1 INTRODUCTION

Research in the field of information systems (IS) has been frequently criticized for its strong allegiance to positivist assumptions and quantitative research methodology. In previous working conferences of the IFIP Working Group 8.2, various authors have criticized the bias toward positivist philosophy and empirical, hypothesis-testing methods. Research published in mainstream U.S. journals has been especially singled out for this criticism. One team of 8.2 researchers argued that

> Information systems and information technology are so new that it is positively dangerous to allow them to be researched using only one methodology....We should currently be generating ideas, theories and hypotheses, rather than simply testing them, and that anything which restricts or constrains this process is inappropriate.
>
> It is often argued that the degree to which the problem exists differs from geographical area to area...in Europe and perhaps in Canada more freedom exists to choose something other than a purely natural science form of enquiry, [and] alternatives are sometimes tolerated and live almost happily side-by-side....However, in the United States, this appears to be even less common, and a study of doctoral programmes confirms this. A worrying aspect of this being that the United States is...the most influential, and potentially the most successful IS society. The rest of the world needs the United States to widen its methods of enquiry in order for this success to be fully realised. [Fitzgerald et al. 1985, pp. 5-6]

Thus, for over a decade there has been a call for greater "methodological pluralism" in IS research, and participants in IFIP 8.2 have been some of its staunchest advocates. Given the emerging position that such pluralism is needed, the options for providing it abound. Several alternative research approaches have been proposed, and many have recently become more common in IS publications – even in U.S.-based mainstream journals. These include a greater frequency of research that is interpretive (Walsham 1995; Orlikowski 1993, 1996), research that combines positivist and interpretivist approaches (Lee 1991), and research that involves qualitative analysis of case studies (Eisenhardt 1989; Leonard-Barton 1990).

While each of these research approaches pose one solution to the problem that Nissen (1985) labeled a "methodological quagmire," this paper focuses on another alternative: research employing quantitative and qualitative research methods to develop or to test theory. This type of research has been widely prescribed, but rarely implemented. More than seventeen years ago, Jick claimed that "research designs that extensively integrate both fieldwork (e.g., participant observation) and survey research are rare" (Jick 1979, p. 604). We begin with the assumption that little has changed in terms of the frequency of mixed quantitative and qualitative research during the years since Jick's observation. This paper seeks answers to the following questions: In the IS field, how prevalent is mixed quantitative and qualitative methods research – both in raw numbers and as a proportion of published papers? Why do IS researchers conduct such research? What are some attributes of mixed quantitative and qualitative research that may explain its unique contribution? These questions are explored in this paper, leading to a framework which classifies different types of mixed methods research. Mixed methods papers are not homogenous, but basically fall into two categories: applying quantitative analyses and qualitative analyses *independently* or *sequentially*. A contribution of this paper is to characterize these two categories of mixed-methods research and to discuss the outcomes associated with each.

2 DEFINITION OF MIXED, QUANTITATIVE AND QUALITATIVE RESEARCH

Merely invoking the phrase mixed methods research opens a pandora's box of questions and issues. First, the phrase *mixed methods* connotes different techniques to different researchers. For example, it may indicate research employing two or more different ways of measuring the *same* phenomenon, such as two survey scales for capturing user involvement in system implementation. Using two measures based on the same research method is excluded from the definition of mixed methods used here, since that is merely "within-method triangulation" (Denzin 1978; Jick 1979). Similarly, studies that employ two variations of qualitative research – such as longitudinal and retrospective case studies (Leonard-Barton 1990) – are also excluded.

The definition of mixed methods in this study refers to the mixing of quantitative and qualitative methods. This definition derives from Denzin and from Jick and their notion of *triangulation between or across methods* – in particular, qualitative and quantitative research. It is not the mere *collection* of data by two different methods that is relevant here, but also the analysis of such data. Jick defined mixed methods as "research designs that *extensively integrate* both fieldwork and survey research" (emphasis added). The significance of the word "extensively" implies that both qualitative and quantitative data must be collected and analyzed in the study. Based on the concepts of Denzin and of Jick, concepts, this refers to studies that are both conducted *and published* as mixed methods research. Mixed methods research is thus defined as empirical research[1] that meets the following conditions:

- at least two different methods are used for collecting data

---

[1]There have been numerous conceptual review articles describing the strengths and weaknesses of various research methodologies (McGrath 1982; Benbasat 1984; Wynekoop and Conger 1991; Wynekoop and Russo 1993; Nissen 1985) and the variety of available qualitative methods (Lacity and Janson 1994). This paper does not include papers about methodology – even those discussing mixed method research – unless an empirical study is presented in the paper.

- at least one of the data collection methods is qualitative (e.g., interviews)
- at least one of the data collection methods is quantitative (e.g., surveys)
- both qualitative and quantitative data are presented
- both qualitative and quantitative data are analyzed
- the research addresses a theoretical question rather than providing description only

A published study must meet all six criteria in order to satisfy the definition of mixed quantitative and qualitative research. One class of research papers that is clearly excluded by this definition is studies where interviews were conducted simply as a precursor to developing a survey, and where the qualitative results are not presented. It has become commonplace to engage in qualitative interviews prior to conducting a survey; however, in many studies, the qualitative data are omitted from the results or mentioned only to provide anecdotes to support the survey results. This has been decried as "pseudo-triangulation" (Maxwell 1993) or using qualitative evidence as mere "window dressing" (Jick 1979).

Several studies were found that achieved four or five of the above criteria, but they were excluded from this paper for failing to meet *each and every one* of the criteria. For example, studies excluded were those that *collected* both types of data but did not *present* or *analyze* results of the quantitative data (Leonard-Barton 1990) or the qualitative data (Grant and Higgins 1991; Smith, Milberg and Burke 1996). Also excluded were studies that presented *raw* survey data without any quantitative analysis (Tyran et al. 1992) or studies that did not answer a theoretical question, such as descriptive Delphi studies (Watson 1990). Other definitions of mixed quantitative and qualitative research are certainly possible; however, the definition used here is faithful to Jick's definition as research that "extensively integrates both field work and survey research" to answer an empirical research question.[2]

Before presenting results from a structured review of the IS literature, it is important to underscore that this paper focuses on the type of data (qualitative and quantitative), rather than the type of theory or the epistemological assumptions used in analyzing the data. Although the terms qualitative and quantitative are often conflated with two other dimensions – epistemology (interpetivist and positivist) and logical structure of theories (process and variance) – these other dimensions are neither perfectly correlated with nor independent of the qualitative-quantitative distinction. The definition of mixed methods research used here assumes nothing about whether the

---

[2]One other category of articles that initially appeared to meet the definition of mixed methods research was those studies that collected all data through one method – qualitative interviews – and then coded and analyzed the data as quantitative results (Earl 1993; Reich and Benbasat 1996). Although such studies employ both qualitative *collection* and quantitative *analysis* of data, they are not mixed method studies, because only a single data collection method (interviews) and data analysis method (quantitative analysis) were used. No triangulation is possible on a single set of data.

researcher seeks to combine positivist and interpretivist approaches or process and variance theories. These issues are distinct from the type of data that are analyzed and have been addressed by other researchers (Lee 1991; Markus and Robey 1988; Soh and Markus 1995; Mohr 1982). The definition of mixed methods research allows for methodological pluralism, permitting the data to be analyzed from either a positivist or an interpretivist perspective, and the theory to be constructed as either variance or process theory. Although some researchers believe that qualitative or "Qualitative" research (with an upper-case "Q") implies an interpretivist perspective (Kidder and Fine 1987; Maxwell 1996), no such assumption is made here.[3]

As stated above, we began with the assumption that mixed methods research has not increased in frequency since Jick's statement in 1979. Two pieces of evidence contributed to this assumption. The first was the observation by Orlikowski and Baroudi (1991) that only 3% of papers published in a set of U.S. journals were mixed methods studies.[4] Second, the *Proceedings of the Fourtheenth International Conference on Information Systems* (DeGross, Bostrom and Robey 1993) were examined, since "valuing diversity through information systems" was the theme of that particular annual conference. No examples of empirical, mixed methods research were identified in the *1993 Proceedings*, despite the diversity theme. Although this finding was disappointing, it confirmed the assumption regarding the scarcity of mixed methods and also prompted a more structured review of the IS literature. This structured review of four U.S. journals that publish IS research was conducted for the years 1988 to 1996. Since the prior literature review by Orlikowski and Baroudi covered the period from 1984 to mid-1988 in four leading U.S. journals, this review focused

---

[3]Qualitative research *tends* to be interpretivist and process-oriented, and quantitative research *tends* to be positivist and variance-oriented. Although research studies tend to cluster at one or the other end of these three dimensions, there are enough exceptions to recognize that the dimensions are somewhat independent of each other. In view of such independence, this paper does not seek to address the two related questions of whether researchers can combine positivist and interpretivist epistemologies or variance and process-oriented research. The definition of mixed methods research encompasses data that are analyzed under either a positivist or interpretivist paradigm, thus avoiding the "epistemological debate" (Sabherwal and Robey 1995). This definition includes research that combines mixed methods, whether the theory is a factor or process theory, or whether the researcher uses positivist or interpretivist philosophy. The debate as to whether different theories and epistemological assumptions are complementary, incompatible, or reconcilable is avoided here. These issues are subjects of debate among researchers (Lee 1991 1989; Markus and Robey 1988; Mohr 1982).

[4]In their review, Orlikowski and Baroudi classified only 3.2% of the articles as "mixed methods," based on four U.S. publications from the period 1984 through mid-1988. The journals they reviewed were *MIS Quarterly, Management Science, Proceedings of the International Conference on Information Systems*, and *Communications of the ACM*. Orlikowski and Baroudi did not specifically define mixed methods, although their category of mixed methods publications would appear to overlap the definition used here.

on the subsequent period (1988-1996), based on similar U.S.-based journals, but a slightly different subset. All papers published in three IS journals (*MIS Quarterly, Information Systems Research,* and *Journal of Management Information Systems*) were reviewed, as well as IS papers published in *Organization Science*.[5]

A total of 583 papers from these four journals were reviewed, with eleven papers meeting the definition of mixed quantitative and qualitative research. The frequency of such papers is only 1.9% across these four journals. Table 1 shows that *MIS Quarterly* published a higher ratio of such papers, while *Information Systems Research* and *Journal of Management Information Systems* published fewer such studies. In addition to the structured review, other examples of mixed methods research were sought by following references from two review articles of IS methodology – one from IFIP 8.2 (Wynekoop and Conger 1991) and another from ICIS (Wynekoop and Russo 1993). This helped to identify other mixed methods studies, even those published in other journals.[6] A total of five additional papers were located by following citations from these papers, resulting in a total of sixteen mixed methods studies that were reviewed and analyzed in order to develop a conceptual framework, described below.

3 CONCEPTUAL FRAMEWORK

All sixteen mixed methods papers were analyzed and found to differ along several dimensions. A preliminary classification of these papers revealed that they differed in terms of

- whether the initial results of the qualitative and quantitative analyses were complementary, contradictory, or unrelated to each other;
- whether the paper's final theoretical contribution required the separate insights of both methods, or whether the theoretical insights could have been reached from one method alone.

Analysis of these papers revealed that half (eight papers) identified a contradiction in their results. Of the remaining papers, two did not identify any contradiction, but they

---

[5]*MIS Quarterly* was the only journal included in both this study and in the Orlikowski and Baroudi review. *Management Science* was not reviewed here, since it now publishes fewer papers related to IS research, compared to the past. Two new journals, *Information Systems Research* and *Organization Science*, were reviewed here but not in the study by Orlikowski and Baroudi because these journals started publication in 1990. *Journal of Management Information Systems* was also included in this literature review.

[6]The term *other* journals refers to journals *other* than those in which the structured literature review was conducted. For example, Barley's two papers (1986, 1990) are included here because they are widely cited as mixed methods studies, although *Administrative Science Quarterly* was not one of the journals included in the structured literature review.

Table 1 Mixed Method Studies Located through Structured Review of IS Publications.

Journal Title	Review Start Date	Review End Date	Number of Mixed Method Papers	Total Papers Published	Percent Mixed Method Papers
Information Systems Research	1990	1996	2	124	1.6%
Journal of Management Information Systems	1988	1996	1	253	0.4%
MIS Quarterly	1988	1996	6	206	2.9%
Organization Science	1990	1996	2	—*	—*
Total Papers	1988	1996	11	583	1.9%

Table 1a Mixed Method Studies Found in Other Publications.

Journal Title	Number of Mixed Method Papers
Administrative Science Quarterly	2
Communications of the ACM	1
ICIS Proceedings	1
Sloan Management Review	1
Total Papers	5

*Only IS publications in *Organization Science* that employed mixed methods were reviewed. It is therefore misleading to calculate a percentage of mixed method papers as a ratio of total papers.

emphasized the importance of the two sets of findings (the quantitative and the qualitative) in providing a synergistic analysis of their data. The latter papers specifically emphasized that the resulting theory required integration of both the qualitative and quantitative findings. Finally, there were six papers without either of these attributes (they found no contradictions nor did they emphasize a synergy between the two sets of data).

Since Robey (1995) recently provided a framework for understanding contradictions in IS research, his terminology was used to as a starting point, although it was expanded. Robey's categories are contradictions *within* a single research study, contradictions *among* research studies, and studies with no contradictions. In the spirit of Robey's terminology, but acknowledging that the categories required here were necessarily more complex (due to the need to also recognize contradictions between the two sets of data within the same study), the following five categories were identified:

1. A study with contradictions that appear within it, due to the use of mixed methods.
2. A study with contradictions that appear within it, but where the contradiction was identified based on a single method alone (rather than due to the mixed methods).
3. A study without an inherent contradiction, but where some results are inconsistent with prior studies.
4. A study without any contradiction, and where a synergy exists between the results of the mixed methods.
5. A study without any contradiction, and where results are parallel but not synergistic between the mixed methods.

Papers were analyzed and classified according to these five categories, with the results shown in Table 2. Most papers were classified in rows 2 and 5 (five and six papers, respectively). Only five papers were classified in the other three rows of the table. Summaries of selected papers are described below, in order to illustrate the classification, and also to identify the theoretical contributions of mixed methods research.

4 LITERATURE REVIEW OF SELECTED PAPERS

Contradictions that appear within a study due to the use of mixed methods. In their study of the effect of computerized laboratory systems in hospitals, Kaplan and Duchon (1988) separately analyzed the results of interviews and surveys, which yielded two key contradictions. First, whereas quantitative analyses based on job characteristics theory (Hackman and Oldham 1980) revealed high levels of satisfaction and acceptance of the new system, the qualitative analyses revealed strong user dissatisfaction. Second, the qualitative analyses revealed patterns of intergroup dif-

Table 2 Classification of Mixed Methods Articlesby Theoretical Outcomes.

Outcomes of Data Analysis	Authors (Year)	Journal*	Methods Used*
Contradictions that appear within a study due to use of mixed methods	Kaplan and Duchon (1988)	MISQ	P-O, S
	Wynekoop (1992)	ICIS	I, S
Contradictions that appear within a study but which were identified based on a single method alone	Barley (1986)	ASQ	P-O, C-O
	Liker, Roitman and Roskies (1987)	SMR	I, S
	Kraut, Dumais and Koch (1989)	CACM	I, S
	Barley (1990)	ASQ	P-O, C-O
	Zack and McKenney (1995)	Org. Science	I, S, O, A
Contradictions among studies No inherent contradiction but some results are inconsistent with prior studies	Markus (1994)	Org. Science	I, S, A
Papers without a contradiction but where a synergy exists between the results of the mixed methods	Blanton, Watson and Moody (1992)	MISQ	I, S
	Sabherwal and Robey (1995)	ISR	I, CCS
Papers without a contradiction and where the results are parallel but not synergistic between the mixed methods	Jobber et al. (1989)	MISQ	I, S
	Moynihan (1990)	MISQ	I, S
	Deans et al. (1991)	JMIS	I, S
	Trauth, Frawell and Lee (1993)	MISQ	I, S
	Leidner and Jarvenpaa (1993)	ISR	O, S
	Brown and Magill (1994)	MISQ	I, S

Legend: ASQ = *Administrative Science Quarterly*; CACM = *Communications of the ACM*; ICIS = *Proceedings of the International Conference on Information Systems*; ISR = *Information Systems Research*; JMIS = *Journal of Management Information Systems*; MISQ = *MIS Quarterly*; SMR = *Sloan Mnagement Review*.
A = archival data; C-O = coded observations; CCS = coded case studies; I = interviews; O = observation; P-O = participant observation; S = survey

ferences in system acceptance (at the departmental level), however, such patterns were obscured in the survey data.[7] After recognizing these contradictions, Kaplan and Duchon searched for an integrative explanation, ultimately identifying the new, group-level construct of *work orientation* as explaining users' acceptance of the system. Two work orientations were defined, with work groups labeled as either *process-oriented* or *results-oriented.* The process-oriented work groups perceived the system as interfering with their real work (conducting lab tests), whereas the results-oriented groups perceived the system as streamlining their work (communicating lab results to other departments). This group-level construct – work orientation – successfully predicted individual workers' attitudes toward the system. Thus, the qualitative and quantitative methods independently generated contradictions that could only be resolved by developing new theory and validating it with existing survey data, through a novel procedure for computing sums and differences between existing items. The authors were highly motivated to resolve the contradiction between the divergent findings without negating either set of findings. Iterating between the two sets of results, the work orientation construct was operationalized and found to explain significantly the differences in individuals' reactions to the system.

A second study that reflected contradictions between mixed methods in the same study was Wynekoop's (1992) study of the implementation of CASE tools in seven firms. She employed both interviews and surveys to identify the factors and processes associated with successful adoption, leading to several contradictions: 1) the firms that were shown to have the strongest managerial support for CASE tools (in the field studies) had the lowest levels of user acceptance and actual usage (in the survey); 2) the firm in which the level of management support was lowest showed the highest levels of user acceptance and usage (in the survey); 3) the amount of positive communication about the benefits of CASE tools was inversely related to user acceptance across all firms studied. These were puzzling findings, since they were internally inconsistent and also contradicted prior evidence showing the importance of managerial support (Jarvenpaa and Ives 1991) and high levels of communication about the benefits of an innovation to potential adopters (Rogers 1983; Ives and Olson 1984).

Due to these contradictions among her results, Wynekoop reconciled them by identifying new constructs in the qualitative data, and then used them to explain anomalies in the survey data. The qualitative data suggested the importance of *bottom-up* and well as top-down management support for the innovation. The data also suggested the importance of *accurate and complete communication* about the benefits of CASE tools if they were to be successfully implemented and accepted by users. The importance of accurate and complete communication explained certain contradictions, because the survey data alone had only analyzed the *amount* of

---

[7]Differences between departments, in terms of user acceptance of the technology, were obscured in the survey data because the quantitative analysis captured only individual means and variances but did not aggregate the data by department to identify group-level differences.

positive communication about CASE tools in each firm, but not its accuracy. Where such information was biased, the users rejected the technology after initial use. Similarly, the paradox of strong management support leading to user rejection was an artifact due to the fact that, in one firm where an overzealous IS manager championed the technology, he did so autocratically, so that grass roots support among users was stifled. In summary, the contradictions led to a re-examination of the qualitative data to identify new constructs (*accurate and complete communication* and *bottom-up support*), and then using them to reinterpret the survey data to resolve the contradictions.

Contradictions that appear within a study, but where the contradiction was identified based on a single method alone (rather than due to the mixed methods). Barley (1990, 1986) identified the inconsistent results of medical CT (computerized tomography) scanning technology in two hospitals. Using a mixed methods data collection strategy as well as a *mixed-level* analysis (focusing on both micro- and macro-level changes[8]), Barley showed that the opposite macro-level outcomes in the two hospitals could best be explained by differences in micro-level phenomena. In one paper, Barley (1990) showed that when the same technology was adopted within two different organizational contexts, it exerted different effects on organizational structure and patterns of interaction. One hospital became much more decentralized while the other hospital showed no changes in level of centralization (Barley 1986). In a related study, Barley (1990) showed that the same technology exerted different effects on communication patterns *within* the same hospital, depending on the age of physicians and the number of years they had been in practice. In the latter study, Barley employed quantitative sociometric data[9] to show that different "relational role patterns" developed between the radiologists and the technicians using the new technology, but these patterns were influenced by the recency of physicians' specialty training and their use of the CT scanners.

---

[8]Barley (1990) used sociometric data to conduct a network analysis (communication frequency analysis), focused on both the frequency and duration of interactions among the radiologists and other paraprofessionals, including technicians. Quantitative network analyses verified that the CT scanner altered role relationships such that younger doctors, who used the CT scanner, had much stronger relationships with the radiology technicians, compared to the older physicians, who rarely used it. The analysis also showed that the radiology technicians who used the CT scanner became "structurally equivalent" to the radiologists in their communication patterns, whereas the technicians who did not use the CT scanner retained a traditional communication pattern, similar to other ancillary health workers.

[9]Markus and Robey (1988) describe the advantages of using mixed-level (or multi-level) research, which is facilitated by, but does not required mixed methods. Mixed-level research collects data at multiple levels of analysis (e.g., individual, group, organizational, or industry). Additional comments about mixed-level data are deferred until the paper's conclusion.

No inherent contradiction but some results are inconsistent with prior studies. Markus (1994) collected data about managers' actual usage of e-mail and their reasons for using e-mail instead of other media. Markus used interviews, surveys, and analysis of sample messages. While her results did not show an inherent contradiction, the overall results were inconsistent with prior theory – namely media richness theory (Daft, Lengel and Trevino 1987). The three categories of data were internally consistent, showing that managers were not primarily influenced by media richness considerations, but rather by social influences which shaped their e-mail usage (Fulk, Schmitz, and Steinfield 1990). This contradicted the conventional wisdom that managers' choice of appropriate media (based on its richness[10]) influences their performance. Markus showed that media richness theory is a poor predictor of either managers' choices or how these choices correlate with their job performance.

Papers without any contradiction, but where a synergy exists between the results of the mixed methods. Sabherwal and Robey (1995) independently tested two theories, based on field studies of fifty system implementation projects. Although both the variance and process theories they developed were grounded in the same set of case studies, Sabherwal and Robey concurrently developed a quantitatively-oriented variance theory, which emphasized the *amount* of involvement by various stakeholders during implementation, as well as a qualitative process theory, which emphasized the sequences of events that occurred during system implementation.[11] The qualitative data were then analyzed using optimal matching, a quantitative analytic technique. Rather than generating contradictory results, the qualitative and quantitative analyses were consistent with each other, but the independent analyses from the two theories were jointly combined to create a more powerful, *synergistic* theory than that possible with either method alone: "To demonstrate the benefits of joint applications of both [research] strategies, we also provided interpretations that could only have been drawn from using both together" (Sabherwal and Robey 1995, p. 321).

Papers without any contradiction, and where results are parallel but not synergistic between the mixed methods. Most papers in this category conducted field inter-

---

[10]Markus (1994, p. 505) paraphrased the definition by Daft and Lengel (1986) of media richness as "the ability of information and media to change human understanding, overcome differing conceptual frames of reference, or clarify ambiguous issues in a timely manner."

[11]Note that the distinction between the terms *process* and *variance* theory is not analogous to the distinction between qualitative and quantitative methods – a point that Sabherwal and Robey emphasize in their paper. In this particular study, however, the variance theory utilized quantitatively-coded data, and the process theory utilized qualitative data (based on event listings). The qualitative data were used to generate a process theory, and this theory was tested through optimal matching – a computerized quantitative analysis method based on dynamic programming. Although their analysis of the process theory has both qualitative and quantitative aspects, the study is included because it met the definition of mixed methods used here: both qualitative and quantitative data were presented and analyzed.

views or observations as a precursor to administering a survey. For example, Brown and Magill (1994) developed case studies of six firms, examining the drivers of a firm's decision to centralize or decentralize its IS function. The authors also collected survey data from the same companies to capture the beliefs of additional respondents regarding the relationship between these drivers and structural decisions. Their findings included analyses of both types of data – which were consistent with each other – but did not involve a synergy. Their paper is labeled as having *parallel results* because the data from both methods were consistent with each other.

As these papers were analyzed to understand whether the authors identified a contradiction and also how they attempted to integrate the two sets of findings, a second important distinction was identified: whether the authors collected and analyzed the two sets of data independently of each other or sequentially. In conducting the study, mixed quantitative and qualitative data may have been collected and analyzed *independently*, with a separate researcher (or separate teams of researchers) collecting and analyzing each set of data. Alternatively, the process of collecting and analyzing the two sets of data may have been *sequential*, that is, where use of one method preceded the other, and hence the insights from one set of findings (e.g., qualitative data) were available for the researcher to elaborate upon or refute with the second method (e.g., quantitative analysis).[12] This distinction between independent and sequential data collection and analysis was used as a second criterion with which to classify the same set of papers. The dimension is labeled the *process* of analyzing mixed methods data. Using this new criterion as one dimension and the rows of Table 2 as a second dimension, these papers were classified into a two-dimensional matrix (see Table 3). Most papers followed a sequential process for collecting and analyzing the data (twelve papers), but four studies analyzed the data independently. Each of these approaches to combining qualitative and quantitative data is discussed below.

5 RESEARCH EMPLOYING MIXED METHODS *INDEPENDENTLY*

In the studies that used mixed methods independently, there was emphasis on the importance of the two sets of data in generating a synergy, whether or not a contradiction was identified. Not only were the findings that emerged from the independent quantitative and qualitative analyses interesting when compared with each other, but the authors stated that the integration between both sets of results was critical in producing the study's insights. The papers that used both methods independently

---

[12]Other researchers have used terms such as *joint, concurrent*, and *separate* to describe research in which the qualitative and quantitative data were collected and analyzed independently (Sabherwal and Robey 1995; Maxwell 1993). Studies where the two sets of data were iteratively analyzed are also classified as *sequential*, for reasons of simplicity.

Table 3 Classification of Mixed Methods Studies.

	PROCESS **OF CONDUCTING MIXED METHODS RESEARCH**	
	Independent	***Sequential***
Contradictions that appear within a study due to use of mixed methods	Kaplan and Duchon (1988) Wynekoop (1992)	*no studies found*
Contradictions that appear within a study but which were identified based on a single method alone	*no studies found*	Barley (1986) Liker, Roitman and Roskies (1987) Kraut, Dumais and Koch (1989) Barley (1990) Zack and McKenney (1995)
***OUTCOMES* OF MIXED METHODS RESEARCH**		
Contradictions among studies No inherent contradiction but some results are inconsistent with prior studies.	*no studies found*	Markus (1994)
Papers without a contradiction but where a synergy exists between the results of the mixed methods	Blanton, Watson and Moody (1992) Sabherwal and Robey (1995)	*no studies found*
Papers without a contradiction and where the results are parallel but not synergistic between the mixed methods	*no studies found*	Jobber et al. (1989) Moynihan (1990) Deans et al. (1991) Trauth, Farwell and Lee (1993) Leidner and Jarvenpaa (1993) Brown and Magill (1994)

generated novel constructs or theories which required the integration of the qualitative and quantitative findings, either to resolve an inherent contradiction between the results from the two analyses (Kaplan and Duchon 1988; Wynekoop 1992) or to provide a synergistic theory which integrated the separate results (Blanton, Watson and Moody 1992; Sabherwal and Robey 1995).[13]

What is it about employing independent data analyses that leads to theoretical conclusions which draw upon both sets of data synergistically? Is there something about the process of independently collecting and analyzing two sets of data before combining them which actually increases the likelihood of significant theoretical contributions? These questions are explored by examining authors' statements about the importance of the independent analyses in providing their study's insights. These researchers suggest that, had they known about the one set of findings before undertaking the other analysis, their insights might not have been so rich – or so trustworthy.

First, Kaplan and Duchon (1988, p. 582) argued

> Our tenacity in holding to our initial independent analyses of the different data...and the increased respect each of us developed for the other's approach, in fact, were positive aspects of our research....A strong determination to accommodate each approach and to reconcile apparently conflicting data resulted in an interpretation that synthesized the evidence.

Consider Wynekoop's (1992, p. 187) statement that "Case studies were written from information gathered through semi-structured interviews...*before* the quantitative analysis was undertaken. Quantitative and qualitative data were analyzed *independently* and synthesized *only after* separate findings and conclusions had been reached" (emphasis added).

Sabherwal and Robey (1995) stated that they conducted their qualitative and quantitative analyses independently or "jointly." They specifically designed the research process to

> implement the two strategies independently, making sure to avoid any overlaps between them....This method [joint application] is perhaps the most powerful way of combining...[different research] strategies because it preserves the distinctive strengths of both strategies by using them *independently* before combining their insights. Reconciliation of the different strategies using this method does not blur the important distinctions between them and offers potential synergy in interpreting results. [Sabherwal and Robey 1995, pp. 308, 323]

---

[13]Even some of the titles of these papers emphasize the integration between both methods: "Combining Qualitative and Quantitative Methods in IS Research: A Case Study" (Kaplan and Duchon 1988) and "Strategies for Implementation Research: Combining Research Methods" (Wynekoop 1992).

Taken as a whole, the studies where researchers independently analyzed qualitative and quantitative data generated novel theoretical constructs: *work orientation* (Kaplan and Duchon 1988), *accurate and complete communication* (Wynekoop 1992), and the importance of both the *level* of participation and the *timing* of various stakeholders' actions during system implementation (Sabherwal and Robey 1995). Each of these novel constructs was developed to integrate the two sets of findings, whether to explain an inherent contradiction between the two sets of findings or to develop a synergy between the data. In fact, these novel constructs, which emerged from the research, were later elaborated in subsequent research, such as the importance of CASE tool adopters' *work orientation* to their acceptance of the technology (Orlikowski 1989, 1993), and the problems associated with not receiving accurate and complete communication about a technology (Griffith and Northcraft 1996).

6 STUDIES EMPLOYING MIXED METHODS SEQUENTIALLY

Turning now to the *sequential* process of conducting mixed methods research, twelve studies were identified in which the researchers collected and analyzed the qualitative and quantitative data sequentially. In most cases, these papers employed a traditional sequence of conducting interviews or observations prior to developing and administering a survey (although there were some exceptions where the survey data were collected first). Each paper's abstract, introduction, discussion and conclusion section was examined for any articulation of the relationship between the study's mixed methodology and its theoretical findings. Although all studies in the *sequential* category employed both qualitative and quantitative data collection and analysis, the importance of triangulating between the two sets of data was not emphasized in these papers. Indeed, it was possible that each paper's theoretical insights could have been reached on the basis of either the qualitative data or the quantitative data alone.

7 DISCUSSION

The prior examples showed that studies employing mixed methods *sequentially* neither generated inherent contradictions between the results from the two methods of the study nor strongly emphasized the need to integrate the findings resulting from the two methods. Why has less attention been focused on the opportunity or the need to integrate findings for those papers that employed mixed methods *sequentially*, compared to those studies employing them *independently*? Are the findings of the independent mixed methods studies truly more significant than the sequential studies, or have the authors chosen to emphasize the importance of independent analysis in generating their conclusions?

The evidence above suggests a possible connection between the process and the outcomes of mixed methods research: independent mixed methods studies appear to be associated with an integration of the qualitative and quantitative findings, perhaps by not constraining one analysis (e.g., quantitative) by the findings that emerged from the other analysis (e.g., qualitative). In examining the factors that influence whether "stories converge," Kidder and Fine (1987, p. 55) argued that "the independent conduct of qualitative and quantitative evaluations is a greater challenge for triangulation, but it also holds promise for greater discovery."

The above examples and statements from researchers demonstrated their belief that independent mixed methods research can lead to greater synergies between the two sets of data, and possibly to more significant contributions, compared to sequential mixed methods research. The underlying mechanism between the two approaches for combining qualitative and quantitative data and their outcomes, however, is still unclear: why does independent analysis have this "promise for greater discovery"? Given the asymmetric patterns of studies in Table 3, it is obvious that *some* relationship exists between the two dimensions of the framework, but what is the nature of this relationship?

This relationship between the process and the outcomes of mixed methods research may be partially explained by Davis' (1971) argument that research which is considered *interesting* by readers is that which develops and then resolves a contradiction. The use of mixed methods independently may be more likely to generate *inherent* contradictions between the two sets of results within a single study, whereas sequential mixed methods studies may generate other types of unexpected findings, but not contradictions between two methods used in the same study. This is because when research collects and analyzes data using two methods independently, the findings are more likely to diverge or to contradict each other – at least initially. In contrast, when researchers collect and analyze two types of data sequentially, they have the opportunity to modify their procedures or to focus their analyses to ensure that their results more consistent, thus decreasing the likelihood of finding inherent contradictions. Inherent contradictions between two methods in the same study are one type of contradiction which, if resolved, lead to more interesting and significant findings (Davis 1971; Poole and Van de Ven 1989; Robey 1995). Davis' argument about the antecedents of interesting research is, at best, a partial explanation for why independent mixed methods research is more likely to lead to significant findings. There are, of course, other types of contradictions that may occur, as shown in Table 3 (rows 2 and 3).

8 DO INTERESTING FINDINGS LEAD TO CLAIMS OF METHOD INDEPENDENCE?

So far, it has been hypothesized that research which employs mixed methods independently is more likely to generate results that require integration across the two sets of data, compared to sequential mixed methods research. In examining this claim, however, note that the implicit direction of causality runs from the *process* of collecting and analyzing the data (independent or sequential mixed methods) to the study's *outcomes*, in terms of synergy across the two types of data. A rethinking of this association between the two dimensions of the framework (Table 3) raises the possibility that the true "causal link" between them runs in the opposite direction. Instead of the research process (independent or sequential) leading to more significant findings, it may be that the nature of the findings influences how researchers choose to frame the research process – either independent or sequential analysis of the data.[14]

---

[14]*Due to the speculative nature of the following material, the program co-chair, Allen Lee, recommended that it be removed from the main body of the paper. Although some examples of independent mixed method research have been presented, the issues raised in here go beyond the available data, posing questions that may only be answered with further research.*

One possibility is that researchers emphasize their independent use of mixed methods as a type of impression management to persuade the reader that their conclusions are more reliable because they are based on independent corroboration. For example, it may be that where an integration or synergy between the qualitative and quantitative findings is required to explain the study's results, researchers attempt to persuade readers of the independence of the two sets of findings in order to refute the notion that the insights from one analysis (i.e., quantitative) may have biased the other (i.e., qualitative). Conversely, where no such integration between the two sets of findings is necessary to understand the study's theoretical contributions, authors may portray their data analysis as being sequential, or not bother to mention the timing of the analyses at all. In the latter case, authors may even downplay one set of results, by treating one method as merely "subordinate or supplementary" to the other (Maxwell 1993).

Is it the case that some researchers engage in "impression management" by stressing the independent analyses of their data to persuade readers of the lack of bias in their findings? The quotes from the authors who independently employed mixed methods show that they do strongly emphasize the independent nature of their qualitative and quantitative analyses as a critical element in generating the paper's conclusions. Claiming that these analyses were conducted independently appears to add rhetorical force to the conclusions, even when the two types of data analysis (quantitative and qualitative) may have overlapped and provided insights for each other.

It may be that researchers believe that when one set of data (e.g., survey data) is analyzed after knowing the results from the other analysis (e.g., qualitative) their findings may be somehow tainted or less reliable. There also appears to be an implicit concern that the admission of sequential analysis may undermine readers' confidence in the findings, since researchers themselves believe that, when analyzing two sets of data, the results from one type of analysis may influence the other. Kidder and Fine (1987, p. 66) state that "We suspect that any researcher is more motivated to find agreement across conclusions within his or her study than are two or more researchers working independently."

This paper has focused on combining qualitative and quantitative research methods, without making any assumptions about the researchers' epistemological stance (positivist or interpretivist); however, the assumption that "independent" validation of results is necessary and valuable is itself a positivist tenet. The very concept of independent analysis and verification is a mainstay of positivist research, designed to ensure the reliability and convergent validity of findings. In contrast, interpretive researchers use a variety of other techniques to persuade readers of attributes such as "plausibility, criticality, and authenticity" (Golden-Biddle and Locke 1993), but not the accuracy or reliability of their findings. Despite

This raises the possibility that the nature of the findings and conclusions in the paper may lead researchers to emphasize the independent nature of their research process. For example, studies that require an integration or synergy between the results of mixed methods may be more often portrayed as using mixed methods independently, rather than sequentially.

This provides a possible explanation for why there were no studies that correspond to the lower left cell in Table 3 (parallel findings based upon independent analyses). This cell implies a weaker set of findings, since it represents consistency – but no synergy – between the two sets of results. The absence of papers in this cell may be explained by the authors' decision 1) to reframe the results to highlight the synergy or contradictions between the two sets of data (moving up to another row on the left side of the framework), 2) to describe the research process as sequential, or 3) to publish the results as a single-methodology study, thus slighting one set of methods and results. Several examples of the latter case were found – where the authors used both methods to collect their data, but then omitted any analysis of either the quantitative data (Leonard-Barton 1990; Tyran et al. 1992) or qualitative data (Smith, Milberg and Burke 1996). This is consistent with Jick's argument that researchers often publish their results in such a way that one research method and its results are omitted (Jick 1979; Konsynski 1993).

> It is probable that the triangulation approach is embedded in many doctoral theses that, when *packaged* into articles, tend to highlight only the quantitative methods....Moreover, journals tend to specialize by methodology, thus encouraging purity of method. [Jick 1979, p. 604-605]

Such studies, when published, would thus not appear to have employed mixed methods at all and would not be included in this paper's literature review or framework (Table 3).

9 CONCLUSION

This paper has shown that studies that employ mixed quantitative and qualitative methods are not homogenous, but differ on two dimensions: the process of combining the two methods and the study's outcomes. There is value in conducting mixed methods research, whether the two methods are combined sequentially or independently. Although there appears to be an assumption held by researchers that independent analyses of such data generate more reliable findings, this assumption requires more in-depth examination. Given the greater number of studies which combine mixed methods sequentially, this indicates that the sequential approach has certain benefits to researchers. Sequential mixed methods research allows researchers to collect qualitative data either in anticipation of or following a quantitative study. Such a process permits researchers to gain insight into the organizational and histori-

---

employing research methods which were qualitative (and often grounded in interpretivist assumptions), some researchers may believe that their results are more convincing to readers if these results are framed as resulting from independent analyses.

cal context within which the quantitative variables are captured, whether the qualitative data is collected prior to the quantitative data (common in IS studies), or subsequently (Trend 1979; Sutton and Rafaeli 1986). Sequential mixed methods research has the advantage that the researchers can modify their procedures, assumptions, propositions and even their research sites, based upon the first set of results. The disadvantage of independent mixed methods research is that it does not permit such refinements to the propositions and data collection procedures since, in principle, the results from one set of data are not available for the other method to exploit. Perhaps the greatest risk of independent mixed methods research is "not so much that the methods will produce contradictory conclusions as that they will simply diverge – leading to noncomparable rather than incompatible ends" (Kidder and Fine 1987, p. 64). Given these potential risks of independent analyses, the offsetting advantages are the fact that the qualitative and quantitative analyses are not constrained by each other and the presumed greater plausibility of the results. The grounds for this latter assumption, however, are called into question by this paper and require further analysis to identify whether they are supported.

Advantages of Both Types of Mixed Methods Research. In articulating the conceptual framework in Table 3 and focusing on *differences* among mixed methods studies, this paper has necessarily minimized many common features of all mixed methods studies. Mixed methods studies do share certain characteristics. One advantage of mixed methods studies is the opportunity to gather mixed-*level* data, which can be especially beneficial for linking the individual to the organizational level of analysis. Particularly in studying the effect of new technologies on organizations, such a mixed-level approach can provide benefits. According to Markus and Robey (1988, p. 594):

> Technologies such as office automation are neither strictly micro nor macro in character....We believe that mixing levels of analysis may be useful in research and theory on IT and organizational change....Mixed-level research should abound in an interdisciplinary field where mixed-level phenomena are the inevitable subject of study.

There is a clear advantage for researchers studying the impact of IT on organizations to evaluate a technology's influence on micro-level processes before analyzing its ultimate influence on macro processes, as Barley's research demonstrated (1986, 1990). When researchers choose only a single method and single level of analysis to understand IT impacts, problems may result; for example, using firm-level surveys to evaluate IT's impacts at the organizational level, while ignoring changes in micro-level processes that underlie these macro-level changes (Markus and Robey 1988; Leavitt and Whisler 1958).[15]

---

[15]The benefits of mixed-*level* theory are not always present in mixed *method* studies. Employing mixed methods is neither necessary nor sufficient to ensure mixed-*level* studies. For example, mixed methods may be used so that quantitative and qualitative data may be collected at a single level (e.g., at the company level only). Conversely, if mixed-level theory is the objective, it may be achieved through other means than mixed-method research, for

A second advantage of mixed methods research is that it has the possibility of reaching both positivist and interpretivist researchers. To positivist researchers, it offers a way of triangulating on multiple perspectives – a technique with a long tradition in the positivist literature (Campbell and Fiske 1959). To qualitative and interpretivist researchers, it offers the opportunity to collect quantitative data to corroborate their field studies. Given these potential benefits of mixed methods research, we return to the earlier observation that mixed quantitative and qualitative research continues to be scarce. Only 1.9% of published IS studies across a set of leading journals were found to meet the definition of mixed quantitative and qualitative research. Some researchers believe that the research question should dictate the appropriate methods to use and, by extension, that the paucity of mixed methods studies proves that few research questions will benefit from mixed methods. This justification for the scarcity of mixed methods studies is too simplistic. Rather than assuming that the research problem determines the methodology to be followed, an alternative model, such as the "garbage can model" of the research process reverses the direction of causality, claiming that personal preferences, such as "methodological considerations often determine which theoretical problems are addressed" (Martin 1982, p. 30). This "garbage can model" suggests that the researcher's choice of a particular methodology, as well as other "personal concerns of the researcher" (Grady and Wallston 1988; Maxwell 1996), will shape the topics that researchers choose to study, and not vice-versa. This argument suggests that there are obstacles posed by mixed methods research that cause researchers to avoid questions that might benefit from their use, and not a scarcity of suitable research questions that would profit from mixed methods research.

Challenges of Using Mixed Methods. Beyond the obvious challenges, such as the time and expense of collecting and analyzing two sets of data, one important obstacle is researcher training, since the disciplinary preparation of researchers is likely to favor one research paradigm and its associated methods over another (Cook and Reichardt 1979). Even if researchers have learned how to collect and analyze data through both methods, performing the triangulation analysis can be difficult. The real challenge often begins when both analyses are completed and found to contradict each other, and many studies that analyze both types of data often fail to explain how the triangulation analysis was actually conducted (Jick 1979).

Limitations of this study. There are certainly limitations to this work. The framework developed here is preliminary, both in terms of the dimensions of the framework (Table 3) and also the classification of papers into its cells. The review of the IS literature included only four U.S.-based publications. It is possible that different conclusions would be drawn if the literature review included European IS publications, or even another sample of U.S. publications. Further research based on a

---

example, through research employing a single method to generate data at multiple levels (e.g., analyzing archival data at the individual, the workgroup, or the company level).

broader set of journals should be conducted to evaluate both the evidence for the scarcity of mixed methods research and the classification of these articles into a theoretical framework.

Further elaboration is also possible on the argument that researchers, when seeking to persuade readers of the significance of their findings, will attempt to convince them of the independence of their analyses. The argument raised here that researchers engage in impression management is novel, but it is supported only with evidence from the authors' perspective and should be supplemented with evidence from the perspective of readers and journal editors. For example, it may be possible to identify biases in readers' perception and judgment that predispose them to be more strongly convinced by mixed methods studies only if the results were generated by independent analyses. Perhaps cognitive studies of how readers evaluate the plausibility of research conclusions can explain why they are less trusting of studies when collection and analysis of one set of data sequentially preceded the other. A deeper understanding of this phenomenon from a cognitive psychology perspective may explain why researchers frame their studies as having followed a certain process.

Although the IFIP 8.2 community has long been one forum for criticizing the preponderance of quantitative, positivist methods, it is also likely to be the strongest channel for broadening the scope of research approaches in IS journals. Like our predecessors who have called for methodological pluralism, my focus on the contributions of mixed methods studies is not intended to replace any other approach, but instead to highlight its unique challenges and benefits. Without expecting to "win over" researchers from the dominant quantitative, positivist tradition or those steeped in purely qualitative research traditions, the belief here is that there are potential benefits to IS researchers in understanding the value of mixed methods in advancing theory development. The objective is that a better awareness of mixed methods research, as an alternative approach, can inform and influence both mainstream quantitative researchers and the increasingly visible qualitative research community (Walsham 1995) in the same way that any minority view normally influences the outlook of the dominant majority. Social psychology research on the effects of minority perspectives on the majority group's information-seeking and decision-making behaviors were summarized by Nemeth (1986), "Minority viewpoints are important, not because they tend to prevail but because they stimulate divergent attention and thought. As a result...they contribute to the detection of novel solutions and decisions that, on balance, are qualitatively better."

10 ACKNOWLEDGMENTS

I wish to thank Allen Lee, Wanda Orlikowski, Jon Turner, and three anonymous reviewers for many helpful suggestions on previous drafts of the paper. I also wish to thank Sivakumar Viswanathan of New York University for his assistance in conducting the literature review.

11 REFERENCES

Barley, S. R. (1986). "Technology as an Occasional for Structuring: Evidence from Observations of CT Scanners and the Social Order of Radiology Departments." *Administrative Science Quarterly*, Volume 31, pp. 78-108.

Barley, S. R. (1990). "The Alignment of Technology and Structure through Roles and Networks." *Administrative Sciences Quarterly*, Volume 36, pp. 61-103.

Benbasat, I. (1984). "An Analysis of Research Methodologies." In W. McFarlan (Editor), *Harvard Colloquium on Information Systems Research.* Cambridge, Massachusetts: Harvard University Press, pp. 47-88.

Benbasat, I.; Goldstein, D. K.; and Mead, M. (1987). "The Case Research Strategy in Studies of Information Systems." *MIS Quarterly*, Volume 11, Number 3, pp. 369-386.

Blanton, J. E.; Watson, H. J.; and Moody, J. (1992). "Toward a Better Understanding of Information Technology Organization: A Comparative Case Study." *MIS Quarterly*, Volume 16, Number 4, pp. 531-555.

Brown, C. V., and Magill, S. L. (1994). "Alignment of the IS Functions with the Enterprise: Toward a Model of Antecedents." *MIS Quarterly*, Volume 18, Number 4, pp. 371-397.

Campbell, D. T., and Fiske, D. W. (1959). "Convergent and Discriminant Validation by the Multi-trait -Multi-method Matrix." *Psychological Bulletin*, Volume 56, pp. 8-105.

Cook, T. D., and Reichardt, D. S. (1970). *Quantitative and Qualitative Methods in Evaluation Research.* Newbury Park, California: Sage Press.

Daft, R. L., and Lengel, R. H. (1986). "A Proposed Integration among Organizational Information Requirements, Media Richness, and Structural Design." *Management Science*, Volume 32, Number 5, pp. 191-233.

Daft, R. L.; Lengel, R. H.; and Trevino, L. K. (1987). "Message Equivocality, Media Selection and Manager Performance: Implications for Information Systems." *MIS Quarterly*, Volume 11, Number 3, pp. 355-366.

Davis, M. S. (1971). "That's Interesting! Towards a Phenomenology of Sociology and a Sociology of Phenomenology." *Philosophy of Social Science*, Volume 1, pp. 309-344.

Deans, P. C.; Karwan, K. R.; Goslar, M. D.; Ricks, D. A.; and Toyne, B. (1991). "Identification of Key International Information Systems Issues in U.S.-Based Multinational Corporations." *Journal of Management Information Systems*, Volume 7, Number 4, pp. 27-50.

Denzin, N. K. (1978). *The Research Act*, Second Edition. New York: McGraw-Hill.

DeGross, J. I.; Bostrom, R. P.; and Robey, D. (Editors) (1993). *Proceedings of the Fourteenth International Conference on Information Systems.* Orlando, Florida.

Earl, M. (1993). "Experiences in Strategic Information Systems Planning." *MIS Quarterly,* Volume 17, Number 1, pp. 1-24.

Eisenhardt, K. M. (1989). "Building Theories from Case Study Research." *Academy of Management Review,* Volume 14, Number 4, pp. 532-550.

Finlay, P. N., and Mitchell, A. (1994). "Perceptions of the Benefits From the Introduction of CASE: An Empirical Study." *MIS Quarterly,* Volume 18, Number 4, pp. 353-369.

Fitzgerald, G.; Hirschheim, R.; Mumford, E.; and Wood-Harper, T. (1985). "Information Systems Research Methodology: An Introduction to the Debate." In E. Mumford, R. Hirschheim, G. Fitzgerald and T. Wood-Harper (Editors), *Research Methods in Information Systems.* Amsterdam: North-Holland, pp. 3-12.

Fulk, J.; Schmitz, J.; and Steinfield, C. (1990). "A Social Influence Model of Technology Use." in J. Fulk and C. Steinfield (Editors), *Organizations and Communication Technology.* Newbury Park, California: Sage Press, pp. 117-140.

Golden-Biddle, K., and Locke, K. (1993). "Appealing Work: An Investigation of How Ethnographic Texts Convince." *Organization Science,* Volume 4, Number 4, pp. 595-616.

Grady, K. A., and Wallston, B. S. (1988). *Research in Health Care Settings.* Newbury Park, California: Sage Press.

Grant, R. A., and Higgins, C. A. (1991). "The Impact of Computerized Performance Monitoring on Service Work: Testing a Causal Model." *Information Systems Research,* Volume 2, Number 2, pp. 116-142.

Griffith, T. L., and Northcraft, G. B. (1996). "Cognitive Elements in the Implementation of New Technology: Can Less Information Provide More Benefits?" *MIS Quarterly,* Volume 20, Number 1, pp. 99-110.

Hackman, J. R., and Oldham, G. (1980). *Work Design.* Reading, Massachusetts: Addison-Wesley.

Ives, B., and Olson, M. H. (1984). "User Involvement and MIS Success: A Review of Research." *Management Science,* Volume 30, Number 5, pp. 586-603.

Jarvenpaa, S., and Ives, B. (1991). "Executive Involvement and Participation in the Management of Information Technology." *MIS Quarterly,* Volume 15, Number 2, pp. 205-228.

Jick, T. (1979). "Triangulating on Mixing Qualitative and Quantitative Methods: Triangulation in Action." *Administrative Science Quarterly,* Volume 24, pp. 602-611.

Jobber, D.; Saunders, J.; Gilding, B.; Hooley, G.; and Hatton-Smoker, J. (1989). "Assessing the Value of a Quality Assurance Certificate for Software: An Exploratory Investigation." *MIS Quarterly,* Volume 13, Number 1, pp. 19-31.

Kaplan, B., and Duchon, D. (1988). "Combining Qualitative and Quantitative Methods in Information Systems Research: A Case Study." *MIS Quarterly,* Volume 12, Number 4, pp. 571-586.

Kidder, L., and Fine, M. (1987). "Qualitative and Quantitative Methods: When Stories Converge." In M. M. Mark and R. L. Shotland (Editors), *Multiple Methods in Program Evaluation.* San Francisco: Jossey-Bass, pp. 57-76.

Konsynski, B. R. (1993). "A Perspective on the 'Case Study Approach' in Evaluating the Business Value of Information Technology." In R. D. Banker, R. J. Kauffman, and M. Mahmood (Editors), *Strategic Information Technology Management.* Harrisburg, Pennsylvania: Idea Group Publishing, pp. 15-24.

Kraut, R.; Dumais, S.; and Koch, S. (1989). "Computerization, Productivity and the Quality of Work Life." *Communications of the ACM*, Volume 32, Number 2, pp. 220-238.

Lacity, M. C., and Janson, M. (1994). "Understanding Qualitative Data: A Framework of Text Analysis Methods." *Journal of Management Information Systems*, Volume 11, Number 2, pp. 137-155.

Lee, A. S. (1989). "A Scientific Methodology for MIS Case Studies." *MIS Quarterly,* Volume 13, Number 1, pp. 33-50.

Lee, A. S. (1991). "Integrating Positivist and Interpretivist Research Approaches: Approaches to Organizational Research." *Organization Science*, Volume 2, Number 4, pp. 342-365.

Leidner, D. E., and Jarvenpaa, S. L. (1993). "The Information Age Confronts Education: Case Studies on Electronic Classrooms." *Information Systems Research*, Volume 4, Number 1, pp. 24-54.

Leonard-Barton, D. (1990). "A Dual Methodology for Case Studies: Synergistic Use of a Longitudinal Single Site with Replicated Multiple Sites." *Organization Science,* Volume 1, Number 3, pp. 248-266.

Leavitt, H. J., and Whisler, T. L. (1958). "Management in the 1980s." *Harvard Business Review*, November-December, pp. 41-48.

Liker, J. K.; Roitman, D. B.; and Roskies, E. (1987). "Changing Everything All at Once: Work Life and Technological Change." *Sloan Management Review*, pp. 29-47.

Markus, M. L. (1994). "Electronic Mail as the Medium of Managerial Choice." *Organization Science,* Volume 5, Number 4, pp. 502-527.

Markus, M. L., and Robey, D. (1988). "Information Technology and Organizational Change: Causal Structure in Theory and Research." *Management Science,* Volume 34, pp. 583-598.

Martin, J. (1982). "A Garbage Can Model of the Research Process." In J. McGrath, J. Martin and R. Kulka (Editors), *Judgment Calls in Research.* Beverly Hills: Sage Press, pp. 17-40.

McGrath, J. (1982). "Dilemmatics: The Study of Research Choices and Dilemmas." In J. McGrath, J. Martin, and R. Kulka (Editors), *Judgment Calls in Research.* Beverly Hills: Sage Press, pp. 69-102.

Maxwell, J. A. (1993). "Combining Qualitative and Quantitative Methods." Unpublished manuscript, Harvard University Graduate School of Education.

Maxwell, J. A. (1996). *Qualitative Research Design: An Iterative Approach.* Thousand Oaks, California: Sage Press.

Mohr, L. B. (1982). *Explaining Organizational Behavior.* San Francisco: Jossey-Bass.

Moynihan, T. (1990). "What Chief Executives and Senior Managers Want From Their IT Departments." *MIS Quarterly*, Volume 14, Number 1, pp. 15-26.

Nemeth, C. J. (1986). "Differential Contributions of Majority and Minority Influence." *Psychological Review*, Volume 93, Number 1, pp. 23-32.

Nissen, H-E. (1985). "Acquiring Knowledge of Information Systems Research in a Methodological Quagmire." In E. Mumford, R. Hirschheim, G. Fitzgerald and T. Wood-Harper (Editors), *Research Methods in Information Systems.* Amsterdam: North-Holland, pp. 39-51.

Orlikowski, W. J. (1989). "Division among the Ranks: The Social Implications of CASE Tools for System Developers." In J. I. DeGross, J. C. Henderson, and B. R. Konsynski (Editors), *Proceedings of the Tenth International Conference on Information Systems.* Boston, Massachusetts, pp. 199-210.

Orlikowski, W. J. (1993). "CASE Tools as Organizational Change: Investigating Incremental and Radical Changes in Systems Development." *MIS Quarterly*, Volume 17, Number 3, pp. 309-340.

Orlikowski, W. J. (1996). "Improvising Organization and Transformation Over Time: A Situated Change Perspective." *Information Systems Research*, Volume 17, Number 1, pp. 63-92.

Orlikowski, W. J., and Baroudi, J. J. (1991). "Studying Information Technology in Organizations: Research Approaches and Assumptions." *Information Systems Research*, Volume 2, Number 1, pp. 1-28.

Poole, M. S., and Van de Ven, A. H. (1989). "Using Paradox to Build Management and Organization Theories." *Academy of Management Review*, Volume 14, pp. 562-578.

Reich, B. H., and Benbasat, I. (1996). "Measuring the Linkage Between Business and Information Technology Objectives." *MIS Quarterly*, Volume 20, Number 1, pp. 55-77.

Robey, D. (1995). "Theories that Explain Contradiction: Accounting for the Contradictory Organizational Consequences of Information Technology." In J. I. DeGross, G. Ariav, C. M. Beath, R. W. Hoyer, and C. Kemerer (Editors), *Proceedings of the Sixteenth International Conference on Information Systems.* Amsterdam, The Netherlands, pp. 55-63.

Rogers, E. M. (1983). *Diffusion of Innovations*, Second Edition. New York: Free Press.

Sabherwal, R., and Robey, D. (1995). "Reconciling Variance and Process Strategies for Studying Information System Development." *Information Systems Research*, Volume 6, Number 4, pp. 303-327.

Smith, H. J.; Milberg, S. J.; and Burke, S. J. (1996). "Information Privacy: Measuring Individuals' Concerns about Organizational Practices." *MIS Quarterly*, Volume 20, Number 2, pp. 167-196.

Soh, C., and Markus, M. L. (1995). "How IT Creates Business Value: A Process Theory Synthesis." In J. I. Degross, G. Ariav, C. Beath, R. Hoyer and C. Kemerer (Editors), *Proceedings of the Sixteenth International Conference on Information Systems*. Amsterdam, The Netherlands, pp. 29-41.

Sutton, R. I., and Rafaeli, A. (1986). "Untangling the Relationship between Displayed Emotions and Organizational Sales: The Case of Convenience Stores." *Academy of Management Journal,* Volume 31, Number 3, pp. 461-487.

Trend, M. G. (1979). "On the Reconciliation of Qualitative and Quantitative Analyses: A Case Study." In T. D. Cook and D. S. Reichardt (Editors), *Quantitative and Qualitative Methods in Evaluation Research.* Thousand Oaks, California: Sage Press, pp. 68-86.

Trauth, E. M.; Farwell, D. W.; and Lee, D. (1993). "The IS Expectation Gap: Industry Expectations Versus Academic Preparation." *MIS Quarterly*, Volume 17, Number 3, pp. 293-303.

Tyran, C. K.; Dennis, A. R.; Vogel, D. R.; and Nunamaker Jr., J. F. (1992). "The Application of Electronic Meeting Technology to Support Strategic Management." *MIS Quarterly*, Volume 16, Number 3, pp. 313-334.

Walsham, G. (1995). "The Emergence of Interpretivism in IS Research." *Information Systems Research*, Volume 6, Number 4, pp. 376-394.

Watson, R. T. (1990). "Influence on the IS Manager's Perceptions of Key Issues: Information Scanning and the Relationship With the CEO." *MIS Quarterly*, Volume 14, Number 2, pp. 217-231.

Wynekoop, J. L. (1992). "Strategies for Implementation Research: Combining Research Methods." In J. I. DeGross, J. D. Becker, and J. J. Elam (Editors), *Proceedings of the Thirteenth International Conference on Information Systems*. Dallas, Texas, pp. 185-193.

Wynekoop, J. L., and Conger, S. A. (1991). "A Review of Computer Aided Software Engineering Research Methods." In H-E. Nissen, H. K. Klein and R. Hirschheim (Editors), *Information Systems Research: Contemporary Approaches and Emergent Traditions*. Amsterdam: North-Holland, pp. 301-327.

Wynekoop, J. L., and Russo, N. L. (1993). "System Development Methodologies: Unanswered Questions and the Research-Practice Gap." In J. I. DeGross, R. P. Bostrom, and D. Robey (Editors), *Proceedings of the Fourteenth International Conference on Information Systems*. Orlando, Florida, pp. 181-190.

Yin, R. K. (1994). *Case Study Research: Design and Methods*, Second Edition. Newbury Park, California: Sage Press.

Zack, M. H., and McKenney, J. L. (1995). "Social Context and Interaction in Ongoing Computer-Supported Management Groups." *Organization Science*, Volume 6, Number 4, pp. 394-422.

22

Qualitative Research in Information Systems: Time to be Subjective?

L. Garcia
Department of Social Psychology
London School of Economics and Political Science
London WC2A 2AE, England
Tel: 44 171 955 7695
Fax: 44 171 955 7565
E-mail: l.garcia@lse.ac.uk

F. Quek
Department of Information Systems
London School of Economics and Political Science
London WC2A 2AE, England
Tel: 44 171 955 7403
Fax: 44 171 955 7565
E-mail: f.k.quek@lse.ac.uk

Abstract

The starting point of a researcher's methodological choice within information systems is not so much a problem of how many methods we employ or if those are of a quantitative or a qualitative nature, but the ability to identify the philosophical and theoretical assumptions which leads to the choice of the appropriate methodology. In practice, despite the recognition of the virtues and the role of qualitative methods in information systems research, explicit institutional barriers and implicit functionalistic assumptions within the field have prevented much progress in their application. There is the danger in not recognizing the resulting side-effect where researchers use qualitative methods in a quantitative manner and pass it off as qualitative research. Using qualitative methods implies allowing and acknowledging the subjectivity of the research process, which should be looked upon as a strength rather than as a weakness.

1 INTRODUCTION

This paper is the result of a seemingly impossible (ad)venture. It is a shared reflection about the use of one research paradigm within a field traditionally recognized for the use of another. It has been a common work based on two different cultural, academic and research backgrounds. As such, it has proven difficult and been plagued with obstacles, but at the same time, it has been full of relevant and highly illuminating discussions.

Although sometimes we have fallen into the trap of a "paradigm incommensurability" (Kuhn 1970), i.e., the impossibility of translating different paradigms into each other and assessing results of different paradigms (not only between the two authors, but also between the two topics covered in this conference: qualitative research and information systems), we have followed the tendency to regard at least some debate and discussion between various proponents of paradigms as possible (Reed 1985). We have worked in a metaphorical way,, transferring ideas and associations from one system or level of discourse to another. In this way, each system can be perceived anew from the point of view of the other. In the process, certain aspects have been illuminated whereas others have been shadowed.

We cover three main points in the paper. First, we stress the need for further critical awareness: reviewing what we are importing into the information systems field and why. Borrowing methods is not a simple task and, without critical awareness, runs the danger of the methods becoming stereotyped or distorted. Second, we consider that the direction promoted from the previous conference in 1990 on qualitative research about the quest for methodological pluralism and more alternative approaches, as well as the debate on quantitative versus qualitative methods, is somehow out of focus. The problem of applying research methods within information systems is not so much a problem of how many methods we employ or if those are of a quantitative or a qualitative nature, but rather to achieve a coherence over the whole research process. The starting point is to identify our philosophical and theoretical assumptions which will lead us to the choice of the appropriate methodology. Third, to comment that using qualitative methods implies allowing and acknowledging the subjectivity of the research process. The lack of this allowance leads researchers to use qualitative methods in a quantitative way. Methods developed mainly in a hermeneutic-dialectical school of meta-science are thus used from a logical-empirical perspective, and therefore the proposed paradigm shift is not fully achieved. From this standpoint, it is not appropriate to talk about coherence or rigour in the research process.

2 CRITICAL AWARENESS

In the field of psychology, we learn how a particular philosophical commitment becomes taken for granted within the history of the discipline (Oppenheimer 1954; Danzinger 1979). Issues which should be opened to clarification and public debate are transformed into certainties, producing a cleavage between theory, method and their corresponding philosophical foundations. The consequence is the absence of a debate about philosophical foundations underlying the choice of methods and theory, to such an extent that few within the discipline are concerned with unearthing the assumptions guiding one alternative or another.

This absence of reflection is what Markova (1982) calls "the unjustified generalizations across different subjects." By overlooking the problems, conceptual frameworks or methods of research in different sciences – which are essentially different, crude generalizations – flourish unchallenged. If generalizations on such fundamental issues are possible, why not import successful models? The appropriateness of importing models is not even considered given the general lack of awareness regarding their presuppositions.

As Nissen, Klein and Hirschheim (1991) pointed out, "no field can avoid assumptions on the nature of its research approaches." However, in the domain of science, the importance of acknowledging the presuppositions on which every domain of human existence is based has great significance. Innocence with respect to our existing assumptions in scientific research is clearly associated with potential dangers (Markova 1982). The dangers are diverse but of the same kind. If a scientist is not aware of the foundations of the work, then the scientist is deprived of an occasion to reflect upon his or her actions, and tends to maintain the existing practice without the possibility of considering alternatives.

This seems to be the case regarding information systems. As a field, information systems is a relatively new one without a research tradition that it can claim to be its own. Its research frameworks and techniques are very much borrowed or imported from other disciplines (Bikson 1991). This reliance on a number of different areas for the development of a theoretical framework or research methods and the need to legitimize them has imported assumptions from those disciplines without a reflection upon the emergence of those assumptions or "upon the context within which attempts are made to operationalize them" (Preston 1991). There is no doubt that borrowing theoretical or methodological models from another discipline can lead to important innovations; however, there is the danger that, in doing so, the model becomes stereotyped or distorted.

As Guerreiro-Ramos (1981) suggests, there is an important distinction between the "displacement" and the "misplacement" of a model from its original discipline. The concept of system, for instance, was successfully displaced from its origins in cybernetics to study organizations. According to Guerreiro-Ramos, the misplacement of a model occurs when it is used inappropriately outside its discourse of origin, usually when there is no effort to understand the wider context where the model has been developed and therefore people only select that suit their concrete interests or way of thinking at a particular point in time. Thus, the misplacement occurs when the debates carried out about the different meanings and uses of the model during its historical evolution are not taken into account.

The past decade has seen the information systems field starting to undergo this kind of self-examination, raising philosophical issues associated with doing research in information systems and debating which philosophical traditions should guide work and which could serve as a legitimate basis for grounding research methods (Klein, Hirschheim and Nissen 1991; Preston 1991). There have been calls for a multidisciplinary approach and methodological pluralism, as well as rigor and relevance in research (Nissen, Klein and Hirschheim 1991).

Developing pluralism in information systems research has received increasing support. It is expected that the use of multiple methods to correspond with the complexity of research investigations will allow the apprehension of the different aspects involved in the constitution of the object under investigation. The concern is about the adoption of more and newer methodologies in order to better explore the object of study and how rigorous the use of those methodologies. The concern with more methods or more methodological rigor in a discipline is not ill-placed but it can disguise an absence of theoretical elaboration (Elejabarrieta 1990). As Baskerville (1996) points out, it is like "leaning against the lamppost for support rather than for illumination." While adopting new methodologies may contribute to the general development of the field, they are still used as a "comfort factor" to reassure the participants that proper practices are being followed to cope with the complexity associated with the field.

In a sense, this "need" of using more and "better accurate" methods in order to develop the field mirrors the Enlightenment notion of human betterment developed in social sciences, that with improved knowledge about our world (or about the object of study) and increased abilities to make rational decisions (on which is the best method), we will be able to design a world fit to live in.

3 STARTING POINT OF METHODOLOGICAL CHOICE

Historically, information systems research inherited the natural sciences paradigm (Mumford 1991) and, as a consequence, there are a number of underlying problems associated with information systems research (Cooper 1988). The major criticism in the past was that research tends to be dominated by scientific approaches (Nissen 1985; Mumford 1991). The models borrowed from natural sciences, suited to science laboratories, were transferred directly to information systems (Galliers and Land 1987) in an attempt to gain recognition and legitimization as a research area (Backhouse, Liebenau and Land 1991). However, they have proven to be "almost always doomed to fail" (Galliers and Land 1987).

This background was borne out of the fact that information systems as a field has its origins in business schools in North America, where there has always been a tradition of functionalist and positivist approach (Orlikowski 1991). Promotion and tenure, which concerns a researcher's career, has a formula which is entrenched in doing the right type of research and publishing in the right type of journals. Academic respectability implies an approach to treat research as a science, with much of the effort placed on laboratory-based experimentation or on field surveys (Vogel and Wetherbe 1984). This seems to be "part of the American system of academic statuses" (Kling 1991, pp 738), and as a consequence, has contributed to the deeply rooted positivistic tradition in information systems research. Another example of this kind of institutional constraint is the doctoral program that follows the American model. There is certainly a divide between America and Europe in terms of the emphasis on traditional research methods in the doctoral curriculum. Much debates have surfaced about the virtues and shortcomings of this model.

However, the 1984 conference on qualitative research – precursor to the 1990 conference in Copenhagen – questioned the traditional approaches to research and criticized the so-called scientific method not only for its emphasis on quantification but also for the commitment among some researchers to a narrow paradigm that "assumes away much of the richness and complexity of information systems"(Weill and Olson 1989). As a result, we are beginning to see research that covers other areas of the information systems spectrum, from purely technical perspectives of systems design and implementation, to social perspectives of the structural and social consequences of information systems at the individual, organizational, and societal levels. The growing recognition and popularity of the information systems field as multidisciplinary within the social sciences and the humanities (Olaisen 1991) has opened the doors for the softer approaches (or qualitative approaches) and the use of methodologies imported from those fields. Currently, the field is still at the theory-building stage (Madon 1994), and the objective seems to be a search for increased understanding of the information systems phenomena in order to strengthen its theoretical base.

It can be said that there is an attempt to change paradigms, to perceive information systems not as a field that covers only the technical and measurable aspects but also the context within which the information system is being developed. Researchers in the field have started to rely on other disciplines from the social sciences to throw light on the problems faced by those designing and implementing information systems in a variety of organizational contexts (Backhouse, Liebenau and Land 1991). This involves being able to interpret or decipher the social phenomenon's basic characteristics. The social sciences may help in this endeavor since they have developed ways of seeing (or creatively discovering) some of those characteristics in a meaningful manner (Alvesson 1995).

However, its uptake in mainstream information systems research is scarce, or somehow misguided. So far, research in information systems is synonymous with the study of advanced quantitative procedures, with the emphasis on the development of a methodology scholar expertly versed in the knowledge and use of such procedures (Olaisen 1991). Alternative approaches such as action research, critical research, interpretivism and semiotics are rare.

The main criticism against traditional methods in favor of methodological pluralism and alternative approaches is that the research problems are looked at using the scientific paradigm as a base (Klein and Lyytinen 1985). Methodological bias in research has been reported in the information systems literature, between 50% and 90% of published material uses only three methods (laboratory experimentation, surveys and case studies) (Cash and Nunamaker 1989, 1990, 1991; Orlikowski and Baroudi 1990; Vogel and Wetherbe 1984). This led Klein, Hirschheim and Nissen to comment that "the most commonly held attitude in the information systems research community is not methodological pluralism, but the belief in the supremacy of a particular set of methodological postulates favoring certain methods and discriminating against others."

Morgan and Smircich (1980) propose that we look at other research modes for established frameworks of observation that can offer a unique range of insights unobtainable by existing methods, such as one that constitutes a specific hermeneutic mode located at the subjective end of the spectrum. However as Mumford (1991) quite rightly pointed out, we should avoid creating a situation whereby researchers either take the quantification route for its own sake, or undertake qualitative research simply to avoid handling numerical data.

This often opens up the debate on quantitative methods versus qualitative methods. Such debates have been at the center of much controversy in both the social and the natural sciences. Most of the time the discussion equates qualitative methodologies with positivistic postulates and qualitative methods as the monopoly of those who criticize those methods. In our view, this is an inadequate way of discussing the issue. The relationship between qualitative and quantitative is not a static one. Frequently, quantity and quality feed back into one another. The chasm between quantitative and qualitative techniques seems to be associated with a tradition of conducting research where the imperative of measurement displaced a concern with theory. The content of theoretical presuppositions can remain unclear under the formulation of hypothesis that, through sophisticated statistical methods, acquire the value of scientific findings. There is no doubt that those practices should be criticized, but the critique should not be out of focus.

Quantitative techniques have been extremely useful in identifying specific phenomena. Moreover there will always be research that relies on a heavy emphasis on use of statistical analysis, with the consequent need for exact measurement of the factors being studied. The question is not whether quantitative techniques can offer the researchers what qualitative techniques cannot and vice versa, but rather on the theoretical and philosophical assumptions that guide the research and therefore determine which methodology one uses. We argue that it is necessary to qualify the use of specific techniques in both the underlying assumptions guiding the research and in the theoretical framework.

4 THE OBJECT OF STUDY

As within many other fields, the origins of the methodological debate in information systems can be found in the difficulties encountered in identifying the object of study (Kuutti 1996). Nissen, Klein and Hirschheim point out that the discussion should be centered around two basic issues: "i) the nature of what is investigated (ontology) and ii) the nature of human knowledge and understanding that can possibly be acquired through different types of research and the appropriateness of the methods of investigation (epistemology)." These two issues may be distinct but in our view they are nevertheless interrelated.

Information systems research has been said to be about the study of improving the effectiveness of information systems design, implementation and use in organizations, and to assess their impact on individuals, organizations and society at large (Keen 1987; Baskerville and Wood-Harper 1996; Galliers and Land 1987). As a highly applied field, it covers a broad spectrum, from practice-biased disciplines such as engineering and management, to soft disciplines such as psychology and sociology (Galliers and Land,1987; Banville and Landry 1989; Achterberg, Van Es and Heng 1991; Baskerville and Wood-Harper 1996).

We can hardly talk about the field as a paradigm in the commonly accepted sense of the concept: that is to say, a theoretically well-structured, broad and extensive research orientation, with a common view of the world, a methodological approach, definition of the research object and common theoretical ancestors and sources of inspiration (Kuhn 1970). Instead, the research field is characterized by a multitude of views and perspectives. According to an IFIP WG8.2 survey carried out in 1986 (quoted in Nissen, Klein and Hirschheim 1991), there are as many as thirty-two reference disciplines involved in information systems.

This broad spectrum creates problems when it comes to a homogeneous or even coherent definition of what information systems as a discipline should be studying. Is the object of research in information systems of a technological or a social nature? Is it the organization, an information system or a social system? As Kuutti asks, "If an organization is too broad and vague, an information system too narrow, and a social system too hazy and one-sided, then what is it that we are actually going to analyze and change?"

We believe that there is a need to bridge the analytical split between human and non-human, organizational life and the information system implemented or developed within the organization. The critical issue to be remembered in doing information systems research in organizations is that the world is composed of hybrids rather than discrete elements, either social or non-social (Grint, Case and Willcocks 1996). There is no condition where humans exist but in networks with humans and non-humans. It is the network of ideas, machines and people developed through an accommodation to each other that should be the focus of our inquiries (Latour 1988). In epistemological terms, to focus on those hybrids instead of discrete elements, run counter to the analytic position set up under the rules of the enlightenment and posit formidable problems of analysis. Our understandings are posed mainly between people and/or things but not on the agglomerations.

Consequently, the tradition in research, has been that one specific effect of one variable can be readily assessed. Therefore, it has been assumed that because we can assess the capacity of the technology, it is possible by the same means to assess its effects upon the organization or the human beings using it. The avoidance of studying single variables can actually help to obtain a more accurate understanding of the effects of technology if the focus is on the total situation instead: the mix of variables, including new technology, that comes together and interacts to produce certain consequences (Mumford 1987). Furthermore, even though it may be possible to measure and grasp the objective side of technology, it is still necessary to remain subjective on the human element. If the analysis is to be focused on the result of interactions between the network of human and non-human within the context of organization (Grint, Case and Willcocks 1996), we will need to take into account not only the objective, visible and measurable factors but also the changing environment in organizations and their dynamic and symbolic features, as well as the subjective or symbolic processes inherent in the process of doing information systems research (Zuboff 1996).

5 QUALITATIVE RESEARCH IN INFORMATION SYSTEMS

There is a push for more qualitative research, as witnessed by the success of the Orlikowski's (1993) employment of grounded theory and the forthcoming special edition of *MIS Quarterly* on intensive research. What exactly is qualitative research? Does the use of recognized qualitative methods qualify as qualitative research?

According to Van Maanen (1979, p. 520),

> The label qualitative methods has no precise meaning in any of the social sciences. It is at best an umbrella term covering an array of interpretative techniques which seek to describe, decode, translate and otherwise come to terms with the meaning, not the frequency, of certain more or less naturally occurring phenomena in the social world.

Qualitative research has been defined in many ways and means different things to different people. Essentially, it is both a certain commitment to some versions of the naturalistic or interpretative approaches to its subject matter, and an ongoing critique of the politics and methods of positivism. Qualitative implies an emphasis on the processes and meanings that are not examined or measured in terms of quantity, amount, intensity or frequency.

Spielberg (1972) argues that using quantitative or qualitative methods of analysis implies a different perspective on human interaction and behaviour. The quantitative approach implies that there is an objective truth existing in the outside world which can be revealed through the use of the scientific method of measuring relationships between different variables systematically and statistically. The concern in this methodology is essentially that the measurements are reliable, valid and generalizable in their predictions of cause and effect. On the other hand, qualitative techniques emerging from phenomenology and interpretative paradigms emphasise a constructive approach where there is no clear-cut objectivity or reality. Social life is perceived as emerging from the shared creativity of individuals (Filstead 1978). The use of qualitative research stresses this socially constructed nature of reality, the intimate relationship between the researcher and what is being explored and the situational constraints which shape the process. Whereas in the positivistic approach, theory is deduced by testing hypothesis, in the phenomenological approach, theory is generated from the data collected, thus, it is grounded in the data (Glaser and Strauss 1967).

Qualitative research is also multi-method in focus, usually the choice of which methods to use or tools to employ is not decided in advance. The choice of research practices depends upon the questions that are asked, and the questions depend on their context (Nelson, Treichler and Grossberg 1992). Therefore, as a contrast with quantitative methods of research, the use of a qualitative framework is unlikely to impose restrictive a priori classifications in the collection of the data. Research is less driven by the testing of a specific hypotheses and categorical frameworks and more concerned with emergent themes and idiographic discussions. As a result, qualitative researchers are more likely to be aware of (and feel the need to explain) the epistemological stance they are taking, whereas few researchers working on the positivist tradition feel the need to do so. In the latter case, the research process becomes normative; it is usually the way research "is done."

However, the upshot in qualitative research is that qualitative researchers might find themselves explaining the paradigm they are using in terms of a paradigm they are not using, thus explaining the use of an interpretative approach in terms of a quantitative one using positivist terms such as reliability, generalizability and validity. The use of alternative approaches such as more qualitative methods in information systems research is therefore beset with the question of not achieving a complete shift in paradigms.

Toraskar (1991), for instance, utilized a field study approach via in-depth personal interviews to evaluate a class of decision support systems from an organizational and user oriented perspective. In his research, he had adopted grounded theory (Glaser and Strauss 1967) approach to the data analysis, where he claimed to be well suited for analyzing the vast amount of qualitative data generated through field-study. In his conclusion, he said that "the research strategy and the methods used here cannot be expected to offer the same degree of precision and reliability of results as the traditional causal-mechanistic methods" and that there is a "need for greater precision in research." It begs the question why he acknowledges the above as limitations of qualitative research, running contrary to what it is all about (see Glaser and Strauss 1967 and Strauss and Corbin 1990).

Calloway and Ariav (1991) also use grounded theory to interpret data gathered from studying the relationships of developers with their tools. They utilize exploratory studies, which are often used to generate hypotheses that can be subjected to quantitative methods, and their objective was to fashion a precise methodology that could be used elsewhere. Again, the opportunity is missed to use qualitative methods the way they were intended to be used.

Another example is case studies research, which has become popular and acceptable, due in part to the work of authors like Yin (1994), which simply treats it as another functionalist research approach (cf. Burrell and Morgan 1979; Lee 1989 and Galliers 1991). This is particularly evident in Lee's utilization of case studies to show how controlled observations and deductions, replicability, and generalizability can be achieved to test hypotheses. His objective was to satisfy the standards of the natural science model of scientific research.

In the examples given above, the objectives of the authors are admirable. But is not this a case of using qualitative methods in a quantitative fashion? The authors tried to explain the use of an interpretative approach in terms of a quantitative one, yielding to a tendency to apply directly in qualitative research the methods developed to assess reliability and validity in quantitative research (Flick 1992).

We acknowledge that the problem of validity has become increasingly important in research processes dealing with qualitative methods. The discussion of credibility and of generalizing data increases along with the use of qualitative methods. One concern of quantitative research is that the measures used will produce the same results when applied to the same subjects by different researchers: "The same 'yardstick' applied to the same individual or object in the same way should yield the same value from moment to moment, provided that the thing measured has itself not changed in the meantime" (Guildford and Fruchter 1978, p. 407), for the characteristics of the researcher to influence the way in which subjects respond to the instruments in a research process would endanger the reliability of the research. Qualitative research, on the other hand, seeks to describe and understand how people make sense of their world and, as such, does not require researchers to strive for this kind of objectivity or to distance themselves from research participants. Indeed, to do so would make qualitative research impossible, as the researcher's subjectivity is an essential part of the research process.

This does not mean that in interpreting qualitative data the issue of possible researcher bias should be ignored. We consider it just as important as in quantitative research that the interpretations are not a simple product of the researcher's biases and prejudices. A first step to revise and improve this is the recognition of the researcher's self consciousness of being an actor in the research process. This leads us to the issue of validity. In quantitative research, a valid instrument is one which actually measures what it claims to measure. Similarly, in qualitative research, a study is said to be valid if it truly examines the topic which it claims to have examined. It could be said then that, in essence, the concept of validity is the same in both research approaches. Where the approaches differ is in the quantitative research's notion of validity, which is centered on the methods, i.e., the validity of the items in a questionnaire as opposed to the focus on the validity of interpretations. Thus, whether a researcher's conclusion that X is the main theme to emerge from the analysis is valid.

There is a considerable debate of what constitutes good interpretation in qualitative research (for a detailed account of the different positions, see Hammersley 1992). Our position is that, as long as we try to base our claims of social processes on data of any kind, we must have a logic for assessing and communicating the interactive process through which we, as researchers, have acquired the research experience and information. If, as we claim, we want to include in our analysis and to expand our understanding of the "detailed means through which human beings engage in meaningful action and create a world of their own or one which is shared with others" (Morgan 1983, p. 397), we need to recognize that "insufficient attention has yet to be devoted to evolving criteria for assessing the general quality and rigour of interpretative research" (Morgan 1983, p. 399).

In information systems, case studies have been evaluated in order to assess their rigour and validity (Yin 1994; Benbasat, Goldstein and Mead 1987; Walsham 1993, 1995). For example, while Lee's work provided the principles and guidelines for case studies by analyzing them from the philosophical perspective of positivism, Klein and Myers (1995) undertook a similar endeavour from the philosophical perspective of hermeneutics for the interpretive field research, in which they propose a systematic list of principles for conducting and evaluating interpretive research.

Qualitative researchers propose the triangulation of methods as one way to achieve this rigour. However, the use of multiple methods or triangulation reflects an attempt to secure an in-depth understanding of the phenomena in question. Triangulation is not a tool or strategy of validation but rather an alternative to validation. The combination of multiple perspectives, methods, empirical materials and observations in a study is, therefore, best understood as a strategy that can add rigour, breath and depth to any investigation (Flick 1992).

Researchers may choose to use different kinds of materials as their data, either quantifiable or of a qualitative nature, but that does not change the fact that the researchers are observers of a world in which they also participate. The research is mediated by a concrete framework of symbols and cultural meanings given by aspects of the life story that the researcher brings to the observational setting. In this sense, all research methods are "essentially qualitative and are for that matter essentially objective; the use of quantitative data or mathematical procedures does not eliminate the intersubjective element that underlies social research" (Vidich and Lyman 1994). Thus, the researcher always remains at the center of the research process.

The question about relying on and emphasizing on quantification was posed to the Information Systems Doctoral Mailing List discussion (MISDOC-L 1996) by one of the authors of this paper to get a feel of how doctoral students perceived and are affected by any of the research traditions. Surprisingly, there was no argument about the use of both quantitative and qualitative methods. Indeed it was encouraging to hear comments such as "regardless of whether quantitative or qualitative methods are used for a research project, I think the qualitative grounded theory approach is a critical research tool. In social science, even a large effect size is still small in absolute [terms]. One should use [the] qualitative approach to understand the context and complexity of the social phenomena in question" (a respondent).

Even the advocation for qualitative research to be used only to supplement quantitative methods is a non-issue. However, there was still a major problem in employing qualitative methods in research. Despite a recognition for its role, the problem stems from the fact that, in practice, quantitative research pays off more. "I cannot help focusing more on quantitative data consciously" (a respondent). In this respondent's case, he has used both quantitative and qualitative methods for his dissertation, but found that researchers and practitioners are more impressed that he surveyed 20,000 households than anything he found in in-depth interviews: "I think it [qualitative methods] provides more 'human-touch' to the study. Even when I analyze questionnaire data, I keep thinking about the people I interviewed. Their voice, their life stories, etc., remind me that I am studying real people and the responses on questionnaires are not just numbers, but it represents thoughts, opinions, and feelings of real people."

With the recognition of qualitative methods in the information systems field, there are now new research methods (Mumford et al. 1985) to help access the symbolically structured object domain of inquiry that were not developed in the natural sciences. In this light, qualitative research has now gained in-roads into the information systems research arena. Nonetheless, despite recognizing the limitations of traditional scientific methods and the negativity associated with this scientific tradition, the irony is that it still dominates all research done in the field (Klein and Lyytinen 1985). Galliers and Land pointed out that 85% of published IS research undertaken by leading US institutions is of the traditional kind.

Such institutional barriers to research practices have been recognized in the past (Orlikowski 1991). The use of the tools for research unfortunately still end up being a political choice translatable to economics dollars and cents. On a positive note, we know it will be a slow and even long process, but at least the wheels have been set in motion, as evidenced by the theme of this conference and the works of Myers, Klein and others.

6 RESEARCHER'S SUBJECTIVITY AS A STRENGTH

Using qualitative methods in the research process is a reflexive activity, constantly informing the researcher's actions. The tools of interpretation are learned through experience (see the debate between Boland and Jonsson in Nissen, Klein and Hirschheim). A researcher's subjectivity enables penetration of the fronts individuals and groups represent which, in turn, permits deeper understanding of actors' perspectives and ways of living. It is a myth that the researcher can claim value neutrality in social research. Even the way we represent the research data is a political choice (Said 1989).

Qualitative methods allow for that subjectivity in the research process and that is clearly their advantage. Within the qualitative research tradition, there is an acceptance of the inherent subjectivity of the research endeavour (Bryman 1988). There are the participant's perspectives on and the interpretations of the situation which are of value in understanding behaviour, therefore a search of objectivity in this type of research will be somehow misguided. In other words, verification cannot be considered to be of decisive significance in assessing the value of the research (Alvesson 1995). But if researchers in information systems still insist in the objectivity of the research process, then according to Mumford (1987), "research must be objective, but it can never be value-free."

This opens the debate between the objective knowledge or subjective knowledge in the research process. The claim for objectivity is an old and debatable issue in the social sciences. It is more than a technical question. It relates to the very nature of the relationship between the elements of the research process, namely the object, the researcher, the subjects (actors) and the results. In information systems, this ontological distinction between objectivism and subjectivism pervades its development methods. When combined with epistemological issues, this distinction leads again to a seemingly implacable dualism of scienticism and interpretativism.

However, the object of investigation is a subjective domain comprising the subjects of social life. The researcher is not usually separated from the object of inquiry but rather exposed to the very same conditions which gave rise to the problem under inquiry (Thompson 1990). There is a relation of potential exchange between the outcome of the social inquiry and the reality from which the outcome emerges. Human beings know and undergo the effects of knowledge they develop about themselves. Objectivity in social sciences assumes a meaning only in relation to a subjective domain which confirms and supports the claim of an objective reality.

As Latour (quoted in Vidgen and McMaster 1996) argues,

> The separation of an objective and given natural world from a socially-constructed social world...contains a paradox in so far as it exposes separation of natural and social worlds while relying upon their inseparability for success....[As such, we do not need to] attach our explanations to the two pure forms know as the object or subject/society, because these are, on the contrary, partial and purified results of the central practice that is our sole concern.

Acknowledging the inherent subjectivity of the research process implies a reconciliation of subject and object, which takes place through a dialectical logic. The knowledge of the world and the knowledge of one-self are co-constitutive of each other rather than as separate categories. The empirical datum and the human mind co-determine each other in such a way that both are transformed through the very activity that their encounter engenders. "It is neither subjective, nor 'objective knowledge'. It is knowledge based on interaction between the knowing subject and the object of its knowledge" (Markova 1982, p. 112).

7 RESEARCH AS A CULTURAL EXPERIENCE

Because of the stress on using qualitative methods in natural settings, Kirk and Miller (1986) suggest that qualitative researchers are engaged in interacting with people in their own language and in their own terms. There is a shift in the description of the people involved in the study as participants and not as subjects. The agreements between the researcher and the participants in the study about the meaning in particular situations or events being studied has led in some cases to more participative research situations. There is not only a recognition of the autonomy of the participant in the research but also a recognition of the role the researcher plays in the study. This is one of the main thrusts of action research (Antill 1985; Wood-Harper 1985; Baskerville and Wood-Harper 1996). Rather than being an involved bystander observing the organizational action, the researcher has an impact on the behaviour and expectations of those around (Cassell and Symon 1994).

Westrup (1996, p. 167) refers to system developers as constituting the organizations they seek to develop information systems for and that what will be fruitful is investigation of the practices of the developers themselves. Likewise, systems analysts are not simply engaged in analyzing an organization (using traditional or refined tools) but use analysis as a resource to construct a representation of the organization that requires the use of an information system.

Indeed, it would be absurd to assume the researchers themselves operate free of a cultural context of any kind; rather it is too obvious that we, too, belong to various thought worlds. Paradigms reflect fashions in the professional time-collective, but the space-collective also leaves its mark. "It is an illusion that we can escape our thought world and immerse ourselves, naked of prejudice into another one" (Czarniawska-Joerges 1991, p. 295). The best we can try to do is to expand our thought world by understanding the possibility of other worlds or "sub-universes of meaning" (Berger and Luckmann 1966).

For instance, Madon says that research into the organizational context of information systems reveals a substantial difference between developing and industrialised countries. In her investigation into the adoption of information systems and technology transfer in India, she found that it is not a matter of replicating the institutions and approaches of the developed countries, but of adapting them to the priorities and contextual characteristics of the developing country in question, in terms of its lack of resources, infrastructure, and the constraints imposed by the social and political context (Felts 1987; Bell and Sheppard 1988; Madon 1994). Hammersley and Atkinson (1983) also support this view:

> We are part of the social world we study....This is not a matter of methodological commitment, it is an existential fact. There is no way in which we can escape the social world in order to study it; nor fortunately, is that necessary. We cannot avoid relying on "common-sense" knowledge nor, often, can we avoid having an effect on the social phenomena we study.

Research, therefore, should be regarded as the activity where the researcher's subjectivity has an unavoidable impact (Alvesson 1995). The observations of the researcher are always guided by world images that determine which data are salient and which are not. Thus, there are no ready-made data waiting for the researcher to be collected, but rather a prestructured selection of the data to be gathered which will influence their later interpretation and understanding. The development of knowledge in a discipline cannot be regarded only as based on epistemological or methodological concerns but also based on the researcher's views and opinions. An act of attention to one object rather than another can reveal a dimension of the researcher's commitment to concrete values, as well as his or her own value-laden interests. Data as such is the result of and is principally determined by interpretation and theory.

As such, research activity should consist of abandoning the taken-for-grantedness of the research context in order to problematize the practices of the actors performing in such a context. It soon becomes clear that this is not a one-way process, as the researcher's practices become problematized in turn. And if the researcher takes a neutral stance by "play(ing) naive we can get acceptance in strange worlds but probably wouldn't understand them (playing naive requires a non-problematic stance towards what is happening taken for granted what it is)" (Czarniawska-Joerges 1991). If we want the understanding, we must ask by posing questions, we problematize by problematizing, otherwise we will reveal ourselves as not really belonging.

Even writing the reports or descriptions becomes an interpretative endeavour as researchers' ideas rarely if ever occur in a systematic, structured way. As Geertz (1988) says, the descriptions filtered through the researcher are second or third order fictions. Clifford and Marcus (1986) argue that the various blindness, evasions, and fictions that were created in order to produce ethnographic insights essentially require new vocabularies and new modes for describing the social and cultural worlds being studied. Stated simply, there is no object of study "out there" to be accurately represented by observers; rather, the observer creates fictions in the process of investigation (Riley 1991).

Methodologies inevitably embed the creator's philosophical paradigms. According to Polanyi (1964), the researcher has the perogative to reserve judgement on finding a good problem, and of the surmises to pursue it, as well as the recognition of a discovery that solves it. This is inspite of following the rules of a scientific inquiry:

> In each such decision the researcher may rely on the support of a rule; but he is then selecting a rule that applies to the case, much as the golfer chooses a suitable club for his next stroke. His choosing will depend on his background and training – and his world view.

In summary, the research process should not be thought of as following an explicit bureaucratic procedure and a clear account of the methods employed, but rather one that is based more on being aware of theory and meta-theory, continuously reflecting on the current position and future developments when reading and conducting empirical work, open to ideas and suggestions. The data is as much an artificial construction as it is a reflection of empirical reality (Alvesson 1995).

Using qualitative methods implies that more attention should be paid not only to multiple narratives that give voice to and allow the construction of multiple worlds, but also to the role of the researcher, of his understanding, insights, experiences, interpretations, etc. A good researcher will be one who can bring such subjectivity to the fore, backed with quality arguments rather than just a display of statistical exactness, precision or confidence.

Multiple narratives will not give us any one representation but they may "give us more interesting ways to think about the organization, ethics, and aesthetics of work than the search for such true systems has" (Boland and Schultze 1996, p. 332). However, as we have seen so far, the narrative in information systems is one of a progress toward clarity, simplicity and purity. Boland and Schultze blame the aura that surrounds information technology, as if it has some magical power to make clear what is blurred and purify what is contaminated. As a result, despite the efforts to date in using qualitative methods, information systems still tend to be fixated by data and a quest for quantification.

8 CONCLUSION

We would like to reiterate that methodological questions do not relate simply to technical procedures and are not a matter of either applying a quantitative or qualitative method. Although the debate is centred around the presumed opposition of qualitative versus quantitative methodologies, it seems that such an opposition is entirely false and does not touch upon the fundamental issues. Methodology relates and actually depends upon theoretical issues which in turn are bound to philosophical conceptions. It is the close connection between the three that guides research options. Therefore, we have tried to challenge the assumption that just an increased adoption of methodologies would help address the problems inherent in information systems research.

In the final analysis, there is probably no such thing as a single, simple and clear road regarding research methods in information systems. As Westrup (1996, p. 170) stated, "adopting a [new approach] to systems development may lead to several advantages though it is unlikely to afford the luxury of yet a better technique of systems development." A better approach would be to use them as suggested frameworks, or guidelines, rather than as dogma (Baskerville 1996). As for doing qualitative research in information systems, that will be the day when we start using qualitative methods in a qualitative way, the day when we dare to be subjective.

9 ACKNOWLEDGMENTS

The authors would like to thank Professor Jonathan Liebenau for his encouragement and guidance on our work, and also to the different blind reviewers for their excellent and detailed critique of our paper. We hope that we have done justice to them all.

10 REFERENCES

Acterberg, J. S.; van Es, G. A.; and Heng, M. S. H. (1991). "Information Systems Research in the Postmodern Period." In H-E. Nissen, H. K. Klein, and R. Hirschheim (Editors), *The Information Systems Research Arena of the 90s, Challenges, Perceptions and Alternative Approaches*. Amsterdam: North-Holland.

Alvesson, M. (1995). *Management of Knowledge-Intensive Companies*. Berlin: De Gruyter.

Antill, L. (1985). "Selection of a Research Method." In E. Mumford, R. Hirschheim, G. Fitzgerald, and A. T. Wood-Harper (Editors), *Research Methods in Information Systems*. Amsterdam: North-Holland.

Backhouse, J.; Liebenau, J.; and Land, F. (1991). "On the Discipline of Information Systems." *Journal of Information Systems*, Volume 1, pp. 19-27.

Banville, C., and Landry, M. (1989). "Can the Field of MIS be Disciplined?" *Communications of the ACM*,, Volume 32, pp. 48-61.

Baskerville, R. (1996). "The Second-Order Security Dilemma." In W. J. Orlikowski, G. Walsham, M. R. Jones, and J. I. DeGross (Editors), *Information Technology and Changes in Organizational Work*. London: Chapman and Hall.

Baskerville, R. L., and Wood-Harper, A. T. (1996). "A Critical Perspective on Action Research as a Method for Information Systems Research." *Journal of Information Technology*, Volume 11.

Bell, S., and Sheppard, I. (1988). *Application of a Systems Development Methodology in Less Developed Countries*. Norwich, England: University of East Anglia.

Benbasat, I.; Goldstein, D. K.; and Mead, M. (1987). "The Case Research Strategy in Studies of Information Systems." *MIS Quarterly*, Volume 11, Number 3, September, pp. 369-386.

Berger, P., and Luckmann, T. (1966). *The Social Construction of Reality*. London: Penguin.

Bikson, T. (1991). "Relevance versus Rigor in Information Systems Research: An Issue of Quality." Panel Discussion chaired by J. A. Turner. In H-E. Nissen, H. K. Klein, and R. Hirschheim (Editors), *Information Systems Research: Contemporary Approaches and Emergent Traditions*. Amsterdam: North-Holland.

Boland, R. J, and Schultze, U. (1996). "From Work to Activiy: Technology and the Narrative of Progress." In W. J. Orlikowski, G. Walsham, M. R. Jones, and J. I. DeGross (Editors), *Information Technology and Changes in Organizational Work*. London: Chapman and Hall.

Bryman, A. (1988). *Quantity and Quality in Social Research*. London: Unwin Hyman.

Burrell, G., and Morgan, G. (1979). *Sociological Paradigms and Organizational Analysis*. London: Heinemann.

Calloway, L. J., and Ariav, G. (1991). "Developing and Using a Qualitative Methodology to Study Relationships among Designers and Tools." In H-E. Nissen, H. K.

Klein and R. Hirschheim (Editors), *Information Systems Research: Contemporary Approaches and Emergent Traditions*. Amsterdam: North-Holland.

Cash, J., and Nunamaker, J. (1989). *The Information Systems Research Challenge, Vol I: Qualitative Research Methods*. Boston: Harvard Business School Press.

Cash, J., and Nunamaker, J. (1990). *The Information Systems Research Challenge, Vol II: Qualitative Research Methods*. Boston: Harvard Business School Press.

Cash, J., and Nunamaker, J. (1991). *The Information Systems Research Challenge, Vol III: Qualitative Research Methods*. Boston: Harvard Business School Press.

Cassell, C., and Symon, G. (1994). *Qualitative Methods in Organizational Research*. London: Sage.

Clifford, J., and Marcus, G. E. (1986). *Writing Culture: The Poetics and Politics of Ethnography*. Berkeley: University of California Press.

Cooper, R. (1988). "Review of Management Information Systems Research: A Management Support Emphasis." *Information Processing and Management*, Volume 24, Number 1, pp. 73-102.

Czarniawska-Joerges, B. (1991). "Culture is a Medium of Life." In P. J. Frost, L. F. Moore, M. R. Louis, C. C. Lundberg and J. Martin (Editors), *Reframing Organizational Culture*. London: Sage.

Danzinger, K. (1979). "The Positivistic Repudiation of Wundt." *Journal of the History of the Behavioral Sciences*, Volume 15, pp. 205-230.

Elejabarrieta, F. (1990). "La Rigurosidad metodologica y la precariedad teorica en Psicologia Social." *Quaderns de Psicologia*, Volume 10, pp. 143-160.

Felts, R. A. (1987). *The Development of Information Systems in the Third World*. M.Sc. Dissertation, London School of Economics.

Filstead, W. J. (1978). "Qualitative Methods: A Needed Perspective in Evaluation Research." In T. D. Cook and C. S. Reichardt (Editors), *Qualitative and Quantitative Methods in Evaluation Research*. Beverley Hills, California: Sage.

Flick, U. (1992). "Triangulation Revisited: Strategy of Validation or Alternative?" *Journal of the Theory of Social Behavior*, Volume 22, pp. 175-198.

Galliers, R. D. (1991). "Choosing Appropriate Information Systems Research Approaches: A Revised Taxonomy." In H-E. Nissen, H. K. Klein and R. Hirschheim (Editors), *Information Systems Research: Contemporary Approaches and Emergent Traditions*. Amsterdam: North-Holland.

Galliers, R. D., and Land, F. L. (1987). "Choosing Appropriate Information Systems Research Methodologies." *Communications of the ACM*, Volume 30, Number 11, pp. 900-902.

Geertz, C. (1988). *Works and Lives: The Anthropologist as Author*. Stanford, California: California University Press.

Glaser, B., and Strauss, A. L. (1967). *The Discovery of Grounded Theory: Strategies for Qualitative Research*. Chicago: Aldine.

Grint, K.; Case, P.; and Willcocks, L. (1996). "Business Process Reengineering Reappraised: The Politics and Technology of Forgetting." In W. J. Orlikowski,

G. Walsham, M. R. Jones, and J .I. DeGross (Editors), *Information Technology and Changes in Organizational Work.* London: Chapman and Hall.

Guerreiro-Ramos, A. (1981). *The New Science of Organization.* Toronto: University of Toronto Press.

Guilford, J. P., and Fruchter, B. (1978). *Fundamental Statistics in Psychology and Education.* London: McGraw-Hill.

Hammersly, M. (1992). *What is Wrong with Ethnography? Methodological Explorations.* London: Routledge.

Hammersly, M., and Atkinson, P. (1983). *Ethnography Principles in Practice.* London: Routledge.

Keen, P. G. W. (1987). "MIS Research: Current Status, Trends and Needs." In R. A. Buckingham, R. A. Hirschheim, F. F. Land and C. J. Tully (Editors), *Information Systems Education: Recommendations and Implementation.* Cambridge, England: University Press.

Kirk, J., and Miller, M. L. (1986). *Reliability and Validity in Qualitative Research.* Qualitative Research Methods Series, Volume 1. Beverley Hills, California: Sage.

Klein, H. K.; Hirschheim, R.; and Nissen, H-E. (1991). "A Pluralist Perspective of the Information Systems Research Arena." In H-E. Nissen, H. K. Klein and R. Hirschheim (Editors), *Information Systems Research: Contemporary Approaches and Emergent Traditions.* Amsterdam: North-Holland.

Klein, H. K., and Lyytinen, K. (1985). "The Poverty of Scientism in Information Systems." In E. Mumford, R. Hirschheim, G. Fitzgerald and A. T.Wood-Harper (Editors), *Research Methods in Information Systems.* Amsterdam: North-Holland.

Klein, H. K., and Myers, M. D. (1995). "The Quality of Interpretive Research in Information Systems." Department of Management Science and Information Systems, University of Auckland, Working Paper No. 89, May.

Kling, R. (1991). "Social Analyses of Computing: Theoretical Perspectives in Recent Empirical Research." *Computing Surveys,* Volume 12, Number 1, pp. 61-110.

Kuhn, T. S. (1970). *The Structure of Scientific Revolutions.* Chicago: University of Chicago Press.

Kuutti, K. (1996). "Debates in IS and CSCW Research: Anticpating System Design for Post-Fordist Work." In W. J. Orlikowski, G. Walsham, M. R. Jones, and J. I. DeGross (Editors), *Information Technology and Changes in Organizational Work.* London: Chapman and Hall.

Latour. B. (1988). "The Prince for Machines as Well as for Machinations." In B. Elliot (Editor), *Technology and Social Processes.* Edemburg: Edemburg University Press.

Lee, A. (1989). "A Scientific Methodology for MIS Case Studies." *MIS Quarterly,* Volume 13, Number 1, pp. 33-50.

Madon, S. (1994). *Designing Information Systems for Development Planning.* Henley-on-Thames, England: Alfred Waller Ltd.

Markova, I. (1982). *Paradigms, Thought and Language*. Chichester, England: John Wiley and Sons.

MISDOC-L (1995). IS Doctoral Mailing List. http://web.bu.edu:80/SMGMIS/misdoc-l.

Morgan, G. (Editor) (1983). *Beyond Method*. Beverley Hills, California: Sage.

Morgan, G., and Smircich. L. (1980). "The Case for Qualititative Research." *Academy of Management Review*, Volume 5, Number 4, pp. 491-500.

Mumford, E. (1987). "Managerial Expert Systems and Organizational Change: Some Critical Research Issues." In R. J. Boland and R. A. Hirschheim (Editors), *Critical Issues in Information Systems Research*. Chichester, England: John Wiley & Sons, pp. 135-156.

Mumford, E. (1991). "Information Systems Research-Leaking Craft or Visionary Vehicle?" In H. E. Nissen, H. K. Klein, and R. Hirschheim (Editors), *Information Systems Research: Contemporary Approaches and Emergent Traditions*. Amsterdam: North-Holland.

Mumford, E.; Hirschheim, R.; Fitzgerald, G.; and Wood-Harper, A. T. (Editors) (1985). *Research Methods in Information Systems*. Amsterdam: North-Holland.

Nelson, C.; Treichler, P. A.; and Grossberg, L. (1992). "Cultural Studies." In L. Grossberg, C. Nelson and P. A. Treichner (Editors), *Cultural Studies*. New York: Routledge.

Nissen, HE. (1985). "Acquiring Knowledge of Information Systems: Research in a Methodological Quagmire." In E. Mumford, R. Hirschheim, G. Fitzgerald and A.T. Wood-Harper (Editors), *Research Methods in Information Systems*. Amsterdam: North-Holland, pp. 39-51.

Nissen, H-E., Klein, H. K.; and Hirschheim, R. (Editors) (1991). *Information Systems Research: Contemporary Approaches and Emergent Traditions*. Amsterdam: North-Holland.

Olaisen, J. (1991). "Pluralism or Positivistic Trivialism: Important Trends in Contemporary Philosophy of Science." In H-E. Nissen, H. K. Klein and R. Hirschheim (Editors), *Information Systems Research: Contemporary Approaches and Emergent Traditions*. Amsterdam: North-Holland.

Oppenheimer, J. R. (1954). "Analogy in Science." *American Psychologist*, Volume 11, pp. 127-135.

Orlikowski, W. J. (1991). "Relevance versus Rigor in Information Systems Research: An Issue of Quality." Panel Discussion chaired by J. A. Turner. In H-E. Nissen, H. K. Klein, and R. Hirschheim (Editors), *Information Systems Research: Contemporary Approaches and Emergent Traditions*. Amsterdam: North-Holland.

Orlikowski, W. J. (1993). "CASE Tools as Organizational Change: Investigating Incremental and Radical Changes in Systems Development." *MIS Quarterly*, Volume 17, Number 3, pp. 309-450.

Orlikowski, W. J., and Baroudi, J. (1990). "Studying Information Technology in Organizations: Research Approaches and Assumptions." Sloan Management School, Massachusetts Institute of Technology, Working Paper.

Polanyi, M. (1964). *Science, Faith and Society: A Searching Examination of the Meaning and Nature of Scientific Inquiry*. Chicago: University of Chicago Press.

Preston, A. M. (1991). "The 'Problem' in and of Management Information Systems." *Journal of Accounting, Management and Information Technology*, Volume 1, Number 1, pp. 43-69.

Reed, M. (1985). *Redirections in Organizational Analysis*. London: Tavistock.

Riley, P. (1991). "Cornerville as Narration." In P. J. Frost, L. F. Moore, M. R. Louis, C. C. Lundberg and J. Martin (Editors), *Reframing Organizational Culture*. London: Sage.

Said, E. W. (1989). "Representing the Colonized: Anthopology's Interlocutors." *Critical Inquiry*, Volume 15, pp. 205-255.

Spielberg, H. (1972). *Phenomenology in Psychology and Psychiatry: A Historical Introduction*. Evanston, Illinois: Northwestern University Press.

Strauss, A., and Corbin, J. (1990). *Basics of Qualitative Research: Grounded Theory Procedures and Techniques*. London: Sage.

Thompson, J. B. (1990). *Ideology and Modern Culture*. Cambridge, England: Polity Press.

Toraskar, K. V. (1991). "How Managerial Users Evaluate Their Decision Support: A Grounded Theory Approach." In H-E. Nissen, H. K. Klein and R. Hirschheim (Editors), *Information Systems Research: Contemporary Approaches and Emergent Traditions*. Amsterdam: North-Holland.

Van Maanen, J. (1979). "Reclaiming Qualitative Methods for Organizational Research: A Preface." *Administrative Science Quarterly*, Volume 24, pp. 520-26.

Vidgen, R., and McMaster, T. (1996). "Black Boxes, Non-human Stakeholders and the Translation of IT Through Mediation." In W. J. Orlikowski, G. Walsham, M. R. Jones, and J. I. DeGross (Editors), *Information Technology and Changes in Organizational Work*. London: Chapman and Hall.

Vidich, A. J., and Lyman, S. M. (1994). "Qualitative Methods: Their History in Sociology and Anthropology." In N. K. Denzin and Y. S. Lincoln (Editors), *Handbook of Qualitative Research*. London: Sage.

Vogel, D. R., and Wetherbe, J. C. (1984). "MIS research: A Profile of Leading Journals and Universities." *DataBase*, Volume 16, Number 3.

Walsham, G. (1993). *Interpreting Information Systems in Organizations*. Chichester, England: Wiley.

Walsham, G. (1995). "Interpretive Case Studies in IS Research: Nature and Method." *European Journal of Information Systems*, Volume 4, pp. 74-81.

Weill, P., and Olson, M. H. (1989). "An Assessment of the Contingency Theory of Management Information Systems." *Journal of Management Information Systems*, Volume 6, Number 1, pp. 59-86.

Westrup, C. (1996). "Transforming Organizations Through Systems Analysis: Developing New Techniques for Organizational Analysis in IS Development." In W. J. Orlikowski, G. Walsham, M. R. Jones, and J. I. DeGross (Editors), *Information Technology and Changes in Organizational Work.* London: Chapman and Hall.

Wood-Harper, A. T. (1985). "Research Methods in Information Systems: Using Action Research." In E. Mumford, R. Hirschheim, G. Fitzgerald and A. T. Wood-Harper (Editors), *Research Methods in Information Systems.* Amsterdam: North-Holland.

Yin, R. K. (1994). *Case Study Research, Design and Methods*, Second Edition. Newbury Park, California: Sage Publications.

Zuboff, S. (1996). "The Emperor's New Information Technology." In W. J. Orlikowski, G. Walsham, M. R. Jones, and J. I. DeGross (Editors), *Information Technology and Changes in Organizational Work.* London: Chapman and Hall.

11 BIOGRAPHY

Lucia Garcia is a Ph.D. candidate in the Social Psychology Department at the London School of Economics (LSE) working on Organizational and Cultural Change. She also teaches Organizational Psychology and Qualitative Research Methods at the Methodology Institute at LSE. She has participated in a number of research projects in Latin America and Eastern Europe regarding organizational transformation in those countries. Currently she is a Research Officer at LSE acting as coordinator for the WHO Healthy Cities Evaluation Project as well as for the US based SRDI Telecommunications Network. Her interests are mainly in organizational transformation from a social psychological perspective focusing on community building, inter- and intra-organizational networks and the role of telecommunications on the transformation process as well as in social research methods.

Freddie Quek is an Information Systems Manager at Electronic Press Ltd. (UK), which is the electronic publishing arm of the Current Science Group, a medical publishing company. He received a Masters of Science from the London School of Economics and is currently pursuing his Ph.D. in Information Systems at the same institution. He is the Professional Activities Division Editor of ISWorld Net, and the Editorial Director of Connect-World Latin America, a publication dedicated to the discussion of liberalization of telecommunications in Latin America. His current research interests include decision support systems, electronic publishing, databases, the use of web-based technologies to support collaborative work and liberalization of telecommunications.

23

Actor-Network Theory and IS Research: Current Status and Future Prospects

G. Walsham
The Judge Institute of Management Studies
University of Cambridge
Cambridge CB2 1AG, England
E-mail: gw10@eng.cam.ac.uk

Abstract

An increasing interest is being shown, not least by IS researchers, in the socio-technical approach known as actor-network theory. The purpose of this paper is to assess the current and potential future contribution of the theory to IS research. A brief review of key concepts of the theory is given, some IS literature which uses the theory is described, and significant criticisms of the theory are examined in some detail. Finally, implications are drawn on the potential value of the theory for IS research in the future, with the broad conclusion being that it has much to offer in both theoretical and methodological terms.

1 INTRODUCTION

The initial development and application of actor-network theory was concerned with the sociology of science and was pioneered at the École des Mines in Paris by Michel Callon (1986) and Bruno Latour (1987). Later work has included a focus on technology (Latour 1996a) and information technology (Latour 1996b) and, in these areas, the theory can be considered to be a development of one strand of the wider school of thought on the social construction of technology (Bijker, Hughes and Pinch 1987). Actor-network theory is concerned with investigating the social and the technical taken together or, putting it another way, with the creation and maintenance of coextensive networks of human and nonhuman elements which, in the case of information technology, include people, organizations, software, computer and communications hardware, and infrastructure standards.

An interest in viewing information systems from the perspective of socio-technical theory has a long pedigree in information systems research, and in IFIP Working Group 8.2, particularly associated in its early days with the work of Mumford (1981) on participative design. However, this approach treated the social and the technical as relatively separate elements, while acknowledging the importance of addressing both elements seriously. In contrast, actor-network theory treats the social and the technical as inseparable, and indeed argues that people and artefacts should be analyzed with the same conceptual apparatus. This point will be discussed in further detail later in the paper, but Latour (1996b, p. 302) illustrates the rationale for symmetric treatment in the following observation on the relationship between "technical" computer systems and "social" organizations:

> It is no longer clear if a computer system is a limited form of organization or if an organization is an expanded form of computer system. Not because, as in the engineering dreams and the sociological nightmares, complete rationalization would have taken place, but because, on the opposite, the two monstrous hybrids are now coextensive.

This description of an aspect of the contemporary world, radically different from the world of computing in the 1970s which gave rise to socio-technical design, suggests a reason for the emergence of actor-network theory, and the rationale as to why it may offer an important contribution to the IS field. We need new methodological and theoretical devices to enable us to think about hybrids of people and information technology: pilots and computer-controlled planes; computers and people playing chess; the Internet; medical diagnosis systems; electronic tagging for prisoners; robots in surgery. The symbolic boundary between people and information technology is in a constant state of flux across a wide spectrum of contemporary work and leisure activities, and actor-network theory offers one way to investigate the issues and dilemmas in this new world.

The purpose of this paper is to review the current status of actor-network theory in IS research, to critically consider the theory's advantages and disadvantages, and thus to offer some views on its relevance and importance to future IS research. In the next section, a brief introduction to the theory is given, mainly for the benefit of those readers who are unfamiliar with its ideas and concepts. This is followed by a review of the literature to date on the application of the theory in the IS field. Next, criticisms of the theory are examined, and the relevance of these criticisms to IS research is discussed. The final section draws together the previous material by offering a personal view of the utility of the theory for IS research.

2 SOME KEY CONCEPTS IN ACTOR-NETWORK THEORY

A first point to note is that actor-network theory is not a stable and unified body of knowledge which can be drawn on by researchers, since its developers frequently revise or extend elements of the theory. Indeed, the author of this paper recently attended a seminar by Latour in which he expressed the view that he would like to "recall" the theory like a defective car. However, the theory also has its strengths, and this section will highlight some key elements of the theory which have remained relatively stable over the last decade or so of its development and use (see Law (1992) for a fuller description). Table 1 provides a brief summary of key concepts in the theory.

Table 1 Summary of Some Key Concepts in Actor-Network Theory.

Concept	Description
Actor (or actant)	Both human beings and nonhuman actors such as technological artefacts
Actor-network	Heterogeneous network of aligned interests, including people, organizations and standards
Enrolment and translation	Creating a body of allies, human and non-human, through a process of translating their interests to be aligned with the actor-network
Delegates and inscription	Delegates are actors who "stand in and speak for" particular viewpoints which have been inscribed in them, e.g., software as frozen organizational discourse
Irreversibility	The degree to which it is subsequently impossible to go back to a point where alternative possibilities exist
Black box	A frozen network element, often with properties of irreversibility
Immutable mobile	Network element with strong properties of irreversibility, and effects which transcend time and place, e.g., software standards

Actor-network theory examines the motivations and actions of groups of actors who form elements, linked by associations, of heterogeneous networks of aligned interests. A key feature of the theory is that actors are taken to include both human beings and nonhuman actors such as technological artefacts. This perspective has created considerable controversy; for example, Collins and Yearley (1992a) argue that the failure of the theory to make a distinction between human action and the behavior of things is an abdication of human responsibility. Callon and Latour (1992) respond that they do not deny differences, but that they refuse to consider them *a priori* and to hierarchy them once and for all into humans and nonhumans. They prefer to treat them all as "actants" who form a part of hybrid networks. Collins and Yearley (1992b) say that they "now concede that the term 'actant' does make a difference," but they continue to argue that the differences between actors and actants are vital. We will return to this important debate again later in the paper.

A major empirical focus of the theory when applied in particular contexts is to try to trace and explain the processes whereby relatively stable networks of aligned interests are created and maintained, or alternatively to examine why such networks fail to establish themselves. Successful networks of aligned interests are created through the enrolment of a sufficient body of allies, and the translation of their interests so that they are willing to participate in particular ways of thinking and acting which maintain the network. Bloomfield et al. (1992) point out that the analysis of the various stratagems employed, such as the use of persuasive rhetoric, to construct and maintain network allegiances draws much from Machiavelli. However, they note the addition in actor-network theory that nonhuman resources, such as a graph in a scientific paper, can be used to "stand in or speak for," or be delegates for, particular viewpoints or truth-statements which help to maintain a particular network of alliances. Bowker and Star (1994, p. 187) make a similar representational point with respect to computer systems and software:

> Modern information technologies embed and inscribe work in ways that are important for policy-makers, but which are often difficult to see... arguments, decisions and uncertainties and processual nature of decision-making are hidden away inside a piece of technology or in a complex representation. Thus values, opinions, and rhetoric are frozen into codes, electronic thresholds and computer applications. Extending Marx, then, we can say that in many ways, software is frozen organizational discourse.

The idea of software as frozen discourse is an example of an inscription which resists change and displays properties of irreversibility. Callon (1991) says that the degree of irreversibility of a particular element of a network depends on the extent to which it is subsequently impossible to go back to a point where alternative possibilities exist, and the extent to which the particular frozen element, or black box, shapes and determines subsequent inscriptions. Actor-network theory uses the term immutable mobiles to describe network elements which display strong properties of irreversibility and are mobile across time and space; various software standards provide illustrations of immutable mobiles.

It is important to note that actor-network theory, in contrast to many social theories, is both a theory and methodology combined. In other words, it not only provides theoretical concepts as ways of viewing elements in the real world, it also suggests that it is exactly these elements which need to be traced in empirical work. So, the researcher is led to investigate and document network elements, both human and nonhuman, processes of translation and inscription, the creation of black boxes or immutable mobiles, and the degree of stability and irreversibility of networks and their elements. This is, of course, no small task for a complex network, and we will return to this point again in our later critical discussion of the theory.

3 ACTOR-NETWORK THEORY IN THE IS LITERATURE

Actor-network theory has become much more widely known in recent years, and an increasing number of IS researchers are making explicit use of the theory in their work. Although there is considerable variety in these applications, all the authors cited below are supportive of the view that the theory offers new concepts and ideas for the understanding of the socio-technical nature of information systems. The purpose of this section is to critically review some of this work, and to examine the ways in which actor-network theory contributed to the authors' methodology or analysis.

Bloomfield et (1992) provide an interesting case study of the development of a particular set of resource management information systems in the UK National Health Service, and they use concepts from actor-network theory to analyze their findings. They point out how the actor-network approach does not privilege either social aspects or technology, which reflects the situation in the case study itself where arguments about social structures and technology are interwoven within the discourse of actors as they attempt to persuade others to align with their own interests. The paper emphasizes the interpretative flexibility of information technology and systems, in the sense that seemingly similar systems result in radically different outcomes in different locations, due to the specific processes of translation and network-building which took place. They argue against the view of technology as a given, but instead illustrate how the boundary between the technical and the social, and the relationship between them, is the subject of ongoing struggles and trials of strength in creating the facts. A related discussion of boundary disputes between the technical and the social, illustrated by cases in the NHS and in an IT systems planning consortium, is given in Bloomfield and Vurdubakis (1994). These two papers provide valuable examples of the use of actor-network theory for case analysis, although it is not clear from the papers whether the theory was used as a methodology for the empirical work as well as for analytical purposes.

A second set of illustrative applications of actor-network theory in IS research is contained in the proceedings of the preceding IFIP Working Group 8.2 Conference in Cambridge (Orlikowski et al. 1996). In addition to a short plenary paper by Latour (1996b), five other papers explicitly use aspects of the theory. Boland and Schultze (1996) adopt the vocabulary of the theory to describe activity based costing as an accounting technology that has been made true, and has been established as a wide-spread practice, through a process of translation in which allies have been enrolled, black boxes have been constructed to enshrine the approach, and arguments have been built up into many layered defenses against adherents of traditional cost accounting techniques. The authors undermine the certainties of this fact construction process by telling a different story, or anti-narrative, where the merits of the two techniques are reversed. They conclude that we need to allow multiple inscriptions and representations of organizational work involving information technology. Bowker, Timmermans and Star (1996) pursue a similar theme of the inscription of work, using an empirical example of a classification scheme for understanding nursing work. They describe how such a classification scheme can be considered to be a political actor, and how the processes in its creation are difficult to retrace once it has been black-boxed.

Two further empirical papers using actor-network theory were presented at the conference cited above. Monteiro and Hanseth (1996) focus on the role of standards, particularly those embedded in infrastructures, in prescribing and proscribing forms of interaction with information technology. Their examples involve EDI systems in the Norwegian health sector, and concern the definition of a message standard for identifying a drug prescription and one for exchanging test results. In both cases, they illustrate the processes of translation and inscription which were taking place, and they contrast the relative successes of the network-building in the two cases. Vidgen and McMaster (1996) describe a case study of an innovative car parking system which was both an information system and an access control point. They carry out a stakeholder analysis of both human and nonhuman interests, and describe how the attempted translation of these interests into the black box of fact was not achieved due to weaknesses in the network of associations between stakeholders. The two papers described in this paragraph are interesting illustrations of the application of actor-network theory in IS research, although their laudable emphasis on explaining the technology seemed to be at the expense of explaining the social interactions in some cases.

To conclude this brief literature review, mention is now made of four other papers, illustrating different areas of application of the concepts in actor-network theory to IT-related areas. Bowers (1992) discusses computer-mediated communication, and notes that the mixture between the human and the nonhuman is being named and welcomed here. He argues, following Latour and others, that if we are to take computer technology seriously, then we will have to abandon innocent humanism in favor of the world of cyborg politics (Haraway 1991). Kavanagh and Araujo (1995) discuss the nature and social construction of time, using actor-network theory as a basis for examining field material from a longitudinal study of the replacement of a control system in a pharmaceutical plant. Hine (1995) describes an information system for botanical plant categorization, and argues that the system came to represent both the plants being described and the taxonomists doing the work. The black-boxing of the taxonomy arose as a result of the social, political, organizational and scientific work that went into the project. Finally, Walsham and Sahay (1996) describe the attempt at the creation of a network of aligned interests for the development and use of GIS for district-level administration in India. The GIS technology inscribed interests of its Western developers, and the paper describes how and why the attempts at translation and alignment of the interests of local-level administrators were a relative failure. In contrast to the comment at the end of the preceding paragraph, this latter paper contains a reasonable degree of detail on aspects of social interaction, but perhaps at the expense of a detailed description of the technological inscriptions.

4 CRITICAL APPRAISALS OF THE THEORY

Any new social theory which receives significant attention tends also to attract criticism, and actor-network theory is no exception to this. It is important that IS researchers who are thinking of using the theory should be aware of these criticisms, and should thus be able to generate an informed view of the usefulness and limitations of the theory in their own work. As far as this author is aware, no similar critical appraisal is available in the IS literature to date. Four broad strands of critique will be considered in this section. In each case, the nature of the criticism will be articulated, responses made by proponents of actor-network theory will be considered, and a personal view on the relevance of this debate for IS research will be offered.

4.1 Limited Analysis of Social Structures

A major strand of criticism of actor-network theory is that it addresses the local and contingent, but that it pays little attention to broader social structures which influence the local. Reed (1995) provides an example of such a critique. He focuses on the description of actor-network theory in Law (1994) and argues that the theory

> engages in a form of analysis that concentrates on how things "get done" to the virtual exclusion of the various ways in which institutionalized structures shape and modify the process of social interaction and the socio-material practices through which it is accomplished. [Reed 1995, p. 332]

Habers (1995, p. 273) makes a similar point, when reviewing Latour (1993), that Latour provides an "asymmetrical reading of the mediation process, which is overly oriented towards the contribution of things to the production of the social order, almost neglecting the reverse, that is, the 'sociality' of the stability of things."

What do proponents of the theory say in response to these criticisms? Latour tackles the issue head-on, saying that

> Network analysis and field work have been criticised for giving interesting demonstrations of local contingencies without being able to take into account the "social structures" which influence the course of local history. Yet...the macro-structure of society is made of the same stuff as the micro-structure. [Latour 1991, p. 118]

Latour goes on to say that it is possible to use the actor-network methodology to move between levels of analysis and that macro-structures can thus be investigated with the same methodological tools as micro-structures. These are bold claims and it is clear that organizational theorists such as Reed remained unconvinced that the substantial prior work of sociologists on the nature and influence of social structures on micro-events and processes can be dismissed so readily. Law (1991) also defends actor-network theory against the above criticism in noting that social structures do not simply reside in the actions of people or in "memory traces" (Giddens 1984), but in a network of heterogeneous material arrangements. Yes, but this argument can be turned around, to note that we need to analyze not just material arrangements but also the memory traces and their implicit social structures.

The author of this paper shares some of the concerns expressed in the critique above, and is not convinced by the exclusivity arguments of the proponents of actor-network theory. One approach then for IS researchers is to combine the methodological approach and conceptual ideas of actor-network theory with insights and analyses drawn from theories of social structure. The work of Giddens was briefly referenced above, and structuration theory (Giddens 1984) and his later work linking levels of analysis from the individual to the global (Giddens 1990, 1991) offer sophisticated models of social action and structure at multiple levels. A major limitation of Giddens' work, from the perspective of an IS researcher, is that it offers little in the way of methodological guidelines, and that the material world of technology is not treated in any depth. A combination of this work with the methodology and concepts of actor-network theory would offer more than either one. Giddens (1984) argued that he did not set out to "wield a methodological scalpel" and he would thus probably be comfortable with this theoretical eclecticism. It is unlikely that the proponents of actor-network theory would accept a similar compromise, but their own theory recognizes the way in which ideas are translated by others and emerge in a different form, so at least the suggestions here would be compatible with that analysis.

4.2 An Amoral Stance

A second broad area of criticism of social constructivism in general, and actor-network theory in particular, concerns its stance on moral and political issues. This criticism was most forcefully articulated by Winner (1993). In this paper, Winner notes positive aspects of theories which break down arbitrary distinctions between the social and the technical spheres, and considers that they open up new possibilities for those who want to understand the place of technology in human experience. However, he goes on to criticize the "almost total disregard" of the social constructivists "for the social consequences of technical choice." He echoes some of the previously articulated concerns on social structure, but with a moral and political emphasis, in the following passage:

> Social constructivism seems not to have noticed the problem of elitism, the ways in which even a broad, multicentred spectrum of technical possibilities is skewed in ways that favour certain social interests while excluding others....Although it succeeds in finding contingency rather than necessity in the course of technological change, it seems so far to have little to say about the deep-seated political biases that can underlie the spectrum of choices that surface for relevant social actors. [Winner 1993, p. 370]

Bijker (1993) responds directly to the critique of Winner by arguing that an amoral stance is not a necessity of the social constructivist approach. The paper appeals to researchers in science and technology studies to be concerned with its implications for society. The paper briefly indicates some directions for this, such as ethical studies and ethnoaccounting studies, designed to show interpretive flexibility, to suggest alternative technological choices, and thus to "debunk the socio-technical ensembles constructed by the powerful." Bijker does admit that "not many of our studies have been presented with this explicit aim."

Perhaps the best defense against the charge of amorality then is to produce studies that demonstrate an ability to carry out what Bijker suggests, and the paper by Star (1991) can be thought to provide one. She uses the example of her own allergy to onions and the indifference to it of outlets in the McDonalds food chain to illustrate how the networks of the powerful can discriminate against various disadvantaged groups. She generalizes this experience as follows:

> A stabilised network is only stable for some, and that is for those who are members of the community of practice who form/use/maintain it. Any part of the public stability of a standardised network often involves the private suffering of those who are not standard – who must use the standardised network, but who are also non-members of the community of practice. [Star 1991, p. 43]

A further example of a paper using the concepts of actor-network theory to make points that are certainly not amoral or apolitical is the paper by Boland and Schultze, cited earlier, where they explicitly examine the political and moral agendas and networks of the proponents of activity based costing. Similarly, Monteiro and Hanseth deliberately engage with the political implications of the EDI standards which they have investigated.

Despite the above examples, the charges of an amoral stance continue to be aimed at actor-network theory, and Latour (1991, p. 130) responds as follows:

> Finally, we are left with the accusation of immorality, apoliticism, or moral relativism. Refusing to explain the closure of a controversy by its consequences does not mean that we are indifferent to the possibility of judgement, but only that we refuse to accept judgements that transcend the situation....Domination is an effect not cause. In order to make a diagnosis or a decision about the absurdity, the danger, the amorality, or the unrealism of an innovation, one must first describe the network.

There is no problem here with "first describing the network" but what comes after this? Where do the moral judgements come from if not from ideas that transcend the situation? If the Internet is examined, we do not need actor-network theory to tell us that the African continent is almost totally excluded. We cannot make a moral judgement on this on the basis of the network alone, but need political and ethical theories concerning socio-economic development.

So, what is the conclusion here for IS researchers who wish to use their studies to examine ethical and moral implications related to information systems? The personal view of this author is that actor-network theory does not offer explicit help in this area. On the other hand, the use of the theory does not preclude such an analysis, as the studies cited above briefly illustrated. As in the previous sub-section, it is the exclusivity arguments of actor-network proponents that are most problematic; if these are ignored, Latour's suggestion that we should first describe the network is a valuable injunction. Moral and political issues should be debated from a solid empirical base, and actor-network theory offers a contribution to the latter if not directly to the former.

4.3 the Problem of Generalized Symmetry

We have already seen how the symmetric treatment for humans and nonhumans in actor-network theory has been the cause of considerable controversy. The description of both as actants rather than actors was thought by Collins and Yearley (1992b) to go some way toward eliminating this problem, but other writers express more serious reservations. For example, Pels (1995) notes that Latour's (1993) symmetric embrace includes science and politics, society and nature, in addition to humans and nonhumans. Pels has this to say in opposition:

> Spokespersons may indeed symmetrically speak for both people and things, but only humans can act (can be *permitted* to act) as spokespersons. Perhaps we moderns have gone way too far in digging epistemological fences between ourselves and the remainder of nature, between science and politics, and between facts and values. But in the century which is presently drawing to a close, we moderns have also gone way too far in *erasing* all such distinctions, in totally politicizing culture, science and society, in massively reducing other people to the status of things, and in degrading ourselves to killing beasts of prey. [Pels 1995, pp. 138-139]

It does not need much imagination to see the type of things to which Pels is referring, such as IT-enabled modern warfare. Less dramatically, but arguably of even greater potential impact, is the IT-based vision of the virtual organization where an objective central group controls the company's global operations, moving people, jobs and societies like pawns on a chessboard (e.g., Mowshowitz 1994). Pels argues in favor of weaker asymmetries, retaining some crucial analytical distinctions between humans and nonhumans for example, and he considers that Latour's contribution is to provide an extreme position, which he does not agree with, but which forces us to rethink these issues.

Where does this philosophical debate leave the IS researcher? This author has found it valuable to think of things as actants and to consider whose interests they inscribe, represent, and speak for. This is not the same as assuming a symmetric position for people and things, but rather can be considered to be a valuable analytical device. The challenge of actor-network theory to the rigid separation of humans and nonhumans is a very valuable one in this age of hybrids and blurred and negotiable boundaries, but this does not imply an acceptance of the extreme position of symmetry.

4.4 Problems of Description

This last category of criticism concerns the major problem of description that arises from a study which follows the methodological guidelines of actor-network theory. It can be considered to be a rather more mundane issue than those discussed above, and there has been no great debate between critics and proponents. Nevertheless, we have noted it before in referring to limitations of some of the paper-length IS applications that used the theory. The problem is that such studies produce a veritable mass of detail, and the response of Latour, among others, is to produce book-length output (e.g., Latour 1996a). Even with this approach, Latour (1996b) is aware of problems. He discusses the limitations of trying to identify all of the heterogeneous associations between the human and nonhuman actors in the network. Instead, he proposes that one should examine the networks by tracing how an indefinite number of entities grasp one another in a limited number of ways. He illustrates this idea (1996b) with an amusing example of Anglo-French cooperation.

What advice can be offered to the IS researcher in this domain? In one sense, the problem is not particular to studies based on actor-network theory, but relates to any in-depth IS case study. However, the theory emphasizes the importance of detail, and thus the problem of selection for presentational purposes tends to be magnified. Three observations may provide a useful starting point for future work. First, it is noticeable that the IS field is singularly lacking in research-based books, rather than articles, and studies based on actor-network theory could offer a contribution here. Of course, many of the disciplinary mechanisms of tenure and promotion ascribe small value to books in relative terms, and individuals are not immune to these pressures. Nevertheless, the disciplinary mechanisms themselves are social constructions and thus not immutable. A second observation is that it would be desirable for IS journal editors to exercise discretion on paper length, and to allow the possibility for longer papers where they were based on in-depth case studies. Finally, we need to experiment with different ways to describe case studies in paper-length format; Latour's suggestion above is one possibility in this regard.

5 FUTURE PROSPECTS FOR THE THEORY IN IS RESEARCH

Actor-network theory has not arisen by chance at this particular point in history, but instead represents an attempt to address the increasingly complex socio-technical world in which we live. Hybrids of human and nonhuman elements continue to proliferate, and the boundaries between the technical and the social, and between human and machine capabilities, are frequently contested and always negotiable. IS research should be centrally concerned with these areas, and the primary conclusion of this paper is that actor-network theory has much to offer the IS researcher in both theoretical and methodological terms. Concepts such as those in outlined in Table 1, and their linking within the broader philosophy of the theory, provide a valuable analytical tool, as the IS studies reported in section 3 illustrated. A further point to note with respect to these studies is that they covered a wide range of contexts, including the health sector, transport applications and government administration; and a considerable variety of information system types, including accounting systems, plant categorization systems and GIS. No particular context or information system type can be excluded as a possible application area for the theory.

Authors such as Latour have described applications of the actor-network approach where the theory was used as a basis throughout the research work, encompassing methodology, method, data collection, analysis and write-up (e.g. Latour 1996a). However, it is noticeable that the authors of the IS studies reported earlier, while they all used the theory for analytical purposes, did not normally appear to use it as the basis for their field research. Does this represent a failing on their part? The view of this author is that it does not, since if actor-network theory can be used to illuminate the results from field research, that is sufficient justification for its inclusion in published work. Nevertheless, there must be concern that, if the full conceptual apparatus of the theory is not applied during the field research, important aspects and processes may not have been studied and documented. The implication in this author's view is that it would be valuable to see some full applications of the theory in the IS area in the future, so that we are able to assess the additional benefits which may be derived from this approach.

What of the criticisms of the theory which we discussed at some length in the previous section? None of the conclusions that we reached prohibit the use of the theory in the IS field, but they do suggest some cautions or qualifications to the IS researcher. The theory can be complemented by other social theories which take better account of broader social structures, such as the work of Giddens. Moral issues are not a direct focus of actor-network theory, and thus an IS researcher addressing such issues may find the theory valuable for empirical purposes, but will need to draw from other areas to supplement the theory. With respect to the two other criticisms discussed earlier, the conclusions can be summarized that we do not have to accept the full symmetry hypothesis of humans and nonhumans in order to make use of the theory, and that the problems of writing up indepth case studies based on the theory are not unique to actor-network theory, but that we need further experimentation here to improve our ways of reporting such studies.

A final word on actor-network theory relates to the more general point of the role of theory in IS research, particularly in the increasing body of work which can be broadly labeled interpretive studies. This author still encounters requests from reviewers and editors for justification as to why a particular theory was the best one to use for a given study. There is not, and never will be, a best theory. Theory is our chronically inadequate attempt to come to terms with the infinite complexity of the real world. Our quest should be for improved theory, not best theory, and for theory that is relevant to the issues of our time. Actor-network theory can be considered to satisfy both these criteria, and its use for a wide range of IS studies in the future offers considerable potential for increased understanding of the socio-technical systems which are the focus for IS research.

6 REFERENCES

Bijker, W. E. (1993). "Do Not Despair: There is Life after Constructivism." *Science, Technology and Human Values*, Volume 18, Number 1, pp. 113-138.

Bijker, W. E.; Hughes, T. P.; and Pinch, T. J. (Editors) (1987). *The Social Construction of Technological Systems*. Cambridge, Massachusetts: MIT Press.

Bloomfield, B. P.; Coombs, R.; Cooper, D. J.; and Rea, D. (1992). "Machines and Manoeuvres: Responsibility Accounting and the Construction of Hospital Information Systems." *Accounting, Management and Information Technologies*, Volume 2, Number 4, pp. 197-219.

Bloomfield, B. P., and Vurdubakis, T. (1994). "Boundary Disputes: Negotiating the Boundary between the Technical and the Social in the Development of IT Systems." *Information Technology and People*, Volume 7, Number 1, pp. 9-24.

Boland, R. J., and Schultze, U. (1996). "From Work to Activity: Technology and the Narrative of Progress." In W. J. Orlikowski, G. Walsham, M. R. Jones, and J. I. DeGross (Editors), *Information Technology and Changes in Organizational Work*. London: Chapman & Hall.

Bowers, J. (1992). "The Politics of Formalism." In M. Lea (Editor), *Contexts of Computer-Mediated Communication*. Hemel Hempstead, England: Harvester Wheatsheaf.

Bowker, G., and Star, S. L. (1994). "Knowledge and Information in International Information Management: Problems of Classification and Coding." In L. Bud-Frierman (Editor), *Information Acumen: The Understanding and Use of Knowledge in Modern Business*. London: Routledge.

Bowker, G.; Timmermans, S.; and Star, S. L. (1996). "Infrastructure and Organizational Transformations: Classifying Nurses' Work." In W. J. Orlikowski, G. Walsham, M. R. Jones, and J. I. DeGross (Editors), *Information Technology and Changes in Organizational Work*. London: Chapman & Hall.

Callon, M. (1986). "Some Elements of a Sociology of Translation: Domestication of the Scallops and the Fishermen." In J. Law (Editor), *Power, Action and Belief: A New Sociology of Knowledge?* London: Routledge & Kegan Paul.

Callon, M. (1991). "Techno-Economic Networks and Irreversibility." In J. Law (Editor), *A Sociology of Monsters: Essays on Power, Technology and Domination.* London: Routledge.

Callon, M., and Latour, B. (1992). "Don't Throw the Baby Out with the Bath School! A Reply to Collins and Yearley." In A. Pickering (Editor), *Science as Practice and Culture.* Chicago: University of Chicago Press.

Collins, H. M., and Yearley, S. (1992a). "Epistemological Chicken." In A. Pickering (Editor), *Science as Practice and Culture.* Chicago: University of Chicago Press.

Collins, H. M., and Yearley, S. (1992b). "Journey into Space." In A. Pickering (Editor), *Science as Practice and Culture.* Chicago: University of Chicago Press.

Giddens, A. (1984). *The Constitution of Society.* Cambridge, England: Polity Press.

Giddens, A. (1990). *The Consequences of Modernity.* Cambridge, England: Polity Press.

Giddens, A. (1991). *Modernity and Self-Identity.* Cambridge, England: Polity Press.

Habers, H. (1995). "Book Review: 'We Have Never Been Modern' by Bruno Latour." *Science, Technology and Human Values*, Volume 20, Number 2, pp. 270-275.

Haraway, D. (1991). *Simians, Cyborgs, and Women: The Reinvention of Nature.* London: Free Association Books.

Hine, C. (1995). "Representations of Information Technology in Disciplinary Development: Disappearing Plants and Invisible Networks." *Science, Technology and Human Values*, Volume 20, Number 1, pp. 65-85.

Kavanagh, D., and Araujo, L. (1995). "Chronigami: Folding and Unfolding Time." *Accounting, Management and Information Technologies*, Volume 5, Number 2, pp. 103-121.

Latour, B. (1987). *Science in Action: How to Follow Scientists and Engineers through Society.* Cambridge, Massachusetts: Harvard University Press.

Latour, B. (1991). "Technology is Society Made Durable." In J. Law (Editor), *A Sociology of Monsters: Essays on Power, Technology and Domination.* London: Routledge.

Latour, B. (1993). *We Have Never Been Modern.* Hemel Hempstead, England: Harvester Wheatsheaf.

Latour, B. (1996a). *Aramis or the Love of Technology.* Cambridge, Massachusetts: Harvard University Press.

Latour, B. (1996b). "Social Theory and the Study of Computerized Work Sites." In W. J. Orlikowski, G. Walsham, M. R. Jones, and J. I. DeGross (Editors), *Information Technology and Changes in Organizational Work.* London: Chapman & Hall.

Law, J. (1991). "Introduction: Monsters, Machines and Sociotechnical Relations." In J. Law (Editor), *A Sociology of Monsters: Essays on Power, Technology and Domination.* London: Routledge.

Law, J. (1992). "Notes on the Theory of the Actor-Network: Ordering, Strategy and Heterogeneity." *Systems Practice*, Volume 5, Number 4, pp. 379-393.
Law, J. (1994). *Organizing Modernity*. Oxford: Basil Blackwell.
Monteiro, E., and Hanseth, O. (1996). "Social Shaping of Information Infrastructure: On Being Specific about the Technology." In W. J. Orlikowski, G. Walsham, M. R. Jones, and J. I. DeGross (Editors), *Information Technology and Changes in Organizational Work*. London: Chapman & Hall.
Mowshowitz, A. (1994). "Virtual Organization: A Vision of Management in the Information Age." *The Information Society*, Volume 10, Number 4, pp. 267-288.
Mumford, E. (1981). "Participative Systems Design: Structure and Method." *Systems, Objectives, Solutions*, Volume 1, pp. 5-19.
Orlikowski, W. J.;Walsham, G.; Jones, M. R.; and DeGross, J. I. (Editors) (1996). *Information Technology and Changes in Organizational Work*. London: Chapman & Hall.
Pels, D. (1995). "Have We Never Been Modern? Towards a Demontage of Latour's Modern Constitution." *History of the Human Sciences*, Volume 8, Number 3, pp. 129-141.
Reed, M. I. (1995). "The Action/Structure Debate in Organizational Analysis." *Conference on Structuration Theory and Organizations*. Paris, France.
Star, S. L. (1991). "Power, Technologies and the Phenomenology of Conventions: On Being Allergic to Onions." In J. Law (Editor), *A Sociology of Monsters: Essays on Power, Technology and Domination*. London: Routledge.
Vidgen, R., and McMaster, T. (1996). "Black Boxes, Non-Human Stakeholders and the Translation of IT." In W. J. Orlikowski, G. Walsham, M. R. Jones, and J. I. DeGross (Editors), *Information Technology and Changes in Organizational Work*. London: Chapman & Hall.
Walsham, G., and Sahay, S. (1996). "GIS for District-Level Administration in India: Problems and Opportunities." *University of Lancaster Research Paper SM 02/96*, Lancaster, United Kingdom.
Winner, L. (1993). "Upon Opening the Black Box and Finding it Empty: Social Constructivism and the Philosophy of Technology." *Science, Technology and Human Values*, Volume 18, Number 3, pp. 362-378.

7 BIOGRAPHY

Geoff Walsham is currently Acting Director of the MBA Programme at the Judge Institute of Management Studies, Cambridge University. His teaching and research is centered on the development, use and management of computer-based information systems, and the relationships of these systems to changes in organizations and societies. His last post was as Professor of Information Management at Lancaster University, but he returned to Cambridge in 1996, where he had previously worked for 19 years in the Management Studies Group of the Engineering Department. His publications include *Interpreting Information Systems in Organizations* (Wiley 1993) and *Information Technology and Changes in Organizational Work* (edited with W. Orlikowski, M. Jones and J. DeGross, Chapman & Hall, 1996).

24

Imagine: Thought Experiments in Information Systems Research

L. D. Introna
Department of Information Systems
London School of Economics and Political Science
London WC2A 2AW, England
Fax: 0171 955 7385
E-mail: L.INTRONA@lse.ac.uk

E. A. Whitley
Department of Information Systems
London School of Economics and Political Science
London WC2A 2AW, England
Fax: 0171 955 7385
E-mail: E.A.Whitley@lse.ac.uk

Abstract

In this paper, we will argue that thought experiments can play a significant role in qualitative information systems research. We show the unique role that thought experiments can play in destroying existing belief systems within a community as well as how they can help creating new ones. Because thought experiments have to rely on existing data and concepts, they are particularly effective at providing the shift in perspective needed for a scientific revolution. In the paper, we analyze four thought experiments, relevant to information systems, to show how they are able to bring structure to a muddled discourse in a way that empirical, quantitative research cannot. We conclude with a discussion of the conditions necessary for effective thought experiments that will enable them to be convincing and challenging. In so doing, it is hoped that the result will be further clarity in the types of questions and answers that we should be exploring in the study of information systems.

1 INTRODUCTION

> *Thought experiments have more than once played a critically important role in the development of physical science.* Thomas S. Kuhn

Few would dispute the convincing power of a well designed thought experiment. Its ability to persuade seems to be in the compact, crisp nature of the narrative, or in the use of common everyday terms and concepts. As a result, thought experiments tend to have an appeal way beyond the limitations of disciplinary boundaries. Yet, these same characteristics also tend to trivialize them. They are often seen as nice "stories" to entertain students or add some spice to an otherwise dull lecture. While this may be true, however, there is no doubt that thought experiments have often played decisive roles in creating clarity in a confused and muddled discourse, often creating powerful counterexamples to dislodge, or seriously question, a prevailing theory. Thus, although there are many reasons to believe that thought experiments do not belong in "serious" science, there seems to be equally sufficient reason to believe that they not only belong, but could play a decisive role in advancing understanding in situations where contradiction and confusion exist (Kuhn 1977).

In this paper, we will show how thought experiments can play a significant role in information systems research and how they can be used to change the beliefs of information systems researchers. We will demonstrate, through the analysis of four thought experiments, that they have the potential to bring clarity to a muddled discourse in a way that empirical research often cannot. We will also put forward some guidelines of when and how to apply thought experiments.

Our intention is to provide a background understanding of thought experiments and the role that they can play to enable the information systems discipline to take and develop the idea of thought experiments to further the field.

The paper is structured as follows: first, we will define the notion of thought experiments and present a taxonomy for classifying them. We will also argue, using the work of Kuhn, why we believe them to be important to current information systems research; second, we will analyze four thought experiments to demonstrate their usefulness to developing our understanding of computer based information systems; finally, we will provide heuristic guidelines for the use of thought experiments in the future.

2 ON THOUGHT EXPERIMENTS

2.1 A Taxonomy of Thought Experiments

Thought experiments are experiments that are unrealizable (Bunzl 1996). They are unrealizable as a matter of principle or of practice. For example, Einstein's (1949 p. 53) observer traveling at the speed of light is unrealizable in principle. Many moral issues are similarly raised by considering situations that could not be done in practice, especially not just to make moral/philosophical points.

One may ask whether a thought experiment is not merely a particular form of argument or even a form of scenario analysis. There are obviously some similarities with these; however, the essential difference is in the fact that a thought experiment is explicitly constructed, within the confines of the existing paradigm, *in order to* destroy the existing paradigmatic position, or in order to construct an argument for a new position. One may define a thought experiment as follows:

> It is a coherent narrative of an unrealizable experimental situation, commensurate with the current paradigm, that is explicitly constructed in order to destroy the current paradigmatic position or to support an emerging paradigmatic position.

Thought experiments are not done mentally purely for the sake of convenience. They are thought experiments precisely because they cannot be performed, in principle or in practice, in the empirical world. This ought immediately to raise a number of questions. If they cannot be performed in the empirical world to what extent are their conclusions relevant to the empirical world? Is this not a form of pure speculation? Some attempts at answering this point are provided by Bunzl (1996), Sorensen (1992) and Wilkes (1988), but a detailed discussion is beyond the scope of this paper. However, in this paper we will show, in a less technical way, that it is true that certain thought experiments are relevant to our knowledge of the world. We will do this by combining a taxonomy of thought experiments with the work of Thomas Kuhn on scientific revolutions.

A first step toward understanding the range of roles that thought experiments can play will be by presenting a taxonomy of thought experiments. Brown (1986) argues that thought experiments can be either destructive or constructive, as indicated in Figure 1. Destructive thought experiments can be thought of as directed against an existing theory and are designed to undermine the theory by demonstrating either an inconsistency internal to the theory or its incompatibility with other background beliefs. In contrast, constructive thought experiments are directed at providing support for a contested existing theory or argument (conclusive), directed at clarifying a known and emerging argument (elucidative), or can be an occasion for speculation to open up the debate concerning an emerging theory or argument (conjectural).

The discussion of the taxonomy above indicates that thought experiments may have a unique role to play in changing the shape of perceptions and beliefs within scientific research. The next section will briefly review the work of Thomas Kuhn on scientific revolutions and suggest the role that thought experiments can play in them.

2.2 Thought Experiments and Scientific Revolutions

Kuhn's historical review of scientific stability and scientific change brought the term paradigm shift into popular discourse. To him, a paradigm is much more than just the methods used by a community of researchers. A paradigm is a way of looking at the world. It is a way of deciding what is an interesting question and it is also a way of deciding what is an appropriate answer.

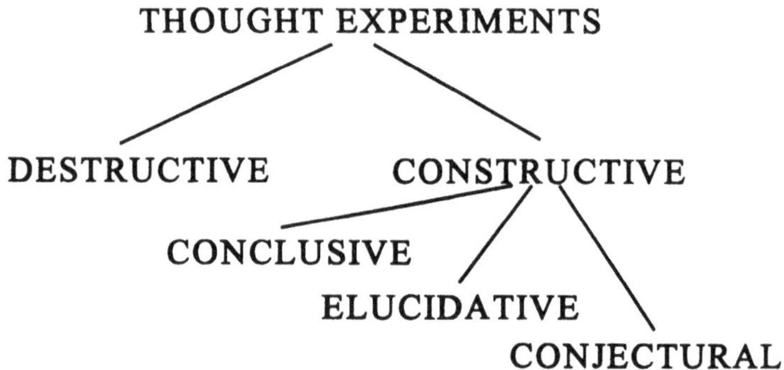

Figure 1 A Taxonomy of Thought Experiment (adapted from Brown 1986).

According to Kuhn, scientific traditions evolve but they do so in discrete rather than continuous steps. Over time, the existing paradigm tends to generate more and more anomalies that cannot be explained within the current framework of beliefs. These problematic results are initially ignored or are attributed to errors in measurement or extraneous variables. At some point, however, they cannot be ignored and, at this point, a scientific revolution occurs and there is a shift to a new paradigm.

It is important to note, however, that a paradigm shift can only occur if there is an alternative emerging paradigm available. This paradigm must do more than just exist, however. It must be able to "explain" the majority of the existing "understood" phenomena as well as a good proportion of the anomalies. The question arises, however, as to how such shifts occur.

Paradigm shifts do not normally arise from spotting new relationships among a large set of anomalies. Instead, as the number of anomalies grows, attention becomes focused on the anomalies themselves and the beliefs that caused the anomalies will come under investigation. Thus, paradigm shifts change the very nature of the scientific work being undertaken. This is normally done through a radical revision of existing beliefs about how the world functions, as seen, for example, in the shift from an earth-centric to sun-centric view of the cosmos by Copernicus.

It thus becomes apparent that the facts in the scientific discipline are not acontextual truths but rather that they are elements of closely interrelated networks of beliefs (Wittgenstein 1969) developed within the scientific community. Thus the scientific beliefs associated with the paradigm shape what are considered to be the facts within the paradigm. In these situations the thought experiment enables the scientist "to use as an integral part of his knowledge what that knowledge had previously made inaccessible to him" (Kuhn 1977 p. 263). By shifting the paradigm, the same problematic phenomena are now viewed with a different conceptual apparatus which emphasizes different aspects of the problem; the viewpoint on the situation has changed.

It seems plausible, therefore, to map the stages of paradigm shift onto our framework for thought experiments. Destructive thought experiments are designed to make explicit the beliefs of the existing paradigm in such a way that they unfreeze (Lewin 1952) the existing situation. Thus, destructive thought experiments play a role in starting a scientific revolution. Constructive thought experiments, thereafter, play a similar role in providing support for the newly emerging paradigm which can then lead to a refreezing of beliefs in the new paradigm (Lewin 1952). This is summarized in the table below.

Stage of change in paradigm	Type of experiment
Existing paradigm has problems dealing with anomalies (unfreeze)	Destructive thought experiment
Attempts are made to find new paradigms (move)	Elucidative thought experiment Conjectural thought experiment
New paradigm is found and becomes dominant (refreeze)	Conclusive thought experiment

2.3 Scientific Revolution in Information Systems?

It is our conjecture that the information systems discipline is now in a Kuhnian crisis. The gap between the expectations raised by the functional/representational paradigm (traditionally at the heart of the discipline) and the growing number of anomalies that "do not respond to minor adjustments of the existing (functional/representational) conceptual and instrumental fabric" (Kuhn 1977, p. 262) is bigger than ever.

There are already signs that researchers are critically analyzing the fabric of their beliefs that have brought the community to its current position. There are papers and conference panels that reconsider the fundamental assumptions behind the way that information systems research is currently being done (Hirschheim, Klein and Lyytinen 1996), on whether information systems can survive as a unique discipline (Markus 1996) (Fedorowicz et al. 1996), on the way that information systems uses research from other disciplines (Adam and Fitzgerald 1996), on the relative merits of different research approaches (Newsted et al. 1996; Myers et al. 1996) and on the effectiveness of current techniques (Fitzgerald 1996).

Kuhn states that during times of crisis "even philosophy will become a legitimate scientific tool" (p. 263) . The 1996 AIS Americas conference had twenty-one papers on the philosophical foundations of information systems. The previous year there had only been a (poorly attended) panel.

Thus there is growing evidence to suggest parts of the discipline are becoming uneasy with the beliefs and assumptions that underlie the dominant paradigm of information systems. In this atmosphere, it is timely to reintroduce the notion of thought experiments to the information systems community as a legitimate method for doing qualitative research and for advancing the field of information systems. Using our framework, thought experiments can help provide the mechanism for making the shift between dominant modes of thought.

3 AN ANALYSIS OF SOME THOUGHT EXPERIMENTS

This section analyzes four thought experiments that are related to information systems research. Each experiment is described and its impact on the field is outlined. Finally, an attempt is made to classify the experiment in the taxonomy given above.

3.1 Searle's Chinese Room

This thought experiment was presented by the philosopher John Searle to examine the notion that computers can understand language (Searle 1980). Searle asks us to *imagine* a room with two slots in the door. People walk up to the room and place two sheets of paper with Chinese writing on them into the upper slot. Then, after a short period of time, they receive a third sheet of paper from the lower slot. Again this sheet has Chinese writing on it. More particularly, the first sheet of paper contains a story in Chinese, the second sheet is a series of questions about the story and the third sheet has the answers to the questions, all written in perfect Chinese. To the outside observer, therefore, the room would seem to understand Chinese. Inside the room, however, is Searle himself who, he assures us, cannot understand a word of Chinese. Instead, he has a series of charts and rule books that say things like "when you get these shapes on the papers respond by writing the following shapes on the sheet." Whenever he receives the story and questions he responds by writing the answers and returns them to the person outside.

The process described here is functionally equivalent to that given by Schank and Childers (1984) when describing their natural language understanding programs. Here the program is given a tale in natural language and a series of questions about the tale and the computer responds with answers to the questions. Schank and Childers claim, therefore, that the computer understands natural language. Not so, argues Searle, based on his thought experiment. Searle, sitting inside the room does not understand Chinese, he is simply manipulating symbols. It is only the external observer who attributes this understanding to the system (see Maturana and Varela (1992) and Winograd and Flores (1986) for further examples of this difference between internal operation and attribution based on observation).

Searle's point with the thought experiment is to clarify the difference between simply manipulating symbols using rules and truly understanding language. Various attempts have been made to try and explain how this situation can lead to an understanding of language, often by explaining that it is not Searle who understands Chinese, but rather it is the combination of Searle, the instruction books and the room. Such explanations, however, do not really help clarify how manipulating symbols can lead to understanding.

Impact of the Chinese Room Thought Experiment. The Chinese Room experiment provoked many responses from supporters of artificial intelligence and its opponents (indeed, the initial publication of the paper was accompanied by a series of commentaries and a response by Searle). Perhaps one of the most interesting consequences is given by Turkle (1996), who states that the experiment suggested a way of dealing with the idea of intelligent machines.

> Searle diffused fears of a cybernetic Frankenstein by reassuring people that even advanced programs, far more complex than those that currently exist, do not embody intelligence in the way human beings do. So accepting machine intelligence became comfortable, because it could be seen as unthreatening to human uniqueness. [p. 124]

In this way, it is apparent that Searle's experiment fits within the destructive category in that it addresses an existing theoretical position and demonstrates that it is incompatible with the background beliefs about human understanding of natural language. It also highlights the existence of conceptual problems that are implicit in the existing view that have not, to date, been fully considered.

3.2 Introna's Transparent World

Introna (1996b) argues that one of the problems with privacy discourse is that it assumes we (society) know why we need privacy, or we know what we would lose if we lose privacy. Introna proposes a thought experiment to help clarify the impact of a loss of privacy on social relationships by proposing a world of absolute transparency.

Imagine a world where there is a comprehensive and complete lack of privacy, complete and immediate access, complete and immediate knowledge, and complete and constant observation of every individual. There will be no private thoughts and no private places. Every thought and every act is completely transparent from motive right through to the actual thought or behavior. Body and mind are immediately and completely transparent to each and every "other." Let us call this world the transparent world.

Let us consider the nature of social relationships in the transparent world with a number of questions. Would differentiated relationships be possible? How would your relationship with your wife or lover differ from your relationship with an official or your manager or your child? What will there be to exclusively *share* since everything is always already known to every "other"? It seems that in the transparent world, notions such as getting to know someone, or being intimate with someone, or sharing yourself with someone just fade into obscurity.

Furthermore, in such a world, how would you differentiate yourself, how would you compete? Competitive advantage requires knowledge of a method, a technique or a way of doing that is not known to the other. Is creativity possible? How is it possible to say "this is my idea" or "this is what I think"? Does it make sense to talk of "my" or "me" at all, since original thought or original action would, in principle, be impossible (or at least indeterminable)?

From this thought experiment it is clear that all social relationships, relationships of collaboration or of competition, require at least some level of privacy.

Impact of Introna's transparent world. This is an example of a constructive conjectural thought experiment. In the experiment, one variable the level of transparency) is increased to its limit. This helps the researcher to think through the issues that may become gray somewhere in the middle. Now, one can protest against such a thought experiment by saying that the transparent world is a useless concept since total transparency is impossible. It is Introna's contention that the issues that are very apparent in the transparent world, as shown in the thought experiment, become issues in the everyday world, where technology erodes our experience or privacy, long before total transparency is reached and it is the thought experiment that allows us to focus on them.

3.3 Varela's Submarine

Cognitive science theory postulates that in order for a system (an individual) to act in a meaningful way in a world, the system must have access to some type of representation of that world. Hence, people have (make/remake) some form of representations of the world "out there" in their heads that functions as the "map" upon which their action is based. The actor would then become aware of certain environmental inputs and would use these inputs and the "map" to decide what the appropriate outputs should be.

Maturana and Varela (1992) argue that this theory is wrong. They argue that the problem is with our epistemological accounting. We are projecting the world of the scientist (as an observer of phenomena) onto the world of the involved actor, in the world. They argue that the involved actor does not take inputs and turn them into outputs. On the contrary, for the involved actor the environmental inputs are merely disturbances (perturbations) that threaten the internal coherence that needs to be maintained if the system is to survive.

To demonstrate this confusion they make use of a thought experiment of a submarine pilot (Maturana and Varela 1992, pp. 136–137). *Imagine* a person who *always* lived in a submarine. The person has never left the submarine but is trained how to pilot it. You (the observer) see the submarine float gracefully through very dangerous reefs and obstacles and surface in the still waters of the bay. On surfacing you contact the submarine pilot and announce: "Congratulations! You avoided the reefs and surfaced beautifully. You really know how to pilot a submarine in dangerous circumstances." The pilot in the submarine is, however, perplexed: "What is this about reefs and surfacing? All I did was push some levers and knobs to establish certain relationships between indicators as I operated the levers and knobs. It was done in a prescribed sequence which I am used to doing. This is what my father taught me, and his father taught him. I did not do any special manoeuver, and on top of that, you talk to me about a submarine. What is that? You must be kidding!" All that exists for the pilot of the submarine are the different indicator readings, their transitions, and sequences of obtaining specific relations between them. It is only for the observer that the dynamic relations between the submarine and its environment exists. These are representations which the submarine pilot does not have or need.

In the example we can see that for the observer there is an input–output model of reality. The model described what actions (by the pilot) created what relationships between the submarine and its environment. For the pilot there is only a closure type description. The inputs from the environment were mere disturbances that had to be dealt with by restoring a particular relationship between certain indicators by applying certain levers or knobs. For the pilot there is an internal coherence that must be maintained. If this coherence is maintained, the submarine world will stay intact; if not, it will disappear.

Impact of Varela's submarine. The argument implicit in the submarine thought experiment has some very important implications for information systems research. If the central doctrine of representationalism used by information systems – imported from the reference discipline of cognitive science – is successfully challenged, then much of what is today seen as the core of the discipline would be under suspicion. For example, it can be used to argue that systems developers do not explicitly attend to method but use method only as part of "getting the job done" (Introna and Whitley 1996). It can also be used to argue that managers do not explicitly attend to information (as an input) but rather see it as perturbations that need to be mediated in "getting the job done" (Introna 1996a).

Varela's submarine is a clear example of a destructive thought experiment (against representationalism). It also serves as a constructive, conclusive thought experiment in support of the theory that meaningful action could be based on local structural coupling (Maturana and Varela 1992).

3.4 The Collins–Turing Test

The issue of intelligent machines is the focus of a second thought experiment, although this time the experiment is more concerned with clarifying misconceptions about *what it means to be a socialized human* than to prove the impossibility of artificial intelligence.

In 1950, the mathematician Alan Turing proposed a test that could be used to address the issue of whether or not a machine was intelligent. Instead of asking what tasks a machine would need to perform in order to be considered intelligent, Turing proposed a test that could be used to examine the claims that a machine was intelligent. Essentially, if a human interrogator could not differentiate between a machine and a human during a period of mediated interaction, the computer would be deemed to be intelligent.

The sociologist of knowledge, Harry Collins (1990), has proposed a thought experiment based on the Turing test which he claims shows the vital role that socialized knowledge plays in being human; knowledge which he argues cannot be explicitly taught to a computer.

When humans interact, they have an overwhelming tendency to compensate for their conversational partners. When people talk, they rarely do so using full, grammatically accurate sentences; their conversations are made up of pauses, mistakes and incomplete sentences. Nevertheless, most conversations do not break down at each of these problems. Instead the dialogue flows smoothly. To counter this tendency for compensation, Collins proposes that the experiment's protocol be tightened up to ensure that the judges are actively looking for the computer and will not make unnecessary allowances for the computer.

Collins' model of human knowledge argues that much of this knowledge is gained through socialization rather than explicit teaching. As such, he argues that unsocialized knowledge can only be spotted during long interactions which allow for the full possibility of interactions.

To demonstrate this, he proposes the following thought experiment. *Imagine* the range of interactions that can take place during a typical Turing test type interaction. Assume that the interaction lasts for one hour and, with both parties typing quickly, a total of 20,000 symbols can be created. If each symbol could be one of 100 possibilities, this gives a total 100 raised to the power of 20,000 possible strings of symbols ($10^{20,000}$). Now *imagine* (this is a thought experiment after all) that all these strings are stored in a computer. One would begin with "Hello how are you"; another would begin "Hello, how are yov," etc. The programmer of the computer now has to select which of these symbol strings to discard and which to keep for the intelligent machine. Many of these strings are simply not sensible (20,000 letter "A's," 20,000 letter "z's," 19,999 "A's" followed by a "B," etc.). However, others are sensible but would not necessarily be used by the programmer. The program works by waiting for the first statement and then picking, at random, one of the responses from the remaining options that match that part of the symbol string. Thus, if the interrogator begins by saying "Hello," the computer responds with one of its preprogrammed choices for following the initiation "Hello."

If the programmer deleted all the responses to a particular question, then the system would crash – it has no from which options to choose. It could, however, be programmed to degrade gracefully by apologizing for not understanding the question. A more difficult problem, however, arises with, for example, conversations that talk about politics. If the interrogator says "I prefer conservatives," what should the programmer do, especially if the programmer's politics are left of center? One option would be to delete all the symbol strings that responded with "So do I" and the like.

By restricting such statements, however, the programmer is not accurately matching the true conversational repertoire of a socialized human. There are occasions when it would be sensible to make statements that give a different political opinion to the programmer's normal one. The canny interrogator would therefore simply have to look out for the conversational partner that never changed its political viewpoint, no matter what the circumstances.

There are further problems if the programmer chooses a more liberal policy. Consider the case of humorous statements and jokes. A more liberal approach would be to include jokes in the list of possible conversations. Unfortunately, a consequence of this would either be a partner who never made jokes (too few jokes were left in the system) or one who made too many jokes, again easily spotted.

The purpose of the Collins–Turing test is to demonstrate the important role that socialized knowledge (such as when it is appropriate to express a different political view or when a joke is called for) is something that cannot be programmed; it is not a rule, it is a learned skill about knowing when to break the rules of conversation.

Impact of the Collins–Turing test. The impact of the Collins–Turing test on the artificial intelligence community is interesting to observe. On the one hand, it is possible to argue that it has had a very limited impact because Turing tests are still being undertaken without taking into consideration the points made by Collins (Shieber 1994a, 1994b; Loebner 1994). On the other hand, Collins has had a far greater impact on the artificial intelligence community at large, most recently as the opening reviewer of the 1992 book by Hubert Dreyfus, *What Computers Still Can't Do,* for the leading journal *Artificial Intelligence.*

The conceptual clarity provided by Collins has been used to address the issue of whether or not it is possible to create false identities on the internet (Whitley 1996). Much has been written about the possibility of creating false identities in cyberspace, where physical cues are no longer present; all that the conversational partner has access to is the linguistic utterances of the speaker. In such a case, however, the person attempting to create a false identity has exactly the same problems as the programmer in the thought experiment. What kind of utterances should the fake character make? In the long run, it will not be possible for the fakers always to make the appropriate utterances because they haven't been socialized into that role. Thus, while it is possible to appear to be a false identity, in the long term this false identity will be spotted, and it is most likely to be spotted by someone who has been socialized into the identity being mimicked.

This is a constructive, conclusive thought experiment in that it proposes a new way of viewing human intelligence in terms of socialized knowledge. As with Searle's experiment, it does not just propose a hypothetical situation but develops the implications of the situation in a variety of ways.

4 ENSURING EFFECTIVE THOUGHT EXPERIMENTS

As the previous examples have shown, in order for a thought experiment to be effective, it must work from within the existing conceptual apparatus of researchers. That is, it must be based on uncontested beliefs (dogmas) of the field. In particular, this means that the experiment must be based on known and accepted terms and concepts, it must articulate all assumptions needed as part of the narrative and these assumptions must also be reasonable to the field as it is. Thus the narrative must ensure that the impact of the thought experiment is not deflected by issues of implausibility (Boland and Schultze 1995). "The imagined situation must allow the researcher to employ his usual concepts in the way he has employed them before" (Kuhn 1977, p. 265).

Based on known and accepted terms and concepts. The terms and concepts employed in the thought experiment must be generally accepted within the current paradigm or must be such that the normal everyday understanding of the terms or concepts will suffice. If this is not true, the revolutionary power of the thought experiment is lost. In Introna's transparent world, the notion of sharing in interpersonal relationships may be too vague and ambiguous to make the experiment convincing, although one of the intentions of the experiment is to help focus on what is meant by sharing in precisely such situations. In contrast, Searle makes every effort to ensure that the "Searle" in the Chinese room acts according to known concepts of computing, and in particular mimics the processes of the computer systems that, it is claimed, can understand natural language.

Background must be specified. As with other experiments, thought experiments should also take care to make explicit background assumptions part of the narrative. Thus, in Varela's experiment, the narrative has the observer speaking effortlessly to the pilot of the submarine even though the pilot does not, by the terms of the experiment, share the life world of the person on the shore (Habermas 1984). Some of the impact of the experiment, about the different epistemological boundaries, is lost as one tries to understand how they could possibly talk together, given their vastly different experiences. If Varela had included an explicit background assumption about their ability to communicate, this problem would not be raised.

The purpose of the thought experiment is not simply to result in a further refinement of the field to cope with yet another anomaly. It is intended to encourage a shift in paradigm. Therefore the full rhetorical tools of discourse must be used to their best effect (Fuchs 1992, p. 30). Unlike traditional experiments, whose results are always under-determined by the data, thought experiments can't be explained away by poor experimental practice or misreading. Either the thought experiment succeeds or it doesn't; it fails in terms of its rhetoric, not its implementation.

5 CONCLUDING DISCUSSION

In this paper, we introduced the notion of a thought experiment as a basis for undertaking qualitative research. It was argued that thought experiments have a particularly important role to play in terms of Kuhnian scientific revolutions.

Next, we sought to classify thought experiments in terms of whether the results they produce are destructive or constructive. A destructive thought experiment seeks to show that existing ways of viewing the world contain conceptual problems that the experiment elicits. Constructive experiments offer new ways of viewing the world.

We then described four thought experiments that could affect our understanding of computer-based systems. These were Searle's Chinese room, Introna's transparent world, Varela's submarine, and Collins' revised Turing test. Each experiment was described and its impact assessed. The experiments were chosen to illustrate the range of uses to which thought experiments have been put. Searle's experiment describes a hypothetical situation and uses it to destroy the belief that simply manipulating symbols is the same as understanding language. Introna, in contrast, offers a more constructive experiment in which the hypothetical situation is used to clarify what is meant by shared relationships.

Thought experiments are effective only rhetorically. It is therefore essential that their rhetorical effect is maximized; in the paper, we reviewed the conditions necessary to achieve this. In particular, the notion that the thought experiment, while proposing a new world view has to be understandable and acceptable from the framework of the existing belief systems.

We have shown how thought experiments can be used to enable paradigm shifts. The information systems discipline, at the current time, seems to be showing symptoms of a Kuhnian crisis. It is becoming clear that the dominant paradigm, based on rationalist and functionalist beliefs, and the main research methods used, namely hypothesis testing and qualitative data analysis, are inappropriate for the full range of phenomena associated with computer-based systems in organizations. Moreover, an alternative paradigm, loosely based around interpretivism (Walsham 1993, 1995), exists with a growing following. It is in this context that we propose that the information systems discipline look more closely at thought experiments as a means of clarifying its conceptual apparatus; of deciding whether it wishes to irreversibly to change its foundational beliefs. If so, we look forward to more published thought experiments in the field to encourage scientific disruption. Perhaps advocates of interpretivism, or any other emerging research approach, should attempt to construct convincing thought experiments to encourage us to follow their approach.

6 ACKNOWLEDGMENTS

The authors would like to thank the representative of the Arizona Highway Police who reminded them of the importance of real world situations as well as thought experiments.

They are also particularly grateful to Steve Sawyer and colleagues at Syracuse University, and Dick Boland and colleagues at Case Western Reserve University who offered many useful recommendations about improving this paper.

7 REFERENCES

Adam, F., and Fitzgerald, B. (1996) "A Framework for Analyzing the Evolution of the IS Field: Can IS Become a Stable Discipline." In J. D. Coelho, T. Jelassi, W. König, H. Krcmar, R. O'Callaghan, and M. Sääksjarvi (Editors), *Fourth European Conference on Information Systems.* Lisbon, Portugal, pp. 17-32.

Boland, R. J., and Schultze, U. (1995). "From Work to Activity: Technology and the Narrative of Progress." In W. J. Orlikowski, G. Walsham, M. R. Jones, and J. I. DeGross (Editors), *Information Technology and Changes in Organizational Work.* London: Chapman and Hall, pp. 308-324.

Brown, J. R. (1986). "Thought Experiments Since the Scientific Revolution." *International Studies in the Philosophy of Science*, Volume 1, Number 1, pp. 1-15.

Bunzl, M. (1996). "The Logic of Thought Experiments." *Syntheses,* Volume 106, Number 2, pp. 227-240.

Collins, H. M. (1990). *Artificial Experts: Social Knowledge and Intelligent Machines.* Cambridge, Massachusetts: The MIT Press.

Dreyfus, H. L. (1992). *What Computers Still Can't Do: A Critique of Artificial Reason.* Cambridge, Massachusetts: The MIT Press.

Einstein, A. (1949). "Autobiographical Notes." In A. Schlipp (Editor), *Albert Einstein: Philosopher-Scientist.* LaSalle, Illinois: Open Court.

Fedorowicz, J.; Lee, D.; Sviokla, J. J.; and Weber, B. (1996). "Are There Barbarians at the Gates of Information Systems?" Panel presented at the Seventeenth International Conference on Information Systems, Cleveland, Ohio, December 16-18.

Fitzgerald, B. (1996) "An Investigation of the Use of System Development Methodologies in Practice." In J. D. Coelho, T. Jelassi, W. König, H. Krcmar, R. O'Callaghan, and M. Sääksjarvi (Editors), *Fourth European Conference on Information Systems.* Lisbon, Portugal, pp. 143-161.

Fuchs, S. (1992). *The Professional Quest for Truth: A Social Theory of Science and Knowledge.* Albany: State University of New York Press.

Habermas, J. R. (1984) . *The Theory of Communicative Action.* London: Heinemann Education.

Hirschheim, R.; Klein, H.; and Lyytinen, K. (1996). "Exploring the Conceptual Foundations of Information Systems." *Accounting, Management and Information Technology.* Forthcoming.

Introna, L. D. (1996a) *Management, Information and Power.* London: Macmillan, forthcoming.

Introna, L. D. (1996b). "Privacy and the Computer: Why We Need Privacy in the Information Society." London School of Economics.

Introna, L. D., and Whitley, E. A. (1996). "Against method." London School of Economics.

Kuhn, T. S. (1977). "A Function for Thought Experiments." In T. S. Kuhn (Editor), *The Essential Tension: Selected Studies in Scientific Tradition and Change.* Chicago: University of Chicago Press, pp. 240-265.

Lewin, K. (1952). "Group Decision and Social Change." In T. Newcomb, E. Hartley, and E. MacCobby (Editors), *Readings in Social Psychology.* New York: Holt, Rinehart & Winston.

Loebner, H. G. (1994). "In Response." *Communications of the ACM*, Volume 37, Number 6, pp. 79-82.

Markus, M. L. (1996). "Thinking the Unthinkable: What Happens if the IS Field as We Know It Goes Away?" Claremont Graduate School.

Maturana, H. R., and Varela, F. J. (1992). *The Tree of Knowledge: The Biological Roots of Human Understanding.* Revised edition. Boston: Shambhala.

Myers, M. D.; Klein, H. K.; Truex, D.; and Wynn, E. (1996). "The Merits of Three Qualitative Research Methods." Panel presented at the Seventeenth International Conference on Information Systems, Cleveland, Ohio, December 16-18.

Newsted, P.; Chin, W.; Ngwenyama, O. K.; and Lee, A. (1996). "Resolved: Surveys Have Outlived Their Usefulness in Information Systems Research." Panel presented at the Seventeenth International Conference on Information Systems, Cleveland, Ohio, December 16-19.

Schank, R. C., and Childers, P. G. (1984). *The Cognitive Computer: On Language, Learning, and Artificial Intelligence.* Reading, Massachusetts: Addison-Wesley Publishing Company.

Searle, J. R. (1980). "Minds, Brains and Programs (with Commentary and Author's Response)." *The Behavioral and Brain Sciences* , Volume 3, Number 3, pp. 417-457.

Shieber, S. M. (1994a). "Lessons from a Restricted Turing Test." *Communications of the ACM*, Volume 37, Number 6, pp. 70-78.

Shieber, S. M. (1994b). Your Article on the Turing Test, June 1994. Personal communication.

Sorensen, R. A. (1992). "Thought Experiments and the Epistemology of Laws." *Canadian Journal of Philosophy*, Volume 22, Number 1, pp. 15-44.

Turkle, S. (1996). *Life on the Screen: Identity in the Age of the Internet.* London: Weidenfeld & Nicholson.

Walsham, G. (1993). *Interpreting Information Systems in Oganisations.* Chichester, England: John Wiley.

Walsham, G. (1995). "The Emergence of Interpretivism in IS Research." *Information Systems Research*, Volume 6, Number 4, pp. 376-394.

Whitley, E. A. (1996). "Is It Possible to Really Play with Identity in Cyber'space'? A Review Based on the Sociology of Knowledge." London School of Economics.

Wilkes, K. V. (1988). *Real people: Personal Identity without Thought Experiments.* Oxford: Clarendon Press.

Winograd, T., and Flores, F. (1986). *Understanding Computers and Cognition: A New Foundation for Design.* Reading, Massachusetts: Addison Wesley.
Wittgenstein, L. (1969). *On Certainty.* Denis Paul and G. E. M. Anscombe, Translators. Oxford: Basil Blackwell.

8 BIOGRAPHY

Lucas D. Introna is a Lecturer in Information Systems at the London School of Economics and Political Science and Visiting Professor of Information Systems at the University of Pretoria. His research interest is the social dimensions and consequences of information technology. He is associate editor of *Information Technology & People* and *The South African Computer Journal.* His practical and consulting experience includes design and implementation of information systems for various large corporations as well as strategic management consulting.

Edgar A. Whitley is a lecturer in Information Systems at the London School of Economics and Political Science. He has a B.Sc. (Econ) Computing and a Ph.D. in Information Systems, both from the LSE. He has taught undergraduate, postgraduate students and managers in the UK and abroad. Edgar was one of the organizers of the First European Conference on Information Systems and is actively involved in the coordination of ECIS conferences. He has published widely on various information systems issues and is currently completing a book on the socio-philosophical foundations of information systems.

25

Legal Case Analysis in IS Research: Failures in Employing and Outsourcing for IT Professionals

S. Ang
Information Management Research Center
Nanyang Business School
Nanyang Technological University, Singapore
Tel: 65 799 5697
Fax: 65 792 2313
E-mail: asang@ntu.edu.sg

A. Endeshaw
Division of Business Law
Nanyang Technological University, Singapore
Tel: 65 799 6242
Fax: 65 791 3697
E-mail: AEndeshaw@ntu.edu.sg

Abstract

In this paper, we introduce readers to the richness of existing legal cases as sources of secondary data for analyzing contemporary issues in the management of information technology. Drawing upon legal research techniques and the principles of typology construction in the social sciences, we describe a method of creating prototypical disputes: synthesizing large masses of qualitative data embedded in past legal cases into summarized descriptions that encapsulate the most commonly found characteristics in those cases. We then demonstrate the development of themes or prototypical disputes on the basis of court decisions on issues arising from employing and outsourcing for IT professionals. We conclude by discussing other domains in the management of IT that may be amenable to the legal case methodology proposed in this study.

1 INTRODUCTION

In the 1990s, information technology, with its three components of hardware, software and people, has infiltrated almost every home, business and major industry. IT has become not only a competitive weapon but also a strategic necessity for organizations in the knowledge-based economy. To date, MIS researchers have made significant inroads into understanding how organizations can design and implement information systems to operate their businesses more efficiently and more effectively.

Although we have accumulated significant knowledge about how organizations use MIS, past MIS research presents a very pro-IT success orientation. Researchers tend toward demonstrating IT success, that is, the positive impacts of the use of IT on decision making, productivity or business value. Unfortunately, research that over-emphasizes successful use of IT has one major unintended consequence: organizations may unwittingly assume that IT failures are rare and therefore forgo important lessons from failure. Yet, we know from the principles underlying control theory of negative feedback that failures provide equal, if not more diagnostic, information than successes. Studying failures is preventive because it helps firms reduce the probability of failures in the future. Performance failure and implementation errors also provide clear signals that something is amiss and must be changed.

Although failures in IS are important, relatively little research focuses on IT (see exceptions in Lucas 1975; Markus 1983; Lyytinen and Hirschheim 1987; Davis et al. 1992; Ang and Toh 1997). One dominant reason is that organizations often keep silent to avoid any publicity of their failures. They restrict access to information on failures because it can potentially damage their image, reputation, and credibility (Sitkin 1992). Consequently, failed cases are kept hidden in organizational closets. Because of the reluctance of firms to expose their failures and weaknesses, researchers and practitioners alike forgo valuable lessons that can be gleaned from failures.

In this paper, we describe a major source of secondary data – legal cases – that researchers can harness for studying failures in IS (see Lee and Belliars [1992] for their argument for adopting law as a reference discipline for MIS). Unlike the typical case study methodology where researchers intrude into organizations to gather primary and secondary data of the phenomenon of interest, legal case studies offer researchers a very rich and unobtrusive secondary data resource. In fact, legal cases arising from use of IT represent the epitome of failures in one major area, namely computer contracting (other areas of dispute being tort and crime). When disputes arise from IT contracts, organizations will typically try to settle the conflicts out of court to preserve the contractual relationship and to avoid unnecessary publicity. However, in cases where informal dispute mechanisms fail, parties will pursue remedies available to them in formal legal litigation (Ang and Beath 1993). Therefore, the legal cases reported often exemplify extreme or heightened circumstances that trigger off conflicts and survive informal private grievance procedures or third-party mediation.

To the best of our knowledge, this paper represents the first effort in IT research to use legal cases to further our knowledge about the use of IT in practice. As with any source of empirical data, there are legitimate concerns about using legal cases. For example, an important question is: what can we learn from legal cases? What could we validly or not validly know or learn about IT from legal cases? What are the boundaries and limits of the knowledge gleaned from legal cases? In this inaugural effort of utilizing legal cases, not all of these issues can be addressed or resolved fully, but some first steps will be taken in that direction.

The paper is divided into two parts. In the first half, we describe the legal case study methodology. This is done by spelling out the sources of, and the techniques for identifying, appropriate legal cases. We also present a method of prototype construction for developing themes characterizing disputes embedded in legal cases.

The second half of the paper illustrates these principles with legal cases on IT failures arising from contracting, employing and/or outsourcing, for IT professionals. We first discuss the unique legal issues that trigger off disputes and then develop constructed types for them. We conclude the article with a discussion of the strengths and weaknesses of the methodology and also other legitimate objections to the methodology that will have to be addressed in future research.

2 METHODOLOGY OF LEGAL CASE ANALYSIS

2.1 Legal Cases as Rich Sources of Data

Traditional legal research uses cases decided by the courts as primary sources of data. Particularly in the Anglo-American legal system, usually called the common law system, decisions of judges are not only important in themselves (as pronouncements of rights and wrongs relative to specific disputes) but serve as guides for future decisions in similar circumstances. The doctrine of precedents and the authority that decisions of higher courts command over lower ones means that judge-made laws have far more significance than is often realized. The laws in force at any one time are not only those issued by the official law makers (Congress or Parliament), but also those laid down by judges.

The succession of judge-made laws (case authorities) that have become dominant and indispensable components in Anglo-American law has, in turn, created the necessity of accurate reporting of cases from about a century ago. In so far as disputants had to prove the law that would support their claims or defenses in courts, possession of records of past cases was both necessary and decisive. In its original meaning, therefore, legal research related to the finding of the law from among the numerous decisions made at the various levels of courts. It took quite a while before this task of finding the law could become relatively easier through the transcription of the judges' decisions and their subsequent collation and reporting on a regular basis. Today, the skills and knowledge required to understand disputes before the courts and to report the decisions (particularly the oral ones) are such that only qualified lawyers undertake this task.

Prior to the availability of IT-based legal databases, cases were reported in thick, paper-based volumes running as serials. The reports continue to be grouped on the basis of the subjects they cover or the geographic area or jurisdiction they originate from. Thus criminal law issues tend to be reported separately from civil law ones. Within civil law too, family cases or commercial disputes appear as distinct reports. On the other hand, as in the United States, cases are reported and organized by States. A more prevalent method is to organize reports by the type of courts which decided the cases; consequently, cases decided in the lower courts are reported in different series than those done by higher ones, such as appeal or supreme courts. It is inevitable that there would be overlaps and some cases find themselves reported in a number of series, partly because of the multiplicity of publishers.

The availability of electronic storage and retrieval of information systems has led to the creation of electronic legal databases. These databases offer lawyers and researchers alike faster and easier access to cases that would otherwise have involved laborious searching. Of the legal databases available, LEXIS services are the most common. One unique feature of LEXIS is that it provides full text reports similar to hard copies available in law libraries (Carrick 1989). The additional advantage of LEXIS is that some unreported cases, that is cases considered not important enough to be included in the regular reports, are also recorded electronically.

2.2 Searching LEXIS

LEXIS organizes legal cases hierarchically (Carrick 1989). The first level, called libraries, are followed by subdivisions (sets of files). Legal cases reside primarily in its MEGA library. Each file in the MEGA library contains all available federal and state cases on the LEXIS service. The MEGA files are either circuit-based or state-based. Circuit-based MEGA files combine federal and state cases from federal and state courts within the geographical area defined by the federal circuit. The state-based MEGA files combine cases from the court of the state and the federal district courts as well as cases from the federal circuit for that state.

A search is initiated by typing in keywords (also known in LEXIS as the "search request"). Cases obtained can be browsed either in full text or in KWIC (Key Words In Context). When one browses cases in KWIC, LEXIS extracts the paragraph that contains the keyword so that one can consider its significance in the context of the case reported. From the information gleaned from KWIC, one can go on to obtain a paper copy of the case and read the full text.

As with any text-based database, keyword searching does not guarantee that all cases extracted are relevant cases. Keyword searching offers an initial extraction of potential cases of interest. Until intelligent search mechanisms are available, one still has to read and judge the relevance of each case extracted.

2.3 Creating a Coding Template for Legal Cases

The most important information residing in legal cases are the facts of the case, the background information of the cases, together with the issues raised in the case, or the nature of the dispute. However, in addition to the facts of the case, there are other salient features of each case that can provide useful background information for legal case analyses. For each legal case, we can code (1) the date in which the case was decided; (2) the state in which the case was heard; (3) the initiating party, that is who started court action (often, the initiating party is the plaintiff; however, in some cases, the initiating party can be an appellant since he will have appealed against a decision of a court in an earlier proceeding); (4) the defendant or responding party whom the initiating party takes action against; (5) the judgment, that is, the decision or ruling of the court in favor of either party; and (6) the rationale – the court's reasons for the judgment. Table 1 presents the coding template listing all the relevant information to be gathered from each legal case.

Table 1 Coding Template for Legal Cases.

Case #	Date Decided	State	Initiating Party	Responding Party	Facts	Issues (Nature of Disputes)	Judg-ment	Rationale

2.4 Coding Legal Cases

With the coding template in place and legal cases searched, one can then proceed to code each case. Depending on the extent of their legal and IT knowledge, coders may have to read up extensively or take a course in computer contracts before coding cases. Prior knowledge in computer contracts is vital to ensure that coders can discern the issues or nature of disputes embedded in each court case.

To ensure inter-rater reliability, at least two coders must be used to code each legal case. Initially, each coder reads and codes the case independently. The coders then come together to compare the results. Inconsistencies are resolved and tacit rules of thumb in the code made explicit. Coders then reiterate the process until they reach an acceptable level of inter-rater agreement. Cohen suggests 80% agreement as computed using the Cohen's Kappa metric as acceptable for nominal scale agreement (Cohen 1960). Cohen's or Krippendorf's (1980) procedures for measuring coder agreement for nominal scales may be adopted. Either procedure measures agreement after random agreement among nominal scales is taken into account.

2.5 Creating Themes and Developing Constructed Types of Disputes

Once the coding is completed, the coded information is then used for further analyses. We propose to rely on the principles of typology construction to summarize the massive qualitative information into constructed types. According to Bailey (1994), a constructed type is a description of the most commonly found characteristics in the subject of interest. A constructed type is thus analogous to a measure of central tendency such as a mean. In our context, constructed types represent themes and prototypical disputes that commonly occur in litigious disputes. With the development of an inventory or typology of constructed types, one can better grasp the breath and depth of failures in IT and the most likely outcome of litigious actions.

3 AN ILLUSTRATIVE EXAMPLE: LEGAL DISPUTES ARISING FROM EMPLOYING AND OUTSOURCING OF IT PROFESSIONALS

To illustrate the power of legal case analysis, we report here on legal cases arising from employing and outsourcing for IT professionals, a major area of IT disputes driven by severe IT skills shortages coupled with the dramatic infiltration of IT in businesses. We first offer a background on the subject of interest: contracting for services of IT professionals followed by an illustration of how the above methodology can be used to derive themes or prototypical cases that represent failures in contracting for IT professionals.

3.1 Employing or Outsourcing for Services of IT Professionals

As a result of the explosive use of IT in all industries, the demand for skilled IT professionals has grown dramatically. Unfortunately, the supply of skilled IT professionals has not kept up with demand (Saxenian 1996). To make matters worse, the pool of competent IT professionals shrinks rapidly by the relentless development of competence-destroying technologies. On average, new IT developments have a useful life span of only about eighteen months. This rapid speed of innovation suggests that whatever skills IT professionals possess today erode very rapidly.

The severe skills shortages coupled with rapid changes in technologies means that organizations face tremendous challenges in developing and managing critical IT operations. Given severe shortages of highly skilled IS workers and rapid erosion of

IT skills, the organizations continue to wrestle with finding and retaining the critical human resources to manage and use IT effectively within their organizations. The severe shortage also means that competent IT professionals are very marketable and highly mobile. The high interfirm mobility of IT professionals also results in organizations outsourcing for IT services (Slaughter and Ang 1996) rather than merely resorting to traditional employment of IT professionals.

Outsourcing can help balance supply and demand for workers by more efficiently allocating the deployment of workers with scarce skills. As illustrated by Slaughter and Ang (1996, p. 49), if five firms need scarce IS skills, such as client-server programming, and each firm chooses to hire a permanent worker, then five programmers will be required. However, if firms opt for outsourcing, fewer programmers will be required as firms can share the services of the programmers from a common pool.

By outsourcing, organizations move away from the traditional long-term employment arrangement (insourcing) to relatively shorter-term, market-mediated arrangement (outsourcing) with their IS workers. Outsourcing reflects the increasing trend toward downsizing and transforming companies into networked forms by "taking the workers back out" (Pfeffer and Baron 1988).

3.2 Legal Ramifications in Managing IT Professionals

Managing IT professionals either by means of traditional insourcing and outsourcing has many legal ramifications. The legal literature identifies three major areas of problems, namely restraint of trade, property rights and the legal status of the professional either as employee or independent contractor (Nimmer 1985; Reed 1990).

Restraint of trade relates to the degree of permitted use of information and skills acquired during the engagement with the employer both during the terms of employment and afterward. Developing software is a highly tacit endeavor. Knowledge about the software developed resides in the heads of software developers and us seldom codified explicitly. Often, the distinction between skills and knowledge acquired on the job, which the professional is allowed to use for his or her own purposes, from the proprietary information, which he or she will have to leave behind for the employer, is blurred. Consequently, employers are keen to protect the information generated with the resources they provide the employee or independent contractor by prohibiting any kind of leakage to competitors, including where the employee sets himself or herself up independently in the line of activity of the employer. Whether the employer will succeed in prohibiting competition and for how long or to what extent have been contested repeatedly. Courts have had to settle these issues by reference to law and public policy. The need to allow skills acquired while under contractual engagements with employers have constantly pushed back the employer's urge to prohibit and constrain contracting parties.

Property rights, usually described as intellectual property rights but not necessarily exclusively them alone, have increasingly become critical in IT employment or outsourcing contracts. The determination of who acquires or retains ownership of such products or information generated has been decided by law in terms that employees in principle do not have rights as such. Where outsourcing is involved and the problem of whether the IT professional has rights is raised, the solution has been arrived at by looking at the provision of materials, facilities and other resources for the performance by the IT professional: if such have been supplied by the employer, property rights can be claimed by the employer; where this is not so, they belong to the employee. However, this has only served as a guideline and no final pronouncements have been possible owing to the shifting nature of the relationship.

Other disputes arise from the changes brought about by IT in the relationship between employees and employers. Such are the disputes as to the status of the hired IT professional and the corresponding rights and obligations he or she has vis-à-vis the employer: the obligations of the employer by law such as in paying benefits on behalf of the professional. The traditional legal test of the existence of control or supervision by the employer over the contracting party has increasingly become irrelevant since IT has made it either redundant or redefined the relationship. The compensation that employers have to pay has also become a bone of contention, linked as it is with the status of the professional.

The above represents legal issues that have been discussed and debated at length in computer law books and journal papers. In the next section, we will examine empirically the nature of disputes embedded in past legal cases using the methodology suggested in the first half of this paper.

Searching Relevant Legal Cases on Employing and Outsourcing for IT Professionals

The first step in the methodology was to find relevant legal cases pertaining to the employment and outsourcing for IT professionals. We gained access to the LEXIS database for the research. In addition to the MEGA library which holds the primary source of all legal cases, LEXIS also contains a special collection on employment issues called the EMPLOYMENT LAW library. This library focuses primarily on public and private section state employment law and contains state and federal cases, fair employment practices, individual employment rights decisions, wage and hour decisions, state and federal codes, state public employee board decisions, employment law treatises, labor arbitration materials, and other relevant employment publications.

In effect, the Employment Law library contains the legal cases pertaining to employment related issues. In the Employment Law library, one can therefore search computer-related employment contracts using strategic keywords such as computer or software. Also, for purposes of this illustrative study, we had restricted our search of the Employment Law cases to the most critical IT related employment cases: cases that appear at the Supreme Courts – the highest and most influential courts in each state. A common search strategy used was to select all cases that contained the key words computer or software and the key word contract within 25 words before or after the former key words. The command used for the LEXIS search was:
COURT (SUPREME) AND (COMPUTER! OR SOFTWARE! W/25 CONTRACT!)

Based on the search strategy, LEXIS identified a total of 249 cases. Of the 249 cases, we narrowed down to 25 cases that have as their central theme disputes arising from the employment and outsourcing of IT professionals. The 25 cases were identified by a careful reading of all the abstracts of the 249 cases and extracting the ones deemed relevant. The other cases were either outrightly irrelevant or tangentially relevant. Extracting 25 cases out of a possible 249 cases seems a very low hit rate (about 10%). This suggests we may have to devise a better search strategy than the command we had used in our original LEXIS search.

Coding the Cases

Two coders were used to code the cases. The coders had working knowledge in IT and were trained by one of the co-authors in legal research methodology. To prepare for the coding process, they also read materials in legal research as well as computer and employment law authorities to ensure that they had sufficient background knowledge to understand the common themes and disputes arising out of computer contracting.

As a first task, the coders photocopied the 25 cases from hard copies of case report found in the Law library. Next, they read the cases independently, and coded information based on the coding template presented in Table 1. The result of the coding is shown in Appendices 1 and 2. Of the elements in the template, the one of greatest subjective contention is the issue or the nature of dispute. Once they had coded each case, they compared notes, discussed the cases, and arrived at a consensus on the facts, issues, judgments, and rationale. To further ensure the validity of their interpretation, one of the co-researchers, who is the computer legal expert, read through the cases and verified their coding.

Developing Themes or Constructed Types

Following formal legal case analysis techniques, the first step in arriving at the themes was to sift the facts and issues in the 25 decided cases and summarize them. This is shown in Appendices 1 and 2, where all the relevant information for each case are entered. The second step involved establishing the recurrence of disputes. This was done by going through the section under issues and determining what areas of law was in contention. Depending on the type of dispute, a tally was made of the overall total for each category. This is shown in Table 2.

As shown in Table 2, the major type of dispute concerns restraint of trade. Typically an employer would have an employee agree to a term in the contract of employment which prohibits the employee, during the period of employment or a few years (one to two) afterward, from engaging in any business (similar to the employer's) that might compete against the employer. Usually this takes the form of noncompetition pure and simple (with indications as to the extent of prohibition – geographic scope as well as duration of time and type of business). Often, the employee may be precluded from using trade secrets or such other information as was particular to the type of business of the employer. Consequently, restraint of trade meshes in with confidentiality clauses.

Table 2 Recurrence of Types of Disputes in the Selected 25 Cases.

Types of Disputes	Recurrence	Cases
Restraint of trade	8	1, 2, 6, 9, 16, 19, 23, 24,
Status of IT personnel	6	5, 7, 10, 11, 12, 21,
Confidentiality	5	6, 9, 19, 20, 24
Procedure	5	4, 14, 15, 17, 22,
Ownership	3	3, 13, 20
Compensation	3	8, 15, 25,
Fiduciary duty	1	18,

Disputes on restraint of trade arise chiefly where (a) the interests to be protected by the employer have not been clearly spelled out; (b) the clauses are too broad and do not stand the test of reasonableness that is used by the courts to determine whether such clauses are valid; (c) the interests of the employee who seeks to use the information and skill acquired in the course of employment and that of the employer who does not to wish to be placed at a disadvantage as a result are in conflict. Courts are likely to give the benefit of the doubt to the employee.

The second major type of dispute relates to the status of the employee. The use of multiple forms of contracting (written, oral, or both written and oral) as well as variations in the degree of control exercised by the employer have produced disputes. The first kind of dispute is as to whether the written contract of employment is conclusive. The second is regarding the relationship between the employer and persons it hires supposedly as independent contractors but restricts in the manner of their work and dealings with clients of the employer. Although these are standard issues in contracts of employment, the changes occasioned by IT in the nature of employer-employee relations (particularly in lessening of control by the former) may have served to rekindle them.

The third most important type of dispute concerns the employer's quest to enforce confidentiality clauses. Usually, this takes the form of an employer seeking to prevent an employee, whether during employment or on termination, using the information made available to him or her by the employer for another employer or for his or her own benefit. The question that would need to be resolved is the confidentiality of the information; that is, whether the information was not publicly available or that it was produced (compiled, invented or otherwise generated) in the employer's business. Courts would refrain from enforcing the obligation of an employee in this regard if they find that the information was widely known or not patentable. At times, the employer's effort to protect its "trade secret" may be similar to, and overlap with, restraining an ex-employee from competing against it.

Procedural issues figure as the fourth important type. These range from preliminary issues as to whether the courts have jurisdiction to receive the cases, the use and type of evidence allowed to prove contracts or claim compensation, the forms of dispute settlement the parties may have agreed to in the contract and the time span within which action can be brought in courts. While these issues may not relate to the substance of the dispute at hand, they would often affect the outcome, if and when the dispute is decided by the courts. The strength of the parties on the underlying dispute may not necessarily determine the court's final ruling where the party concerned did not observe the correct procedural steps and proves it to the court's satisfaction.

Ownership of information generated by employees during employment (whether at the work place or outside) and the compensation they would expect from their work (salaries or commissions) are the last two types of disputes. The use of the employer's facilities and time has generally been the yardstick to determine if the employer can claim proprietorship over the information generated by the employee. On the other hand, the level of compensation due to the employee has been difficult to assess partly because of the combination of oral and written forms in the contract, and partly because of the fluctuating nature of commission.

4 STRENGTHS AND WEAKNESSES OF THE METHODOLOGY

Since in this paper we are chiefly concerned with introducing and illustrating a methodology, we shall presently take up a discussion of strengths and weaknesses as well as the major objections that may be raised against the methodology. These determine when the use of legal cases is the preferred approach and when it is not.

4.1 Strengths

The chief strength of the methodology is the use of very rich, and relatively untapped, legal cases as secondary data. Cases are written in considerable detail by case reporters. Whereas traditional case studies rely primarily on interviews or questionnaires that intrude as foreign elements into the social settings (Webb et al. 1966), legal cases are unobtrusive, do not require cooperation of firms, and they do not themselves contaminate the responses. We have discussed earlier the reluctance of companies to share their failure stories with researchers for fear of loss of reputation and credibility. Legal cases offer an excellent source of data to plug a hole in our existing research that grossly under-rated failures. Legal cases open windows for us to peer into the events that lead to contractual disputes that firms were not able to resolve through informal dispute resolution mechanisms.

The second strength of the methodology is the developing of constructed types from legal cases. Constructed types enable researchers to synthesize large numbers of legal cases which may differ in context but share a number of distinctive features that characterize the legal issue in dispute. Constructed types reduce complexity and achieve parsimony. It allows one to identify both similarities among cases as well as differentiate between them. A full typology of constructed types of issues arising from legal disputes is also an excellent inventory tool for researchers and practitioners. It allows one to locate and position any problem that arises and know at all times what types are available for analysis.

The third strength of the methodology is the breadth of application. One can use the methodology to describe and understand potential causes of failures and disputes in computer contracting. With the heightened awareness and use of outsourcing in the management of IS, a thorough understanding and appreciation of failures that lead to legal disputes can potentially avert costly litigation and disruption of business operations. We have demonstrated the use of the methodology to examine disputes arising from employing and outsourcing for IT professionals. The methodology may be used to understand other IT-related issues such as disputes in software development outsourcing (e.g., see Ang and Toh 1996), disputes in facilities management outsourcing, personal rights to privacy, intellectual property pertaining to electronic sources, etc.

4.2 Weaknesses

Like any method, the methodology of developing constructed types from legal cases has certain weaknesses. First, the methodology calls for good grounding and extensive knowledge in law and IT. Both disciplines have considerably high knowledge barriers, each with a very idiosyncratic set of jargon. The greatest challenge facing researchers is overcoming the high knowledge barriers, particularly the technical jargon embedded in both the fields of law and IT. Unfortunately, relatively few researchers possess competencies in the two areas. IT researchers are typically not trained in law and, similarly, few law researchers have sufficient technical grounding in IT to appreciate and understand the complexities of managing IT. A solution to the problem is for sustained, cross-disciplinary collaboration between IT and legal researchers. First, collaborators must possess declarative knowledge in the fundamental concepts in both law and IT. This knowledge is best learned through formal education: basic courses in business law and information technology. Next, they must also have the motivation and willingness to invest in cross-training and cross-educating each other on the idiosyncratic knowledge of each other's domains. Through the collaborative effort, birds of different feathers learn to flock together.

Second, the ability to develop constructed types is predicated on the nature of the legal disputes. If there are sufficient numbers of cases with similar characteristics, then constructed types make sense. On the contrary, if cases have too few common threads, then developing constructed types will be meaningless as there will be as many constructed types as individual cases.

Third, there are limitations inherent to the sources. The collection of cases depends very much on what is available in reports. It would probably never be possible to have access to all the relevant cases which were disputed by parties before the courts. A large percentage would be settled out of court either because the parties did not consider that going to court would be advisable, financially worth their while or of any importance. Cases which might involve trade secrets or elements of businesses that have critical importance to the operations of those businesses are usually not allowed to develop into full blown disputes enjoying the glare of publicity that would inevitably follow them. Whether as plaintiffs or defendants, companies which do not wish this to happen to them will proceed to resolve their disputes through arbitration or private settlements.

4.3 Major Objections to the Methodology

Apart from the weaknesses iterated above, there are certain legitimate objections that can be raised against the methodology presented. These relate, but are not by any means confined, to the extent to which cases represent reality and incorporate relevant facts, biases introduced into cases by the opposite parties' perceptions, sanitization of cases because of removal by the courts in their decision of the political and social context, the time lag between disputes and judgment, the representative nature of LEXIS records and the sufficiency of the number of cases selected through it for research. Others which might introduce a potentially significant source of noise into the analysis are problems in the coding procedure, the value of generalization of research in IT-related cases where jurisdictional limitations matter, the indeterminable nature of what is or is not reported, and the process of filtering of facts that judges may be felt to undertake in formulating legal rules. We will attempt to examine each of these possible objections below.

All cases start with a complaint, called a claim, by a plaintiff who attempts to state as fully as possible the grounds for such a claim – all allegations and facts that the plaintiff views to be supporting it. The party responding to the claim will in turn either deny the alleged legal infraction, submit its own contrary claims or accept the plaintiff's allegations partly or wholly. Both parties must at the same time set out the evidence (documents or witnesses) they rely upon. It will then be up to the judge(s) to decide whose claims have been borne out by the presented evidence. Judgments so rendered are expected to be based on the proven facts and the arguments presented by the parties. This does not change whether the verdict becomes favorable to the plaintiff or the defendant or that it is written or issued orally – such being a frequent practice, particularly in the trial courts (Stone and Wells 1991).

It follows from this that, normally, a legal case consists of all the relevant data or facts that pertain to a specific dispute or disputes. Any failure in that regard does not prevent judgment from being given as each judgment is commensurate with the extent of proven facts laid before the courts. While all the reports of judgments (when made) may not necessarily record all the facts of a case, the more credible and authoritative ones produced by trained lawyers in the employ of long established publishing houses routinely incorporate all the relevant or (in legal parlance) material facts that were recognized to be such by the judges in the particular case. Sometimes too, the reporters seek the assistance of the courts (either the judges personally or the archivists) to verify the accuracy of their reports. This is particularly so in England.

Consequently, legal cases properly reported or published in the major series do reproduce the relevant facts in each dispute. Those facts that might be omitted for lack of space and in consideration of the great number of cases that have to be reported regularly on a daily basis would in the general course of things be those that are non-material or without consequence to the legal dispute. The summaries made in Appendix 2 of the facts are hence those most important relative to the issues to be resolved by the courts in each case. The brevity of the facts is not because more could not have been said of the parties or the circumstances of the dispute but that such lay at the bottom of the disputes and all else contributed nothing or very little to the decisions of the courts.

The fact that legal disputes are handled by two opposed parties with partisan views of what is right or wrong might suggest that the judgment when given would suffer from a bias. Yet such a view ignores the fundamental role of the conduct of a trial by judges (sometimes supported by the jury): the establishment to the extent possible of objective facts or data supported by incontrovertible evidence. The standard of evidence required of the contestants is such that neither sides' bias could possibly be a basis for any decision no matter the strength of argument it is presented under. In the end, whatever purposes the data so obtained may be put to, there can be no doubt that they provide the background (in a distilled form) for the decision reached by the judges. The use of those data in the decisions could of course be possible for all types of studies. However, our contention is that they can be amenable to IS research, as demonstrated in the particular example of outsourcing of IS professionals. The absence from the judgment of other data, political or otherwise, which might give a different complexion to the reported case (thereby arguably "sanitizing" it) does not prevent us from using the case for our projected purpose. What it means is only that other studies may have to examine the extent of use of the facts given in case reports for their specific objectives. As far as IS research is concerned, it is our finding that the facts as given in the reports are sufficient and do not suffer from any distillation or sanitization that might otherwise reduce their utility.

Viewed differently, too, the existence of bias is true for standard case methodology as well, where the ethnographic ethos of interpretivism is central (Geertz 1983; Van Maanen 1988). As Stake (1994) elegantly puts it, what we perceive, study, and record in any case study are subjective representations and choices :

> One cannot know at the outset (of conducting a case study) what the issues, the perceptions, the theory will be. Case researchers enter the scene expecting, even knowing, that certain events, problems, relationships will be important, yet discover that some actually are of little consequence. *Case content evolves in the act of writing itself.*
>
> Even though committed to empathy and multiple realities, *it is the researcher who decides what is the case's own story, or at least what of the*

> *case's own story he or she will report.* More will be pursued than was volunteered. Less will be reported than was learned. Even though the competent researcher will be guided by what the case may indicate is most important, even though patrons and other researchers will advise, what is necessary for an understanding of the case will be decided by the research. *It may be the case's own story, but it is the researcher's dressing of the case's own story. This is not to dismiss the aim of finding the story that best represents the case, but to remind that the criteria of representation ultimately are decided by the researcher.* [Stake 1994, p. 240; emphasis added]

Therefore, the point about whether legal cases are biased in representing reality does not appear to be a specific deficiency, even were it provable.

Will the variation between the date of filing (presentation) and that of the decision of cases matter? Undoubtedly, the intervening periods after the presentation or filing of a claim before a court may matter if similar cases have appeared elsewhere and decisions have been passed on the pending issues. Decisions by higher courts in the same jurisdiction will have a direct impact as they become binding immediately; other court decisions may be influential and persuasive, depending on their merit. In any case, the value for this study of the decision in any reported case will not become any less simply because time will have transpired between the date of filing and of the decision.

On the other hand, it is true that the dates of original disputes are important for IS research. It is also true that such can be found for all cases, whether they are at appeal levels or before the highest courts. The illustrative examples used in the paper have had to be limited to the Supreme Courts of states not because the value of such an information was ignored but because it would require more time and labor to dig through all the relevant decisions at the lower levels and to weigh the jurisdictional/state legal variations that might have had an impact in each case. The conscious decision to avoid these two elements was taken in order to make the presentation of the methodology simpler and limit the diversionary elements that might bog the reader's mind in unnecessary detail at this inaugural stage. It would be at the stage of full study of the different facets of outsourcing that a comprehensive concern for all the aspects would be necessary.

Otherwise, the illustrative use we have made of cases brought before the Supreme Courts does not limit the pertinent issues to be raised in or the relevance to IS research of such cases. Indeed, the differences between cases in Supreme Courts and those in lower courts in most cases relate to the complexity of issues involved and either the degree of dissatisfaction of the parties with the judgment rendered or their deep pockets. Thus if the type and number of cases appearing before the Supreme Courts can tell us anything distinct about them, it will not be about the nature of the cases. Cases decided at lower courts but not presented before the Supreme Courts would not necessarily have lacked the merit required of them to do so, although some might not be able to make it for procedural reasons. (It is the practice of courts that appeals are allowed on legal grounds and that every appeal beyond the first level must prove the existence of those grounds.)

The objection as to the insufficiency in the number of reported cases expresses what is but widely known. It is readily acknowledged that even with the 4 million or so cases reported up to now since reporting started in 1789 (at appellate levels) and since 1817 (at the US Supreme Court level) and the current annual of 13,000 cases from about 600 courts (Jacobstein, Mersky and Dunn 1994, at 23), no complete reporting of all cases has been possible, for one reason or another. It is therefore obvious that LEXIS cannot be all-inclusive while even the hard-back reports of cases that it is based on are not. Neither do we claim that the legal cases we have investigated represent *all* disputes arising from employment and outsourcing IT personnel. In fact, we have indicated in our introduction that organizations typically try to preserve their contractual relationship and avoid publicity by resorting to informal dispute mechanisms. It is only when all informal means fail that the hard legal court remedy is pursued.

Even then, the number of cases presented for the illustration is an absolute one. No attempt was made to select any number from a larger pool. The process used in determining which were relevant and which not was an open-ended one, without any need to discriminate between cases. Therefore whether or not 25 cases were a low or high number could not arise. Any desire to enlarge the number could lead only to the inclusion of lower court decisions because the 25 arrived at are the maximum possible, at the supreme court levels, using the existing resources of LEXIS.

We recognize that the coding procedure can be enhanced.[1] To avoid the influence of one coder over another, a sequential adjustment procedure may be adopted. In this procedure, coders first code independently a relatively small sample of cases (e.g., ten or twelve). They then compare results and resolve differences, evolving standard rules of thumb for coding subsequent cases. They then independently content code another small sample of cases and results are compared and differences resolved. This process repeats until a satisfying level of agreement is reached among the coders and the coding stabilizes. Only then can subsequent sample cases be coded independently and used for further data analysis. Typically for a novice, a case takes between two to three hours to code. However, once one becomes familiar with the specialized legal vocabulary, and genre of legal case reports, a case takes between fifteen to thirty minutes to code.

5 REFERENCES

Ang, S., and Beath, C. M. (1993). "Hierarchical Elements in Software Contracts." *Journal of Organizational Computing*, Volume 3, Number 3, pp. 329-362.

Ang, S., and Toh, S. K. (1997). Failure in Software Outsourcing." In M. Lacity and L. Willcocks (Editors), *Outsourcing: Theory and Practice*. New York: Oxford University Press, forthcoming.

[1]We are grateful to an anonymous reviewer for the suggestion of this sequential adjustment procedure.

Bailey, K. D. (1994). *Typologies and Taxonomies: An Introduction to Classification Techniques*. Thousand Oaks, California: Sage University Paper series on Quantitative Applications in the Social Sciences, 07-102.
Carrick, K. M. (1989). *LEXIS: A Legal Research Manual*. Dayton, Ohio: Mead Data Central.
Cohen, J. (1960). "A Coefficient of Agreement for Nominal Scales." *Educational and Psychological Measurement*, Volume 20, Number 1, pp. 37-46.
Davis, G. B.; Lee, A. S.; Nickles, K. R.; Chatterjee, S.; Hartung, R.; and Wu, Y. (1992). "Diagnosis of an Information Systems Failure: A Framework and Interpretive Process." *Information & Management*, Volume 23, pp. 293-318.
Geertz, C. (1983). *Local Knowledge*. New York: Basic Books.
Jacobstein, J. M.; Mersky, R. M.; and Dunn, D. J. (1994). *Fundamentals of Legal Research*, Sixth Edition. Westbury, New York: The Foundation Press, Inc.
Krippendorf, K. (1980). *Content Analysis: An Introduction to its Methodology*. Newbury Park, California: Sage Publications.
Lee, A. S., and Belliars, K. (1992). "Law as a Reference Discipline for MIS." Working Paper, Management Information Systems Research Center, University of Minnesota, Minneapolis.
Lucas, H. (1975). *Why Information Systems Fail*. New York: Columbia University Press.
Lyytinen, K., and Hirschheim, R. (1987). "Information Systems Failures: A Survey and Classification of the Empirical Literature." In P. I. Zorkoczy (Editor), *Oxford Surveys in Information Technology*, Volume 4. New York: Oxford University Press, pp. 257-309.
Markus, M. L. (1983). "Power, Politics, and MIS Implementation." *Communications of the ACM*, Volume 26, Number 6, pp. 430-444.
Nimmer, R. T. (1985). *The Law of Computer Technology*. Boston: Warren, Gorham & Lamont.
Pfeffer, J., and Baron, J. (1988). "Taking the Workers Back Out: Recent Trends in the Structuring of Employment." In B. M. Staw and L. L. Cummings (Editors), *Research in Organizational Behavior*, Volume 10. Greenwich, Connecticut: JAI Press, pp. 257-303.
Reed, C. (1990). *Computer Law*. London: Blackstone Press Limited.
Saxenian, A. (1996). "Beyond Boundaries: Open Labor Markets and Learning in Silicon Valley." In M. B. Arthur, and D. M. Rousseau (Editors), *The Boundaryless Careers*. New York: Oxford University Press, pp. 23-39.
Sitkin, S. B. (1992). "Learning Through Failure: The Strategy of Small Losses." In B. M. Staw and L. L. Cummings (Editors), *Research in Organizational Behavior*, Volume 14. Greenwich, Connecticut: JAI Press, pp. 231-266.
Slaughter, S. A., and Ang, S. (1996). "Employment Outsourcing in Information Systems." *Communications of the ACM*, Volume 39, Number 7, pp. 47-54.

Stake, R. E. (1994). "Case Studies." In N. K. Denzin, and Y. S. Lincoln (Editors), *Handbook of Qualitative Research*, Thousand Oaks, California: Sage Publications, pp. 236-247.

Stone, J., and Wells, W. A. N. (1991). *Evidence: Its History and Policies*. Woburn, Massachusetts: Butterworth-Heinemann.

Van Maanen, J. (1988). *Tales of the Field*. Chicago: University of Chicago Press.

Webb, E. J.; Campbell, D. T.; Schwartz, R. D.; and Sechrest, L. (1966). *Unobtrusive Measures: Nonreactive Research in the Social Sciences*. Chicago: Rand McNally & Company.

6 BIOGRAPHY

Soon Ang is Head of the Division of Human Resource and Quality Management. She specializes in human resources and IT management. She graduated from the University of Minnesota in MIS with supporting fields in organizational psychology and strategic management. Soon Ang currently serves as an Associate Editor for *Information Systems Research* and a Consulting Editor for *Journal of MIS Education*. Her current research interests are in information systems outsourcing, managing hi-tech professionals, and cross-cultural management.

Assafa Endeshaw (LLB LLM PhD) is a lecturer in law at the Nanyang Business School. He specializes in intellectual property, information technology and transfer of technology laws as well as in international trade and franchising. He was previously a legal attorney and advisor in government departments and a consultant in a law firm in Ethiopia. Dr Endeshaw has authored *Intellectual Property in China: The Roots of the Problem of Enforcement and Intellectual Property Policy for Non-Industrial Countries*. He is also a regular contributor to the "Information Technology" column of *The Singapore Law Gazette*.

Appendix 1
Coding Template for Legal Cases in Employment and Outsourcing

Case #	Date Decided	State	Initiating Party (A)	Responding Party (R)	Facts	Issues (Nature of Disputes)	Judgment for	Rationale
1	1994	Georgia	Employer	Employee	See Appendix 2		Employee	Employer's restriction not effective because territorial scope not limited
2	1994	Utah	Employee	Employer	See Appendix 2		Employee	Employer acted with improper purpose in interfering and therefore affirmed decision in favor of employee
3	1994	S. Dakota	Employer	Employee	See Appendix 2		Employee	Royalties received were for services as programmer to third party and not as highway superintendent
4	1993	New York	Employee	Employer	See Appendix 2		Employer	Employee denied access to data because his right was not established
5	1993	Idaho	Employee	Employer	See Appendix 2		Employee	Contract vague therefore summary judgment (by District Court) dismissing R's claim (cause employee at will) precluded; reversed and remanded for decision
6	1993	New York	Ex-employer	New employer	See Appendix 2		New employer	R did not tortiously interfere with contract or engage in unfair competition; knowledge of customers readily ascertainable from directories. Ex-employee did not violate her obligation not to compete

Case #	Date Decided	State	Initiating Party (A)	Responding Party (R)	Facts	Issues (Nature of Dispute)	Judgment for	Rationale
7	1992	Vermont	Employee	Employer	See Appendix 2		Employee	Company's right to discharge at will employee modified by allowing grievance procedure (time card falsification not believed by jury); hence trial court's finding of modification of contract, affirmed.
8	1992	Utah	Employee	Employer	See Appendix 2		Employer	Denial of attorney's fees affirmed. (No discrimination between lay and professional attorneys)
9	1991	Alabama	Employer	Employee	See Appendix 2		Employer	Information is available to the public; no exclusion of competition in contract
10	1991	New York	Employer	Government	See Appendix 2		Government	A paid them directly; their activities with clients were restricted; required to submit time sheets to A; sufficient direction and control; hence employees. Decision affirmed.
11	1990	New York	Employer	Government	See Appendix 2		Government	Unemployment Insurance Appeal Board's decision that they were employees rather than independent contractors affirmed
12	1990	New York	Employer	Government	See Appendix 2		Government	Unemployment Insurance Appeal Board's decision that they were employees rather than independent contractors affirmed
13	1990	W. Virginia	Employee	Employer	See Appendix 2		Employee	Court has no authority to enforce arbitration clause in employment contract; arbitration clause could not defeat human rights action. Lower court's decision that arbitral agreement would override reversed.

Case #	Date Decided	State	Initiating Party (A)	Responding Party (R)	Facts	Issues (Nature of Disputes)	Judgment for	Rationale
14	1987	Wyoming	Employee	Employer	See Appendix 2		Employer	R owned original copies of programs it paid for, possessed and used; A could only use ideas, concepts and techniques in future. Confirmed lower court's judgment. Transfer issue not solved owing to lack of facts.
15	1987	Alabama	Employer	Employee	See Appendix 2		Employer	Written agreement unambiguous and parol evidence (to bind owner, Austin) not admissible
16	1986	New York	Employer	Employee	See Appendix 2		Employer	Shareholders/sellers have a duty to refrain indefinitely from soliciting ex-customers; duty survives further sale of business
17	1985	Mississippi	Employer	Employee	See Appendix 2		Employer	Case within proper jurisdiction of court; employment agreement not entire agreement; admission of other evidence justified. Decision for employee affirmed.
18	1982	New York	Employer	Employee	See Appendix 2		Employee	R could prepare for future employment; conduct not actionable; lack of facts prevented a ruling on other claims
19	1982	Utah	Employer	Employee	See Appendix 2		Employer	A's program was secret and worthy of protection; hence lower court's ruling affirmed
20	1980	Oklahoma	Employer	Employee	See Appendix 2		Employee	Program not patentable, only better way of doing things; company cannot claim ownership of invention per employee contract; employee can use system after leaving

Case #	Date Decided	State	Initiating Party (A)	Responding Party (R)	Facts	Issues (Nature of Disputes)	Judgment for	Rationale
21	1980	New York	Employer	Employee	See Appendix 2		Employee	A controlled distribution of work, supplied necessary equipment and under contract could only refuse work for good reason. This showed employee-employer relationship. Decision of Board affirmed.
23	1977	Alabama	Employee	Employer	See Appendix 2		Employee	R had intention to fire Robinson as soon as they had a replacement; inequitable and unreasonable to enforce a contract R did not intend to keep. A not provided same service as R.
24	1974	Pennsylvania	Employer		See Appendix 2		Employee	Prohibition not to be employed by any business R came into contact while in A's employment not reasonable; use of information about former client not unfair competition, if available generally.
25	1972	Massachusetts	Employee	Employer	See Appendix 2		Employee	"Notice" effective against R; non-disclosure of basis of calculations would make settlement voidable; a party cannot waive information containing error unknown to him.

Appendix 2
Summary of IT Employment Contract Cases at State Supreme Court Levels in the United States of America

NO. CASE	FACTS	ISSUES	JUDGMENT
[1] *American Software v Moore* [448 S.E. 2d 206] [1994, Georgia]	Ex-employee provides maintenance and support services to employer's clients	Violation of restrictive covenant	Restriction not effective because territorial scope not limited [A lost]
[2] *John P. Pratt v Prodata Inc et al.* 885 P.2d 786 [1994, Utah]	A hired as computer programmer; contract prohibited him from engaging in competing businesses within 50 miles of R's for one year following his termination. Left and started work as independent contractor. Prodata first reviewed his situation and considered no violation of contract but later complained to ne employer over his employment; latter terminated his relationship. Pratt sued for wrongful interference in economic relations.	The ambit of non-competition clause	Prodata acted with improper purpose in interfering and therefore affirmed decision in favor of A.
[3] *Rural Pennington County Tax Assoc et al. V Jack C. Dier* 515 N.W.2d 841 [1994, S. Dakota]	R an employee of A as highway superintendent. A engaged a third party to develop software on which R (and wife) participated in spare time. R entered into independent contract with third party and received royalties. A claims entitled to proceeds that R received.	Ownership of software; whether R did so as part of his service?	Royalties received were for services as programmer to third party and not as highway superintedent; R owner of software because not invented or developed with A's equipment or on its time.
[4] *Alexander Tsigutkin v Brian Scanlan et al.* 599 NYS 2d 262 [1993, New York]	Ex-employee seeking share in sale of computer programs	Access to documents (contracts) to determine amount	Denied cause his right not established.
[5] *Williams and WIlliams v Computer Resources Inc* 851 P.2d 967 [1993, Idaho]	A offered a job to work as programmer for R. Letter confirming it sent to A; letter stated it constituted the employment agreement. A later asked but refused to sign non-competition and confidentiality agreement; terminated.	R in breach of contract of employment? Was Williams an at-will employee or employed for specific period?	Contract vague therefore summary judgment (by District Court) dismissing R's claim (cause employee at will) precluded; reversed and remanded for decision.

NO. CASE	FACTS	ISSUES	JUDGMENT
[6] *Howard Systems Int v IMI Systems* 596 NYS 2d 48 [1993, New York]	A's executive vice-president entered into non-disclosure agreement concerning A's computer business during or after employment. Quit her job and got a job with R. A claims that R knowingly hired her.	Inducement to breach contract; wrongful use and disclosure of trade secrets and confidential information (plus customer's identity)	R did not tortiously interfere with contract or engage in unfair competition; knowledge of customers readily ascertainable from directories. Ex-employee did not violate her obligation not to compete.
[7] *Fletcher E. Foote v Simmonds Precision Products Co.* 613 A.2d 1277 [1992, Vermont]	A computer operator for many years; sought to use grievance procedures about hired supervisor considered unqualified; poor work evaluation and discharged allegedly for falsifying time card (left early). R alleges relied on policy allowing operators to leave before end of their shifts	Can promissory estoppel (i.e., using grievance procedures) modify employment contract that is otherwise terminable at will?	Company's right to discharge at will employee modified by allowing grievance procedure (time card falsification not believed by jury); hence trial court's finding of modification of contract affirmed.
[8] *S. R. Smith v D. K. Batchelor et al.* 832 P.2d 467 [1992, Utah]	A former employee provided computer service to R; claimed back wages and overtime pay; awarded but denied attorney fees (although an attorney himself).	Does federal law preempt state law on overtime pay?	Denial of attorney's fees affirmed. (No discrimination between lay and professional attorneys.)
[9] *Public Systems v H. Kenneth and SD Adams* 587 So.2d 969 [1991, Alabama]	R ex-employees of A (engaged in financial and technical assistance in obtaining funding); R set up company in competition with A; A sued for misappropriating confidential information and trade secrets (customer lists, pricing information and spreadsheet software)	Customer lists and data trade secrets? Interference with A's business and contractual relations?	Not so; information available to the public; no exclusion of competition in contract; A failed to prove other claims.
[10] *Compu-Tech Software Services Inc v TF Hartnett (Commissioner of Labor)* 570 NYS 2d 374 [1991, New York]	A assessed for additional unemployment insurance contribution for persons working as data processing technicians for their clients. A denies it.	Status of technicians	A paid them directly, their activities with clients were restricted; required to submit time sheets to A; sufficient direction and control, hence employees. Decision affirmed.

NO. CASE	FACTS	ISSUES	JUDGMENT
[11] *Rakam Inc v TF Hartnett (Commissioner of Labor)* 165 A.D. 2d 939 [1990, New York]	A assessed for additional unemployment insurance contribution for computer consultants who were restricted in activities with clients (nondisclosure of home address, telephone number and rates of pay without A's permission).	Status of consultants	Unemployment Insurance Appeal Board's decision that they were employees rather than independent contractors affirmed.
[12] *TSR Consulting Services Inc v. TF Hartnett (Commissioner of Labor)* [1990, New York]	A engaged computer consultants to service clients. Consultants required to keep time sheets and paid by A; their activities were also restricted with clients; A alone solicited clients. A assessed additional unemployment insurance contribution for computer consultants.	Status of consultants	Unemployment Insurance Appeal Board's decision that they were employees rather than independent contractors affirmed.
[13] *JT Copley v NCR et al.* 394 S.E. 2d 751 [1990, W. Virginia]	A employed to sell computer hardware and software. Contract has arbitration clause in cases of dispute. A filed a complaint against NCR alleging age and sex discrimination; fired. Sued for breach of employment of contract, unlawful discrimination and retaliatory discharge.	Could A's claim be overridden by arbitration agreement?	Court has no authority to enforce arbitration clause in employment contract; arbitration clause could not defeat human rights action. Lower court's decision that arbitral agreement would override reversed.
[14] *SN Shauers v Board of County Commissioners of Sweetwater* 746 P.2d 444 [1987, Wyoming]	A employed to develop software programs. R later decided to sell them, A consented on condition. Dispute over ownership arose; R sought a declaration from court.	Ownership of software developed by employee; right to transfer	R owned original copies of programs it paid for, possessed and used; A could only use ideas, concepts and techniques in future. Confirmed lower court's judgment. Transfer issue not solved owing to lack of facts.
[15] *Professional Bus. Systems Inc et al v DC Kaufman and M Kaufman* 507 S0.2d 421 [1987, Alabama]	R employed as computer data processors; company in financial trouble and never got paid 1980 salary; A (through founder, Austin) promised to pay them in future while they continue in employment; still not paid. R sued personally.	Capacity of promisor personal or as agent of company? Parol evidence allowed to establish intention?	Written agreement unambiguous and parol evidence (to bind owner, Austin) not admissible.

NO. CASE	FACTS	ISSUES	JUDGMENT
[16] *Delta Resources et al. v GJ Harkin et al.* 506 NYS 2d 695 [1986, New York}	R was shareholder cum employee of A, later sold; R became employee obliged not to compete within one year of departure unless company made no request of his continued service beyond his contractual term of three years.	Could A permanently restrain R from setting up competing business and soliciting former customers?	Shareholders/sellers have a duty to refrain indefinitely from soliciting ex-customers; duty survives further sale of business.
[17] *Universal Computer Services Inc v BL Lyall* 464 So.2d 69 [1985, Mississippi]	R ex-employee (on salary and commission basis) who sought to claim unpaid commission and salary; A sent check for much lower amount but was rejected. R sought attachment against car he was using; trial court.	Jurisdiction of courts to attach; whether employer liable to pay up?	Yes, proper jurisdiction; employment agreement not entire agreement; admission of other evidence justified. Decision for employee affirmed.
[18] *Calspan Corp v KR Piech et al.* 458 NYS 2d 211 [1982, New York]	R accepted a job before resigning and has his name used by future employer.	Was R in breach of fiduciary duty or conspiring to misappropriate A's trade secrets and property?	R could prepare for future employment; conduct not actionable; lack of facts prevented a ruling on other claims.
[19] *J&K Computer Systems Inc v DT Parrish et al.* [1982, Utah]	Parrish employed as programmer; contract enjoined him from disclosing methods or programs used by A during or after term of employment. Parrish set up company with another ex-employee using accounts receivable programs developed during employment with A.	Whether R can be prevented from using or disclosing program?	A's program was secret and worthy of protection; hence lower court's ruling affirmed.
[20] *Amoco Production Co v RH Lindley* 609 P.2d 733 [1980, Oklahoma]	Employee developed program in his own time but later adopted by company. Employee left.	Ownership of program and preventing ex-employee from disclosing trade secret.	Program not patentable, only better way of doing things; company cannot claim ownership of invention per employment contract; employee can use system after leaving
[21] *Professional Data Services Inc v Carol Caruso and P Ross (Industrial Commissioner)* 433 NYS 2d 273 [1980, New York]	A engaged clerical home workers to work key punch machines. One installed in Caruso's home. Each picked up individual work, finished within deadline and job priced differently. Board decided employee eligible to receive benefits.	Status of Caruso as home clerical worker	A controlled distribution of work, supplied necessary equipment, and under contract could only refuse work for good reason. This showed employee-employer relationship. Decision of Board affirmed.

NO. CASE	FACTS	ISSUES	JUDGMENT
[22] *Read Q Systems v DD Agee* 417 NYS 2d 494 [1979, New York]	R accounts manager entitled to commission on her sales plus additional 4% for consultation fees (allegedly oral agreement) obtained through her. Defendant's motion to strike out case denied.	Oral contract barred by statute of limitation?	Falls within statute of frauds, but discretionary verdict of court granting her leave to reapply. Reversed and motion granted.
[23] *KG Robinson et al v Computer Systems Inc et al.* 346 So.2d 940 [1977, Alabama]	A was a former employee and executive officer of R engaged in data processing; contract forbid noncompetition for two years after termination. Set up consultancy business (in use of equipment) with former client of R.	Would noncompetition clause be effective? Should an injunction have been given against A?	R had intention to fire Robinson as soon as they had a replacement; inequitable and unreasonable to enforce a contract R did not intent to keep. A did not provide same service as R.
[24] *Trilog Associates Inc v Farmularo et al.* 314 A.2d 287 [1974, Pennsylvania]	R had worked for A in data processing business. Left A and set up own company in similar field; contracted with client of A which sought injunction and got it.	Effect of restraint of trade; anti-competition clause in contract.	Prohibition not to be employed by any business R came into contact with while in A's employment not reasonable; use of information about former client not unfair competition if available generally.
[25] *EF Gishen v Dura Corp* 285 NE 2d 117 [1972, Massachusetts]	A branch manager selling computer terminals; employment contract part printed, part handwritten; new contract in force but rate of compensation to stay as in "original agreement" (per "payroll notice" given) A fired before recovering from new sale. Had accepted calculated figure at one stage.	Was compensation to be based on printed one? R contended per handwritten no commission.	"Notice" effective against R; nondisclosure of basis of calculations made would make settlement voidable; a party cannot waive information containing error unknown to him.

26

Balancing Interpretation and Intervention in Information System Research: The Action Case Approach

R. Vidgen
Department of Computation
UMIST
Manchester M60 1QD, England
Tel: +44 161 200 3386
Fax: +44 161 200 3324
E-mail: rvidgen@sna.co.umist.ac.uk

K. Braa
Department of Informatics
University of Oslo
N-0316 Oslo, Norway
E-mail: kbraa@ifi.uio.no

Abstract

Understanding how technical artefacts are created and used within organizations is a central aspect of the IS research discipline. The conduct of research in an organizational setting is thus a major issue for the IS community. A research framework for in-context IS research is presented and used to position purified and hybrid forms of research method. From the framework, theoretical support for an action case research method is presented. The research framework is then used to describe and explain an IS research project from which a practice-based rationale for an action case method is argued. Characteristics of the action case method, a hybrid of interpretation and intervention, are described. Learning at three levels of analysis – concrete, general, and meta – is proposed as a way of reflecting on both the content of an IS research project and the IS research methods employed.

1 INTRODUCTION

A major strength of IS research is the potential to consider technological and organizational issues jointly, spanning the traditions of organization behavior and management through computer science and engineering. We argue that the primary laboratory for IS research is the organization, where the development and use of technical artefacts can be studied in-context and the resulting research findings used to inform both the practice and theory of IS. However, in conducting in-context research we recognize that it is possible for IS researchers to find themselves caught in an uncomfortable space, falling between research traditions which have different notions of relevance and rigor (Keen 1991) as well as different research methods. Thus, a central concern for IS research is the difficulty and challenge of adopting an interdisciplinary approach to research in the organizational laboratory.

The interdisciplinary nature of IS research may mean that we need new concepts and new or hybrid research methods in order to design, control, report and make effective use of IS research. An IS research framework has been proposed by Braa and Vidgen (1997) to assist IS researchers in navigating the space of in-context research. The research framework is based on the assumption that, regardless of the research tradition and method adopted, the organization constrains and enables what research can be done while at the same time recognizing that, to a greater or lesser extent, any research activity has the potential to initiate change in the organizational context. The aim of this paper is to illustrate the use of the IS research framework in practice as a device for planning, controlling, and evaluating IS research projects. One specific outcome of this work is the identification of a hybrid IS research method: action case.

The structure of the paper is as follows. In section 2, the IS research framework is described and a theoretical justification for an action case method advanced. In section 3, experiences of applying the research framework to an in-context IS research project are documented. The action case research method is elaborated in section 4; in section 5, a three-level analysis of learning from research projects is proposed; and in the last section a summary is made, together with ideas for future work.

2 AN IS RESEARCH FRAMEWORK FOR THE ORGANIZATIONAL LABORATORY

Research methods can be classified into two categories: positivist and interpretivist (Galliers 1985, 1992; Galliers and Land 1987). The positivist approach assumes that phenomena can be observed objectively and rigorously; good research is legitimated with reference to the virtues of repeatability, reductionism, and refutability (Checkland 1981). In contrast, the interpretivist approach considers the methods of natural science to be inappropriate where human beings are concerned, recognizing that different stakeholders (including researchers) will interpret a situation in different ways. These two views of research can be characterized as positivism, which is concerned with reducing the area of investigation in order to be able to make reliable predictions and explanations, and interpretivism, which is concerned with making a reading of history in order to gain understanding. With the positivist approach, the researcher is an observer of the laboratory. Any intervention must be controlled such that only the experimental variable changes; the prevailing organizational context is kept constant in order to provide replicability and predictive power. When an interpretivist approach, such as case study, is used, researchers also attempt to minimize their impact on the situation. However, we argue that in both positivist and interpretivist approaches the researcher is making an intervention (observation/interpretation constitutes an intervention) and can therefore affect the organizational context insofar as there may be unintended consequences (Giddens 1984). In some forms of research, such as action research, the aim is to gain knowledge through making deliberate interventions in order to achieve some desirable change in the organizational setting. The ideas of reduction (positivism), interpretivism, and intervention form the basis of the IS research framework.

2.1 The IS Research Framework

The framework is represented by a triangle (Figure 1), which comprises points, sides, and a constrained space (Braa and Vidgen 1997). The points represent intended research outcomes: *prediction* is aligned with the reduction of a positivist approach; *understanding* with an interpretive approach; and *change* with an interventionary approach. The points of the triangle should be viewed as ideal types in the Weberian sense, that is, they are non-moral abstractions that can be used to make comparisons with empirical reality. As such, these ideal type approaches to research are not attainable in practice, which is represented by the constrained space of the triangle.

The dotted lines inside the triangle represent movements toward the ideal types. As the researcher moves toward the prediction point through a process of *reduction* there should be greater explanatory power, predictive power, and statistical generalizability. The traditional approach to explanation and prediction is experimental method. Movement toward the understanding point through a process of *interpretation* is associated with greater richness of insight into the role of IS in organizational settings and is achieved typically through case studies. Baskerville and Wood-Harper (1996) point out that IS as a highly applied field with strong vocational elements (p. 235), which means that a mix of practice and research is needed if relevant and usable knowledge are to be produced. Action research allows the researcher to address the practical aspects of IS and helps the researcher develop a practical compe-

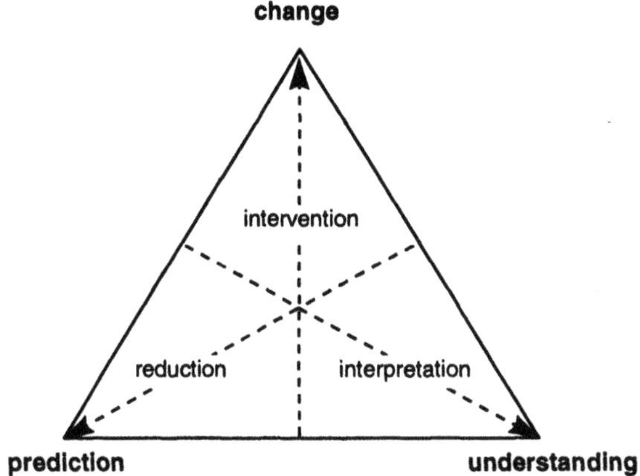

Figure 1 An IS Research Framework for the Organizational Laboratory.

tence that the methods of positivism and interpretivism can only approximate. The change point is achieved through a process of *intervention*, through which the researcher learns at first-hand about the mundane realities of IS and IS development in organizations.

2.2 Research Methods for the Organizational Laboratory

In this section, the different approaches to research adopted in the organizational laboratory are described in brief. We consider three purified forms of research - field experiment, soft case study, and action research – together with three hybrid research methods – quasi-experiment, hard case study, and action case.

With a view to making generalizable statements that are applicable to real-life situations, the motivation for field experiments is to construct an experiment in a more realistic environment (an organizational context) than is possible in a laboratory setting. Field experiments aim at controlling a small number of variables which may then be studied intensively. There are two types of field experiments (Cook and Campbell 1989; Zmud, Olson and Hauser 1989): "true" experimental design which meets the criteria of multiple treatments (or one treatment and a control group), randomization, and experimental control; and "quasi" experimental design, which does not meet these three criteria but rather attempts to preserve as many of the properties of true experimentation as possible, given the constraints of the research setting.

Galliers (1992) classifies case study as scientific, while Iivari (1991) categorizes the case study as an interpretivist method. For the purpose of providing a contrast we thus distinguish between the positivist *hard* case study, in the tradition of Yin (1984) and Lee (1989), and the interpretivist *soft* case study, as described by Walsham (1993, 1995). Soft case studies based on ethnographic methods can involve a variety of data collection techniques, such as videotape, and data analysis might involve techniques from grounded theory (Glaser and Strauss 1967).

Action research has been typified as a way of building theory and descriptions within the context of practice itself (see, for example, Susman 1983; Checkland 1991). Theory is tested through intervention in the organizational laboratory, that is, through experiments that bear the double burden of testing hypotheses and effecting some desirable change in the situation (Argyris and Schön 1991). Drawing from Habermas (1972), we argue that change also involves a critical perspective, as exemplified in the Scandinavian tradition (Bansler 1989; Ehn and Kyng 1987).

In Figure 2a, we align field experiment with prediction, case study with understanding, and action research with change in order to locate the research methods within the research framework. Hard case study and quasi-experiment have a less pure basis with respect to the ideal types of research outcome and are placed in the triangle such that hard case study is represented as a mix of understanding and prediction, and quasi-experiment as a mix of prediction and change.

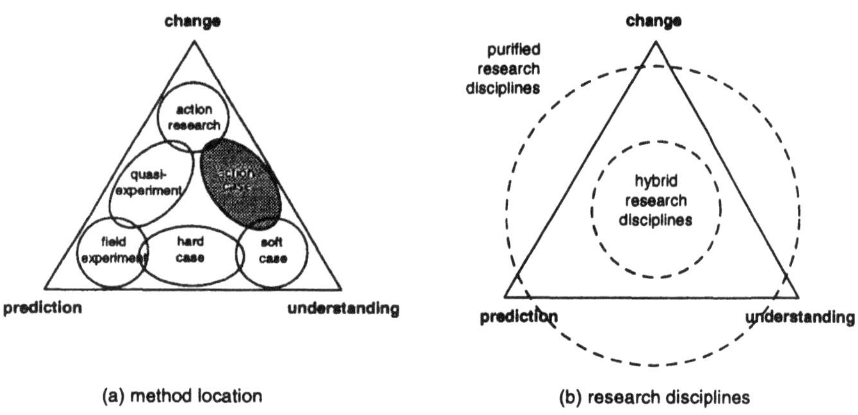

(a) method location (b) research disciplines

Figure 2 Research Methods.

Analysis of the research framework suggests that a further hybrid might be appropriate. The shaded area of Figure 2a has been labeled "action case," which is a hybrid of understanding and change. In Figure 2b, purified disciplines – field experiment, soft case study, and action research – are contrasted with hybrid disciplines: quasi-experiment, hard case study, and action case. In the next section, we consider whether it would be possible to develop a general-purpose IS research method for use in the organizational laboratory. Such a method would need to be a three-headed hybrid that satisfies the requirements of prediction, understanding, and change.

2.3 Dilemmas of IS Research in the Organizational Laboratory

McGrath (1982) introduces the term dilemmatics and states that "the research process is to be regarded not as a set of problems to be 'solved', but rather as a set of dilemmas to be 'lived with'" (p. 69). According to McGrath, experimental research should aim to maximize: generalizability with respect to populations; control of variables; and existential realism. Research might be designed to maximize one of the desiderata, for example, a well-designed and well-executed laboratory experiment may result in a high level of control, but does so at the expense of generalizability and realism. Alternatively, the researcher might try to maximize two of the three desiderata, for example, a field experiment addresses control and realism to some extent but falls down on generalizability. Thus, McGrath presents research as a three-horned dilemma in which one can maximize one of the three desiderata (generalizability, control, or realism), but be impaled on the remaining two horns. Alternatively, one might plan to achieve higher levels of two desiderata but be impaled fully on the remaining horn. McGrath summarizes the three-horned dilemma: "There is no way – in principle – to maximize all three conflicting desiderata of the research strategy domain" (p. 76).

We can take the lessons of McGrath's dilemmatics and apply them to the IS research framework of Figure 2, which manifests the three-horned dilemma in two ways. First, the three purified forms of research (field experiment, action research, and soft case study) each address one horn of the dilemma, but at the expense of the remaining two points of the triangle. Secondly, the hybrid research methods (quasi-experiment, action case, and hard case study) make an uneasy compromise between two points, while being impaled fully on the third point. Thus, it is not possible for a researcher to be involved with IS practice as though she/he were entirely and indistinguishably part of the organization, while also being an outsider who can stand back from the situation and make interpretations, and at the same time produce rigorous results in the positivist tradition. Increasing the proportion of one ideal type of research outcome is counter-balanced by a diminution of one or both of the other ideal types.

Focusing on the sides of the triangle, we can express the dilemmas (trade-offs) between pairs of ideal types of research outcome and thus focus on the hybrid methods:

- *understanding/prediction:* this side highlights the trade-off between a desire to make rich interpretations of complex situations (understanding) and the need to reduce complexity in order to ascribe cause and effect relationships (prediction). The hard case method is an attempt to balance the dilemma of understanding and prediction, of subjectivity and objectivity. This trade-off is made at the expense of practical knowledge (*change*).
- *change/prediction:* a trade-off between making an intervention in the situation (to create change and gain practical knowledge) and a desire to reduce the number of experimental variables in the interests of predictive power. In action research, the

aim is to support desired change in an organizational setting while field experiments are geared toward hypothesis testing and a desire to keep the organizational context constant. The difficulty of conducting true experiments in an organizational laboratory is reflected in a survey conducted by Zmud, Olson and Hauser of the use of field experimentation within IS research in which they found only seven such studies reported. Thus, quasi-experiments (designed and natural) are more likely to be used than true field experiments in IS research. This trade-off is made at the expense of richness of insight (*understanding*).
- *understanding/change:* a trade-off between being an outside observer who can make interpretations (understanding) and a researcher involved in creating change in practice. Case study methods attempt to minimize changes caused by the research activity, while in action research the aim is to support desirable change in an organizational setting. However, when doing case studies, researchers contribute to change by questioning events and applying new concepts. On the other hand, full-scale action research projects are often not appropriate due to organizational constraints or the nature of the topic to be investigated. Small scale intervention with a deep contextual understanding is one way of balancing this dilemma - this is the area labeled action case. This trade-off is made at the expense of explanatory power (*prediction*).

In summary, the points of the triangle are characterized by action research, field experiment, and soft case study. Of the three dilemmas of IS research highlighted by the sides of the triangle, two are addressed currently, by quasi-experimentation and hard case study. The third dilemma we posit is not currently addressed by IS research theory and we have labeled this area action case. In the next section, the research framework is used to analyze an IS research project and to gather empirical evidence concerning the action case method.

3 APPLYING THE RESEARCH FRAMEWORK IN PRACTICE

The fieldwork was conducted in a European aerospace organization (which we shall call Eurospace) involved in all aspects of the design and manufacture of aircraft. The research was sponsored by Eurospace's Software Quality Directorate. The terms of reference for the project called for the development and application of an IS quality method that could be used alongside the structured systems analysis methods (for example, SSADM (CCTA 1990) and object-oriented methods (for example, Rumbaugh et al. 1991)) that were currently in use within the organization. For the purposes of this paper, we focus on the research method adopted for the project and the context in which the research was conducted; we do not present details of the research content, i.e., the development and application of an IS quality method, this being described elsewhere (Vidgen 1996). The fieldwork was divided into three phases and spanned an elapsed time of just over two years, allowing for gaps between phases. The three phases are presented in chronological order.

3.1 Phase 1: Study of the Development Organization

The first phase of the research lasted five months. At the outset of the first phase, the empirical research was loosely structured, being organized around the general objective of finding out about the system development process within Eurospace and the quality issues perceived by system development staff. All of the interviews were carried out with personnel from the technical computing department, who develop and manage applications software for aircraft documentation systems and computer-aided engineering (CAE) (see Dean and Susman [1989] and Liker, Fleischer and Arnsdorf [1992] for experiences of integrating CAE software into the manufacturing process). As the interviews progressed, common themes began to emerge that formed a basis for semi-structured interviews. In phase 1 of the research project, an understanding of the system development environment in technical computing was acquired through interviews and inspection of source documents. The researcher's interpretation of the phase 1 data highlighted the technology-based and process-centered perspective of system developers and gave an indication of the difficulties development managers might face in adopting a quality and customer-centered approach to system development.

3.2 Phase 2: Analysis of Specific Information Systems

The aim of phase 2, which had a duration of nine months, was to understand better the context in which IT applications were used. Two computer systems were chosen for in-depth investigation: one was a planning system for aircraft electrical systems and the other a design quality monitoring system. Stakeholder analysis was used by the researcher to identify those affected by and affecting the computer system being studied and, as in phase 1, a series of interviews were conducted. Different stakeholders, including developers and various categories of users, were then brought together in a workshop in order to explore different conceptions of quality. This brought together primary and secondary users with the system developers and constituted an intervention insofar as prior to the research there had been no formal channel for the developers and secondary users to communicate. As a result of the workshop and the report produced at the end of the phase, changes to the operation and management of the electrical planning system were initiated. Following the completion of phase 2, a provisional approach to incorporating quality methods within the IS development process was proposed.

3.3 Phase 3: Application of the IS Quality Method

The IS quality method developed at the end of phase 2 was now to be tested and developed further through action research. The researcher met with the head of technical computing to discuss potential projects, the result being that a software development project concerned with the automation of wind tunnel operation and the collection and processing of aerodynamic data was identified. The researcher joined the project team and introduced the use of quality techniques, including quality function deployment (King 1989; Slabey 1990) and soft systems methodology (Checkland 1981; Checkland and Scholes 1990). In the third phase, which lasted ten months, there was a considerable degree of intervention initiated by the researcher: a series of quality requirements workshops were held with wind tunnel customers; there was close working with wind tunnel staff in producing an IS quality plan (this incorporated a quality questionnaire which was distributed to the user community); liaison with system developers in defining a computer system architecture, object model, and process model; and a work study of wind tunnel operation was made. Together these activities constituted a considerable intervention in the problem situation from which the IS quality method could be evaluated and made operational.

3.4 Using the Research Framework: Explanation and Reflection

The three phases described above were mapped retrospectively (the research framework was not available until a point in time after the project had started) into Figure 1: the research design allowed for a general study of the system development context, more specific studies of particular computer systems and the development of an IS quality method which was to be tested through action research (Figure 3a). In practice it seemed that the case studies of phase 2 contained a greater element of intervention than had been envisaged. This intervention can be attributed in part to the workshop and to the end of phase report, both of which relate to improved communication between stakeholders. Thus, we consider that there was a higher degree of intervention than would occur with a "pure" case study, although in this instance the resultant change was largely an unforeseen consequence.

Phase 3 of the project, although having a quite considerable degree of intervention, did not result in the level of intervention and assimilation of methods that might have resulted from a commercial exercise with senior management backing and consultancy support. We attribute this to the project being perceived by the organizational participants as primarily a research exercise that would not change to any great extent the way system development was conducted. This was due in part to organizational factors. For example, the research project sponsors reported through a different part of the organization from the system development and wind tunnel departments, which meant that any access had to be negotiated on an informal basis; this could be difficult since all personnel time had to be accounted for and allocated against a budget code – participants could easily and legitimately decline to be involved. However, despite this the researcher was able to gain significant access to different parts of the organization and to conduct quality workshops. Phase 3 resulted in changes to the way the role of the wind tunnel department was perceived by its customers, the way in which the wind tunnel department perceived its role, and in a significant revision of the wind tunnel department's IT strategy.

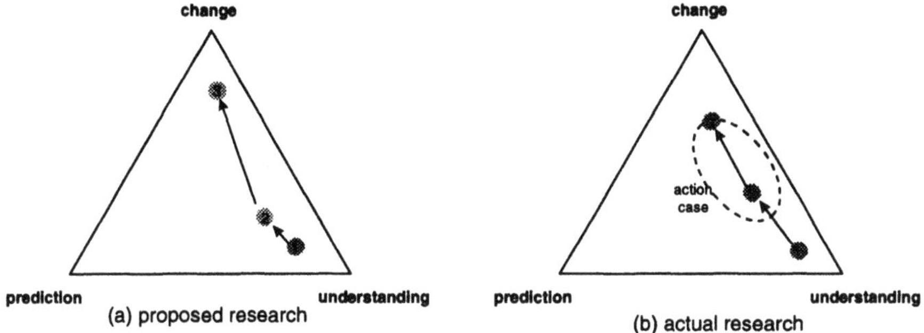

Figure 3 Proposed and Actual Research Illustrated.

Our concern is that phase 2 does not seem to be a "pure" case study, due to the change element, while phase 3 does not quite constitute "pure" action research, due to the perception of the project as largely academic. Thus, in Figure 3b we show the research as it unfolded as being better typified on the boundaries of the action case area. The comparison afforded by Figure 3 can be used to help explain how the research unfolded in practice, particularly the unforeseen consequences that are characteristic of any activity in the organizational laboratory. The framework can also be used to monitor and take control action as the research unfolds.

4 ACTION CASE ELABORATED

The area labeled action case in Figures 2a and 3b represents a mix of interpretation/ understanding and intervention/change. In Figure 2a we argued for action case on the basis of dilemmas in the research framework and in Figure 3b we argue for action case on the more pragmatic grounds of unintended consequences and organizational constraints in the organizational laboratory. In practice the dilemma between intervention and interpretation is significant. For example, when doing a case study in a development context it is hard not to affect solutions on a concrete level, by bringing people together, stating critical questions, as happened in the fieldwork when workshops were conducted. However, if the aim of the research is to bring in new methods and concepts and to study their effect on the development process, what then is being studied in actuality? The researcher's ability to diffuse new ideas and solve problems or the appropriateness of the method? These issues need to be framed, not as an either/or choice, but as a deliberate space for action. Thus the action component reflects the potential for research to change organizations resulting in changes to the social world and the case component reflects the necessity of weighing the understanding gained from the findings. With respect to the action component, we follow Checkland's (1991) seven-stage model of action research in making a framework of ideas explicit (a theory to be tested): enter the problem situation; establish roles; declare methodology and framework of ideas; take part in the change process; rethink roles, methodology and framework of ideas and take part in further change processes; exit from the problem situation; reflect and record learning in relation to the framework of ideas, the methodology, and the area of application. With purer forms of action nearer to the change point of the research framework this requirement might be relaxed, typically in situations in which a strongly critical perspective is taken.

From the fieldwork described above a number of practical lessons have been extracted, which serve to better delineate action case as well as providing further practical support for such an approach to IS research. The issues that have arisen from the fieldwork have been categorized under the headings of *suitability* (is action case a suitable method according to the research question investigated), *interpretation* (will sufficient depth of understanding be achieved), *intervention* (what degree of intervention can be achieved and managed), and *practicability* (what organizational constraints might impede the research). Each of these has been divided into a number of subheadings and an example from the fieldwork provided by way of illustration (Table 1).

4.1 Characteristics of the Action Case Method

We recognize that the demands of the interpretation and intervention perspectives of action case might conflict (e.g., richness versus scale) and prefer to address such issues directly. However, it might be argued that action case, being a hybrid method, will inherit the weaknesses of the contributing "purified" research approaches, namely case study and action research. Thus, an action case might be subject to the criticisms of case study, such as generalizability, replicability, and control (Lee 1989) and of action research, such as paying insufficient attention to the ethical implications of change (Galliers 1992). However, we argue that action case should be seen as a response to the dilemma of interpretation and intervention as well as providing a pragmatic response to the issues of manageability of in-context research. Similarly, quasi-experiments and hard case studies represent approaches for dealing with the dilemmas of reduction and intervention, and interpretation and reduction respectively. Labeling the area of the research framework "action case" provides a basis for delineating the characteristics and usefulness of such an approach.

We see the characteristics of the action case approach as follows. First, the scope of the investigation is restricted such that small-scale interventions are made in the interests of gaining practical knowledge of IS use at the same time as achieving a rich, albeit proscribed, understanding of the context in which change takes place. Second, the timescale will typically be of a short to medium duration rather than the long durations associated with full-scale action research. Third, the intervention will be focused and deliberate such that the effects of the change can be studied in detail, per-

Table 1 Characteristics of the Action Case Method.

Factor	attribute	action case concern	example from the Eurospace fieldwork
Suitability	Research design	Is action case appropriate to the research question to be investigated?	The action case method was appropriate to phase 2 (formulation of an understanding of what constitutes IS quality) and phase 3 (learning how the quality management can be incorporated in IS development).
	Researcher skills	Does the researcher have the skills and experience to make an intervention?	The researcher had a number of year's experience as a practitioner and as a consultant in the area of IS development.
Interpretation	Richness	Is the scope of the research wide enough to provide understanding?	The scope of the research project was widened to include multiple stakeholders to ensure sufficient richness of context.
	Focus	Is the research question sufficiently focused?	The focus of the research was reduced to testing a framework of ideas related to a specific aspect of IS development - the role of quality management.
Intervention	Scale	Is the scale of the subject for research manageable?	The time-scale of phase 3 was of medium duration (10 months), limited to a single system development project for one department, and involved change on a small-scale.
	Participation style	What level of participation can be expected from the organization members?	User personnel did not wish to be involved in the development of the IS quality method, but were happy for it to be applied as long as it did not disrupt users or developers. Full-scale action research would have been difficult.
	Critical impact	Is a critical approach required?	The current situation was not perceived as requiring a critical intervention and the small-scale intervention of the research was expected to change working practices significantly.
Practicability	Economics	Is sufficient financial support and researcher time available?	The researcher was available two days per week and had funds available for travel and equipment.
	Access	Can access be negotiated with stakeholders (e.g., users, managers, developers, customers, business partners)?	Negotiation of access to an appropriate project for action-oriented research proved to be problematical. A series of smaller scale interventions (phases 1 and 2) were needed to gain the confidence of users and developers.
	Politics	Does the research conflict with the organizations politics? Is there sufficient backing for the action and case components?	The research was not perceived to be politically sensitive from a corporate perspective, but the sponsors had no direct leverage with senior user management and thus access was negotiated bottom-up.
	Control	Can the research project be controlled?	The research focus, scope, and scale contributed to a reduction of complexity such that the research could be monitored against the research plan (using the research framework) and compensating action taken.

haps involving pre- and post mini-case studies. Although there is a flavor of experimental design in which the researcher seeks to control variables, in action case this will be rather less formal and is related to the issue of scope; in this sense action case involves a quasi-reduction of complexity. Fourth, action case will take from the tradition of action research a concern with building the future through purposeful change, while maintaining an interest in the historic conditions in which the research is set.

5 ORGANIZING THE LEARNING FROM THE RESEARCH

Learning from research is a combination of learning about the content of the research and learning about the process of enquiry. In order to talk about the learning from research, we propose that three levels are distinguished: concrete, general, and meta level learning. The motivation for adopting this approach is grounded in systems theory; three levels of analysis provides a powerful way of organizing our thoughts such that one can look up a level to (more) basic assumptions and down a level to practical results. Although it is often difficult to set the level of resolution appropriately (and the levels are potentially infinite in their upward and downward extent), the process of defining the levels promotes reflection and provides a vehicle for the organization of learning. Bateson (1972) provides similar levels of learning originated in communication theory and cybernetics (Star and Ruhleder 1994). Bateson differentiated between first, second, and third order learning. The first level emphasizes learning something, such as learning to use a tool. The second level is concerned with learning about something, such as the ability to choose between categories of tools. The third level addresses theories of categorization: learning about the assumptions that underlie the different categories of tools. We similarly adopt a three level approach to learning, referring to the three levels as concrete, general, and meta levels. Furthermore, we apply the three levels to both the content and process of IS research.

5.1 Learning from the Content of the Research

Although the details of the content of the IS research project are excluded from this paper, it is relevant to comment on how the learning achieved in the project might be assessed. At the first level, the research could be evaluated in terms of practice. For example, the experiences of running and facilitating IS quality workshops and the mechanics of applying quality function deployment (QFD) to the IS domain were reflected on in terms of practical learning (*concrete* level). At the second level, the implications of combining quality methods with mainstream IS development methods were considered from a methodological perspective (*general* level). At the third level, the research was considered from the viewpoint of basic assumptions about quality and information systems development (e.g., objectivism and subjectivism, conflict, and ethics): the *meta* level. This three-level approach to the analysis of the research was found to be a useful way of structuring the learning and is orthogonal to the research framework of Figure 3.

5.2 Learning About the Research Process

The three levels of learning can also be applied to the research process. Practical experience of using individual research methods is gained (concrete). Learning is made about the research framework (Figure 3), including the identification of the action case method (general). The third level is concerned with the assumptions on which the research framework is based (meta) and in this instance is associated in part with the problems of inter-disciplinary working, an issue that we consider to be central to both IS and IS research. It would be reasonable to expect there to be some justifiable relationship between the three levels of analysis of the content of a research project and the three levels of analysis of the research process employed, particularly at the assumptional (meta) level. This relationship need not necessarily be a one to one correspondence as shown by Clegg (1990), who uses modernist methods to study post-modern forms of organization, but the assumptions underpinning the research method and the assumptions under-pinning the research topic should be expected to have some degree of consistency.

6 SUMMARY AND FUTURE WORK

Some of the challenges and difficulties of being part of an interdisciplinary field consisting of often contradictory values, assumptions and methods have been highlighted in this paper. An IS research framework has been presented in order to provide language and concepts to support researchers navigating the organizational laboratory. The aims of IS research are presented as prediction and explanation, understanding and insight, change and practical knowledge. We recognized that these three aims constitute a three-horned dilemma represented by purified (one-point) research approaches – field experiment, soft case study, action research – and hybrid (two-point) research approaches – quasi-experiment, hard case study, and action case. We believe that a particular strength of IS research is the integration of theory and practice, intervention and interpretation, and that the elaboration of how these interests can be balanced will help in making IS research more professional.

An IS research project was analyzed using the research framework and it was proposed that learning from the content of the project be considered using three levels of analysis: concrete, general, and meta. The three-level analysis of learning is also recommended for evaluation of the learning achieved with respect to research methods. At the concrete level, we have gained experience of applying the action case method and have identified some of the characteristics of the method, which were elaborated using the categories suitability, interpretation, intervention, and practicability. Action case is typified as involving a mix of interpretation and intervention with a sufficiently rich context; a focused research question; a framework of ideas to be tested; less than full participation by members of the organization; a low planned level of critical impact; small-scale interventions that are achievable given the researcher's experience and resources; and a short to medium duration. Clearly, further work is needed in developing an action case method and it is recognized that this requires the method to be adopted and developed by others. At the general level, the action case method was identified and the usefulness of the IS research framework for guiding and managing an IS research project has been reported; the research framework needs also to be applied in further research projects by others to assess whether it might have wider usefulness.

The meta level addresses the inter-disciplinary nature of IS research, where the assumptions at this level may be based on different schools of thought. For example, the meta level might be based on paradigmatic closure (Burrell and Morgan 1979), which would suggest that research methods should be developed faithfully within their paradigms. We tend toward more recent developments such as structuration theory (Giddens 1984) and actor network theory (Callon 1986; Latour 1987) where there is symmetric treatment of object and subject worlds. Given that these basic assumptions influence the content of IS research projects (for example, Hirschheim and Klein (1989) use the Burrell and Morgan's four paradigm model and Orlikowski (1992) uses structuration theory) we would expect these ideas to affect also research approaches and methods. We suggest that IS research methods need to be developed at all three levels of analysis and, although it is not possible to address the issues associated with a meta-level discussion of IS research in this paper, we consider that this is an important and continuing area for further work.

7 ACKNOWLEDGMENT

We thank the IFIP 8.2 referees for their valuable and constructive comments. This paper has benefited also from being the subject of an Internet Project discussion group and we wish to thank everybody who participated for their thorough and helpful criticism. We acknowledge the financial support provided to the Internet Project by the Swedish Transport and Communications Research Board (Kommunikationsforskningsberedningen). See http://internet.adb.gu.se/ for further details of the Internet Project.

8 REFERENCES

Argyris, C., and Schön, D. A. (1991). "Participatory Action Research and Action Science Compared." In W. F. Whyte (Editor), *Participatory Action Research.* Newbury Park, California: Sage.

Braa, K., and Vidgen, R. (1997). "An IS Research Framework for the Organization as Laboratory." In M. Kyng and L. Mathiassen (Editors), *Computers in Context: Joining Forces in Design*. Cambridge, Massachusetts: MIT Press (forthcoming).

Bansler, J. (1989). "Systems Development Research in Scandinavia: Three Theoretical Schools." *Scandinavian Journal of Information Systems*, Volume 1, pp. 3-20.

Baskerville, R., and Wood-Harper, A. T. (1996). "A Critical Perspective on Action Research as a Method for Information Systems Research." *Journal of Information Technology*, Volume 11, pp. 235-246.

Bateson, G. (1972). *Steps to an Ecology of Mind*. New York: Ballantine.

Burrell, G., and Morgan, G. (1979). *Sociological Paradigms and Organizational Analysis*. London: Heinemann Educational Books.

Callon, M. (1986). "Some Elements of a Sociology of Translation: Domestication of the Scallops and the Fishermen of St Brieuc Bay." In J. Law (Editor), *Power, Action and Belief*. London: Routledge and Keagan Paul, pp 196-233.

CCTA, (1990). *SSADM Version 4 Reference Manual*. Oxford: NCC Blackwell.

Checkland, P. (1981). *Systems Thinking, Systems Practice*. Chichester, England: Wiley.

Checkland, P. (1991). "From Framework through Experience to Learning: the Essential Nature of Action Research." In H.-E. Nissen, H. K. Klein, and R. Hirschheim (Editors), *Information Systems Research: Contemporary Approaches and Emergent Traditions*. Amsterdam: North Holland.

Checkland, P., and Scholes, J. (1990). *Soft Systems Methodology in Action*. Chichester, England: Wiley.

Clegg, S. (1990). *Modern Organizations: Organization Studies in the Postmodern World*. Newbury Park, California: Sage.

Cook, T. D., and Campbell, D. T. (1989). *Quasi-Experimentation: Design and Analysis Issues for Field Settings*. Chicago: Rand McNally.

Dean, J., and Susman G. (1989). "Organizing for Manufacturable Design." *Harvard Business Review*, January-February, pp. 28-36.

Ehn, P., and Kyng, M. (1987). "The Collective Resource Approach to Systems Design." In G. Bjerknes, P. Ehn, and M. Kyng (Editors), *Computers and Democracy: A Scandinavian Challenge*. Aldershot, England: Avebury, pp. 17-58.

Galliers, R. D. (1985). "In Search of a Paradigm for Information Systems Research." In E. Mumford, R. Hirschheim, G. Fitzgerald, and A. T. Wood-Harper (Editors), *Research Methods in Information Systems*. Proceedings of the IFIP WG 8.2 Colloquium, 1 - 3 September, 1984, Manchester Business School. Amsterdam: North Holland.

Galliers, R. D. (1992). "Choosing Information Systems Research Approaches." In R. D. Galliers (Editor), *Information Systems Research: Issues, Methods and Practical Guidelines*. Oxford: Blackwell Scientific.

Galliers, R. D., and Land, F. F. (1987). "Choosing Appropriate Information Systems Research Methodologies." *Communications of the ACM*, Volume 30, Number 11, pp. 900-902.

Giddens, A. (1984). *The Constitution of Society*. Cambridge: Polity Press.

Glaser, B., and Strauss, A. (1967). *The Discovery of Grounded Theory: Strategies for Qualitative Research*. Chicago: Aldine.

Habermas, J. (1972). *Knowledge and Human Interests*. London: Heinemann.

Hirschheim, R. A., and Klein, H. K. (1989). "Four Paradigms of Information Systems Development." *Communications of the ACM*, Volume 32, Number 10, pp. 1199-1216.

Iivari, J. (1991). "A Paradigmatic Analysis of Contemporary Schools of IS Development." *European Journal of Information Systems*, Volume 1, Number 4, pp. 249-272.

Keen, P. (1991). "Relevance and Rigor in Information Systems Research: Improving Quality, Confidence, Cohesion and Impact." In H.-E. Nissen, H. K. Klein, and R. Hirschheim (Editors), *Information Systems Research: Contemporary Approaches and Emergent Traditions*. Amsterdam: North Holland.

King, R. (1989). *Better Designs in Half the Time: implementing QFD*. Methuen, Massachusetts: GOAL/QPC.

Latour, B. (1987). *Science in Action*. Cambridge, Massachusetts: Harvard University Press.

Lee, A. S. (1989). "A Scientific Methodology for MIS Case Studies." *MIS Quarterly*, Volume 13, March, pp. 33-50.

Liker, J.; Fleischer, M.; and Arnsdorf, D. (1992). "Fulfilling the Promises of CAD." *Sloan Management Review*, Spring 1992, pp. 74-85.

McGrath, J. (1982). "Dilemmatics: The Study of Research Choices and Dilemmas." In J. McGrath, J. Martin, and R. Kulka (Editors), *Judgement Calls in Research*. Beverly Hills: Sage, pp. 69-102.

Orlikowski, W. (1992). "The Duality of Technology: Rethinking the Concept of Technology in Organizations." *Organization Science*, Volume 3, Number 3, pp. 398-427.

Rumbaugh, J.; Blaha, M.; Premerlani, W.; Eddy, F.; and Lorensen, W. (1991). *Object-Oriented Modeling and Design*. Englewood Cliffs, New Jersey: Prentice-Hall.

Slabey, R. (1990). "QFD: A Basic Primer." *Transactions from the Second Symposium on Quality Function Deployment*, June 18-19, Novi, Michigan.

Susman, G. (1983). "Action Research: A Sociotechnical System Perspective." In G. Morgan (Editor), *Beyond Method: Strategies for Social Research*. Newbury Park, California: Sage.

Star, S. L., and Ruhleder, K. (1994). "Steps Toward an Ecology of Infrastructure: Complex Problems in Design and Access for Large-Scale Collaborative Systems." *Proceedings of the CSCW'94: Transcending Boundaries*. New York: ACM Press, pp. 253-265.

Vidgen, R. (1996). *Multiple Perspectives of Information System Quality*. Unpublished Ph.D. Thesis, April, University of Salford.

Walsham, G. (1993). *Interpreting Information Systems in Organizations*. Chichester, England: Wiley.

Walsham, G. (1995). "Interpretive Case Studies in IS Research: Nature and Method." *European Journal of Information Systems*, Volume 4, pp. 74-81.

Yin, R. K. (1984). *Case Study Research: Design and Methods*. Second Edition. Thousand Oaks, California: Sage.

Zmud, R. W.; Olson, M.; and Hauser, R. (1989). "Field Experimentation in MIS Research." In I. Benbasat (Editor), *The Information System Research Challenge: Experimental Research Methods, Volume 2*. Cambridge, Massachusetts: Harvard Business School Research Colloquium.

9 BIOGRAPHY

Richard Vidgen has a first degree in Computer Science accounting Accounting and an M.Sc. in Accounting, both of which were awarded by the University of Manchester. He then developed and supported financial applications software for MSA Inc. (now Dunn & Bradstreet Software). This was followed by a number of years working as a freelance consultant engaged in the design and implementation of information systems in the financial sector. In 1992, he was appointed to a lectureship at the University of Salford, where he completed a Ph.D. in Information System Quality. He is currently a lecturer in the Department of Computation at UMIST with research interests in IS development methods, requirements analysis and process modeling, and group-working technologies.

Kristin Braa received her Ph.D. in computing science from the University of Oslo in 1995. She now holds a position as associate professor at the Department of Informatics at the University of Oslo. She does most of her research in the Internet project (http://internet.adb.gu.se/).

27

Using Case Study Research to Build Theories of IT Implementation

G. Paré
École des Hautes Études Commerciales
3000 chemin de la Côte-Ste-Catherine
Montréal, Québec, Canada
Tel: (514) 340-6812
Fax: (514) 340-6132
E-mail: Guy.Pare@hec.ca

J. J. Elam
Florida International University
Miami, Florida, United States
Tel: (305) 348-2719
Fax: (305) 348-3278
E-mail: Elamj@servax.fiu.edu

Abstract

In this paper, we present and illustrate how the approach proposed by Eisenhardt (1989) for building theories from case study research can help researchers understand and explain the inherently dynamic nature of numerous IT phenomena. The approach, which adopts a positivist view of research, relies on past literature and empirical data as well as on the insights of the researcher to build incrementally more powerful theories. We describe in some detail how this methodology was applied in a particular research study on IT implementation and how the use of this approach contributed to the discovery of a number of new perspectives and empirical insights. Furthermore, we discuss when it is appropriate to follow, to ignore, or to modify the suggestions made by Eisenhardt.

Overall, using Eisenhardt's approach as a starting point, our objective is to provide a more complete and detailed guide for using case studies to build theories within the MIS field.

1 INTRODUCTION

Information technology (IT) implementation has constituted a central and growing issue of research in the IS field. There is extensive literature on IT implementation dating back to the 1970s (e.g., Swanson 1974; Robey and Zeller 1978; Lucas 1978) with a growing number of studies conducted in the late 1980s and early 1990s (e.g., Srinivasan and Davis 1987; Leonard-Barton 1988; Lucas, Ginzberg, and Schultz 1990; Sabherwal and Robey 1993). The IT implementation stream of research consists primarily of studies, often referred to as "factor studies," which have tried to identify factors believed to be relevant to IT implementation success. Even though these studies have substantially contributed to our understanding of IT implementation, there are limitations inherent in the factor approach employed. First, these studies can only realistically handle a subset of the pieces of the implementation puzzle (Swanson 1988) and hence have caused a greater fragmentation of our understanding of the phenomenon (Kwon and Zmud 1987; Wynekoop 1992). Second, and most important, the factor approach has not provided much insight into the dynamics of the implementation process, that is, how and why independent variables interact and affect project outcomes (Newman and Robey 1992; Elam, Prescott and Wasala 1994).

In short, researchers have built models that identify a limited set of critical factors affecting IT implementation success, but we know very little about *how* and *why* the factors included in these models interact and work together to produce success or failure. As a result, MIS researchers lack a full understanding of the IT implementation process that is necessary to guide practitioners to attain positive outcomes. It thus appears important to ask ourselves, as researchers, how to improve not only our research models, but also our methodologies so that the results of our work can be of greater value to practitioners.

IT implementation is a complex, dynamic process involving diverse groups of key actors and activities. Researchers, tired of conflicting, ambiguous results, are seeking new methods with which to explore this process. For instance, Newman and Robey introduced an episodic-mapping methodology and demonstrated how it could be used to study the development of computer-based information systems. This methodology was then applied to a fifteen year systems implementation effort within a single organization, demonstrating its value in identifying and tracking important events, and highlighting patterns that recurred over time (Robey and Newman 1996). These researchers were motivated by the desire to utilize a methodology specifically designed to accommodate the intricacies of the IT implementation process, and they did indeed succeed in capturing the interplay of diverse groups and perspectives.

As another example, Elam, Prescott and Wasala conducted an in-depth case study that followed the implementation of an emerging IT over an eighteen month period. The study assessed the extent to which characteristics traditionally associated with successful implementation efforts were present in this implementation. It was found that only some of these characteristics were present at only certain times during the implementation period. To explore why this particular implementation was successful, a model was developed that showed the ways in which these ideal characteristics interacted. This interaction model was then used to explore how the presence of some characteristics compensated for the absence of others. Importantly, findings from this study revealed how mixed patterns involving factors at different levels complicate traditional statistical analysis that conceives of a direct association between implementation predictors and outcomes.

From these "innovative" studies, it clearly appears that further progress will require more complex, realistic research models and the development of alternative perspectives for viewing IT implementation. In this paper, we present and illustrate how the approach proposed by Eisenhardt (1989) for building theory from case study research can help researchers understand and explain the inherently dynamic nature of the IT implementation process. Several pieces of the approach proposed by Eisenhardt are borrowed from extant literature. In this regard, the approach includes key ideas and concepts from the work of Glaser and Strauss (1967) on grounded theory, Yin (1984) on case study research, Miles and Huberman (1984) on qualitative data analysis, Van Maanen (1988) on ethnography and Jick (1979) on triangulation of data types, to name a few. While these previous writings provide pieces of the process and focus on defending building theory from cases, the work of Eisenhardt focuses on *how* to actually build theory from cases. The approach relies on past literature and empirical data as well as on the insights of the researcher to build incrementally more powerful theories. It adopts a positivist view of research in that it is based on predefined research questions, a consideration of a priori constructs, and "it is directed toward the development of testable hypotheses and theory which are generalizable across settings" (Eisenhardt 1989, p. 546). Importantly, the final product of this approach may be the discovery of one or more emerging concept, the development of a new conceptual framework or the refinement of an existing one, or the development of a set of research propositions or possibly a mid-range theory.

In order to provide a practical demonstration of how the approach proposed by Eisenhardt can be used in studying IT implementation, this paper illustrates it with extensive material taken from an actual, published IT implementation case study (Paré 1995; Paré and Elam 1996; Paré, Elam and Lima forthcoming). This in-depth case study examines the implementation process, use, and consequences of three clinical information systems at a large tertiary care teaching hospital.

We show that the Eisenhardt approach to theory-building using case study research can be successfully applied in an IT context and can contribute to the discovery of new phenomena. In addition, we provide insights into the many choices that a researcher must make when adopting this approach. We discuss when it is appropriate to follow, to ignore, or to modify the suggestions made by Eisenhardt. Using Eisenhardt's approach as a starting point, our objective is to provide a more complete and detailed guide for using case studies to build theory within the IS field.

2 A CASE STUDY APPROACH TO STUDYING IT IMPLEMENTATION

This section describes the "roadmap" proposed by Eisenhardt for building theories from case study research and illustrates how this methodological framework can serve as a useful guide to researchers interested in studying the complex and dynamic nature of IT implementation. The roadmap is summarized in Table 1.

2.1 Step 1: Getting Started

According to Eisenhardt, three issues are of great importance in getting started: the initial definition of research questions, the *a priori* specification of constructs, and the consideration of *a priori* theory or hypotheses. Each of these issues will be examined in turn.

Initial Definition of Research Questions

First, an initial definition of one or more related research question, in at least broad terms, is as important in building theory from case studies as it is in hypothesis-testing research. Without a research focus, it is easy to become overwhelmed by the volume of qualitative data.

The ultimate intent of our study was to broaden and strengthen our understanding of IT implementation by researching the dynamic nature of the implementation process. More specifically, efforts were directed toward opening the black box and providing the story that explains *how* and *why* contextual conditions and implementation tactics and strategies interact and work together to produce project outcomes. In pursuit of this objective, two interrelated research questions were initially stated:

> *To what extent is the "ideal" implementation scenario a necessary condition to success? Referring to Swanson's metaphor (1988), to what extent should all the pieces of the "puzzle" be present and "fit" together to ensure implementation success?*
>
> *What are the laws of interaction which characterize the dynamic nature of IT implementation? How do contextual conditions and implementation tactics interact and work together to ensure system success?*

These research questions provided a well-defined focus to our research study and permitted us to specify the kind of data to be gathered.

Table 1 Process Building Theory from Case Study Research (Eisenhardt 1989).

Step	Activity	Reason
1. Getting started	Definition of research questions Possibly a priori constructs Neither theory nor hypotheses	Focuses efforts Provides better grounding of construct measures Retains theoretical flexibility
2. Selecting cases	Specified population Theoretical sampling	Sharpens external validity Focuses efforts on cases that replicate or extend theory
3. Crafting instruments and protocols	Multiple data collection methods Qualitative and quantitative data combined Multiple investigators	Strengthens grounding of theory by triangulation of evidence Synergistic view of evidence Fosters divergent perspectives and strengthens grounding
4. Entering the field	Overall data collection and analysis Flexible and opportunistic data collection methods	Speeds analysis and reveals helpful adjustments to data collection Allows investigators to take advantage of emergent themes and unique case features
5. Analyzing data	Within-case analysis Cross-case pattern using divergent techniques	Gains familiarity with data and preliminary theory generation Forces investigators to look beyond initial impressions
6. Shaping hypotheses	Replication, not sampling, logic across cases Search evidence of "why" behind relationships	Confirms, extends, and sharpens theory Build internal validity
7. Enfolding literature	Comparison with conflicting literature Comparison with similar literature	Builds internal validity Sharpens generalizability
8. Reaching closure	Theoretical saturation when possible	Ends process when marginal improvement becomes small

A Priori Specification of Constructs

With respect to the issue of using existing theoretical constructs to guide theory-building research, two different approaches may be taken (Anderson and Aydin 1994). In the first, the researcher works within an explicit conceptual framework. A conceptual framework "consists of a selection of concepts and relations among them, grouped so as to enable its users to easily see the major concepts simultaneously in their relations to one another" (Kochen 1985, p. 93). Therefore, a conceptual framework becomes a "researcher's first cut at making some explicit theoretical statements" (Miles and Huberman 1994, p. 91). In the second, the researcher tries not to be constrained by prior theory and instead sees the development of relevant theory, hypotheses, and concepts as a purpose of the project. In the present study *both approaches* were combined since the main intent was *to provide freshness in perspective to an already researched topic.* Importantly, given that this study was aimed at theory building, not theory testing, the conceptual framework (and its constructs) was used solely as a starting point. Basically, it helped make sense of occurrences, ensured that important issues were not overlooked, provided a set of constructs to be investigated, and guided our interpretation and focus. Specifically, using the research questions as a guide, a conceptual framework (see Appendix 1) was developed that grouped constructs related to the *contextual conditions* surrounding most implementation situations (e.g., resources availability, top management support, user attitudes, system characteristics), the *tactics* and *strategies* aimed at launching the project, managing the development of the new system and preparing organizational members for the new computer application, and the different criteria commonly adopted to evaluate *system success* (e.g., system use, user satisfaction with system, individual consequences, satisfaction with overall implementation process). In this light, the conceptual framework developed in our research provides an insightful way to study the process of implementing information technologies. Specifically, it suggests that researchers should pay careful attention to contextual conditions, human actions (both those of the implementers and the actions of those who are the targets of the implementation), and their interaction in order to better understand IT implementation success. However, as stressed by Eisenhardt, although early identification of possible constructs allows them to be explicitly measured in interviews and questionnaires, it is equally important to recognize that the identification of constructs is tentative in theory-building research. We found this to be true as new factors were found during data collection that needed to be added to the analysis.

Consideration of A Priori Theory or Hypotheses

The objective of our research study was to develop a *process theory* of IT implementation. Eisenhardt suggests that theory-building research must begin as close as possible to the ideal of no theory under consideration and no hypotheses to test since preordained theoretical perspectives may bias and limit the findings. However, as stressed by Eisenhardt, it is quite impossible to achieve the ideal of a clean theoretical slate. Hence, although we followed her suggestion in terms of not identifying specific relationships between the constructs identified in our conceptual framework, we found it necessary to make use of a process meta-theory called the teleological view (Van de Ven and Poole 1995). Indeed, a caveat for existing process models raised by Mohr (1982) seems particularly relevant to IT implementation studies. Precisely, Mohr argues that it is not enough for such models to supply the succession of events (such as in stage models). Rather, he posits that process models must provide the external forces and probabilistic processes constituting the means by which events are understood to unfold. In accord with Mohr, we believe process explanations become more meaningful when situated within a broader or higher level of process theory. The adoption of a particular meta-theory, namely, teleological theory, reflected our basic assumptions about the nature of the phenomena being studied, assumptions that were supported by strong evidence in the data.

The teleological view of process theory shaped our study of IT implementation in three important ways. First, the implementation of a computer-based information system was conceived as a purposeful endeavor which involved movement through different states toward attaining a specific goal or desired end state. Second, there were many possible paths that could be adopted in order to fulfill a specific end goal. Third, human actions were viewed as based on the actors' perceptions of how likely it was that a particular action would move the process closer toward goal achievement. In sum, by adopting a teleological view, our theory of IT implementation cannot specify what trajectory implementation will follow. At best, we can rely on norms of rationality to prescribe certain paths. Consequently, by adopting a teleological view of IT implementation, we focused our research efforts on understanding how courses of action were selected, developing process explanations related to the movement toward attaining a desired end state, and accessing the role of human perception in making progress toward goal achievement.

The adoption of the teleological process meta-theory was of great help in focusing our research efforts at the outset of the project since it provided the frame through which we could observe the IT implementation process and identify the key events of interest out of numerous ones that were occurring. As a final remark, it should be stressed that the data gathered in this study could have been analyzed using concepts such as punctuated equilibrium, conflict, and gradualism belonging to other types of process meta-theories such as life-cycle, dialectic, and evolution. For instance, the adoption of a dialectical perspective would have encouraged the study of issues such as politics and conflict within the IT implementation process. Using this perspective, a researcher would recognize the existence of subgoals and self-interest, and would examine how participants build, maintain, lose, and challenge power bases and whether they strive to resolve conflict through open communication or whether they resort to threats and coercion.

2.2 Step 2: Selecting Cases

Selection of cases represents another important aspect of building theory from case studies (Lee 1989; Benbasat, Goldstein and Mead 1987; Eisenhardt 1989). Such research relies on theoretical sampling (i.e., cases are chosen for theoretical, not statistical, reasons). The cases may be chosen to replicate previous cases or extend emergent theory, or they may be chosen to fill theoretical categories and provide examples of polar types (Eisenhardt 1989).

Given the nature of our research, we adopted a literal replication strategy where similar, not contrasting, results were predicted for each case. The number of replications is a matter of discretionary and judgmental choice (Yin 1984; Eisenhardt 1989). It depends upon the certainty a researcher wants to have about the multiple-case results. Three distinct organizational units at a large tertiary care teaching institution agreed to participate in our research project. Consequently, three independent IT implementation projects became the objects of our research.

2.3 Step 3: Crafting Instruments and Protocols

Theory-building researchers typically combine multiple data collection methods. The rationale is the same as in hypothesis-testing research; that is, the triangulation made possible by multiple data collection methods provides stronger substantiation of constructs and hypotheses (Eisenhardt 1989). Several MIS researchers (e.g., Wynekoop 1992; Lee 1989; Benbasat, Goldstein and Mead 1987; Kaplan and Duchon 1988) recommend that both quantitative and qualitative data be used in any study if at all possible. Collecting different types of data by different methods from different sources produces a wider scope of coverage and may result in a fuller picture of the phenomena under study than would have been achieved otherwise (Bonoma 1985).

We collected both qualitative data and quantitative data in our study. Qualitative data were primarily collected through face-to-face semi-structured interviews. As stressed by Kaplan and Maxwell (1994), the primary goal of interviews is to elicit the respondent's views and experiences in his or her own terms rather than to collect data that are simply a choice among preestablished response categories. The first step in the research design was to interview individuals who participated in the development of each of the IT implementation projects along with a small group of user representatives. Each interview started with a brief discussion of the research project, carefully designed to arouse the attention and interest of the interviewee, while not biasing the responses by providing too much information about the conceptual framework. The core of the interviews was semi-structured. Interview guides had been developed and were used during each interview. Basically, each interview guide contained the specific issues to be discussed with the respondent and questions to be kept in mind during each interview. An excerpt of an interview guide used in our study is presented in Appendix 2.

We also encouraged open discussions toward the end of each interview allowing interviewees to ask any questions and add any comments they might want. A total of 95 interviews were conducted over a period of six months. Interviews were conducted for one IT implementation project before proceeding to another. The average length of each interview was approximately 60 minutes with individuals involved in the IT implementation project and 30 minutes with user representatives producing a total of 812 pages of transcripts. Appendix 3 presents a profile of the interviewees.

Each project had been implemented within the last four years, making real time data gathering impossible. Recognizing this limitation, two tactics were adopted in our study to increase construct validity: reconstruction of events using multiple respondents and having key informants review final versions of reports.

Documents and texts also can be valuable sources of qualitative data (Miles and Huberman 1994; Kaplan and Maxwell 1994). For instance, in Kaplan's studies of the acceptance and diffusion of medical information systems (1983, 1987, 1988), the author read closely original source documents such as published research papers, popularizations in medical magazines, newsletters and books, and conference reports. In line with Kaplan's work, all documents relevant to the present study, including organizational charts, annual reports, special reports and/or administrative documents, newsletters and other internal publications, user manuals and/or training material, and software vendor marketing kits were collected and analyzed. In one of the three cases, the researchers read a series of three scientific papers that had recently been published by two of the key actors involved in the implementation process. These papers present the results of a post-audit evaluation effort which took place before, during and after an anticipated four-day system failure. These documents provided precious quantitative information that could be compared with the responses of the interviewees in regard to the value of the electronic charting system over the hand-written method.

Finally, whenever possible, observation completed the qualitative assessment. Observation in qualitative studies produces detailed descriptive accounts of what was going on. Such observation often is crucial to the assessment of a system. For example, Kaplan and Duchon (1988) went to the laboratories to observe what technologists actually did, rather than simply depend on verbal reports or job descriptions. In our own study, observation took place during several training sessions and meetings involving IT implementation project team members, user representatives and external parties. Direct observation of a few clinicians using the different computer-based information systems was also possible in all three organizational units. Detailed notes were taken during all observations in order to capture the researchers' impressions and insights.

The second and last step in the research design was to gather quantitative data. As stressed by Eisenhardt, quantitative data "can keep researchers from being carried away by vivid, but false, impressions in qualitative data, and it can bolster findings when it corroborates those findings from qualitative evidence" (p. 538). Questionnaire items are often developed after the researcher has analyzed a series of interviews, observations, and documents (Kaplan and Duchon 1988). This strategy reflects a fundamental difference between case studies and alternative methods (e.g., survey, laboratory experiment, field studies). In the former, the researcher may have less a priori knowledge of what the variables of interest will be and how they will be measured (Eisenhardt 1989).

In our study, qualitative data were used primarily to develop or suggest theoretical arguments which could then be strengthened (or weakened) by quantitative support. Survey instruments were developed to collect data that would either confirm or refute our interpretation of the data. Respondents were the identified key informants, namely, the individuals actively involved in the three IT implementation projects who had been interviewed earlier. To ensure that the responses were valid, the surveys were administered toward the end of data collection, although complete analysis of the interview data had not been completed. The survey contained questions that were based on the preliminary data analysis and therefore had not been discussed during the interviews.

In sum, the gathering of both quantitative and qualitative data from multiple sources helped to demonstrate the extent of congruity and consistency between the researchers' and key informants' evaluations of the IT implementation projects. However, because the analysis of the interview data could not be completed prior to the administration of the surveys, some important and relevant constructs were not captured in the survey instruments developed for each case. As recommended by Leonard-Barton (1990), sufficient time should be allowed for analysis between waves of data collection in order to eliminate this problem.

2.4 Step 4: Entering the Field

A striking feature of research to build theory from case studies is the frequent overlap of data analysis with data collection (Eisenhardt 1989). The analytical techniques adopted in the first stage of data analysis in our own research are presented below. Note that these techniques were used to help us identify themes, develop categories, and explore similarities and differences in the data, and relationships among them.

First, field notes were an important means of accomplishing this overlap in our study. As described by Van Maanen (1988), field notes are an ongoing stream-of-consciousness commentary about what is happening in the research. By reviewing our field notes frequently, important issues or conflicting answers provided by different individuals were identified immediately. Selected key informants were interviewed again to clear up any questions and to provide any additional information that was missing. The field notes also were useful in revising the interview guides as the study progressed. Second, once an interview was transcribed, reflective remarks were directly entered into the transcripts within brackets. These remarks were ways of getting ideas down on paper and of using writing as a way to facilitate reflection and analytic insight. They were a way to convert the researcher's perceptions and thoughts into a visible form that allows reflection (Strauss and Corbin 1990; Miles and Huberman 1994). In short, reflective remarks helped us start thinking, making deeper and more general sense of what was happening, and explaining things in a conceptually coherent way. Finally, a document summary form was created for each document collected and then filled out in the database. This form put the document in context, explained its significance, and gave a brief content summary (Miles and Huberman 1994).

In sum, overlapping data analysis with data collection not only gives the researcher a head start in analysis but, more importantly, allows researchers to take advantage of flexible data collection. Indeed, a key feature of theory-building case research is the freedom to make adjustments during the data collection process. In our study, adjustments included adding questions to interview guides, reviewing more data sources, observing meetings when the opportunity arose to do so, and interviewing previously unknown individuals who were identified during the study as important actors in the IT implementation projects.

2.5 Step 5: Analyzing Data

Analyzing data is the heart of building theory from case studies, but it is both the most difficult and the least codified part of the process (Eisenhardt 1989). Qualitative studies tend to produce large amounts of data that are not readily amenable to mechanical manipulation, analysis, and data reduction (Yin 1984). Therefore, the basic goal of qualitative data analysis is understanding, i.e., the search for coherence and order (Kaplan and Maxwell 1994). Inspired by the work of Eisenhardt, our data analysis included two aspects: "Within-Case Analysis" and "Cross-Case Analysis." The analytical techniques adopted during each of these two phases are briefly examined below.

Analyzing Within-Case Data

Within-case analysis typically involves detailed write-ups for each case. These write-ups are often simply pure descriptions, but they are central to the generation of insight because they help researchers to cope early in the analysis process with the often enormous volume of data (Eisenhardt 1989). However, there is no standard format for such analysis. The procedure followed to analyze each of the IT implementation projects in our study is summarized in Table 2.

As a first step, we needed to develop a database for each IT implementation project. The database organized and documented the data collected for each IT implementation project. Each of the three databases (one for each project) contained the following elements: (1) raw material (including interview transcripts, researcher's field notes, documents collected during data collection, and survey material); (2) coded data; (3) coding scheme; (4) memos and other analytic material; (5) data displays; (6) general chronological log of data collection; and (7) document summary forms.

Coding in qualitative research involves segmenting the data into units (Hammersley and Atkinson 1983) and rearranging them into categories that facilitate insight, comparison, and the development of theory (Strauss and Corbin 1990). Codes serve as retrieval and organizing devices which allow the rapid retrieval and clustering of all the segments related to a particular question, concept, or theme. To be consistent with our conceptual framework, the coding scheme developed in our study was divided into three broad categories: (1) contextual conditions, (2) implementation tactics, and (3) implementation success criteria. Appendix 4 shows an excerpt of the coding scheme developed in our study.

Table 2 Within-Case Analysis Procedure.

Step 1: Development of a database	
1.1	Gather reflective remarks and observation notes
1.2	Codify and extract data from the transcripts using a validated coding scheme
1.3	Group extracted segments under categories (codes and pattern codes)
1.4	Perform descriptive statistical analyses on quantitative data
Step 2: Development of a logical chain of evidence	
2.1	Evaluate the contextual conditions surrounding the implementation project a) perform a qualitative assessment b) perform a quantitative assessment c) verify consistency between qualitative and quantitative assessments d) explain any significant inconsistency
2.2	Evaluate the extent of implementation success a) perform a qualitative assessment b) perform a quantitative assessment c) verify consistency between qualitative and quantitative assessments d) explain any significant inconsistency
2.3	Establish a logical chain of evidence between implementation context and success a) identify the challenges b) provide the story that explains the extent to which each challenge was overcome c) build a summary table

Specific rules had to be established to ensure the reliability of the coding scheme and the overall quality of the coding process. First, an initial list of codes was developed based on our conceptual framework. The original list was then used to codify and extract the data from the transcripts associated with case one. As a result of this process, we found the need to add a few codes. Once all transcripts associated with the first project were codified, two coders were selected to determine inter-rater reliability. After a ten minute initial briefing by the researchers, each coder was instructed to read coding instructions to become acquainted with the coding scheme. Each coder was asked to assign codes to a series of segments representing contextual conditions, implementation tactics and implementation success criteria. The selected segments were randomly selected from all the segments included in the same category. It is worth noticing that the segments used as examples in the instructions were not selected for the validation process. Once each coder completed the task, the researchers' original coding was supplied and each coder was instructed to discuss any differences with the researchers. On a pairwise basis, the coders' responses and the researchers' codes were compared. Results revealed a fairly strong agreement among the coders.

Although most coding categories are drawn from existing theory or prior knowledge of the setting or system, others can be developed inductively by the interviewer. In addition to predefined codes, our study identified and defined pattern or inferential codes during data analysis (Eisenhardt 1989). Pattern codes are ones that identify an emergent theme, pattern, or explanation that the site suggests to the researcher (Miles and Huberman 1994). Pattern coding is, for qualitative researchers, an analogue to the cluster-analytic and factor-analytic devices used in statistical analysis (Miles and Huberman 1994). Pattern coding served two main functions in our study. First, it reduced large amounts of data into a smaller number of analytic units and, second, it helped us build a cognitive map, an evolving schema for understanding what was happening in each case. Four pattern codes were used in each of the three IT implementation projects analyzed in this study. These codes reflected perceived relationships among constructs included in the conceptual framework. More specifically, these codes reflected: (1) the influence of a contextual condition (e.g., beliefs of key actors) on the way a specific tactic was implemented (e.g., internal integration); (2) the direct influence of a contextual condition (e.g., system complexity) on an aspect of the success of a project (e.g., system acceptance); (3) the effect of a coping tactic (e.g., incremental implementation) on a contextual condition (e.g., users' attitudes); and (4) the direct effect of a coping tactic (e.g., external integration) on an aspect of the success of a project (e.g., project progress).

In order to understand the *how* and *why* associated with each IT implementation project and hence to provide answers to our research questions, a logical chain of evidence (Yin 1984) needed to be established. This chain of evidence was built in several steps. The first task was to identify the challenges encountered during the implementation process. Challenges were identified through an in-depth analysis of the contextual conditions surrounding the implementation project. In turn, for each challenge, we described the tactics adopted to cope with the encountered problems, anticipated or not. The extent to which each challenge was overcome was explained by (1) providing evidence of the effectiveness of each coping tactic, (2) identifying and explaining how certain contextual conditions enhanced the effectiveness of coping tactics, and (3) explaining how other conditions prevented the adoption of tactics by acting as compensatory mechanisms. As recommended by Yin, each chain of evidence was established by having sufficient citations in the report to the relevant portions of the case study database and developing a case study protocol that clearly indicates the links between the content of the protocol and the initial research questions.

The adoption of displays such as matrices, flowcharts, and conceptual maps was also useful in several ways during data analysis. For one thing, they made ideas visible and permanent. For instance, besides indicating who has formal authority over whom and what the role names are among actors, context charts (Miles and Huberman 1994) were useful in telling us about the quality of the working relationships between actors (or groups of actors) involved in each IT implementation project. Importantly, these charts showed who the *key actors* were as well as the role played by every individual. Figures and charts also served two other key functions: data reduction and presentation of data that allows it to be grasped as a whole (Miles and Huberman 1994). For instance, checklist matrices were used to synthesize the overall evaluation (qualitative and quantitative) of 1) the implementation situation or context and 2) the extent of implementation success. A short glance at these tables allowed us to clearly identify the challenges that were encountered over the course of each project and the extent of project success. Importantly, comparison of matrices showing qualitative and quantitative evidence revealed a large extent of congruity and consistency between the researchers' and the key informants' evaluations. In sum, the use of displays allowed us to draw and verify valid conclusions because each display was "arranged coherently to permit careful comparisons, detection of differences, noting of patterns and themes, seeing trends" (Miles and Huberman 1994, p. 92).

Searching for Cross-Case Patterns

As stressed earlier, the ultimate intent of our research was to gradually build a new theory of IT implementation. This iterative process started with the development and presentation of an initial set of theoretical propositions based on evidence from the first IT implementation project and the theoretical assumptions associated with the teleological process meta-theory. The initial propositions then became a vehicle for generalizing to the other two projects. As a second step, the emergent propositions from the first project were systematically compared with evidence from the second project. The theoretical propositions were either supported by the evidence, revised, or not supported for lack of sufficient evidence. As a third and final step, the process was repeated when refined theoretical propositions were systematically compared with evidence from the third project. The central idea was to iterate toward a theory that fits the data, where projects that supported the emergent theory enhance confidence in its validity, while projects that did not support the theory often provide an opportunity to refine and extend the theoretical model (Eisenhardt 1989). Step 6 describes how the series of propositions were derived.

2.6 Step 6: Shaping Research Propositions

The next step of this highly iterative process is to compare systematically the emerging theory with the evidence from each project in order to assess how well or poorly it fits with the data. The central idea is that researchers constantly compare theory and data — iterating toward a theory that closely fits the data (Eisenhardt 1989).

Based on the teleological process meta-theory, our study proposed a series of research propositions reflecting the complex and dynamic nature of IT implementation. Each proposition addressed a specific aspect related to the dynamic nature of IT implementation. For instance, the teleological process meta-theory incorporates the systems theory assumption of equifinality; that is, a given end goal can potentially be achieved via a number of paths, all tending toward the same endpoint. Importantly, the teleological view stipulates that human agents are rational actors, that is, choices are made based on the actors' beliefs of how likely it is that a particular action or decision will move the process closer to goal achievement. Evidence from all three projects supported both of these contentions. Overall, the seven propositions developed in this study (see Appendix 5) defined a preliminary set of laws of interaction which characterizes the dynamic nature of the IT implementation process. As presently constituted, these propositions are at least one step short of theory formation. At minimum, they are empirical generalizations; that is, they summarize observed uniformities of relationships between predictors and outcomes. At best, they suggest a rudimentary model of IT implementation process.

Again, it is important to note that the above analysis and prescriptions only hold when IT implementation is studied within a teleological view. The adoption of a "dialectical" or an "evolutionary" view would have certainly led to a totally different set of theoretical propositions, since those types of process meta-theories address different aspects of the IT implementation process.

The process of shaping propositions is more judgmental in theory-building research because researchers cannot apply statistical tests. The research team must judge the strength and consistency of relationships within and across cases and also fully display the evidence and procedures when the findings are published, so that readers may apply their own standards. Consequently, qualitative data are particularly useful for understanding why or why not emergent relationships hold. When a relationship is supported, the qualitative data often provide a good understanding of the dynamics underlying the relationship, that is, the why of what is happening. This is crucial in the establishment of internal validity. Consequently, having sufficient citations and quotes in each of the three IT implementation project reports was an important way of ensuring internal validity in our study. Another way of validating researchers' interpretations is by systematically gathering feedback about one's conclusions from participants in the case being studied (Guba and Lincoln 1989). Two tactics were therefore adopted to further increase the validity and reliability of our research. First, the draft of each IT implementation project report was reviewed by key informants. Second, a site analysis meeting for each project took place at the end of data analysis. Participants in these meetings were those in a position to reflect on the project's "big picture."

2.7 Step 7: Enfolding Literature

An essential feature of theory building is comparison of the emergent concepts, theory, or hypotheses with the extant literature (Eisenhardt 1989). This involves asking what is it similar to, what does it contradict, and why. In pursuit of this objective, for each proposition, we indicated the extent to which it was supported by previous research and the extent to which we have added some new perspective or new idea when thinking about the management of the IT implementation process. For instance, one proposition posits that the selection and effectiveness of implementation tactics and strategies depend on the background, skills, and beliefs of key people involved in the implementation effort. While previous research has acknowledged the importance of having individuals with specific characteristics involved in an implementation effort (Fossum 1986; Schultz, Slevin and Pinto 1987; Hunsucker and Loos 1989; Joshi 1990), our study has shown how these characteristics affect both the selection and effectiveness of various implementation tactics employed. This implies that no one set of normative implementation tactics can or should be applied to all projects. Rather, project leaders should ensure that the implementation tactics adopted complement the experiences, skills, and beliefs brought by each player in the implementation effort.

Another proposition stipulates that successful implementation requires identifying and addressing implementation challenges. This evidence adds support to previous research that has found that most unsuccessful IT implementation projects are the result of poor management, not technical problems (Waldrop 1984; Lyytinen and Hirschheim 1987; Ewusi-Mensah and Przansnyski 1991). While much of the implementation research has equated good management with knowing *what to do* (Schultz, Slevin and Pinto 1987; Leonard-Barton and Deschamps 1988; Lorenzi and Riley 1995), we suggest that good management must also focus on *what to look for and think about*. In short, we found that tying the emergent theoretical propositions to existing literature enhances internal validity and generalizability of theory building from case study research as suggested by Eisenhardt.

2.8 Step 8: Reaching Closure

An important issue in reaching closure is when to stop adding cases. Ideally, researchers should stop adding cases when theoretical saturation is reached (Eisenhardt 1989). Theoretical saturation is the point at which incremental learning is minimal because the researchers are observing phenomena seen before (Glaser and Strauss 1967). In practice, however, theoretical saturation often combines with pragmatic considerations to dictate when case collection ends. In fact, it is not uncommon for researchers to plan the number of cases in advance.

For pragmatic reasons of time, money, and opportunity, this study involved only three IT implementation projects. Clearly, theoretical saturation cannot be attained with such a small number of cases. Therefore, additional case studies of IT implementation projects must be conducted to increase the validity and reliability of the theoretical propositions developed in our research. The theoretical propositions would benefit not only from being tested in other organizational contexts and using other information technologies but also from being tested against recent project failures where projects were abandoned at some point or where systems were not used at all.

3 CONCLUDING REMARKS

The objective of this article was twofold. First, our aim was to present and critique the methodology for building theories from case study research proposed by Eisenhardt within the context of the MIS field. Our second intent was to describe in some detail how this methodology was applied in a particular research study on IT implementation and how the use of this methodology contributed to the discovery of a number of new perspectives and empirical insights. In light of these objectives, this article makes two contributions to the literature. The first is to operationalize the "roadmap" presented by Eisenhardt and to document the specific decisions that a researcher must make in order to build theories from case study research. The second is to show how previously-defined techniques (e.g., Yin 1984; Miles and Huberman 1984) can be used in applying Eisenhardt's approach.

Little MIS research has been focused on the development of theory. Rather, the MIS field has borrowed heavily from the theories of other disciplines. However, there are numerous IT phenomena in addition to IT implementation whose underlying dynamics are unknown and thus are good candidates to study using a case study research strategy. We hope that we have provided a detailed guide for carrying out such a research strategy.

There is still an issue of legitimacy when conducting qualitative studies. Qualitative studies are gradually becoming more accepted; meanwhile, researchers will have to work harder, be more creative, and come up with new and more robust methodological tools to have their work recognized and accepted in a community that tends to be skeptical of qualitative studies. Applying a well-defined methodology along the lines described in this paper will help to position qualitative studies more in the mainstream of IT research.

It is also important to consider the overall demand of this methodological approach on the researcher. For instance, process research usually results in the collection of large amounts of data vulnerable to subjective interpretation and surpassing human ability to compile. Because of the demands and problems encountered during qualitative research, researchers must have a great interest in and dedication to the object of research (Barley 1990; Leonard-Barton 1990). While it is important to gain the trust and confidence of organizational members, it is also important to remain sufficiently detached so as to be objective. Importantly, researchers should not underestimate the time and effort required to conduct these kinds of studies. From this research it was also learned that one must often be willing to spend lunches, evenings, and weekends collecting data at the site. Despite these constraints, qualitative studies remain, we believe, the best approach available for studying complex phenomena such as IT implementation. The reward clearly appears to be a deeper and broader understanding of IT implementation and the ability to contribute significantly to cumulative knowledge in the field.

4 REFERENCES

Anderson, J. G., and Aydin, C. E. (1994). "Overview: Theoretical Perspectives and Methodologies for the Evaluation of Health Care Information Systems." In J. G. Anderson, C. E. Aydin, and J. J. Stepen (Editors), *Evaluating Health Care Information Systems, Methods and Applications*. Thousand Oaks, California: SAGE Publications, pp. 5-29.

Barley, S. R. (1990). "The Alignment of Technology and Structure Through Roles and Networks." *Administrative Science Quarterly*, Volume 35, pp. 61-103.

Benbasat, I.; Goldstein, D. K.; and Mead, M. (1987). "The Case Research Strategy in Studies of Information Systems." *MIS Quarterly*, Volume 11, Number 3, September, pp. 369-385.

Bonoma, T. V. (1985). "Case Research in Marketing: Opportunities, Problems, and a Process." *Journal of Marketing Research*, Volume 22, pp. 199-208.

Eisenhardt, K. M. (1989). "Building Theories from Case Study Research." *Academy of Management Review*, Volume 14, Number 4, pp. 532-550.

Elam, J. J.; Prescott, M.; and Wasala, C. (1994). "Making it Work: How Organizations Succeed in Implementing Emerging Information Technologies." Working Paper, Florida International University.

Ewusi-Mensah, K., and Przasnyski, Z. H. (1991). "On Information Systems Project Abandonment: An Exploratory Study of Organizational Practices." *MIS Quarterly*, Volume 15, Number 1, March, pp. 67-88.

Fossum, B. (1986). *A Normative Model for CIM Implementation*. Unpublished Doctoral Dissertation, University of Texas at Austin.

Glaser, B., and Strauss, A. (1967). *The Discovery of Grounded Theory: Strategies of Qualitative Research*. London: Wiedenfeld and Nicholson.

Guba, E. G., and Lincoln, Y. S. (1989). *Fourth Generation Evaluation*. Newbury Park, California: Sage.

Hammersley, M., and Atkinson, P. (1983). *Ethnography: Principles in Practice*. London: Tavistock.

Hunsucker, J. L., and Loos, D. (1989). "Transition Management, an Analysis of Strategic Considerations for Effective Implementation." *Engineering Management International*, Volume 5, pp. 167-178.

Jick, T. (1979). "Mixing Qualitative and Quantitative Methods: Triangulation in Action." *Administrative Science Quarterly*, Volume 24, pp. 602-611.

Joshi, K. (1990). "Reorganization of the Work System for Successful Information Systems Implementation: A Case Study." *Information and Management*, Volume 19, pp. 271-284.

Kaplan, B. (1987). "Initial Impact of a Clinical Laboratory Computer System: Themes Common to Expectations and Actualities." *Journal of Medical Systems*, Volume 11, pp. 137-147.

Kaplan, B. (1988). "Development and Acceptance of Medical Information Systems: An Historical Overview." *Journal of Health and Human Resources Administration*, Volume 11, pp. 9-29.

Kaplan, B. (1993). "The Computer as Rorschach: Implications for Management and User Acceptance." In R. E. Dayhoff (Editor), *Proceedings of the Seventh Annual Symposium on Computer Applications in Medical Care*. Silver Spring, Maryland: IEEE Computer Society Press, pp. 664-667.

Kaplan, B., and Duchon, D. (1988). "Combining Qualitative and Quantitative Methods in Information Systems Research: A Case Study." *MIS Quarterly*, December, pp. 571-586.

Kaplan, B., and Maxwell, J. A. (1994). "Qualitative Research Methods for Evaluating Computer Information Systems." In J. G. Anderson, C. E. Aydin, and S. J. Jay (Editors), *Evaluating Health Care Information Systems, Methods and Applications*. Thousand Oaks, California: Sage Publications, pp. 45-68.

Kochen, M. (1985). "Are MIS Frameworks Premature?" *Journal of Management Information Systems*, Volume 2, Number 3, Winter 1985-1986, pp. 92-100.

Kwon, T. H., and Zmud, R. W. (1987). "Unifying the Fragmented Models of Information Systems Implementation." In R. J. Boland and R. A. Hirschheim (Editors), *Critical Issues in Information Systems Research*. Chichester, England: John Wiley and Sons, Ltd., pp. 227-251.

Lee, A. S. (1989). "A Scientific Methodology for MIS Case Studies." *MIS Quarterly*, Volume 13, Number 1, March, pp. 33-52.

Leonard-Barton, D. (1988). "Implementation and Mutual Adaptation of Technology and Organization." *Research Policy*, Volume 17, Number 5, 1988, pp. 1-17.

Leonard-Barton, D. (1990). "A Dual Methodology for Case Studies: Synergistic Use of a Longitudinal Single Site with Replicated Multiple Sites." *Organization Science*, Volume 1, Number 3, pp. 248-266.

Leonard-Barton, D., and Deschamps, I. (1988). "Managerial Influence in the Implementation of New Technology." *Management Science*, Volume 34, Number 10, October, pp. 1252-1265.

Lorenzi, N. M., and Riley, R. G. (1995). *Organizational Aspects of Health Informatics: Managing Technological Change*. New York: Springer Verlag.

Lucas, H. C. Jr. (1978). "Empirical Evidence For a Descriptive Model of Implementation." *MIS Quarterly*, Volume 2, Number 2, June, pp. 27-42

Lucas, H. C. Jr.; Ginzberg, M. J.; and Schultz, R. L. (1990). *Information Systems Implementation: Testing a Structural Model*. Norwood, New Jersey: Ablex.

Lyytinen, K., and Hirschheim, R. (1987). "Information Systems Failures: A Survey and Classification of the Empirical Literature." *Oxford Surveys in Information Technology*, Volume 4, pp. 257-309.

Miles, M. B., and Huberman, A. M. (1984). *Qualitative Data Analysis*. Beverly Hills: Sage Publications.

Miles, M. B., and Huberman, A. M. (1994). *Qualitative Data Analysis: An Expanded Sourcebook*. Beverly Hills: Sage Publications.

Mohr, L. B. (1982). *Explaining Organizational Behavior*. San Francisco: Jossey-Bass.

Newman, M., and Robey, D. (1992). "A Social Process Model of User-Analyst Relationships." *MIS Quarterly*, Volume 16, Number 2, June, 249-266.

Paré, G. (1995). *Understanding the Dynamics of IT Implementation: The Case of Clinical Information Systems*. Doctoral Dissertation, Florida International University.

Paré, G., and Elam, J. J. (1996). "Understanding the Dynamics of IT Implementation: A Case Study in a Burn Center" *Congrès de l'Association des Sciences Administratives du Canada,* Montréal, Québec, May 25-28.

Paré, G.; Elam, J. J.; and Lima, C. (Forthcoming). "Implementation of an Electronic Medical Records System: How Can Health Care Managers Ensure its Success?" *Journal of Information Technology Management.*

Robey, D., and Newman, M. (1996). "Sequential Patterns in Information Systems Development: An Application of a Social Process Model." *ACM Transactions on Information Systems,* Volume 14, Number 1, January, pp. 30-63.

Robey, D., and Zeller, R. L. (1978). "Factors Affecting the Success and Failure of an Information System for Product Quality." *Interfaces,* Volume 8, Number 2, February, pp. 70-75.

Sabherwal, R., and Robey, D. (1993). "An Empirical Taxonomy of Implementation Processes Based on Sequences of Events in Information System Development." *Organization Science,* Volume 4, Number 4, November, pp. 548-576.

Schultz, R. L.; Slevin, D. P.; and Pinto, J. K. (1987). "Strategy and Tactics in a Process Model of Project Implementation." *Interface,* Volume 17, Number 3, May-June, pp. 34-46.

Srinivasan, A., and Davis, J. G. (1987). "A Reassessment of Implementation Process Models." *Interfaces,* Volume 17, Number 3, May-June, pp. 64-71.

Strauss, A. L., and Corbin, J. (1990). *Basics of Qualitative Research: Grounded Theory Procedures and Techniques*. Newbury Park, California: Sage.

Swanson, E. B. (1974) "Management Information Systems: Appreciation and Involvement." *Management Science,* Volume 21, pp. 178-188.

Swanson, E. B. (1988). *Information System Implementation: Bridging the Gap Between Design and Design and Utilization*. Homewood, Illinois: Irwin.

Van de Ven, A. H. (1992). "Suggestions for Studying Strategy Process: A Research Note." *Strategic Management Journal,* Volume 13, pp. 169-188.

Van de Ven, A. H., and Poole, M. S. (1995). "Explaining Development and Change in Organizations." *Academy of Management Review,* Volume 20, Number 3, July, pp. 510-540.

Van Maanen, J. (1988). *Tales of the Field: On Writing Ethnography*. Chicago: University of Chicago Press.

Waldrop, J. H. (1984). "Project Management: Have We Applied All That We Know?" *Information and Management,* Volume 7, pp. 13-20.

Wynekoop, J. L. (1992). "Strategies for Implementation Research: Combining Research Methods." In J. I. DeGross, J. D. Becker, and J. J. Elam (Editors), *Proceedings of the Thirteenth Annual International Conference on Information Systems*. Dallas, Texas, December, pp. 185-193.

Yin, R. K. (1984). *Case Study Research: Design and Methods* Beverly Hills: Sage Publications.

5 BIOGRAPHY

Guy Paré is assistant professor of information systems at the École des Hautes Études Commerciales in Montréal. He received his Ph.D. in information systems from Florida International University. His research interests center on system implementation, the organizational impacts of IT, and the virtual organization.

Joyce J. Elam is the James L. Knight Professor of Management Information Systems in the Department of Decision Sciences and Information Systems. She was previously an associate professor at the University of Texas and an assistant professor at the University of Pennsylvania's Wharton School. Dr. Elam was a Marvin Bower Fellow at the Harvard Business School during the 1987-1988 academic year. Dr. Elam earned both her Ph.D. in operations research (1977) and her BA in mathematics (1970) from the University of Texas. Dr. Elam has published extensively in the areas of the competitive use of information technology, the management of the information services function, and the use of information technology to support both individual and group decision making.

Appendix 1
Conceptual Framework

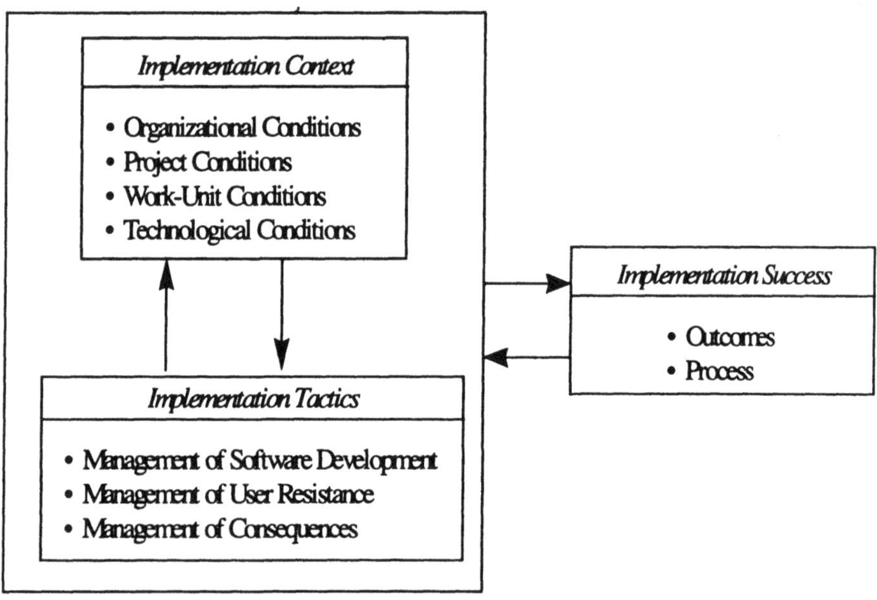

Appendix 2
Excerpt of an Interview Guide

Interview Guide # ___

Health Care Center: ____________ Date: __/__/__
Unit: Burn Unit______ Time: ________

1. INTRODUCTION

Purpose of the meeting: Learn more about the context in which the implementation of the computerized charting system took place as well as the tactics adopted to ensure system success.

2. RESPONDENT

Name: (confidential)________ Phone: ________________
Title: ___________________ Beeper: __________

- How long did you work for the Burn Center?
- Which position(s) did you occupy?

3. IMPLEMENTATION CONTEXT

Previous experience with IT:

- <The director of the medical unit> told me that prior to using the <second system>, nurses and physicians were using a mainframe-based information system. He also told me that there was reluctance from the staff to use this system in the beginning. How had the transition been from paper-based to computer-based?
- How would you describe the Burn Unit experience with the <first> system implementation? Did you go through "chaos" in the beginning? How has the situation evolved? Did people adjust easily? If so, what made them adjust? Were there specific actions taken at a certain point?
- To what extent would you say the experience with the first system affected the implementation of the second computer system? Explain.

Organizational Climate

- How would you describe the work environment in the unit? Explain.
- Had you been aware of any major or minor political issue(s) that took place and were debated during the project? If any, ask for details: What? When? Who was involved? Why?

Organizational Resources

- In your opinion, has the implementation of the <second> system been supported by enough resources in terms of money, people, and equipment. Explain.
- Has the implementation process been affected by a lack of resources at any point in time?

4. IMPLEMENTATION TACTICS

External Integration

- How have physicians, nurses, and administrators been kept informed of the progress regarding the implementation of the <second> system?
- <Director of Burn Center> mentioned that nursing provided some input in the design of the system. To what extent would you say nursing input was critical? What have been the effects associated with this tactic?

Phased implementation (gradualism)

- Many argue that the key to getting nurses and docs to use any computer system is gradualism; that if you start with the full implementation of computer chart, it won't work. Would you say that the phased implementation strategy adopted for both the first and the second systems was an effective strategy?

Championing

- Many argued that any system should be sold to nurses and physicians if they are to use it? How has this happened here in the case of the second system?
- Were the benefits and advantages of the second system over the first system broadly diffused to your staff? Did you emphasize the problems associated with the first system and how the <second> system would solve them?

5. IMPLEMENTATION SUCCESS

- Overall, how successful has the use of the <second> system been?
- In your opinion, what have been the major benefits associated with the use of the <second> system, from an individual or nurse standpoint and from an organizational or unit standpoint?
- Ultimately the most significant beneficiary of electronic patient charts should be the patient. Has this been achieved in your case? Explain.

6. AFTERTHOUGHTS AND COMMENTS: (if any)

Appendix 3
Profile of the Interviewees

Case	System	Site	Interviews with team members	Interviews with users
1	Medical records - Electronic signature	Hospital-wide	Dir. of Medical Records VP Medical Affairs HIS coordinator Education coordinators Systems analysts Programmers Number of interviews: 26	Attending physicians * Nurse liaisons Medical records staff Number of interviews: 13
2	Nursing flowsheet system	Trauma Center	Dir. Clinical Applications Asst. Dir. Soft. Tech. Clinical educators Head nurses Programmers Number of interviews: 19	Registered nurses Number of interviews: 31
3	Electronic patient chart	Burn Center	Medical Director Associate Director Head nurse Clinical educator System administrator Number of interviews: 12	Registered nurses * Physicians Resident staff Physical therapists Dietician Number of interviews: 25
* primary users				

Appendix 4
Excerpt of the Coding Scheme

Contextual Conditions

National Movement toward Computerization (EC/NAT_MOV)
A segment which presents evidence of efforts made by national associations, agencies, and hospitals towards computerization.

Organizational Climate (OC/ORG_CLI)
A segment which reflects one's own perception about his/her organization with respect to commitment to technological and/or management initiatives.

Organizational IT Experiences (OC/IT_EXP)
A segment which refers to the memories or experiences that exist in the organization about prior information technology initiatives.

Availability of Organizational Resources (OC/AVA_RES)
A segment which shows the extent to which the organizational resources needed to support the development and implementation of the system were available. Organizational resources do not only include money, but also time, people, hardware, software, and facilities.

Users Skills/Knowledge (WUC/SKILLS)
A segment which describes one's perception of the extent to which users are familiar with the task being automated, are familiar with the computer system, and/or have experience with computers in general.

Implementation Tactics

External Integration (SD/EXT_INT)
A segment which indicates the adoption of tactic(s) whose objective is to link the project team's work to the users. Examples of external integration tactics include the selection of a user as project leader, the selection of particular users as team members, and the consultation of users on an occasional basis for feedback purposes.

Internal Integration (SD/INT_INT)
A segment which describes the adoption of tactic(s) whose purpose is to ensure that the project team operates as an integrated unit. Well-known internal integration tactics include the selection of experienced IT professionals to be part of the project team; frequent project team meetings; participation of all team members in goal

setting; and selection of a high percentage of team members with significant previous work experience and relationships.

Championing (SD/CHAMP)
A segment which illustrates effort(s) made for providing motivation to the project team; generating enthusiasm for the targeted users; providing crucial political support during periods of important decision making; selling the idea to top management; and/or getting senior managers sufficiently interested in the project, etc.

Incremental Approach (UR/INCREM)
A segment which provides evidence that a strategic decision was to introduce the various modules of the computer system in a gradual, step-by-step manner.

Mutual Adaptation (MC/ADAPT)
A segment which portrays how the organization moved ahead with the introduction of the technology, left existing organizational arrangements (e.g., structure) in place, and subsequently attended to organizational changes on a responsive or adaptive basis.

Implementation Success Criteria

System Acceptance and Use (O/ACCEPT_USE)
A segment which expresses one's perception of users' acceptance and/or use of the computerized information system.

Project Progress (P/PROGRESS)
A segment which provides insights as for how the project evolved or progressed over time. Most IT implementation or development processes are usually evaluated in terms of their respect of deadlines and budgets. IT projects are also subject to unavoidable or unexpected problems of all sorts.

Overall Satisfaction with the Implementation Process (P/SATIS)
A segment which makes a suggestion about one's own satisfaction, perception, reflection, and/or evaluation in regard with the overall development and implementation process.

Appendix 5
Research Propositions

Proposition #1: Pragmatism. The successful implementation of computer-based information systems represents a purposeful process where key actors socially construct envisioned end goals, anticipate challenges ahead, and recognize the presence of and capitalize on opportunities.

Proposition #2: Equifinality/Rationality/Complementarity. The implementation of a computer-based information system is characterized by the systems theory of equifinality; that is, there are likely several equally effective ways to achieve a given end goal. The selection of a particular course of action is a rational process largely influenced by the degree to which key actors can recognize the mediating role of each tactic, can conceive of an alternative beyond the selected course of action, and are motivated to action. Consequently, greater complementarity of key actors' skills and interests is likely to favor a higher quality and more effective implementation strategy.

Proposition #3: Duality of Structure. Key actors' beliefs regarding a course of action that should be adopted are influenced by the contextual conditions which surround a given project. Yet, through the action of reflective actors, effective implementation tactics are likely to become established as standardized practices while ineffective courses of action are likely to be quickly abandoned.

Proposition #4: Supporting Mechanisms. The effectiveness of any given implementation tactic is likely to be enhanced when complemented or supported by the presence of one (or many) contextual conditions.

Proposition #5: Compensatory Mechanisms. Certain favorable contextual conditions surrounding a given implementation project might have a direct effect on its success when acting as compensatory mechanisms.

Proposition #6: Envisioned End Goals and States of "Rest." Actors' decisions and actions are not all independent of each other and hence their order matters in achieving success. The implementation process can be characterized as a movement where temporary states of "rest" are reached and envisioned end goals are ultimately fulfilled. The fulfillment of any envisioned end goal or state of "rest" constitutes a necessary condition but not sufficient condition for success.

Proposition #7: Indeterminacy. The implementation of a computer-based information system is characterized by a certain indeterminacy first reflected through the occurrence of unexpected challenges caused by either uncontrollable events or loose implementation practices. This indeterminacy also means that the implemented system might not have all the effects originally envisioned by key actors or might produce unexpected and undesirable consequences.

28

Panel – Information Systems Qualitative Research in Health Care

B. Kaplan
Quinnipiac College, USA

F. Lau
University of Alberta, Canada

J. Aarts
Fontyns Hogeschölen, The Netherlands

D. E. Forsythe
University of California, San Francisco, USA

Interest in information systems in health care is growing. Information technology is becoming increasingly important as health care organizations feel pressures to improve quality while reducing costs. In addition to the more familiar business and administrative applications, information technology also is used to collect, analyze, and communicate clinical data in support of patient care processes. For example, there are systems for medical records, for communicating treatment orders or laboratory test results, for organizing and disseminating health knowledge as practical guidelines, for enhancing clinical practice through decision support systems, and for real-time monitoring of patient conditions.

An increasing number of information systems researchers throughout the world are carrying out studies in health care organizations. While the information systems field has developed, the discipline of medical informatics also has developed, a discipline that includes interest in organizational aspects as well as other areas.

The panel brings together information systems and medical informatics researchers experienced in different national health care settings. Panelists will draw on a variety of research projects to provide empirically based discussion of why qualitative research is important in health care and how to derive more general lessons for qualitative information systems research in other substantive areas. Panelists will draw on their research experiences to discuss

- the appropriateness of qualitative research in health care;
- issues unique to the intersection of health care and information systems qualitative research; and
- general issues of information systems qualitative research as they are exemplified in health care settings.

Bonnie Kaplan will chair and moderate the panel. She will make introductory remarks that set the panel agenda and closing remarks that tie together panelists' comments and provide a framework for opportunities and experiences in qualitative research in health care. She will raise issues in conducting information systems qualitative research in hospitals, such as legitimacy of the researcher, gaining entry, and presentation of results. She will draw upon research findings from a variety of hospital-based research projects she conducted to suggest topics and theoretical frameworks relevant to the IS research community at large.

Francis Lau will present an example of qualitative IS research in health care. He will discuss a project in which he and other researchers are studying the adoption and use of an Internet-based disease guidance system by physicians, residents, and nurses. The project provides an example of how IS qualitative research can be applied in health care by illustrating the development and refinement of such qualitative methodologies as action research, ethnography, longitudinal research, and phenomenolgy.

Jos Aarts will present a theoretical basis for qualitative research projects in information systems using health care settings as an example. He will discuss the social nature of clinical work. He will present a conceptual model that relates organizational change and the planning, design, and implementation of information systems to clinical work. Based on that, he will present the types of qualitative methodologies most appropriate for assessing the impact of information and communication technology in health care delivery. He will also propose an agenda for IS research in health care settings. The models and methodologies he suggests should be of general interest to the IS community because of the social nature of work in other settings.

Diana Forsythe will discuss what constitutes ethnographic expertise and why it is useful in system design and evaluation based on her nine years of research in software development laboratories where well-known medical informatics developers turned ethnographers. Forsythe's characterization of the misconceptions involved in such do-it-yourself ethnography will be recognizable to IS researchers working in other contextual settings. Her discussion of some do's and don'ts of ethnographic research will shed light on the legitimacy of qualitative research in IS.

Index of Contributors

GPSR Compliance
The European Union's (EU) General Product Safety Regulation (GPSR) is a set of rules that requires consumer products to be safe and our obligations to ensure this.

If you have any concerns about our products, you can contact us on

ProductSafety@springernature.com

In case Publisher is established outside the EU, the EU authorized representative is:

Springer Nature Customer Service Center GmbH
Europaplatz 3
69115 Heidelberg, Germany

www.ingramcontent.com/pod-product-compliance
Ingram Content Group UK Ltd.
Pitfield, Milton Keynes, MK11 3LW, UK
UKHW012141240726
13966UKWH00001B/98